NORTHERN IRELAND ARCHAEOLOGICAL MONOGRAPHS NO 7

HARNESSING THE TIDES

The Early Medieval Tide Mills at Nendrum Monastery, Strangford Lough

THOMAS McERLEAN
NORMAN CROTHERS

Series Editor
BRIAN SCOTT

Thomas McErlean

THE
STATIONERY
OFFICE

ENVIRONMENT
AND HERITAGE SERVICE

A CIP catalogue record for this book is available from the British Library.
A Library of Congress CIP catalogue record has been applied for.

First published 2007

ISBN 978-0-337-08877-3

Printed in Northern Ireland by Graham & Heslip, Belfast, Co. Antrim

Contents

List of Figures

Nendrum in deep winter (Tony Corey)

Foreword

The monastic ruins of Nendrum can be considered one of the most important monuments in state care in Northern Ireland and it gives me considerable pleasure to introduce a new volume of research on the archaeology of this evocative site. In 1925 H.C. Lawlor published the results of his 1922–24 excavations in *The Monastery of Saint Mochaoi of Nendrum* under the auspices of the Belfast Natural History and Philosophical Society. Our new publication presents the results of the Environment and Heritage Service funded excavations from 1999–2001 and brings a new level of interpretation to our understanding of life in an Early Medieval Irish monastery. The exciting and largely unexpected discoveries on the foreshore below the monastery resulted from my Directorate's responsibility for maritime archaeology, a role started in 1992 in relation to historic wrecks, by an agency agreement with the Department of the Environment (England). In 1995 the Historic Monuments and Archaeological Objects (NI) Order extended the remit to include archaeological sites on the seabed from High Water Mark to 12 nautical miles offshore. From this date Environment and Heritage Service embarked on an ambitious programme of 'field survey' of the coastal edge, foreshore and seabed of the three maritime counties of Northern Ireland. During the course of the Strangford Lough survey enigmatic ruins were encountered on the shore at Nendrum and the subsequent intertidal excavations uncovered the splendidly preserved remains of the tide mills of the early monks. Their discovery constitutes a landmark in the Built Heritage Directorate's role in protecting the maritime heritage. It also reminds us that not all the archaeological treasures of the sea derive from ships on the seabed. It is highly probable that many other exciting discoveries will be revealed during our ongoing survey of the intertidal zone of Northern Ireland. Finally, I hope that this volume will have popular appeal, not only to archaeologists, but also to the public at large and that it will enhance appreciation of the great richness of our maritime heritage and culture.

Michael D A Coulter
Director of Built Heritage
May 2007

Preface

Since H.C. Lawlor's seminal excavation of 1922–1924 and its swift publication in 1925, Nendrum has occupied a prominent position in the monastic archaeology of Ireland. After its presentation to the public in 1924, a major project involving some restoration of the ruins, improved road access and the provision of a tea room, the site became a well-visited place of excursion and exploration for the general public. Like many other ancient holy places all over the world, Nendrum, in the 21st century, still possesses that hard to define quality, best described as an aura of sanctity. Some of this atmosphere must derive from the stillness of its island setting, with the quiet waters of Strangford Lough lapping around the exterior of the monastic enclosure and unspoilt views over the gentle green drumlins of Co. Down. Today, like Early Medieval pilgrims before them, visitors come in increasing numbers and most leave spiritually uplifted or culturally enriched. The ruins never fail to stir the historical imagination, and this aspect of Nendrum is finely captured in J.S. Andrew's novel *The Bell of Nendrum* (Andrews 1969), a moving narrative of an accidental time traveller who is transported from the second half of the 20th century to a Nendrum of gentle monks and savage Vikings in the year AD 974. While Andrew's book is a testament to the stimulus invoked by the ruins in imagining the past, this one, based on archaeological evidence is constrained by the solid information retrieved. However, as the people behind the ruins and artefacts and their way of life are central to archaeology it can be claimed that an excavation report such as this also contains major elements of the romance of the past.

The discovery of the tide mills opens a new chapter in the archaeology of Nendrum begun by Reeves in 1844 when he rescued this important monastery from historical obscurity. The excavation has generated new information on many themes. Among these is the story of how man in the past, living on the coast, exploited the resources offered by his maritime environment. We are already well aware of many aspects of early maritime heritage such as the harvesting of fish, shellfish and seaweed and the ability to navigate the sea, but it is rather more surprising that the tides were harnessed for milling at an early date. Foreshore archaeology, that is the evidence of human activity between high and low water, is in its infancy and Nendrum has been the largest intertidal excavation carried out in Ireland to date. It demonstrates the great discoveries to be made in this zone.

The excavation has produced extremely valuable evidence pertinent to the development of technological innovation, improvement and progress. Ireland has produced the largest known number of examples of early mills, and at the time of writing Nendrum stands at the top of this list in being the earliest. The invention of the corn mill and the mechanical use of waterpower with its rapid adoption in the early centuries of the first millennium was one of the great advances in the history of technology. Its impact on food processing was direct, literally relieving a large section of the population of their laborious manual daily grinding of corn for bread.

Monasteries dominated the social landscape of Early Medieval Ireland but archaeological information about their layout and organisation is still severely lacking. It is hoped that this work adds to our understanding of this fascinating period in the Irish story.

The precise dating of the construction of the first tide mill to the years AD 619–621 by tree-ring analysis, demonstrates how far archaeology has come since the 1922–1924 excavation and provides an historical horizon which it is stimulating to contextualise with other events around that date. The mill was built some 20 years or so after the death of St Columba at Iona, four years after the death of St Columbanus, the great missionary monk from Nendrum's monastic neighbour Bangor, in Bobbio in Northern Italy (in AD 615). Further east, Mohammed went to Medina where he founded Islam in AD 622, the year after the first mill was completed.

Since the ending of the excavation in 2001 it was intended, following best practice, that the results should be published as soon as possible so that the information should enter the mainstream of archaeological knowledge. Inevitably many factors, such as funding budgets, staffing and so on, conspired to defeat this aim, and pragmatic decisions had to be taken to facilitate publication within acceptable time limits. Not least of these was that publication should proceed before further work on the environmental sampling, the wood corpus and some other aspects of the excavation were completed. Delaying until such time as funding became came available would have postponed publication for much longer. Although this report attempts to be as comprehensive as possible, it should not be regarded as the last word on the results of excavation and many aspects demand further investigation. Their results will hopefully be exploited in future papers.

The discovery of tide mills at Nendrum contributes to the respect and admiration felt for the achievement of our ancestors and brings us closer to the reality of their lives. Above all else, it highlights that Nendrum still holds many secrets.

Thomas McErlean and **Norman Crothers**
2007

Acknowledgements

The authors and contributors take great pleasure in acknowledging and thanking the large number of people who helped in various ways both during the excavation and bringing its results to publication. In particular a special debt of gratitude is owed to Mr David Chamberlain of Mahee Island, the owner of part of the site, who generously gave permission to excavate and facilitated the work in many ways. Both the excavation and its publication were made possible by generous funding by the Environment and Heritage Service (EHS) and sincere gratitude is owed to Dr Brian Williams who guided the project from its initiation to completion. Thanks are due for the granting of scheduled monument consent for the excavation and for permission to excavate within the Strangford Lough Special Protection Area (SPA).

Pride of place among the acknowledgements must go the small band of dedicated excavators who worked under extremely difficult foreshore conditions during all kinds of weather and unsocial hours imposed by the tidal timetable: Peter Bowen, Niall Dunlop, Samantha Hattrick, Andrew Gault, David Kilner, Stuart McCleary, Paul McCooey, Stephanie McMullan, Shane Maher, Peter O'Halloran, Paul O'Halloran, Keith Oliver and Trevor Rice of Archaeological Development Services Ltd (ADS), some of whom were also involved in the post-excavation work. Thanks are also due to Wes Forsythe and Rosemary McConkey of the Centre for Maritime Archaeology (CMA) of the University of Ulster, who assisted during the early stages of the excavation in 1999.

Much appreciation is owed to James Patience and David Wilkinson of EHS who acted as site surveyors during the three seasons. Furthermore, the former also made a vitally important contribution to the final illustrations and to discussion regarding the site in general. Many thanks are due to Malcolm Fry of EHS for painstaking conservation work on the large corpus of wood and other artefacts and to his assistant Alan Martin.

For their contributions to the illustrations it is a pleasure to thank the following: for photographic work Tony Corey and Gail Pollock of EHS and Nigel McDowell of the University of Ulster, Gillian Gilmour of ADS for the drawing of the artefacts, and Kilian McDaid and Lisa Rodgers of the University of Ulster for their infinite patience and seemingly endless application in preparing all of the final figures for publication.

Thanks are due to the host community of the excavation, the Mahee islanders, for help and hospitality, Max Browne (also a contributor) and Mrs Browne, Peter Browne, the late Patrick Carruthers, Roland Chamberlain, Tracy Hamilton, Mary Lee Jackson, Paddy and Julie Mackie and to Norman Patton of EHS, the diligent caretaker of Nendrum, for his constant assistance.

Warm thanks to Colin Rynne of University College Cork for access to his unpublished groundbreaking thesis on horizontal-wheeled mills and for discussion on various aspects of milling technology, and also to Niall Brady of the Discovery Programme. Appreciation is extended to Chris Lynn and Jackie McDowell for allowing access to their forthcoming, *An Early Christian Settlement at Deer Park Farms, Glenarm, Co. Antrim,* to Nick Brannon for permission to use material from his 1979 and 1982 excavations and for discussion, to Michael Lynch and Joseph Byrne for information and references to tide mills in North County Dublin, to Ken Neill, Declan Hurl, Gary Burrows and Gareth Edwards of EHS, Colin Breen of the CMA, Andrew Cooper, Rory Quinn, Peter Wilson and Bernie Lafferty of the School of Environmental Sciences in the University of Ulster, Mike Baillie of the Department of Archaeology and Palaeoecology, Queen's University Belfast, David Plunkett of Eling Tide Mill Trust, Mike King of Down County Museum, Cláudia Silveira of the Ecomuseu Municipal do Seixal, Portugal, Loïc Ménanteau of the Estuarium Association and Brian and Lesley Black of Byword Production.

A great debt is owed to Brian Scott, the series editor, for his editing of the various drafts of the work and to Sheelagh Hughes of Editorial Solutions for her great patience and skill in proofing the final version and to Julitta Clancy for indexing. Thanks are due to Bryan McCann of Leslie Stannage Design for the graphic layout and finally appreciation is given to Marie Maguire and the team at TSO Ireland for managing the publication process. Some of the contributors have recorded their own acknowledgements separately in the text but inevitably there are many others who helped in various ways and who deserve thanks, but are not mentioned here.

List of Contributors

Principal authors

Thomas McErlean	Centre for Maritime Archaeology (CMA), University of Ulster
Norman Crothers	RSK (Ireland) Ltd, Belfast

Contributors

David Brown	Department of Archaeology and Palaeoecology, Queen's University Belfast
Max Browne	Knockcree, Mahee Island, Comber, Co. Down
Cormac Bourke	Ulster Museum, Belfast
Gifford Charles-Edwards	University of Wales, Bangor
Anne Davis	Museum of London Archaeology Service (MoLAS)
Caroline Earwood	Lydbury North, Shropshire
Colmán Etchingham	Department of History, NUI Maynooth
Damian M. Goodburn	Museum of London Archaeology Service (MoLAS)
Allan Hall	Department of Archaeology, University of York
I.G. Meighan	Formerly of the late Department of Geology, Queen's University Belfast
Eileen Murphy	Department of Archaeology and Palaeoecology, Queen's University Belfast

Chapter 1

Introduction

Thomas McErlean

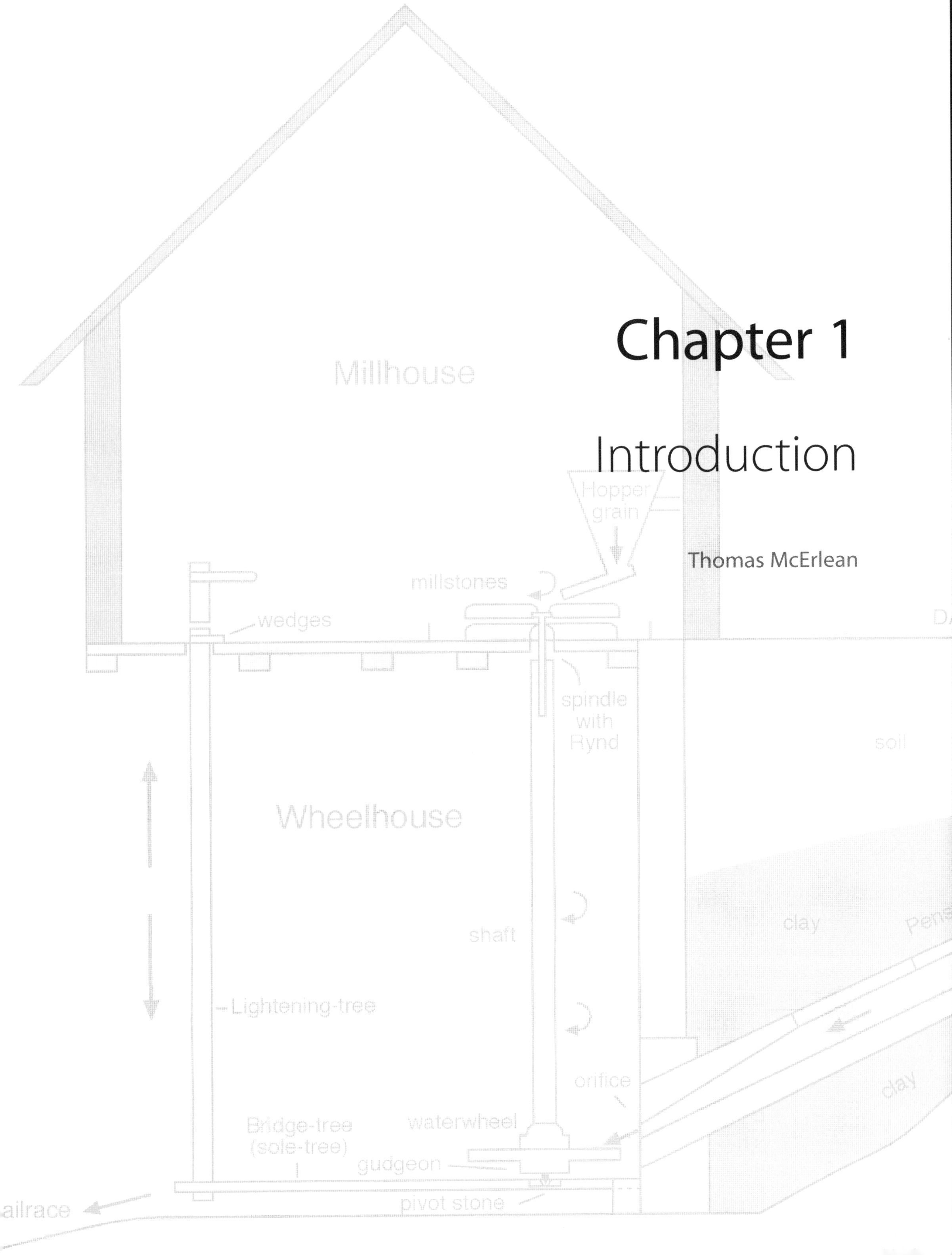

Chapter 1
Introduction

Thomas McErlean

INTRODUCTION

This is the story of the discovery of what is, at the time of writing, the earliest mill in Ireland. It was constructed in the years AD 619-621 to service the Early Medieval monastery at Nendrum, which was at its height as a monastic establishment in the 7th and 8th centuries AD. Accurate dating is crucial in assessing the significance of an archaeological site, and we are singularly fortunate that Nendrum yielded a wealth of oak timbers, which allowed precise dating of structures by dendrochronology. Sited on the foreshore below the island monastery on Strangford Lough, the mill was

Fig. 1.1
View of Nendrum from the north showing the monastic ruins and the visible remains at low tide of the dams of the first and second tide mills on the foreshore below the monastery (Gail Pollock, May 1999)

powered by the tides and has the further distinction of so far being the earliest example of a tide mill anywhere in the world. The first mill was replaced in about AD 789 by a second, which is one of the most complete examples of an Early Medieval mill discovered in Ireland. Both are of the horizontal-wheel type, as are the vast majority of Early Medieval Irish examples known at present. Both have many other claims to distinction and these will be described in the following pages.

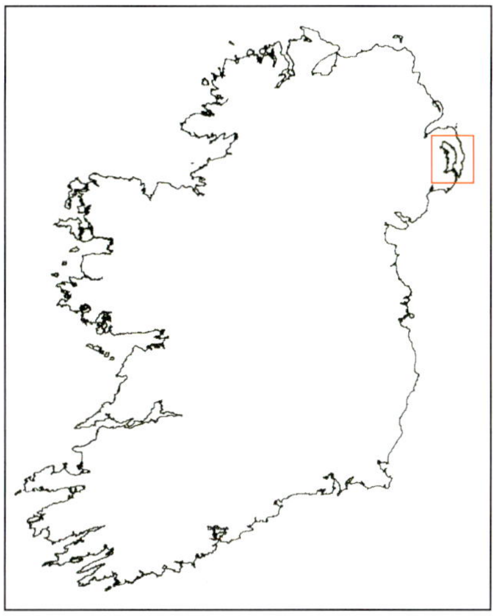

Fig. 1.2A
All Ireland map with inset of Strangford lough

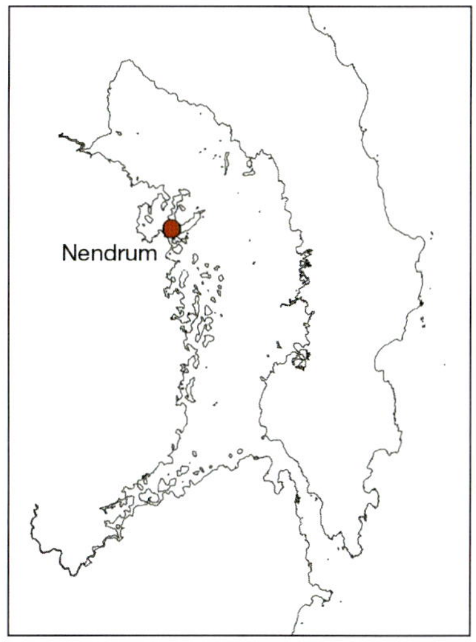

Fig. 1.2B
Strangford Lough

The Nendrum tide mills provide a fascinating insight into the Irish Early Medieval world, with the evidence they provide on hydraulic engineering, mill technology and the social and ecological environment in the 7th and 8th centuries, and the organisation of an early Irish monastery. It is probable that, at the time of construction, both were at the cutting edge of contemporary technology, and that the builders incorporated the latest innovations in water-powered milling. At Nendrum, situated on a tidal island devoid of fresh water streams, the designers of the first mill turned to the latent power of the twice-daily rise and fall of the tides, which washed the shore at the bottom of the monastic enclosure. To harness the power of the tides was not a simple matter. It involved great technological difficulties, and represented a major investment in material and labour.

Mill 1 appears to have been a great success and served for over 150 years. However, during its working life it is likely to have become run down and defects in its design may have emerged. This, combined with advances in mill technology, may have made it seem increasingly out of date, with the result that the old work was decommissioned and a grand new mill was built. Among the many interesting aspects of the excavation was attempting to work out what these design problems might have been and how they were solved, and detecting the technological advances of the period. Though designed in the 7th and 8th centuries, the Nendrum tide mills have a particularly modern appeal. The wheel has come full circle, and sources of green energy latent in wind and tides are once again seen as viable alternative power sources that constitute renewable environmental assets.

Fig. 1.2C
Nendrum and surrounding area

THE EXCAVATION

Excavation commenced early on the morning of Monday April 19th, 1999, with a small team of eight archaeologists, three from the Centre for Maritime Archaeology, University of Ulster, Coleraine and five from Archaeological Development Services Ltd. backed up by the surveying, photography and conservation staff of the Environment and Heritage Service (EHS). The original brief was modest, and this was intended to be one of a number of small-scale excavations to be carried out during the spring and summer of 1999. The aim was to provide information on sites, recorded during the Strangford Lough Survey (McErlean *et al.* 2002), which had presented problems of interpretation, or were under threat from tidal erosion. Previous interpretations of a rectangular tidal pond at Nendrum suggested that it was a fishpond, and that the linear band of stones across the foreshore of the bay was a fish trap. Indeed, the latter had been given statutory protection as such by scheduling. However, survey work carried out during the previous autumn had cast serious doubts on the validity of these interpretations.

The excavation was planned to last for two weeks, after which the team was to move on to investigate other problematical intertidal sites around the lough. In the first few days two small trenches were opened up. The first, Trench 1, measuring 12m by 3m, was located on the foreshore at the eastern end of the large east-west embankment (see Fig. 3.1B). In this area, surface observation showed stone kerbs in the configuration of an open rectangle, with the two long sides running down the shore and superficially resembling some of the many boat slipways around the lough. The second trench, Trench 2, measuring 4m by 2m, was located in the car park immediately adjacent to the monastic complex and in line with the western end of the of the east-west embankment (see Fig. 3.3B). This was intended to ascertain if the embankment here originally extended under the reclaimed land to connect with the monastic precinct. It was also designed to provide an area in which to work when Trench 1 was covered at high tide.

The ground under Trench 2 had been disturbed in the recent past by pipe-laying and no archaeology was encountered. In Trench 1, the stone kerbs proved to be tops of a wall forming a structure like a boat dock, which had been filled in at sometime in the past with a mixed deposit of orange clay and large boulders. By noon on the last scheduled day of the excavation, neither dateable material nor any clear evidence for the function of the structures encountered had been found.

The decision was made in the light of funding and other commitments of the survey project to abandon the excavation. As the last few hours of work were being carried out despondently, two dramatic developments took place. The first was the discovery of a small sherd of souterrain ware and the second, that of a fragment of a granite millstone. These two small items of information, one supplying a date range for the site the other a function, revealed that it was a tide mill of Early Medieval date serving the monastery on the adjacent shore. It was one of those moments which occasionally occur on archae-

Fig. 1.3
View of the dams at low tide from the north west showing the site of both mills under excavation (Gail Pollock, May 1999)

ological excavations when, in the process of painstaking and laborious work producing few results, a vital piece of evidence emerges that changes everything and the excitement of a major discovery takes over. The main effect was that the 'two-week' excavation, due to end on the afternoon of April 30th, continued over the spring, through summer and autumn and into the dark days of winter, finally ending on the day before Christmas Eve 1999. Subsequently, further work was done on the site in the spring and summer of 2000 and in the summer and autumn of 2001.

The tide mills are situated on the sheltered bay below and to the east of the monastery and represent an extension of the monastic precinct onto the shore. Before excavation, the ruins of their millpond embankments or dams were visible as two enigmatic, linear stone features on the foreshore. That of the first mill was prominent at low water as a band of boulders running north-west/south-east across the fluid mud, and at high tide as a ribbon of seaweed enclosing a roughly-triangular millpond (see Fig. 1.4). The second mill was constructed over its predecessor and, to a great extent, destroyed its remains (see Fig. 1.5). It was designed on a different plan, with the construction of a smaller, rectangular millpond enclosed by a large, stone-clad dam running east–west parallel to the southern shore of the bay. Parts of this dam were so well preserved that it had the appearance of being of relatively recent construction.

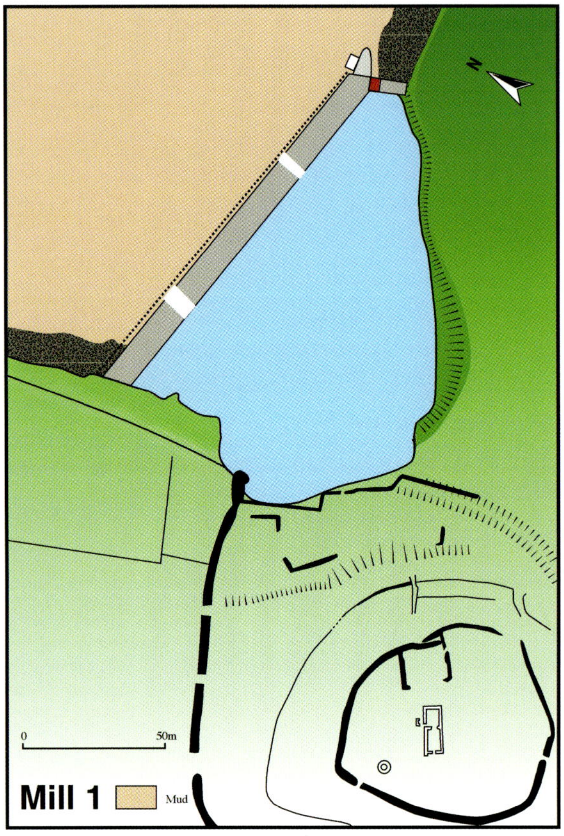

Fig. 1.4
Plan of Mill 1, showing its dam, millpond and the site of the mill (red) with the ruins of the monastery. The millpond is shown at low water when it would have been full of trapped tidal water and milling could commence

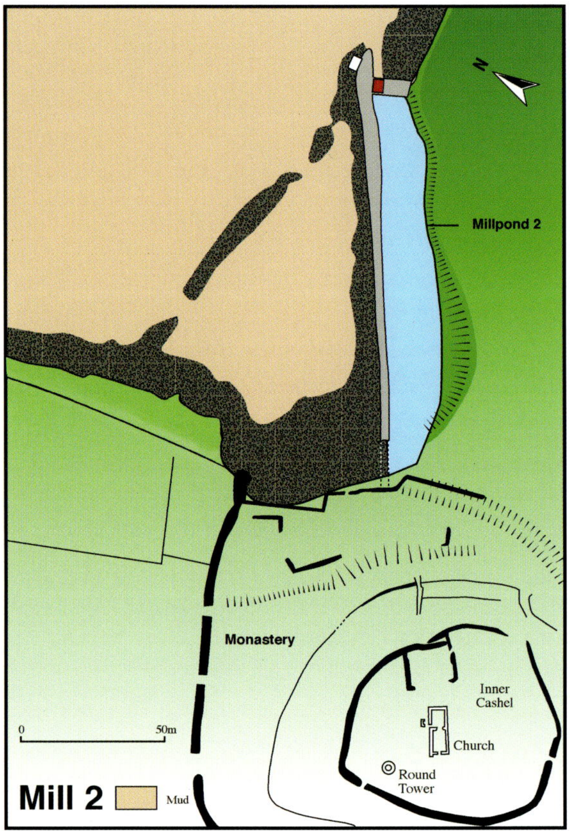

Fig. 1.5
Plan of Mill 2 showing its dam, millpond (and ruins of the dam of Mill 1) and the site of the mill (red) over that of Mill 1

During excavation, it was thought that features and stratigraphy encountered supported the interpretation that there was an intermediate mill between those of AD 619 and AD 789, something that was suggested in a number of interim reports (McErlean and Crothers 2001; McErlean *et al.* 2002). However, subsequent analyses demonstrated that this was not the case and that evidence used to argue for the existence of an intermediate structure can be attributed to either Mill 2 or Mill 1.

During the long months spent working on the foreshore, a special affinity spanning the centuries grew between the excavation team and the original creators and users of the mills. We shared with the labourers who dug the foundation courses of the dam during the months of AD 619, 620 and 621, the discomfort of working in wet, sticky mud and having our labour covered twice daily by the tides. Our working timetable, as theirs, was dictated by the monthly tidal cycle, with its frequently unsociable hours, when low water fell in the early morning or late evening. This too created an empathy with the generations of millers whose working hours were determined by the timing of low water. In attempting to work out the design of the mills and problems of interpretation, we felt close to the challenges faced by the early millwrights who designed the tide mills and solved all of the difficulties of impounding tidal water and transforming it into a power source.

The excavation produced a large body of information about many aspects of the Early Medieval period, which is described and interpreted in the following chapters. Chapter 2 covers the excavated structures and features of Mill 1, while those of Mill 2 are discussed in Chapter 3. The dams and millponds of both mills are discussed in Chapter 4, the penstocks in Chapter 5, the waterwheels in Chapter 6 and the millstone in Chapter 7. Study of the local tidal conditions at Nendrum, together with the excavated information, supply sufficient evidence on which to base estimates of the energy potential and milling capacity of Mill 2, and aspects of its hydraulic engineering and design, which are discussed in Chapter 8. The wet foreshore context of the excavation favoured the survival of a large amount of wood, and the assemblage included many wooden artefacts, wattle fences, structural timbers from the dams and mill parts. These are described in Chapter 9. The excavation also produced an interesting *corpus* of Early Medieval animal bone, discussed in Chapter 10, which provides an insight into the diet and monastic economy of the 7th and 8th centuries.

A revaluation of aspects of the historical sources on Nendrum is provided Chapter 11 and draws attention, in particular, to the presence of bishops in the monastery in the 7th and 8th centuries. The discovery of the tide mills has added a whole new dimension to the interpretation of the monastery, which demands a new assessment of previous work, especially the results of the 1922–1924 excavations, and this is offered in Chapter 12. The body of artefactual material recovered during the 1922–1924 excavations is still the most extensive *corpus* from an early Irish monastic site and in Chapter 13 is given a fresh appraisal in the light of modern research. All strands of information are then brought together in the concluding Chapter 14. As the book covers a number of major themes concerning monastic archaeology and the archaeology of early mills it would seem appropriate, before proceeding, to provide the reader with a basic introduction to the monastery of Nendrum and to the archaeology of Irish Early Medieval mills in general and to horizontal-wheeled mills and tide mills in particular.

NENDRUM MONASTERY

The ruins of the monastery are situated on Mahee Island, the largest of the numerous islands in Strangford Lough (McErlean *et al.* 2002). The island takes its name from the saint Mo-Choí, whose cult was especially promoted at the monastery. Mo-Choí is a shadowy historical figure (see Chapter 11) whose death is recorded in the *Annals of*

Ulster (AU) as having taken place in either AD 497 or 499. His ordination by St Patrick is mentioned in some of the later Patrician sources, but whether or not he was the actual founder of the monastery is uncertain.

In the mid-6th century, Irish society experienced a great monastic movement when many of the major monasteries, which were to dominate Irish society in the 7th and 8th centuries, were founded. It is not possible on present evidence to date the foundation of Nendrum to the 6th century but certainly by the early 7th century, it was sufficiently well-established to undertake the construction of an ambitious tide mill, presumably to service the needs of a large community of monks. By the mid-7th century, some of its abbots and other clerics were sufficiently important to have their deaths recorded in the annals, and a number of bishops are recorded at the monastery in the 7th, 8th and 9th centuries, adding to its status as a religious centre (see Chapter 11). The last reference to Nendrum in the annals occurs in AD 976. Thereafter there are no historical references to the site until the late 12th century, when it was refounded as a Benedictine Priory by the Anglo-Norman, John de Courcy. The site was rediscovered by Reeves in 1844 (Reeves 1847, Reeves 1902), and was extensively excavated in 1922–1924 by H.C. Lawlor (1925a) and swiftly published. Lawlor's excavation methods and interpretations now seem somewhat crude by modern standards, but in terms of structures found and artefacts retrieved, his work still stands as perhaps the most important early monastic excavation to have taken place in Ireland (see Chapter 12).

Since the late 19th century, Mahee Island has been joined to the mainland by causeways, but prior to this date access was by tidal fords. Thus, twice daily, the monastery would have been separated from the outside world by water. Islands, especially tidal islands, were a popular choice for many monastic communities in Early Medieval Ireland. The standing remains at Nendrum are impressive, and have survived largely because — unlike most other Irish monastic sites — they were relatively undisturbed by Later Medieval and Post Medieval burial and continued religious use. The ruins constitute one of the best surviving examples of what an early Irish monastery looked like.

Nendrum is laid out in three concentric, oval divisions, which defined spatially the organisation of the monastic community (see Chapter 12). The inner enclosure with its church, burials and round tower was the sanctified core, with the middle and outer enclosures being devoted to the more materialistic activities of a living community. Mahee, with its neighbouring islands and the adjacent coastal townlands, comprised the monastic estate, and the monastery with its enclosures formed its social and spiritual heart. The monastery, though primarily a religious institution, was part village, part industrial estate, part home farm and was, at its height in the 7th and 8th centuries, a well-organised social unit and nucleated population centre. The large mechanised mills can be seen as the symbols of the monastery as a flourishing and focused community and the administrative centre of a large estate.

IRISH EARLY MEDIEVAL MILLS

Ancient watermills fall into two categories classified by the rotational plane of their waterwheels. These are the vertical-wheeled watermill and horizontal-wheeled watermill. Since the beginning of the 19th century, at least 80 examples of the horizontal-wheeled type have been found in Ireland, in varying states of survival (Rynne 1988). Their distribution is spread throughout the island, from Co. Antrim to Co. Cork and from Co. Dublin to Co. Galway. This fact — in conjunction with their prominence in the Early Medieval Irish documentary sources such as law texts and the lives of saints — suggests strongly that they were a common component of the Irish Early Medieval landscape. In contrast, in the rest of Europe where the discovery of an early mill is a rarity and the large *corpus* of early Irish mill sites is regarded with envy. Irish horizontal-wheeled mills have attracted an extensive literature from the mid-19th century onwards. In 1856, MacAdam published a drawing of the Moycraig waterwheel, which was found in a bog in north Antrim (MacAdam 1856), and subsequently dated by radiocarbon to the 10th century AD (Rahtz and Bullough, 1977, 18). In spite of many subsequent discoveries, Moycraig is still the most complete example of an early horizontal waterwheel and mill shaft found so far and has been used as an illustration in mill literature worldwide (see Fig. 6.9).

Important syntheses of the Irish horizontal-wheeled mill have been carried out by Lucas (1953), Fahy (1956) and Rynne (1988). In his 1988 work and subsequent publications, Rynne has raised research on early Irish mills to a new plane and assessed their significance within a European context. One of his most important contributions has been demonstrating the contemporaneous use here of vertical-wheeled and horizontal-wheeled types, as previous to this it was believed that the vertical-wheeled mill was a part of new technology introduced into the country by the Anglo-Normans in the late 12th century AD. At Little Island, Co. Cork examples of both types of mill dated by dendrochronology (tree-ring dating) to AD 630 were found side by side (Rynne 1988, 1989 a and b).

Before about 1970, most Irish mills remained undated, although many were assigned to an Early Medieval horizon on the basis both of associated finds and general consensus. The major breakthrough came in the 1970s, with the impact of the creation of tree-ring chronologies based on oak (Baillie 1982), and the largely oak-built Irish mills provided ideal candidates for developing this new dating technology. Tree-ring dating, or dendrochronology, has had a major impact upon the study of early Irish mills, and has confirmed that the vast majority belong to the Early Medieval period. The first published mill to be dated by this method was at Drumard, Co. Derry (Baillie 1975), then placed in the 8th century. But with the later completion of a Belfast master tree-ring chronology (Baillie 1995), its construction could be dated with precision to AD 782. To date, 32 mills have been dated by dendrochronology to earlier than the 12th century (see Table 1.1), with three ascribed to the 7th century, nine to the 8th century, fourteen to the 9th century, six to the 10th century and none, so far, to the 11th century.

In the light of current evidence, it is possible to suggest that an initial early horizon of mill building, in the first half of the 7th century, is represented by Nendrum, Co. Down (AD 618 to 621), Little Island, Co. Cork (AD 630) (Rynne 1988, 1989a, 1989b) and Ballykilleen Co. Offaly (*c.* AD 636) (Lucas 1955). It is interesting to note that these early mills have a wide geographical distribution on the island — one from the north, one from the midlands and one from the south — and that two are coastal and one inland. This is sufficient to suggest strongly that it would be premature to formulate any theories about the diffusion of mill building from one area, or to suggest that one part of the country lagged behind another part in the early 7th century.

Currently, following this early horizon, there is a gap of over 60 years between Ballykilleen of *c.* AD 636, and the next site with secure chronology — Ballygormill South, Co. Laois (Lucas 1969, 23) — which is dated to *c.* AD 719. Baillie (1995, 126–127) has drawn attention to a major phase of mill building during the period spanning AD 770 to 850, when 15 sites were constructed. The total now dated to this period, including the second Nendrum mill stands at 16. The succeeding 123 years down to *c.* AD 973 furnish a further nine examples, and this is followed by a total absence of mill sites dated to the 11th century. There are two examples currently dated to the 12th and a further two to the 13th century.

It is important to try to assess the implications of this present pattern of mill chronology. The early 7th-century dates are highly significant and establish clearly that mills, both horizontal-wheeled and vertical-wheeled, were in use in the country, and that their origins may be sought in the 6th century or earlier. The 7th-century dates agree well with the earliest documentation of mills in the law texts and other sources which imply that mills were already an established part of the landscape. Baillie (1995, 125) has pointed out that start dates determined for oak timbers show a very low occurrence of oak that started growing between *c.* AD 720 and AD 840. This would seem to highlight a horizon when the large-scale exploitation of oak woodlands for building resulted in a period in the Irish landscape where few oaks forests where regenerating. It is possible, therefore, to see the rise in mill construction in the late 8th and early 9th centuries as an indicator of a period of a rising population; one when increasing land pressure may have witnessed a major phase of forest clearance and an increase of land being brought into agricultural use for arable crops and grazing. The dendrochronological evidence suggests some oak regeneration in 9th and 10th centuries, but during the same period mill construction was continuing, with nine mills dated to the late 9th and 10th centuries.

The present lack of mills dating to the 11th century is puzzling and, although negative evidence, raises a number of speculations. The seeming lack of mill building in this century might indicate a real decline in mill construction during this period and may suggest a decline in cereal production prompted by falling population levels. But other interpretations are possible. Might there have been a more widespread adoption of the vertical-wheeled mill in the landscape and, since these tend to have less archaeological visibility in comparison to horizontal-wheeled mills, might this have resulted in the apparent absence of mills in this century?

Table 1.1: Dendrochronologically dated early Irish mill sites (Source, the Palaeoecology Centre, Queen's University, Belfast)

Horizontal-wheeled mills			Vertical-wheeled mills		
Site	County	Date AD	Site	County	Date AD
Nendrum Mill 1	Down	619			
Little Island	Cork	630	Little Island	Cork	630
Ballykilleen	Offaly	636±9			
Ballygormill South	Laois	719±9 or later*			
Ballinderry	Londonderry	744±9			
Newcastle Upper	Wicklow	744±9 or later	Morret	Laois	770
Drumard	Londonderry	782	Ardcloyne	Cork	787±9 or later
Nendrum Mill 2	Down	789			
Crushyriree	Cork	799±9			
Cloghbally Upper	Cavan	803±9 or later			
Mullantine	Kildare	804±9 or later			
Cloongowna	Clare	808±9 or later			
Maghnavery	Armagh	810±9 or later			
Boherduff	Galway	810±9 or later			
Ballygearda	Kilkenny	811±9 or later			
Rasharkin	Antrim	822			
Ballynoe	Cork	827±9			
Cloontycarthy	Cork	833			
Ballydowane West	Waterford	841±9			
Keelaraheen	Cork	843			
Farranmareen	Cork	873±9			
Coolboy	Wexford	873±9			
Lowesgreen	Tipperary	890±9			
Brabstown	Kilkenny	913±9			
Clonlea	Clare	914±9			
Newtown	Tipperary	914±9 or later			
Ballyroe	Wexford	916±9			
Rossorry	Fermanagh	926±9			
Knocknarragh	Galway	973±9 or later			
Carrickmines Great	Dublin	1123±9 or later			
Clonlonan	Westmeath	1149±9 or later			
Corcannon	Wexford	1228±9			
Ballymascanlan	Louth	1243±9			

*The term 'later' is used when a sample is missing all the sapwood plus an unknown quantity of heartwood. The Belfast sapwood estimate of 32 +/- 9 years is added to the date of last heartwood ring present and 'later' to signify an estimated date after which the tree could have been felled.

Mills are well documented in the early Irish laws of the 7th and 8th centuries (Kelly 1988), which implies strongly that watermills were an integral part of the social and economic landscape. One of the most important texts for the study of the mill is *Di chetharšlicht Athgabála* which dates to *c.* AD 600 and lists 'the 8 parts of a mill', clearly referring to a horizontal-wheeled mill (MacEoin 1982). This text actually names 12 parts, amongst which are the water-source, the mill-race, the millpond, the upper and lower millstones, the shaft, the point of the shaft and the pivot stone, the penstock or chute, and the sluice gate (MacEoin 1982, 15).

Coibnes Uisci Thairidne, a legal text of probable mid 7th-century date, the title of which translates literally as 'Kinship of conducted water', deals with some of the legal aspects of milling, mill construction, mill-races and water rights (Binchy 1955; Kelly 1997, 245 and 482) and Rynne has pointed out that this is the earliest set of milling laws in Early Medieval Europe (Rynne 1989a, 111). In the early 8th century text *Críth Gablach,* a high-ranking freeman farmer was expected to have his own mill, while one of lower rank might have a share in one (Kelly 1997, 245, 484). It was illegal to grind in someone else's mill without permission, or to build a mill on someone else's land. But a landowner had the right to cut a mill-race over the land of a neighbour if necessary (Kelly 1997, 434, 482). A heavy penalty was imposed for damage to, or destruction of, a mill (Kelly *op. cit.* 484). Legal commentary also refers to a *muilenn túaithe* a mill of the *túath* (territory), which was presumably a large one serving a wide area (Kelly *op. cit.* 484, CIH iv 1211.27; vi 2171.38). The millwright *(sáer muilinn)* was an important professional, who ranked along with the builders of churches and boats, and was afforded the same status as the lowest grade of noble in the text *Uraicecht Becc* (Kelly *op. cit.* 482). That there was a specialised miller is attested by the term *muilleóir* (Kelly *op. cit.* 484).

THE HORIZONTAL-WHEELED MILL

As the Nendrum tide mills (along with the overwhelming number of other early Irish mill discoveries) are of the horizontal-wheeled type, a brief introduction to the horizontal-wheeled mill is required. The defining characteristic of the horizontal-wheeled mill is that its waterwheel rotated in a horizontal plane, in contrast to that of the vertical-wheeled mill which rotates in the vertical. The transmission of power from the waterwheel to the millstones is performed by a vertical shaft and is therefore direct and does not involve any gearing, unlike that required by the vertical type. The mechanism needs only two bearings, one at the base of the waterwheel and the other in the hole at the centre of the lower millstone. A reconstruction of a typical horizontal-wheeled mill is shown on Fig. 1.6, which is based on examples still in use in recent times and on evidence from the large number of known Irish Early Medieval horizontal-wheeled mills. The mill building consisted of two storeys, an upper storey housing the grinding apparatus (the millhouse) and the lower storey or undercroft, which housed the waterwheel assembly (the wheelhouse). The waterwheel with its shaft was positioned directly below the millstones, which were on the floor of the millhouse above. The other major components of the mill complex were the millpond and its dams and sluice gates, the penstock or flume, a wooden chute shaped like a trough, which channelled the water to the waterwheel (see Chapter 5) and the tail-race which channelled the water away from it.

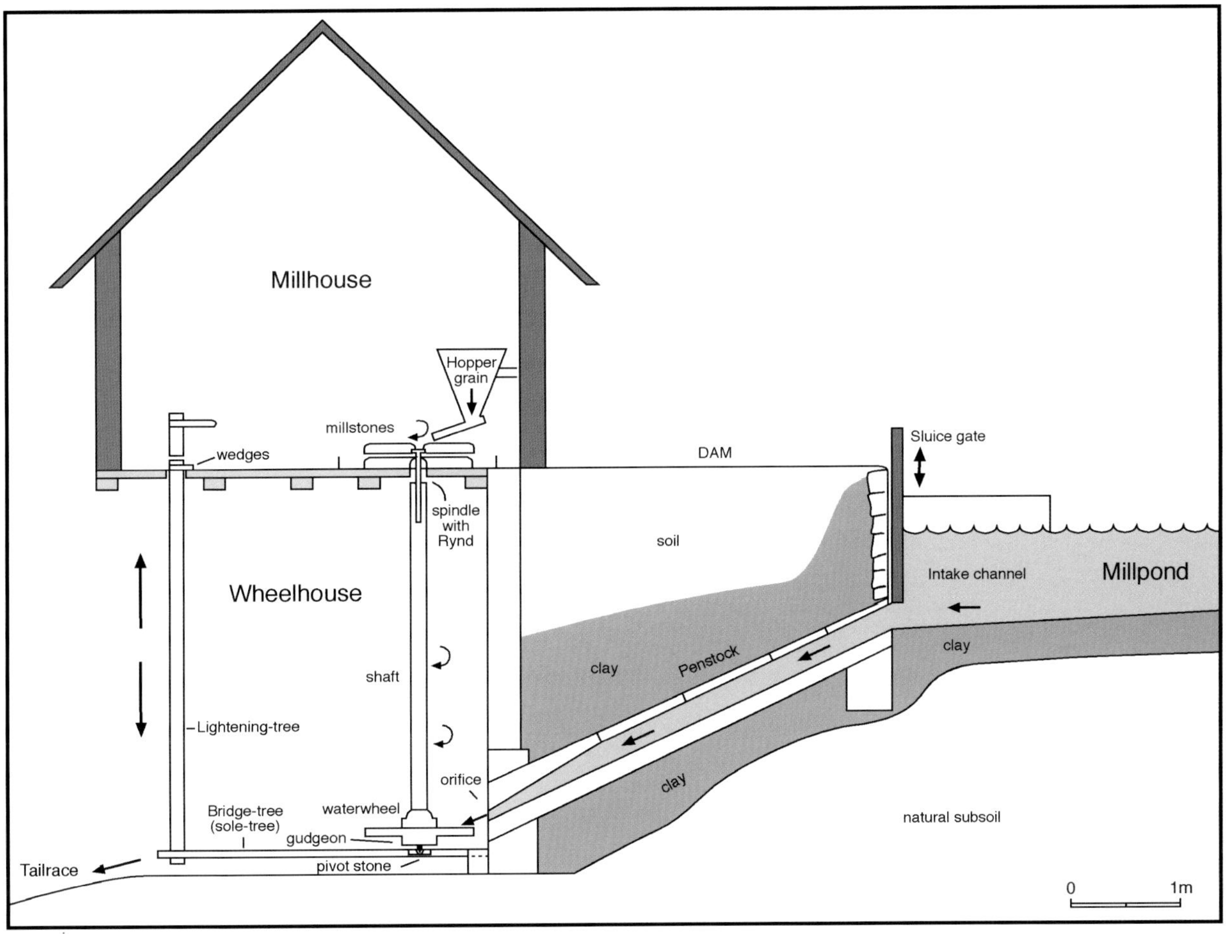

Fig. 1.6
A reconstruction of an Early Medieval horizontal-wheeled watermill showing all its principal working parts. The reconstruction is based on the large number of Irish Early Medieval archaeological examples with some aspects added from horizontal-wheeled watermills of recent centuries. The dimensions are based on Mill 2 at Nendrum.

The operation of the mill was relatively simple. Water was released by opening a sluice in the millpond and flowed through the penstock, which was inclined downwards in the direction of the waterwheel. It emerged through a small hole (the 'orifice') on the wheel-house face of the penstock as a pressure jet. The jet was angled onto the paddles of the wheel causing it to rotate and, by direct power transmission via the shaft and spindle, caused the upper millstone to rotate also. In all known horizontal-wheeled mills, the waterwheel assembly systems were very similar. The waterwheel was positioned a short distance out from and below the orifice of the penstock to receive the maximum impact of the water jet. In the centre of the base of the waterwheel was a pintle or gudgeon, which was inserted into a foot-bearing normally of stone (the 'pivot stone'). The latter was fixed on a horizontal plank (the 'sole-tree' or 'bridge-tree') located just above the floor of the wheelhouse. A shaft and spindle were attached to the centre of the upper side of the water wheel. At the end of the spindle was a T-shaped iron bar (the 'rynd'), which was keyed into a socket on the underside of the upper stone so that when the wheel turned, so did the upper stone. Grain was fed from hopper into the space between the upper and lower stones through a central hole in the upper stone (the 'eye'), and was ground between the moving upper stone and the stationary lower stone. Milling was most commonly a two-stage process, the first being the de-husking or 'shelling' of the grain, the second being the grinding into meal or flour. Differential grinding was achieved by varying the distance between the millstones, with a wide space being used for de-husking and the production of course meal, and a narrow one for the production of finer meal and flour. The process of adjusting the space between the upper and lower stones ('tentering') to produce the desired degree of grinding was achieved by a lever (the 'lightening -tree'), which could be operated from inside the mill. The lower end of the lightening-tree was attached to the end of the bridge tree, and its upper end went through the floor of the mill. Raising the lever lifted the bridge-tree which, in turn, raised the waterwheel and shaft and by means of the rynd, the upper millstone. The upper end of the lightening tree within the mill was fitted with slots into which wedges could be inserted to hold the millstones at the required distance apart.

A number of features of the horizontal-wheeled mill have influenced their survival in the archaeological record and led to the discovery of the large and growing *corpus* of Early Medieval horizontal-wheeled mills in Ireland. In the design of all the Irish examples discovered so far, it appears that the penstock was buried after being positioned when the mill was being constructed. The space above was then backfilled leaving only its open end or 'mouth' through which the water from the millpond entered on the surface, thus rendering it relatively protected from later agents of destruction. Similarly, wheel-houses being largely underground structures were left comparatively undisturbed when mills were abandoned, and survive relatively well. In the period immediately following a mill falling into disuse or being abandoned, some of the material from the millhouse above would have fallen into the wheelhouse below, leading to a gradual filling up of the space. The buildings above ground would have suffered the normal fate of such structures through time, and no examples of a millhouse belonging to an Irish horizontal-wheeled mill has yet been discovered *in situ*.

A significant number of penstocks have been found and are discussed in Chapter 5. In contrast to all previous examples found in Ireland and elsewhere, which have been of wood, the penstock of Mill 2 at Nendrum is constructed from hollowed-out stone blocks.

All of the Irish horizontal waterwheels discovered prior to Nendrum have finely-crafted, scoop-shaped paddles and the waterwheel of the second mill is also of this form (see Chapter 6). In contrast, the wheel of Mill 1 had simple, flat boards or 'vanes' of the type found in the horizontal-wheeled mills of Orkney, Shetland, Scandinavia and parts of northern Europe and Asia. Complete or partial millstones have been found at a large number of sites and are discussed in Chapter 7. Mill 2 produced a matched pair

Fig. 1.7
Remains of the wheelhouse and penstock of a horizontal-wheeled watermill found in 1930 during work at Samuel M'Gladery's Brickworks, Springfield Rd. Belfast. This casual discovery and its state of preservation are typical of many other Irish horizontal-wheeled mill sites. The remains of the oak penstock are visible at the top centre of the photograph. Surviving features of the wheelhouse are the massive oak penstock support beam on the back wall and the two oak sole plates of the side walls. The bridge-tree on which the waterwheel rotated and its support beam have survived in situ on the floor of the wheelhouse (Photograph by R.J. Welsh, courtesy of the Ulster Museum).

comprising an upper stone and lower stone. There has been little research on the mill dams, millponds and mill-races of early Irish mills — with the exceptions of Mashanaglass Co. Cork (Fahy 1956) and High Island, Co. Galway (Rynne 2000) — as at most sites, little above-ground evidence is visible or has survived. One of the great advantages of the Nendrum evidence is that both the mill dam and millpond of the two mills are remarkably preserved.

Distribution

In the recent past the horizontal-wheeled mill had a wide geographical distribution stretching from northern and western China to south-western Asia, and from the Mediterranean basin to northern and western Europe (Rynne 1988, Moog 1994). The technology of the horizontal-wheeled mill is relatively simple, and remained amazingly unchanged and uniform over a long time span. Examples of 19th- and early 20th-century horizontal-wheeled mills in diverse parts of the world are almost identical to those found by archaeology in 7th- and 8th-century Ireland. The post-Medieval *Rodizio* mills of Portugal, for example, are remarkably close in design to the Irish examples (Rynne 1988, 2, 113). This longevity and continuity of technological design is a testament to its efficiency as a grinding machine for grain which served the requirements of society over a long period.

Origin

Whereas the vertical-wheeled mill clearly was in existence from at least the last century BC, since it was described by Vitruvius in *c.* 25 BC (Smith 1984, 72–73), due to the dearth of early archaeological examples and documentary evidence, the date and location of the invention of the horizontal-wheeled mill are presently unclear. To date, the earliest excavated example of the use of a horizontal waterwheel was found in a mill of late 3rd- or early 4th-century AD date, built in the ruins of a Roman bridge at Chemtou in Tunisia, as yet not fully published (Wikander 2000; Smith 1984, 74; Watts 2002, 47, 63, 65, 70). The design of this installation differs considerably from other known early horizontal-wheeled mills, and resembles that of an impulse turbine of 19th-century date. Apart from this somewhat remarkable site, there is little evidence for the use of the horizontal-wheeled mill in the Graeco-Roman world (Wikander 2000, 375–376) where vertical-wheeled mills seem to have been the norm. Although archaeological examples are presently absent, Rynne (1988) has suggested that the horizontal-wheeled mill must have existed in late-Roman or early post-Roman times, from where it was introduced to Ireland in the 6th century. Smith (1984, 73) argues for a possible origin in northern Europe, while noting the early example in Tunisia. Clearly the origins of the horizontal-wheeled mill are still a matter for research and more early examples are needed before any definitive conclusions can be reached (see p. 435). As it stands at the moment, the first mill and its waterwheel at Nendrum, provide the earliest dated example of a horizontal-wheeled mill in western Europe and indeed anywhere in the world.

TIDE MILLS

While the vast majority of known early water mills were powered by freshwater streams and rivers, tide mills in contrast — both horizontal- and vertical-wheeled mills — used the twice-daily rise and fall of the tides as their power source. Often referred to in the past as 'salt mills', 'salt water mills' or 'sea mills', tide mills worked on the simple principle of impounding water at high tide behind a barrier (or dam) on the foreshore. As the tide rose, water entered a tidal millpond through a sluice gate in the dam which closed at high water. When the tide dropped sufficiently to leave the waterwheel free of the water that would impede its rotation, the impounded water in the millpond was released to turn the wheel to allow milling to start. Milling ceased when the rising tide reached the waterwheel again or when the millpond was empty. On most tides, the mill could have worked for about four hours; two hours before and two hours after low water, giving approximately eight hours each day for milling. Once the problem of creating an effective dam was overcome, the tide mill had the great advantage over its freshwater counterpart of having a totally reliable water source unaffected by summer droughts, and its wheel could turn throughout the year. Drawbacks included considerable effort in keeping the dam in good order as it was exposed to damage by storms, tidal surges and occasional abnormally high tides. The same natural events also rendered the millhouses vulnerable to damage. In some areas, relatively fast silting-up of the tidal millpond would have created problems. One of the disadvantages of the tide mill for the miller was having to work frequent night shifts at times when low tides occurred during the hours of darkness.

In Late- and Post-Medieval times, the main concentration of the tide mill was on the Atlantic coastline of western Europe from south-western Spain to southern England (see fig. 1.8). During the period of colonial expansion from the 17th century onwards, tide mill technology was spread to North America and elsewhere. A very small number, presently three known examples, were built in the early to mid-19th century in Australia (Minchinton 1977).

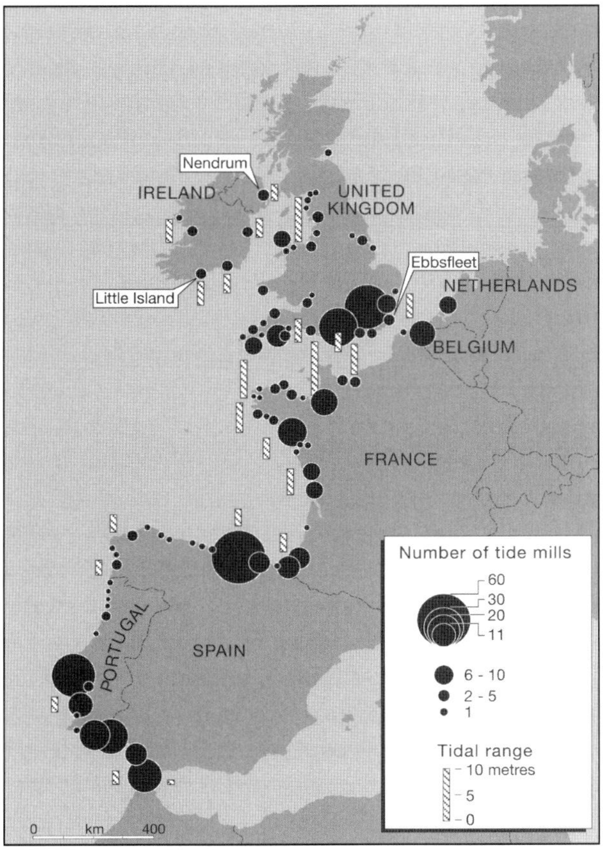

Fig. 1.8
Distribution of Post-Medieval tide mills in Western Europe (source Menanteau and Kostrowicka 2005, 97 with additions) and the location of the three presently known Early Medieval examples

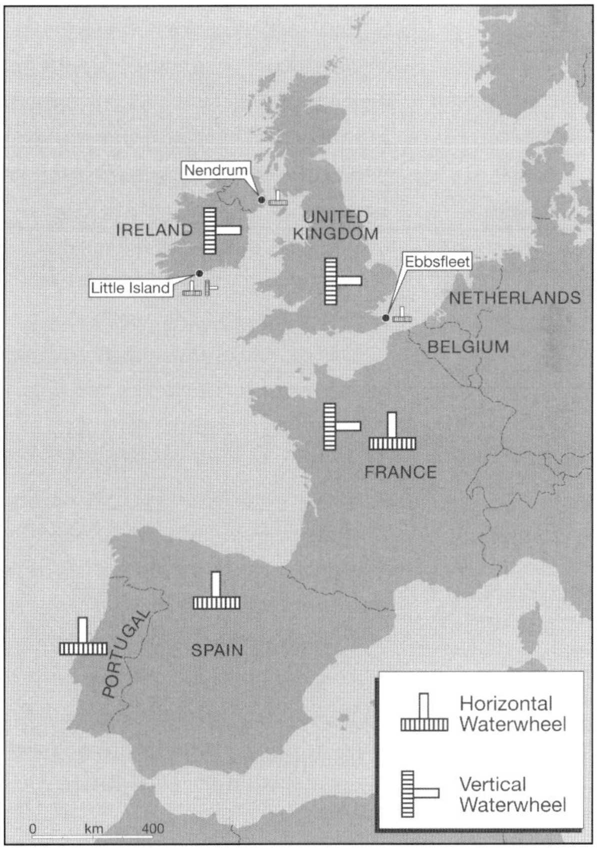

Fig. 1.9
The distribution of the use of vertical and horizontal waterwheels in tide mills. (Source, Azurmendi Pérez and Gómez Carbello 2005, 22 with additions)

Particularly dense and localised concentrations were to be found along parts of the coastlines of Portugal, Spain and in western France where they were a prominent component of the coastal economy down to the beginning of the 20th century. In Spain, notable zones of density include the Bay of Cadiz in the south-west and Cantabria in the north. In Portugal, the estuaries of the Tagus, Sado, Arade and the Formosa in the Algarve had high concentrations too (Seixal 2005; Santos 1992). The Tagus estuary alone had at least 40 examples (Seixal 2005). The Portuguese and many of the Spanish examples are of particular interest to the study of early Irish mills, because of their continued use of the horizontal waterwheel until recent time. In France there was a large concentration of tide mills in Brittany with the estuary of the Rance in the Gulf of St Malo and the Gulf of Morbihan having high local densities (Menanteau and Kostrowicka 2005).

Tide mills in England had a wide distribution stretching from the Solway Firth in the north-west around to the Humber Estuary on the north-east (Wailes 1939, Day 1994). Minchinton (1977, 340) lists 169 tide mills that existed in recent centuries, and this may be an underestimate of the true number. Within this distribution are a small number of areas of concentrated density with the Thames estuary, especially in the vicinity of London, being particularly notable. There were also significant numbers on the coastline around the Solent and Southhampton Water, especially the Portsmouth area and the Isle of Wight. They were also present in significant numbers along the coastlines of Devon and Cornwall, especially in the estuaries of the Tamar and Tavy and around Plymouth. The main concentration along the Welsh coast occurs in Anglesey (Lucy 1939 and 1945), and tide mills were also present in small numbers along the Lancashire and Cumbrian coasts (Minchinton 1977).

Fig. 1.10
Distribution of currently known Irish tide mills

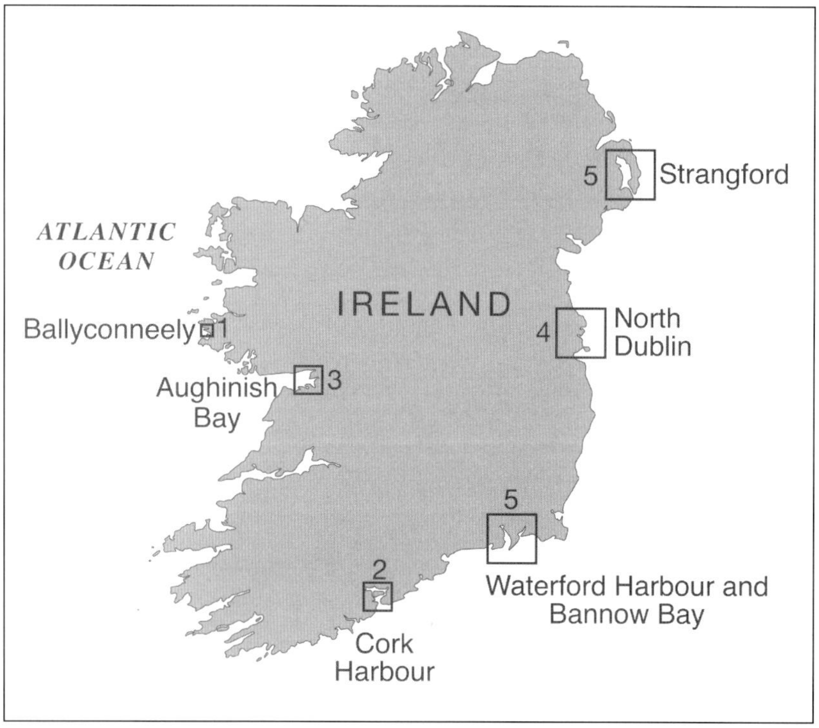

The number of tide mills around the Irish coastline in the past appears to have been relatively small. Provisional research has identified approximately 20 sites (see Fig. 1.10), of which 18 are Post-Medieval. But it is highly probable that further field survey and documentary research will add significantly to this number. Examples are found along the coastlines of counties Down, Dublin, Wexford, Waterford, Cork and Galway. Within this distribution are three areas of concentration — Strangford Lough, Co. Down, the coastline between Balbriggan and Portmarnock in northern Co. Dublin and around Waterford Harbour in Co. Wexford and Co. Waterford.

There are four or possibly five examples in Strangford Lough, commencing with Nendrum (Green 1963, 47, Bowie 1977, 9–10). Writing in 1744, Harris (1744, 41 and 48) mentions two — one at Castle Ward and one at Ardkeen. The dam and sluice gates at Castle Ward are described (*op. cit.* 41) as follows

> A dead wall is carried across the gut, in which there are two arches, and in them two flood gates fixed, the one to admit the tide, and the other to keep it in or let it out, as occasion serves.

There is some confusion surrounding the location of the Castle Ward example (Gribbon 1969, 51 and 52). The estate mill within the farmyard of the Castle Ward demesne, which was first built in the early 18th century, was subsequently remodelled at various dates, and its location near the shoreline suits that given by Harris. This mill was not tidal in the early 19th century, but was served by an elaborate system of freshwater ponds. However, a short distance away at the southern end of Castle Ward Bay at the Black Causeway in Strangford Lower townland (td.) is the site of an 18th-century mill which appears to have used the tides, and this may have been the Black Causeway mill to which Harris is referring. It is possible that the Castle Ward example utilised the tides in the 18th century, and therefore two tide mills may have existed on the bay. Harris (*op. cit.* 48) also mentioned 'a salt-water mill' on a little bay some miles northwards of *Ardchin* (*recte* Ardkeen), on the eastern side of the lough. No trace of this mill could be found on the 19th-century Ordnance Survey maps, but its probable site is in Gransha td. where there are remains of a substantial wall stretching from the shore to the adjacent Horse Island and cutting off a large area of foreshore which may represent its dam (MRD 187:88). The last one to work on Strangford Lough — one of the last to work in Ireland — was built by J.W. Maxwell of Finnebrogue in 1824 (Green 1963; Gribbon 1969, 51 and 52; McCutcheon 1980) at the Saltwater bridge on the Quoile estuary near Downpatrick (see Fig. 1.11). This was in operation into the 20th century, and there are good remains of its dam, millhouse and vertical undershot wheel. It could work for three hours before low water and three hours after.

The north Co. Dublin group comprises at least four known examples which exploited the tides in constricted shallow inlets off the Irish Sea. They are Newhaggard td. near Rush, Baltray corn mill in Kilcrea td. near Donabate, Burrow td. near Portmarnock and Yellow Walls td. at Malahide (*pers. comm.* Michael Lynch, Fingall County Council). One of these mills (Yellow Walls) has 15th-century documentation (*pers. comm* Joseph Byrne) and all four were working in the mid-18th century as they are shown on Rocque's 1760 map of Co. Dublin and may have continued into the 19th century.

In the Waterford harbour and adjacent coastline, five tide mills existed in the past and it is highly probable that more examples will be discovered in this area of Wexford and Waterford. In the townland of Saltmills on Bannow Bay, Co. Wexford, a tide mill with a vertical wheel appears to have been still in use in 1803 (Colfer 2004, 62 and 64) and is the origin of the name of the townland. It was probably a successor to a Medieval one on the same site belonging to the Cistercian abbey of Tintern, a short distance away. In the same locality there is another townland called Saltmills, which is situated on the estuary of the Suir, and adjacent to Dunbrody Cistercian abbey. This can be taken as evidence of the existence of a tide mill most probably belonging to the Dunbrody Abbey. A water mill is mentioned at this location in a land grant of 1611 (CPRJ1, 205). Also on the Suir estuary, there was a tide mill in Ballycanvan Big td. in Co. Waterford (ASI Wa 18–001). In 1611 and 1615 the existence of two 'salt water mills' on a narrow creek off Tramore Bay, in Corbally More td. Co. Waterford is mentioned in land grants (CPRJ1, 193, 281).

Apart from these three areas, no other notable concentration of tide mills has yet emerged, although four other examples are known from around the Irish coastline. In Cork city, the 18th-century St. Francis' Abbey mill used tidal water (Rynne 1999, 79 and 82). At Rineen td. on Aughinish Bay, near Kinvarra, Co. Galway, a tide mill (ASI Ga 112–03701) called 'the Frenchman's mill', built by a Baron de Bastero in the 18th century, was still working the mid-19th and another existed nearby in Moneyscribe or Moneyscreebah td. (ASI GA 112–030). At Carrowmore td. there was a tide mill off Galway Bay (ASI Ga 102–024), and possibly another one at Ballyconneely (ASI Ga 049–001). All of the known Irish examples are on narrow, somewhat constricted, tidal creeks and on sheltered parts of the coast, which have a tidal range of approximately 2.5m to 3.2m.

The tide mill shared, with freshwater mills, a gradual decline in the late 19th and early 20th centuries, culminating in their virtual extinction by the end of the 20th century. By 1938, there were only ten tide mills working in England and Wales and, by the end of World War II, only three remained (Wailes 1938, 1; Day 1994, 3 and 4). The tide mills of western Europe and the United States shared a similar fate. The factors influencing their demise were similar to those which determined the fate of the freshwater mill, and include the use of steam and electrical power and the industrialisation and centralising of grain-processing at the expense of the small local mill. The high cost of maintaining dams, and the silting of millponds, among other things, were added problems. In recent years, as a reaction to their loss and in growing appreciation of their heritage value, a small number have been restored and are open to the public. In Portugal, Corroios on the Tagus estuary and Mourisca on the Sado estuary are fine examples with horizontal waterwheels. Likewise there are good examples in Spain at Pozo del Camino in Andalucia, Pozo do Cachón on the Ria de Muros near Corunna, and Santa Olaja at Arnuero in Cantabria, and in France at Moulin des Loges near Marennes in Charente-Maritime, Indret on the estuary of the Loire near Nantes, Moulin de Berno on the island of Arz in Golf of Moribhan and Moulin du Prat on the Ranche Estuary. Examples can also be seen in Belgium, at Rupelmonde on the Schelde-Mass-Rhine delta, while in England the Eling Tide mill on Southampton Water and The House Mill at Bromley-by-Bow in East London have been restored.

The cultural and topographical factors influencing the origins and distribution globally of tide mills have still to be fully ascertained. Their use in some locations was influenced, no doubt, by the absence of suitable power sources in the form of fresh water rivers and streams. Tidal amplitude can also be seen as an important factor, as their densest concentrations occur on coastlines with middle to high tidal ranges of over 2m, and they are generally absent along coastlines with low tidal ranges, those with less than 1m. Few are found, for instance, in the Baltic and the Mediterranean. Although they occur on a wide range of coastline types, most were sited on narrow tidal creeks and inlets whose constricted tidal flow made it convenient to create a dam and mill pond. Many occur in estuaries, as these combined constricted tide conditions and population concentrations with the attendant need for a mill.

The origin of the tide mill is presently unclear. There is as yet no positive evidence that they formed a component of Roman milling technology (Wikander 2000, 379) although a recent paper has argued that an artificial channel and wooden piling on the river Fleet in London may be evidence of a possible Roman tide mill dating to the 1st century AD (Spain 2005). At present the two earliest examples found so far anywhere are in Ireland, Nendrum, Co. Down, AD 619 and Little Island, Co. Cork (Rynne 1989a and b), dated to AD 630. Another early example is a horizontal-wheeled mill probably powered by the tides recently discovered at Ebbsfleet near Gravesend in northern Kent. It has been dated by dendrochronology to AD 684–720 (MoLAS 2003), and is one of the earliest horizontal-wheeled mills discovered so far in England (C.A. 2002, 193).

While mills are mentioned frequently in early Irish documentary sources, there are no obvious references specifically to tide mills. A solitary and isolated reference to a probable tide mill occurs in an Old English charter of AD 949, where a *Mylenfleotes* 'an estuary mill' is mentioned near Reculver in Kent (Rahtz and Bullough 1977, 24; Watts 2002, 73)). If the known distribution of tide mills in the recent past can be taken as a guide to their origin, the wide area covered by the Atlantic coastline of Portugal, Spain, France, England and Ireland stands out as the maritime zone where it is possible that the use of tidal power for milling emerged. At present there is insufficient information to narrow this down further. At present it is not known whether it can be considered an independent invention in this area or whether it can be seen as adapting Roman milling technology to the potential tidal energy encountered along the Atlantic coast.

An independent development of tide mill technology may have take place in the Middle East, as a 10th-century reference by the Arab geographer Al-Muqaddasi mentions the existence of tide mills at Basra in Iraq, on the Persian Gulf (Haverson, 1993, 15–17). Although it does not follow that all mills located on the coast were powered by the tide, it is probable that some of the coastal mills recorded in the Doomsday Survey of AD 1086 (Hodgen 1939) were tide mills. Documentary references to tide mills become more plentiful from the 14th century onwards, but comparatively little early documentation exists on them in the areas where they were common in the Post-Medieval period. In the Late-

and Post-Medieval periods, the tide mill emerges as a distinctive component of the maritime cultural landscape of the Atlantic coastline of western Europe. However, as practically no archaeological excavation has been carried out it is impossible to demonstrate their antiquity in these areas at present. This makes Nendrum a landmark site for their study and, based on the evidence which the site provides, it is clear that tide mill technology was well advanced in Ireland in the early 7th century and that its origins lie in the 6th century or earlier. As foreshore survey progresses, the number of discoveries of early tide mills is likely to increase.

Fig. 1.11
The dam of the Quoile tide mill at Saltwater Bridge on the Quoile estuary, Strangford Lough. This tide mill was built by John Waring Maxwell of Finnebrogue in c.1824 and was one of the last working tide mills in Ireland. (Photograph by W.A.Green c.1915-1920, WAG 2013, Courtesy of the Ulster Folk and Transport Museum)

Chapter 2

The First Mill *c.* AD 619

Thomas McErlean
and Norman Crothers

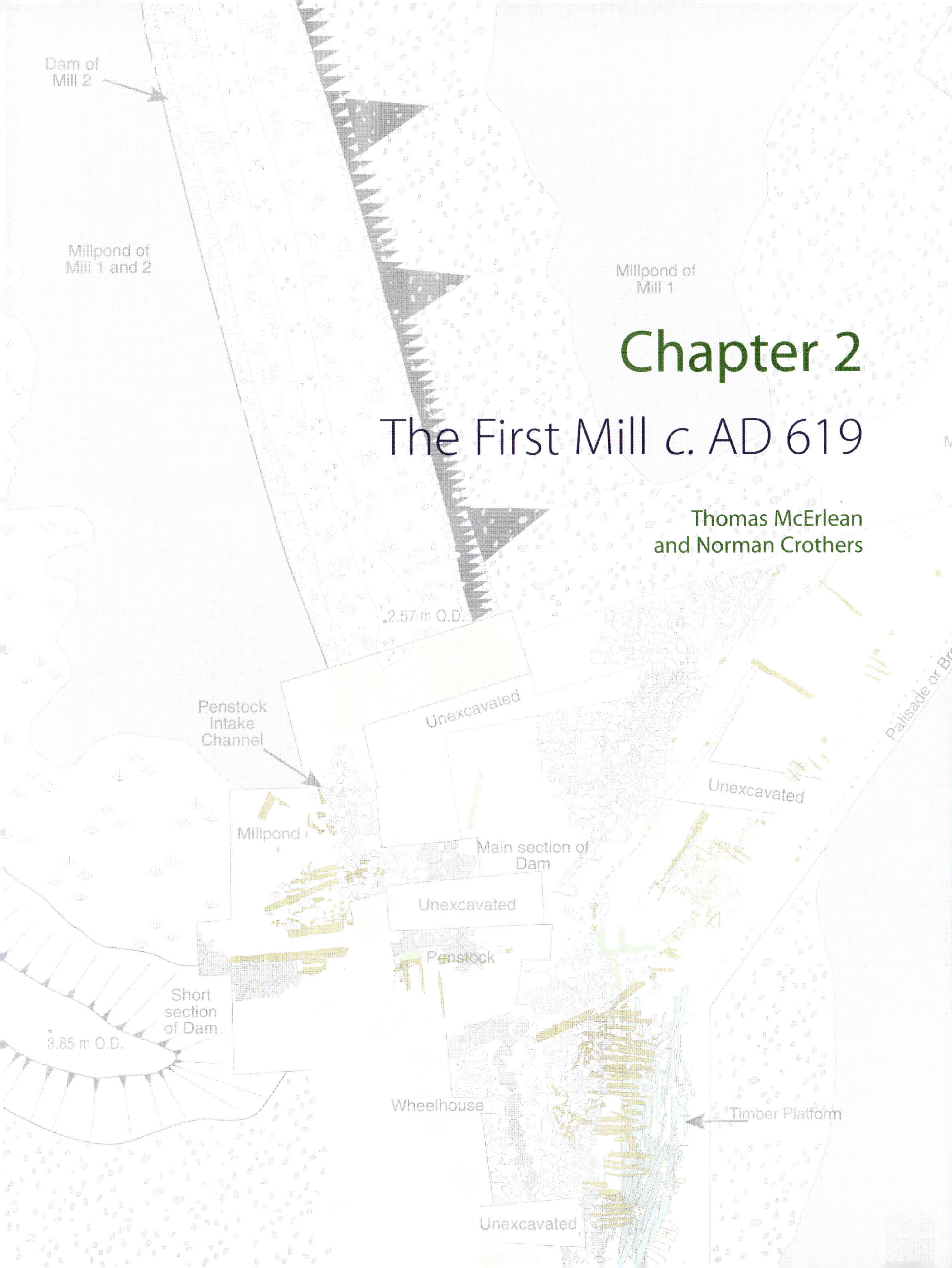

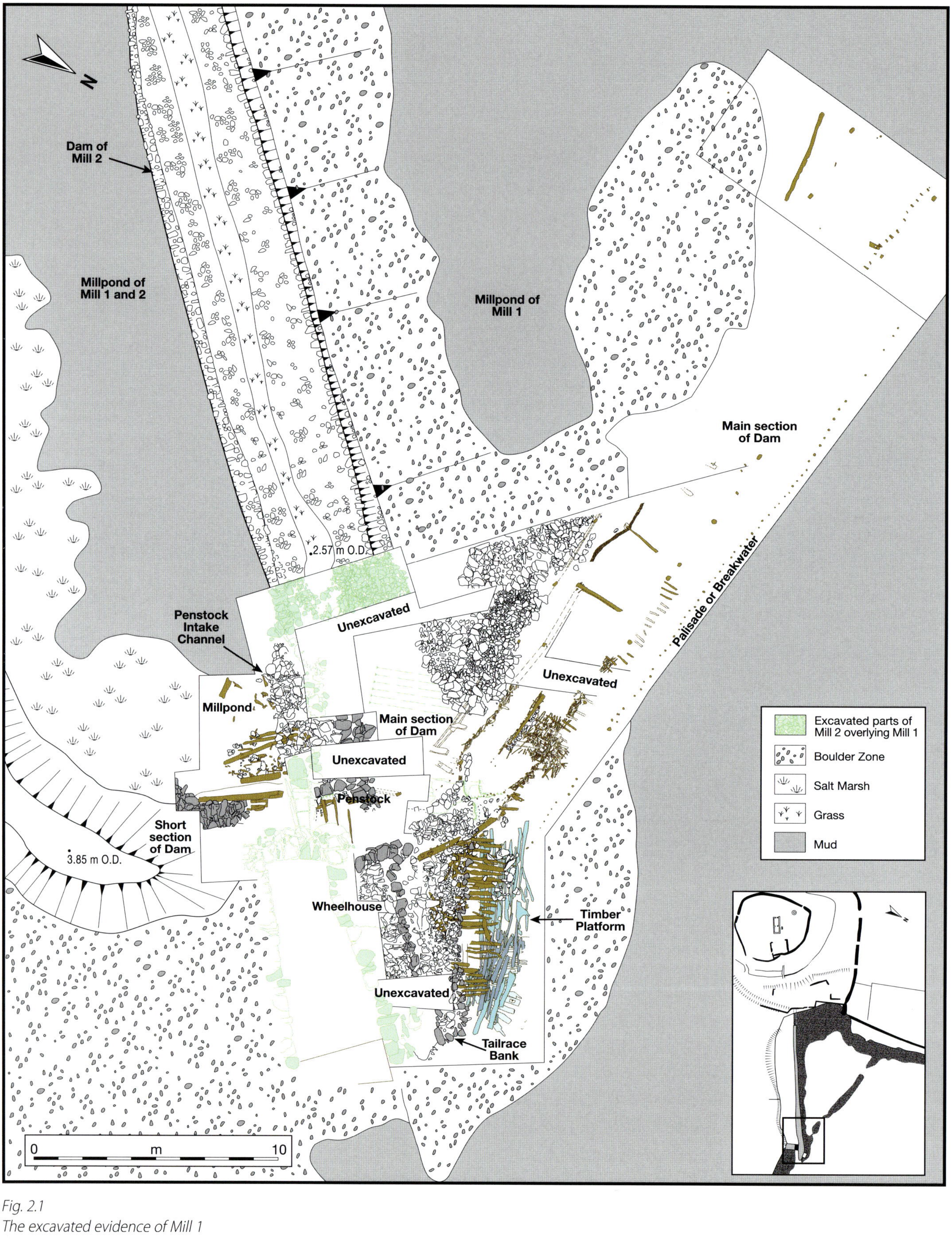

Fig. 2.1
The excavated evidence of Mill 1

Chapter 2
The First Mill *c.* AD 619

Thomas McErlean and Norman Crothers

INTRODUCTION

All of the surviving evidence of Mill 1, apart from the main section of its millpond dam, was buried below Mill 2. The excavation succeeded in revealing most of its main features, which are shown on Figs 2.1 and 2.2. and described below. The structures uncovered comprised the millpond and its dam and outer palisade or breakwater, the penstock intake channel, penstock (and possible evidence for a second penstock), wheelhouse, tailrace, and a wooden platform or landing place. Discussion of the excavation of the mill is presented in general geographic order from south to north, starting from the extant remains of the millpond and the short section of the dam, and proceeding to the penstock, wheelhouse, tailrace and the main section of the dam on the north and ending with the landing place on the north-east (see Fig. 2.2).

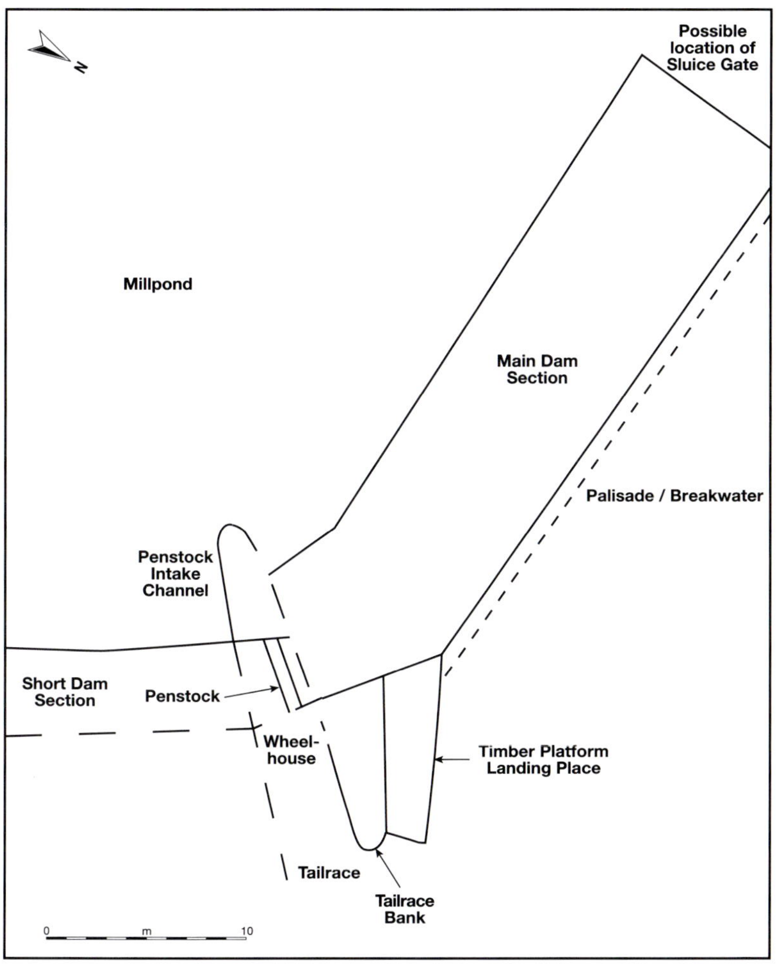

Fig. 2.2 Simplified plan of the main features of Mill 1

THE MILLPOND

Introduction

The tidal millpond of Mill 1 was enclosed by a long dam *c.* 110m in length, composed of two sections and extending from the shore on the north-west to the adjacent shore on the south-east. It enclosed an area of foreshore situated in the roughly right-angled bend of the western end of Mahee Island, forming a triangular-shaped tidal millpond with a surface area of *c.* 6,500m^2 (see Fig. 1.4). At low water, almost all of the bottom surface area of the millpond is exposed and, like much of the surrounding foreshore, consists of liquid mud, which is impossible to walk on. Approximately 14.5m^2 of the millpond was excavated, mainly in Trench 4 (see Fig. 2.4) and, although this was only a very minute part of its total area, work focused on the important, roughly rectangular intake area located immediately in front of the penstock and the site of the mill. The southern side of the intake area was formed by the shore, the eastern by a short length of the dam, approximately 13m long and orientated approximately north-south. The northern side was formed by the termination of the main section of the dam and was approximately 9m wide. On the west, it was open to the main body of the millpond.

Fig. 2.3
The millponds and parts of the dams of Mill 1 and 2 under excavation. In the foreground are the large beam (C34) in the dam of Mill 1 and the stone penstock of Mill 2. The scene conveys some of the difficulties of excavating in the intertidal zone where trenches are flooded twice daily.

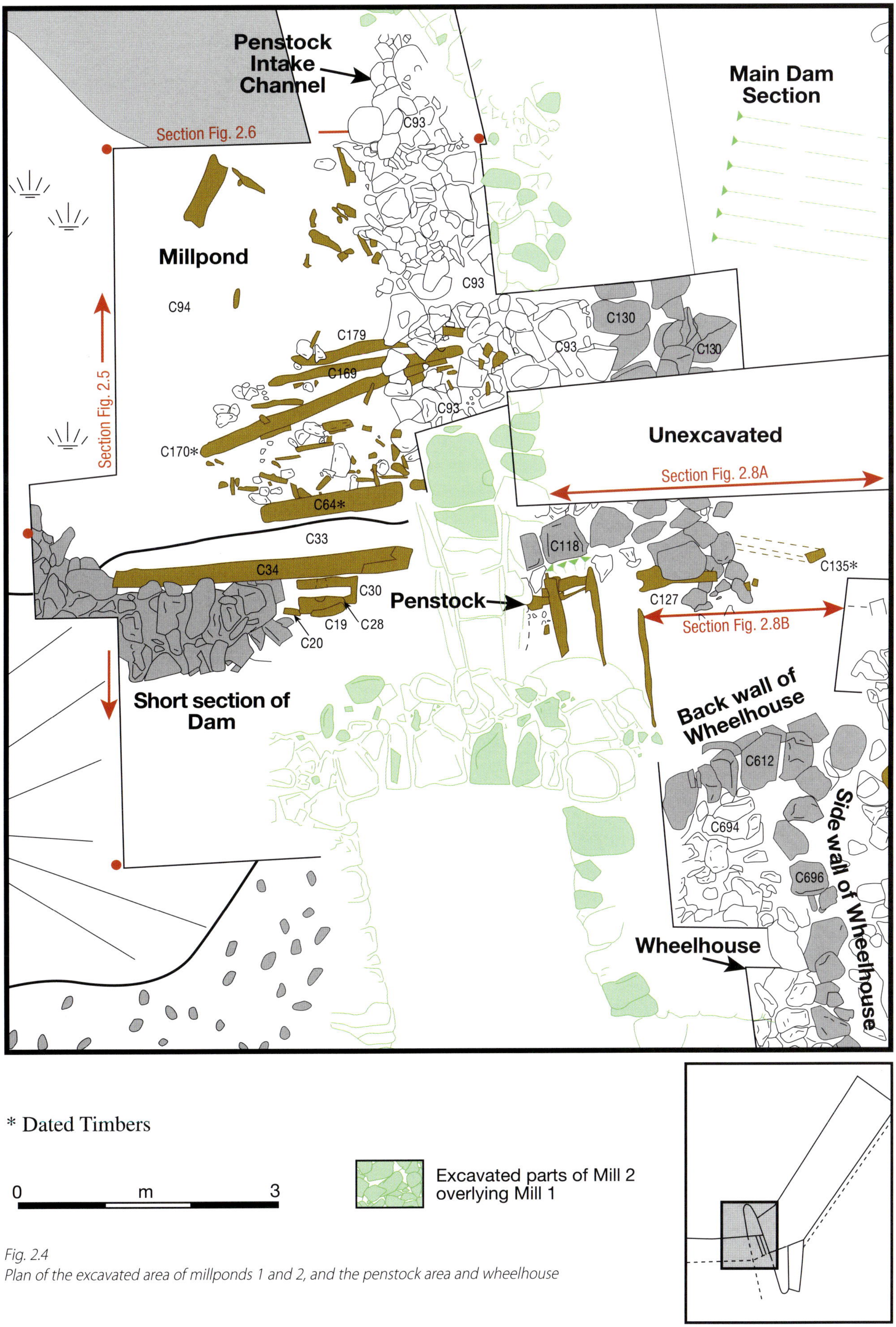

Fig. 2.4
Plan of the excavated area of millponds 1 and 2, and the penstock area and wheelhouse

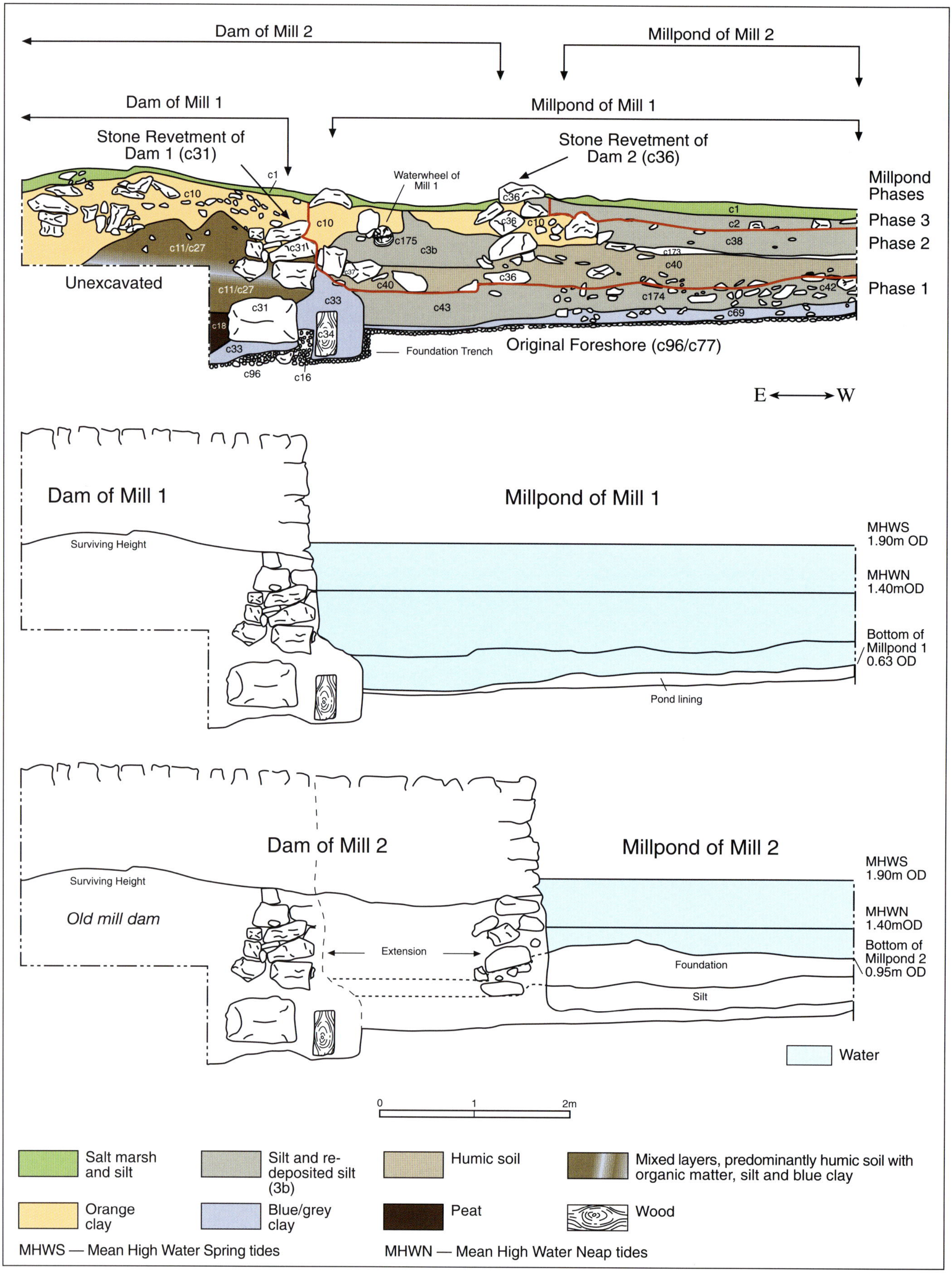

Fig. 2.5

East-west section (north facing) through the dams and millponds of Mill 1 and 2 with interpretative diagrams (for location see Fig. 2.4) Phase 1, Mill 1, Phase 2, Mill 2, Phase 3, post abandonment

The stratigraphy of the millpond was relatively straightforward. On its southern edge (see Fig. 2.5), the modern surface level is approximately 1.3m above the original shoreline and the layers occurring between can be conveniently divided into three phases, discussed here with reference to the sections shown in Figs 2.5 and 2.6 The sequence starts at the base with Phase 1, comprising approximately a 30cm depth of layers associated with the Mill 1 millpond. Above this, and representing Phase 2, lies 30cm of deposits associated with the millpond of Mill 2. The last phase, Phase 3 consists of naturally-deposited silt varying from 60cm to 70cm in thickness and representing silting that took place after the site was abandoned. Phases 2 and 3 are discussed in Chapter 3.

The original foreshore

The original foreshore, contexts C96 and C77 (see Figs 2.5, 2.6 and 2.8), consisted of a natural deposit of gravel, stones and shell material, and its surface sloped very gently from the high water mark located on the south and west down towards the north. On its surface were some small fragments of worked wood and wood offcuts, presumably representing waste debris from the construction phase of Mill 1 and its dam.

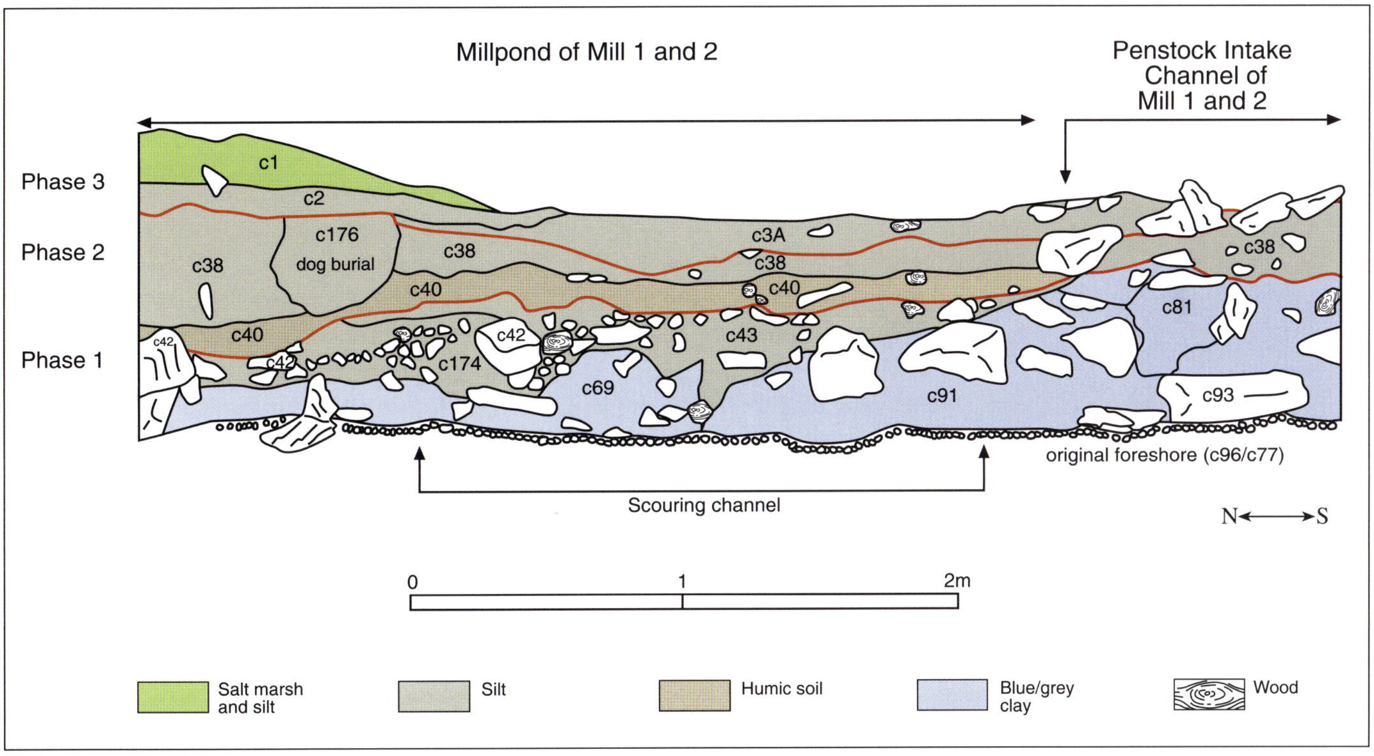

Fig. 2.6
North-south section (east facing) through the millponds, penstock intake channel of Mill 1 and 2 (for location see Fig. 2.4). Phase 1, Mill 1, Phase 2, Mill 2, Phase 3, post abandonment

The pond lining (C69)

On top of the original foreshore was a dumped layer of blue-grey clay with a gravel content (C69). Its thickness varied from *c.* 10cm to *c.* 30cm, becoming progressively deeper as the underlying foreshore sloped down to the north. The surface was largely level, but towards the middle of Trench 4 there was a wide, roughly V-shaped dip filled with silt (see Fig. 2.6), probably formed by scouring during the rapid passage of water released during milling. It is clear that the clay was laid down as a lining to form a water-resistant sealing layer and create a level surface at the bottom of the millpond. The surface of the clay lining, and therefore that of the bottom of the millpond also, was at 0.625m Ordnance Datum (OD).

A large assemblage of worked wood was found both on the surface of, and partially within, the pond lining. The great majority of the 176 pieces found consisted of small oak pieces, on average between 15cm and 30cm long, and including fragments of planks, beams and stakes. Most of the pieces had evidence of having been worked, but their small size prevented identification. A significant number, however, could be identified as offcuts from woodworking activities. The character and context of this assemblage suggests strongly that (like the small sample of wood on the surface of the original foreshore below) it represents largely debris from woodworking activity, associated with the construction phase of the mill. The waste seems to have been casually discarded and was trapped in the clay lining at the bottom of the millpond.

On the surface of the pond lining — and distinguished from the main assemblage of small wood fragments by their greater size — are a number of large oak timbers, which appear to be structural members *in situ* (see Fig. 2.4). Beam C64 was situated at the base of the face of the dam on the east, and was partially embedded in the pond lining. It was 1.60m long, 11cm wide and varied in thickness from 21–28cm. Its position strongly suggests that it was placed at this location to form a revetting element at the grey clay base of the adjacent dam (see below) to protect it from being undermined by water action. This timber produced a tree-ring date of late AD 618 or early AD 619 (Q9931, see pps 68-76).

A plank, C170, was found lying horizontally to the west of C64 (see Fig. 2.4), and measured approximately 2.86m long by 17cm wide and 11cm thick. It was aligned north-west/south-east, with its north-western end underlying the stones of the penstock intake channel (see below). It produced a felling date of late AD 620 or early AD 621 (Q9932, see pps 68-76). This is particularly interesting, as it is at least some 18 to 24 months later than most of the other dated timbers from Mill 1 which belong to AD 618/619 and its later date indicates that construction work continued to then.

Plank C169, also underlying the stones of the penstock intake channel, was adjacent to, and level with, C170 and touched the latter at its northern-western end (see Fig. 2.4). It was 2.3m long, 12cm wide and 5cm thick. To its west was another substantial plank (C179) with a similar alignment and also partially underlying the stones of the penstock intake channel.

The upper surfaces of all of these timbers were badly eroded, probably indicating that they were exposed twice daily between tides when the millpond emptied of water. Their large size and primary context seem to preclude any suggestion that they were simply discarded timbers. The simplest explanation is that they were placed on the surface of the sticky clay to facilitate walking during the construction phase of the mill complex. However, it is equally plausible that they were put in place to stop erosion of the surface of the grey clay when the mill was in operation, and to extend the protection from scouring by fast-flowing water, provided by the stone-lined penstock intake channel adjacent on the north.

The penstock intake channel (C93)

On the northern edge of the intake area, and leading down to the mouth of the penstock (and also the mouth of the possible second penstock), was a stone-lined channel (C93) composed of large stones, the size of which increased with depth, set in a matrix of grey clay, which formed a rough pavement. The channel had a maximum width of 2.2m and was traced for 7m into the millpond to the west. Among the stones were many small fragments of wood, similar in character to those found elsewhere at the bottom of the millpond. The position of this feature and its nature make it clear that it was designed to form a firm base to prevent scouring by the surge of water to the penstock(s). The channel was re-used to form the foundation for the intake channel of Mill 2 (see p. 93).

Built-up silt (C43)

Above the bottom of the millpond was sticky, dark brown silt from 20cm to 30cm in thickness, which contained occasional patches of peaty material and grey clay (see Figs 2.5 and 2.6). This can be interpreted confidently as having built up during the working life of the mill, being brought down by the release of the impounded water during milling. Towards the west of the intake area, and away from the mill site, it became greyer in colour and contained many stones.

Like the underlying surface of the pond lining (C69), this silt contained a significant amount of wood, consisting largely of small fragments. Unlike that found on the bottom of the pond, however, there were no large planks or beams. Interestingly, approximately half of this wood assemblage consists of small offcuts. It is highly probable that this represents a second major phase of woodworking activity, the debris from which was caught in the millpond silt. This activity would seem to relate to the dismantling of Mill 1 and the building of Mill 2. The occasional patches of grey clay and peat are probably also the result this building activity and derived from material used to construct the dam for the millpond of Mill 2. The concentration of medium- to large-sized stones, forming a rough surface (C42) within the silt layer on the western side of the trench, is interpreted as the result of dumping into the millpond silt as a part of the foundation course for the millpond of Mill 2 (see p. 92).

Environmental sampling from C43 produced seeds, mainly from plants of disturbed ground, wet habitats and grassland. These presumably reflect land type and use on the adjacent shore around the mill, and were washed into the millpond. Since the subject of the excavation was a corn mill, it was particularly disappointing that sampling produced relatively little cereal evidence, although the discovery of some grain and awn fragments of oats (*Avena sp.*) was particularly interesting.

The water levels of the millpond

The functioning of a tide mill depends on the rise and fall of the tides. Thus, an essential dimension of its design is the relationship between the levels of its various components to each other, and of the structure overall, to the tidal range in which the mill is situated. Therefore OD levels of all features were carefully recorded during excavation, as this information is important in understanding how the mill functioned. Basically, the level of the water impound in the millpond is governed by the mean high-water level (MHW). At Nendrum, the mean high-water level of the spring tides (MHWS) is at 1.90m OD (see p. 210 and Fig. 2.5). For most of the tidal cycle, this level would be the average maximum height of the impounded water in the millpond and, as the mean high-water neap tide level (MHWN) is at 1.40m OD for most of the tidal cycle, would be the average minimum level. As the level of the top of the pond lining (C69) is at around 0.625m OD, this suggests that the depth of the column of impounded water was in the range of 1.27m on spring tides and 0.77m on neap tides.

Fig. 2.7
Extreme accuracy in recording OD levels during the excavation was of crucial importance for the interpretation of the relationship of all parts of the mills to the local tidal regime

THE SHORT SECTION OF THE DAM TO THE SOUTH OF THE WHEELHOUSE

Introduction

The dam enclosing the millpond is in two distinct sections, the division between the two occurring at the penstock area of the mill (see Fig. 2.2). The main section to the north of the wheelhouse extends north-westerly across the foreshore while the shorter section discussed here, of which approximately 13m survives, lies to the south of the wheelhouse. The major structural elements are shown in the east-west cross-section (Fig. 2.5), the north-south longitudinal section through its core (Fig. 2.8B) and in plan view (Fig. 2.4)

This section of the dam has a north-south orientation and curves around slightly to the west, ending above high water on the shore. Apart from impounding water, this part of the dam joined the site of the mill to the adjacent shore, and would have been used as short causeway to the mill building. It has survived to a much greater height than the main section of the dam, due to its position higher up the shore and its re-use as part of the dam for Mill 2 (Fig. 2.9). But it is clear that much of its upper portion has gone, and

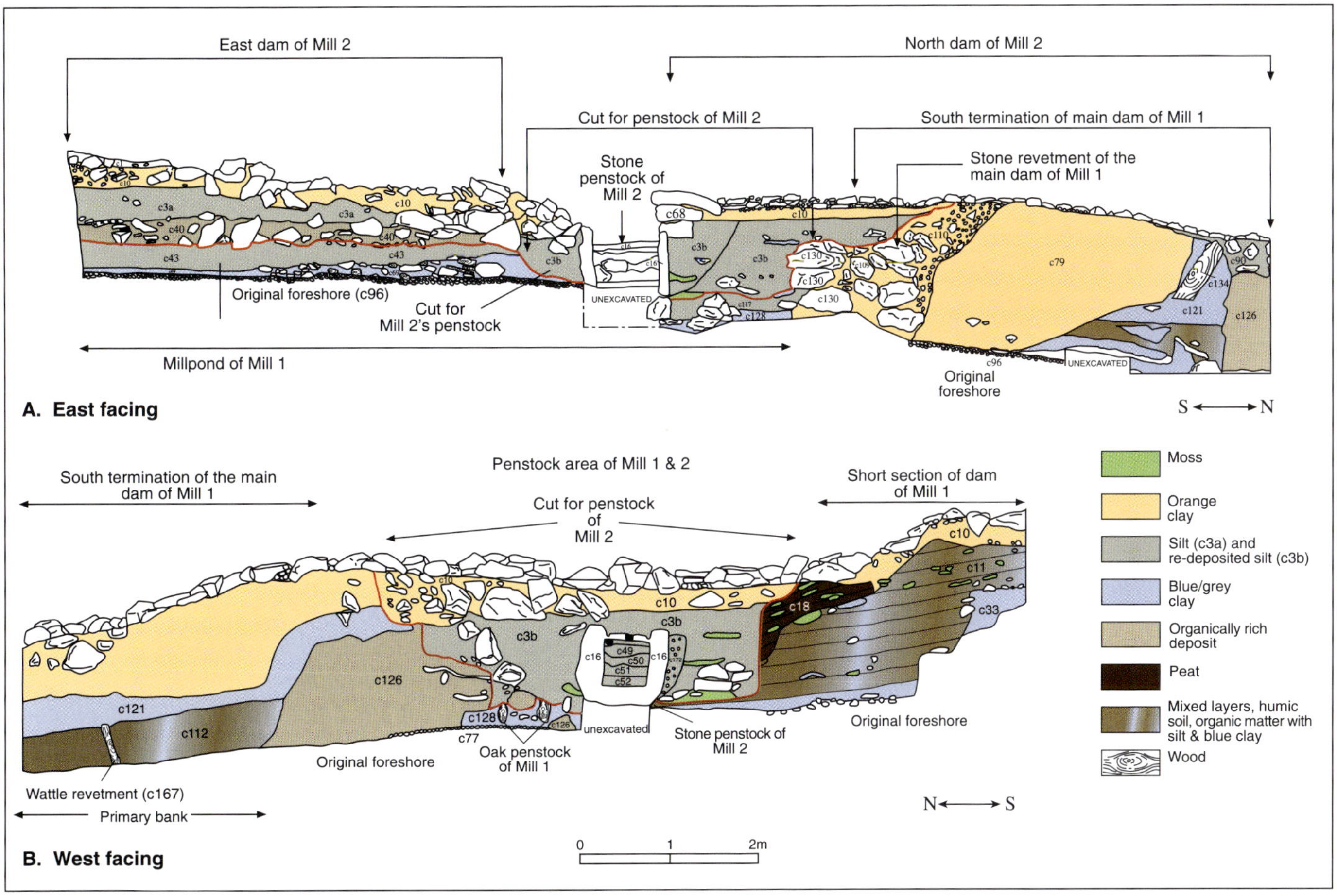

Fig. 2.8A
North-south section (east facing) through the millpond and termination of the main dam of Mill1 and the east dam and stone penstock of Mill 2 (for location see Fig. 2.4)
Fig. 2.8B
North-south section (west facing) through parts of the dams and oak penstock of mill 1 and parts of the dams and the stone penstock of Mill 2 and penstock areas of both mills (for location see Fig. 2.4) .

Fig. 2.9
The surviving portion (east face) above high water of the short section of the dam of Mill 1

also that it was modified considerably for its re-use as part of the dam of Mill 2 (see Fig. 2.5). Towards its northern end, a large cut had been made for the construction of the wheelhouse of Mill 2 and the placing of its penstock.

The first stage of construction was the digging of a narrow and shallow trench into the original foreshore to form a foundation. A large oak beam (C34) was placed in it, and the trench was filled with grey clay. More grey clay was dumped on top to form a low bank, which served as the foundation of a stone revetment wall on the millpond face of the dam. The space behind the clay bank and wall was packed with a mixed deposit of silt and brown earth with occasional lenses of moss and clay (C11/27). Above this was a deposit of peat (C18) and, sealing the whole dam, was a layer of orange clay (C10) on top of which were large boulders. Some of the orange clay and boulders may belong to the Mill 2 phase as it was not always possible to distinguish them from the material used as a component of the first dam. The original width of this section of the dam could not be ascertained as its eastern side had been removed to make the back wall of the wheelhouse of Mill 2. Based on surviving evidence to the south and north, it is estimated to have been originally around 6m or more wide.

The foundation trench

The foundation trench was U-shaped and approximately 60cm wide and 40cm deep (Fig. 2.5). Observable in places adjacent to its eastern side was a low ridge of foreshore gravel and stones upcast from its excavation. It was tightly filled by well-packed grey clay. The large beam (C34) occupied the centre of the trench for all of its excavated length.

The large beam (C34)

This impressive oak beam was the largest structural timber to have survived from the first mill (see Figs 2.4, 2.5, 2.10 A,B,C and 2.12). It was rectangular in section and measured 3.34m long by 28cm wide by 43cm thick. The surface of the beam is at approximately 0.553m OD, and is horizontal, something achieved on the sloping foreshore by filling the trench with a sufficient depth of grey clay to make level the surface on which it was placed. Once positioned, the heavy casing of grey clay and burial beneath the grey clay bank and overlying wall would have held it rigidly in place.

Fig. 2.10A
Beam C34 (from south) with its casing of grey clay (C33) partially excavated. Also visible are beam C64 (in shadow on left), and the stones of the dam revetment (bottom) and stone penstock (top) of Mill 2.

Fig. 2.10B
Beam C34 (from east)

Fig. 2.10C
The northern end of beam C34 (from above) showing sloping rebate and damaged mortise

The surviving northern end of the beam terminated at the cut for the penstock of Mill 2 (see p. 146). It retained a number of worked features including a degraded V-shaped joint or mortise and a sloping rebate on its eastern edge. This joint was present only on the upper portion of the end, the lower part being roughly worked as if it had been hacked away. The presence of this joint suggests that the beam was originally joined to another which would have extended further northwards, but must have been removed when the cut for the later penstock was made. The sloping rebate appears to have been designed to receive the placement of another structural member. In the absence of other evidence, these features are somewhat enigmatic. It is clear, however, that the beam would have served to strengthen the base of the bank. But it will be argued below (see pps 38-39) that possibly it also served as a support for the rear end of a penstock.

The timber was sampled for tree-ring dating but, in spite of the presence of 149 growth rings and complete sapwood, proved impossible to date (Q9896, see p. 72). However, given its structural contemporaneity with other timbers used in the dams of Mill 1, and its close proximity to beam (C64) *c.* 0.45m to the west, its placement must belong to the same horizon as the rest of the structural timbers of the Mill 1. A mould of the beam was taken for recording purposes and after excavation, the beam was re-buried *in situ*.

Fig. 2.11A
View from the south of the surviving top of the stone revetment (C31) of the short section of the dam

The grey clay bank (C33)

More grey clay was dumped above beam C34 to form a low bank *c.* 0.9m wide and 40cm high, above the foundation trench (see Fig. 2.5). The millpond face of the clay bank does not appear to have been revetted by stones unlike the rest of the dam elsewhere, but was faced for a short distance by a beam (C64) at its base. This lack of protection against water erosion was probably responsible for a slight overhang of the clay bank, near its base on the pond side which seems to have been worn away and the space filled with silt.

The stone revetment (C31)

The upper part of the pond face of the dam had a stone revetment of which about 2.1m length was exposed by the excavation. It measured *c.* 1.1m in width and consisted of four courses of large boulders laid in a rough double row, with the spaces between them filled by smaller stones, and survived to a maximum height above the foundation trench of *c.* 1m. It is probable that some of the stones were robbed out for use in the stone revetment of the dam of Mill 2, some 2m to the west. The stone revetment ended abruptly at the junction of the cut made through the dam for the penstock of Mill 2.

Fig. 2.11B
View from the north of the stone revetment (C31) of the short section of dam (on left) with the core of the dam of Mill 2 on the right

The core of the dam (C11/C27)

The main core of this section of the dam was composed of a very compact layer of mixed grey-brown silt and brown, humic soil with occasional lenses of grey clay, peat, sand, moss and other organic matter. The top of this deposit was almost totally sealed by a clay layer *c.* 10–13cm thick, the purpose of which, presumably, was to stop water penetration. This seems to have been particularly effective, as much of the organic material in the core was dry and somewhat desiccated when exposed by excavation. Perhaps the most notable feature of the core of the dam was the presence of a large quantity of moss. On first exposure, the moss had a remarkably fresh appearance, most of it still retaining its green colour. It occurred in lenses and occasionally in lumps, some of which were very thick (up to 10cm). The deposit had been laid down in discernible bands, probably representing the cyclic deposition of the material during different periods of low water when construction work could take place, and subsequent inundation at high tide.

The core contained two large worked pieces of wood (C28 and C30). C30 was found near the base of the dam and immediately adjacent to the large beam C34, while C28 was located approximately 30cm above on the top of the layer (see Fig. 2.12). In spite of the distance, the pieces are perhaps parts of one composite object. C30 was roughly rectangular and measured approximately 66cm by 40cm, and was about 30cm in maximum thickness, tapering to *c.* 24cm. It had a central linear groove *c.* 25cm deep. There was a crude hole cut through one of the long sides, which was matched by a circular depression on the side opposite. One end was damaged and broken off, and it may be that C28 is, in fact, this broken end. Parts of the object were tightly packed around with moss. C28, which also had a central groove running along its length, was roughly square, the sides measuring *c.* 52cm, and was *c.* 11cm thick. Frustratingly, viewing both intriguing pieces together or separately yielded little information as to what type of object or objects they were. Their context, however, makes it clear that they were discard worked wood which had been used as part of the packing for the internal core of the dam, and did not relate to any structural part of the mill *in situ*.

Fig. 2.12
View from the north of wooden objects C30 (to left of beam C34) and C28 (above C34)

The peat deposit (C18)

Above the mixed layer C11/C27, which formed the core of the dam, was a very well-packed deposit of reddish-brown peat (C18) containing large lenses and clumps of moss and occasional patches of grey clay. It was laid in horizontal bands like C11/C27 below. The layer was truncated to the north by the sharp and near-vertical cut for the penstock of Mill 2. The deposit was 1.2m wide and reached a maximum of 80cm in depth. Environmental sampling confirmed that the peat was from a wet area and contained seeds and rhizomes of sedge species and other seeds indicative of this type of habitat. Also present were lenses of decayed organic matter, which may have been derived from a coarse, vegetative matting (perhaps decayed branches). Analyses of the moss from this layer and from other contexts relating to both mills (see Appendix 3) indicated that it was gathered from a forest floor.

Through the peat deposit, and going down through the underlying layer, were two, near-vertical oak piles (C19 and C20) in close proximity. Their function was obviously to strengthen the core of the bank. C19 was rectangular in section and measured 1.11m long and 40.8cm by 88cm at the top, tapering to 45cm at the bottom. It had a rectangular mortise and three dowel holes. C20, which also displayed a mortise hole, was situated approximately 12cm to the south of C19 and was rectangular in section, measuring 1.725m long and 28cm by 19cm at the top, tapering to 88cm at the base. The peat deposit had been packed tightly around the upper portion of both timbers. It is clear that the mortises on both timbers did not relate to their function in the dam.

THE PENSTOCK AREA BEHIND THE WHEELHOUSE

Fig. 2.13
The peat deposit (C18) in the core of the dam under excavation with the top of oak pile C19 protruding. The stones of the back wall of the wheelhouse of Mill 2 are visible on the left edge of the picture.

The penstock area behind the wheelhouse occupied the space between the adjoining ends of the two sections of the dams. Most of this had been removed by the digging of the large U-shaped trench for the penstock and wheelhouse of Mill 2 (Fig. 2.8B). This cut, measuring approximately 5m wide and 1.3m deep, had removed the stratigraphic connection between the two sections of dam and the space above the penstock, but fortunately some basal features had survived, including the remains of a wooden penstock (see below).

The area was defined by the lower courses of the back wall of the wheelhouse of Mill 1 on the east, and the lower courses of the penstock intake wall on the west, the space between being approximately 3.8m wide. The original core material filling this space, and in which the penstock(s) were buried, had been removed for the insertion of the penstock of Mill 2 and back-filled with re-deposited silt (see Figs 2.8A and B). However some of it survived behind the wheelhouse wall, and consisted of a tightly-packed and organically-rich, brown deposit (C126) which extended northwards to form a component of the core of the main dam section where the deposit survived as a bank, which had a maximum height of 1.1m and was *c.* 2.4m wide. (see Fig. 2.8B). Dumped against the base of the northern side of the bank was a mixed layer composed of organic material, silt and grey clay (C112), somewhat similar in composition to deposit C11/C27, which formed the basal layer of the short length of dam to the south of the wheelhouse. The bank was sealed on its sides and top by grey clay (C121), above which was a layer of orange clay (C79).

Environment sampling of C126 demonstrated that it was rich in vegetative matter consisting of moss, bracken, wood and twig fragments. Like the peat deposit (C18) in the dam section to the south of the cut, plants of wet and wooded habitats were well represented.

THE SURVIVING PENSTOCK

The remains of a penstock made from a hollowed-out oak trunk, were found *c.* 1.5m below the present foreshore surface, just below the base of the cut for the penstock of Mill 2. (see Figs 2.4, 2.8B, 2.14 and 5.1). Unfortunately, its western or intake end had not survived and had been probably removed by the cut. The upper surface of the remainder was badly degraded and few detailed features remained (see pps 132-133). After recording, it was covered with a geotextile membrane and re-buried *in situ*.

The penstock was orientated approximately east-west and had an external width of 60cm, while the internal chamber was 36cm wide and was filled with a layer of silty gravel (C1129). Frustratingly, it was only possible to excavate 1.22m of it as the remaining length went under the wheelhouse wall of Mill 2 and further investigation would have entailed the destruction of the latter. However, it must have been an additional 2m in length so that it could reach the back wall of the wheelhouse to deliver a jet of water to the waterwheel, thus giving a total length greater than 3.22m.

The penstock was set in a bed of stones and gravel in a matrix of grey clay (C128/C117), obviously placed on the underlying foreshore to provide a firm foundation to keep it rigidly fixed in position. The level of the foreshore below the penstock was at -0.178m OD. There was a setting of three large stones (C118) in front of its surviving western end, possibly indicating the intake point at its presumed mouth (see Figs 2.4 and 2.14). The central stone of the three sloped down gently towards the surviving end of the penstock, while the two flanking stones had flat surfaces. As the space between the two side stones was just over 60cm, it seems probable that the end of the penstock would have been tightly wedged between them and resting on the sloping middle stone. The approximate level of the top of these stones is at -0.15m OD.

Fig. 2.14
The oak penstock of Mill 1 (from west) with the stone setting C118 in the foreground. The stone penstock of Mill 2 is visable at the top right of the picture.

The base of the mouth of the stone penstock of Mill 2 was set at the level of the bottom of its millpond, and this was probably the practice at most horizontal-waterwheeled mill sites. As the bottom of the first millpond is at 0.625m OD, the level at the mouth of the penstock of Mill 1 must have been very similar. The surface level at the surviving western end of the penstock was at –0.054m OD, approximately half way along its length at -0.105m OD and, where it went through the wall of the wheelhouse of Mill 2 approximately 1.45m to the east, at -0.138m OD. The measurement of the height differential along its surface is sufficient to establish that it was inclined, with the higher end at the pond side and the lower towards the wheelhouse. However, because of the decayed and uneven nature of the surface, these measurements were not sufficiently reliable to estimate accurately the angle of inclination. This was unfortunate, as the angle of the setting of the penstock is an important element in the overall structural design of a mill. However, if the level at the mouth was the same as the bottom of the millpond (0.625m OD), and where the penstock went through the wall of the later wheelhouse at -0.138m OD, this gives an angle of 20°.

A possible second penstock

The evidence for the possible existence of a second penstock — and thus for the existence of two waterwheels serving Mill 1 — is somewhat circumstantial, but nonetheless requires discussion (see Fig. 2.15). It centres to a large extent on the significance of the large beam (C34), buried within the dam to the south of the surviving penstock. This is roughly aligned with the three large stones (C118) in front of the existing remnant of the surviving penstock. The position makes it possible to interpret it as the surviving part of a support beam for the rear or intake end of a second penstock located adjacent to the south of the surviving one. While front support beams for penstocks have been found at quite a few horizontal-wheeled mill sites, rear support beams are relatively rare. However, at the horizontal-wheeled tide mill site at Little Island, Co. Cork, which had two penstocks, a displaced beam 3.24m long by 52cm wide by 15cm thick and with two shallow niches on its surface, was thus interpreted (Rynne 1988, 2, 277–279). The two penstocks would have rested in the niches.

At Cloontycarthy Co. Cork, a displaced beam measuring 2.6m long by 20cm wide and 37cm thick, and which had a central recess, was also interpreted as a rear support beam (Rynne 1988, 2, 303). Rynne (1992, 63) suggests that rear support beams were largely a feature of double-penstock mills, with Cloontycarthy being the only single penstock mill site discovered so far that has produced solid evidence for having one. There are six known Irish examples of horizontal-wheeled mills with two penstocks, these being Bagenelstown Co. Carlow (Corlett 2001, 7), Mount Lucas, Co. Offaly (Rynne 1992, 65), Newton, Co. Tipperary (Lucas 1986; Rynne 1992, 65), and Ballykenly (Rynne 1992, 65), Little Island (Rynne 1988; 1992, 63) and Mushera (Rynne 1992, 63, 65), all in Co. Cork. The Little Island site is of special interest as, like Nendrum Mill 1, it is a tide mill of the early 7th century and demonstrates that double penstocks were present early in the sequence of Irish horizontal-wheeled mills and were being used in tide mills. The probable tide mill at Ebbsfleet, Kent, which is dated to the end of the 7th or early 8th century, also appears to have had two penstocks (MoLAS 2003, CA 2002, 193, Foreman *pers. comm.).*

The contextual link between the surviving penstock and the end of the beam has been removed by the later cut and along with it any physical evidence that may have existed of an additional penstock. However, as the space between the surviving penstock and the end of beam two is 1.6m wide, in theory at least it would have provided ample room for the placement of a second penstock of the same external diameter (60cm).

It seems clear that the northern end of beam C34 was either joined to another member or was of greater length, and that the missing part was removed when the cut for the penstock of Mill 2 was made. The sloping rebate at its surviving end may or may not be significant. However, it is possible to suggest that it was made to fit the base of a penstock, or some other structural member, for its support. The level of the surface of the beam is at approximately 0.56m OD, while that of the bottom of the millpond is at 0.625m OD. This close agreement is hardly coincidental and must have been planned deliberately. If the end of a sloping penstock was placed on the surface of the beam, the base of its mouth or intake end would have been at or very near the level of the bottom of the millpond.

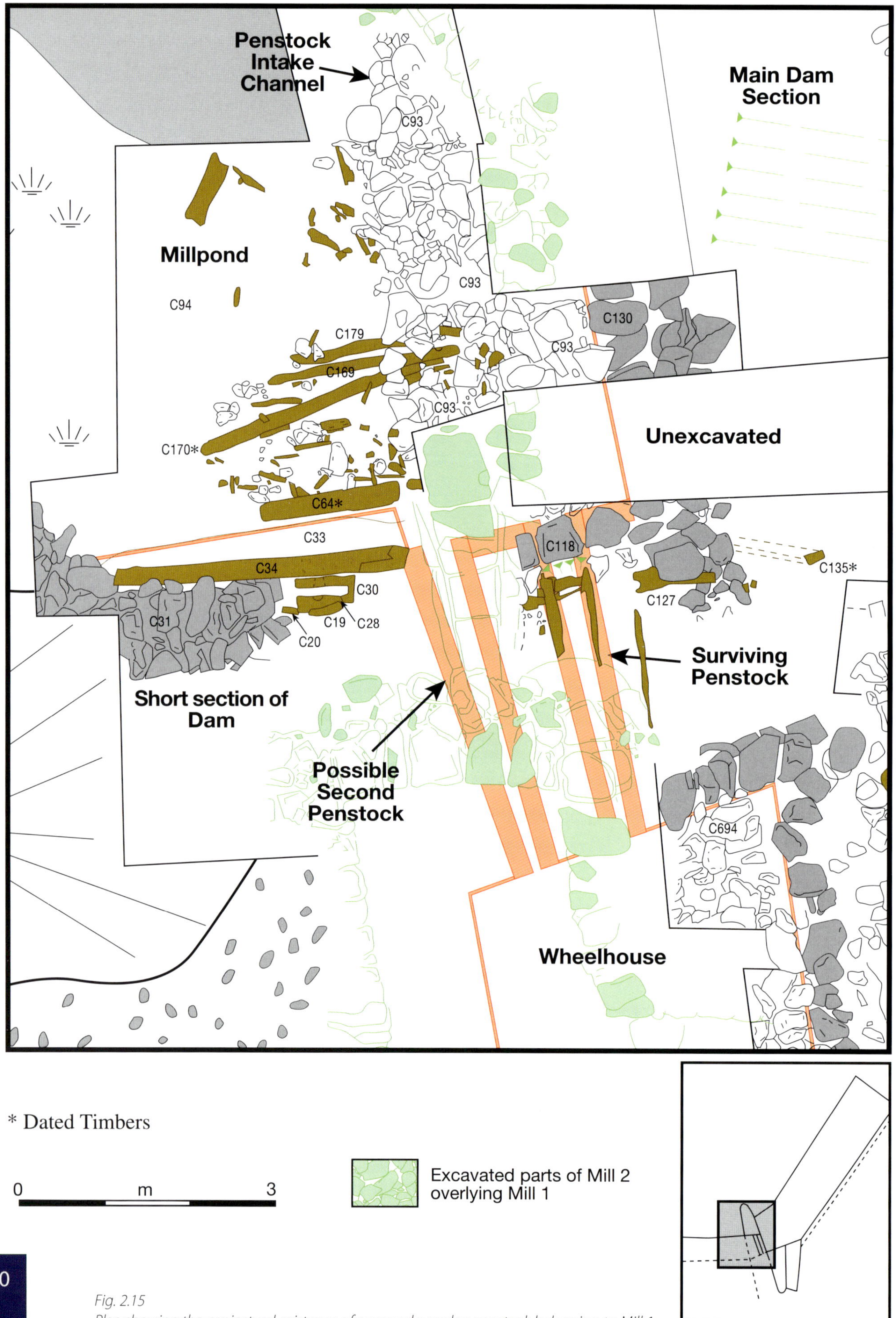

Fig. 2.15
Plan showing the conjectural existence of a second wooden penstock belonging to Mill 1

THE WHEELHOUSE

Sadly very little evidence remained of the wheelhouse of Mill 1, and it is clear that to a large extent it had been removed for the construction of the wheelhouse of Mill 2. The space it had occupied had been back-filled with orange clay and large boulders. Some features survived of its floor, basal courses of its back wall on the west and side wall on the north, but all trace of its south side wall appears to have been eradicated completely by the building of the wheelhouse of Mill 2 (see Figs 2.16, 2.17 and 2.18).

The foundation for the floor of the wheelhouse consisted of a deposit of large stones (C694) laid on the original foreshore. Remains of the back wall consisted of a linear stone setting (C612), 2.5m in length and oriented north-south, which survived to a height of three courses of large boulders but unfortunately this did not include the part of the wall where the front face of the penstock or penstocks were located. The northern side-wall was defined by a basal course of large stones (C696), which revetted a well-defined bank to the north (C613: see below). Many of the stones of this wall appear to have been pushed in deliberately to fill the wheelhouse and tailrace as a part of the construction work on Mill 2. The bank continued on eastwards beyond the wheelhouse to form the northern side of the tailrace of Mill 1. It was not possible to ascertain where the eastern end of the first wheelhouse terminated and the western end of its tailrace started. No structures or finds were recovered from the floor of the wheelhouse. However, the water-wheel which was originally located in it was found out of context in the core of the dam of Mill 2 a short distance to the south, where presumably it had been casually dumped during the dismantling of Mill 1 and the construction of Mill 2 (see Fig. 2.5).

It is important to state that very little solid information pertaining to the first wheelhouse, and the millhouse that would have been situated above, was retrieved. It may be observed, however, that the wheelhouse of Mill 1, like that of Mill 2, appears to have been constructed in stone, as evidenced by the surviving stone basal courses of the back wall and northern side-wall. Thus, the Nendrum wheelhouses differ from the majority of those of other Irish horizontal-wheeled mills, whose wheelhouses were built in wood. The overall dimensions of the wheelhouse of Mill 1 cannot be accurately ascertained from the surviving evidence, but it is possible to infer, albeit on the basis of scant information, that it was in the region of 4m wide from north to south and perhaps 3m east-west. The location of the wooden penstock suggests that it entered the wheelhouse chamber towards the centre or perhaps to the left of centre of its back wall. This is a different arrangement to that of Mill 2 and to almost all of the other known examples of Irish wheelhouses, where the penstock enters to the right of centre of the back wall (see Chapter 5). This may suggest that its waterwheel turned in an anticlockwise direction unlike the clockwise rotation of the waterwheel of Mill 2 and of other early Irish horizontal-wheeled mills.

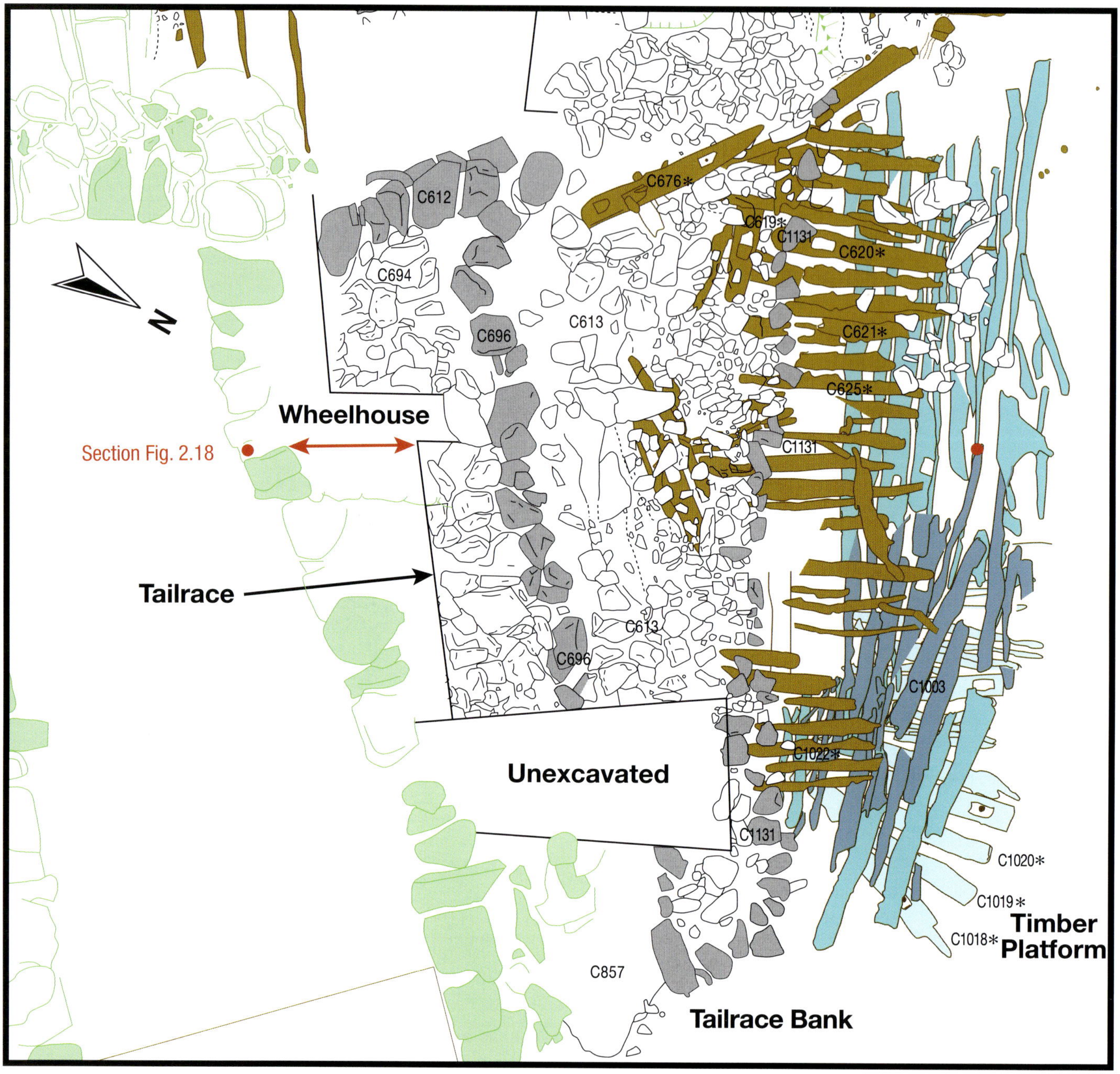

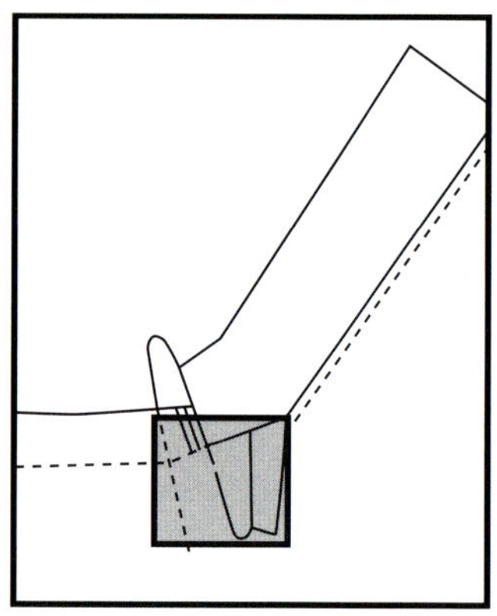

Fig. 2.16
Plan of the remains of the wheelhouse, tailrace, tailrace bank and timber platform or landing place of Mill 1

THE TAILRACE

Part of the northern side of the tailrace could be traced for a considerable distance (Fig. 2.16), but its southern wall had been removed as a part of the construction of the later mill. Like the wheelhouse, the tailrace had been filled in with a spread of medium to large boulders in orange clay (C605). At the base of the infill, and representing the original floor of the tailrace, was a layer of small stones (C857) approximately 50cm deep (Fig. 2.18). Presumably this had been laid to form a hard bottom to the channel to facilitate efficient run-off of the spent water and to prevent scouring of the underlying sleech. This layer extended to the east, beyond the observable trace of the northern side of the tailrace.

THE WHEELHOUSE BANK AND TAILRACE BANK (C613)

A prominent feature of the plan of the mill complex is a low, roughly tongue-shaped bank, which extends for approximately 8m eastwards at an angle from the main dam section (see Fig. 2.16), and forms the northern side of the wheelhouse and tailrace of the mill. At its western end, it partially overlies the lower core of dam, while its northern edge partially overlies the timber platform or landing place to the north-east of the mill complex (see pps 65-68). Immediately to the north of the wheelhouse, the bank is *c.* 3m wide and has a surviving height of 1.1m. As it goes eastwards and forms one side of the tailrace, it gradually reduces in height to *c.* 80cm high and 2m wide. The surviving maximum height of the tailrace bank is between 0.618m and 0.633m OD. It may not have been much higher originally, and so it is probable that most of it would have been submerged at high water. As its function was to facilitate the run-off of spent water from the waterwheel — something that only took place at low water — there would have been no need to have it above the high-water level. On the southern edge (the tailrace side), the bank was revetted by a kerb of large stones (C696) and, on the external side, by one of smaller stones (C1131).

The base of the bank on the original foreshore surface consisted of a layer of grey clay with some stone and occasional pieces of wood. Above this was a layer of more substantial boulders set in grey clay, above which — and forming the main core of the bank — were large boulders in a matrix of orange clay (see Fig. 2.18). The western end of the bank overlaid slightly the main dam and had a higher component of stones. At the interface, a layer of grey clay (C1074) was placed, separating the tailrace bank with its make-up of orange clay and stones, from the underlying organic core (C626) of the main dam. On the surface of the organic core was a large timber (C676), orientated north-south and parallel to the dam. It was held in place by two posts driven into the underlying organic core (see Fig. 2.16).

Fig. 2.17
View (from east) of the wheelhouse and tailrace of Mill 1. Remains of the back wall of the wheelhouse (top centre) and northern side wall of the wheelhouse and tailrace (centre right). The rear of the northern side wall of the wheelhouse of Mill 2 on left edge.

During the construction of the dam and tailrace bank of Mill 2, the tailrace bank was retained to form the foundation of the new tailrace bank. A layer of orange clay was laid over the top of the old bank (C606) and surfaced with stones.

Fig. 2.18
North-south section (west facing) through the tailrace, tailrace bank, wooden platform of Mill 1 and part of the stone platform or landing place of Mill 2 (for location see Fig. 2.16)

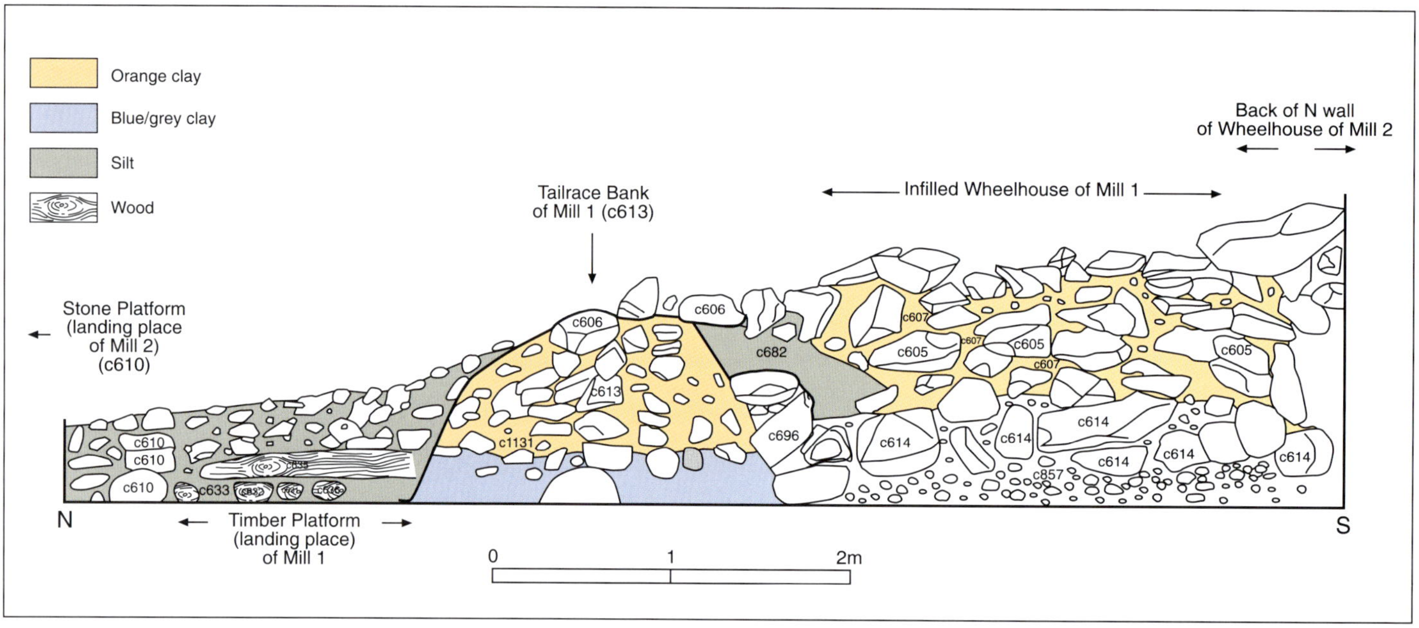

Fig. 2.19
View of wheelhouse bank and tailrace bank (from north) of Mill 1 partially overlying the timber platform. Rear of the north side wall of the wheelhouse of Mill 2 visible on top left.

THE MAIN DAM SECTION

Introduction

By far the most impressive surviving part of Mill 1 is its main dam section, the foundation and basal courses of which are still visible at low tide as a linear band of stones and seaweed c. 110m long and orientated north-west/south-east across the foreshore below the monastery (Figs 2.20A and 2.37). Using information gained from a number of excavation trenches, it was possible to build up a composite picture of its complex nature, and this is probably best understood by reference to the interpretive plan (Fig. 2.21A) and section (Fig. 2.21B). The dam can be seen as a major piece of engineering work, remarkable in a single-phase foreshore structure for the range of construction techniques used.

Fig. 2.20A (above)
View of the main dam section from the south-east near the site of Mill 1

Fig. 2.20B (below)
View of the main dam section from across the bay on the north-west

The principal structural features of the main dam are listed below from the millpond side of the structure on the west to its sea-facing side on the east:

1 Inner stone revetment or wall set in a matrix of orange clay set in a foundation trench, terminating in a stone revetted bank of orange clay at the wheelhouse
2 Grey clay sealing layer
3 Timber revetment of piles and planks
4 Primary core or bank of mixed clay, silt, organic material and sand
5 Wattle revetment with timber bracing over a foundation trench
6 Core of organic material
7 External palisade or breakwater
8 Two gaps, the possible original locations of sluices

Overall, these elements combine to make up a dam with an overall width at its base of approximately 8.8m. While excavation focused on the south-eastern section near the wheelhouse and the site of the mill, it seems highly probable that the features revealed were representative of the remaining visible 100m or so which was not excavated.

The foundation trenches

The base of the dam was formed by two roughly parallel foundation trenches cut into the old foreshore surface, and leaving a narrow, upstanding platform between them. The inner trench, situated on the millpond side, had a flat bottom and an almost vertical profile on the millpond side on the west. It was approximately 4.4m wide and had been dug *c.* 1.24m into the underlying surface. The outer trench, situated on the seaward side, was *c.* 2.2m wide and *c.* 1m deep. Its inner side, towards the core of the dam, had a relatively vertical profile, while the profile of the outer side sloped gently.

Inner stone revetment and orange clay bank

The excavation of the linear band of stones visible on the surface of the foreshore mud showed it to be the base of a stone wall or revetment, approximately 4m wide. It was set in the inner foundation trench and formed the millpond face of the dam. The bottom and sides of the trench had been lined with a thick layer of relatively pure, grey-blue clay and, on top of this and filling the trench, were placed large stones bonded in a matrix of orange clay. Most of the stones were tightly packed, some being wedged together with their long sides placed vertically. As the revetment approached the wheelhouse to the south-east, the orange clay content in the stone revetment gradually increased, eventually becoming a bank of orange clay (C79). This bank was approximately 9.5m long and, on the millpond side, had a revetment (C130) approximately 2m wide, consisting of large stones bonded by orange clay (see Figs 2.22A and 2.8A). In this area, some of the upper section of the dam had survived — being crossed by and incorporated as part of the foundation for that of Mill 2 — rising up to 1.65m in height above the old shoreline. As the present maximum height of the surviving top of the main dam section is at 1.049m OD, it is clear that perhaps it was up to 1m or more higher originally.

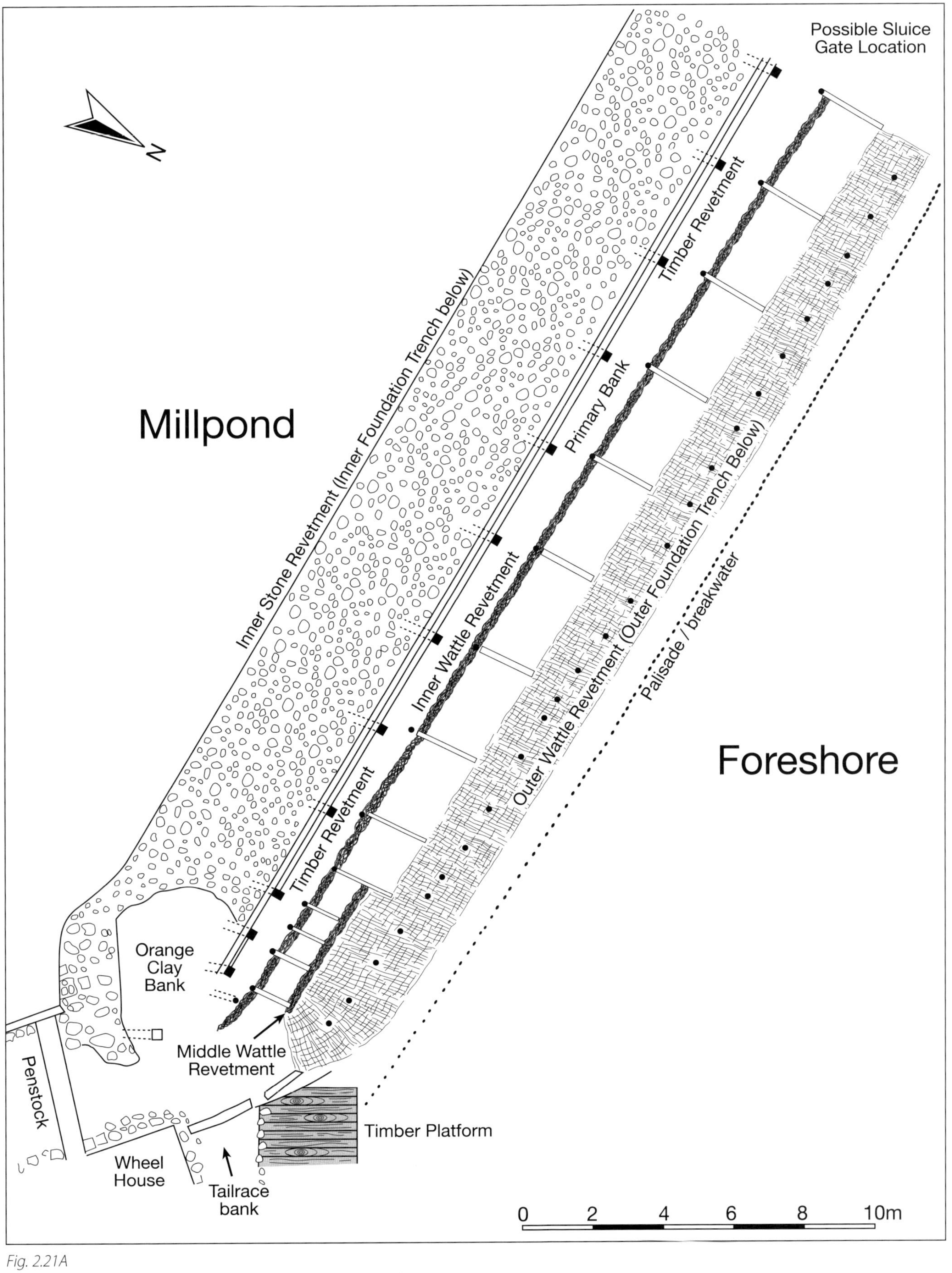

Fig. 2.21A
Interpretive plan of the main structural features of the main dam

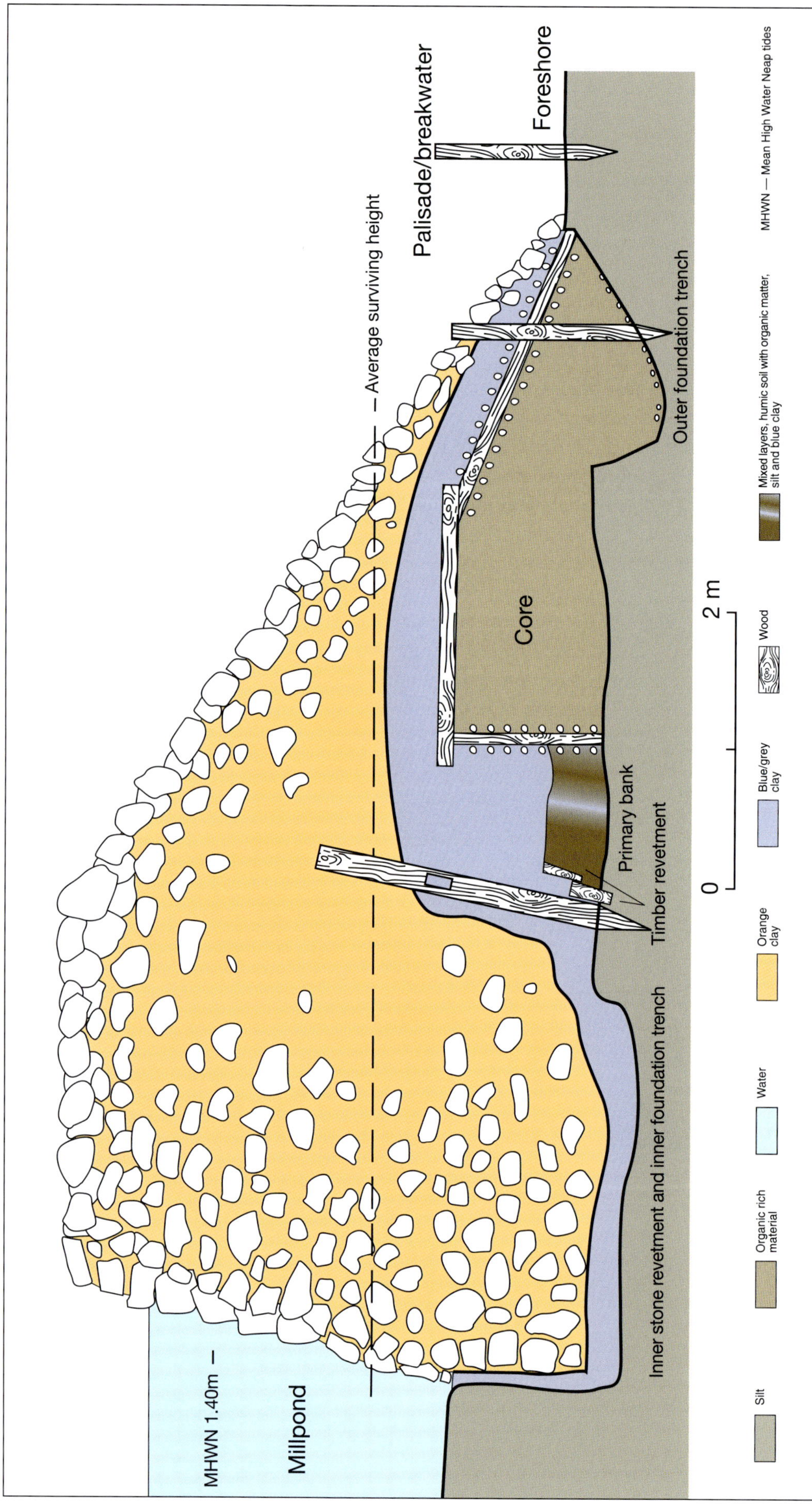

Fig. 2.21B
Interpretive section across the main dam

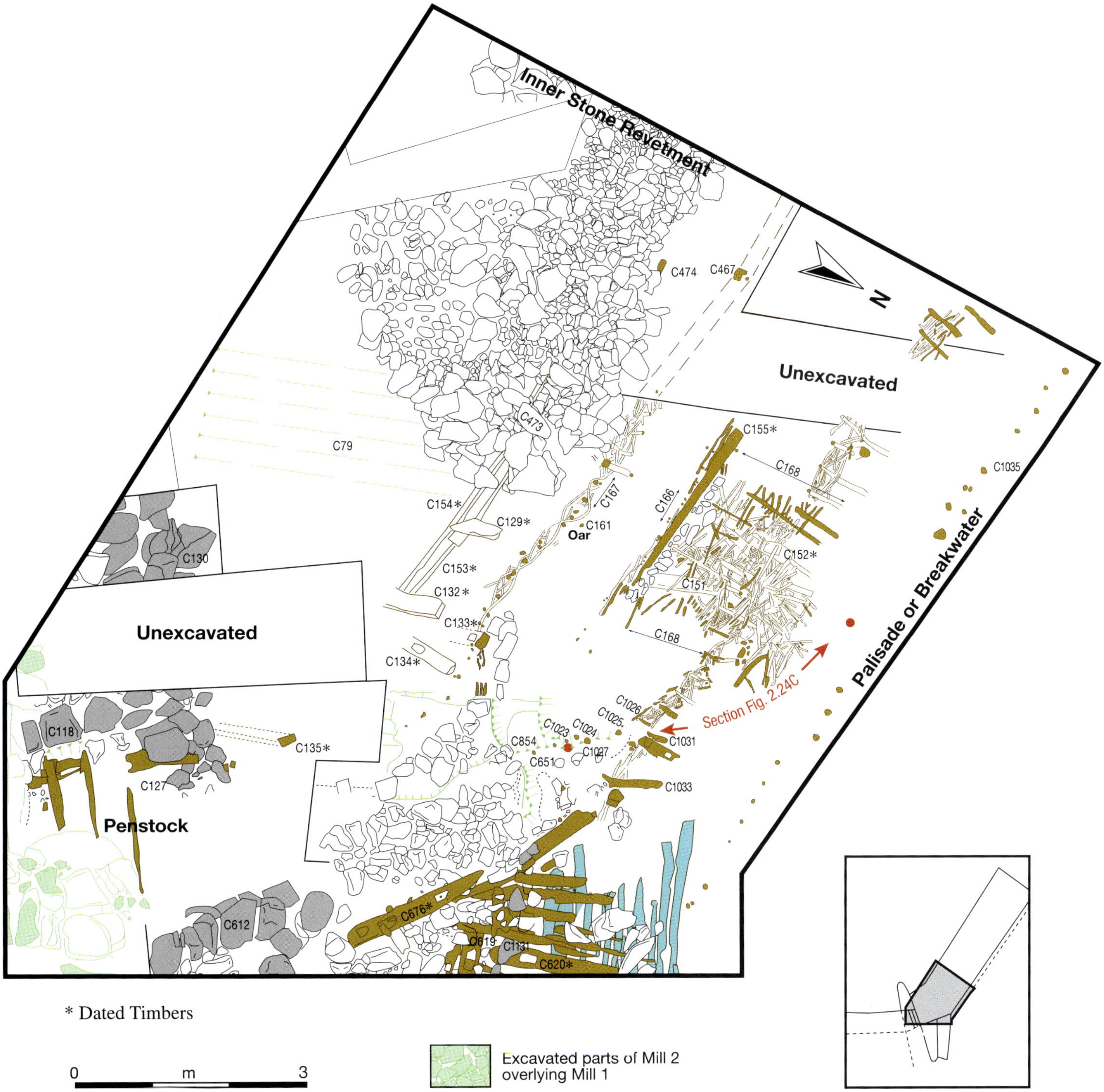

Fig. 2.22A
Plan of excavated features of the main dam section in Trench 4

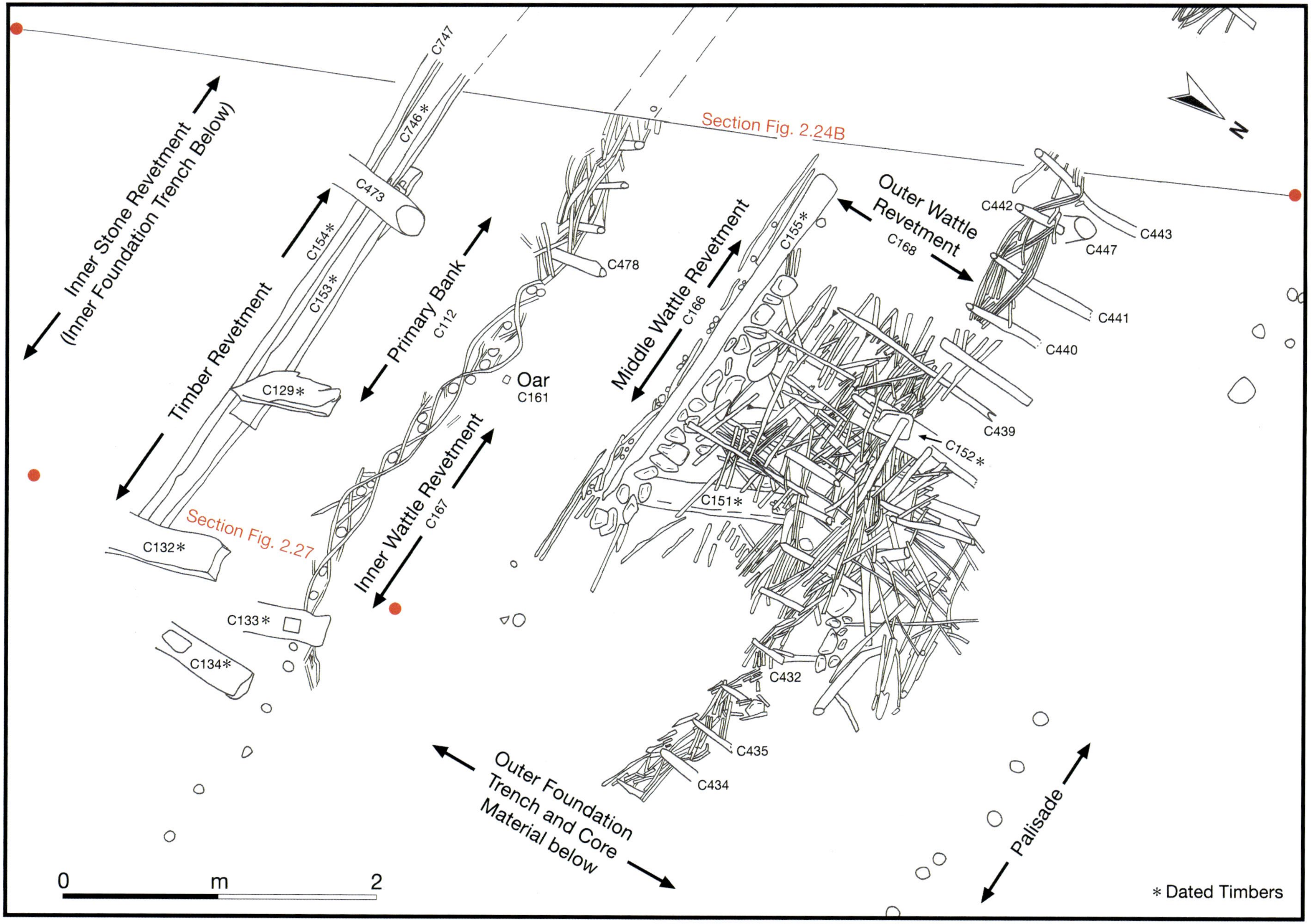
N
Section Fig. 2.24B
Section Fig. 2.27
Inner Stone Revetment
(Inner Foundation Trench Below)
Timber Revetment
Primary Bank
C112
Inner Wattle Revetment
C167
Middle Wattle Revetment
C166
Outer Wattle
Revetment
C168
Outer Foundation
Trench and Core
Material below
Palisade
Oar
C161
C747
C746*
C473
C154*
C153*
C129*
C132*
C133*
C134*
C478
C155*
C151*
C152*
C439
C440
C441
C442
C443
C447
C432
C435
C434
0
m
2
* Dated Timbers

Fig. 2.22B (left)
Detailed plan of excavated features of the main dam section in Trench 4

Fig. 2.23A (below)
Plan of excavated features of the main dam section in Trench 5

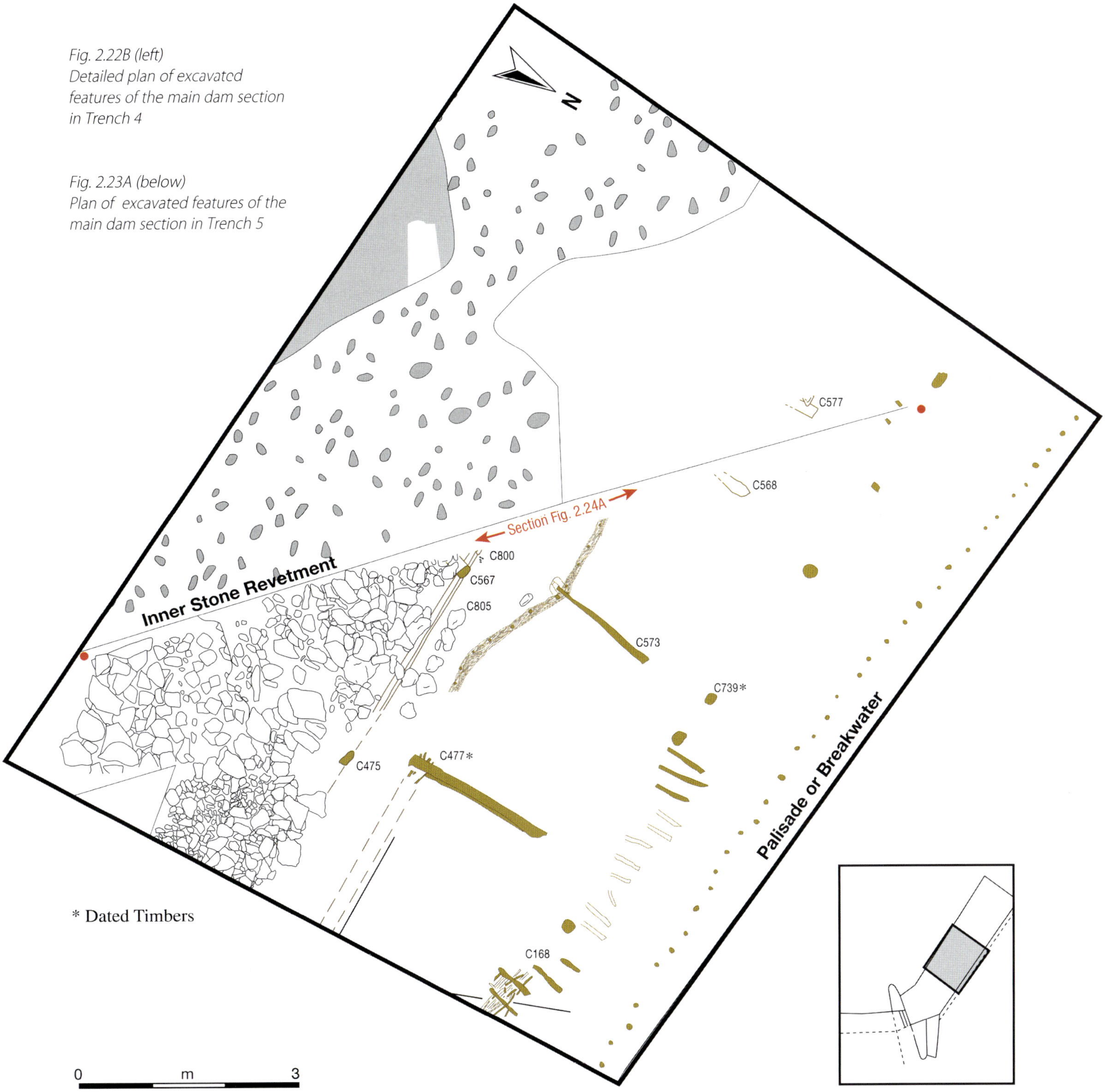

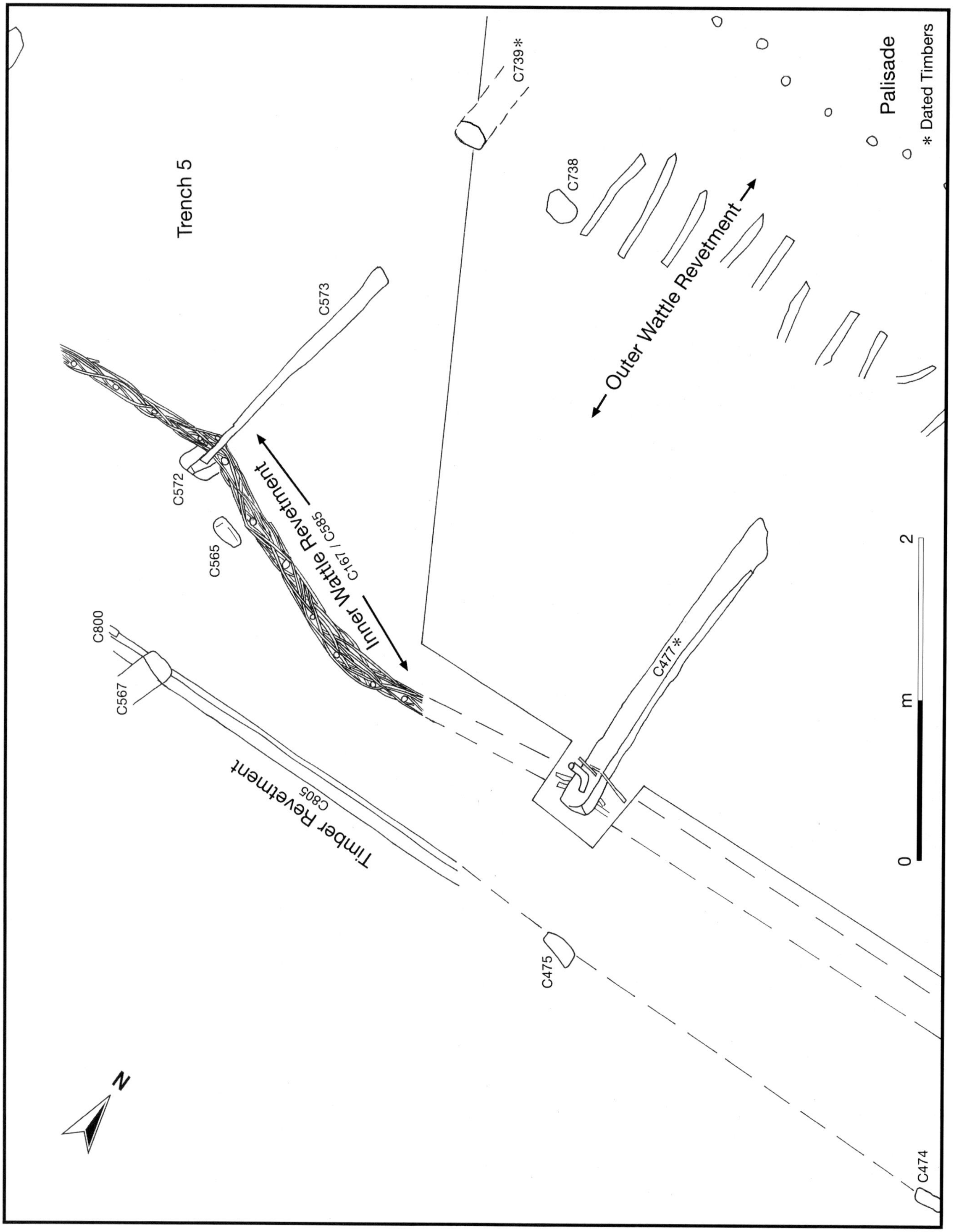

Fig. 2.23B
Detailed plan of excavated features of the main dam section in Trench 5

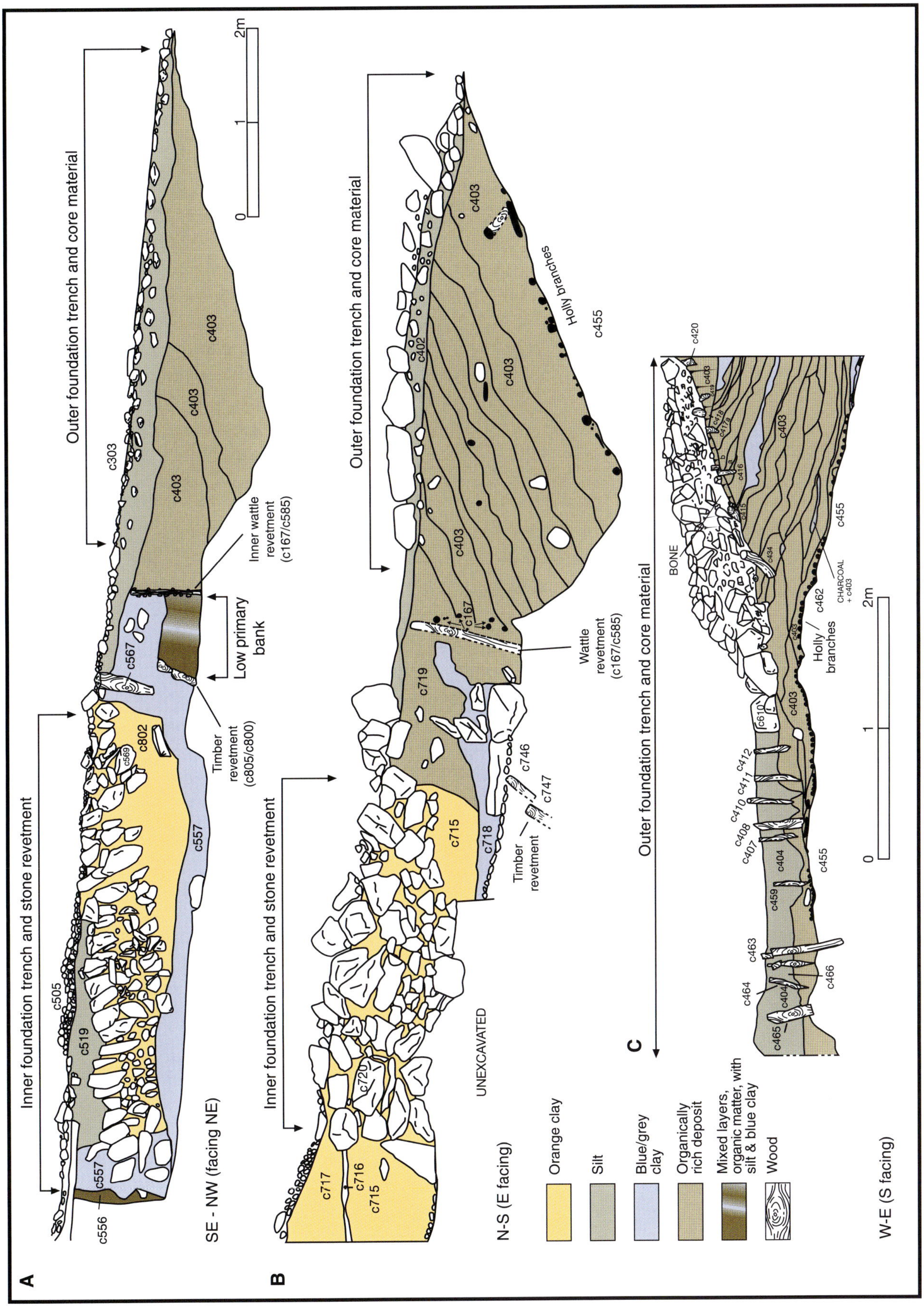

Fig. 2.24
Sections across the main dam (for locations see Figs 2.22A, 2.22B and 2.23A)

Driven through the body of the orange clay bank, near its junction with the wheelhouse, was a large pile C135 (see Fig. 2.22A), which yielded a date of AD 625+9 (Q9919: see pps 68-76). It was not vertical, but leaned to the north and towards the inner core of the bank. The pile was roughly rectangular in section, measuring 1.12m long by 24cm by 12cm. Its width tapered from the top to a point at the base. A rectangular mortise had been cut out some 8cm from the top, but this was badly eroded.

Underlying the stone revetment at the termination of the orange bank, and adjacent to the penstock area, was a partially-worked segment of tree-trunk or stump (C127) lying horizontally on the original foreshore. It was in poor condition and measured approximately 51cm long by 33–40cm, and one end had been worked to an L-shaped profile, but otherwise it was largely unworked (see pps 68-76: Q9914). Its function may have been to act as a stabilising foundation timber for the wall.

The grey clay lining

The grey clay lining (C121) of the bottom and sides of the inner trench was, on average, 40cm thick and extended upwards out of the trench and over the inner core of the dam on the east (see Figs 2.24A and 2.8B) to overlay the timber revetment and primary foundation bank (see below). Although only the inner section now survives, it was obviously placed to seal the entire basal core of the dam (see Fig. 2.21B). The uprights or piles supporting the timber revetment were driven through this layer. In the south-eastern area, where the dam has survived to a greater height, the grey clay is overlain by a thick deposit (up to 1m in depth) of orange clay, a continuation of the orange bank C79 (Fig. 2.8B).

The timber revetment

This was a low timber revetment or plank shuttering for the inner side of the basal core of the dam. It consisted of a row of large oak piles placed at intervals of approximately 3m, with the space between their bases closed by two courses of horizontal planking. From the evidence recovered, it is clear that the timber revetment was designed to retain the low basal core or primary bank (C112) described below, on top of which the upper parts of the dam were constructed.

The line of the revetment was traced for approximately 13.6m, to the point where it terminated on the south-east some 4.5m from the wheelhouse (Figs 2.22A and B, Figs 2.23A and B). The evidence suggests that it probably continued the full length of the dam, across the bay to the north-west. Its continuation could be inferred from the protruding tops of piles. On top of the revetment, on the millpond side, there was a sealing layer of grey clay, while on the seaward side was a contrasting brown-coloured, mixed deposit of redeposited silt, humic soil, blue clay and organic material (C112).

In Trench 4 (see Figs 2.22A and B), two courses of planking composed of timbers C153 and C154, C746 and C747, associated with three uprights (C132, C129 and C473) were

Fig. 2.25A
The timber revetment from the west showing pile C473 with planks C746 and C747 (on left) and C153 and C154 (on right)

Fig. 2.25B
View from southeast of overlapping planks of timber revetment C153 (left) and C154 (right)

Fig. 2.25C
View from west of overlapping planks of timber revetment C153 (top) and C154 (bottom)

revealed. None of the planks was fixed to any other or to the associated piles, but they were held in place by the surrounding deposits. They were placed on their sides and leant slightly into the inner core of the dam. The top of the bottom plank in the lower course slightly overlapped the base of the plank in the course above. Likewise, their ends slightly overlapped the adjoining plank in the same course.

Timber C154 had been placed on the old foreshore surface to form part of the bottom course of the revetment and overlapped part of the base of C153 in the course above. Its south-eastern end rested against upright C132, while its north-western end rested against upright C473. It measured approximately 3m long by 24cm by 7cm and had a small mortise hole near its south-eastern end. This proved to be the second largest surviving timber found in the dam and produced a felling date of AD 603+9 (Q10017: see pps 68-76).

Timber C153 was wedge-shaped in section and measured approximately 91cm long by 22–26cm by 3–6cm. It produced a felling date of AD 611+9, but definitely after AD 608 (Q9920: see pps 68-76). The north-western ends of C153 and C154 partially overlapped a similar pair — C747 and C746 — of which C746 produced a date of AD 560+9 (Q10020). However, all of the sapwood and a large amount of the heartwood had been removed to make the plank, and it is thought to be from the inner section of a tree felled probably at around the same time as the main timbers used in the dam.

Upright C132, a large square-sectioned pile, was the last upright in the revetment at the wheelhouse end and produced a date of AD 625+9 (Q9916: see pps 68-76). Upright C129 was an oak plank *c.* 99cm long and only around 6cm in width. It had two circular holes of 2.5cm in diameter, one with a peg *in situ* suggesting strongly that it was re-used timber from an other structure.. This upright was dated to AD 513+9 (Q9915: see pps 68-76). However, as it had been fashioned from the central section of a tree, the absence of the outer section of the tree made it impossible to date the time of felling, but, like C746 discussed above, it is probably much later than the early 6th century. Just beyond the end of the timber revetment, on the south-east, was a large oak pile, C134, which had been driven through the orange clay bank and underlying grey clay. It was rectangular in section and, like pile C135, leaned in the direction of the inner core of the dam. A sub-rectangular mortise was situated some 40cm below its eroded top (see Figs 2.22B and 2.26A). The presence of sapwood and spring vessels allowed it to be dated precisely to April or May of AD 619 (Q9918: see pps 68-76).

Fig. 2.26A
View (from west) of the piles of the timber revetment, C129, C132, C133 and C134 under excavation

Fig. 2.26B
View (from south) of piles of the timber revetment, C129, C132, C133 and C134 under excavation

The continuation of the revetment, revealed in Trench 5 to the north-west (see Figs 2.23A and B), consisted of two horizontal planks (C805 and C800) placed against an upright (C567) in exactly the same fashion as those in Trench 4. In Trench 5, and at the end of Trench 4 — and observable in other areas — the grey clay overlying and sealing the revetment was undisturbed and intact (see Figs 2.24A and B). From this it can be concluded that the revetment consisted originally of two horizontal courses of timber only — in some places only one — and that it probably had a maximum height of *c.* 50cm.

Low primary bank (C112)

This low bank was retained by the timber revetment and the inner side of wattle framework (C167), and formed a primary core to the dam as a whole. It was approximately 1m wide and 45cm high, and was composed of mixed layers of a predominantly dark-brown, organically-rich soil mixed with redeposited silt, sand and clay, which had been dumped in discernable bands. The top of the deposit was sealed by a continuation of the grey clay layer (Fig. 2.27). It ended at the junction of the wheelhouse area and the dam (Fig. 2.8B), and resembled closely, in terms of its composition, deposit C11/C27, which formed the basal layer of the short section of the dam to the south of the penstock area.

A large upright or pile, C133, which produced a date of April or May of AD 619 (Q9917: see pps 68-76), had been driven through the deposit near its end on the south-east. It was approximately rectangular in section and measured some 1.13m long by 21cm by 10cm, and had a sub-rectangular mortise *c.* 34cm from the top.

Outer foundation trench and core material

The outer foundation trench, organic core and wattle framework combined to form the outer, or seaward, side of the surviving base of the dam. The outer foundation trench, which terminated a short distance from the wheelhouse, was on average *c.* 2.2m wide

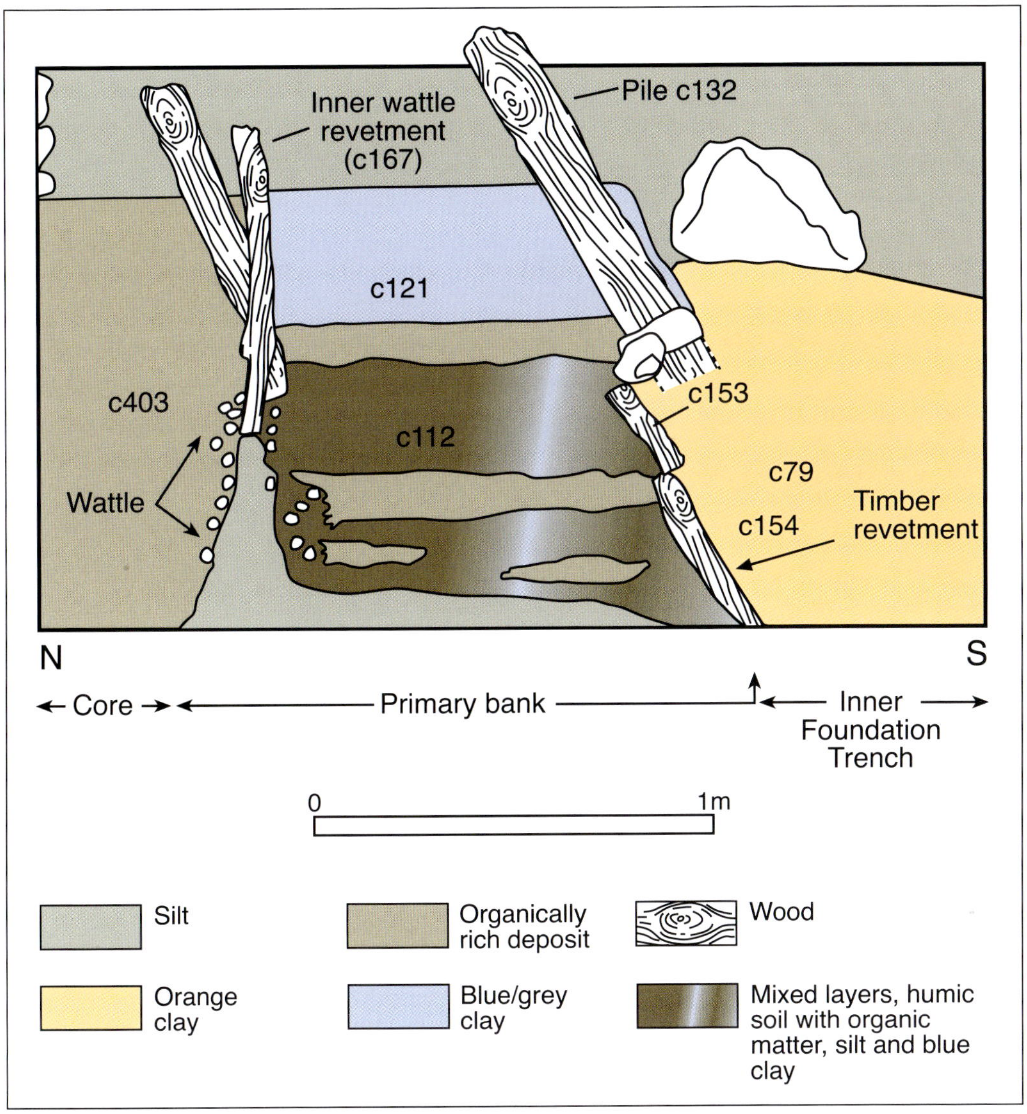

Fig. 2.27
North-south (west facing) section through part of the orange clay bank, timber revetment, primary bank, inner wattle revetment C167 and part of the core of the dam (for location see Fig. 2.22B)

Fig. 2.28A
Holly branches lining the base of the outer foundation trench

Fig. 2.28B
Freshly excavated holly leaf from the lining of the outer foundation trench

and had been cut to a depth of *c.* 1m into the original shoreline. The inner face of the trench was nearly vertical, while the base and outer side sloped gently up to the exterior. On the surfaces of the base and outer side, and extending out over the space between the trench and the outer palisade, was a layer of brushwood, composed of holly branches (see Figs 2.24B and C, 2.28A). When first exposed, the holly leaves were still green. The obvious interpretation of the brushwood is that it was to provide a working platform on the soft mud during construction.

The trench was filled with a very well-packed, desiccated, organically-rich deposit (C403) laid in sloping bands. The tipping lines within this deposit were very well pronounced and made it clear that the material was dumped into the trench from the north-eastern side, the outside of the dam (see Figs 2.24). It extended over the trench and into the central part of the dam, and the top and sides of the deposit were encased in a retaining framework made of wattle work and timber.

Fig. 2.29A
The outer foundation trench and core material from south east.

Fig. 2 29B
The outer foundation trench and core material from north west.

The wattle and timber framework
For most of its uncovered length, this structure lay just below the present foreshore surface, covered by a layer of greyish-brown silt over a compact layer of stones. Towards the wheel-house end of the dam, however, some of the original overlying deposits survived to a greater height and demonstrated that, originally, it had been sealed beneath the layer of grey clay (C121), over which a thick layer of orange clay with stones had been deposited (Fig. 2.8B).

The structure was composed of three main elements (see Figs 2.21A, 2.22A and 2.22B). On the south-western (or millpond) side of the dam was an inner wattle revetment (C167), braced on the pond side by spaced, vertical piles. On the seaward side was a sloping, outer wattle revetment placed over the fill of the outer trench of the dam and similarly braced by vertical piles. The third element — of which only fragmentary evidence survived — was a series of horizontal timbers connecting the tops of both revetments. Near the wheelhouse end of the dam, for a short distance, was an additional length of wattle forming a middle fence (C166). The inner wattlework (C167) survived comparatively well, but the sloping outer part of the structure, which faced the incoming tide, was badly eroded and fragmentary.

Inner wattle revetment (post lines C167 and C585)
The inner wattle revetment was located approximately 80–100cm to the north-east of the timber revetment (see Figs 2.22 A and B, 2.23A and B), and two well-preserved sections were excavated in Trenches 4 and 5. The section uncovered in Trench 4 (C167) was approximately 5.4m long and survived to a maximum height of 1.2m. Its continuation in Trench 5 (C585) was approximately 3m long, surviving to a maximum height of *c.* 93cm. In some areas, the wattlework appears to be relatively complete so that the original height of the structure may have been around 1.2–1.3m.

The posts in the wattlework were spaced between 20cm and 30cm apart and were, on average, 5–6cm in diameter. Analysis of both uprights and wands showed not only that

Fig. 2.30A
View of the west side of wattle revetment C167

Fig. 2.30B
View of surviving top wattle revetment C167 from west

holly was the most common species used, but also that the assemblage included one example of an oak upright and four examples of willow wands (see Appendix 1). At its maximum height, the wattlework was made in four courses, and analysis of the weave pattern showed that in general, the wands were woven by placing their ends behind one upright, then bending them in front of two uprights and returning behind the next upright. Alternatively, depending on their position within the structure, the wands were woven behind two uprights and in front of the next two and so on.

Associated with the revetment was an almost complete oar of estimated original length of 2m (C161) made from split ash (see Figs 2.22A and B, 2.31, and p. 228). It had been inserted vertically on the north-eastern side with the blade downwards, and presumably was placed at a point of weakness as reinforcement.

Fig. 2.31
The oar (C161) used as a bracing element in the inner wattle revetment (C167) under excavation

The revetment was supported on the pond side by large posts spaced at intervals of approximately 3m. These were mostly rectangular in section and typically measured about 20cm by 10cm, surviving to *c.* 1m in length. On the top of the wattle, and resting horizontally on the surface of the core, were two timbers (C477 and C573, see Figs 2.23A and B). Their ends were slotted into the tops of two of the posts supporting the inner wattle. Partial evidence for the existence of two others was uncovered on the north-west (C568 and C567), but they were not excavated fully. It seems clear that these timbers constituted tranverse horizontal bracing members at the tops of the wattle revetting framework.

C477 was a roughly triangular–sectioned beam which measured 2.1m long by 18cm by 11cm by 5cm, and had a mortise approximately 19cm from one end. The southern end of the timber rested on top of one of the larger upright posts and on the top of the wattle fence, while the northern, or seaward, end was badly eroded. This timber produced a date of AD 616+9 (Q10015: see pps 68-76). Beam C573 was triangular in section and was approximately 90cm long by 10cm by 6cm by 5cm and tapered in thickness towards the inner side of the dam with the narrow end slotted into a V-shaped groove on top of post C572 (see Fig. 2.23B).

Short section of middle wattle revetment (C166)

This was discovered near the wheelhouse end of the dam and 1m to the east of the inner wattle line, just above the inner side of the outer trench (Figs 2.22A and B). This section of revetment was 3.6m in length and no trace of its continuation north-westwards was encountered. Its top was connected to the outer wattle fence by two horizontal bracing

Fig. 2.32
View (from west) of the middle wattle revetment (C166) and horizontal beam C155

timbers. The spacing of posts was very similar to that of the inner wattle revetment, as indeed was that of the outer one (C168). Sampling again showed that holly was, by far, the predominant species used for both uprights and wands, along with a few examples of willow and single specimens of oak, hazel and alder (see Appendix 1).

Against the seaward side was a large, triangular–sectioned beam (C155), *c.* 2.5m long and tapering in width from 20cm at its northern western end to 6cm at its south-eastern end and with a badly-eroded mortise at its broader, north-western end. This produced a date of AD 616+9, but is thought to be after AD 614 (Q10018: see pps 68-76).

Outer sloping wattle revetment (C168)

To a large degree, the outer sloping wattlework survived in a badly-degraded condition, but a relatively well–preserved section remained in Trench 4 (Figs 2.22A and B). Here,

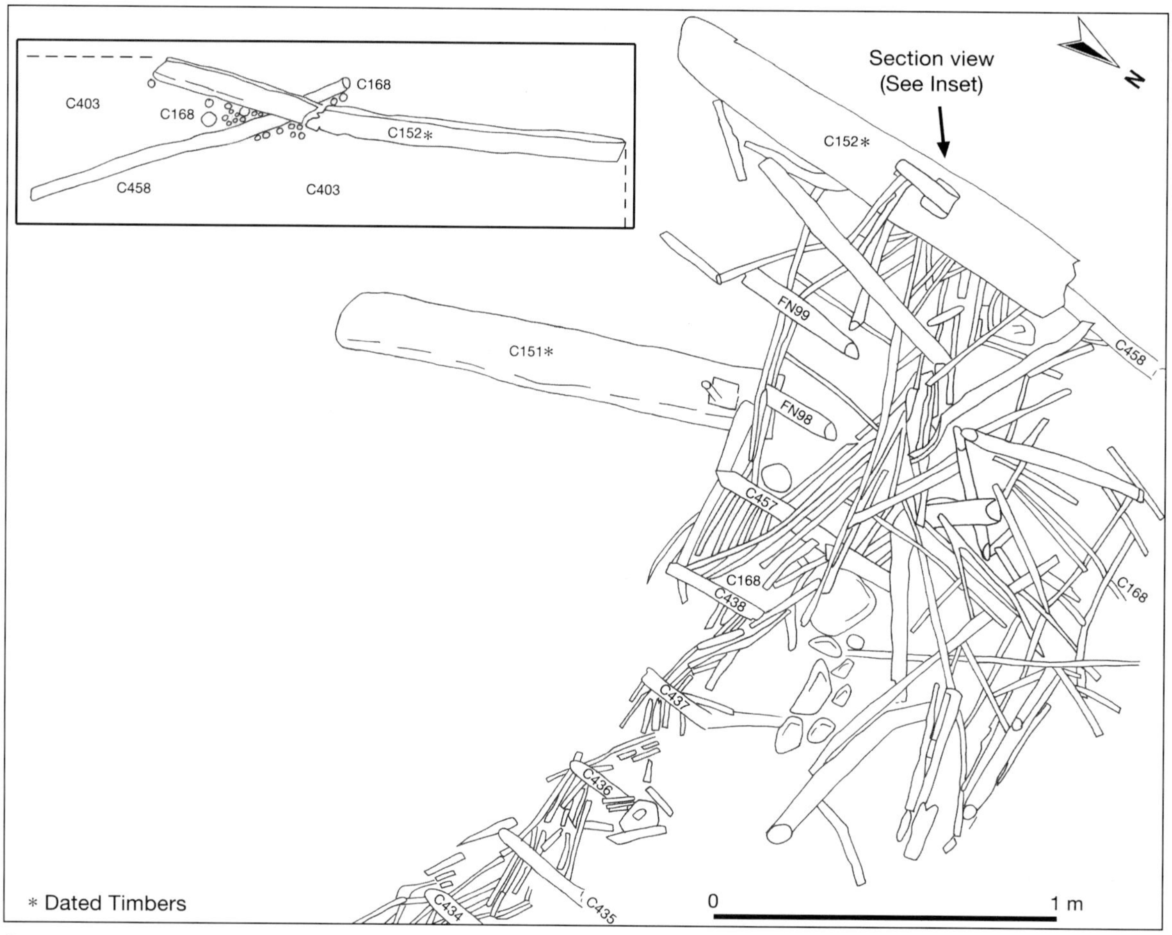

Fig. 2.33
Detail plan of outer wattle revetment showing timbers C151 and C152.

the wattle had been placed resting at an angle of about 20° over the ditch and its fill on the outer and sea-facing side of the dam. In the best-preserved section, it rested on two spaced timbers (C152 and C151, see Figs 2.22B and 2.33) set on the underlying surface of the core deposit and acting as bracing members. C152 was a radially-split plank that produced a date of late AD 618 or early AD 619 (Q10013: see pps 68-76). It measured *c.* 1.32m long by 20cm by 45–51cm and had a sub-rectangular mortise about one third along its length from its seaward end (Fig. 2.33). A sloping stake had been driven through this and into the underlying core, pinning the plank in place. Both timbers were waterlogged and in very poor condition, with evidence of weathering and worm attack.

Fig. 2.34
Timbers C152 (bottom) with post C458 through mortise and C151 after excavation

C151, a beam, also in poor condition, was located approximately 60cm to the south. It is possible that it was cut from the same tree as C152. It was also dated to late AD 618 or early AD 619 (Q10014: see pps 68-76). It was roughly triangular in section and measured 1.22m long by 16cm by 6cm. Like C152 it had a sub-rectangular mortise, through which a slender stake had been driven deep into the underlying core.

Fig. 2.35A
View from south east of the sloping outer wattle revetment

Three posts, located near the south-eastern end of the structure, had well-preserved tool marks on their points, which demonstrated the use of an axe with a broad face (C1031, C1033 and C1037: see p. 441). Four horizontally-placed bracing timbers were set on top of the revetment, and two of these were connected into the short length of middle fence (C166). Study demonstrated that most of the wood used in the outer revetment, like the other two wattle revetments, consisted of holly with a small content of willow and one example of an oak upright (see Appendix 1).

Line of bracing posts and piles

Along the outer lip of the trench was a line of large, vertical posts or piles, spaced roughly 3m apart which acted as bracing members for the revetment (see Figs 2.23A, 2.36A). One of these (C739, Fig. 2.23B) was a large, rectangular-sectioned pile some 2.69m long, which tapered to a wedge-shaped point, and leaned inwards in the direction of the dam. The top, which was badly weathered, measured 17cm by 7cm, and some 1m from the top was a rectangular-shaped mortise. This timber produced a date of AD 618±2 (Q10016: see pps 68-76).

Fig. 2.35B
View from south east of part of the sloping outer wattle revetment showing C152 (bottom left) and bracing pile C447 (top centre)

Fig. 2.36A
Two of the spaced bracing piles of the outer wattle revetment in the outer foundation trench

Fig. 2.36B
Bracing pile in the outer foundation trench under excavation

Fig. 2.36C
Bracing pile in the outer foundation trench after excavation

General observations on the wattle framework

A relatively complete picture of the original interconnected nature of the three wattle structures can be built up from the evidence. It is clear that their function was to form a retaining frame or cage for the basal core of the bank. They were buried under a deposit of clay and stone as shown in the interpretative schematic section (Fig. 2.21B). A vertical fence formed the inner or pond side of the frame, and the inner core, towards the mill end of the dam, was given added strength by an additional short stretch of vertical fence. The outer side of the frame consisted of a sloping face, like a batter, at the outer base of the dam. This side of the dam faced the tides and the slope would have lessened tidal attrition. The three structural elements were tied together on the top by spaced, horizontal timbers, only a few of which survived. It is probable that when Mill 1 was decommissioned, much of the material above the framework, including probably many of the horizontal bracing members, was removed to provide construction material for Mill 2.

North-south post line and associated short north-west/south-east post line

At the south-eastern end of the dam at its junction with the wheelhouse area, was a short line of posts orientated approximately north-south. The line was *c.* 4.3m long, but there was a gap of *c.* 1.6m near its centre. At its northern end the posts had been driven into the surface of the underlying trench deposit. It would seem that the post line may have been placed on the top of the dam and ran down its outer sloping face, and unlike the wattlework, was not buried in the foundation core of the dam. The posts were spaced at the same distance as those of the wattlework, although no trace of wattle was found. Presumably, however, they were uprights in a wattle fence from which the wattle element had been eroded away. Associated with the post line was a shorter one which diverged from it in a north-westerly/south-easterly direction. Five of the posts of the north-south line were sampled for wood identification and three were found to be of hazel and two of holly, while four of those sampled from the north-west/south-east line were of holly (see Appendix 1). The points of some of the posts had well-preserved tool marks (see Appendix 2). The function of these post lines is not entirely clear, although one possible interpretation is that they formed a barrier preventing access onto the main part of the dam.

The location of the sluice gates: the two gaps

Two conspicuous gaps can be seen in the surviving line of the stones of the dam on the present foreshore surface (see Fig. 2.37). These may possibly represent the location of the dam's sluice gates, which would have been opened to admit the incoming tide and closed at high water. It was hoped to determine if gaps represented original breaks in the dam and therefore the probable location of sluices, or if they were simply breaches resulting from erosion. The gap nearest the wheelhouse end was investigated under very difficult conditions, as the foreshore at this location consisted of extremely fluid mud.

Fig. 2.37
Aerial view of the dam from the north-east showing two gaps possibly indicating the location of sluice gates. (Gail Pollock)

The highly dangerous conditions made proper investigation impossible and the results were inconclusive. There was some indication of an apparent break in the organic-rich core deposit and inner stone-lined trench, but the true nature of both gaps remains an enigma. The excavation failed to locate any other possible trace of sluices. This problem is discussed further in Chapter 4.

THE PALISADE OR BREAKWATER (C1035)

A line of post stumps was uncovered approximately 1m out from the external base of the dam and running parallel to it (see Figs 2.22A, 2.23A and 2.38). It commenced on the south-east at the timber platform (see below) and, with the exception of a small gap, could be traced for about 26.5m. On the south-east, the stumps were overlaid by the general surface stone spread, below which was deposited marine silt. Below this, and surrounding the surviving upper parts of the posts, was a deposit of organically-rich silt, possibly derived from seaweed trapped along the post line. Further along the line to the north-west, the posts were overlaid only by naturally-deposited silt.

Approximately 63 post stumps were uncovered, and these ranged in thickness from 7cm to 9cm in diameter. They were spaced fairly uniformly between 30cm and 40cm apart and had been driven some 20cm to 30cm into the underlying sleech. Most survived to about 20cm above the original foreshore level and the levels of the tops ranged between –0.22m to –0.32m OD, with most between –0.25m and –0.27m OD. This indicates a relatively uniform rate of attrition of the posts by tidal action and decay. From the excavated evidence it seems highly probable that the post line extended the full length of the seaward-side of the dam and was thus a prominent element in the overall layout.

Fig. 2.38
The posts of the palisade/breakwater looking north-west from near its termination adjacent to timber platform

More than half of the stumps, taken from different parts of the line, were sampled for wood identification. This demonstrated that, as with the wattle revetments, the great majority were of holly. The sample also identified a few oak posts, as well as single examples of willow, ash and birch. As the line was largely composed of holly, a link between it and the layer of holly branches lining the bottom of the external ditch seems probable. It is possible to conclude that the line was placed at the same time as the lining of the ditch, with the operation involving the stripping of the branches from the holly posts. For this and other reasons, it is clear that the post line belonged to the original construction phase of the site. No evidence of wattling was found between the posts, but as only the basal part of the structure survived, it is possible that wattlework, which might have been present, has been eroded away entirely. This was the case in almost all of the Early Medieval fish traps in the lough (McErlean and O'Sullivan 2002), where only the basal stumps remained.

It is apparent that the post line was not a retaining structure on the face of the dam. There is no evidence of larger spaced posts or piles acting as bracers along its line as were found in association with other revetting elements in the dam; for example the wattle frame work and the timber revetment. The surviving remains appear to provide firm evidence for the existence of a major free-standing barrier placed in front of the seaward base of the dam. The most obvious interpretation of its function is that it acted as a breakwater protecting the seaward face of the dam. With or without wattling, this palisade would have diffused some of the force of the incoming tide against its base. The original height would have been required to be no greater than that of the average high tide level and may therefore have been around a maximum of *c.* 2m or less, with the structure largely submerged at high tide.

THE TIMBER PLATFORM OR LANDING PLACE

This structure was a major component of Mill 1, and consisted of a timber platform laid on the foreshore mud, on the seaward side of the mill complex (Figs 2.1 and 2.16). It was located to the north-east of the wheelhouse, adjacent and roughly parallel to the tail-race bank which partially overlaid it. The platform was bounded on the west by the millpond dam, on the north and east by the open foreshore and on the south by the tail-race bank. The external palisade terminated at its north-western corner.

The platform measured approximately 9m in length, was 3m broad and 70cm deep and was orientated approximately east-west. It was constructed with tightly-packed timbers laid in courses one on top of the other. Two courses were found at the western end, the timbers of the top course having been laid transversely to rest on those of the lower course which were laid longitudinally. Towards the eastern end, the number of the courses increased to four, the top laid transversely, the next two longitudinally and the bottom transversely again. Those laid transversely ranged in average length from *c.* 1.2–2m, while those in the longitudinal courses were up to 4m in length. Some of the timbers in the bottom course at the eastern end had been fixed into the foreshore mud by posts driven though mortises. The courses were laid in a stepped fashion, with the lower layers commencing and extending further to the north than the upper ones.

Approximately 135 substantial timbers were uncovered. All were of oak and comprised a mixed assemblage of worked and unworked wood. The worked pieces constitute a significant component of the assemblage and consisted of some with mortises, a small number with mortises and tenons, beams, planks and miscellaneous examples. The unworked examples encompassed logs and branches. Much of the timber showed evidence of advanced erosion by marine organisms, and by tidal action that had eroded the ends of many of the timbers and hollowed out the centres of some of the logs. Degradation was at its most severe along the northern edge of the platform which faced the incoming tide, with much of the top layer here having been lost completely (see Fig. 2.16). It is possible that one complete course on the top of the structure may have been totally eradicated, as some very degraded timber was found resting on the present top surface. The best-preserved pieces were located on the bottom layer at the eastern end, these having been protected by the overlying layers. The pattern of erosion strongly suggests that the platform was exposed to the dry and wet daily cycle of the foreshore for a considerable period. The surviving surface of the platform was level and at a height of 0.10m to 0.13m OD and thus would have been submerged at all high tides (from 1.40m to 1.90m OD).

Nine timbers were selected for dendrochronological dating, four from the bottom layer at the eastern end, one from the second layer at the same location and four from the middle and the west end of the top layer (for their locations, see Fig. 2.16). Eight were dated successfully, demonstrating that they belonged to the same felling horizon as the other timbers used in the construction of the Mill 1 complex — between the springs of AD 619 and AD 621 (see pps 68-76). The four dated timbers from the bottom layer consisted of a squared beam with an eroded mortise Q10227 (C1020) which dated to late spring AD 619, an unworked log Q10214 (C1019) dated to spring AD 620–621, Q10445 (C1022) a timber with a mortise hole and a tenon, which dated to AD 619/620 and another with a mortise hole and a tenon Q10446 (C1018) which dated to late AD 619 or early AD 620. It was not possible to date the sample from the second row Q10213 (C1003).

The four timbers from the top row comprised: a mortised beam with tenon Q10226 (C620) dated to AD 620, and unworked logs: Q10217 (C621) dated to spring AD 619, Q10216 (C625) dated to spring AD 619 or 620, and Q10215, (C619) dated to spring AD 620. It is clear therefore that the platform was constructed from the same stock of felled timbers as the rest of the mill complex. The platform produced four examples of beams with mortise holes and tenons, two coming from the well-preserved bottom layer and two from the top layer (see Fig. 2.16). The context would suggest that they were re-used timbers from another structure, and it is possible that they may have been originally fashioned to serve as door jambs (see pps 243-245). However, three of them Q10226, (C620), Q10445, (C1022) and Q10446 (C1018) have been dated to AD 619–620 and have complete sapwood, and one, Q10446, has bark, making it extremely unlikely that they were ever used for this purpose. This observation agrees well with the many other examples of timber with mortises or other signs of working which have been used in the structure of the dam. The implications of this are discussed on pps 71-72.

The stratigraphic position of the structure, partially underlying the tailrace bank, together with the dating bracket of AD 619–621, suggests strongly that its construction belonged to the primary phase of the mill complex. It seems clear that its function was to provide a firm platform on the foreshore mud, best interpreted as a landing place for boats arriving at high tide at the mill and monastery. The platform would have formed a hard stand for craft to rest on without sinking in the foreshore mud at low water. Its role as a landing place, perhaps the principal one for the monastery, seems to have continued during the life of the second mill when the platform was consolidated by a spread of

Fig. 2.39A
View of the timber platform/ landing place from above after the tailrace bank has been removed by excavation (spoil heap of stones on right)

Fig. 2.39B (far left)
View (from east) of top layer of the timber platform/landing place under excavation

Fig. 2.39C (left)
View (from east) of the timber platform under excavation

Fig. 2.39D (far left)
View (from north) of the eastern end of the bottom layer of the timber platform

Fig. 2.39E (left)
View (from the west) of the eastern end of the bottom layer of the timber platform

Fig. 2.40
One of the four examples of beams with mortise holes and tenons possibly fashioned to serve as door jambs found in the timber platform

stones laid on top, and extended northwards over the mud with a low bank (C610: see p. 109). Similar structures are familiar from the Early Medieval period in crannógs and trackways.

THE SMALL FINDS FROM MILL 1

Rather disappointingly, apart from parts of structural features and part of the waterwheel (see Chapter 6), very few small finds can be definitely assigned to the Mill 1 phase of the site. None of the small number of sherds of souterrain ware nor any of the metalworking debris and slag recovered during excavation can be demonstrated to belong to this phase.

THE DATING OF MILL 1 – Thomas McErlean and David Brown

Introduction

As has been seen the large amount of oak timber used in the construction of the first mill complex provided an excellent opportunity for the tree-ring dating (dendrochronology) of the site. This was carried out by the Palaeoecology Centre, Queen's University, Belfast. The methods used for measuring the samples are those described by Baillie (1982) and English Heritage (1998). The tree-ring series obtained from the samples from Nendrum were compared with a suite of site and regional chronologies from Ireland. Where significant and consistent correlations values were found, a start date, an end date and a felling date could be assigned.

Sampling

All possible timbers from the excavation were examined for their potential for dating purposes, and the selection of suitable timbers was carried out both during the excavation and after it had ceased. Twenty-eight wood samples from Mill 1 contexts were selected (see Table 2.2). This comprised 15 from the main section of the dam and two from the short section, two from the millpond and nine from the timber platform (or landing place). Each sample was given a unique number beginning with Q. For cross-correlation the site context number is also given in the discussion below. The character of the Nendrum samples differs somewhat from that from previous horizontal-wheeled mills in that none was from the wheelhouse or mill building, and it is probably the first site to have dam revetment timbers present. It also differs in terms of the large number sampled and successfully dated. Previously, at most mill sites only one to five samples were available or taken.

Results and interpretation

Many of the samples had complete sapwood, with their final growth rings before felling having survived. Thus, a felling date for the tree from which the timber was fashioned could be ascertained for 25 out of the 28 examples taken. It was possible to date 16 of these precisely and to estimate nine within a relatively close date range. These form a tree-ring chronology some 299 years long dating from AD 322 to AD 620/21.

The dating of individual timbers has already been given within their relevant contexts and a summary of the these is provided in Tables 2.1 and 2.2. Table 2.1 gives the results from the 16 precisely-dated examples – divided into five dating brackets – their location in the mill complex and the nature of the timber. The results from all the samples are shown in Table 2.2 including information on the three samples that proved impossible to date.

The 16 precisely-dated examples (see Table 2.1) extend over the period late AD 618/early AD 619 to late AD 620/early AD 621, and thus give clear evidence that timber used in the construction of the mill complex was felled over these two years. Bark and

Table 2.1: Precisely-dated samples

Dating Brackets	Location	Timber
Late AD 618/Early AD 619		
Q10013 (C152)	Main dam section (outer wattle revetment)	Plank with mortise hole
Q10014 (C151)	Main dam section (outer wattle revetment)	Beam with mortise hole
Q9931 (C64)	Short dam section (pond side revetment)	Beam
Spring AD 619		
Q9917 (C133)	Main dam section (organic core)	Beam with mortise hole used as an upright
Q9918 (C134)	Main dam section (orange clay bank)	Pile with mortise hole
Q10217 (C621)	Timber platform (top layer)	Unworked log
Q10227 (C1020)	Timber platform (bottom layer)	Beam with mortise hole
Q10228 (C676)	Main dam section (junction of dam and tailrace bank)	Irregular-shaped timber
Late AD 619/Early AD 620		
Q10216 (C625)	Timber platform (top layer)	Unworked log
Q10445 (C1022)	Timber platform (bottom layer)	Beam with mortise hole and tenon
Q10446 (C1018)	Timber platform (bottom layer)	Beam with mortise hole and tenon, possible door jamb
Spring AD 620		
Q10215, (C619)	Timber platform (top layer)	Unworked log
Q10226 (C620)	Timber platform (top layer)	Beam with mortise hole and tenon, possible door jamb
AD Late 620/Early AD 621		
Q9932 (C170)	Millpond (bottom)	Plank
Q10019 (C156)	Millpond (bottom)	Pile used horizontally
Q10214 (C1019)	Timber platform (bottom layer)	Unworked log

sapwood are fragile and easily damaged so often do not survive intact. Thus, when the sapwood is complete and in good condition it indicates that the timber was used shortly after felling. The presence of complete sapwood in these samples suggests strongly that the construction of the mill was being carried out over this two year period.

This dating bracket is further re-enforced by the age determinations for a further six samples (see Table 2.2), in which some of the sapwood (the outer rings) was damaged. Age determinations for these are assessed within a range of plus or minus nine years. Their felling dates are within the dating bracket AD 607–634. In the case of these samples, felling is estimated to have occurred after AD 614. Given the firm felling horizon between AD 614 and 621 established from the precisely-dated samples it seems highly probable that these six samples with some missing sapwood rings were felled in the same years.

As a result of the large number of successfully dated samples, it was possible to detect five dating brackets (see Table 2.1), and therefore to propose a dating sequence or phasing of construction of the individual components of the mill complex between the years AD 619 and 621.

Dating brackets late AD 618 or early AD 619 and spring AD 619

Three samples, all from the dam, had precise felling dates of late AD 618 or early AD 619. They are Q11013 (C152) and Q100014 (C151), (possibly from the same tree) from the outer wattle revetment of the main section of dam, and Q9931 (C64) a horizontal beam from the junction of the base of the short section of dam and millpond. These demonstrate that trees were being felled during the winter months of AD 618–619 for use in building the dam. Q9931 (C64) has complete sapwood and, as possibly the earliest sample in the assemblage, may provide evidence to support the interpretation that the short section of the dam adjacent to the land, was constructed first. Five samples had precise felling dates of spring AD 619, probably April or May. These are Q9918 (C134) from the orange clay component of the main section of dam, Q9917 (C133) from the organic core, Q10228 (C676) from the junction of the dam and the tailrace bank and two samples from the timber platform (landing place), Q10227 (C1020) from the bottom layer and Q10217 from the top layer. They appear to demonstrate that tree felling for timber for the construction of the dam continued during spring AD 619. As there are no later-dated timbers from the dam, it may be deduced that its construction had been completed by the end of AD 619.

Dating bracket late AD 619 to early 620 and spring AD 620

Three samples could be assigned to the period late AD 619 to early 620. They are Q10216, Q10445 and Q10446 all from the bottom layer of the timber platform. Two samples could be assigned to the bracket of spring AD 620, Q10215 and Q10226, both from the timber platform. These demonstrate that tree felling continued or was resumed during the winter and spring months of AD 619–620.

Dating bracket late AD 620 to early 621

Three samples could be dated to late AD 620/early AD 621. They are Q9932 and Q10019 from the bottom of the millpond and Q10214 from the bottom layer of the timber platform. The two dated timbers, Q9932 and Q10019, used in the lining of the bottom of the millpond appear to have been felled up to 18–24 months later than those used in the dam, and would seem to demonstrate that work on the millpond was carried out towards the end of the building programme. This appears logical from the building sequence, since work on lining the millpond could only proceed after the dam had been constructed.

The eight dated samples from the timber platform (see Table 2.2) include timbers from AD 619, AD 620 and possibly AD 621. The one timber dated to late AD 620/early AD 621 (Q10214) was found on the bottom layer so the creation of the timber platform cannot predate this. It would seem to suggest, therefore, that the timbers used in its construction were a gather-up of lumber, perhaps leftovers from the stockpile used in the construction of the main mill complex. As with the millpond, the timber platform appears to have been one of the last structures put in place. This also appears logical in the building sequence.

Three samples – Q9917 (C154), Q10020 (C747) and Q9915 (C129) – all from the timber revetment of the main dam, produced potentially earlier dates than the AD 618–621 bracket and raise the possibility of the common practice of using timbers recycled from another structure. Q9917 (C154), a beam, which had incomplete sapwood, was dated to AD 603+9. It is possible that the number of missing sapwood rings may be underestimated and its true felling date may not be incompatible with the AD 618–621 felling episode. Samples from Q10020 and Q9915 have possible 6th century dates and are therefore of great interest in that they may constitute evidence of activity at the monastery in that century, and thus predate all of the other current archaeological evidence. Q10020 (C746), a plank from the timber revetment of the dam, was estimated to date to AD 560+9. It consists of heartwood with all the sapwood having been removed and could possibly have come from the inner section of a tree felled about AD 619. Q9915 (C129), also a plank from the timber revetment with an estimated date of AD 513+9 is from the inner section of the tree and the felling date could have been considerably later. Therefore, on dendrochronological grounds neither of these two timbers can be conclusively used as evidence for the presence of 6th-century re-used wood. However, Q9915 (C129), the plank used as an upright in the timber revetment of the dam has two complete peg holes (one with a peg *in situ*) and one unfinished one suggesting that it was originally not only prepared for use but actually used for some purpose.

Whereas the dendrochronological evidence cannot be used unambiguously to support the case for re-used timber, a large number of the dated timbers in addition to plank Q9915 (C129) mentioned above, have a character that seems to constitute evidence of re-use. The clearest manifestation is the presence of many timbers with mortise holes or other features, which play no part in the way they were employed in the structures of the mill complex. The most obvious examples of this are the timbers with mortise holes and tenons (Q10445, Q10446 and Q10226), which may possibly have been door jambs. They were found making up the layers in the timber platform and all had complete sapwood dating to AD 619/620. Others include the examples with unused mortise holes, many of which also have complete sapwood and, in some cases, bark suggesting strongly that they were never used for the purpose for which they were prepared and therefore cannot be demonstrated to have been actually from an earlier structure. This presents a major problem for interpretation which is further discussed in Chapter 9.

It remains to discuss the three samples among the 28 taken which proved impossible to date dendrochronologically – Q9896 (C34), Q9914 (C127) and Q10213 (C1003). The most important of these is sample Q9896 (C34), the large beam encased in grey clay and buried in the foundation trench of the short section of the dam, and possibly functioning as the rear-support beam for the penstock or penstocks of the mill. This has 149 annual growth rings, complete sapwood with its final spring vessels present and the under-bark surface visible, and was probably felled in late April or May. There were no major problems associated with the measurement of the tree-ring pattern on the sample but in spite of being measured at least five times none of these measurements nor a combination of them provided acceptable correlation values with existing tree-ring chronologies. With complete sapwood it was expected that the tree from which this timber was taken would have fallen into the range AD 619 to AD 621 determined for most of the other timbers from the site. This was not, however, the case. At an early stage in the excavations, it was suggested that it might be part of an intermediate mill between Mill 1 and Mill 2 (dated dendrochronologically to AD 788), but it was later confirmed stratigraphically to be a part of Mill 1.

This poses the question of why a sample with 149 clear annual growth rings and complete sapwood failed to provide an adequate dendrochronological date. One possible answer is that its growing environment was somewhat different from most of the other samples. It may have been growing in wetter conditions near the coastal margins, or in a boggy patch of ground. The possibility that it is a re-used timber from another building or structure seems very unlikely considering that the sample showed complete sapwood as, in most cases, timbers lose sapwood during re-use. In any case a re-used timber would be expected to produce an earlier date. The other possibility is that it came from afar, but this is unlikely considering its condition. If the tree came from a different part of Ireland, it would be expected to date with, and have consistent correlation dates with regional and local site chronologies from its general location. If imported from England or Scotland, then it should give good correlation values with chronologies from these countries. Extensive checking failed to produce any consistent or significant correlation values.

The other two samples that failed to yield dates are Q9914 (C127) and Q10231 (C1003). Q9914 seems to be a largely unworked stump and was used as a foundation timber in the main section of the dam. It had complete sapwood, but was only 70 years in length and had many and varied problems in the tree-ring pattern. Sample Q10213 from the middle-layer of the timber platform had 125 rings, including 60 sapwood rings, but again posed serious problems in trying to extract an intelligible ring pattern. Other aspects of the information derived from the dendrochronological analyses are discussed in Chapter 10.

Table 2.2: Results of all the samples from Mill 1

The timber revetment

Sample and context no	Description	No of years	Start date	End date	Date (felling date or estimated felling date range)
Q9920 (C153)	Horizontal member plank, radially split, incomplete sapwood	276	AD 333	AD 608	AD 611 ± 9 but after AD 608
Q10017 (C154)	Horizontal member beam with mortise hole, incomplete sapwood	262	AD 330	AD 591	AD 603 ± 9
Q10020 (C746)	Horizontal member plank, heavily truncated, no sapwood	258	AD 271	AD 528	AD 560 ± 9 or later (probably inner section of tree felled AD 619)
Q9915 (C129)	Upright, plank, has two peg holes, one with peg *in situ*, radially split and heavily truncated, from inner section of tree. No sapwood	160	AD 322	AD 481	AD 513 ± 9 or later
Q9916 (C132)	Upright, squared pile, partial sapwood	129	AD 478	AD 606	AD 625 ± 9

The orange clay bank (C79) at end of dam near wheelhouse

Sample and context no	Description	No of years	Start date	End date	Date (felling date or estimated felling date range)
Q9918 (C134)	Upright pile with mortise hole, complete sapwood and final spring vessels	136	AD 484	AD 619	April/May AD 619
Q9919 (C135)	Upright pile with mortise hole, partial sapwood	133	AD 484	AD 616	AD 625 ± 9
Organic core					
Q9917 (C133)	Upright, beam with mortise hole, complete sapwood	121	AD 499	AD 619	April/May AD 619
Inner wattle revetment (C167)					
Q10015 (C477)	Horizontal bracing timber, beam with mortise hole, incomplete sapwood	123	AD 485	AD 607	AD 616 ± 9 years
Middle wattle revetment (C166)					
Q10018 (C155)	Bracing member, beam with mortise hole, incomplete sapwood	182	AD 433	AD 614	AD 616 ± 9 but after AD 614
Outer wattle revetment (C168)					
Q10016 (C739)	Upright, rectangular pile with mortise hole, complete but damaged sapwood	88	AD 529	AD 616	AD 618 ± 1-2 years
Q10014 (C151)	Horizontal bracing timber, beam with mortise, hole, complete sapwood	180	AD 439	AD 618	Late AD 618 or AD 619
Q10013 (C152)	Horizontal bracing timber, radially split plank with mortise hole (stake through mortise), complete sapwood	189	AD 430	AD 618	Late AD 618 or early AD 619

Undated		No of rings
Q9914 (C127)	Stump used as foundation timber, complete sapwood.	70

Junction of dam and tailrace bank (C613)

Q10228 (C676)	Irregular, complete sapwood	141	AD 461	AD 619	Late spring 619

Short section of dam south of the wheelhouse

Q9931 (C64)	Pile (pointed end) used as a horizontal beam, junction of the base of the short section of dam and millpond, complete sapwood	160	AD 459	AD 618	Late AD 618 or early AD 619

Undated		No of rings
Q9896 (C34)	Large beam in core of short section of dam possible penstock rear support beam. 31 sapwood rings, pith missing	149

The millpond

Q9932 (C170)	Horizontal plank, radially split, complete sapwood	139	AD 482	AD 620	Late AD 620 or early AD 621
Q10019 (C156)	Pile laid horizontally on surface of grey clay lining, radially split, complete sapwood	122	AD 499	AD 620	Late AD 620 or early AD 621

Sample and context no	Description	No of years	Start date	End date	Date (felling date or estimated felling date range)
The Timber Platform					
Bottom layer					
Q10214 (C1019)	Unworked log, complete sapwood	138	AD 483	AD 620	Late AD 620 or early AD 621
Q10227 (C1020)	Mortised beam, complete sapwood	92	AD 528	AD 619	Late spring AD 619
Q10445 (C1022)	Mortise hole and tenon, (stake through mortise) almost complete sapwood	141	AD 476	AD 616	AD 619 or 620
Q10446 (C1018)	Mortise and tenon (stake through mortise). Possible door jamb, complete sapwood and some bark present	140	AD 480	AD 619	AD 619 or early AD 620
Top layer					
Q10215 (C619)	Unworked log, complete sapwood	104	AD 516	AD 619	Spring AD 620
Q10216 (C625)	Unworked log, complete sapwood	141	AD 479	AD 619	Late AD 619 or early AD 620
Q10217 (C621)	Umworked log, complete sapwood, cut with bow saw.	105	AD 515	AD 619	Late spring AD 619
Q10226 (C620)	Mortised beam, possible door jamb, complete sapwood	144	AD 476	AD 619	Early spring AD 620
Middle layer – undated					
Q10213 (C1003)	Unworked, complete sapwood	125 rings			

THE END OF THE FIRST MILL

There is no compelling evidence to suggest lack of continuity between the two mills although this is difficult to demonstrate with certainty. Therefore it is possible to postulate that Mill 1 had a working life approaching 167 years, spanning the period from AD 621 when it appears to have been completed, to AD 789 when it was replaced by Mill 2. It is to be presumed that by the late 8th century the design of a mill laid out in the early 7th century would have become outdated and overtaken with improved mill technology. As will be seen, some aspects of more sophisticated technology can be detected in the archaeology of the second mill.

Chapter 3

The Second Mill *c.* AD 789

Thomas McErlean
and Norman Crothers

Chapter 3
The Second Mill *c.* AD 789

Thomas McErlean and Norman Crothers

INTRODUCTION - THE NEW MILL

Towards the end of the 8th century, Mill 1 was replaced by a new mill, Mill 2. Tree-ring dating of one its structural timbers found *in situ* at the base of its wheelhouse, suggests that this took place around AD 789. To allow for this new work, most of the old mill dam was dismantled and its penstock intake channel, wheelhouse and tail-race were filled in. Mill 2 was built to a different, and improved, design to that of Mill 1, but on a similarly ambitious scale, which showed that the monastery was as vibrant a community at the end of the 8th century as it had been at the beginning of the 7th. Its outstandingly well-preserved remains constitute probably the most complete example of an Early Medieval tide mill complex to have been discovered so far anywhere in the world.

Many of the main features of Mill 2 were visible above ground before excavation, although not recognised as such. These included the millpond and its enclosing dams, the surviving top of the stone wheelhouse and the tailrace walls. Most of the excavation work on it took place during the 1999 season and its features were uncovered mainly in Trenches 1, 3, 4, 5 and 6. The main features discovered are shown on Figs 3.1A and B and include the millpond, dams, the penstock and its intake channel, the wheelhouse, tailrace, platform and a landing place. Trench 1 was located over the wheelhouse and part of the eastern dam, while the adjacent Trench 4, on the west, covered parts of the eastern and northern dams, the penstock, the penstock intake channel and part of the millpond. Trenches 2 and 5, further to the west, provided sections through the northern dam, and part of Trench 6 covered the tailrace, the platform and landing place.

Discussion of the excavation is presented from west to east, starting from the extant remains of the millpond and its dams and proceeding to the wheelhouse, tailrace and other features on the east.

THE MILLPOND DAMS

The millpond is enclosed by two dams, parts of which are very well preserved. It was the existence of these features that first attracted attention to the site during the Strangford Lough intertidal survey in 1997 (McErlean *et al.* 2002). The northern dam runs slightly south-west to north-east (but for convenience, is referred to in the text as the

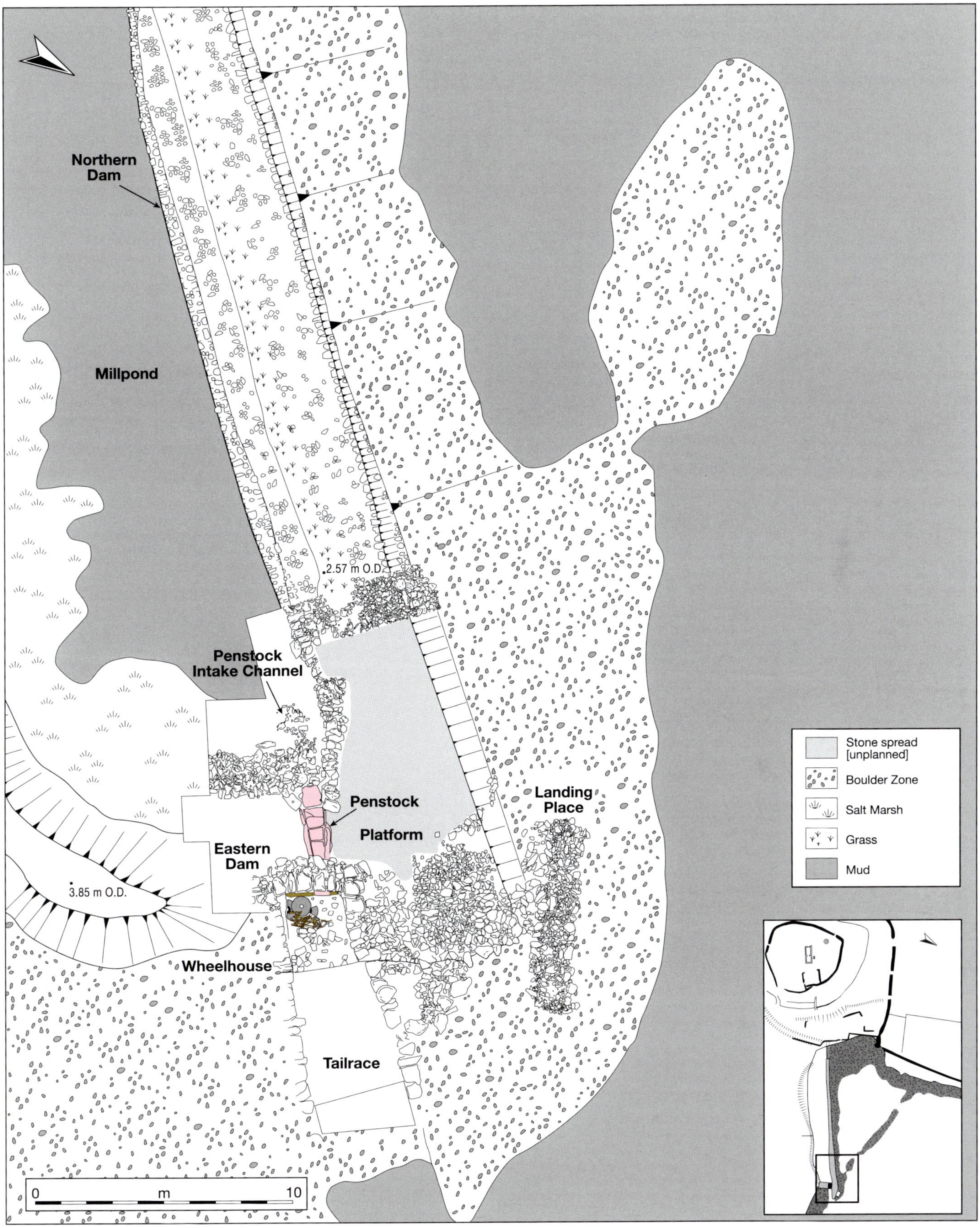

Fig. 3.1A
Plan of the main features of Mill 2

'northern' dam), and the eastern dam runs slightly south-east to north-west (referred to for convenience as the 'eastern' dam), and together they form the sides of the rectangular millpond.

The northern dam

The northern dam is prominent on the foreshore as a linear bank of stones approximately 125m long and extending out from the high-water mark near the base of the monastic enclosure (see Fig. 3.1A). In an attempt to ascertain if it extended westwards beyond its visible remains and under the road to connect with the outer monastic enclosure at this location, a trench (Trench 2, see Fig. 3.3B) was excavated immediately outside the modern boundary wall of the site. Unfortunately this area had been completely disturbed by service pipes and road construction, and nothing of significance was encountered.

The dam is poorly preserved for its first 32m from the western end, and has been reduced to a linear band of stones *c.* 3m wide and some 30cm high above the surface of the millpond. The height of its top surface is at 1.9m OD. Based on an estimated figure discussed later (p. 105), the original height of the dam is thought to have been at

Fig. 3.1C
View of the dams and millpond of Mill 2 (centre right) from the northeast (Gail Pollock)

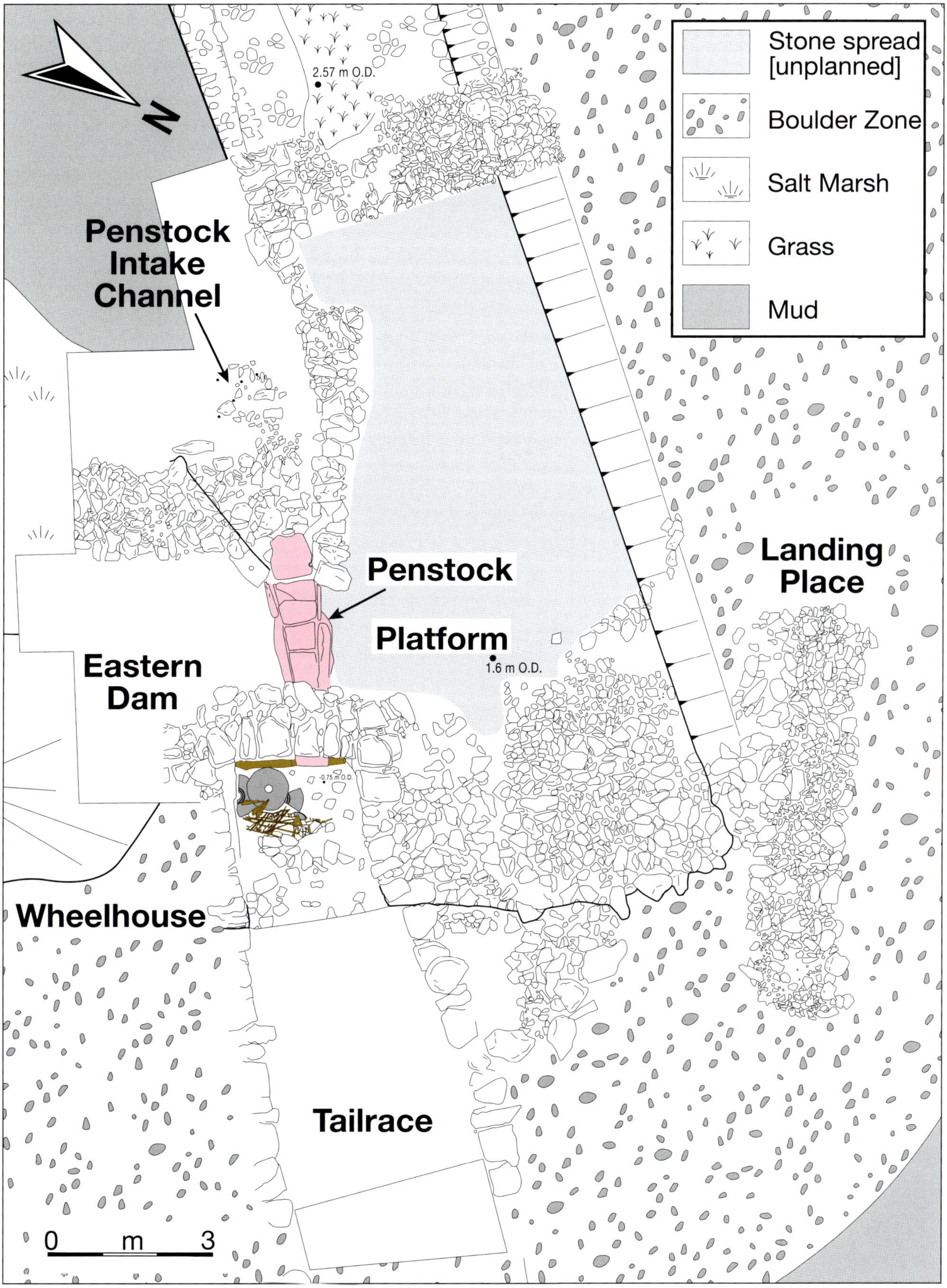

Fig. 3.1B
Plan of the excavated features of Mill 2

c. 3m OD and therefore some 1.1m of its height may have been lost in this section. For the next 62m, it becomes gradually more substantial and increases in width to *c.* 4m at the base and *c.* 3m at the top, and is up to 1m high above the surface of millpond. The height of its top surface is at 2.17m OD and therefore *c.* 83cm have been lost. This is followed by an extremely well-preserved section consisting of two wall faces with a core of clay between them and grass growing on the top. It is 28m long and from *c.* 5m to 5.8m wide at the base, 4m wide at the top, and stands *c.* 1.3m above the present foreshore level of the millpond (see Fig. 3.2A). The top of dam here is at 2.57m OD and is therefore well above the high tide range (mean high water springs level at 1.9m), and may have lost only about 43cm of its original height. This section ends abruptly in a tidally-eroded scarp *c.* 1m high. The upper level of the eastern end of the dam has been largely destroyed by erosion and probably also by human activity, and has been reduced to the level of the millpond at 1.6m OD, thus having lost *c.* 1.4m of its height. The surface of the top dam widens out from 4m to 6m at this location and merges with a platform adjacent to the wheelhouse and site of the mill.

Three trenches were excavated across the line of the northern dam (Trenches 3, 4 and 5). Trench 3 was a small cutting across the surviving basal layers towards the western end (see Figs 3.3A and 3.3B). This showed the dam to be 3.6m wide at this point, and to consist of an external stone revetment wall on the seaward side 1.6m wide, and an inner stone revetment wall on the millpond side *c.* 80m wide, with a core made up of sandy, orange clay between. The base of the outer revetment wall was built directly on top of the surface of the foreshore, and its inner and outer faces were constructed neatly using large boulders, the space between being filled with smaller stones. Below the inner revetment wall and the clay core was a foundation trench with a U-shaped section, *c.* 80cm wide and 30cm deep, excavated into the foreshore and filled with pink clay.

Trench 5 was cut through the best-preserved length of the dam (see Figs 3.4A and 3.4B), and provided an extremely good picture of its construction. Excavation confirmed the features observed in Trench 3, which showed that the dam was composed of an inner core of clay and earth held in place by stone revetment walls on the inner and outer sides.

At this location, it survives to 2.1m in maximum height above the original pre- millpond foreshore and measuring 5.8m wide at the base and 4m on the top (the latter surface is at 2.57m OD). The external revetment wall is approximately 2.2m wide and 2m high. Its outer face is neatly constructed (see Figs 3.1B and 3.4A) with very large, sub-rectangular boulders up to 70cm wide and 40cm high (C552) placed to give it a slight batter. The face of its inner wall face is similar, and the intervening space between the two is tightly filled with smaller stones and pebbles.

Partly leaning against the outer revetment wall, and forming the first component of the core of the dam, was an extensive deposit of grey clay (C530) up to 1.5m wide and 1.2m

Fig. 3.2A
The well-preserved section of the north dam looking back westwards towards the monastic enclosure

Fig. 3.2B
The north dam at low water looking eastwards from the monastic enclosure

Fig. 3.2C
Outer face of the north dam wall (from east) on a rising tide

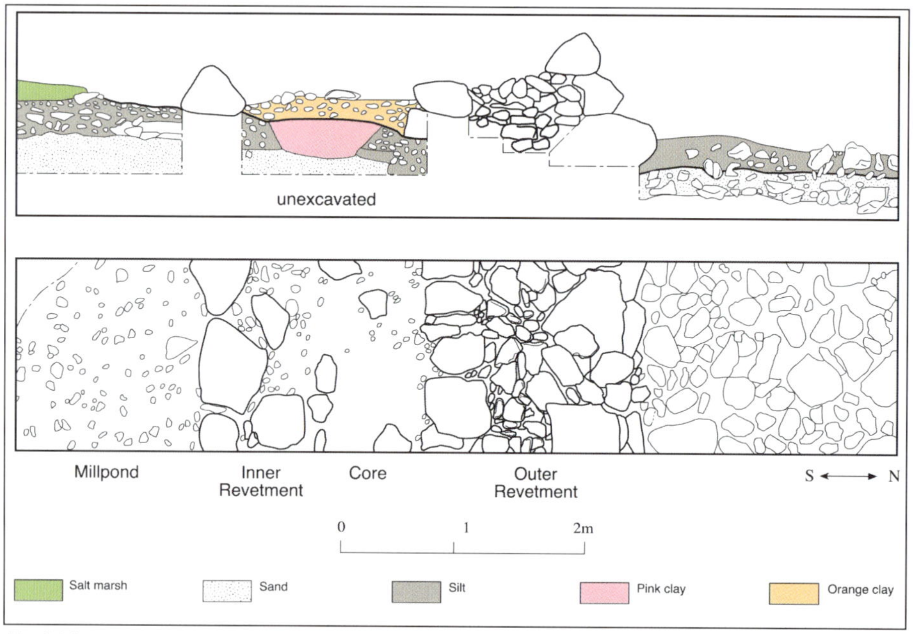

Fig. 3.3A
Excavation plan and section of the north dam in Trench 3

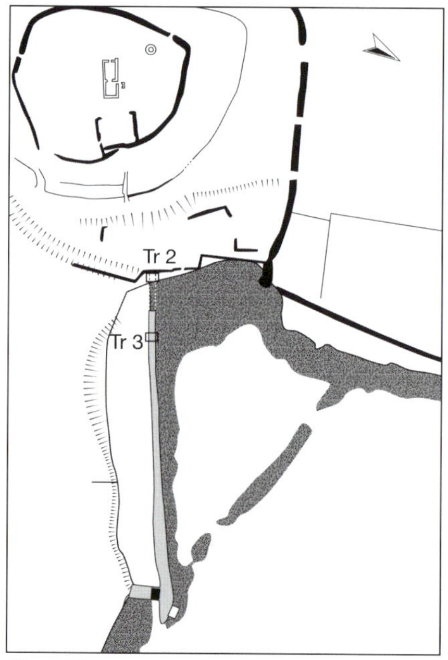

Fig. 3.3B
Location of Trenches 2 and 3

high. The second component was a deposit approximately 1.4m wide and 1.4m high, composed of interleaved lenses of brown, humic soil and grey clay (C529). This was nicknamed 'the zebra layer' because of the appearance of its contrasting colours. Overlying this and the grey clay was a deposit of orange clay (C504) *c.* 1.7m wide and 70cm high, which, at this location, has grass growing on its surface.

The revetment wall forming the inner, or millpond, side of the dam is well constructed and is 1.4m wide and 1.6m high. Its inner and outer faces are formed by medium to large boulders, and there is a core of smaller stones and pebbles in between. The most interesting feature of this wall is that the spaces between the stones have been densely and solidly packed with moss.

Fig. 3.4A
North-south section (east facing) through the north dam in Trench 5

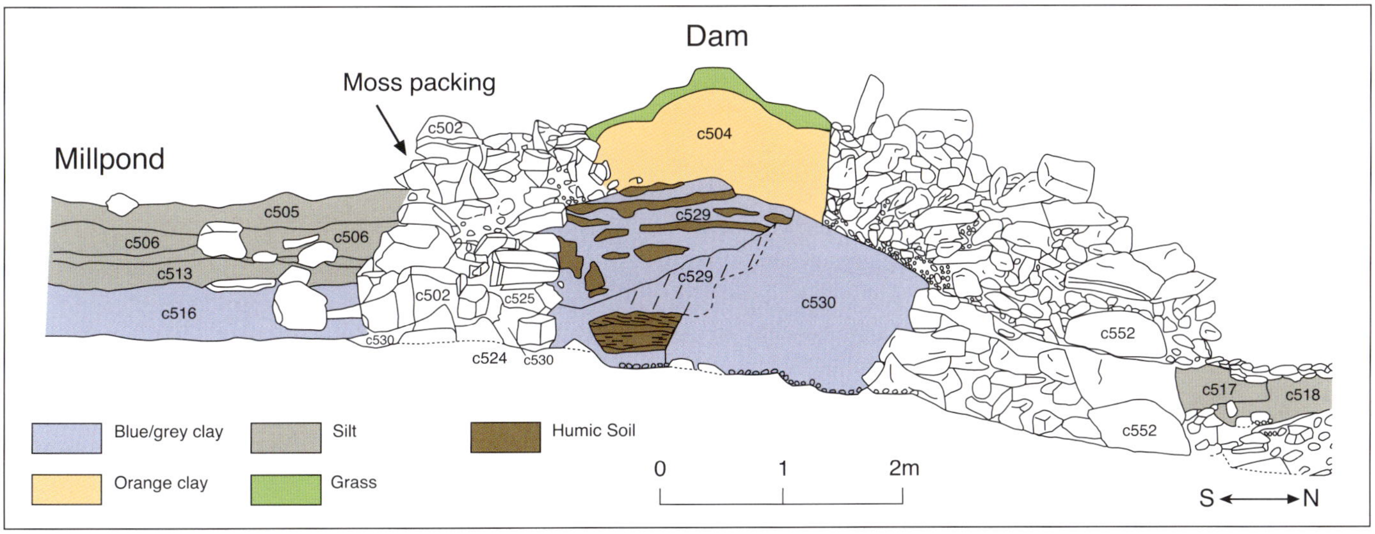

The eastern dam

The eastern end of the millpond is enclosed by a short length of dam approximately 16m long, which commences above the shore on the south and runs approximately from the south-east to terminate on the north-west at the junction with the northern dam. The section extending out from the adjacent shore, approximately 12m long, is well preserved and is covered by a dense growth of blackthorn. It is 6m wide at the base and stands *c.* 1.66m above the present level of the millpond. Its top surface is at 3.85m OD and probably sloped down to the site of the millhouse. The upper layers of the northern end have been largely destroyed and are reduced in height almost to the same level as the millpond at 1.6m OD.

Fig. 3.4 B
North dam under excavation from north

The basal layers of the northern end, adjacent to the wheelhouse and site of the mill, were excavated in Trench 4 where it could be demonstrated that part of the dam of Mill 1 was reutilised (Figs 2.5 and 2.8B). The old dam was given additional width on the western side by building a stone retaining wall (C36) *c.* 3m in front of the old work and the intervening space was filled in largely with silt (see Fig. 2.5). This retaining wall, like that of inner one of the northern dam, was caulked with moss. The base of the space between the new and the old dam retaining walls was filled with a humic layer (C40). Above this was dumped a layer of silt (C3b), some 50cm thick, which was capped with a thick layer of orange clay (C10). Part of a waterwheel belonging to the first mill, which consisted of the hub with remains of two paddles *in situ* (see pps 156-159), was found at the junction of C3b and C10. The context of its deposition suggests that it was casually dumped here during the dismantling of Mill 1, which went hand-in-hand with the construction phase of Mill 2. The north-south surviving basal layers through the east dam are shown on Fig. 2.8.

Location of the sluice gate

The one key element for which no evidence was found in either dam was the intake sluice gate or tide gate. This would have been opened during the rising tide to fill the millpond and closed at high tide to impound the water. Its possible location can be narrowed down from the existing remains. A location on the eastern dam is highly unlikely as there is no trace of a gap in the extant remains, some of which survive well above the tidal heights. It is possible — but unlikely — that it was located on a channel underneath the millhouse, near the top of the back wall of the wheelhouse and that all trace has been obliterated. But it seems much more probable that its location was somewhere along the northern dam. The lowest point on the two dams around the wheelhouse where they have been lowered by erosion is at 1.6m OD, and provides a minimum level for the base of the sluice. The better-preserved parts of the northern dam range in height from *c.* 1.9m OD to 2.6m OD and are devoid of any obvious gap where a sluice may have been placed. This narrows down the possible location of the sluice gate to a relatively short space about 4m in length between the well-preserved portion of the northern dam and its northern-eastern end (Fig. 3.5). A sluice gate at this location has the advantage of close proximity to the mill from where it could be supervised. Based on the minimum surviving height of the dams at 1.6m OD, Browne (see Chapter 8) suggests that only tides over this height were impounded in the configuration of Mill 2. Further aspects of the missing sluice gate are discussed in Chapters 4 and 8.

THE MILLPOND

The millpond still retains it original sub-rectangular shape and measures *c.* 125m long by 16m in maximum width, giving it a surface area of *c.* 2000m^2 (Fig. 3.1A). Some two-thirds of its interior is occupied by salt marsh, which presumably invaded the pond gradually as it silted up, and now covers the entire western end and most of the southern margin.

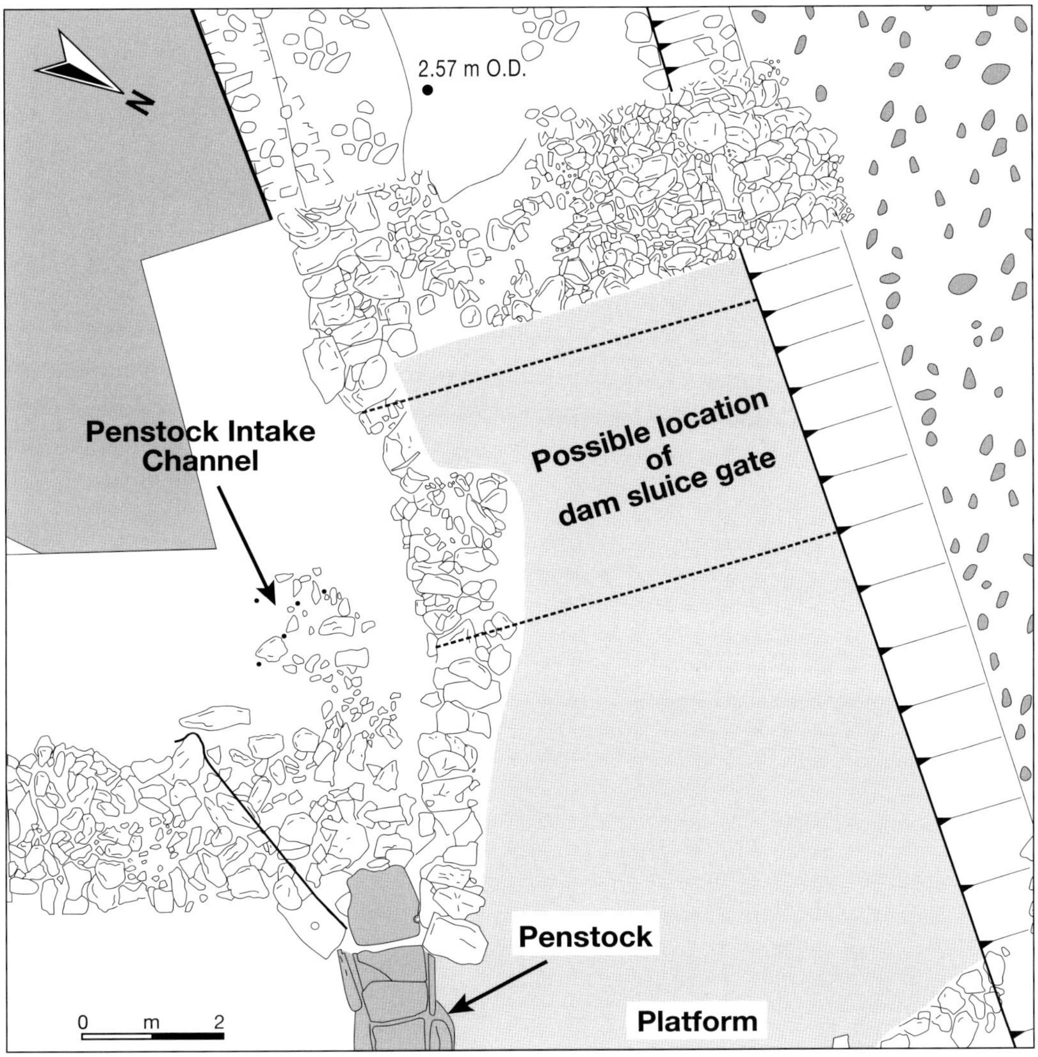

Fig. 3.5
Possible location of the dam sluice gate

The areas free of salt marsh have a muddy foreshore surface with occasional stones and are still covered with water at high tide, while at low tide, all of the water drains out of the pond.

Towards the western end of the millpond are two low cross-walls formed by lines of boulders, one extending over the line of the northern dam and continuing on down to the mud zone of the foreshore. A third wall is located on the seaward side of the northern dam near its western end. It is clear that these features post-date its use as a millpond and probably date to the 18th century, and are associated with the subdivision of the foreshore to regulate seaweed exploitation. Small, single-line boulder walls in the intertidal zone are a prominent feature of the Strangford Lough foreshore (McErlean *et al.* 2002, 345–346).

Fig. 3.6A
The millpond at approaching low water from the site of the mill looking westwards towards the monastic enclosure

Fig. 3.6B
The millpond at approaching high water from the site of the mill looking westwards towards the monastic enclosure

The flat surface of the millpond when empty contrasts sharply with the adjacent sloping upper foreshore on the north and east, suggesting strongly that its creation entailed the terracing of the original profile of the shore. The steep and probably largely artificial carp forming the coastal edge along its southern boundary, again in contrast to the much gentler adjacent local coastal-edge topography, further strengthens this interpretation. It would seem therefore that the construction of the millpond involved the modification by excavation of a large area of the foreshore and coastal edge.

Fig. 3.6C
The millpond of Mill 2 at high water looking eastward from inside the monastic enclosure

Approximately 14.4m^2 of the eastern end of millpond 2 was excavated in Trench 4, along with a small area along its northern edge in Trench 5. Although this constituted less than 1% of the total area, it succeeded in demonstrating some of its most important features.

The stratigraphy of the second millpond

The stratigraphic sequence in the millpond is explained by reference to (Figs 2.5 and 2.6). Some of the layers in these sections have already been discussed with reference to the first millpond.

Below the salt marsh on the southern side of the pond (Fig. 2.5) was approximately 60cm of naturally-deposited silt consisting of three distinct layers (C1, C2 and C38), differentiated by consistency and slightly varying shades of grey. C1 was *c.* 10cm thick on average and consisted of a sticky, semi-fluid muddy silt, while C2 was *c.* 20cm thick and is drier and sandier. C38 was darker in colour, purer in consistency and *c.* 30cm thick, representing the slow and gradual build up of silt in the millpond during the working life of the mill and after it went out of use. In places at the base of C38 was a very thin deposit of fine, light-grey sand (C173). Below the silt layers, the stratigraphy changed radically to a 40cm-thick layer of brown, humic soil (C40), which ran under the stone revetting wall of the eastern dam and ended at the base of the revetment wall of the dam of Mill 1. Underlying this was a layer of stones (C42) in a matrix of silt (C174) about 30cm thick. The former represents the division between the ponds of Mills 1 and 2 (the layers associated with the first mill pond are discussed in Chapter 2).

Below the area of the pond not covered by salt marsh, towards the central and northern part of the excavated part of the millpond, was another natural silt or mud deposit (C3a). It was distinguishable from C1 and C2, being more fluid in consistency, darker grey in colour and containing some gravel (visible on the north-south, east-facing section of

Trench 4, Fig. 2.6), and directly overlaid silt C38. Cut into the surface of C3a was a pit (C176) *c.* 40cm wide by 40cm deep, which contained the skeleton of a dog in a hessian sack (see p. 282). The humic or soil layer (C40) below C38 extended over three-quarters of the excavated area of the millpond surface, ending at the wall of the intake channel and the area in front of it. Below this again were the layers associated with first the millpond, silt layer C43 and the underlying deposits of dark- and light-grey clays (C69 and C91), which formed the lining of the intake channel for Mill 1 and were re-used for that of Mill 2 (see Chapter 2).

The millpond layers in Trench 5 (see Fig. 3.4A.) were similar to those further to the east in Trench 4. The top 55–60cm consisted of naturally-deposited grey silt in which three distinct bands could be observed. The first *c.* 20cm (C505) had a slightly sandy texture characteristic of silt with a growth of salt marsh vegetation, while the next 25cm (C506) had some clay content and overlaid some 10cm of darker grey silt (C513). Below the silt layers was a thick deposit of grey estuarine clay (C516), up to 40cm deep, which contained some stones. This rested on the natural foreshore and can be interpreted as an artificial lining placed on the bottom of the millpond in the area leading to the penstock intake channel.

Interpretation of the stratigraphy of the upper layers of the millpond of Mill 2 is relatively straightforward. Layers C1, C2, C3 and C38 are naturally-deposited silt, which built up within the millpond over the many centuries since the mill went out of use. Beneath the natural layers of silt deposit lay two man-made deposits, C42 and C40, associated with the making of the millpond of Mill 2.

Fig. 3.6D
The stratigraphy on the south side of the millpond

The first stage of construction was the dumping of a stone spread (C42) over the silt of the pond of Mill 1 (C43, C174). This deposit was obviously placed as a foundation layer to consolidate the silt of the old millpond. It contained occasional patches of grey clay and some wood, which can be interpreted as construction debris deposited during the building phase of the adjacent dams and mill buildings. The dump of stones (C42) was followed by a second foundation layer consisting of a thick layer of humic soil (C40) the surface of which represents the bottom of the new millpond. As this ran under the new dam revetment wall, terminating at the base of the earlier one to the east, it clearly was laid down in the primary stages of construction before the new revetment wall was built. The purpose of these foundation layers, apart from their function as a lining for the bottom of the millpond, seems to have been to raise its level to a pre-determined height in relation to the configuration of the working of the mill and the heights of the tides (see Chapter 8).

THE PENSTOCK INTAKE CHANNEL

The stone-lined penstock intake channel (see Figs 3.7A and B), of which only the basal courses of its sides survive, is located at the right-angle formed by the northern and eastern dams and leads from the millpond to the mouth of the penstock. It is funnel-shaped and measures 2.8m long and 2.6m wide at its opening from the pond, narrowing to 80cm at the sill-stone at the mouth of the penstock. Its southern side is formed by the termination of the eastern dam and splays out from the penstock in a south-westerly direction, while the northern side is formed by the line of the northern dam.

The bed of the channel base is at approximately 1.27m OD and was stone-lined with small and medium-sized stones (C93), this lining sloping down to, and under, the penstock. Under this was a large deposit of grey clay belonging to the underlying penstock intake channel of Mill 1, which was reused as the foundation course with the addition of more grey clay. The stone lining and grey clay continued westwards beyond the opening of the channel into the millpond for a further 3.9m. On the surface of the bed of the channel was a layer of obviously water-deposited gravel (C61), within which, near the mouth of the penstock, one sherd of souterrain ware was found.

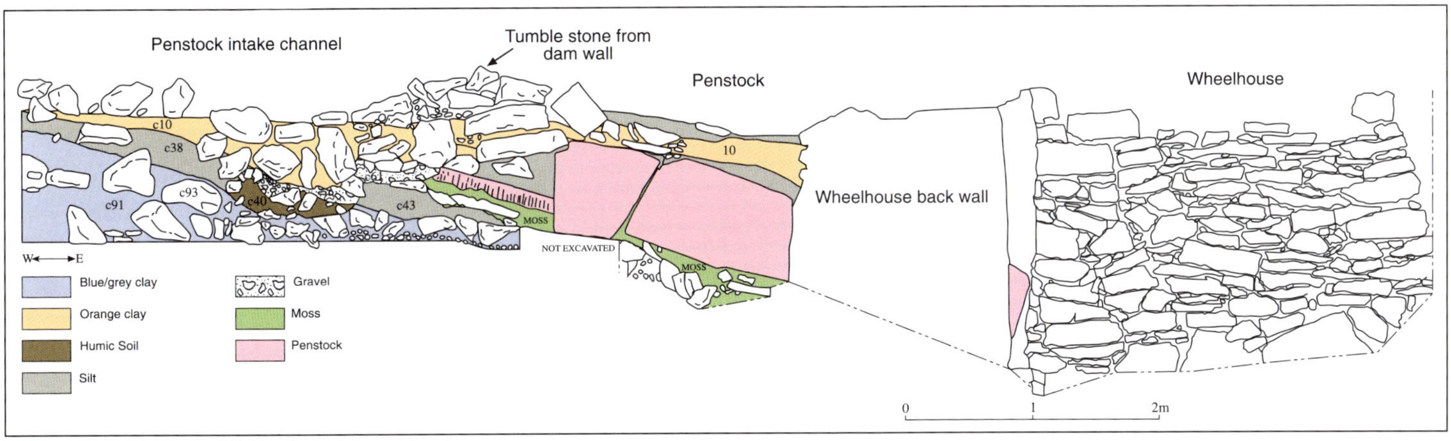

Fig. 3.7A
East-west section (south facing) through of the penstock intake channel, penstock and wheelhouse

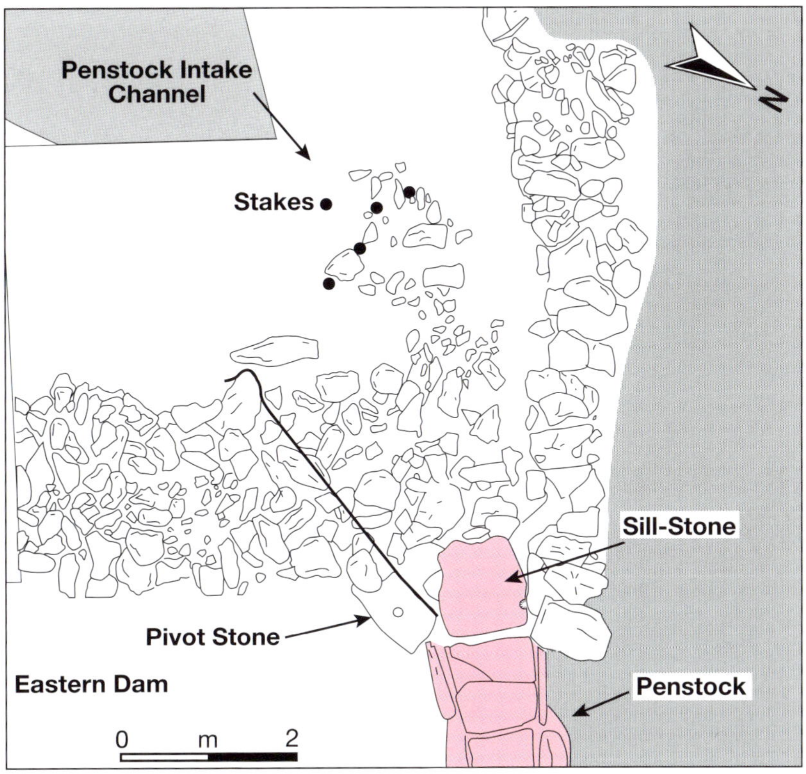

Fig. 3.7B
Plan of the penstock intake area of the millpond

In outline, the intake channel is similar to that found at the vertical-wheeled mill site of Morett, Co. Laois. This consisted of a funnel-shaped, timber-lined channel measuring 4.76m long, 1.88m wide at the mouth and 86cm wide leading to the wheelhouse (Lucas 1953, 16).

THE PENSTOCK SLUICE GATE

A very important surviving feature of the channel is the probable pivot stone (C23) for the penstock sluice gate. This gate controlled the discharge of water from the millpond into the penstock (see Fig. 3.8A). The pivot stone is the first evidence found for the existence of a penstock sluice gate at any early Irish mill site. It was found, still *in situ,* just beneath the present surface, immediately to the south-west of the penstock mouth, within the base of the southern wall of the penstock intake channel. It is a large, flat and approximately sub-rectangular slab of local shale and measures *c.* 85cm long by 45cm wide by 15cm thick. On its surface, towards the penstock end and in line with the middle of the penstock sill-stone, is a circular depression *c.* 10cm in diameter and 3cm deep, which, presumably, was the pivot for the sluice gate. The surface of the stone at 1.32m

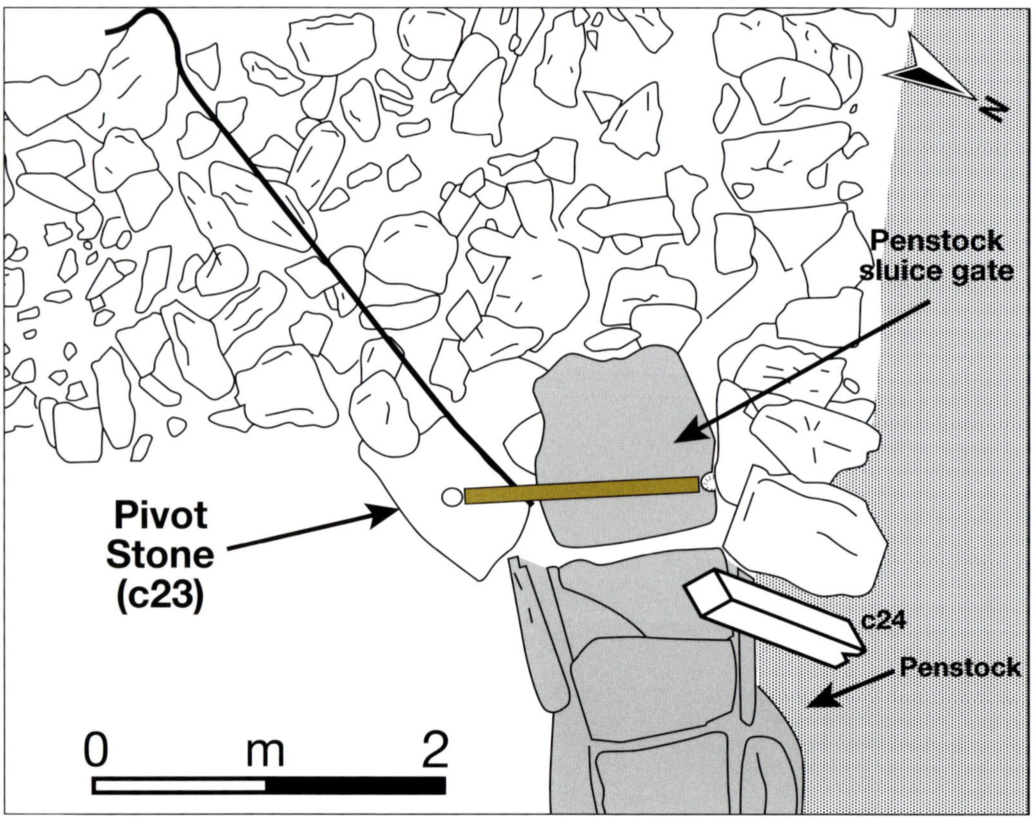

Fig. 3.8A
Possible configuration of the penstock sluice gate

OD is therefore just slightly above the level of the adjacent base of the penstock intake channel at 1.27m OD. Opposite the pivot stone, on the northern edge of the surface of the sill-stone, is a semi-circular depression.

On the northern side of the channel, lying in the destruction layer, was a square-sectioned stone in the shape of a small column (C24). It was not *in situ* and lay at a sloping angle above the mouth of the penstock (see Fig. 3.8A and C). It was approximately 20cm square in section and 70cm long. At the end away from the channel was a shallow, V-shaped groove approximately 2cm wide at the top and 2cm deep. Given its context in close proximity to the mouth of the penstock and its shape, it is possible to interpret this as a stone post for the northern side of the sluice gate, the groove being for the top bar and handle of the gate to lock into. One other possible item of evidence for the existence of the sluice gate is the discovery of a small lead object in the gravel layer (C61) at the mouth of the penstock, very near to the pivot stone. This is possibly the setting for the base of an iron bar and may have originally been in the pivot hole.

Fig. 3.8B
The pivot stone

We can gain an impression of the probable dimensions of the sluice gate, as being about 80cm to 1m wide. This would make it of sufficient size to close the width of the penstock intake channel at this point. An idea of its height can be ascertained from the varying heights of the tidal water trapped in the millpond. From the figures given on p. 213, the probable maximum level of water within the pond over the tidal cycle would have been at 2.2m OD. However, for most of the time within the tidal cycle, the maximum levels would have been at 1.90m OD (mean high water spring levels). Given that the level of the base of the channel is around 1.27m OD near the pivot stone, a gate between 70cm and 90cm high would have been sufficient to block off the water. The gate would have been closed as the tide flooded into the millpond and opened to release the impounded water to power the waterwheel when the tide had receded and milling commenced.

Fig. 3.8C
The pillar stone (C24)

The design of the intake channel can be seen to be well-planned to allow it to fulfill its function of funnelling the impounded water into the penstock and to concentrate water pressure. The stone lining over the grey clay counteracted scouring of its base.

In the upper, silted-up part of the channel near the mouth of the penstock, a fan-like arrangement of three flat stones was found. These were laid to slope down into the largely silted-up mouth of the penstock. It seems clear that these were placed long after the mill ceased operation and may relate to an attempt to drain the millpond.

Fig. 3.9A
Overview of penstock and wheelhouse

Group of stakes

In the millpond, a short distance from the mouth of the intake channel, are the stumps of five stakes. Three of these, each *c.* 40m apart, form a roughly north-south line in front of the intake channel. The other two are orientated towards the south-east (see Fig. 8.7B). It is envisaged that some provision was made to stop material like seaweed, leaves, branches and other debris from entering the channel and clogging the penstock and the stakes may represent the remains of a wattle grill across the opening from the millpond to prevent this.

THE PENSTOCK

The stone penstock is by far the most impressive component of Mill 2 to have survived and is discussed in detail later (see Chapter 5), with this section concentrating on putting it in context in relation to other features of the mill.

The penstock was located at the eastern end of its intake channel and at the right angle made by the junction of the northern and eastern dams and was buried underneath the termination of the latter. Outside the mouth of the penstock was a large slab of shale functioning as the penstock sill-stone (described in detail on pps 144-145). The penstock is 3.78m long and was inclined at an angle of 15°, with its lower, or orifice end merging in the back wall of the wheelhouse. Much of the overlying material in which it was originally buried had been removed but its depth can be estimated approximately. Above its western or intake end, the original depth of overlying material was probably in the region of 1–1.4m, increasing to 3.2–3.6m at its eastern, or orifice end (approximately 2.2m at this location survives). The surviving stratigraphy (Fig. 3.7A) above the western half of the structure shows that its upper surface was covered by redeposited silt with interleaved layers of moss. Above this was the normal upper-dam make-up of orange clay capped with stones. The eastern half was buried within the back wall of the wheelhouse. The base rested on a layer of moss, below which was a sloping ramp of stones.

During its working life, it would have been essential to keep the penstock clear of washed-in material, as any blockage would have seriously reduced the efficiency of the water jet acting on the waterwheel. It is probable that the penstock silted up relatively quickly after the mill ceased working. When excavated, its interior was completely filled by silt. The first stage in this silting process would have been the blocking of the orifice. On discovery, this was clogged with worked wood fragments, some of which were probably offcuts from the salvage of wood from the millhouse, and suggesting that the penstock started to fill up immediately after the mill went out of use. Within the penstock chamber, four distinct layers of silt could be recognised (Fig. 3.9B). The primary silt at the bottom of the chamber (C51) was approximately 12cm thick, was dark-grey and had a high content of loose grit and a few medium-sized stones. Above this was a layer of silt (C50) about 15cm thick, with a lens of iron pan which had stained the silt an orange colour, and a small number of stones. This layer was overlain by approximately 13cm of very gritty silt (C49), which produced one sherd of souterrain ware. The top layer was *c.* 6cm thick and consisted of a heavily iron-panned orange clay (C48) below the lid.

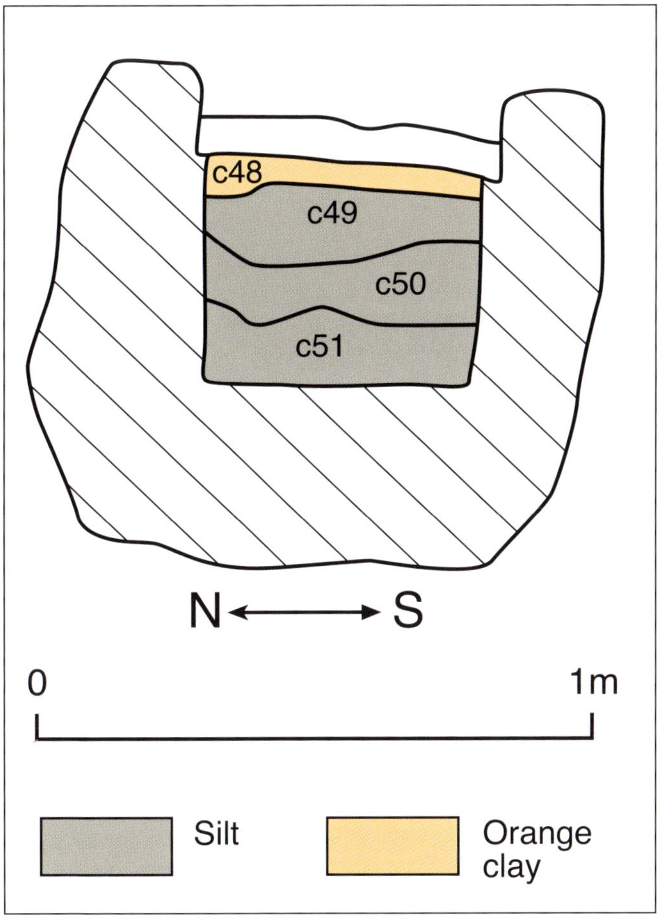

Fig. 3.9B
Section (west facing) through penstock showing silting layers

These layers would seem to represent some four stages in the gradual blocking up of the penstock. The discovery of a sherd of souterrain ware may suggest that the near-

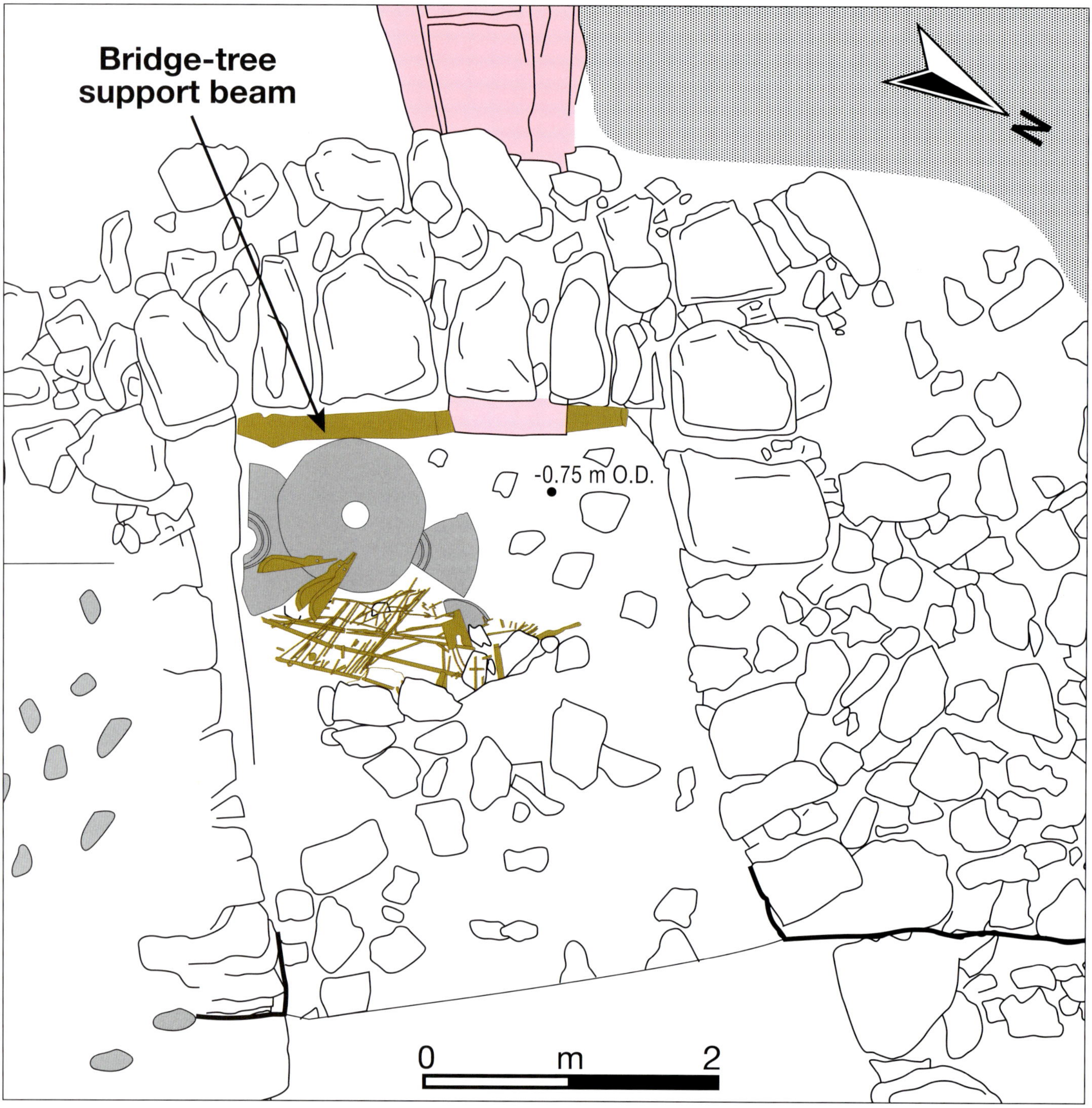

Fig. 3.10A
Plan of the wheelhouse

complete silting up had taken place before the end of the Early Medieval period. This observation is reinforced by the discovery of fragments of two lathe-turned alder bowls (see p. 225 and Figs 9.1 and 9.2) of Early Medieval character found within the silts. Other finds included a possible wooden handle (see p. 232 and Fig. 9.8a). Perhaps the most interesting find, from mid-way down the penstock, was a short length of post, 34cm long and of rectangular section, with a tenon at one end and grooves or slots along both of its narrow sides (see Fig. 9.15 and p. 245), which probably came from the dismantled mill building.

THE WHEELHOUSE

The tops of surviving walls of the stone-built wheelhouse and tailrace were visible on the surface of the foreshore before excavation as a slipway-like feature with a back wall and two side walls, the latter sloping down the foreshore. Large boulders and stones, some of considerable size, filled the area between by the walls. Excavation (Trench 1) commenced with the removal of the stones and boulders and the exposed stratigraphic sequence is shown on Fig. 3.10B.

Below the surface, the stone and large boulders were contained in a matrix of orange clay (C1132) which continued down for approximately 75–80cm. Lying underneath this was a layer of almost stone-free grey silt (C1133), containing within it a layer of silt with a noticeably greater shell content (C1134) than that of the silt layer above. Together, these layers were *c.* 60–65cm in depth. Below this was a basal layer of silt (C1135) over the bottom of the wheelhouse, which contained a dense concentration of archaeological material. This included many fragments of worked wood, two wattle panels, a complete lower millstone, three large pieces of an upper millstone, three waterwheel paddles, one large structural timber *in situ* and a small amount of souterrain ware. Excavation of the floor of the wheelhouse was extremely difficult because of constant flooding. Even when the pump was kept continuously running, seeping water from the sides of the trench ensured that the bottom 10cm or so was never free of water.

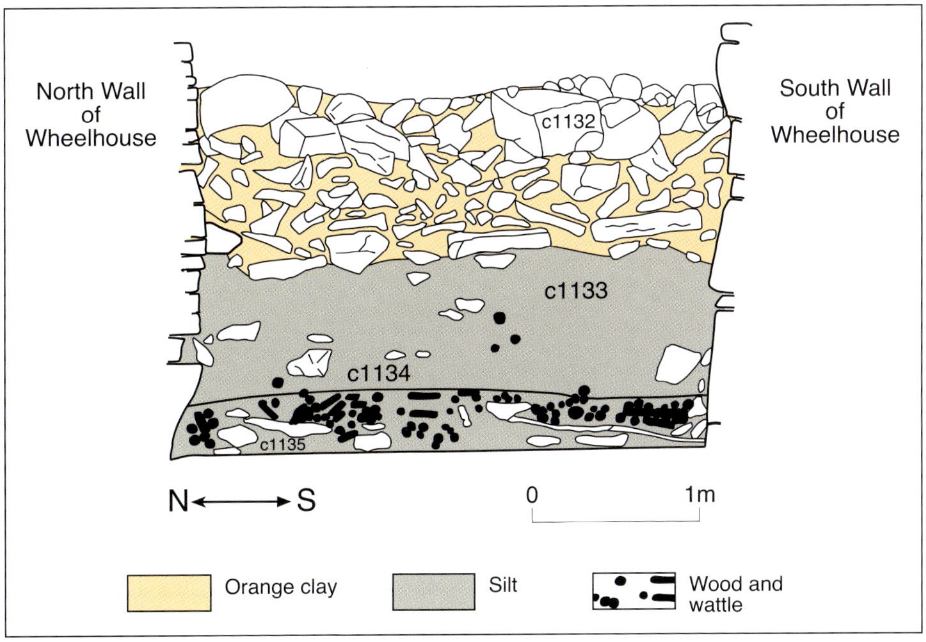

Fig. 3.10B
North-south (west facing) section through the wheelhouse

It is possible to interpret the depositional sequence of layers between the surviving walls of the wheelhouse with relative certainty. When the floor of the millhouse above collapsed, material from there, including the millstones and some stones, fell onto the wheelhouse floor below. Natural silting for a considerable period (C1135, C1134 and C1133) subsequently covered this. The layer of stones and boulders in orange clay (C1132) forming the upper surface is recognisable as an artificially-placed deposit, one which represents an episode of deliberate infilling. The ruin of the wheelhouse with its steep sides must have been a safety hazard on the foreshore for man and animals for a considerable period, and action was taken eventually to fill it in with material derived from the surrounding ruins of the upper part of the wheelhouse walls and dams. This act seems responsible, in part, for the surrounding damage to this area of the site and would have initiated the active tidal erosion that can be observed at the eastern end of the complex. No artefactual evidence has been discovered to indicate when the infilling took place, but judging from the depth of underlying silt, which probably took a long time to accumulate, it is likely to have occurred in recent centuries.

Fig. 3.10C
The infilled wheelhouse and tailrace (from east)

The wheelhouse walls

The lower courses of the walls of the wheelhouse — a back wall and two side walls (the north and south walls) — are splendidly preserved and stand up to 2.36m high, merging with those of the tailrace. They are largely of dry-stone construction, but some of their inner cores are bonded with orange clay. They were built using undressed stones of local shale, which naturally forms straight faces along bedding planes.

The back wall

The back wall (C1136), which is 2.45m wide and 1.4m thick and survives to a maximum height of 2.36m (see Figs 3.11A and B), incorporates the front face of the penstock. It is constructed from large sub-rectangular blocks of local shale, some up to 1m long, laid roughly in horizontal courses with the spaces between the larger blocks infilled with smaller stones. A rectangular opening, through which the penstock protrudes, is located to the right of the centre of the wall. It is approximately 86cm high and 70cm wide. A large lintel, approximately 1.2m long and up to 30cm high, bridges the top of this opening. The wall is relatively vertical but leans a little outwards towards the top. Its line veers slightly to the north-east towards its northern end. Given that the ends of the back wall are not bonded into the sidewalls of the wheelhouse, and that these appear to continue on behind its face, it seems obvious to conclude that the side walls were built first and the back wall was constructed after these walls were in place.

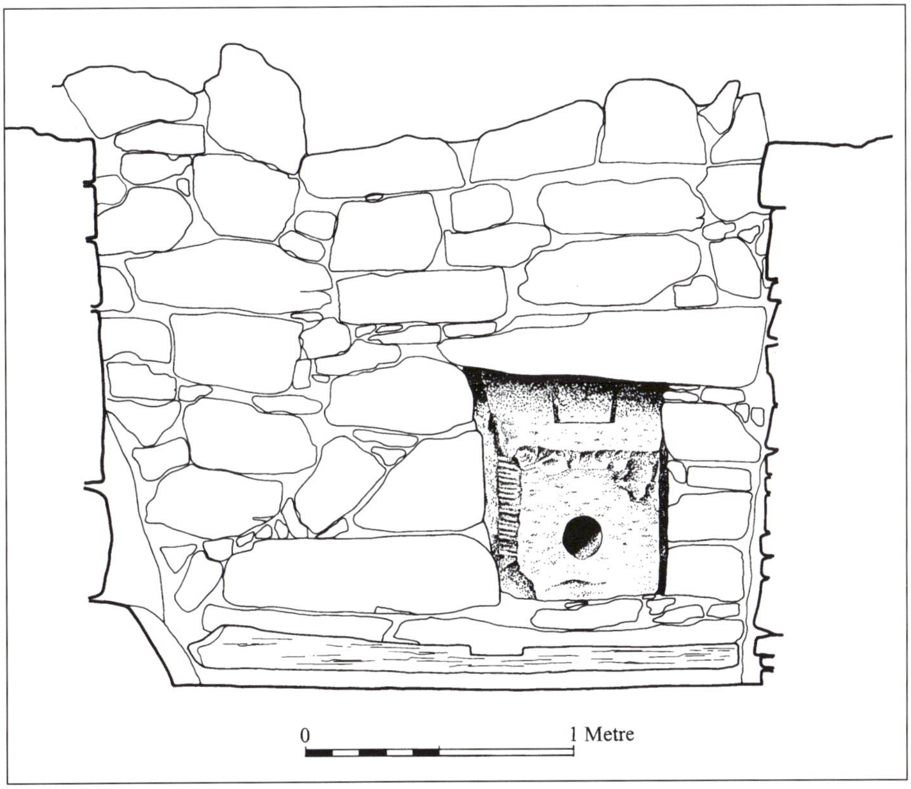

Fig. 3.11A
Elevation of the back wall of the wheelhouse with the protruding penstock, orifice and bridge-tree support beam (J. Patience)

Fig. 3.11B
The back wall of the wheelhouse with the protruding penstock, orifice and bridge-tree support beam

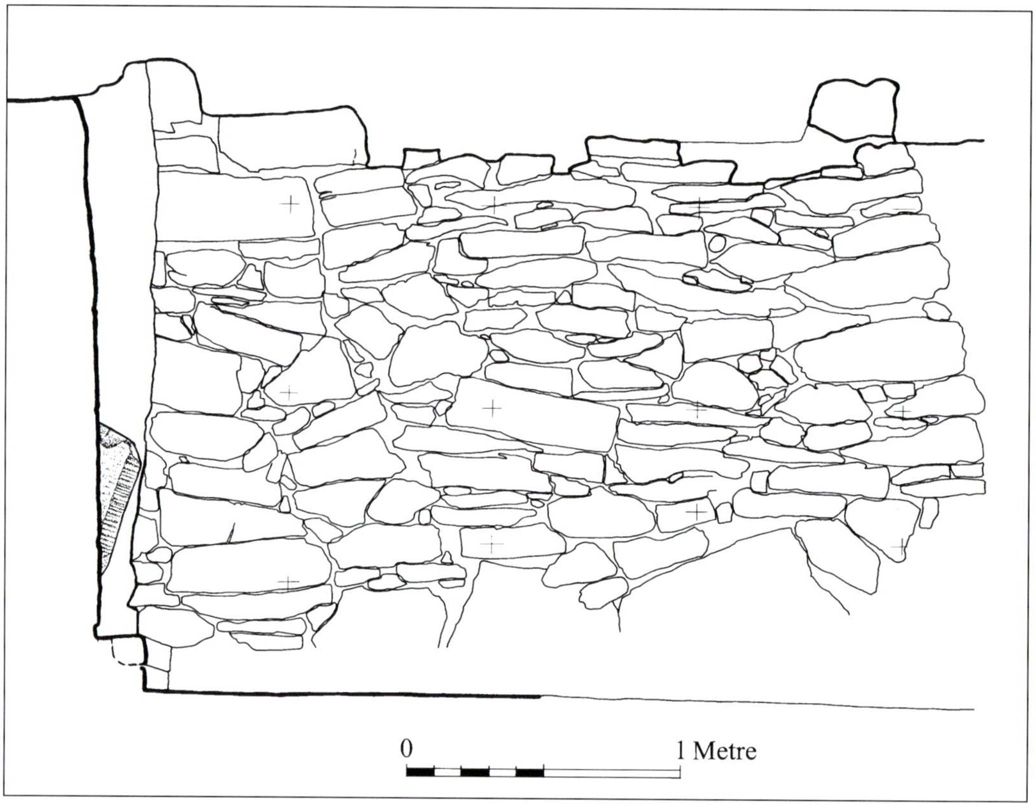

Fig. 3.12A
Elevation of the north wall of the wheelhouse (J. Patience)

Fig. 3.12B (below right)
The north wall of the wheelhouse at its junction with the back wall

Fig. 3.12C (below left)
The north wall of the wheelhouse at its junction with the tailrace

The north wall (C1075)

The north wall is 90cm thick and survives to height of 2.34m above the wheelhouse floor. At approximately 2.21m from the back wall is a slight return, which appears to mark the end of the wheelhouse and start of the tailrace. At 3.3m from the back wall, there is a more pronounced return to the north of about 25cm, which marks the end of the adjacent platform. Visual inspection of the joints in the stone of the wall suggests that it was built in five vertical sections, starting at the western end

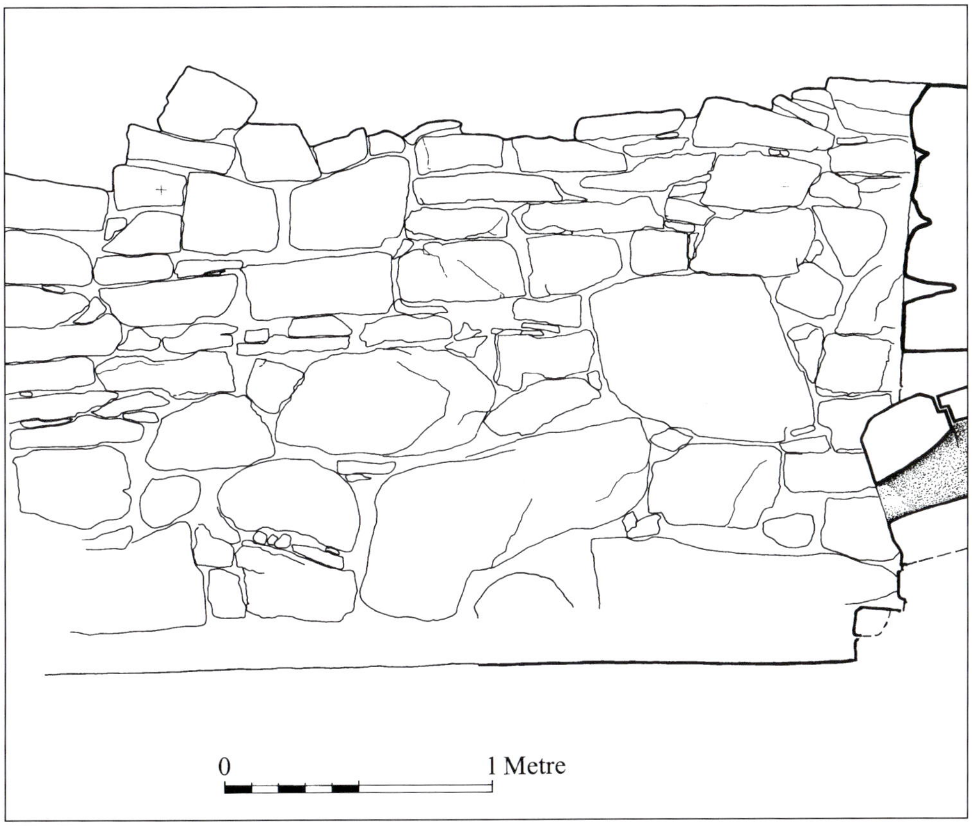

Fig. 3.13A
Elevation of the south wall of the wheelhouse (J. Patience)

Fig. 3.13B
The south wall of the wheelhouse at its junction with the back wall

and proceeding eastwards, with each section partially leaning on the preceding one. Towards the eastern end, there is a bulge at the surviving top of the wall causing a slight overhang. This may be an original feature to minimise any spray from a rising tide and to prevent splashes from the waterwheel wetting the millhouse floor above.

The south wall (C1076)

The south wall of the wheelhouse survives to a height of 2.25m and includes some massive boulders, up to 1.1m wide and 65cm high. Discernible horizontal coursing is present in its upper portion. This wall merges with the southern wall of the tailrace, with no clear demarcation.

The wheelhouse floor

Practically all of the area of the wheelhouse floor was excavated, but it was only against the back wall, and especially in the south-western corner, that undisturbed archaeological material survived (see Fig. 3.10A,). Stretching across the base of the back wall, and *in situ,* was the beam that supported the bridge-tree (or 'sole tree') on which the waterwheel rotated. In the south-western sector underneath some fallen stones, all grouped together and embedded in silt, were the millstones, the wheel paddles and the remains of two wattle panels. Presumably the fallen stones had held them in position and prevented the lighter pieces from being carried away by the tide.

Fig. 3.14
Fallen wattle panel on the floor of the wheelhouse

Two large segments of a broken upper millstone were found at the base of the silt, with the upper face upwards and underlying a complete lower millstone with its lower face upwards (see Fig. 7.1). Two other portions of the upper millstone stone were found a short distance away. Partially overlying the millstones were three scoop–shaped horizontal waterwheel paddles. Partly sandwiched between the upper millstone fragments and the complete lower stone was a section of relatively well-preserved wattle panel, which extended north-eastwards across the wheelhouse floor, and had a number of oak offcuts on top of it. The panel was approximately 1.2m long by 65cm wide and consisted of four rods, some 15cm apart, with the fragmentary remains of woven wands in between. Remains of another wattle panel, in a much more fragmentary condition, were also found. Within the silt itself was a dense concentration of small fragments of worked oak.

It is obvious that the millstones fell from the floor of the millhouse above and, from context of their deposition, it seems clear also that they fell in one episode along with the wattle panels, which also seemed to come from above. From the proximity of the fragments of the upper stone to the south wall, it is possible that the upper stone hit the wall during its fall and broke into large pieces. The fall of the upper millstone was followed by that of one of the wattle panels, then by the lower stone, which turned at least once during its fall to land on top of the panel upside-down, and finally by another panel. The millstones seem to have hit part of the waterwheel as they fell, knocking off some paddles, which landed towards the south wall.

The basal silt throughout the wheelhouse produced 79 sherds of souterrain ware and two bone pins, the finds being concentrated mostly in the western sector. In spite of the relatively large number of sherds, they represent only a small number of vessels. One large piece was located wedged in the narrow space between the bridge-tree support beam and the wall.

The remainder of the floor area outside the western area contained no large or *in situ* material, but did produce approximately 190 fragments of oak, as well as a very large deposit of broken wattle debris. A significant proportion of the oak fragments were small offcuts. This suggests that the millhouse above, unlike the wheelhouse, was made of wood and furthermore seems to constitute evidence that it was systematically salvaged for wood, leaving a lot of debris to fall into the wheelhouse below. Most of the wood was found below the wattle debris, demonstrating that the latter was also derived from above and was not a part of any wattle flooring of the wheelhouse. The floor itself was paved with a rough surface of stones, but because of the constant flooding it was not possible to record all of these.

The level of the wheelhouse floor is at -0.75m OD. This is well above both the mean low-water neap tides level, which is -1.06m OD and that of the mean low-water spring level at -1.5m OD. This means that the floor of the wheelhouse would have been dry at low water. The level of the original foreshore, as revealed by excavation *c.* 4.m to the west and beneath the dam, is at –0.121m OD. Thus it would appear that the original foreshore was excavated to a depth of *c.* 56.9–62.5cm to make the floor of sufficient depth in relation to the fall of water from the millpond.

An essential feature of tide mills is that the millhouse should be placed at a safe height above all but the most freak high tides. The mean high-water spring tide level at Nendrum is at 1.9m OD, while that of mean high-water neap tides is at 1.4m OD. A number of observations make it clear that a considerable part of the upper portion of the wheelhouse has been destroyed. At present the surviving wall tops are at 1.56m OD and are covered by water on most high tides. Therefore, if the floor of the millhouse was near the present height of the walls, it would have been frequently flooded. However, it is highly probable that the base of the mill building was at the same level as that of the dams.

The maximum surviving height of the eastern dam, immediately adjacent to the south of the wheelhouse, is 3.85m OD, while that of the northern dam is 2.6m OD, suggesting that the floor of the millhouse may have been at a level between 3.85m OD maximum and 2.6m OD minimum. The former height is probably not representative of the height of the dams in general, as it is located at a point where the adjoining shoreline, with which it connects, is high and this section probably sloped down somewhat. The height of the roadway at the foot of the monastery and at the end of the millpond — on average around 3m OD — is, in a general way, a good guide to a safe height above various high waters. However, it should be noted that an occasional high tide has occurred above this height in the last 50 years (see p. 214). It is postulated that, originally, the level of the millhouse floor was at *c.* 3m OD. This figure suggests strongly that the original height of the walls was in the order of *c.* 3.75m and that therefore some 1.3m or more of the wheelhouse walls has been lost.

The bridge-tree support beam (C1137)

The only structural mill timber that remained *in situ* in the wheelhouse was the bridge-tree support beam; the bridge-tree itself was not found (see Fig. 1.6). In a horizontal-wheeled mill, the bridge-tree support beam was positioned below the orifice of the penstock and parallel to the back wall of the wheelhouse, forming a component of the waterwheel assembly and of the tentering mechanism (see Chapter 6). Its function was to support the bridge-tree on which the waterwheel was pivoted and which could be raised or lowered to adjust the space between the millstones above. The beam was roughly rectangular-sectioned, measuring 2.02m long, and approximately 16cm wide (increasing to 20cm at its southern end) and 9cm thick.

The lower surface retained about one-third of a rounded profile, along with bark of the small oak tree from which it had been cut. Halfway along its length on its upper surface was the mortise for the bridge-tree. This was quite shallow, being 3cm deep, and measuring 21cm by 16cm, and its centre was approximately 30cm to the left of the centre of the orifice. The support beam was not fixed to the floor of the wheelhouse, but rested on a number of stones and was positioned some 5cm out from the base of back wall. Other examples of support beams have been found at Drumard, Co. Derry (Baillie 1975) and Mashanaglass Co. Cork (Fahy 1956). The importance of the beam was greatly increased by its supplying a dendrochronological date for the construction of Mill 2. A sample cut from its southern end gave a felling date of AD 788+1 (Q9803) (see pps 110-111).

The tailrace

The tailrace channel extends down the foreshore from the eastern end of the wheelhouse and dams for a traceable distance of approximately 11.7m. Where it ends was not ascertained, but it is likely to extend much further to the east, under the foreshore silt. On the surface it appears as a linear, stone and silt-filled depression enclosed by two lines of low wall that slope down the foreshore as continuations of the walls of the wheelhouse. These walls survive to heights of 2.2m at the wheelhouse end, falling to *c.* 1.2m at 6m eastwards of this point, to disappear beneath the mud further down the foreshore. The southern wall runs in a straight line, while the northern one splays outward towards the north-east. The tailrace, where it starts at the end of the wheelhouse, is 3m wide, but widens out to *c.* 4m towards its visible eastern end.

Due to time constraints the tailrace was left largely unexcavated, except for a small trench 1.5m wide across part of the eastern end. This demonstrated that the sequence of layers within the channel was similar to those observed in the wheelhouse, reflecting a primary stage of natural silting, lasting a considerable time, followed by an episode of artificial infilling. The basal layer consists of a hard, gravelly surface with stones, probably artificially laid down to line the bottom of the tailrace to prevent scouring. Above this was a layer of largely stone-free, soft silt with shells, approximately 60cm thick (C1073), which contained fragments of wattle and wood and some bone. This represents the primary silting-up of the tailrace during the working life of the mill and the initial stage after it

Fig. 3.15A
The bridge-tree support beam in situ

Fig. 3.15B
The bridge-tree support beam after removal

had been abandoned. Above this was a soft grey silt (C1072) with stones, some up 50cm in maximum thickness, and including a small quantity of animal bone. In this layer, especially at the sides adjoining the walls, were large boulders (C1071), most probably derived from tumble from the walls of the tailrace, but including some that had been deliberately dumped to infill the channel. The southern wall was much better preserved than the northern, the latter appearing to have been more extensively robbed to infill the channel. Above the infill and constituting the modern foreshore was a black, shelly layer of silt approximately 10cm thick (C689).

The purpose of the tailrace was to ensure the effective run-off of spent water to prevent any back-up from flooding the wheelhouse and impeding the rotation of the wheel. To form the tailrace, a trench was excavated into the sloping foreshore and the sides revetted by stone walls backed by low banks. Gravel and small stones were then deposited to line the base of the channel. Although the end of the tailrace was not located, it is probable that it extended sufficiently far eastwards to connect with a tidal channel that flows to the east on this side of the bay.

THE PLATFORM AT THE END OF THE DAM AND ADJACENT TO THE SITE OF THE MILL

The embankment forming the northern dam extends beyond the millpond for approximately 8m to form a platform, which flanked the northern side of the wheelhouse and the site of the mill building. This part of the embankment can be regarded as functionally different from the dam, as it was not involved in holding back water in the millpond. The platform, now reduced to its foundation layers, overlies part of the wheelhouse, dam and tailrace of Mill 1. These foundations were formed by filling in the old wheelhouse and tailrace with a deposit of large boulders in a matrix of orange clay. Beyond the termination of the platform, a sloping down spread of stones extends down the foreshore.

The platform has a maximum width of *c.* 6m. Much of its seaward end has been damaged by erosion, but evidence of its original character is provided by a short length of very large boulders, orientated north-south and traceable for 2m, which form a batter for the platform. The platform survives to a height of approximately 1.6m OD, but originally it would have been the same as the associated dams. As the adjacent top of the dam on the west is at 2.6m OD, it can be deduced that it has lost a minimum of about 1m of its surface. However, as it was probably at the same height as that postulated for the floor of the millhouse at 3m OD, it may have lost *c.* 1.4m.

It is possible to speculate that the platform provided space for many of the activities associated with the mill. But with the erosion of a large depth of its surface, it is clear that all traces of any structures that may have been on it have been eradicated.

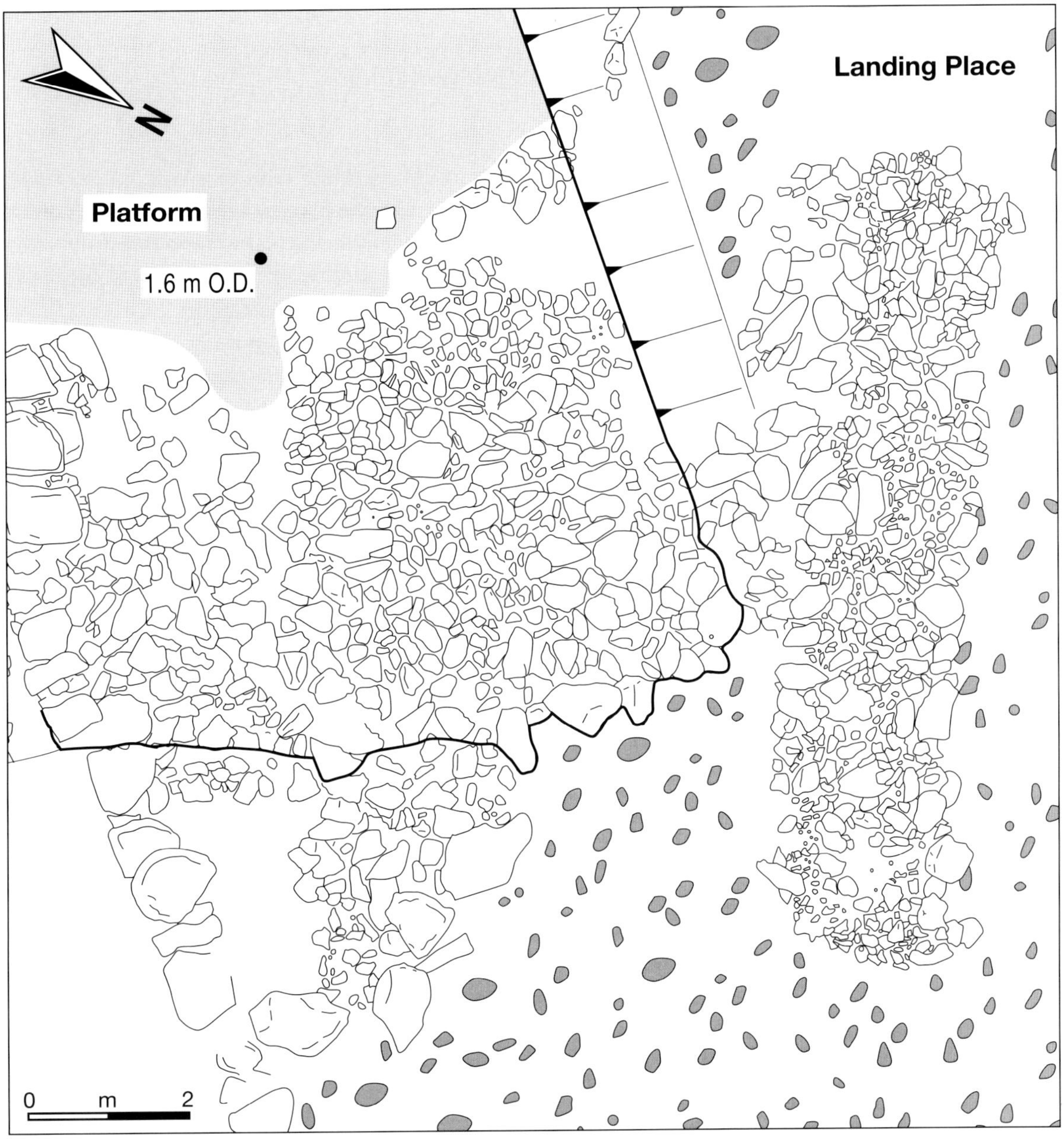

Fig. 3.16
Plan of the platform and landing place

THE LANDING PLACE

The area of the wooden platform, which functioned as a landing place for Mill 1 (see Chapter 1), was remodelled to act as a landing place for sea craft for Mill 2. A layer of stones was placed on top of the old wooden platform and, in the area adjacent to the north, it was extended with a low platform of stone and gravel (C610) *c.* 0.5m high placed on the foreshore mud. The platform is orientated approximately east–west (Fig. 3.16) and measures *c.* 7.4m long, tapering in width from *c.* 2.4m at its western end to *c.* 1.8m at its eastern end. It has a surrounding kerb of medium- to large-sized stones acting as a revetment for an internal area filled with smaller stones and gravel, and consolidated with a packing of redeposited dark-grey, sandy silt (C690). It seems highly probable that some of the top surface of the platform has been eroded away by tidal action.

The material making up the platform was comparatively rich in small finds. These included three small pieces of souterrain ware, a bone pin, several scraps of leather, some small wooden pieces including a wedge, a peg and an offcut, some bone and about 21 worked flints. There was also metalworking debris in the form of 19 lumps of slag, six small pieces tentatively identified as tuyère and two small lumps of burned clay. A layer of grey, gritty sand, which abutted the northern and eastern edges of the platform (C692 and C818), produced another bone pin, two small fragments of slag and tuyère and some worked flint. In comparison to other parts of the site, the density of occupational material found on and around the platform is exceptional, and the most likely explanation is that it was made up with a deposit brought in from an occupation layer on land. It is probable that the humic content of this has been eroded leaving the stones, gravel and artefacts. It seems clear that the stone and gravel platform served the same function as the timber platform of Mill 1 and was constructed to provide a firm landing place ('a hard') for boats on the soft foreshore mud.

THE DATING OF THE SECOND MILL

All of the wood associated with Mill 2 contexts was examined for its potential for tree-ring dating, including the large collection of small pieces of oak, although practically all of these were too small for dating. The only sample that proved suitable was the bridge-tree support beam found *in situ* at the bottom of the wheelhouse (see Fig. 3.15A). This contained 125 growth rings and retained its centre, or pith. Included in the measurement were 32 sapwood rings. These are possibly complete, but an extra crushed ring at the outside may be present. The tree-ring series obtained from the timber was compared with a suite of regional and local site chronologies and consistent correlation values were found. As the sapwood is possibly missing its final year, the best estimated felling date for the tree from which the support beam was fashioned is AD 788+1 giving AD 789. The presence of possibly complete sapwood suggests that the timber was not reused from elsewhere and was probably incorporated into the structure shortly after felling.

Table 3.1

Sample and context no	Description	No of years	Start date	End date	Date (felling date or estimated felling date range)
Q9803 (C1137)	*In situ* bridge-tree support beam at the bottom of the wheelhouse Sapwood complete	125	AD 664	AD 788	AD 788 +1 year giving AD 789

Thus, in contrast to the large number of dated timbers from Mill 1, the dating of the construction of the second mill rests solely on the dendrochronological determination of one timber. This is unsatisfactory, but greater confidence can be placed on its value in providing a foundation date for the construction of Mill 2, by the nature of the dated timber itself, the bridge-tree support beam. This member, found *in situ,* played a fundamental role in the working of the mill, being an integral part of the waterwheel assembly and tentering mechanism (see Fig. 1.6). It would have been the first timber in the whole apparatus to be put in place during construction. It can be argued that once in place, it would not have been necessary to replace it, unlike perhaps, some of the other members such as the bridge-tree itself which, due to the stress placed on it, may have needed replacement several times during the working life of the mill. It is therefore possible to regard the bridge-tree support beam as a reliable indicator that the second mill was constructed around AD 789.

Fig. 3.17
Sample Q9803, from the bridge-tree support beam of Mill 2

To a large degree, the lack of dateable wood retrieved during the excavation of Mill 2 is a reflection of oak not having been used in the construction of the dams, the penstock and the wheelhouse. It may also be an indication that most of the large timbers from the millhouse — if it was, in fact, a wooden building — and from elsewhere around the site, were salvaged for reuse when the mill ceased to function. The presence of offcuts and small wood fragments in the primary silt of the wheelhouse, millpond and penstock suggest that the mill building was dismantled and its timber salvaged soon after it went out of use.

Ancillary relative dating evidence in the form of closely-dateable small finds is lacking. Some souterrain ware was found in the makeup of the landing platform, which can be argued as belonging to the constructional phase of Mill 2. Though not closely dateable, souterrain ware is generally assigned to the 8th to the 12th centuries. Therefore it at least does not contradict the dendrochronological date. A sample of charred wood found at the bottom of the wheelhouse was submitted for radiocarbon dating and produced a date of 1600+20 BP, 420–533, cal AD (GrN-25434). This date is clearly unacceptable as it would make the second mill earlier than the first and presumably is an example of 'old wood effect' and the sample may have come from the heartwood of a tree growing in the late 5th or early 6th century.

THE DEMISE OF THE SECOND MILL

In the absence of a date for the end of the working life of Mill 2, it is extremely difficult to work out the length of time during which it was in use. If Mill 2 had a similar working life as that postulated for Mill 1, it would have lasted into the mid-10th century. Some sherds of cordoned souterrain ware were deposited in the wheelhouse, presumably dropped from the millhouse above either during its working life or when its floor collapsed depositing the millstones and other material below. This decorated form, though not closely dateable, is thought to be later in the series than the undecorated forms and may have been current after the 9th century (Lynn 1978b, 69).

The excavation failed to produce any direct information to elucidate the nature of the demise of the mill or the date when it occurred. A number of options can be considered for the end of the second mill, including deliberate destruction, or accidental destruction by a tidal event, storm, high tide or fire. The simplest explanation is that the mill may have been abandoned and, with neglect, was gradually reduced to a ruin.

In the history and archaeology of mills, a number of recurrent causes for the destruction of a mill can be found, one of the most prevalent being fire. The milling operation includes a high risk of accidental fires. Mill dust is highly combustible, and a spark from badly positioned rotating millstones can cause an explosion leading within seconds to a raging inferno. A fire was considered to be the cause of the destruction of the horizontal-wheeled freshwater mill at Drumard Co. Derry (Baillie 1975, 30) dated to AD 782 and therefore a near contemporary of Nendrum Mill 2. The mid- or late-9th century horizontal-wheeled mill at Tamworth, Staffordshire was also destroyed by fire (Rahtz and Meeson 1992, 31). Probably the earliest historical reference to the burning of a mill in Early Medieval Ireland is found in the mid-7th century *Life of St Brigit* by Cogitosus (Connolly and Picard 1987, 25), where it is recounted that the entire millhouse at her monastery in Kildare was destroyed by fire, but the millstone left unharmed. No evidence was found that fire caused the end of Mill 2, but it cannot be ruled out.

The second possible cause, and one of direct relevance to a tide mill, is destruction caused by an abnormally high tide. It would have been normal practice to construct a tide mill to be well above the height of the normal range of spring high tides. However, it would still have been very vulnerable to freak weather conditions that could result in an abnormally high tidal surge. The bay in which the mill is situated, is off the main body of the lough and surrounded on three sides by drumlin islands. Although sheltered from the westerly and south-westerly prevailing winds and having a weak wave action due to limited fetch, circumstances can arise which might have led to damage by a high tide. The combination of a north-easterly storm during a spring tide and a deep depression could have resulted in a high storm tide causing major damage to the mill building.

To these two possible factors can be added the pattern of warfare and raiding endemic in early Irish society, in which monasteries, as important social and economic centres, were often targets. The monastic mill may have been destroyed in one of these offensives.

The key question, however, is why Mill 2 was not rebuilt or replaced, and the answer to this must lie in the history of the monastery which it served. It seems logical to conclude that it was not replaced because the need for it had gone. A mill would have been a necessity to grind a large volume of grain to supply the daily quantity of bread needed for a sizeable monastic community. If the population of the monastery had fallen below a certain level or, indeed, if community life had ceased completely, there would have been no need to build another mill. Considering the evidence from both the mill excavation and that of the monastery, together with the historical evidence, it is possible to reach the conclusion that community life at Nendrum may have ceased by the 11th century. The lives of the two mills span the 7th and 8th centuries, possibly extending through the 10th century, thus corresponding well with the documentary history of the monastery (see Chapter 11). The monastic estate, which survived the demise of community life, would have been more conveniently served by a mill on the mainland. In Late Medieval times there was almost certainly a mill at Ardmillan on the adjoining mainland. The existence of this mill can be surmised from the placename 'Ardmillan', which can be translated as 'the promontory or peninsula of the mill' and from the presence of a mill there in the Post-Medieval period.

Chapter 4

The Dams and Millponds

Thomas McErlean

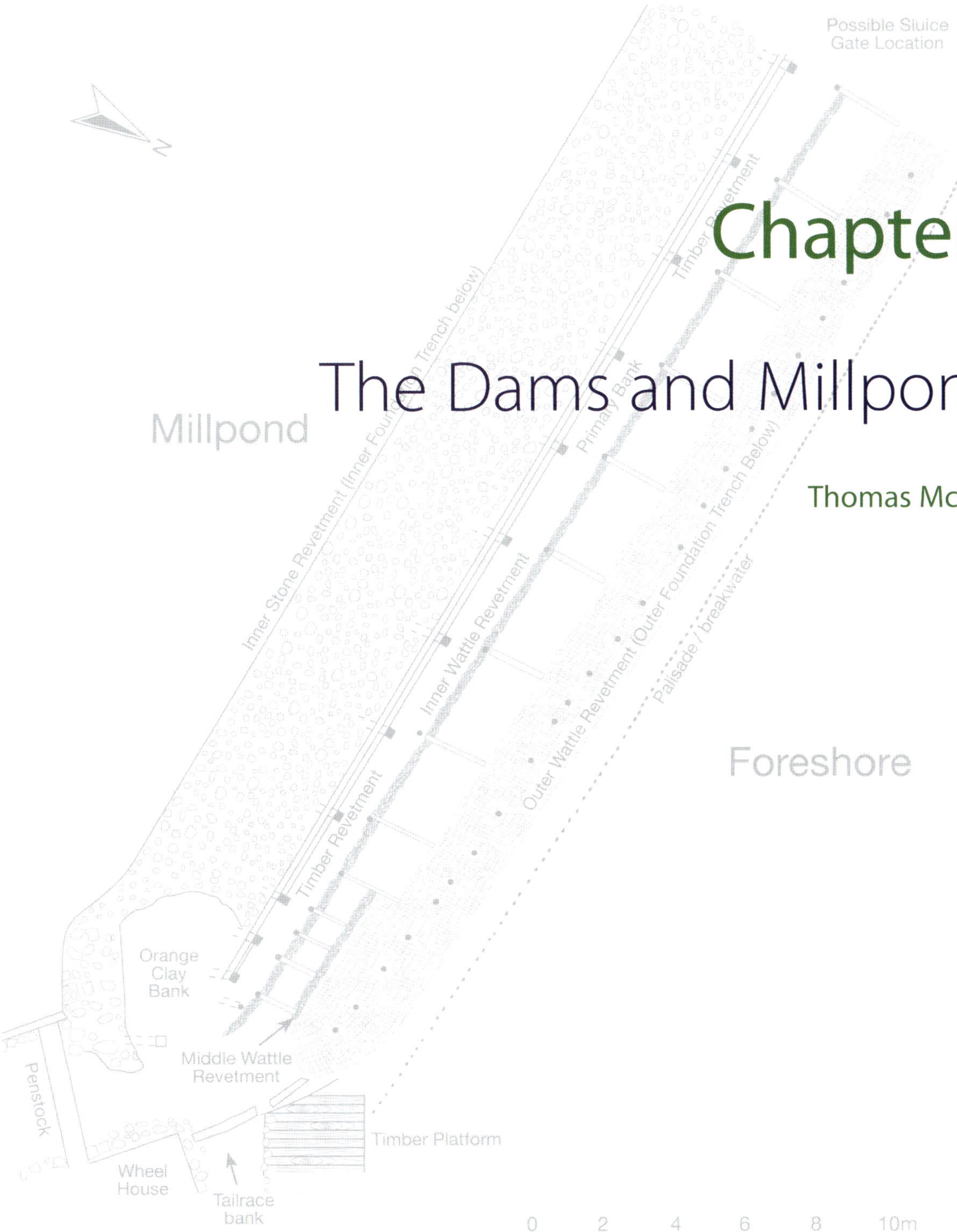

Chapter 4
The Dams and Millponds

Thomas McErlean

INTRODUCTION

Fundamental to the working of a watermill was the presence of a water source with a fall in its course causing a flow, the energy of which was used to turn the waterwheel. Where a natural fall of water was not available, it could be created by building an artificial barrier (a dam) to raise the water level behind, forming a reservoir (the millpond) and thus increasing the flow and providing a fall (the head).

At most watermill sites, the building of a dam and the creation of a millpond was the single most labour-intensive feature in the mill complex. In spite of the large number of known early Irish mills, excavation and field survey to date have provided surprisingly little information regarding their dams and millponds. In many cases it is probable that their traces above ground have been obliterated, but more focused field survey followed up by excavation is likely to reveal much. The evidence from Nendrum, where the dams and millponds of both mills have survived well, is of great interest given the relative absence of information at other mill sites.

The main structural features of the dams of Mill 1 and Mill 2 and their millponds have been described in Chapters 2 and 3, and their design aspects and constructional details are discussed here. Builders and designers of tidal and freshwater dams faced similar problems, but tidal dams presented additional challenges. At high tide, both sides of the dam are surrounded by water, but with the retreating tide the outer side is left dry and the impounded water exerts enormous pressure. Tidal dams, like freshwater ones, therefore have to be of sufficient strength to withstand the pressure exerted by the impounded water, but unlike them, have to be of sufficient height to trap high tides. Like freshwater dams, they have to be waterproof to prevent seepage of the impounded water, as apart from causing loss of waterpower, seepage would weaken the structure and lead to severe and rapid damage. Unlike freshwater dams, tidal dams had to be robust enough to withstand tidal action on their seaward sides, which were exposed to erosion. In addition, the builders had to face the difficulties of erecting a structure on the foreshore, an environment inundated by water twice a day. Responses to all of these challenges can be observed in the structural design of both dams at Nendrum.

THE STRUCTURAL DESIGN OF THE DAM OF MILL 1

The first dam is a complex, composite structure and it is tempting to interpret some of its components, which used a variety of constructional materials and techniques, as possibly belonging to different structures, which were added to over time. The first question that needs to be considered therefore — if only to dismiss it — is whether or not the excavated evidence supports the interpretation that the structure was of more than one phase rather than a single design concept executed in one go. It is clear, however, that the dating evidence establishes that the dam constitutes one single structure made up of various components constructed at one time.

The design of the structure consists of a central basal core comprising an interlocking framework or box structure of timber and wattlework filled with earth, covered by clay and revetted and capped with stones (see Fig. 2.21A). With an approximate width of 8.8m, length of *c.* 11m and a probable height of over 2m, the main section of the dam of the first mill, when complete, would have been an impressive structure on the foreshore. In its original state it would have had the outward appearance of a stone-clad embankment and given little impression of the complex nature of its internal structure as shown on Fig. 2.21B.

The wooden framework

Probably the most difficult task facing the builders was creating the initial core structure on the foreshore on which the body of the dam rested. The elaborate framework of a wattle and timber revetment enclosing a core of organically-rich earth is one of the most interesting aspects of the design of the dam. It is possible that the high content of organic material in the core of the dam may represent sods and the more fibrous material, faggots. To ensure stability, considerable effort was expended on securing the structure to the bed of the foreshore. This was achieved by the provision of foundation trenches and by pinning the inner core to the foreshore bed using piles and posts. The posts also acted as supports and bracing for the box frame structure of the inner core.

The use of timber may reflect the availability of a plentiful supply of wood, especially oak, in the locality when the dam was built in the early 7th century (see further discussion of this issue at p. 252.) It also represents a considerable investment in labour and materials, and it seems obvious that the designers regarded this element of the structure as a vital component in the creation of an effective dam. It is somewhat difficult to ascertain its effectiveness, since this form of construction was not used in the design of the dam of the second mill. This may imply that it was not a total success, or that the same degree of stability could be achieved by other means.

The outer structure

While the loss of most of the upper structure of the first dam presents major problems of interpretation, a relatively good picture of its composition could be built up from surviving elements at various locations, especially the short, better-preserved parts towards the south-eastern section of the main dam near the site of the mill. These demonstrate that the inner core, with its wooden framework, was completely sealed with a thick deposit of grey clay. This in turn was sealed by a very thick bank of orange clay, with the whole structure being surfaced with boulders as shown on Fig. 2.21B. The main structural strength was concentrated on the inner or millpond side where the pressure of the impounded water was greatest. Here, a stone revetment wall, on average 4m wide, was constructed of tightly-packed stones and boulders bonded in orange clay. The probable profile of the dam is shown on Fig. 2.21B and consists of a vertical face on its pond side and a sloping face on the seaward side. The latter seems probably to have been designed to disperse the wave energy acting against the outward face of the dam.

The original height of the dam

As the excavations demonstrated that, in the main, only the base or foundation of the original structure has survived, it was not possible to ascertain the original height of the structure. On the best-preserved section — located on the southeast where it was incorporated into the base of the dam of Mill 2 — it survives up to a height of 1.1m OD. But elsewhere the surviving surface is at a maximum of 0.32m OD, and mostly is well below this level. It is highly likely that it was constructed to be, at the very least, above the bi-monthly spring tides which locally reach 1.9m OD (see Chapter 8) to impound the maximum volume of water. Thus, a minimum height of at least 2m OD can be envisaged. Using this minimum assessment it can be deduced that at least 1.68–2m is missing from the main body of the dam, and at least 90cm from the highest surviving part of the bank on the south-east, near the site of the mill. It is probable, however, that the dam was much higher and designed to be well above almost all but the exceptional and very infrequent high tides and provide dry access along the top, which would have been desirable to work the sluices and other activities. The maximum highest surviving height of the dam of Mill 2, at 2.6m OD, provides a useful indication of the possible height of that of Mill 1. It is very probable that the original height of the dam above the foreshore was in the region of 2–2.5m.

Waterproofing

The builder went to great effort to render the dam waterproof to prevent penetration of water into the core of the structure. If this had occurred, not only would it have defeated the sole purpose of the dam, which was to impound water, but it would have also weakened the structure and led to its rapid deterioration. The main material used to prevent seepage of water through the dam and render it relatively impermeable was clay. It would seem that in its original state, the whole of the inner core of the structure was sealed in an envelope of this material, with two types — grey and orange — used. The two clays are used differentially in the structure. In general where the two clays occur together, the orange clay is placed overlying the grey form. The grey form has a higher content of clay particles than the orange and therefore is presumably more impervious to water penetration. It was used for parts of the foundation layers and to seal the inner core of the dam and in places was packed around some of the piles and other wooden members. The orange clay was used as a matrix or bonding agent for the stonework. Moss was used in the inner core and may have been used extensively in the outer part of the structure. However, evidence for its presence was lacking, in contrast to the second dam where it was used as a caulking agent in the interstices between the stones of the inner revetment wall. It was probably used in this way in the first dam also, but as the upper part of the latter has not survived this cannot be demonstrated.

Protection from tidal erosion

The first line of defence against tidal erosion adopted by the builders was the placing of a palisade breakwater in front of the dam to disperse some of the wave energy acting on the base of the dam. Further measures to lesson tidal attrition included the stone-faced batter which sloped outwards. Parallels in the form of similar palisade-like breakwaters have been found in prehistoric and Medieval waterfronts in some of the ports on the Rhine and its tributaries, and at the Viking port of Haithabu (Ellmers 1981, 93) and within an Irish freshwater context many of the palisades surrounding crannógs may be interpreted as having functioned as breakwaters.

THE CONSTRUCTION MATERIALS AND THEIR SOURCES

One of the most interesting aspects of the dam of Mill 1 is the variety of materials used and the large quantities of each needed. The inventory includes orange and grey clays, which were of major importance, brown organically-rich soil, and wood. In general, the use of clay does not figure prominently in the Irish archaeological record in comparison to wood and stone, and may have been overlooked. Thus, its presence as a major component at Nendrum is of special interest.

The most obvious source of both the grey and the orange clays is the adjacent shoreline. At the southern edge of the millpond is a steep scarp, which appears to be artificial, and this may have been excavated for both types. Another possible source may have been the deep ditch forming the south-eastern boundary of the monastic enclosure (see p. 382).

Clay has been found as a constructional material in a small number of other mill sites. At Mashanaglass, a deposit of blue-grey clay *c.* 1.3m in depth was found over the penstock (Fahy 1956, 17). At the probable 9th-century horizontal-wheeled mill at Tamworth, clay was used as packing around the penstock and lower parts of the mill (Rathtz and Meeson 1992, 29).

The grey clay

Covered under this descriptive term is very visually distinct clay that ranged in colour from light-grey, to blue-grey, to darker shades. In some contexts it was mixed with gravel and stones, and had a stiff, sticky consistency when wet, drying out to a hard substance with an almost cement-like quality. This clay, which is found at various locations around the shores of Strangford Lough, is normally described as grey estuarine clay and regarded as a marine deposit of post-glacial origin. Analyses of a sample from the dam of Mill 2 (Peter Wilson, *pers. comm.*), where it was also used extensively, showed it to consist of 42.50% clay (particle size < 0.002mm), 44.50% silt (particle size 0.002mm–0.0625mm) and 13.00% sand (particle size 0.0625mm–2.00mm). Observation on the locations where it was found in the dam demonstrates that its main use was as an impervious sealing agent to prevent the seepage of water from undermining structures, and to seal more porous deposits such as soil and organically-rich material. Placed on the foreshore, it also formed a foundation layer for the millpond. Individual structures, such as the penstock and its support beam, were embedded in it, while some other structural wood was packed around with it.

The orange clay

Like the grey clay, this is very distinctive visually, and where the two occurred in close proximity in the dam, as they often did, there was a striking contrast in colour. Covered under the term 'orange clay' is a substance which ranges in colour from red, to reddish-brown, to orange, with occasional iron staining, and it is possible that clays of two different origins are present in this deposit. The orange-coloured form is undoubtedly boulder clay of glacial origin, which forms a large component of the drift material in the region. However, some of the darker-red forms may be red marine clay of Late Glacial date. The orange clay was used similarly to the grey clay as a bonding agent between stones and as a sealant, but to a large degree its use was confined to the outer part of the structure.

The organic-rich deposits

Organic-rich deposits were encountered at various locations during the excavation (C151/C403, C126, C18, C27 and other minor layers), all located in the inner core of the dam. They are characterised by their brown colour and fibrous nature, and by having visible vegetable matter in the form of leaves, moss and twigs. A general assessment of samples taken for environmental study would seem to indicate that deposits used in these layers came from several sources. This seems particularly evident from the seeds, which represent a wide variety of habitats including woodland, disturbed ground, cultivated land and wasteland, wet habitats, and grassland. The peat deposit (C18) and, to a lesser extent C11/C27 (found in the short section of the dam to the south of the wheelhouse), was recognisable as having a high content of dark, reddish-brown peat (see Figs 2.5 and 2.13) containing moss, root material and many seeds of sedges (*Carex sp.*). Many decayed leaves and branches were also present, and some branches may have formed a rough matting layer in places.

C126, which was found around the penstock area and the area behind the wheelhouse, was similar to C18 and C11/C27, and had a recognisable content of peat and many sedge seeds and root fragments, indicative of a wet habitat. C151/C403 was a very extensive deposit filling the outer trench and the outer core of the dam. It had a high content of moss, wood fragments, plant stems and well-preserved holly leaves, as well as small fragments of charred wood. Also included were seeds of plants from wet habitats, woodland and disturbed ground. The presence of leaves suggests an origin in a wooded environment with an accumulation of leaf litter, although they also may be derived from the debris from wood working, during the initial dressing of timber from felled trees.

While the reasons for using stone for structural strength and clay for its waterproofing qualities and as a bonding agent are clear, the choice of organic material is less obvious. One interpretation is that it was used as bulking-up material, with the stone and clay reserved for the inner and upper portions of the dam.

Stone

Of the different types of material used, stone was the most easily obtained, as it is to be found in abundance in the boulder zone forming the upper foreshore all around the site. Bonded with clay it was used for the retaining walls and capping material.

Timber

The dam is characterised by the large amount of structural wood used. Of special note is the prominence of oak. This would seem to imply that there was a plentiful supply of oak in the vicinity. The wattlework also represents a major amount of wood, with a high proportion of holly, and all of this points to the exploitation of woodland in the vicinity of the site. An intriguing feature of the wood used in the dam and in the landing place is the possible presence of worked pieces prepared for another use but not employed for it. This is discussed on pps 250-251.

COMPARATIVE EVIDENCE

There are no other examples of excavated early tidal dams with which to compare the structure at Nendrum. No traces of the tidal dam were observed at Little Island, Co. Cork. In the extremely sparse body of information on the freshwater dams of the many early mill site, Mashanaglass, Co. Cork represents the only published Irish mill excavation where part of the dam was explored. At this site the partial remains of the dam measured 14 feet (4.27m) wide and 3 feet 9 inches (1.14m) high and consisted of a stone-revetted earthen bank. Three substantial posts, *c*. 1 foot (30cm) diameter, set deeply into the ground, were found in front of both faces of the dam, one on one side and two on the other (Fahy 1956, 15–16). Rynne (2000, 187 Fig. 141, 194–195) has interpreted these posts as the remains of a possible wooden revetment with horizontal planking on both faces of the dam. Remains of the mill dam at High Island, Co. Galway were revetted with upright slabs (Rynne 2000, 187). The use of clay has been observed at a few sites, for instance at the horizontal-wheeled mill site at Milverton, Co. Dublin, the dam was composed of yellow clay (O'Donovan 1858–9, 252).

One must look further afield for comparative information, although no exact parallels are apparent. The oft-quoted description by St Gregory of Tours (dated to towards the end of the 6th century) of the building of a mill dam at the monastery at Loches mentions stakes being inserted across the river bed and packed with large stones (Horn 1975, 229; Rahtz and Bullough 1977, 20; Wikander 1985, 151; Rynne 2000, 196). Water-retaining embankments are present in the archaeological record as components of later Medieval millponds and fishponds, and in both the use of clay is evident. A succession of Medieval and Post-Medieval millpond dams excavated at Rothwell, Yorkshire, shows a variety of construction techniques including a clay bank revetted with very large oak piles, and horizontal planks with a core of clay, stones, turves and faggots (Youngs. *et al.* 1987, 173 and Faul and Moorehouse 1981, 713–715). A clay dam of Late- or Post-Saxon date with internal timber revetting was excavated at Wharram Percy (Youngs. *et al.* 1982, 213-214; 1983, 209).

BUILDING ON THE FORESHORE AND THE SEQUENCE OF CONSTRUCTION

The building of the first mill complex was a major project, with the construction of the dam being the biggest component of the work, requiring a large workforce. The first part of the project consisted of sourcing and assembling the materials needed, something that would have involved digging and moving a large volume of clay and stones, felling and working a large number of oak trees, and cutting material for the wattlework. The next stage — the building of the dam — similarly would have needed a sizeable team of craftsmen and labourers. While in many of the early Irish monasteries the monks performed manual labour, it may be presumed that the building of the dam involved the input of a large workforce over and above those normally resident in the monastery. Oxen or horses may have been used for the carriage of materials. Work on the foreshore could only have taken place during each of the two daily periods of low water and the position of the dam on the foreshore would have permitted only four to five hours per low tide before the incoming high tide stopped activity. Work on the foreshore also would have been limited to periods of low tides occurring during daylight. The summer months would have provided the optimum period of coincidence of low water and daylight, as well as more clement working weather, and it is probable therefore that most of the work was carried out then. Even during the long hours of summer daylight, it would have been only on rare occasions that two low tides could have been worked on the same day. Once the dam reached above the level of high tide, however, the constraint of tidal submergence would have been removed.

Considerable experience was gained during the excavation, of the practicalities faced by the builders in working in the foreshore conditions. Wood, in the form of piles, beams, planks and material for wattle, unless of considerable mass or firmly weighted down, will be displaced and dispersed by the incoming high tide. Therefore no stockpiling of wooden material could have taken place on the foreshore itself, and it must have been assembled on the nearest adjoining part of the shore above the high water mark. At least a part of this problem could have been reduced by building the dam in sections, with one part being built to near final height and used as the platform for further progress. No evidence for this was observed, but nevertheless it remains a possibility.

The stratigraphic information makes it possible to work out with reasonable accuracy the sequence of construction of the various elements in the dam which the tree-ring dating evidence suggests strongly commenced in spring AD 619 and may have been completed in the same year (see p. 70). The foreshore at Nendrum — like most of the foreshore in Strangford Lough — is composed of an upper shore of boulders, the result of erosion of the surrounding drumlins, which slopes down to a middle shore consisting of a flat expanse of fluid mud overlying sleech. Much of the dam is built on the mud and sleech, and required the digging of foundations to stabilise it. Construction work appears to have commenced on the external side of the dam with the digging of the outer trench. There is no direct evidence in the form of pure, redeposited silt, for where the excavated material spoil was disposed of, and presumably much was mixed with the other deposits making up the basal core of the bank. The bottom and outer sides of the trench were then lined with holly branches and the posts of the palisade were placed. Given the great quantity of holly used for the posts in the palisade, it is possible that the holly branches in the ditch are largely derived from the preparation of the holly posts in the palisade. Also at this stage the large piles were driven and the spaced line of large posts was probably placed in the outer trench and, quite possibly, the two other parallel rows as well.

The next major operation involved the construction of the wooden framework. The first stage in this was erection of the inner and middle wattle revetments and it is probable that these were woven on the foreshore. Analyses of the weave-pattern suggest that they were set in place from the north-west and progressed towards the mill. The space between them and the outer trench was then tightly packed with the organically-rich layers (C151/C403 and C126). The tipping lines in the sections through the outer trench in (see Fig. 2.24) show that they were filled by dumping the material in from the outside. The sloping outer wattle was then put in place, holding the ditch fill in. On the top of the deposit in the main part of the dam, horizontal timber bracing was placed to hold the whole framework together.

The inner trench appears to have been excavated next. Some of its spoil, mixed with grey clay and organically-rich soil and other material (C112), was deposited against the inner wattle revetment forming a low bank which was shuttered with planks placed against its pond-side face (see Fig. 2.27). When this was complete, the basic foundation core of the dam was in place. The bottom and sides of the inner trench, the sides and top of the timber revetment, top of the wattle framing and probably the whole of the basal core of the dam were sealed by a thick layer of grey clay. Most of the grey clay over the core had gone, but enough evidence remained to demonstrate its presence.

Following the sealing of the core, the inner stone revetment wall was constructed. The inner trench was packed with boulders and stones in a matrix of orange clay. The orange clay was also placed to cover the grey clay and the core below. Most of the upper layer of orange clay had also gone but, as with the grey clay layer, there was sufficient evidence to show its former existence. As the final stage, the inner stone face of the millpond side of the dam was made, and the whole upper portion of the dam capped with stone.

CONCLUSION

It is clear that considerable effort went into creating a strong and effective dam. The design does not appear to be a 'first effort', but shows accumulated experience and expertise in dam building were present in early 7th-century Ireland.

It is highly probable that the first dam was deliberately demolished to supply a convenient source of stone and clay for the construction of the adjacent new dam for Mill 2. This, however, left a substantial and ruinous structure on the foreshore, which was subject to 14 centuries of tidal attrition to reach the condition observed at the time of excavation. Although sufficient remained to provide a relatively clear picture of the character of the dam, some aspects remain unclear and only further excavation can resolve them. The most important of these is the location of the intake sluice gates or tide gates. Current interpretation is that it seems highly probable that the apparent gaps in the structure represent their location, but this remains to be verified. It is only possible to speculate about the type of sluice used, although this may well have been the flap-gate type used in later tidal mills and other tidal sluices which are opened automatically by pressure from the rising tide and closed by the pressure of the falling one. As the dam of Mill 2 is different to that of Mill 1, both in its structural design and its location on the foreshore, we may conclude that among the factors influencing the construction of the new mill were defects identified in Mill 1. Among the factors leading to the need for a new mill may have been the failure of the dam, or the cost of maintaining a dam of this large size.

THE STRUCTURAL DESIGN OF THE DAMS OF MILL 2

The rectangular millpond belonging to Mill 2 is enclosed by two dams: a long main dam on the northern side and a short dam at 90° to it at its eastern end. Only a small part of the eastern dam was excavated and much of its upper part had not survived. Fortunately, however, part of the northern dam had survived in excellent condition, and it consists of an embankment wider at the base than the top composed of thick stone revetting walls enclosing a clay core (see Fig. 3.4A). It is *c.* 125m long and becomes progressively broader as it projects out from the shore, widening from *c.* 3m here to 6m in the vicinity of the mill. This presumably reflects the need for a greater thickness in the dam towards the mill or discharge end of the millpond where the pressure of impounded water was greatest. The dam has a flat top, and it is highly probable that it was used as a walkway from the monastic enclosure to the mill. Kiln-dried and granary stored grain to be ground in the mill was probably transported from inside the monastery enclosure along the top of the dam. In addition, people arriving at high tide in boats at the landing stage beside the mill may also have used it as an access route to the monastery.

The inner core

The core of the dam is composed of tightly-packed clay. The lower layers consist of grey clay, some of which is interleaved with lenses of brown earth, the upper of orange clay, which completely seals the grey clay deposit below. Although the upper surface of the dam has not survived, it seems probable that it was capped with stones.

The outer structure

The seaward face of the dam consists of a wide stone revetment wall built with a slight batter. The wall is made up of an inner and outer line of large boulders, with smaller stones packed and set in a matrix of clay behind them (double boulder-and-fill method). The millpond face of the dam was similarly constructed, but is narrower, and the interstices between the boulders and stones were packed with moss.

Original height of the dam

The maximum highest surviving height of the main dam is at 2.57m OD, thus well above the mean high water spring level at 1.9m. It has been argued earlier (see p. 105) that its original height may have been at *c.* 3m OD. This latter figure suggests that it may have stood around 2m above the foreshore. It is to be noted that a small part of the eastern dam adjacent to the shore near the site of the millhouse is very well preserved, and that its top surface is at 3.85m OD. It seems unlikely, however, that this height is representative of the general height of the dams. As there is a high coastal scarp at this location, it seems probable that the surface of the dam would have sloped down here to the mill.

Protection from tidal erosion

The single biggest factor in combatting tidal erosion was the positioning of the main section of the dam perpendicular to the direction of the incoming tide, rather than facing it directly as was the case in the dam of Mill 1. This would have acted to greatly lessen the impact of wave action. Further protection was provided by the relatively massive seaward stone revetment, which was built with a batter.

Waterproofing - the moss caulking

In like manner to the dam of Mill 1, considerable effort was expended in waterproofing the dam of Mill 2. As is the case with the dam of Mill 1 the main impermeable material used was grey and orange clay. Also the same technique of sealing the grey clay in the inner core with a cap of orange clay was employed. Moss was used as the first line of defence against water seeping into the core of the dam, with the interstices between the surface stones on the sides of the dam being tightly packed with it. On contact with water, moss acts like a sponge, swells and becomes saturated, forming a highly effective barrier to penetration. The value of moss as a caulking material appears to have been recognised globally early in prehistory. It is probably best seen in the caulking of the spaces between timbers of prehistoric boats, such as those from North Ferriby and Dover which date to *c*. 1300–1350 BC (Parfitt 1993; Clarke 1997), and its use for this purpose continued to Late Medieval times. The use of moss has been noted also at some other mill sites. At the 7th-century Little Island mill, and the 9th-century Cloontycarthy mill, both in Co. Cork, moss was used to line the headrace (Rynne 1988, 64), while at Kilmagar, Co. Kilkenny, it was used to caulk the lids of the penstock (Byrne 1851, 158; Rynne 2000, 187).

When uncovered during excavation, most of the moss was in a remarkable state of preservation and appeared fresh and green. It is evident, therefore, that it was put in place a very short time after collection and would have been saturated by the next incoming tide. Examination showed that it had been pulled in lumps with the roots still in place. The species range and the presence of oak buds and bud scales and also hazel nuts show that it was gathered from a shady habitat on a woodland floor (see Appendix 3). The quantity uncovered during the excavation was impressive and represented only a minute sample of the total amount that would have been required to caulk the dams.

BUILDING ON THE FORESHORE, THE SEQUENCE OF CONSTRUCTION AND MATERIALS USED

From the section shown in Fig. 3.4A, it is possible to demonstrate the sequence of construction of the main portion of the dam. The first stage was the building of the bases of the outer and inner faces of the revetment wall on the seaward side, with large boulders being laid on the original foreshore. When these had reached a height of *c*. 1m, the space between the faces was filled with smaller stones. Then a bank of well-packed grey clay was placed against this, forming the base of the inner core of the dam. Next, a mixed deposit of earth and grey clay was placed against and partially overlying the grey clay bank, and the first metre of the revetment wall on the millpond side was built. The next stage, evident from the stratigraphy shown in Fig. 3.4A was the completion of the revetment walls to the full height of the dam, and the sealing of the basal section of the inner core by placing a thick deposit of orange clay over it. The building of the dam was a major project and would have involved a large labour input. However, in comparison to that of Mill 1 it would have required much less effort, as all parts of it were much closer to the shore and it had no wooden component to put in place. But it did require an enormous amount of material including a massive volume of stones, orange and grey clay, and earth. It would seem obvious that much of this was derived from the systematic dismantling of the upper part of the dam of Mill 1. Additional stone was available from the boulder zone around the shoreline, and more clay was probably dug from the steep and probably artificial scarp edging the southern side of the millpond.

CHANGES IN DESIGN BETWEEN THE DAMS OF MILL 1 AND MILL 2

Positioning

The dam of Mill 1 faced the incoming tide while dam of Mill 2 was largely perpendicular to it, and this constitutes an important improvement in design that would have resulted in much lessened tidal erosion. The dam of Mill 1 was largely built on the foreshore mud, while that of Mill 2 was for the most part located on the fringing boulder zone higher up the shore giving it a firmer foundation.

Structural design

The dam of Mill 1 had a significant timber framework, which included wattlework, planks and piles, whereas that of Mill 2 was built almost completely of clay and stone. No wood was used, and it is an example of a 'gravity dam' held in place by its own mass. The abandonment of the elaborate wattle and timber box framing structure used in the dam of Mill 1 is intriguing. The straightforward explanation is that it was not needed and that it was possible to construct a stable dam without this component. Both dams were probably much the same height, but as their height is directly related to the tidal range, which was appears to have been constant during the 7th and 8th centuries, there would have been no reason to vary this. The dam of Mill 1 is wider than that of Mill 2 but as it impounded less water it did not need to be as massive.

Waterproofing

In terms of waterproofing, both dams, with the use of grey and orange clay, are very similar. It is possible, however, that greater use was made of moss as a waterproofing agent in the dam of Mill 2, although as much of the upper part of the dam of Mill 1 has been lost it is not possible to be certain on this point.

It is of interest to consider the motivation for the changes in design between the dams of the two mills. In comparison to the composite nature of the dam of Mill 1, the dams of Mill 2 are relatively simple examples of a gravity dam of the embankment type whose solid mass was capable of withstanding the pressure of impounded water. Comparison of the two designs may suggest that the elaborate construction details of Mill 1's dam were overkill, and experience may have proved them to have been unnecessary. It may have proved too costly to maintain and so the decision was made to replace it completely with a simpler type of dam, rather than to repair it. It is a tribute to the structural strength of the dam of Mill 2 that a significant portion still survives on the foreshore today and has withstood approximately 1200 years of tidal attrition.

THE MILLPONDS

Introduction

There is very little information on the millponds attached to early Irish mill sites, as previous excavations have tended to focus heavily on the sites of the wheelhouses and have rarely explored the millpond. Likewise, documentary evidence is sparse, although the text *Di chetharšlicht Athgabála,* which dates to *c.* AD 600 and lists the parts of the mill (MacEoin 1982, 14, 15), mentions the millpond as the *tír linde,* literally translated as 'the land of the pond' and also refers to the water source (*topur*) and the mill race (*tuidin*). One of the many exciting aspects of the Nendrum evidence is the relatively complete nature of its millponds and, although only a very small area of these was investigated, they provide, in the absence of other sources, important information.

The first millpond

The first thing to be observed about the millpond of Mill 1 is its size. With a surface area of *c.* 6,500m^2, it is impressive, and becomes more so when compared to the much smaller area of that of Mill 2 with its surface area of *c.* 2000m^2. It had, therefore, the capacity to impound a large volume of tidal water. As the shape of the island takes an approximately right-angled bend at this location, the construction of the dam across the foreshore has resulted in the millpond having an almost triangular shape.

One of the most important features is the lining of the bottom of the pond with grey clay, at least in the small but important area excavated in the vicinity of the mill. This represents a serious effort to make the bottom of the pond impervious and to provide it with a flat base on the sloping foreshore. Furthermore, it appears also that in the vicinity of the penstock intake area, planks were placed on the grey clay presumably to protect against degradation by scouring.

The second millpond

The second millpond is rectangular in shape and, whereas the shape of the first was largely based on natural topography, its shape contains a strong element of artificial landscaping and the terracing of an area of the foreshore and coastal edge to create a rectangular, level platform on the upper shore. In the small area excavated, no attempt had been made to line the bottom with grey clay, except in a narrow area in front of the penstock intake channel. Instead, a foundation of stones and earth was placed over the silt of the underlying earlier millpond. It may have been that the underlying grey clay foundation of the first pond was still effective. Assessment of the potential energy of the volume of impounded water in the millpond of Mill 2 is discussed in Chapter 8.

Changes in design between millpond 1 and 2

The primary difference between the two millponds is the larger size of that belonging to Mill 1 and therefore its capacity to impound a greater volume of water than the millpond of Mill 2. On a superficial level this appears a somewhat retrogressive development.

However, experience may have demonstrated that the first millpond had a greater storage capacity than needed. The entrapment of a larger volume of water may have been counterproductive in terms of the longer time taken to discharge it through its penstock(s) when the mill was working during low water. There were also advantages in having a smaller millpond, which would have been much easier to manage, and would have had fewer problems caused by silting. Indeed, as much of the bed of millpond 1 was sited on a large expanse of foreshore mud, silting up of parts of it could have been a problem. It seems clear that in contrast to the first millpond, the second millpond was the result of more considered planning. Its smaller size was probably deliberately designed to retain a sufficient volume of impounded water as a part of the overall efficient working of the mill.

Chapter 5

The Penstocks

Thomas McErlean

Chapter 5
The Penstocks

Thomas McErlean

INTRODUCTION

The function of the penstock in a horizontal-wheeled mill was to deliver a high-pressure water jet to the waterwheel, and the configuration of its internal chamber was designed for this. Many early Irish examples have survived (see Table 5.2), all of which follow closely the same design. Each consists of a box-like structure, with an open, or intake, end and a closed end perforated by a small opening (the orifice). The open end functioned as the 'mouth' of the structure through which the water from the millpond entered the chamber, and was then ejected as a pressure jet directed onto the waterwheel through the orifice in the closed end. To build up pressure, the penstock chamber progressively narrowed from the mouth to the orifice, and to cope with the build up of pressure, it was buried and kept stable by the weight of the overlying material. All of the Irish penstocks examples display evidence of having been fitted with lids and there are no clear examples of open chutes. Again, all of the known Irish examples were placed on a sloping plane down from the intake end to the orifice end. The orifice end or façade in almost all Irish examples emerges to the right of centre of the back wall of the wheelhouse and at a short height above the wheelhouse floor. The splendidly-preserved stone penstock of Mill 2 has all of these features, and it seems most likely that the poorly-preserved wooden penstock of Mill 1 had them also.

THE WOODEN PENSTOCK OF MILL 1

Interpretation of the features uncovered around the penstock area of Mill 1 suggests the possible original existence of two penstocks (see pps 38-40) although only the remains of the one have survived. It was in a very degraded condition and few detailed features remained (see Figs 2.14 and 5.1), but it was clearly made from a hollowed-out oak trunk. The intake end had not survived, and the area of its orifice end was buried in the wheelhouse wall of Mill 2 and was not excavated to avoid damaging the wall. It was estimated (for reasons put forward on p. 38) that its total original length was greater than 3.22m, but only over one third, 1.22m, of its length was uncovered. The surviving section towards its intake end had an external diameter of 60cm, narrowing to 54cm towards the orifice end. Only one side of the internal chamber had survived appreciably above internal base (see Fig. 2.8B), to a height of *c.* 25cm, and it was impossible to ascertain how much above this had been lost. The internal width of chamber was *c.* 36cm. The interior base had a rounded profile, but it is unclear how much of this is due to degradation of a straight base or if it is original. The few features which were ascertained can be compared to those of other wooden penstocks summarised in Table 5.2.

Fig. 5.1
The oak penstock of Mill 1 from west

The disturbed area of the penstock(s) of Mill 1 and the degraded state of the surviving one make it difficult to glean information about this very important early example. Evidence for the penstock or possibly two penstocks (see pps 38-40), is extremely limited compared to that for the splendid stone penstock of Mill 2. The presence of two penstocks at tide mill sites may reflect the secure water resource offered by the tides. It has been claimed that at the Bagenalstown, Co. Carlow, horizontal-wheeled mill site (Corlett 2001, 7), both penstocks were angled to serve one waterwheel. However, in all known examples of horizontal-wheeled mill sites with two penstocks in Europe and Asia, they were employed to power separate wheels (Rynne 1992, 65). Thus, the first mill at Nendrum may have had two sets of millstones.

THE STONE PENSTOCK OF MILL 2

Introduction

The massive stone penstock of Mill 2 is very impressive, and has a superficial resemblance to a large stone sarcophagus. To date, it is the only Irish example of a penstock made in stone, all of the others being of oak. Except for some damage around the intake area, it has survived relatively intact and is the most complete example of a penstock to have survived on any Irish site. In common with the large number of examples from other Irish horizontal-wheeled mill sites listed in Table 5.2, the interior of the Nendrum penstock consists of a wedge-shaped box, open at one end and closed at the other.

Description

The exterior is roughly wedge-shaped and has an external overall length of 3.78m. It is 1m wide and approximately 85cm high at the mouth, and 60cm wide and 55cm high at the orifice end. The orifice end protrudes beyond the back wall of the wheelhouse by 15cm and is at a right angle to the inclined longitudinal plane of the penstock and therefore slants outward from the base. The external surfaces of the sides are roughly dressed and have many chisel marks visible. In contrast, the main area of the orifice façade (Figs 5.3A and B) has been worked to a smooth face, especially around the orifice itself. The angle between the bottom and the right-hand side is sharp, but the left-hand side has been worked to a chamfer. The top right-hand corner has either been knocked off or left undressed. The base and both sides of the orifice façade are tightly bonded with the wall of the wheelhouse. As it was decided to leave the penstock *in situ,* the layers underneath

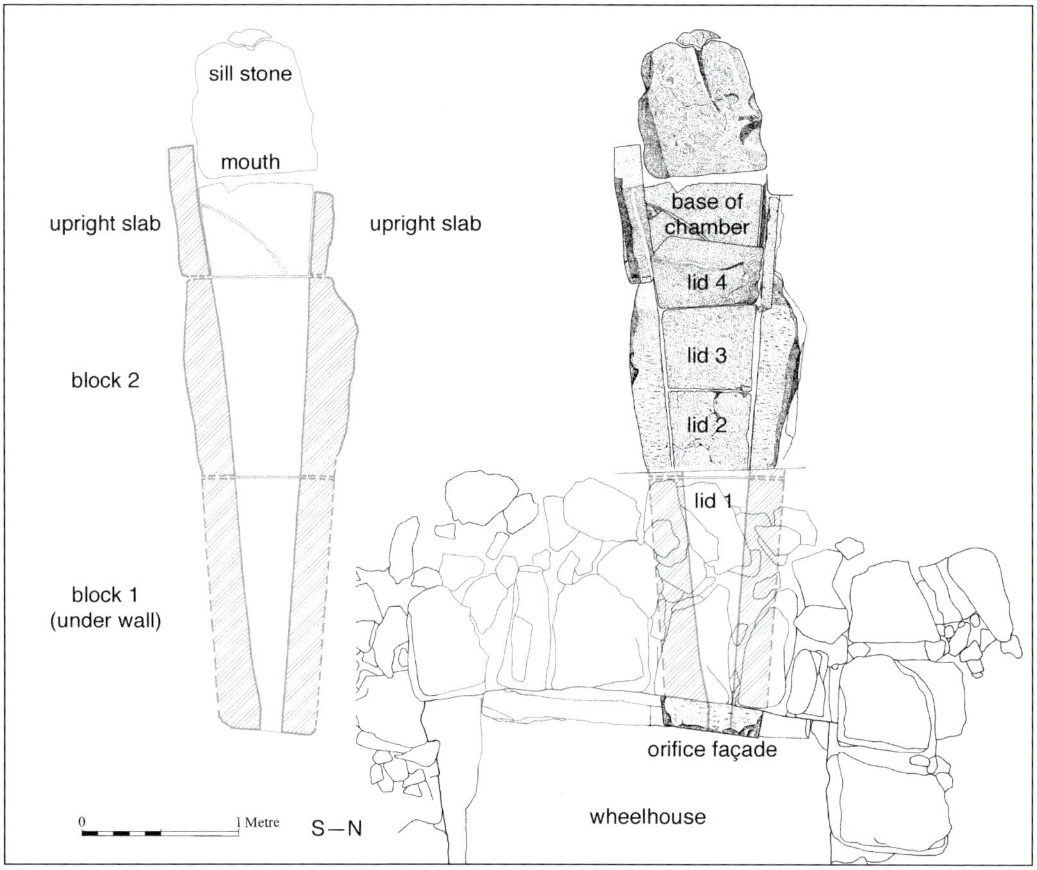

Fig. 5.2A
Explanatory plan of the parts of the penstock (J. Patience)

Fig. 5.2B
Side view of the penstock from north

were not excavated. This meant it could not be ascertained if or how the penstock was fixed into the wall to stop it from subsiding.

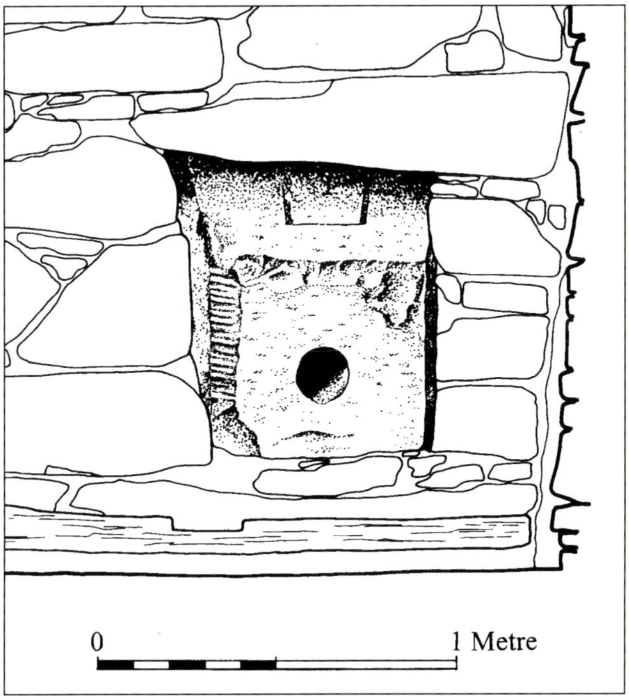

Fig. 5.3A
The orifice façade of the penstock in the wheelhouse (J. Patience)

Fig. 5.3B
The orifice façade of the penstock in the wheelhouse with the bridge-tree support beam below

Fig. 5.3C
Detail of the orifice

The penstock was constructed in three sections, all butt-jointed together (see Fig. 5.2A). The first two consist of large stone blocks, (blocks 1 and 2), with their interiors hollowed out to a rectangular section. The third component, which forms the mouth or intake section, consists of two upright slabs forming the sides and one horizontal slab forming the base. Four tightly-fitting lids formed by heavy stone slabs closed the top of the structure. Block 1 is located at the orifice end and, with the exception of the small portion protruding into the wheelhouse, is buried in its back wall. It is 1.41m in length, and is 83cm wide at its broad end and 60cm at the narrow end. Its height is probably close to that of Block 2, which is *c.* 66–71cm. The side walls are in the region of 20cm thick, while the orifice end is 35cm thick.

Block 2, which abuts the western end of Block 1, is 1.47m long. It is 1.025m wide at the broad end and 82.5cm at the narrow end, and ranges in height from 66–71cm. Approximately 20cm of its length is buried in the back wall of the wheelhouse. A prominent feature of the second block is the presence of two cracks, one on each side face (see Figs 5.5A and B, 5.6A and B and 5.7B and C). That on the southern side is a major one and extends externally from the western end of the block eastwards for *c.* 1.20m, disappearing into the wall of the wheelhouse. Its origin is clearly at the western end where it is widest, and would seem to be the result of a misguided chisel blow during the dressing of

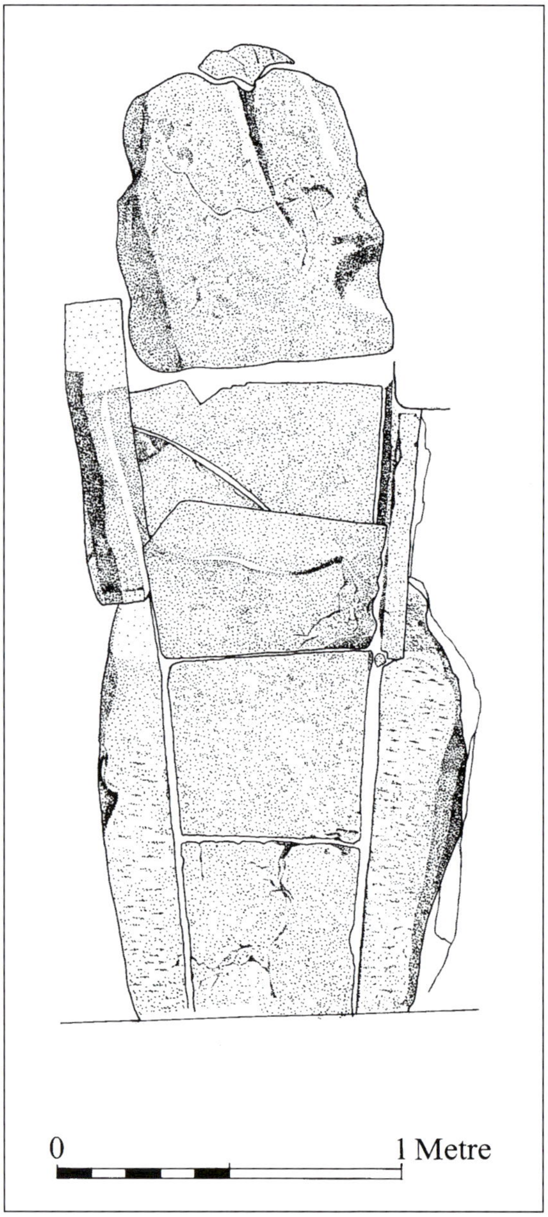

Fig. 5.4A
Plan of the top view of the penstock west of the wheelhouse wall (J. Patience)

Fig. 5.4B
Top view of the penstock with the lids in place and the intake and mouth area not fully excavated

Fig. 5.4C (far right)
Top view of the penstock with the lids removed and the intake and mouth area excavated exposing the penstock sill stone

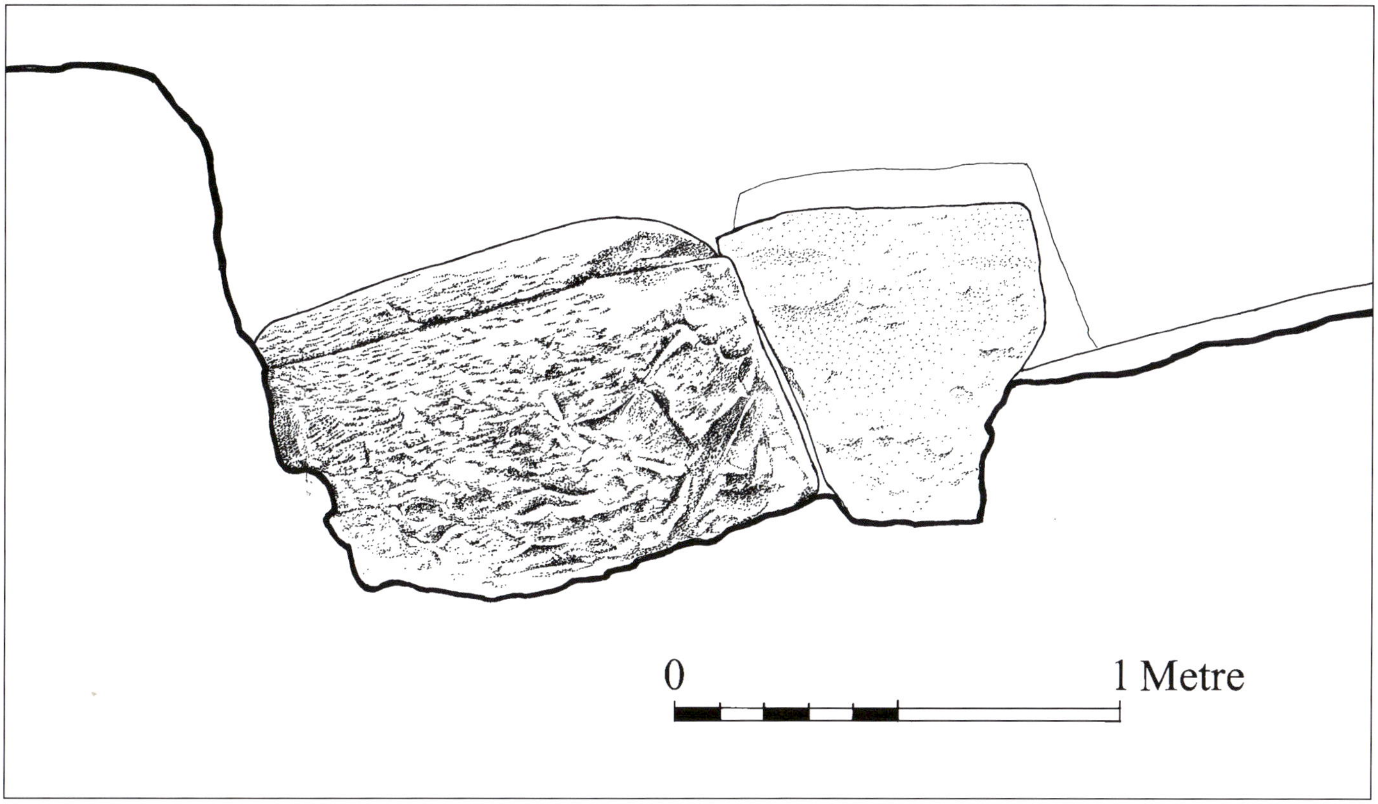

Fig. 5.5A
The north side of the penstock (J. Patience)

Fig. 5.5B
The north side of the penstock showing block 2

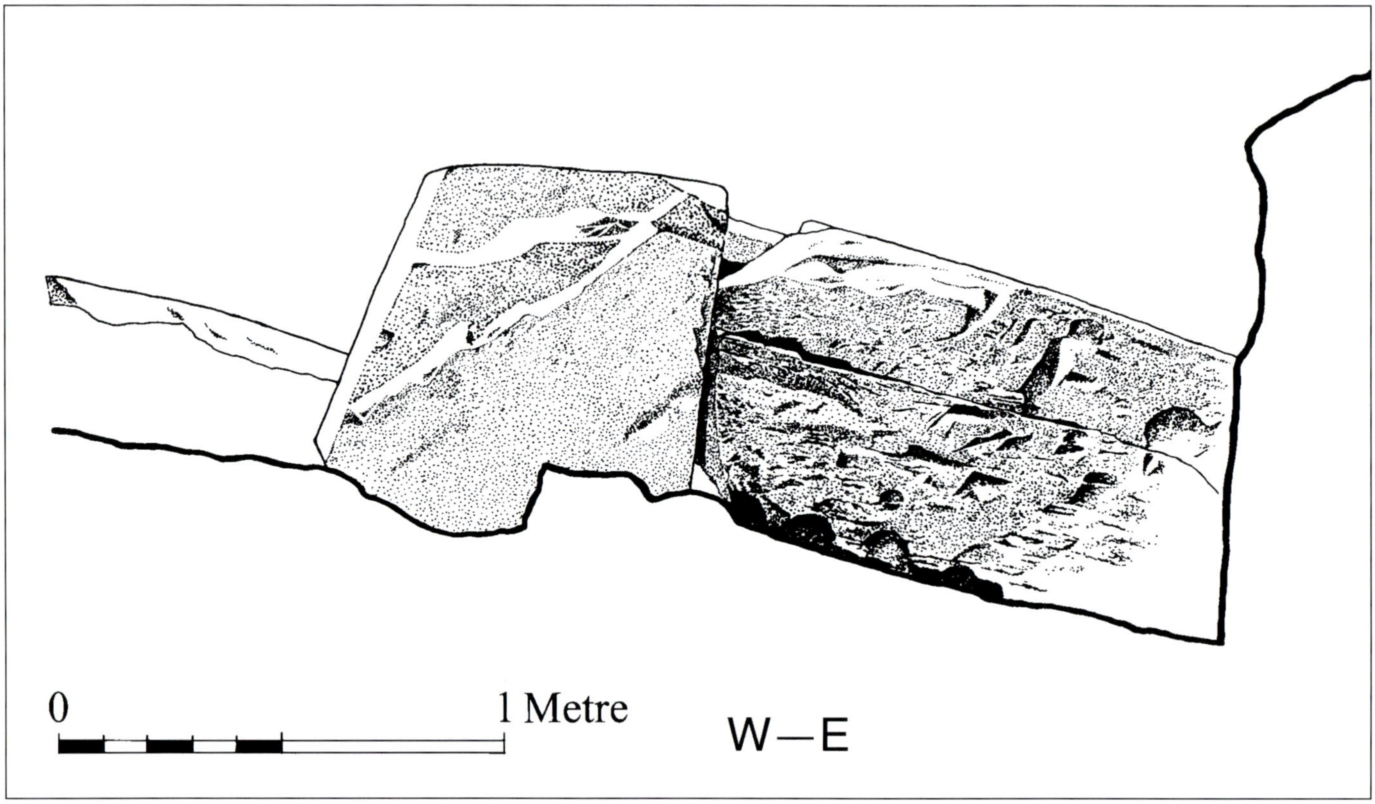

Fig. 5.6A
The south side of the penstock
(J. Patience)

Fig. 5.6B
The south side of the penstock
showing block 2

the stone. It is unlikely that any dressing took place after the penstock was put it position, as this would have upset the careful and critical positioning of the structure in relation to the waterwheel and other parts, so it may have occurred before it was brought to the site.

For the first 45cm from the western end, this crack is a substantial crevice, which gradually diminishes towards the east. It penetrates the interior face of the chamber (see Fig. 5.7C and 5.9), but is very narrow at this location. No evidence of it having been caulked was noted during excavation. However, caulking may have been present originally, given that the surrounding external area of the penstock was well caulked with moss (see p. 97). It is unlikely that the crack leaked water or led to any reduction of the water pressure through the chamber.

The rim and ledge

Around the top of the penstock is a prominent rim defined by a right-angled rebate cut to form a ledge to support the lids. The rim is 20.3cm wide on the southern side and 18.6cm on the northern. The ledge on which the four heavy, wedge-shaped stone lids rest is located *c.* 14.0cm below the top of the rim. Its width varies, but is 4.2cm on average. There is a crack at the junction of the rim and the ledge on the northern side (see Figs 5.5A and B, 5.7B), which extends through the full thickness and length of the rim. As a result, the whole rim section of this side of the block can be moved slightly sideways, pivoting around its eastern end which is held in place by the weight of the wall. When the penstock was uncovered, this section of rim was observed to overhang slightly the external side of the structure. This crack may have been the result of an accident during the carving of the rim or when it was being moved. It is also possible that it was deliberate and was made to rectify an initial miscalculation of the width of the ledge, the original ledge perhaps having been too narrow to support the heavy lid.

Fig. 5.7A
View of the top of the penstock from the south showing detail of Lids 3 and 4 in situ

Fig. 5.7B
View of the top of the penstock from the south with Lids 3 and 4 removed showing the rim and lid ledge

Fig. 5.7C
View of the top of the penstock from the north with Lids 3 and 4 removed showing the rim and lid ledge and the rebate on Lid 2 to lock into similar on Lid 3

The lids

The lids are not fixed, but depended on their own weight and that of the material placed on top to keep them in place. When the material above was removed by excavation, it was possible to lift them off. The middle lids interlocked at the ends with their neighbours, by a rebate forming a type of lap-joint, as shown on Fig. 5.9.

Fig. 5.8A
Lids 3 and 4

Fig. 5.8B
East end of Lid 3 showing rebate (joined with Lid 2 when in situ)

Three of the four lids survive intact, but the one at the mouth end has been damaged and only approximately half remains *in situ*. A small fragment of the missing portion was found nearby. Lid 1 (numbered from the orifice end) is buried within the back wall of the wheelhouse and, apart from a small section visible from there, could only be inspected from below within the penstock chamber. It is approximately 1.36m in length, 58cm wide at its broad end and 22cm at the narrow end, and is 12cm thick. Lid 2, which is thicker than its two neighbours and with a higher upper surface, is 15cm thick, 71cm long, and 51cm wide at the broad end, 40cm at the narrow end. Lid 3, has sides of unequal length, one measuring 55cm, the other 50cm long.

The broad end is 58cm wide, the narrow end 52cm. The surviving portion of lid 4 is 45cm long, 71cm wide at its broad end and 62.5cm at its narrow end, and is 9cm thick. It is possible to estimate closely its original dimensions, which show it to be the largest of the four, at 77.5cm long, 82.5cm at its broad end and 62.5cm at its narrow end. The surfaces of the lids are recessed below the surface of the rim and all of the lower surfaces are flush with each other.

The penstock chamber

The penstock chamber has a much more pronounced wedge-shaped plan in comparison to the external outline of the structure, and measures 76cm wide at the mouth narrowing to 20cm where the orifice commences. The dressing of its interior surfaces is remarkably smooth compared to the rough dressing of the exterior. The mouth of the chamber is rectangular and is 41cm high (measured from the floor to the ledge for the lid) and 76cm wide. As the main design feature of the penstock is that it narrows progressively from mouth to orifice, this is probably best appreciated by observing the cross-section area at a number of locations from the mouth to the orifice as shown in Table 5.1 and Fig. 5.10. At the mouth, the cross-section area is 0.31m^2 which reduces to 0.019m^2 at the orifice.

Table 5.1: Reduction of cross-sectional area in the penstock from the mouth to the penstock

Location	Height by breadth dimensions	Cross-sectional area
Mouth	41cm by 76cm	0.31m^2
1m from mouth	40cm by 55cm	0.22m^2
2m from mouth	31cm by 37cm	0.12m^2
3m from mouth	31cm by 21cm	0.7m^2
Orifice	15cm by 16cm	0.019m^2

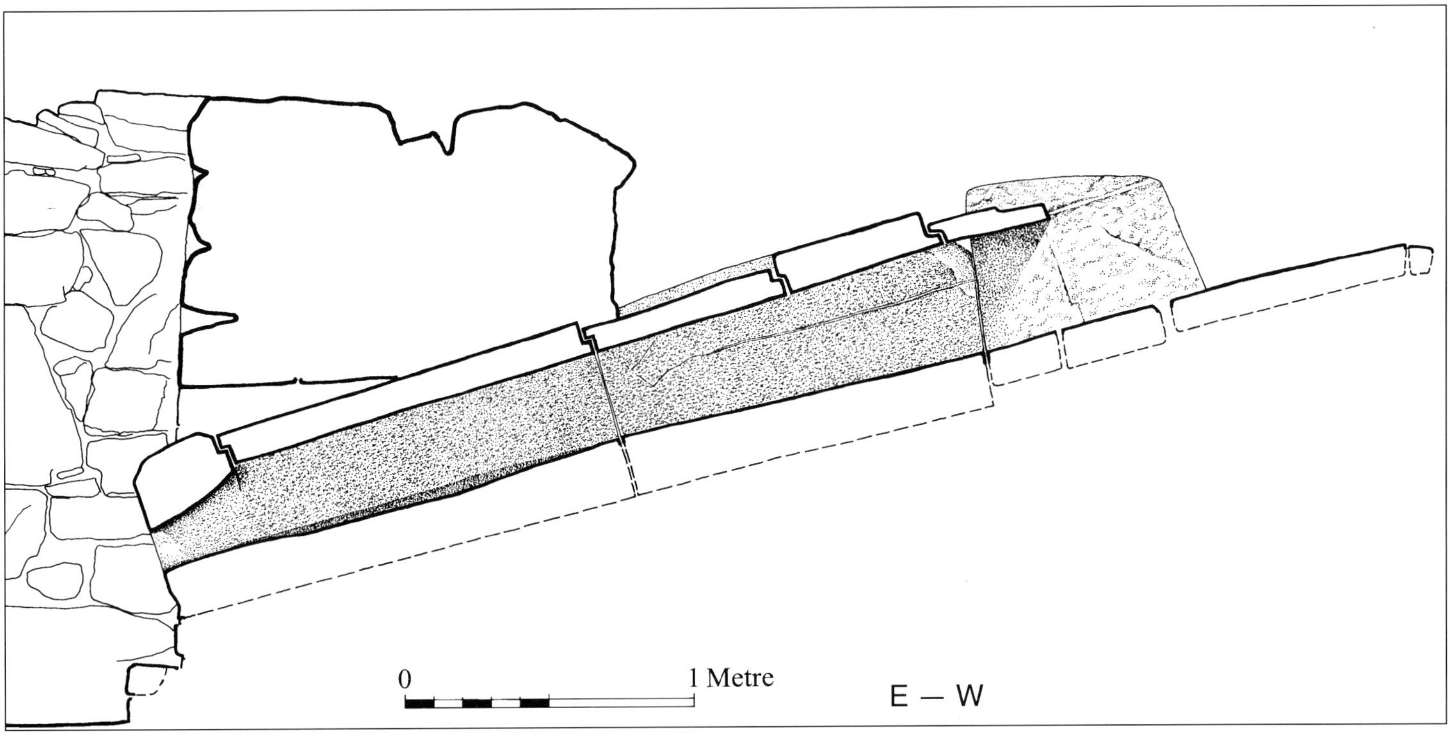

Fig. 5.9
Section (north facing) through penstock chamber (J. Patience)

This reduction was achieved by splaying the side walls of the chamber inwards from the mouth to the orifice, and by a more gradual reduction in height (see Figs 5.9 and 5.10). The southern wall has a slightly wider splay than the northern one. The orifice is oval and has a cross axis of 15cm and vertical axis of 16cm. Its base is flush with the base of the chamber, which is inclined at 15° to the horizontal and has a fall of 95cm from the mouth to the base of the orifice.

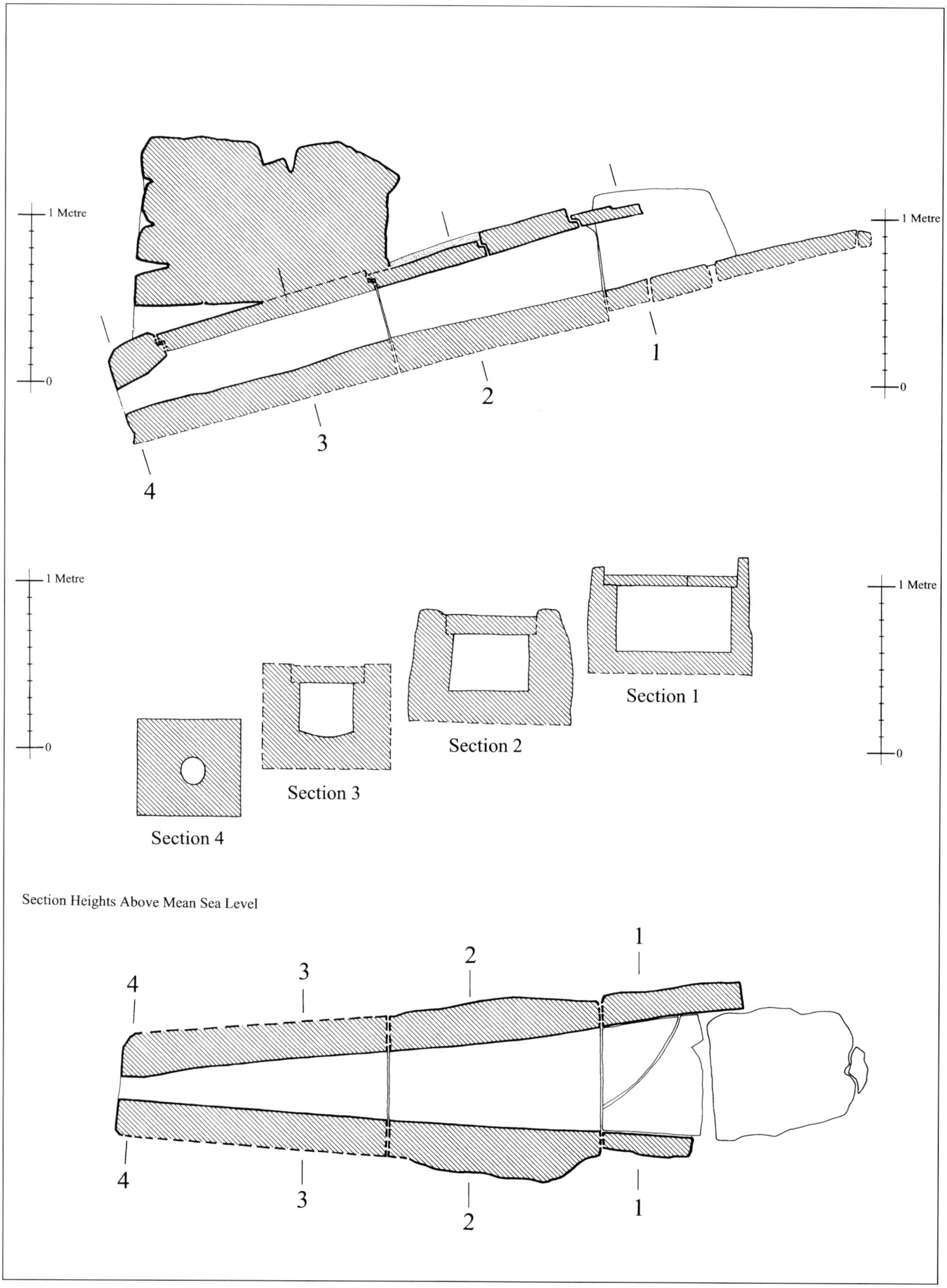

Fig. 5.10
Cross sections through the penstock chamber (J. Patience)

Fig. 5.11A
The mouth of the penstock before clearance

Fig. 5.11B
The mouth of the penstock after clearance

Fig. 5.12A
The excavation of the penstock chamber (excavator Shane Maher)

Fig. 5.12B
The penstock chamber with Lids 3 and 4 removed

Fig. 5.13A
View down through the penstock chamber from the mouth to the orifice

Fig. 5.13B
View up through the penstock chamber from the orifice to the mouth

THE PENSTOCK SILL STONE AND PENSTOCK INTAKE CHANNEL

Situated immediately outside the mouth of the chamber (see Figs 5.2A. 5.14A and B), and at the end of the penstock intake channel, and set in the same sloping plane as the base of the penstock chamber, is the penstock sill stone which can be considered a functional part of the structure. No other Irish site has produced evidence of the presence of a sill stone outside the mouth of a penstock.

The southern side of the sill stone is partially between the side-walls of the penstock which projects beyond the chamber at this point. It consists of a large, approximately tongue-shaped slab of shale measuring 92.5cm long by 75.3cm wide and 11cm thick. Its base is embedded in thick layer of moss and its surface is smooth, perhaps as the result of water erosion. There is a

Fig. 5.14A
Side view (from south) of the penstock sill stone in its bed of moss and the upright slab forming the south side of the mouth of the penstock

Fig. 5.14B
Top view of the penstock sill stone

gap of 6.5cm between it and the base of the chamber (see Fig. 5.4A). Evidence for the position of a penstock sluice gate is discussed at pps 94-95.

In preference to 'headrace channel', 'feeder channel' and 'sluice', the term 'penstock intake channel' is used here for the short and narrow channel which brought the water from the millpond to the penstock. In discussing the term *brágit na linne,* found in an early source and literally translated as 'the neck of the pond', MacEoin (1982, 16) erroneously identifies it with the penstock, but it seems much more plausible to see it as a term for the penstock intake channel (Rynne 1988, 1, 146). The well-defined example at Nendrum is characterised by its short length and the short distance between the millpond and the penstock. This is in contrast to the penstock intake or 'headrace channel' at Mashanaglass, Co. Cork (Fahy 1956, 17) which is *c.* 46m long.

THE MAKING OF THE PENSTOCK

At the time of writing, the type of rock from which the penstock is made has not been definitively identified. It is pink to orange in colour and resembles sandstone in texture, but it is likely to be Castle Espie limestone, which it resembles very closely. This localised outcrop of carboniferous limestone is on the shoreline approximately three miles to the north of Nendrum. It was worked from at least the 16th century for, amongst other things, grave slabs and doorways, and later, in the 18th century, was exploited as a source of lime. Apart from the outcrop, boulders of Castle Espie limestone occur around the shores of the lough as glacial erratics.

The sheer dimensions of the two blocks which made up most of the penstock, before their interiors were hollowed out, would have been impressive. To make Block 1, a boulder of minimum measurements 1.74m long by 1.025m wide by 71cm high would have been required, while for Block 2 minimum dimensions would have been 1.47m long by 1.025m wide and 71cm high. It is improbable, though not impossible, that boulders of these dimensions would have been found around the shoreline as glacial erratics, but it seems more likely that the stone was quarried. It is highly likely that to reduce transport weight, the shaping and dressing of the stones — especially the hollowing-out of the interior — was carried out at the quarry site and in such a way that the structure could be reassembled at the mill. This seems especially obvious in the case of the easily-removable lids.

The controlled carving of the penstock chamber and orifice is impressive and implies the presence of good stone-carving tools with steeled edges. It has been suggested that a dramatic improvement in stone carving noticeable in the 9th and 10th centuries must reflect a similar improvement in masonry tools (Gelly 1995, 158). The precision of the cutting of the orifice suggests drilling, probably carried out from both sides. Evidence for the contemporary use of drills is also present on some high crosses (*ibid.*

158). The Nendrum stone penstock is one of the few examples of a major piece of Irish Early Medieval stone-carving, carried out specifically to produce an object having a non-religious function.

THE POSITIONING OF THE PENSTOCK

The positioning of the penstock was critical to the overall design of the mill, requiring a high level of hydraulic engineering and forward planning. It had to be set at a level compatible with the local tidal range and in a precise position in relation to other components of the mill. If the intake level at the mouth was set too high, it would miss out on the lower tides in the tidal range. If set too low, problems would have emerged in the wheelhouse in keeping the waterwheel free of water at low tide, to prevent its rotation from being impeded. The level at the top of the mouth is at 1.09m OD and, as the mean high-water neap tide level at Nendrum is 1.4m OD (see p. 210), it evidently was set at a level which takes account of this. The angle of incline of 15° was probably predetermined by calculation of the potential volume of tidal water impounded in the millpond and the maximum fall to supply a sufficient operational head which could be achieved within the tidal range. The level of the orifice was also critical to the overall working of the mill and obviously had been precisely calculated.

It is possible to work out the sequence of placement of the components. The first stage, carried out at the same time as the excavation of the wheelhouse, involved the excavation of a large cut in the pre-existing dam of Mill 1. A stone ramp was made to a predetermined slope and height on which to place the penstock, and the basal layers of the back wall of the wheelhouse were laid. The surface of the ramp was lined with a bed of moss from 10–20cm thick. The second stage comprised the placing and the assembling of the component parts. Block 1 was brought down the ramp and put in position at the predetermined angle of incline and the back wall of the wheelhouse was built up around its sides. Above the block, a large stone lintel was placed to bridge the top of the opening on the back wall. This also served to take some of the weight imposed by the overlying wall, off the narrower end of the penstock, and contributed to fixing it rigidly in place. Block 2 was positioned butting against Block 1, and this was followed by the placing of upright slabs and base at the intake end. In the final stage the wheelhouse wall was finished and the surrounding cut filled with layers of silt interleaved with layers of moss. The penstock was buried with layers of redeposited silt, clay and stones to a depth of approximately 1.2m over the mouth and just over 2m near the orifice end. The moss packing below and around the penstock served two functions, the more important being to prevent seepage of water beneath the penstock which would have destabilised it, the other to provide a soft bed for the base. An amber pendant (Fig. 5.15A and B) was uncovered in the material surrounding the penstock and fill of the cut made for its placement and was, presumably, lost by someone involved in the work.

Fig. 5.15A
Amber pendant found in the fill of the cut for the stone penstock (T.Corey)

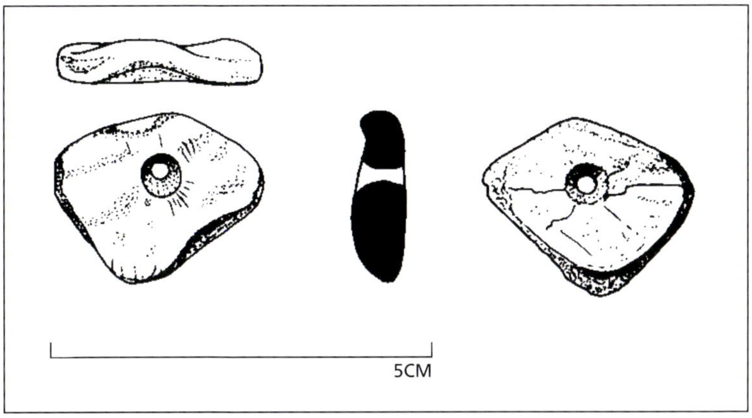

Fig. 5.15B
Drawing of amber pendant (G.Gilmour)

THE NENDRUM PENSTOCKS COMPARED TO OTHER IRISH PENSTOCKS

Examples of penstocks are known from some 41 Irish horizontal-wheeled mill sites (see Table 5.2). At some other mills, however, the penstock has not survived or has not been recovered, as was the case at Ballykilleen Co. Offaly (Lucas 1955), and at many others, like Mill 1 at Nendrum and at Drumard Co. Londonderry (Baillie 1975), they survive only in a very fragmentary condition. Unfortunately in the majority of cases where they did survive well, their recording in the past tended to be very general and was normally confined to external length and breadth measurements with little other detail being provided. With the exception of Nendrum Mill 2, all of the previously-discovered examples are made of oak. Again, with this one exception, all are of one-piece construction, leaving the stone-built Nendrum penstock standing in dramatic contrast to all other penstocks discovered so far, not just in Ireland, but in any other region.

In the older literature, there is a tendency to describe the wooden penstocks of horizontal-wheeled mills pejoratively as mere hollowed-out logs. This is somewhat unfair, as analysis shows that they are finely-crafted objects. Rynne (1992) has defined two basic types of Irish horizontal-wheeled mill penstocks. The first, represented only by the two examples found at the tide mill site at Little Island, Co. Cork (Rynne 1988, 2), consists of an oak log hollowed to an oval section and having a slot for a lid. These two, dated by dendrochronology to AD 630, are the nearest contemporary examples to that of Nendrum Mill 1. The second type, which comprises all other examples known previously, is made of oak, has a rectangular internal cross-section, a lid or lid-rebate, and has the orifice face cut to be flush with the back wall of the wheelhouse. With the discovery of the Nendrum stone penstock, a third type can now be considered to exist.

Table 5.2: Irish horizontal-wheeled mill sites where the penstock has survived

Sites with penstocks	External dimensions	Penstock chamber	Orifice
Ballindeasig, Co. Cork, (Rynne 1988, 2 , 324)	c. 4.27m long No further details		
Ballygeardra, Co. Kilkenny, (Lucas 1969, 20, Baillie 1982, 192) AD 811+9	Slanted orifice face No further details		
Ballydowane West, Co. Waterford (Lucas 1969, 20) AD 841+9	Slanted orifice face No further details	Lid	
Ballykenly, Co. Cork, (Rynne 1988, 2, 324–325, Rynne 1992, 65)	Two penstocks No further details		
Ballylough, Co. Cork (Berry 1893, 250)	No further details		
Banagher, Co. Derry (Stokes 1868, 125–126)	Two penstocks No further details		
Bantry Co. Cork (Windele 1844; Fahy 1956, 55)	c. 4.27m long No further details	Inclined 30-40°	
Breenymore, Co. Cork (Windele 1843, Rynne, 1988, 2, 336))	4.57m long No further details	Lid	
Clonickilvant, Co. Westmeath (Lucas 1969, 20)	Slanted orifice face No further details	Lid rebate	
Cloontycarthy, Co. Cork, (Rynne 1988, 2, 312-314, 1992, 56) AD 833	Rear support beam, Slanted orifice face	Lid rebate Inclined 25-29°	Oval 21cm x 18cm
Coolnannav, Co. Waterford, (Lucas 1969, 20)	Slanted orifice face No further details	Lid chamfer	
Corcannon, Co. Wexford, (Inv. Wexford, 45) AD 1228+9	3.87m long, No further details		
Coumshinagaun (Kilclooney td.) Co. Waterford, (Fahy 1956, 56, Waterford Inv 155)	3.66m long 61cm wide 61cm high		
Crushyriree, Co. Cork (Cotter 2003) Early 9th century	Very damaged, surviving dimension: 1m long Slanting orifice face	Lid rebate Internally 22cm wide 21cm high Inclined 21°	Circular 16cm
Donoughmore, Co. Cork (TKAS* 1849–1850, 159)	c. 4.27m long		
Dawstown, Co. Cork (Rynne 1988 2, 328, 1992, 56)	3.25+ m long Slanting orifice face	Lid rebate	12cm

* Trans, Kilkenny Archaeol. Soc.

Sites with penstocks	External dimensions	Penstock chamber	Orifice
Drumard, Co. Derry (Baillie 1975) AD 782	Fragment 3.00 m +		
Fennagh, Co. Carlow (Corlett, 2001,7)	Two penstocks No further details		
Great Island, Co. Wexford (Lucas 1969, 20)	No further details	Lid rebate	
Inchydoney, Co. Cork (Byrne 1849–1851)	c. 4.27m long No further details	Lid	
Killbarry, Co. Cork (Fahy 1956, 39–40)	No details		30.5cm
Killyscolban, Co. Down (MacAdam 1856)	No details		
Kilkenny Castle, Co. Kilkenny (Robertson 1860–61, 347)	2.44m long 96cm wide at mouth 74cm wide at orifice end 35cm high at broad end Slanting orifice face		Two rectangular orifices 1) 15.2cm x 30cm 2) 23cm x 30cm
Kilmagar, Co. Kilkenny (Byrne 1849–51, 58)	4.27m long	No further details	Lid
Kilnagross, Co. Cork (Byrne 1849–51, 159–160; Fahy 1956, Rynne 1988, 2, 330–331)	c. 4.27m long	Inclined 30-40°	
Killynumber, Co. Derry (Mawwhinney, 1992)	No details		
Killphillibeen Co. Cork (Rynne 1988, 2, 330, Rynne 1992, 56) c. AD 827	3.40 m+ long 80cm external width at mouth 61cm external height at mouth Slanting orifice face No further details	Lid rebate 71cm wide at mouth 38cm high at mouth	Level with floor Fitted orifice? 23cm x 13cm
Knocknagranshy, Co. Limerick (Lucas 1969) C14 AD 8th – 9th centuries	2.08m long 70cm wide at mouth end 36cm wide at orifice end 39cm high at mouth end 29cm high orifice end Slanting orifice face	Lid rebate Length of chamber c. 1.80m Mouth 57cm wide 29cm high	Circular 16cm in diameter
Knocknacarragh, Co. Galway Inv Galway 1,171) AD 973+9	Two penstocks No further details		
Knockrour, Co. Cork (Ó'Conlon 1926)	4.11m long 79cm wide at mouth end 51cm wide at orifice end 61cm high at mouth end 55cm high at orifice end Slanting orifice face	Lid. Chamber 3.81m long Mouth 50cm wide 38cm high Inclined at 40°	Circular 20cm in diameter

Sites with penstocks	External dimensions	Penstock chamber	Orifice
Little Island, Co. Cork, (Wallingstown td) (Rynne 1988, 2, 364–396, 1989) c. AD 630	Two penstocks 1) 2.10m long 2) 2.03m long 81cm high at both mouth ends	Oval section	34cm 25cm
Mallow, Co. Cork (Byrne 1849–1851)	4.27m long	Inclined 30-40°	
Mashanaglass, Co. Cork (Fahy 1956)	2.44m long 56cm wide at mouth end 56cm wide at orifice end 56cm high at mouth end 56cm high at orifice end Slanting orifice face	Stone lids Mouth 31cm high 22cm wide Inclined 30°	Sub-rectangular 12cm x 18cm
Moneyleck, (Rasharkin) Co. Antrim (Baillie 1982, 192, SMR Ant 26:23), AD 822	3.125m long 52cm wide at mouth end 52cm wide at orifice end 60cm high at mouth end 46cm high at orifice end Slanting orifice face angles.	Lid, pegged Chamber length 2.76m Mouth 38cm wide 32cm high	Sub-rectangular 23cm x 13cm Fitted
Mount Lucas, Co. Offaly, (Rynne 1992, 65)	Two penstocks No further details		
Mushera (Muskerry), Co. Cork (Windele 1844)	Two penstocks each 3.66m long and 53cm high		
Nendrum, Co. Down Wooden penstock AD 619–621	Wooden penstock 3.22m + long	Inclined 20°	
Stone penstock AD 788	Stone penstock 3.78m long 1m wide mouth face 60cm wide orifice end Orifice face at right angle to base	Four stone lids Mouth 76cm wide 41cm high Inclined at 15°	Oval 15cm x 16cm
Newtown, Co. Tipperary (Lucas 1986, 22) 8th century AD	Two penstocks Slanting orifice face	1) Lid 2) Lid rebate	
Rossory, Co. Fermanagh, (Wakeman 1873, 16; McGrail 1978, ii, 11, 125 Fig. 24) AD 926+9	No details	Lid rebate	
Shanacashel, Co. Cork, Trans. Kilkenny Archaeol. Soc., Rynne 1988, 333)	c .3.66m long No further details		
Toberaquill, Co. Westmeath, (Lucas 1969, 20)	Slanting orifice face No further details	Lid	

The lengths of 23 penstocks are listed in Table 5.2. These range from three very short examples of 3.03m and 2.1m at Little Island, Co. Cork (Rynne 1992) and 2.08m at Knocknagranshy, Co. Limerick (Lucas 1969, 18), to seven examples the lengths of which are given as 4.27m, reflecting a number of 19th-century descriptions where the length was estimated to be '14 feet' (4.3m). The measurements in Table 5.2 give an average penstock length of 3.48m, but this is slightly misleading, as the few short examples distort the pattern. A breakdown of the figures shows that eight penstocks were over 4m long, while five were over 3.5m long, four over 3m, and five between 2m and 2.5m. Over half, therefore, were longer than 3.5m. In terms of length, the stone penstock at 3.78m can be seen as lying within the 'normal' range. However, the external length is only a crude index of the capacity of a penstock, and it is the volume of the chamber which is of central significance. Comparative data on the cross-sectional area of other penstock chambers is difficult to obtain as these are seldom provided in published descriptions and the small scales of published plans do not help. Further research is needed, but it seems clear that the Nendrum penstock chamber is considerably larger than most known examples.

The evidence suggests that all Irish Early Medieval penstocks were provided with lids. These have not survived in the majority of cases, but their former existence is indicated by the presence of a prominent rebate below the rim. The nearest parallels to the stone lids of the Nendrum penstock are the sandstone lids on the wooden penstock at Mashanaglass (Fahy 1956), but it is not known if these were interlocked in the manner of those at Nendrum.

Many penstocks appear to have had a one-piece oak lid, an example of which survived in place at Knockrour, Co. Cork (Ó'Conlon 1926, 96), where it rested on a ledge 7.6cm wide carved 10cm below the rim. Similarly, one-piece lids were found at Kilmagar, Co. Kilkenny (Byrne 1849–51) and Moneyleck, Co. Antrim (Baillie 1982, 192: SMR Ant 26:23) penstocks. It is clear that, apart from being carved in stone, the rim form and ledge of the Nendrum example are exactly similar to those found in wooden penstocks. In most cases, it seems that lids were held in place solely by the weight of the overlying material as at Nendrum, but some, for instance the penstocks from Newton, Co. Tipperary (Lucas 1986a) and Knocknagranshy Co. Limerick (Lucas 1969) have produced evidence of pegs or clamping devices to fix them in position (Rynne 1988, 1, 41–43).

Orifice shape varies, and while one would tend to expect that oval and circular types, such as Nendrum, would have been standard, this seems not to be the case as there are examples of rectangular or sub-rectangular forms. The circular orifice in the penstock at Knocknagranshy (Lucas 1969) had a diameter of 16cm, thus very similar in size to the Nendrum one. The damaged orifice of the early 9th-century Crushyriree, Co. Cork penstock (Cotter 2003, 109) is described as being 16cm square. However, the setting of the orifice in line with the bottom of the penstock chamber seems to have been a standard feature.

In the treatment of the orifice face, the Nendrum example differs from all previously known examples, which have this face cut back at an angle of less than 90° to the longitudinal plane of the structure. Fahy (1956, 27) suggested that this was done so that it was flush or on the same plane as the vertical back wall of the wheelhouse. At Nendrum this was not done and the orifice face protrudes beyond the wall.

The Nendrum wooden penstock was inclined at approximately 20° to the horizontal, while the stone penstock is at 15°. The latter is at a much lower incline than has been recorded or inferred at many other sites, where most have been set relatively steeply at 30°–40°. The nearest setting to the Nendrum penstock is the 21° recorded for that at Crushyriree, Co. Cork (Cotter 2003, 109). As Rynne (1992, 61–62) has noted, when the incline of a penstock has not been ascertained *in situ* — which is the case with the overwhelming majority of Irish sites — it can be calculated from the angle of the slanting orifice face. The magnitude of the angle of the setting of the penstock is a reflection of the relative height between the bottom of the millpond and the level of the waterwheel. The greater the height of the water in the millpond relative to the waterwheel, the higher the angle.

It seems beyond doubt that the wooden type of penstock was used as the prototype and it is possible to see here the direct translation into stone of a design previously executed in wood. Indeed, some of the features where the design differs may have resulted from the use of stone. The composite nature of the stone penstock, in three parts as opposed to the one-piece construction of the wooden penstocks, is the prime example. There would have been difficulty in obtaining a block of stone 3–4m in length and 1m in section. Even if available, the weight would have presented extreme difficulties in transporting it to the site and setting it into position.

It is possible that the use of stone for the penstock of Mill 2 and the non-use of oak in its dams — in contrast to its abundance in the dam of Mill 1 — indicate a scarcity of oak in the Strangford region as early as the late-8th century, considerably earlier than observed elsewhere. Mill 1 reveals that in the early 7th century, the monastery had an abundance of exploitable oak. Baillie, however, has demonstrated (1995, 125–126) that between AD 720 and 840, there was an intense phase of building activity in Ireland, using oak, which resulted in a severe lack of the timber by the end of the 9th century.

However, this interpretation may not be so straightforward. A wooden penstock of the same dimensions as the stone penstock, would have required a piece of timber approximately 4m long by 1m wide. It would seem probable that an affluent 8th-century monastery like Nendrum would have had the wherewithal to source a timber of this size for a penstock if so desired. Therefore other reasons for the change to stone should be entertained. It may have been part of the general movement, which becomes evident in the 9th century, towards building in stone rather than wood, perhaps expressing a perceived view of and desire for, the greater permanency which stone provides. This is evidenced from the first references to stone churches in the documentary sources, although this itself may have been a reflection of the diminishing oak resource.

There were possibly also practical reasons behind the choice. Experience gained in Mill 1 of using a wooden penstock in a foreshore environment may have shown that the exposed face of the wooden penstock, alternatively wet and dry twice daily over the tidal cycle, was prone to cracking and erosion. It may also have been discovered that a wooden one did not stand up to the pressure of the volume of impounded tidal water and became unstable. Any movement of its position would have caused enormous problems for the whole mechanism of the mill, and the solution found was to make it of stone. It remains to be seen from future discoveries if this solution was confined to Nendrum or if it was adopted elsewhere in Ireland.

Fig. 5.16
With the clearance of the penstock chamber, tidal water was able for the first time in perhaps well over one thousand years to issue through the orifice

Chapter 6

The Waterwheels of Mill 1 and Mill 2, the Waterwheel Assembly, the Tentering System and the Wheelhouse

Thomas McErlean

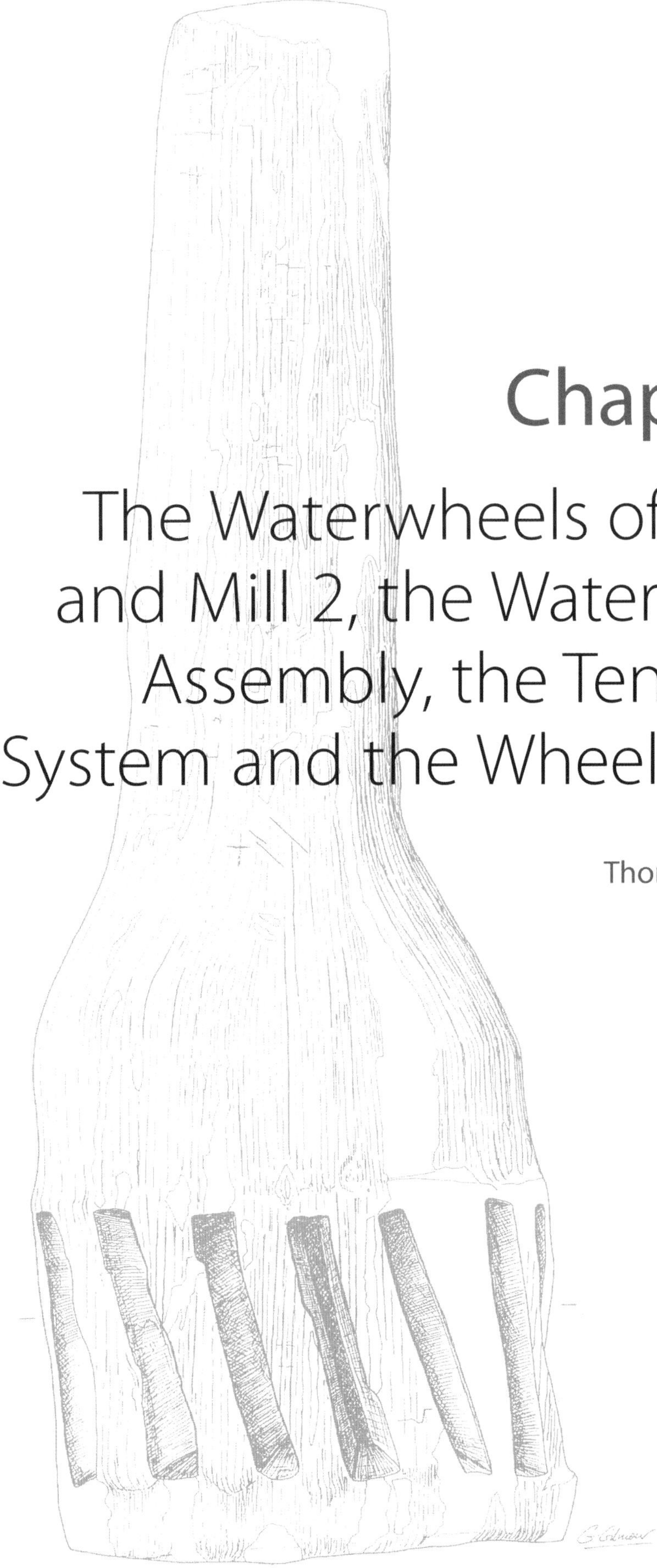

Chapter 6
The Waterwheels of Mill I and Mill 2, the Waterwheel Assembly, the Tentering System and the Wheelhouse

Thomas McErlean

INTRODUCTION

This chapter proceeds from the penstock discussed in the last chapter, into the wheelhouse of the mill to analyse the evidence concerning the waterwheels. The waterwheel is the heart of the mill and converts the latent power of the impounded water into an energy source. The horizontally-set waterwheel is the defining component, which differentiates the horizontal-wheeled mill from the vertical-wheeled mill. It consists of a central hub from which paddles radiate and is connected by a shaft and a spindle to the upper millstone in the millhouse. The base of the hub rotates on a timber called the bridge-tree at the bottom of the wheelhouse. All the known Irish horizontal waterwheels are made from oak. Built into the waterwheel assembly is a mechanism — the tentering system — for adjusting the space between the upper and lower millstones to perform different grades of grinding.

THE WATERWHEEL OF MILL 1

The evidence for the waterwheel of Mill 1 consists of a hub with a portion of shaft and a paddle *in situ* with a fragment of another paddle (Figs 6.1 A, B and C, 6.2 A and B). The paddle is of the simple flat-blade form and the first of its kind found in Ireland. The hub and its surviving paddle are dated, by association with Mill 1, to the early 7th century and are thus the earliest examples of waterwheel parts found so far in Ireland. As such they are of great importance in tracing the evolution of horizontal waterwheel types in Ireland and have much wider implications for waterwheels elsewhere.

The hub

The hub was discovered lying horizontally in the redeposited silt in the core of the dam of Mill 2 (see Fig. 2.5). Its context strongly suggests that it had been casually deposited here during the construction of Mill 2, but this does not necessarily imply that it was in use at the time of the demise of Mill 1. It may have been discarded long before and derive from silt used in making the new dam. Three other badly-degraded wooden objects of cylindrical shape (wood catalogue numbers, 860, 918 and 967), which may have been hubs but were in too poor and fragmentary a condition to be positively identified as such, were found in contexts associated with Mill 1.

Fig. 6.1A
The waterwheel hub and paddle of Mill 1 under excavation (from north)

Fig. 6.1B
The waterwheel hub and paddle of Mill 1 under excavation (from above)

Fig. 6 .1C
The waterwheel hub of Mill 1 after conservation

The hub was fashioned out of an oak trunk and consists of a cylindrical section separated by a shoulder from a remaining length of shaft (see Figs 6.2 A and B). It has a total height of 95.5cm, of which the hub comprises 30cm, the shoulder section 13.8cm and the shaft 51.7cm. Approximately half of the hub portion is well preserved, the other half, which was facing upwards on discovery, was unfortunately almost completely removed by decay. In its original state the hub was cylindrical and had an average diameter of 30.9cm. The base is flat and badly decayed making it impossible to ascertain if it had a central hole into which a gudgeon (footstep bearing) may have been inserted. The shoulder had a gentle curve, which tapers to its junction with the shaft.

The hub has a sequence of inclined slots for the paddles (see Fig. 6.2A), seven of which are well preserved and 11 or possibly 12 others can be traced, giving a wheel of probably 18 or 19 paddles. The slots begin at approximately 5cm above the base of the hub. They are at an angle of approximately 15° from the vertical and are spaced 3–4cm apart on average and inclined to the left. They vary from 16.5cm to 17.1cm in length and from 2.4cm to 3.2cm in width and are on average 9cm deep. The slots are roughly V-shaped in section, with rounded bases. There are no indications of dowels, or their peg holes, having been used to hold the paddles in place.

The shaft is circular in section and is *c.* 16.5cm in diameter at its base. It tapers gently to 13.1cm to its surviving top end which is badly eroded. It is impossible to decide if it had been cut at this location, or if its present form constituted the junction of the shaft and spindle.

The paddle

The better-preserved paddle found *in situ* in one of the slots (see Fig. 6.2B) survives to a length of 24.8cm and is 16.5cm wide, with a maximum thickness of 2.2cm. The external end of the paddle has been damaged and has lost some of its length, leaving 15.8cm of surviving blade. The section mortised into the hub is 9cm long and tapers slightly in thickness as it goes inwards.

Table 6.1: Dimensions of the flat-blade paddle from the waterwheel of Mill 1.

Total length (cm)	Blade length (Incomplete) (cm)	Mortised section	Height (cm)	Thickness (cm)
24.8	15.8	9	16.5	2.2

When found, the paddle had a crack at the junction of the blade and mortised section. This would appear to be a point of weakness, as the other paddle fragment had broken off here also, leaving only the mortised section. As neither the mortised section of the

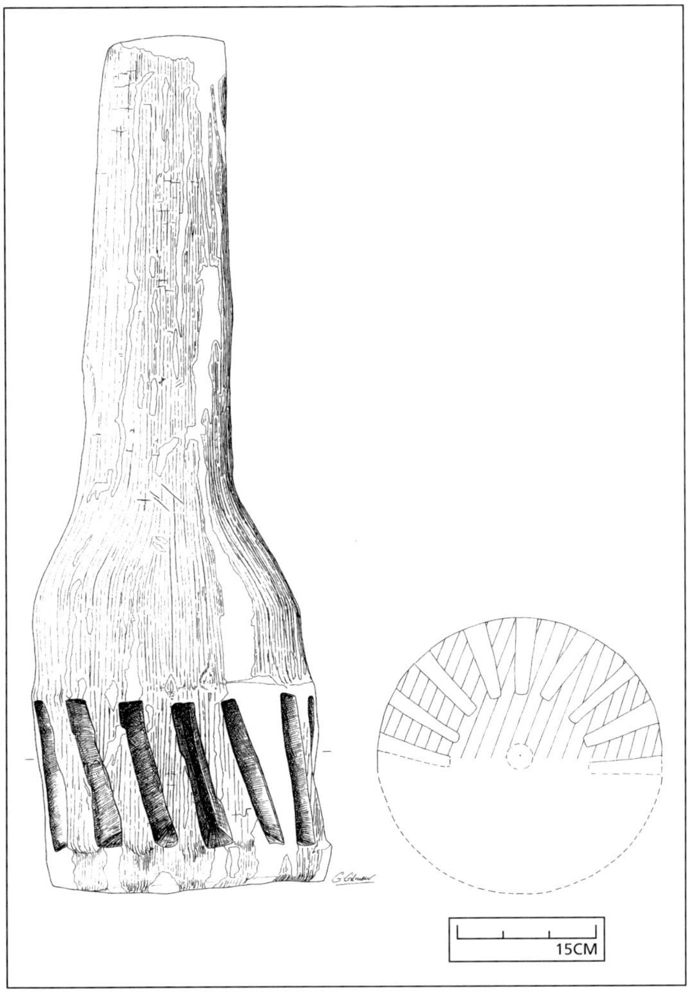

Fig. 6.2A
The well-preserved side of the waterwheel of Mill 1 with section through the paddle slots (G. Gilmour)

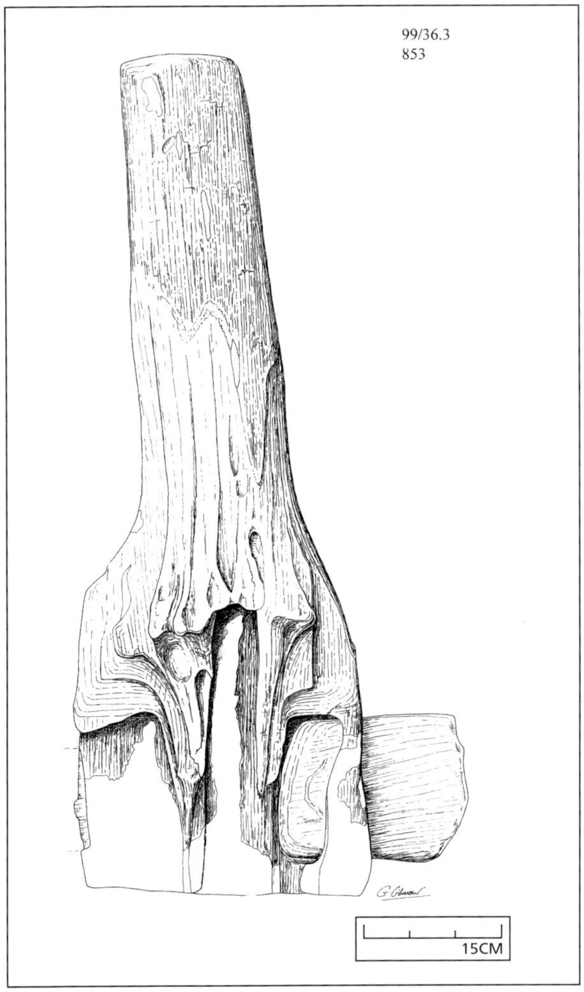

Fig. 6 2B
The decayed side of the waterwheel of Mill 1 with paddle (G. Gilmour)

paddle, nor the sides of the slots had dowel holes, it seems clear that the paddle was secured only by being tightly wedged into the slots in the hub.

Because of the loss of some of the blade length, it is impossible to estimate accurately the diameter of the waterwheel beyond stating that it was in excess of 62.5cm (hub-diameter plus two blade lengths). However, using the parallels with a paddle from Ballykilleen Co. Offaly (Lucas 1955, 105–110) discussed below, it is possible to suggest an approximate size for the waterwheel (see pps 169-170). The main features of the waterwheel of Mill 1 are its simple flat, board-shaped paddles (18 or 19 in number) inserted at an inclined angle into the hub to present an inclined face to the water jet. As the slots are inclined to the left, the wheel would have rotated in a clockwise direction.

THE WATERWHEEL OF MILL 2

The paddles

While the hub associated with the waterwheel of Mill 2 was not recovered, a vital part of its waterwheel, is represented by three paddles of 'scoop' form found beside the mill-stones at the bottom of the south-western corner of the wheelhouse. A possible fourth paddle was found on the wheelhouse floor, to the east of the others, but was in a very degraded state and fragmentary condition. The well-preserved paddles were carved from blocks of oak and are still in remarkably good condition. When uncovered, they were lying topside up and immediately adjacent to each other, so that it is clear that all three belonged to the same waterwheel (see Fig. 3.10A). From their context, it is fairly certain also that they all must have snapped from the hub of the waterwheel together in one destructive event. As may be expected, since they are derived from the same waterwheel, the paddles are extremely similar in design and minor detail, but have slight and interesting variations.

The paddles resemble closely other horizontal waterwheel paddles found at a number of Irish mill sites, and belong to a form that has been classified as 'scoop–shaped' (Moog 1994, 13, 48). The surviving Irish scoop paddles follow a nearly identical design (see Fig. 6.8) in which the paddle can be divided into three well-defined sections comprising a blade, a block and a tenon. The blade is at the outer end of the paddle from the hub, and its scoop-shaped front face is hit by the water jet. The next section consists of a rectangular block through which dowels were driven to attach the blades to each other and to the hub. The third section comprises a tenon, which was inserted into a mortise in the wheel hub. The plan of these paddles, viewed from the top, shows the front face of the whole length of the paddle as a straight line. The back face has a curved profile, which terminates at the inner end of the blade, which is followed by the rectangular outline of the block projecting out at an oblique angle.

Paddle 1 (Figs 6.4A and 6.5A and B) is the best preserved of the three. It is 40.5cm long and has probably survived to almost its full original length. The blade is 24.2cm long, the block 9.7cm long and the tenon 6.6cm long. It has six dowel holes, four of which (Fig. 6.4A numbers, 1, 6, 4 and 5) are cut through the front face of the block, the other two from the side of the top. Some have remains of the pegs *in situ*. There is a large hole, *c.* 2.5cm in diameter, cut through the face of the tenon.

Paddle 2 (Figs 6.4B and 6.5C) has lost some of its tenon and has an overall surviving length of 36.5cm. The blade and block are well preserved, the blade measuring 23.5cm in length and the block 9cm. The remaining section of tenon is 4cm long, and shows evidence of two holes. This paddle, while very similar to the other two, is distinctive in having a block section which is 7.2cm wide, as compared to 4.8cm in Paddle 1 and 4.5cm in Paddle 3. It has six circular holes cut through the front face of the block, two of which have pegs *in situ*.

Fig. 6.3A
The waterwheel paddles of Mill 2 (top view)

Fig. 6.3B
The waterwheel paddles of Mill 2 (bottom view)

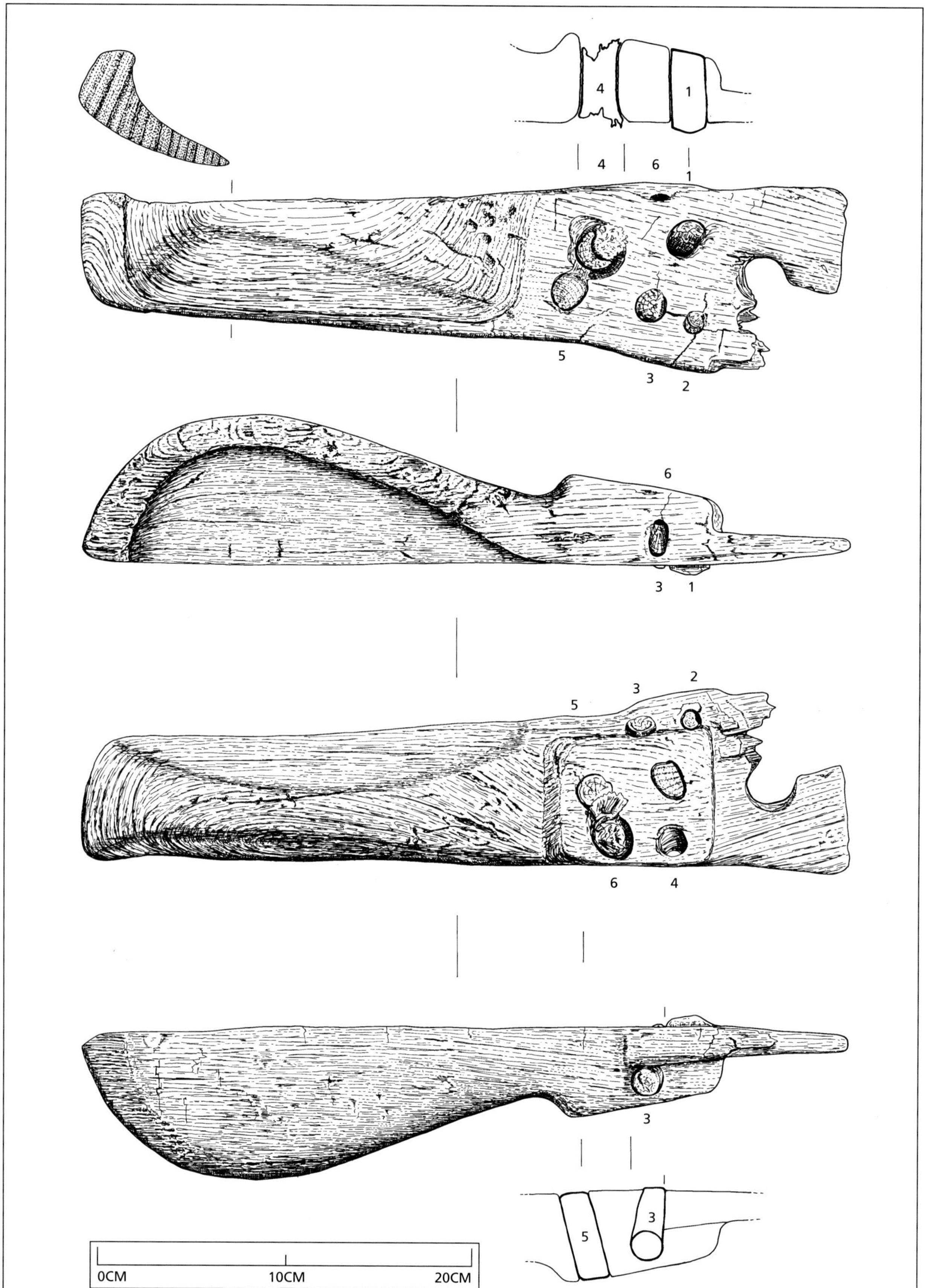

Fig. 6.4A
Paddle 1 of the waterwheel of Mill 2 (G. Gilmour)

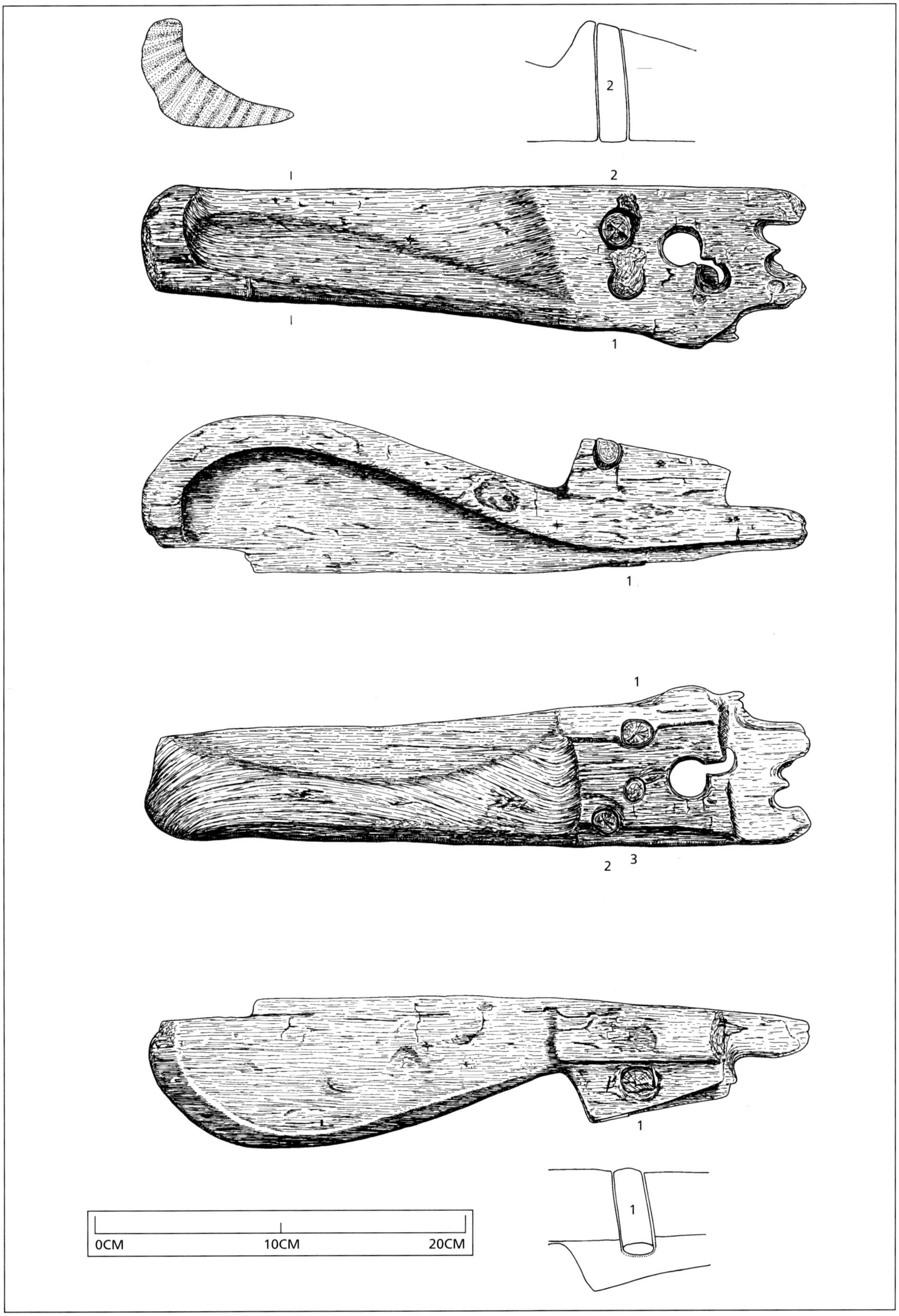

Fig. 6.4B
Paddle 2 of the waterwheel of Mill 2 (G. Gilmour)

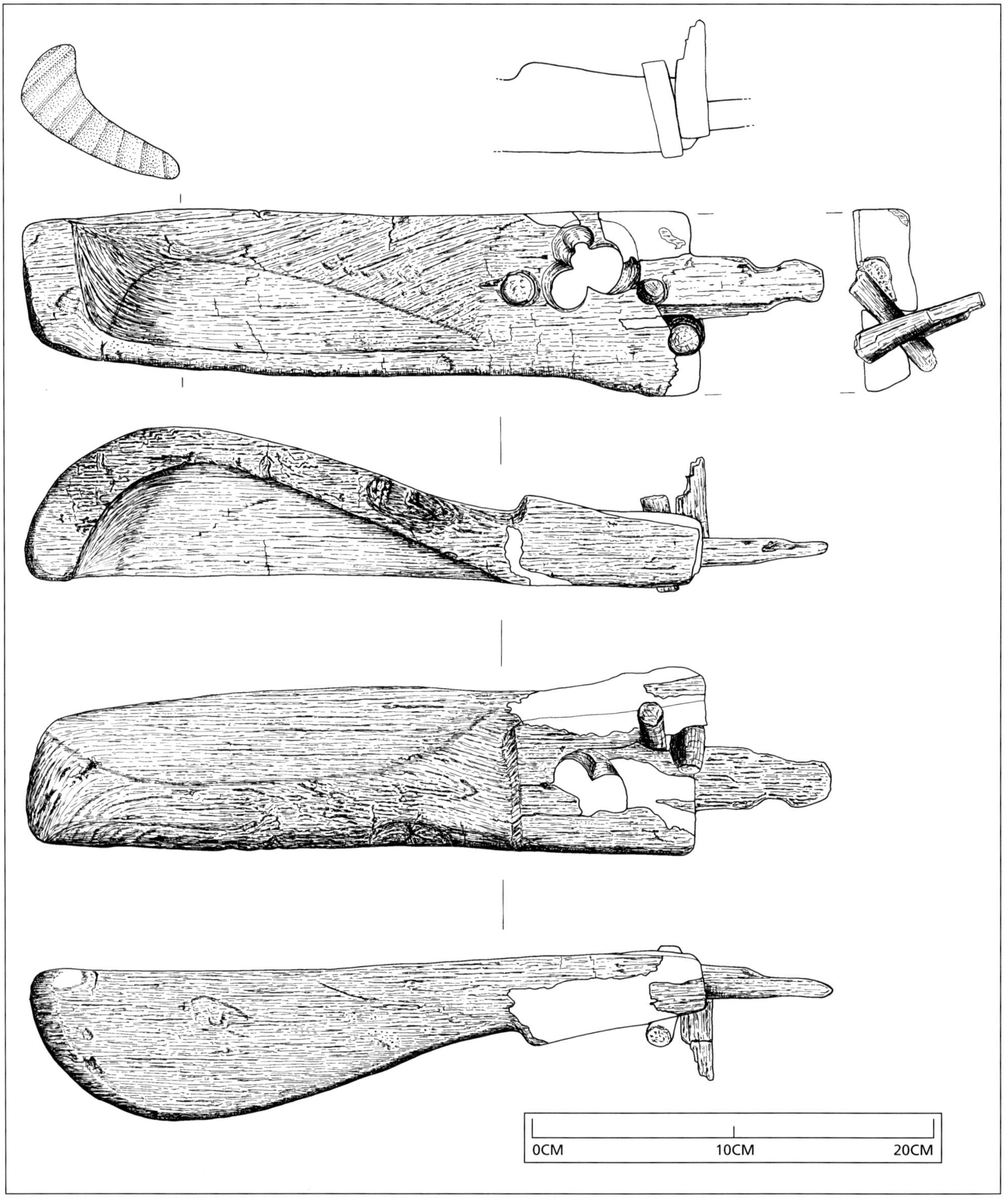

Fig. 6.4C
Paddle 3 of the waterwheel of Mill 2 (G. Gilmour)

Paddle 3 (Figs 6.4C and 6.5D and E), apart from some superficial damage to the block section, has survived to nearly its original length and is 40.3cm long. The blade is 24.6cm long, the block 9.5cm long and the tenon 6.2cm. The block section has six holes, five of which, when it was found, contained fragments of pegs, four of roundwood and one of splitwood.

Fig. 6.5A
Paddle 1 (front face)

Fig. 6.5B
Paddle 1 (back face)

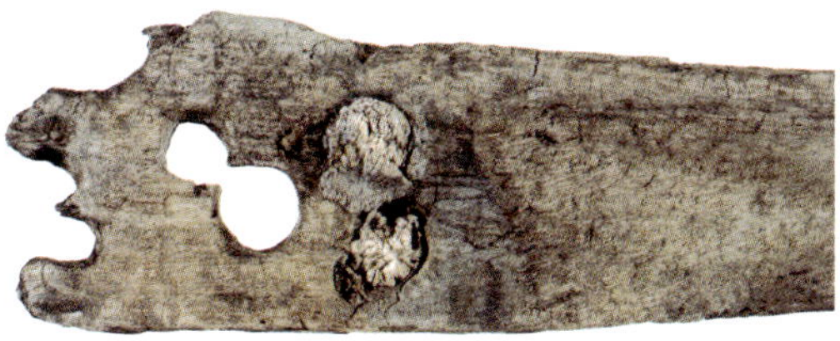

Fig. 6.5C
Paddle 2 (detail of front face)

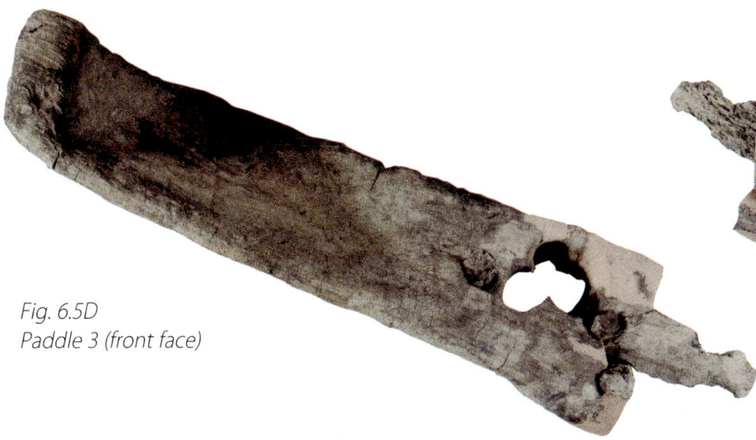

Fig. 6.5D
Paddle 3 (front face)

Fig. 6.5E
Paddle 3 (back face)

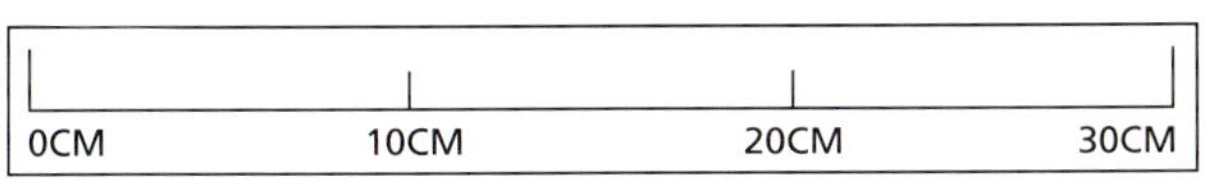

Table 6.2: Comparative analyses of the dimensions of the three paddles of the waterwheel of Mill 2

	Total length (cm)	Blade overall length (cm)	Blade, inner length (cm)	Block length (cm)	Tenon length (cm)
Paddle 1	40.5	24.2	22.0	9.7	6.6
Paddle 2	36.5	23.5	21.5	9.0	4.0
Paddle 3	40.3	24.6	22.7	9.5	6.2

	Blade maximum thickness (cm)	Blade inner thickness (cm)	Block thickness	Tenon thickness
Paddle 1	8.1	6.5	4.8	1.7
Paddle 2	8.7	7.0	7.2	2.6
Paddle 3	7.6	5.6	4.5	1.5

	Blade maximum height (cm)	Block height (cm)	Tenon height (cm)
Paddle 1	6.2	7.8	9.1
Paddle 2	6.1	7.6	8.6
Paddle 3	6.8	7.9	3.2

The overall lengths of Paddles 1 and 3, at 40.5cm and 40.3cm respectively, differ only by 2mm. This implies that Paddle 2, which has lost some of its tenon length, was probably very similar. The heights of all the three paddle blades vary by only a few millimetres, as do their maximum blade widths. The inner blade-thickness measurements are extremely similar for Paddles 1 and 2, while the heights of the blocks are practically the same on all three paddles. The greatest difference in the paddles is in the greater thickness of the block of Paddle 2, which is 2.4–2.7cm thicker than the other two. The much shorter tenon length of Paddle 2 is the result of the damage visible at this end. The thickness of the surviving tenon sections of Paddles 1 and 3 are almost identical, but they are from 9mm –1.1cm thinner than those of Paddle 2. This difference may be due to damage, but may also possibly indicate that the tenons of the paddles in the wheel varied in thickness.

All three paddles have identical cross-section profiles through the blades. The front faces of the blades are concave and set at an angle to meet the inclined water jet at 90°. The underside and back faces of the blades are also curved, but have more angled profiles, while the backs of the blades are much thicker than their bases. Scoop blades are well designed to maximise the torque imparted by the water jet. The front faces of the Nendrum blades, with their gently curving surfaces and the angles at which they face the water jet, can be seen as having been designed to maximise the energy of the impact of the water jet, which would have hit the blades directly and drained away immediately. If water was retained for any length of time, this would reduce torque. Similarly, the profiled backs of the blades were designed to minimise splashing from the blade behind.

Attachment to the hub

Although the hub to which the paddles belonged has not survived, evidence provided by the tenons and dowel holes allows interpretation of how the paddles were placed in the assembly of the waterwheel. As the diameters of the holes are greater on the front faces of the paddles, it is clear that the pegs were driven in from this side. Thus, it appears that the paddles were inserted into the hub in an anticlockwise sequence. To receive the dimensions of the well-preserved tenon in Paddle 1, for example, the hub mortise must have been slightly over 9.1cm high and 2.6cm wide. From the evidence of the widths of the tenons of Paddles 1 and 3, it is possible that there were two widths of mortise — the larger being a minimum of 2.6cm, the smaller a minimum of 1.7cm.

After a paddle was inserted in its mortise, one peg (possibly two) was driven in at an angle through the tenon to fix it to the hub. Each paddle has six dowel holes of varying size driven through the block at a variety of different angles. From this, it is clear that the paddles were also attached to each other by dowels through their blocks. The sequence is not entirely clear, but it seems likely that two holes were bored in each block and through the blocks of the next two paddles. Thus, each block received two dowels from each of the preceding two paddles making four, and had an additional two made in it, giving a total of six in each.

The paddles are finely crafted objects and present a great contrast to the relatively simple and crude paddles of Mill 1. The degree of precision of the workmanship is remarkable and provides solid evidence of the very high level of craftsmanship of the millwright, who made the waterwheel.

Number of paddles on the waterwheel

There is no evidence to suggest that there was a space between the blocks on the paddles when joined together, and each block appears to be jointed against the back face of the paddle in front. In Paddle 2, the front and back of the faces of the block are set at an angle of 15°. If all of the paddle-blocks were of this configuration, which they are not, it would imply a wheel of 24 paddles. The same angle in Paddles 1 and 3 is 10° and, if all the blocks of all of the paddles were the same as these, which they are not, it would imply a wheel of 36 paddles. Following the evidence of the surviving three paddles, the reality probably is that a mixture of paddles with slightly differing block-widths was used.

A pragmatic decision on the width of block required for the overall number of paddles intended for the wheel was probably made as the work of assembly proceeded. This appears to have been the case in the near-complete example of the Mashanaglass waterwheel (Fahy 1956, 23–24). The work of varying the block-widths would have been a simple matter, as they could be trimmed down with little effort without affecting the dimensions of the paddles. On balance, it can be suggested that the wheel probably had about 24 paddles.

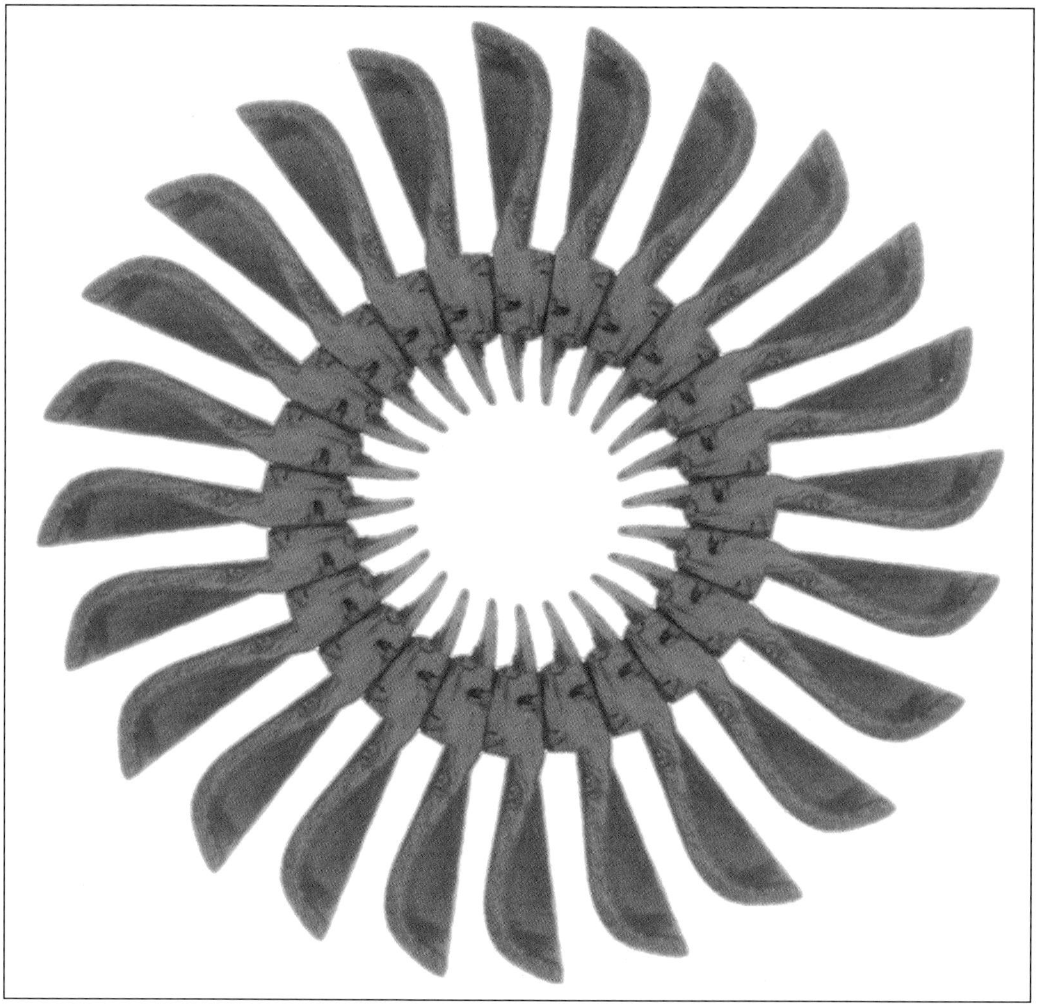

Fig. 6.6 Reconstruction of the configuration of the 24 probable paddles on the waterwheel of Mill 2

THE WATERWHEEL PADDLE FROM MILL 1 AND OTHER IRISH HORIZONTAL WATERWHEEL PADDLES

The paddle from Mill 1 has the distinction of being the only Irish example of the flat-blade type and demonstrates that in the early 7th century, this form was in use and in Ireland at least, preceded the scoop form. The simplicity of the paddle form from Mill 1 contrasts greatly with the sophisticated scoop paddles of Mill 2. The discovery of two dated examples of waterwheel paddles of different forms at Nendrum is of great significance in demonstrating increasing technical improvements in horizontal waterwheel design taking place during the 7th and 8th centuries.

Geographically, the nearest examples of the simple, inclined flat-blade form of horizontal waterwheel are from 19th century horizontal-wheeled mills in the Shetland Islands, and possibly some of the outer Western Isles of Scotland (Goudie 1886). The latter examples are at the north-western end of a wide distribution of the form, which stretched in recent centuries from the Himalayas and south-western Asia, through Russia and the Alps and northern Europe to Scandinavia (Rynne 1988; Moog 1994).

The paddles of Mill 2 conform to almost all previously-known examples found in Ireland, and are of a form whose distribution is found in recent centuries in the northern Mediterranean region, through Spain and Portugal. The importance of the Nendrum evidence is that the relationship between the two forms is shown, on this site at least, to be chronological and not geographical. This suggests that at the beginning of the 7th century a waterwheel with simple flat blades was used, but that by the end of the 8th century a much more sophisticated scoop-shaped paddle had been adopted. The latter form can absorb almost twice the energy of the flat type (Rynne 1989, 1, 68), and represents, therefore, a significant improvement in horizontal waterwheel design.

Fig. 6.7
7th-century horizontal waterwheel paddle from Ballykilleen, Co. Offaly (Lucas 1955, 106)

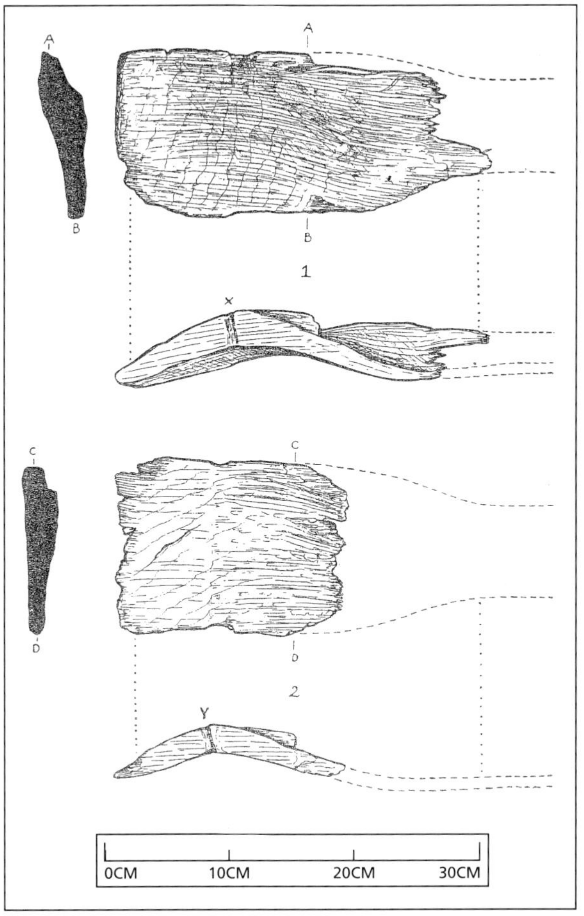

This raises the question of why the simpler form was retained over a wide area of the distribution of the horizontal-wheeled mills when it was less efficient. The only other 7th-century waterwheel paddles presently known are the two examples from Ballykilleen, Co. Offaly (Lucas 1955, 105–108) and dated to AD 636+9 (Baillie 1982). These are in the form of a dished blade lacking the fully-developed scoop (see Fig. 6.7), and are considered by Rynne (1998, 92) to be the earliest known examples of their type in Europe. The blade of Ballykilleen paddle form is rectangular in outline and has a concave or 'dished' profiled front face and convex profiled back. It is considerably different from the scoop form. The paddle has a tenon section which would have been wedged vertically into a hub, but the blade was carved to give its face an angle to the water jet (Lucas 1955, 105–110). No other Irish site has yet produced a parallel to the Ballykilleen paddle, although a similar dished blade was found at Dalswinton in Dumfriesshire, Scotland (Maxwell, 1955, 1956), where the similarity to the Ballykilleen paddle was noted.

Comparison of the dimensions of the Nendrum 1 and Ballykilleen paddles (Table 6.3) shows a relatively good degree of similarity except in their blade lengths, and this can be accounted for by the loss of some of the original length from the Nendrum paddle.

With the discovery of the flat blade form at Nendrum dated to earlier in the 7th century, it is possible to view the slightly later Ballykilleen paddles as a more developed form of the flat-blade type of Mill 1. It can also be interpreted as intermediate between the latter and the fully developed scoop blades of the Nendrum Mill 2 paddles, and similar ones from Cloontycarthy, and Mashanaglass, Co. Cork, Killinchy Co. Down, Drumard Co. Derry, Deer Park Farms and Moycraig Co. Antrim and Tamworth Staffordshire in England. As no 7th-century examples of the scoop form have yet been discovered in Ireland, it is reasonable in the light of current information to question its existence in the country at this time. The two earliest dated mills with associated scoop paddles are Nendrum Mill 2 and the near-contemporary mill at Drumard, Co. Derry, dated respectively to AD 789 and AD 782+9. This suggests that by the end of the 8th century, the scoop form was well established in the northern part of Ireland at least. The evidence of the Nendrum 1 paddle of flat blade form, and the Ballykilleen paddle of dished blade form and the later examples of the scoop form, suggests a development sequence of increasing technical sophistication in paddle design. In the light of current knowledge, it is impossible to decide if this took place in Ireland, or was adopted from elsewhere in the later 7th or early 8th centuries.

Table 6.3: Comparison between the waterwheel paddles from Nendrum Mill 1 and Ballykilleen, Co. Offaly (Lucas 1955 105–110)

	Total paddle length	Blade length	Blade height	Mortised section length	Blade thickness
Nendrum 1 AD 619–621 (incomplete)	24.8cm	15.8cm	16.5cm	9.0cm	c. 2.2cm
Ballykilleen AD 633±9	30.0cm	20.0cm	13.5cm	10.0cm	c. 2.5cm

ESTIMATE OF THE SIZE OF THE WATERWHEEL OF MILL 1

The diameter of a horizontal waterwheel is made up of the diameter of its hub and the length of two paddle blades. Direct measurement of the size of the waterwheel of Mill 1 is not possible because some of the length of the blade of its better preserved paddle is missing. However, considering the similarity between the dished blade paddle from Ballykilleen and the flat blade paddle from Nendrum Mill 1, in terms of their heights, thicknesses and the lengths of their mortised sections, it is possible to deduce that the original length of the flat blade of Nendrum paddle was very similar. The Ballykilleen blade is approximately 20cm in length, the incomplete Nendrum blade 15.8cm.

Therefore, it is probable that the original length of the Nendrum specimen was around 20cm also. This would imply that it has lost only about 4.2cm of its original length. Using the measurements shown in Table 6.4, together with this estimated original blade length, gives a probable diameter for the waterwheel of Mill 1 of *c.* 71cm.

Table 6.4: The possible diameter of the first waterwheel using the evidence from the Ballykilleen paddle

Hub diameter	Two blade lengths	Diameter of waterwheel	Number of paddles
30.9cm	40cm	71cm	18/19

THE WATERWHEEL PADDLES FROM MILL 2 AND OTHER IRISH HORIZONTAL WATERWHEEL PADDLES

In contrast to the lack of parallels to the flat blade paddle form from Mill 1, four Irish sites and one English site, (see Table 6.5 and Fig. 6.8) have produced good examples of paddles of very similar form to those of Nendrum Mill 2. The Nendrum scoop paddles are almost identical in design to those from Deer Park Farms, Co. Antrim (Lynn and McDowell *forthcoming*), Cloontycarthy, Co. Cork (Rynne 1988, 2, 310–312) and Killinchy, Co. Down (MacAdam 1856; Baillie 1975). The paddle from the horizontal-wheeled mill site of Drumard, Co. Londonderry, is badly warped, but seems to be similar (Baillie 1975). To the Irish examples can be added that from the 9th-century horizontal-wheeled mill at Tamworth, Staffordshire (Rahtz and Meeson 1992, 100–104). In all of these, the paddle design consists of a scoop-shaped blade, followed by a block and a tenon. Further examples are the scoop paddles of the Moycraig Co. Antrim (MacAdam 1856) and Mashanaglass Co. Cork (Fahy 1956) waterwheels which are also very similar. However, in the case of Moycraig, there is a short shaft between the blade and the block and, in the Mashanaglass paddles, the outer tip of the blade has a block-shaped rim segment (see Fig. 6.8).

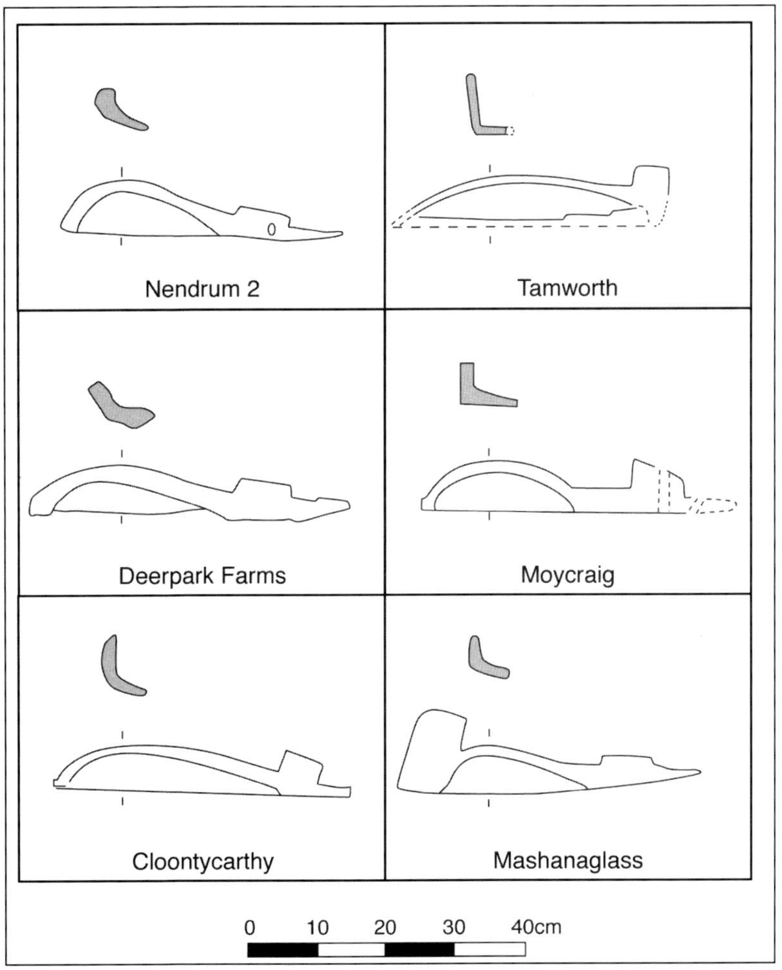

Fig. 6.8
The scoop paddles from Nendrum 2, Co. Down; Deer Park Farms, Co. Antrim (Lynn and McDowell forthcoming), Cloontycarthy, Co. Cork (Rynne 1988, 2, 310–312); Tamworth, Staffs (Rahtz and Meeson 1992, 100–104); Moycraig, Co. Antrim (MacAdam 1856) and Mashanaglass Co. Cork (Fahy 1956).

Comparisons of the measurements of the paddles from these sites with those from Nendrum is given in Table 6.5. The total length of the paddles, including the often-damaged tenon sections, ranges from 40.4cm for Paddle 1 at Nendrum to 46cm in the example from Deer Park Farms. Inner blade lengths range from 20.3cm at Moycraig to 25.5cm at Deer Park Farms. Block lengths vary from 7.6cm at Moycraig to *c.* 10cm at Killinchy. The lengths of surviving tenons vary from 6.6cm at Nendrum to 9cm at Killinchy. In all of the examples, the maximum width of the blade varies very little, the range being 6.4cm at Moycraig to 8.1cm at Nendrum.

The inner thicknesses of the blades vary even less, from 5cm at Cloontycarthy and Deer Park Farms to 6.5cm at Nendrum. As this is the part of the paddle designed to engage with the water jet, it can be considered to be one of the most important features of the wheel assembly and it is interesting to note the very close agreement between the different paddles. Block thicknesses range from 4.3cm at Cloontycarthy to 7.6cm at Moycraig, block heights from 4.6cm at Cloontycarthy to 7.8cm at Nendrum, and tenon heights from 5.1cm at Mashanaglass, Cloontycarthy and Deer Park Farms to 9.1cm at Nendrum. Tenon thickness varies from 1.7cm at Nendrum to 4cm at Deer Park Farms. The maximum height of blades varies from 5cm at Cloontycarthy to 9cm at Tamworth.

Table 6.8: Comparative dimensions of the Nendrum 2 scoop form paddles and those from other sites

	Total length (cm)	Blade inner length (cm)	Block length (cm)	Tenon length (cm)
Nendrum 2	40.5	22.0	9.7	6.6
Mashanaglass	43.9	22.2	8.6	6.7
Moycraig	45.7	20.3	7.6	7.6
Cloontycarthy	42.0	25.0	9.0	6.6
Deer Park Farms	46.0	25.5	9.0	7.2
Killinchy	45.0	23.0	10.0	9.0
Tamworth	40.0+	c. 33.0	c. 6.0	Tenon missing

Mashanaglass rim segment 6.3cm long, Moycraig shaft between blade and block 7.6cm long. Cloontycarthy, measurements as given in Rynne (1988, 1, 310).

	Blade maximum thickness (cm)	Blade inner thickness (cm)	Block thickness (cm)	Tenon thickness (cm)
Nendrum 2	8.1	6.5	4.8	1.7
Mashanaglass	7.6	5.1	5.1	2.5
Moycraig	6.4	5.1	7.6	2.5
Cloontycarthy	7.0	5.0	4.3	c.2.5
Deer Park Farms	c.8.0	5.0	6.0	4.0
Killinchy	Nk	Nk	Nk	Nk
Tamworth	Nk	Nk	Nk	Nk

	Blade maximum height (cm)	Block height (cm)	Tenon height (cm)
Nendrum 2	6.2	7.8	9.1
Mashanaglass	5.0	5.9	5.1
Moycraig	7.0	7.0	7.0
Cloontycarthy	5.0	4.6	5.1
Deer Park Farms	7.0	5.1	5.1
Killinchy	Nk	Nk	Nk
Tamworth	9.0	Nk	Nk

BLADE PROFILES

The treatment of the cross-section profile of the blade has a number of variations (see Fig. 6.8). The Moycraig blades have a sloping floor and a vertical back. The Tamworth example is somewhat similar, but the back is at a slightly oblique angle to the floor. The Deer Park Farms, Cloontycarthy and Mashanaglass examples resemble the concave profile of the Nendrum paddles, but lack the greater thickness of the back section.

METHOD OF ATTACHMENT

In the Deer Park Farms examples (Lynn and McDowell *forthcoming*), the blocks have no dowel holes, but large holes are present through the tenons. The Moycraig specimen (MacAdam 1856) has three dowel holes through the block and one through the tenon.

The Cloontycarthy paddle (Rynne 1998, 93–94) has no dowel holes through the block, but one through the tenon. The Mashanaglass paddles (Fahy 1956) have one dowel hole through the block and one through the tenon. The Nendrum paddles, with evidence of six dowels through the block and one or two through the tenons, stand out as being very securely attached to each other and to the hub.

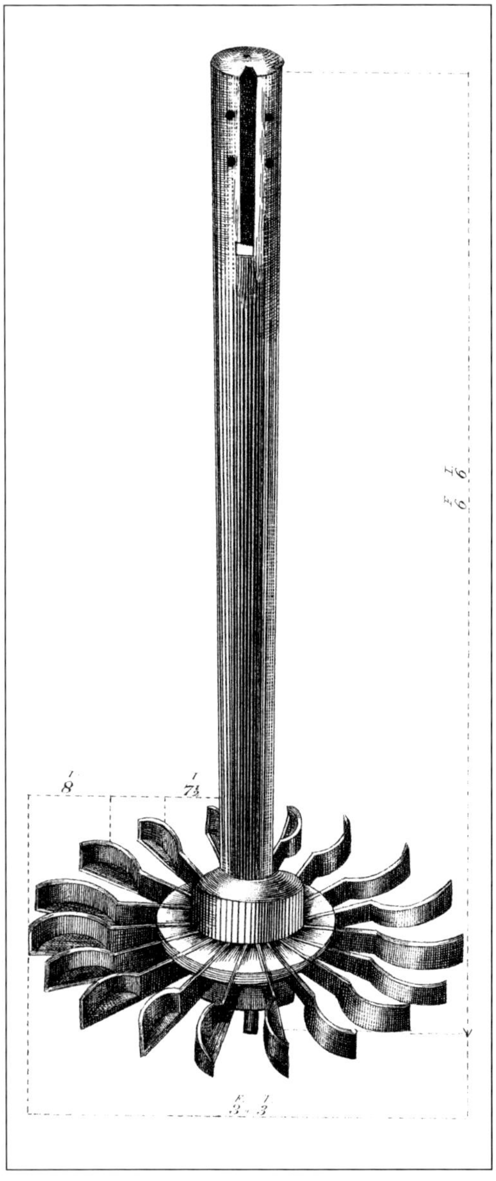

Fig. 6.9
The Moycraig waterwheel and shaft (MacAdam 1856)

HUBS AND WATERWHEELS

Comparative examples for the missing hub and configuration of the waterwheel of Mill 2 are available from a small number of other sites. Moycraig Co. Antrim (MacAdam 1856) is the most complete early horizontal waterwheel (Fig. 6.9) discovered so far anywhere and, since its publication in 1856, has been used as the model for a typical horizontal mill waterwheel. Mashanaglass, Co. Cork (Fahy 1956), produced an almost-complete wheel, and Cloontycarthy, Co. Cork (Rynne 1988) a relatively good example. A small number of sites have produced waterwheel hubs, including Mill 1 at Nendrum, and their details are shown in Table 6.6. The Nendrum 1 hub is of early 7th-century date, Deer Park Farms is probably 8th century, and Cloontycarthy is from the early 9th century. A radiocarbon determination suggests that the Moycraig hub may belong in the 10th century (Rahtz and Bullough 1977, 18, 1000+110 BP, Birm.-491) while Mashanaglass is undated, but probably Early Medieval (see Fig. 6.10 and Table 6.9).

Comparison of these five hub examples demonstrates that their shapes vary. The Nendrum 1 hub has a cylindrical profile, and a high shoulder separating it from a remaining section of shaft. The Cloontycarthy and Moycraig hubs are similar in section, and have shoulders between their hubs, their shafts being made from single pieces of oak. The Deer Park Farms specimen is all in one piece and is also cylindrical, but has no shoulder between the hub and remaining section of shaft. The shaft on the Moycraig wheel has survived intact and the hub still has *in situ* a stone gudgeon, or 'footstep bearing', on which the waterwheel rotated on the bridge tree. This is the only wheel so far discovered that has retained this component. The Deer Park Farm example, however, has a cavity on the base suggesting the position of a similar bearing.

The Mashanaglass hub is quite different, and Fahy has aptly described its shape as resembling a giant spinning top (Fahy 1956, 22). Its shaft, which did not survive, was a separate piece and appears to have been mortised into the top of the hub. There was no evidence of a gudgeon and it was concluded that the hub rotated on its pointed base.

Table 6.6: Irish horizontal waterwheel hub dimensions

Site	Hub diameter	Hub height	Paddles	Wheel diameter
Nendrum 1	30.9cm	30.0cm	18/19	est. 71.9cm
Cloontycarthy	32.0cm	23.3cm	19	96.4cm
Deer Park Farms	26.0cm	22.0cm	18	1.04m
Mashanaglass	29.2cm	31.8cm	23	1.03m
Moycraig	30.4cm	22.9cm	19	1.05m

The shape of the hub that housed the Nendrum 2 paddles is unknown and could, in theory, be similar to any of the hubs listed above. Given the close similarity of the paddles to those from Deer Park Farms, it could be that the hub of the Nendrum 2 waterwheel was of this form.

ESTIMATE OF THE SIZE OF THE NENDRUM MILL 2 WATERWHEEL

Lacking the hub to which the Nendrum paddles were attached, it is not possible to be definite about the diameter of the waterwheel. However, an estimate can be made from the length of its surviving paddles and information from the other hub examples. The total length of Paddle 1 with its tenon is 40.5cm, giving 81cm for two. The solid part (not pierced by mortises) of the hubs ranges from 15cm at Moycraig, through 15.5cm at Nendrum Mill 1, 15.8cm at Mashanaglass and 16cm at Deer Park Farms, to 18cm at Cloontycarthy. This gives an average for the solid core of these five hubs of 16.2cm. Using this as a guide to the size of the Nendrum Mill 2 hub, added to the total length of two paddles, gives an estimate of 97.2cm for the overall diameter of the wheel. Alternatively, using the average hub diameter of those listed in Table 6.6, 29.7cm, and the maximum blade and block lengths of the paddles from Nendrum Mill 2, gives a similar Figure of 98.3cm.

Fig. 6.10
Irish horizontal waterwheel hub profiles: 1. Nendrum, Co. Down, early 7th century, 2. Deer Park Farms, Co. Antrim, possibly 8th century (Lynn and McDowell forthcoming), 3. Cloontycarthy, Co. Cork, mid 9th century (after Rynne 1988), 4. Moycraig, Co. Antrim, possibly 10th century (after MacAdam 1856), 5 Mashanaglass, Co Cork, (after Fahy 1956).

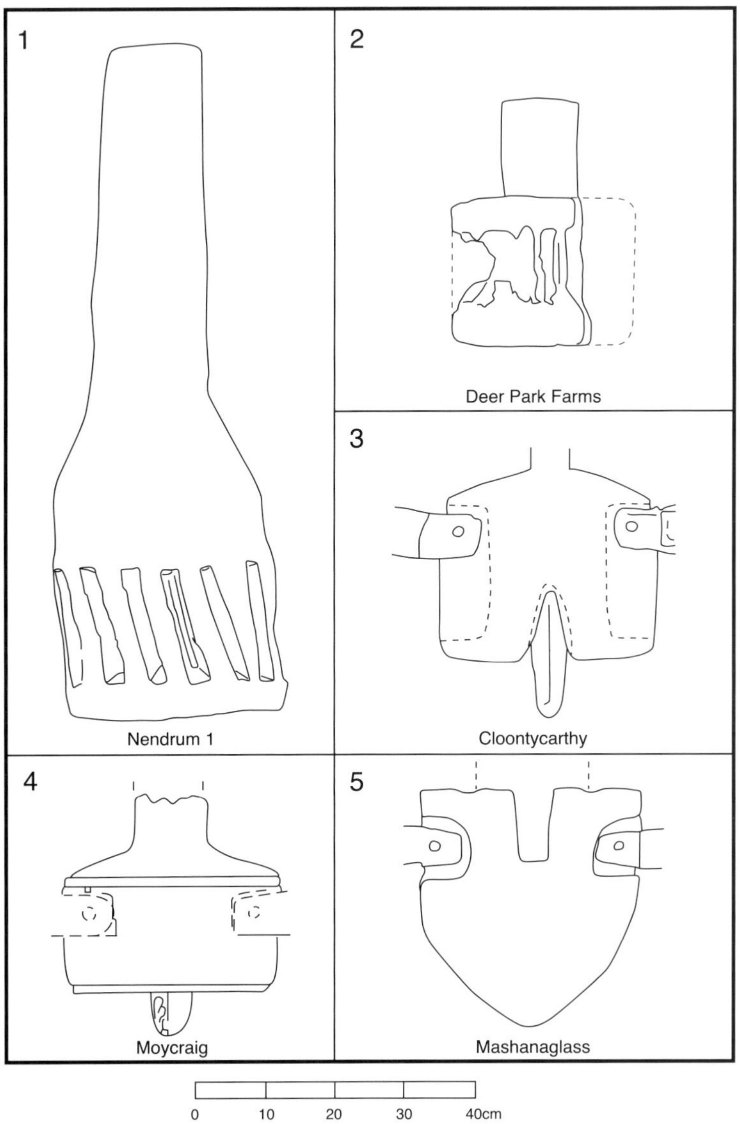

Table 6.7: Estimated diameter of the waterwheel of Mill 2 based on its paddle measurements and comparative hub measurements from other Irish sites shown on Table 6.6

	Hub diameter (cm)	Paddles	Wheel diameter (cm)
Nendrum 2	est. 29.7	est. 23/24	est. 97.2–98.3

As the 7th-century Nendrum Mill 1 waterwheel is estimated to be about 71cm in diameter, and that of the Mill 2 of late 8th-century date to be *c.* 97.2–98.3cm, this together with information in Table 6.8 below suggests that waterwheel size may have increased during the 7th and 8th centuries.

Table 6.8: The estimated size and number of paddles of the waterwheels from Mill 1 and 2 and other Irish sites

Site	Paddles	Wheel diameter	Date
Nendrum 1	18/19	est. 72cm	Early 7th century
Nendrum 2	23/24	est. 97–98cm	Late 8th century
Cloontycarthy	19	96cm	Mid 9th century
Deer Park Farms	18	1.04m	Poss. 8th century
Mashanaglass	23	1.03m	Undated
Moycraig	19	1.05m	Poss. 10th century

Comparison of the range of diameters of early millstones (discussed in the next chapter) with the horizontal waterwheel diameters given in Table 6.8, would seem to indicate that the waterwheels in early horizontal-wheeled mills were slightly larger than the millstones that they powered.

The measurements of the various parts of the waterwheels given here cannot be regarded as absolutely representative of their original dimensions, as some allowance should be made for varying states of survival and differentials in shrinkage of the oak from which they were fashioned. However, the surviving Irish examples of waterwheels, hubs and paddles suggest that from the 8th century at least, waterwheel dimensions were very similar. This indicates strongly that throughout the country, Irish millwrights at this time, and in the following centuries, employed a standard size of waterwheel, centring on 1m in diameter. Present evidence also suggests that from at least the early 7th century, waterwheels had a minimum of 18 or 19 paddles, as evidence for any waterwheel with fewer paddles has not yet come to light.

THE SHAFT AND SPINDLE

No evidence of the shaft belonging to the waterwheel of Mill 2 was recovered during the excavation. Indeed, apart from the Moycraig example, and where small portions have survived on hubs, information about the shafts of Irish horizontal waterwheels is poor. Details from five sites where a fragment of shaft has survived attached to the hub or, as in the case of Mashanaglass, where some evidence of its diameter was preserved (Fahy 1956, 22), are given in Table 6.9. Apart from Mashanaglass, where there is evidence that the shaft was mortised into the top of the hub (Fahy 1956, 22), the others were made in one piece with the hub. In all the examples, the shafts are circular in section and their diameters range from 9.5cm to 16.5cm.

Table 6.9: Shaft dimensions

	Surviving length of shaft	Diameter
Nendrum 1	51.7cm	13.1–16.5cm
Cloontycarthy	51.5cm	9.5cm
Deer Park Farms	14.0cm	11.3cm
Moycraig	1.76m	10.2cm
Mashanaglass		15.2cm

As the shaft connects the waterwheel with the upper millstone, its length (minus the length of the spindle) is directly related to the depth of the wheelhouse below the floor of the millhouse. Thus, the length of the complete Moycraig example at 1.76m suggests that at this site the wheelhouse was relatively low in height, unless its spindle was of a significant length. In contrast, the floor of the millhouse of Nendrum Mill 2 is estimated to have been at a height of *c.* 3.75m above the floor of the wheelhouse. Taking into consideration the small space of a few centimetres below the bridge-tree and the floor of the wheelhouse, and the probable height of the hub itself, the implication is that a very long shaft, in the region of *c.* 3.3m, was required for the Mill 2 waterwheel. But again, the caveat must be added that the length of the spindle is unknown.

No spindle from an Irish horizontal-wheeled mill has yet been found, and information on their character is scant. The immediate question to arise concerns the relative length of the shaft to that of the spindle in horizontal waterwheel assemblies. It is highly probable that all spindles employed in Irish horizontal-wheeled mills were made of iron. Some evidence for the thickness of the spindle of the waterwheel of Mill 2 is provided by the survival of the wooden bearing in the lower millstone (see pps 187-189). This has an aperture with a diameter of 2.9cm, suggesting a spindle of slightly smaller diameter. At the top of the spindle was the rynd (power-transfer bar), which was fitted into a socket, or chase, around the eye on the bottom surface of the upper millstone, causing it to turn with the rotation of the waterwheel. Much more evidence is available about the types of rynds employed in Irish horizontal-wheeled mills due to the survival of rynd sockets on millstones, and this is discussed in the next chapter.

THE TENTERING SYSTEM

In horizontal-wheeled mills, the mechanism for adjusting the space between the millstones — the tentering system — is relatively simple but effective (see Fig. 1.6). A vertical timber called the 'lightening-tree' extended from the floor of the millhouse to connect with a horizontal timber called the 'bridge-tree' at the bottom of the wheelhouse on which the base of the waterwheel rotated. Raising or lowering the lightening-tree resulted in a similar movement of the bridge-tree and the waterwheel and, via the shaft and spindle, ultimately the upper millstone via the rynd on top of the spindle.

Unfortunately, very little evidence of the tentering system from either mill was recovered. A possible 'sword', or lever which would have been attached to the upper end of the lightening-tree of Mill 1 was recovered from the silt in its millpond (see p. 231) and was tentatively identified as such because of its similarity to one found at Mashanaglass (Fahy 1956, 32). In Mill 2, the only part of the tentering system recovered was the beam on which the bridge-tree rested (the 'bridge-tree support beam' or 'bolster head beam'. This was found *in situ,* at the base of the back wall of the wheelhouse and is discussed on p. 106.

POSITION OF THE WATERWHEEL WITHIN THE WHEELHOUSE

The accurate positioning of the waterwheel, and especially of the paddles in relation to the water jet issuing from the penstock, is the central factor in the efficiency of the whole mill. Loss of efficiency would result if the paddles were set too high or too low, or at too great a distance from the source of the water jet. Fortunately, for Mill 2 it is possible from a number of key measurements, to work out relatively accurately the positioning of the waterwheel and its paddles.

The height of the paddles above the wheelhouse floor and below the orifice

The survival of the bridge-tree support beam *in situ* at the base of the back wall of the wheelhouse and immediately below the orifice is a vital piece of information in ascertaining the height of the paddles. The bridge-tree itself had not survived (or was not found), but has left its footprint in the form of the mortise in the middle of the support beam and to the left of the orifice. This establishes the east-west and north-south horizontal planes for the base of the gudgeon or footstep bearing on the centre of the base of the hub. The thickness of the bridge-tree, from examples from other sites where this component has survived (Mashanaglass, Drumard and Tamworth), can be suggested to have been in the region of 5cm.

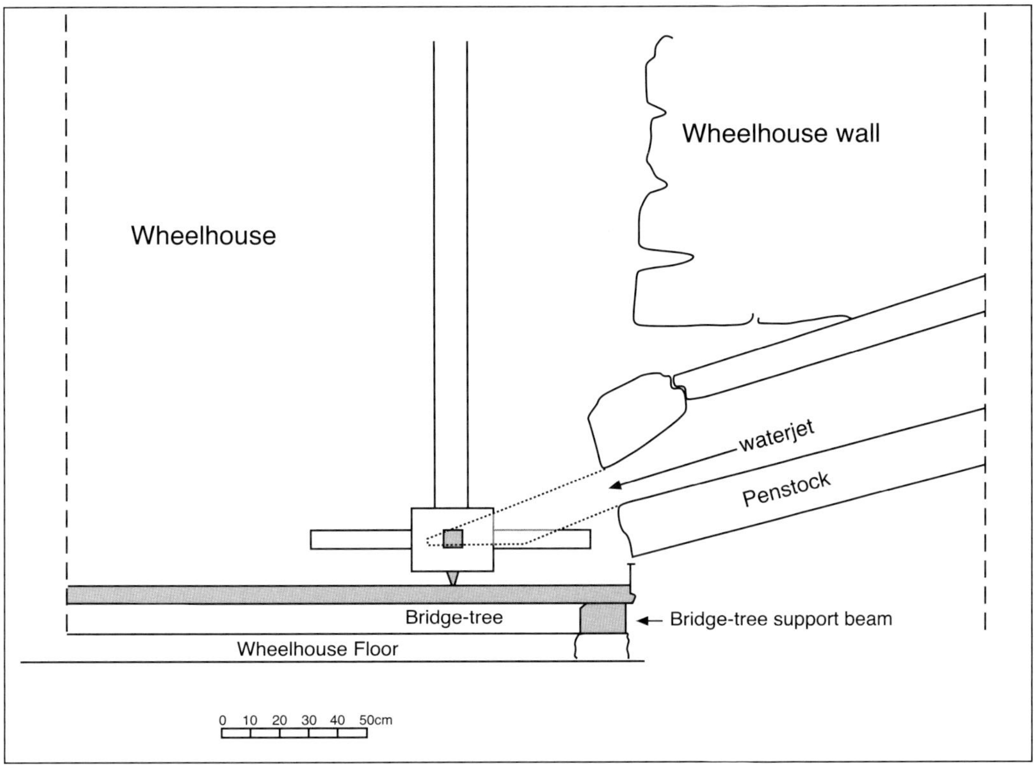

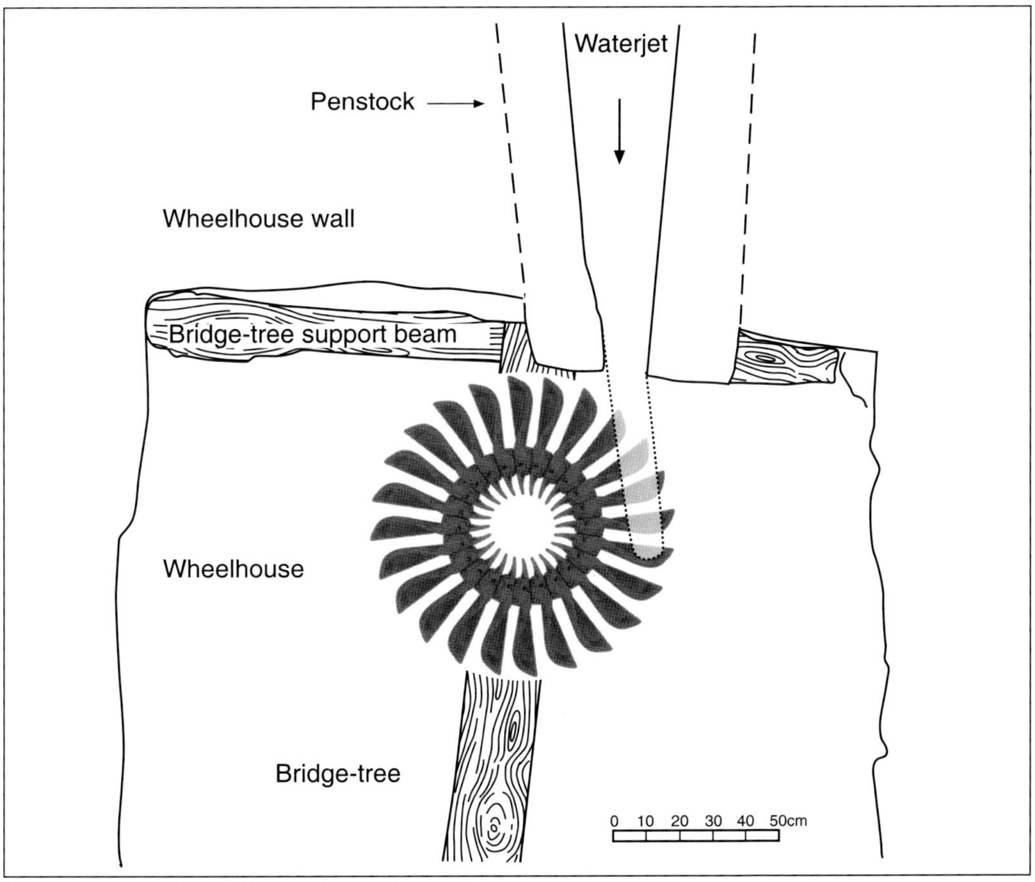

Fig. 6.11A
Positioning of the waterwheel of Mill 2 in the wheelhouse, section view

Fig. 6.11B
Positioning of the waterwheel of Mill 2 in the wheelhouse, plan view

Similarly, the gudgeon has survived on the hub from Moycraig, indicating a height for this of *c.* 5cm. The distance from the base of the hub to the centre of the paddles, based on surviving hubs, is about 10cm. This gives an approximate height for the centres of the paddles of around 20cm above the support beam, which suggests that they were approximately 17cm below the centre of the orifice (for a slight alternative estimate of the latter measurement see p. 216). The position of the bridge-tree to the left of the orifice establishes that the waterwheel turned in a clockwise direction.

Distance of the centre of the wheel out from the orifice

An approximate position for this can be ascertained by the trajectory of the water jet as it issued from the orifice. The water emerged at a downward angle of 15° from the horizontal and its trajectory is shown in Fig. 6.11A The waterwheel has been estimated as being *c.* 97cm in diameter and, if a wheel of this size is positioned as suggested above, the probable point of impact with the paddles is shown on Figs 6.11A and B.

The setting of the wheel

The setting of the wheel as shown in Figs 6.11 A and B is based on the estimate that the centre was approximately 64cm out from the back wall of the orifice, leaving a clearance of only some 15.5cm between it and the wall.

In this reconstruction, it can be seen that the paddles of the wheel were positioned as closely as possible to the orifice to maximise the energy from the jet. The waterwheel was positioned well above the wheelhouse floor, as it was important to keep it above any water accumulating there, which would have impeded rotation of the wheel. The positioning of the penstock to the right of centre of the wheelhouse conforms to all other known examples of Irish horizontal-wheeled mills and confirms the clockwise rotation of the Nendrum Mill 2 waterwheel and millstone. There are no known advantages inherent in clockwise as opposed to anticlockwise movement, but it appears to be a deeply-entrenched technical preference in Irish mills.

THE WHEELHOUSE OF MILL 2

The plans of the wheelhouses of both mills correspond closely to that of all other known Irish examples. In all of these, the wheelhouse is an undercroft structure located below the floor of the millhouse and is square to rectangular in plan. Apart from part of the ground plan, little information was recovered concerning the wheelhouse of Mill 1. Like that of Mill 2, it appears to have been built of stone, or at least no structural timber remained. It is possible, however, that it was built in wood with stone footings and that the timber was salvaged for use elsewhere when it was filled in during the construction of the second mill.

The splendid state of preservation of the stone wheelhouse of Mill 2 provides an almost complete example of the wheelhouse of a horizontal-wheeled mill. Unlike the majority of Irish examples, with the exception of Mashanaglass, which were largely wooden structures, it was built in stone. Therefore it lacks the large structural foundation timbers, the sole-plates and back wall beams familiar from other horizontal- and vertical-wheeled mill sites. A rough stone paving took the place of a planked wooden floor, the latter regarded by Rynne as virtually a standard feature of Irish horizontal-wheeled mills (1988, 1, 61). Very good examples of this survived at Mashanaglass, Co. Cork and Ballykilleen Co. Offaly. The wattle panels and the large amount of wattlework fragments found around the floor appear to derive from above, not from a wattle mat lining the floor.

It is possible at a number of sites (listed in Table 6.10) to ascertain the floor areas of their wheelhouses.

Table 6.10: The Nendrum wheelhouse compared with other wheelhouses in order of area

	Back wall	Side walls	Area	Height	
Crushyriree, Co. Cork (Cotter, 2003, 108)	2m	2m	$4m^2$		Wood
Drumard, Co. Derry (Baillie, 1975)	2.1m	2.50m	$5.25m^2$		Wood
Nendrum 2	2.45m	2.21m	$5.41m^2$	est.3.75m	Stone
Ballymartin Co. Kilkenny TKAS, 1849-51, 154)	1.83m	3.35m	$6.13m^2$		Wood
Knocknagranshy Co. Limerick (Lucas 1969)	2.16m	3.60m	$7.78m^2$		Wood
Mashanaglass, Co. Cork, (Fahy 1956)	1.98m	4.11m	$8.14m^2$	c. 3.73m	Stone
Cloontycarthy, Co. Cork	2.50m	4.0m	$10m^2$		Wood and stone
Bramblestown, Co. Kildare	c.3.5m	3.35m	$11.22m^2$		Wood
Tamworth (Staffs) Rahtz and Meeson 1992	2.63m	5m	$13.50m^2$ $21.25m^2$		Wood

The Irish examples range in size from $4m^2$ to $11.22m^2$. All are smaller than the $13.50m^2$ recorded for the wheelhouse of the horizontal-wheeled mill at Tamworth in Staffordshire (Rahtz and Meeson 1992). Some are of approximately square in plan while others are rectangular. The Nendrum Mill 2 wheelhouse is in the smaller size range and has an almost square plan. At only a few sites is it possible to ascertain the original heights of the walls. Interestingly, both Nendrum Mill 2 and Mashanaglass where this is possible, have very similar heights at *c.* 3.75m and 3.73m respectively.

Chapter 7

The Millstones and Millhouses

Thomas McErlean

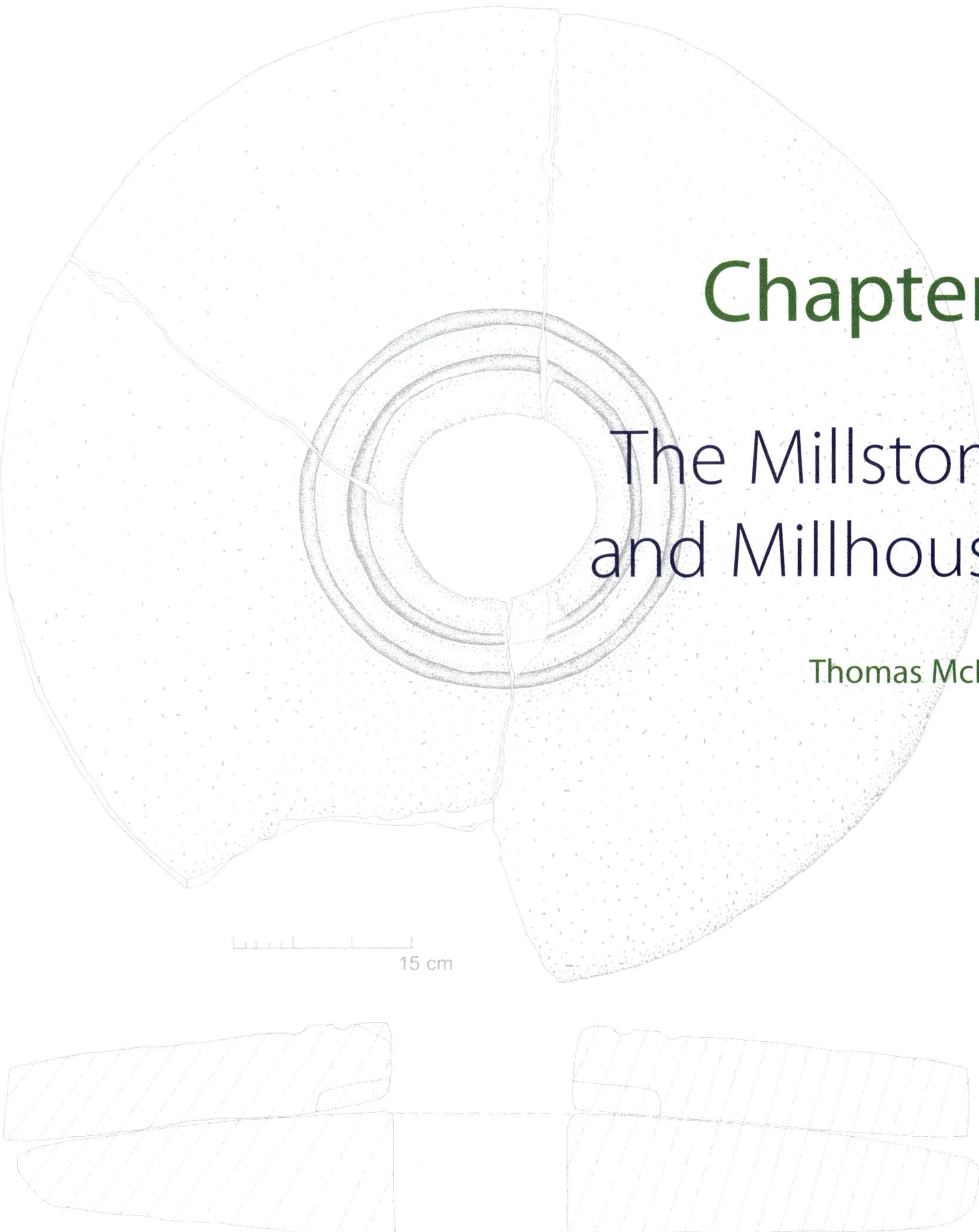

Chapter 7
The Millstones and Millhouses

Thomas McErlean

INTRODUCTION

The granite millstones of Mill 2, found where they fell from the floor of the mill-house to the floor of the wheelhouse below, are impressive (see Figs 7.1 and 7.2) and match the high quality of the other components of the mill.

Only a few other early Irish mill sites have produced millstones. None was found at Knockrour Co. Cork (Ó Conlon 1926), Ballykilleen, Co. Offaly (Lucas 1955), Morret, Co. Laois (Lucas 1953), Knocknagranshy Co. Limerick (Lucas 1969), Little Island Co. Cork (Rynne 1988, 2), Ardcloyne Co. Cork (Cleary 1999), or Crushyriree Co. Cork (Cotter 2003) for example. Similarly, no millstones were recovered from Mill 1 at Nendrum, although

Fig. 7.1
The millstones (in situ) as found at the bottom of the wheelhouse of Mill 2. The lower stone complete with its wooden bearing was found with its lower surface upwards and the large fragment of the upper stone was found with its upper surface upwards

six small granite fragments that were found, may possibly derive from millstones but retain no diagnostic features. Cloontycarthy Co. Cork (Rynne 1988, 2, 314–316) produced a fragment of an upper stone, while Drumard, Co. Londonderry (Baillie 1975, 29) produced a lower stone and Newton, Co. Tipperary (Lucas 1986a, 24; Rynne 1990, 26) produced a fragment of another. Mashanaglass Co. Cork (Fahy 1956, 27–30) produced four millstone fragments, three from upper stones and one from a lower stone, and Glenwood Co. Cork (Fahy 1956, 57) produced six fragments, of which two could be identified as upper stones and two as lower. However, before Nendrum, no Irish site has produced a contemporary matching pair of upper and lower stones.

Fig. 7.2
The lifting of the lower stone from the bottom of the wheelhouse

THE UPPER OR 'RUNNER' STONE

The upper stone was found in three pieces leaving only a small fragment of the outer perimeter not recovered. One large fragment made up approximately one half (see Fig. 7.3) of the stone. Together the three pieces allow reconstruction of almost the entire millstone, including the area around the central aperture or 'eye' and approximately 314° of the circumference. The upper stone measures 84.3cm in diameter and has a maximum thickness of 8cm around the eye, narrowing to 6cm at the rim.

The top surface is gently convex in profile, making an angle of approximately 8° from the edge. The eye is 16cm wide, cylindrical in profile and 8cm deep. The most prominent features of the upper surface are two raised, concentric bands or collars around the eye, that are defined by two shallow and concentric incised grooves in the stone. This surface has been dressed to a smooth finish and the rim shows little signs of wear or damage.

The lower, or grinding, surface has a slightly rough texture and is gently concave in the central area, but flat in the final few centimetres towards the rim. Concentric striations from wear are visible in the central zone, while the area immediately around the eye is smooth. The most interesting features of the lower surface are the rynd sockets facing each other at 180° on either side of the eye. They are 7cm in length by 7cm in width and 2.5cm deep, and have gently rounded ends.

Fig. 7.3A
The large fragment of the upper stone (upper surface) in situ at the bottom of the wheelhouse

THE LOWER OR 'BED' STONE

The lower stone is complete and is 82cm in diameter. It is 11cm thick at the rynd or spindle aperture which is cylindrical in profile and has a diameter of 15cm. The stone narrows to a thickness of 6cm at the rim, and is slightly smaller in diameter (only by approximately 2.3cm) and slightly thicker over all (by 3cm) than the upper stone. The upper or grinding surface is gently convex, approximately matching the curve of the lower surface of the upper stone. Towards the rim, the angle of the curve becomes slightly steeper. The grinding surface shows a pattern of concentric striations which are most pronounced in the central zone. The lower surface is roughly dressed and is partially flat and partially slightly convex.

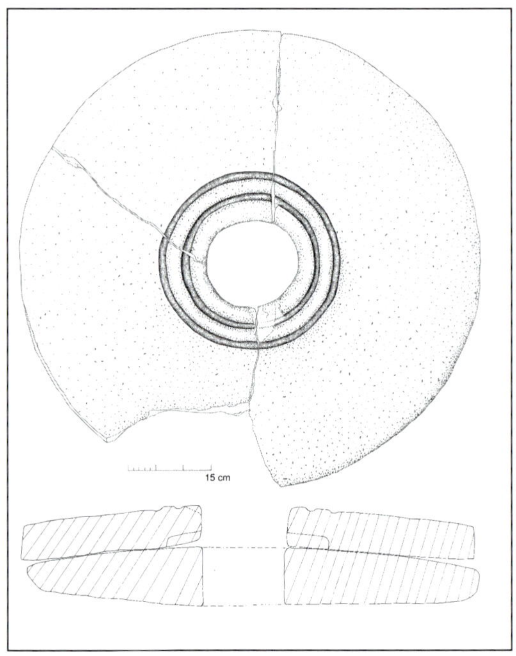

Fig. 7.3B
The upper surface of the upper stone (G. Gilmour)

Fig. 7.4A
The lower surface of the upper stone showing the rynd sockets

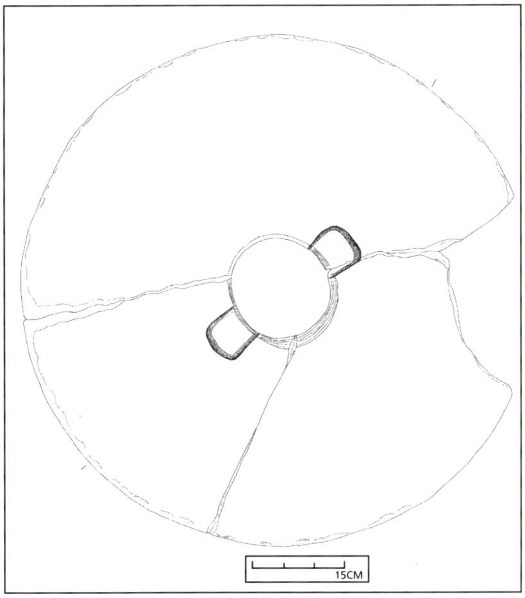

Fig. 7.4B
The lower surface of the upper stone with the rynd sockets (G. Gilmour)

Fig. 7.5A
The upper surface of the lower stone

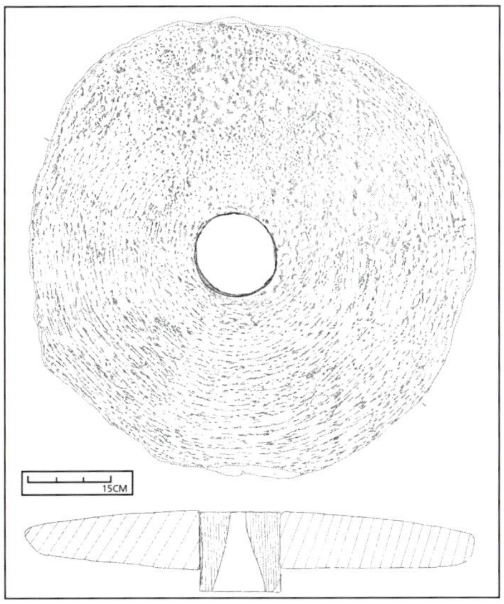

Fig. 7.5B
The upper surface of the lower stone with a section drawing showing the placement of wooden bearing for the spindle and rynd (G. Gilmour)

THE WOODEN BEARING OR 'BUSH'

The outstanding feature of the lower stone is the survival, *in situ*, of the wooden bearing or 'bush' through which the spindle on the top of the shaft bearing the rynd passed to engage the upper stone. This is the only known early Irish millstone where the bearing has survived. It was made from a length of oak roundwood, from which the sapwood had been removed and much of interior carved out. Except for the presence of four cracks on the inner surface, it has survived in excellent condition (see Figs 7.6A-F).

Externally, the bearing is cylindrical in shape, with an outside diameter of 14.5cm and a height of 14.5cm. The interior has an inner 'pipe-and-funnel' profile, the 'pipe' being 2.9cm in diameter and the funnel 9.9cm. The diameter of the 'pipe' gives an indication of that of the spindle, which must have been only slightly less thick. The diameter of the bearing was slightly less than that of the aperture of the lower stone and a tight fit was achieved by placing wedges between it and the stone (see Figs 7.6 F and G).

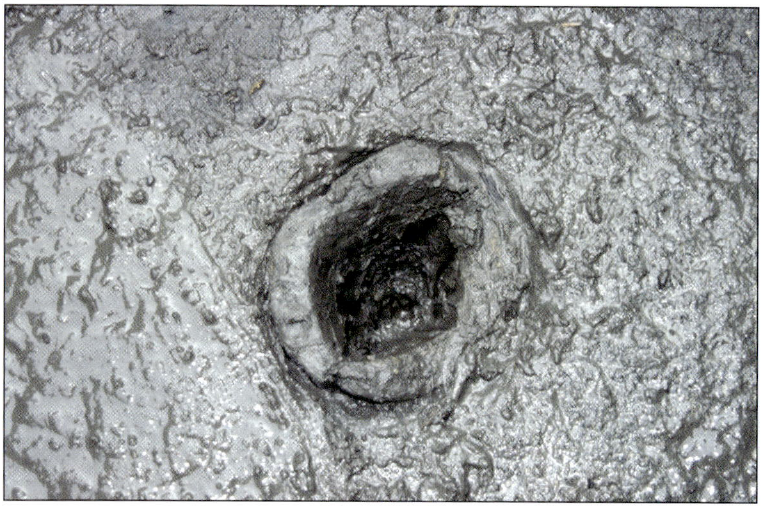

Fig. 7.6A (above) Close-up view of the wooden bearing in situ, when excavated (lower surface of the lower millstone)

Fig. 7.6B (left) Side profile of the wooden bearing (T. Corey)

Fig. 7.6C (right) Bottom and side profile of the wooden bearing (T. Corey)

Fig. 7.6D Top profile of wooden bearing (T. Corey)

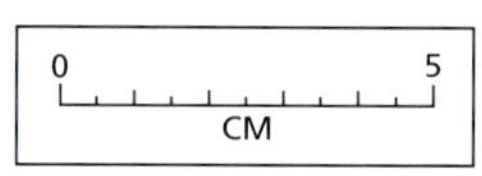

Fig. 7.6E
Bottom profile of wooden bearing (T. Corey)

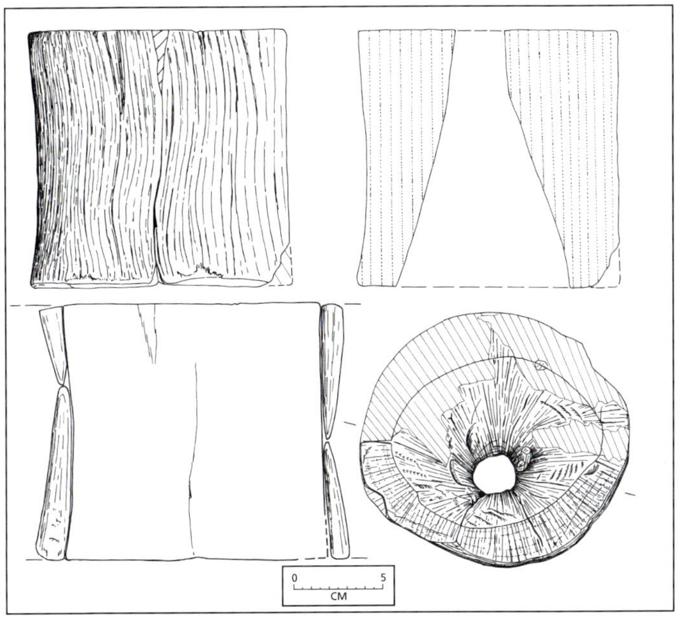

Fig. 7.6F
Profiles and section of the wooden bearing (G. Gilmour)

DISCUSSION

The Nendrum millstone pair follow closely the simple, classical design of most rotary millstones. They are circular and the upper stone has a central eye, with rynd sockets on the lower face. The grain was introduced through the eye and ground between the two stones. The ground material gravitated under centrifugal force towards the edge of the stones, and the concave profile of the upper stone and the matching convex profile of the lower were designed to aid this movement. Towards the perimeter of both stones, their profiles change slightly to leave a wider space between them, thus facilitating the dispersal of the meal or flour for collection in the surrounding area. In an ideal situation, the upper stone never touched the stationary lower stone when in motion. If this happened, it could cause extensive damage to the grinding surfaces, as well as creating sparks, which would constitute a serious fire hazard. Mill dust is highly combustible and the historical record provides many incidents of mills catching fire. As previously noted perhaps the earliest mention of such an occurrence in Ireland is the 7th-century reference in Cogitosus' *Life of St Brigit* (Connolly and Picard 1987, 25), to the destruction by burning of a mill belonging to a monastery of St Brigit, probably at Kildare itself. There is no evidence of damage on either grinding surfaces of the Nendrum millstones.

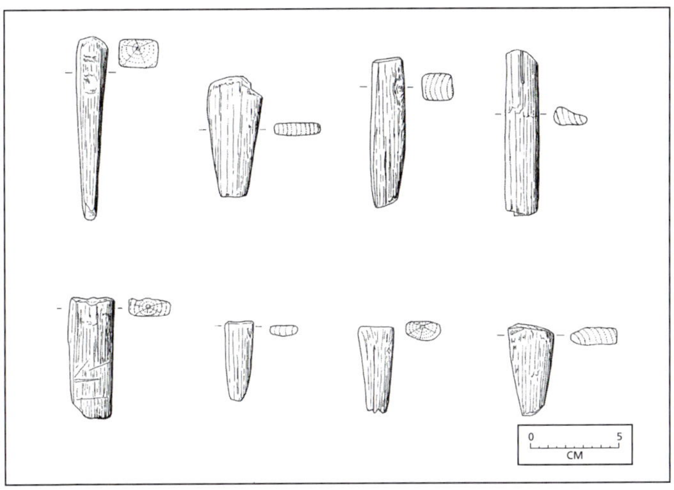

Fig. 7.6G
The wedges inserted to hold the wooden bearing tightly in place (G. Gilmour)

Rynd sockets are a standard feature of upper millstones and are also found in some examples of rotary querns. The Nendrum rynd sockets are two-winged, conforming to an approximately T-shaped rynd. Their primary function is to key the rynd or power transfer bar at the top of the spindle into the upper stone. In horizontal-wheeled mills, each complete turn of the waterwheel is matched by a complete turn of the upper stone, by virtue of the rynd at the top of the spindle and shaft. Its other function, shared by some more sophisticated examples of hand-operated rotary querns, was to permit the raising and lowering of the upper stone to vary the space between it and the lower stone. This was achieved in horizontal-wheeled mills by the tentering mechanism previously outlined (see p. 14) and for rotary querns by devices discussed by Curwen (Curwen 1937). The tentering mechanism allowed for different grinding regimes for different products. Thus, a wide space was used for the first milling or shelling of grain, and for the production of bran and course meal or grain for malting, while close grinding was required for fine flour.

Raised bands and recessed grooves similar to those around the eye of the Nendrum upper stone have been found on a small number of other millstones and on some querns. Mashanaglass millstone C (Fahy 1956, 27–30), and those from Cloontycarthy (Rynne 1990, 25), Glenwood (Fahy 1956, 87) and Castlefreke (Inv. Cork 1, 290) have a concentric lip or collar or a raised band around the eye. A fragment of an upper stone of unknown diameter from Desert, Co. Cork is described as having 'stepped concentric rings' (Inv. Cork 2, 166) a feature which may be similar to the Nendrum example. Raised bands or rings are found on some later Romano-British and Anglo-Saxon querns (Watts 2002, 37 and 38). They are also present on a number of Irish querns, notably the examples from Church Island, Co. Kerry (O'Kelly 1958) and Inniskea North, Co. Mayo. An example from Dunadd, Argyle has three concentric bands similar to those on the Nendrum example (Lane and Campbell 2000, 181, 185, no. 2224). Their function is not thought to be purely ornamental, but may have stopped the grain flowing into the eye from the hopper, from dispersing around the upper surface of the stone. Any grain landing in this area would have been periodically brushed into the eye.

Fig. 7.7A (left)
Bottom millstone left, upper Millstone, right (Tony Corey)

Fig. 7.7B (right)
Upper and lower millstones in position (Tony Corey)

COMPARISON OF THE NENDRUM MILLSTONES WITH OTHER EARLY IRISH MILLSTONES

It is important to place the design of the Nendrum millstones within the context of other Irish Early Medieval examples. The main characteristics of a representative number of other early Irish millstones are shown in Table 7.1. This list is not exhaustive and is compiled from published reports of early millstones recovered from other horizontal-wheeled mill sites, or found during excavation of settlement sites, and of stray finds which are likely to be Early Mediaeval in date. Where early finished millstones are found in a non-mill context, it is generally safe to assume the presence of a mill in the locality. The table includes some stones that may have belonged to early vertical-wheeled mills since, in the light of current information, there is no compelling evidence to suggest that in the Early Medieval period, these differed from those of horizontal-wheeled mills.

In archaeological literature, considerable problems exist in distinguishing between large rotary quern stones and small millstones, and the two types have often been confused one with the other. Scrutiny of the published sources suggests that any stone over *c.* 55cm in diameter and certainly any over 60cm, unless having strongly diagnostic features to suggest otherwise, should be viewed as a probable millstone, rather than a rotary quern stone. Hand-operated rotary querns appear first in the archaeological record in the last centuries BC, when they largely replaced the saddle quern. From the beginning, two types are present in Britain and Ireland, the disc quern (Curwen 1937) and the beehive quern (Caulfield 1977). Disc querns are flattish and circular, while the upper stone of the beehive quern is somewhat dome shaped, has a rounded profile and is sometimes oval in shape.

The extensive study by Caulfield (1977) of the beehive quern in Ireland has shown that the type was largely confined to the northern half of the island and that it had gone out of use probably by the 6th century AD or slightly before. Ninety per cent of the 180 upper stones of beehive querns studied by Caulfield had diameters between 28 and 36cm. Their rounded profiles and handle sockets present little difficulty in distinguishing them from millstones. In contrast to the relatively short time-span of the beehive quern, the disc quern lasted down to the 19th century in many places and was used for the grinding of cereals alongside watermills. It is one of the most common finds on Early Medieval sites, and its presence is sometimes taken as suggesting the absence of mills from the local landscape. It is clear that it is erroneous to see disc querns and mills as mutually exclusive, and that the hand quern probably complemented the workings of a mill. For example, many granite disk querns were found during the excavation of the monastic site at Nendrum (Lawlor 1925a, 18 and 137). Unfortunately none of these appears to have survived, and little information is given about them, apart from the fact that one was inscribed with a cross, and that all, except for one lower stone, appeared to have been deliberately smashed.

There has been no recent comprehensive study of Irish disc querns, even though their number has increased enormously with the accelerated rate of excavation in recent years. Most have diameters ranging from *c.* 30–50cm, and at the upper end of their range they can be very similar in diameter to small millstones. The presence of rynd sockets (for adjusting the space between the stones) on some of the lower surfaces of their upper stones can sometimes cause confusion with power-operated millstones. Most disc querns have sockets for handles on the upper surface of the upper stone. This feature, while generally diagnostic of a hand-operated rotary quern, can sometimes be a feature of millstones where the socket was for a 'damsel' or agitator to cause the hopper to dispense

Table 7.1: Early millstones' dimensions ranked in order of descending diameter size of the upper stone

Site	Stone diameter (cm)	Maximum thickness (cm)	Rynd socket (cm)	Diameter of eye (cm)	Rock type (if known)
Rathmullan, Co. Down, (Lynn 1982, 111, 114-115, 136-138)	U 106 (B)	5 (average)	Slighty curving X-shaped rynd sockets Depth 2.0	15	Sandstone (possibly Scrabo, Co. Down)
Rathmullan, Co. Down, (Lynn 1982 114-115, 136–138)	U 95 (A)	10	Slighty curving X-shaped rynd sockets	18-14	Sandstone
Glendalough (Brockagh td), Co. Wicklow (Inv Wicklow, 201)	U 94	7		12	Granite
Nendrum, Co. Down	Pair U 84.3	8 L 82.0	Bar form: linear 11 Width 7 Depth 2.5	16 Length 7	Mourne granite
Mashanaglass, Co. Cork (Fahy 1956, 27-30)	U est 84–102 (C) L est 76.2–102 (A)	14 31	Bar form: dove-tailed Depth 2.4	15	Red sandstone
Arundelmills, Co. Cork (Inv Cork 1, 289)	U 82	19	Bar form: linear	15	
Connor, Co. Antrim (SMR 7/Ant 38:30)	U 78	11	Cruciform Length 9.4 Width 8.0 Depth 2.0		
Glenwood, Co. Cork (Fahy 1956, 57)	U 76 L 80 L 76	15.2 17.8 35.5	Bar form	14	
Bramblestown (Byrne 1851, 156)	U 73.7				
Inishrush Co. Derry (Day and McWilliams 1993, 95, 120-121)	U 73	17.8	Cruciform	6.4	
Ballinderry, Co. Westmeath (Hencken, 1936, 162-163)	L 71	29			Sandstone
Ballynarry, Co. Down (Davison 1962, 72-74)	U 71	6.4		12.7	Mourne granite

Site	Stone diameter (cm)	Maximum thickness (cm)	Rynd socket (cm)	Diameter of eye (cm)	Rock type (if known)
Brahalish, Co. Cork (Inv Cork 1, 406)	U 71	13	Bar form Length 11 Width 4	13	
Newton, Co. Tipperary (Lucas 1986a 24, Rynne 1990, 26)	L c. 70	26			
Cloonamore, Co. Galway, (Inv Galway 1, 169)	U 70	25			Granite
Cloontycarthy, Co. Cork (Rynne 1988, 2, 314-316	U est 70	7.5	Bar form: dove-tailed Length 5.2 Depth 1.5 at eye 1.4 at closed end	19-10	Red sandstone
Caherolickane, Co. Cork, (Inv. Cork 1, 406-407)	L 68	18		12	
Cronavan, Co. Cork, (Inv Cork 2, 165-167)	U 67	11	Bar form	10	
Knockageehy (Castlefreke) Co. Cork (Inv. Cork 1, 290)	U 65	13	4-D-shaped Length 4 Width 4 Depth 3	12	
Curraghgorm, Co. Cork (Rynne, 1988, 1 79)	U 65	8		10	
Kilnagross, Co. Cork (Byrne 1849-1851, 160)	U 61	38.1			
Mashanaglass Co. Cork (Fahy 1956, 27–30)	U 61 (C)	12	Bar form dove-tailed Length 8.89 Breadth 5.72 (at eye) Breadth 7.62 (at closed end)	11	Red sandstone
Shannacashel, Co. Cork (Byrne 1851, 161)	U 61	c. 20.3			Sandstone
Ballinderry, Co. Westmeath (Hencken, 1936, 162–163)	L 60	6			Sandstone
Lisduff (Inv Cork 1, 290)	L 60			10	
Knockanpower, Co. Waterford (Inv Waterford 155)	U 56		Bar form		Sandstone
Drumard, Co. Derry (Baillie 1975, 29)	L 55	c. 15		12	Sperrin granulite
Rathruane More (Inv. Cork 1, 290)	U 55	13		10	

Site	Stone diameter (cm)	Maximum thickness (cm)	Rynd socket (cm)	Diameter of eye (cm)	Rock type (if known)
Not identified as upper or lower					
Kilbeg, Co. Wicklow (Inv. Wick 201)	108 Unfinished			16	
Milverton Co. Dublin (O'Donovan 1859. 252)	c. 107				
Dunboyke, Co. Wicklow Inv. Wicklow, 201	87	25			Granite
Milverton, Co. Dublin (O'Donovan 1859, 252)	c. 81.3				
Timaconway, Co. Derry, (Day and McWilliams 1993, 119)	71	12.7		15	

KEY

U= upper millstone, L= lower millstone, est.= estimated,

(A) and (B) after Rathmullan examples refers to Lynn (1982, 111, 114-115, 136-138) references

(A), (B) and (C) after Mashanaglass to Fahy (1956, 27–30) references.

Inv followed by a county name refers to the published archaeological inventories by the Archaeological Survey of Ireland.

grain as the stone rotated. A further complication in interpretation is where millstones, presumably damaged, have been cut down in size to form querns. An example of this practice was found during the excavation of a rath at Ballynarry Co. Down (Davison 1962, 72–74) and has been suggested for some of the querns found at Dunadd, Argyle (Lane and Campbell, 2000, 185).

It is instructive to compare the diameters of millstones from different periods. Most millstones from the Classical world have diameters between 55cm and 85cm, and none has been convincingly shown to have been smaller than 48cm or larger than 1.09m (Wikander 2000, 392). Interestingly, the diameters shown in Table 7.1 indicate that Irish Early Medieval stones also fall comfortably within this range. Unfortunately, there are no published examples of Late Medieval millstones from Ireland with which to compare those of Early Medieval date. During the 17th and 18th centuries, millstones grew in size and it is not uncommon to find stones in the range of 1.83m to 2.14m. But during the early 19th century, improvements in mill technology led to a reduction in millstone size, to a range of *c.* 1.22m to 1.42m (Sass 1990, 28).

For comparison with Irish Post-Medieval millstones, the Ordnance Memoirs of the 1830s provide some information. While those compiled for the northern Irish counties make a point of recording the statistics of watermills, they tended to concentrate on waterwheel measurements and only occasionally provide information on the millstones. An exception to this is the much more detailed information contained in the accounts of some Co. Londonderry parishes, especially those in the Roe Valley (Day and McWilliams 1991). These show that the millstones of 18 small rural corn mills had diameters ranging from 1.22m–1.47m. This gives an average diameter of 1.38m, showing them to be considerably larger than Early Medieval examples.

One of the largest diameters recorded for a finished early Irish millstone is that of an example found in the middle of the 19th century. It was re-used as a grave slab in a graveyard adjoining the site of a horizontal-wheeled mill at Milverton, Co. Dublin (O'Donovan 1859, 252). The diameter was estimated at 1.07m, but, unfortunately, whether it was an upper or lower stone was not recorded. Two impressive upper millstones, the largest early examples so far from Ireland, were found during the excavation of the motte and raised rath at Rathmullan, Co. Down (Lynn 1982, 111, 114–115, 136–138). One had been re-used as the base for a hearth, the other as the base of a wall on a layer probably dating to the late-12th or early-13th centuries. Both had X-shaped rynd sockets with curving arms. Similar rynd sockets have been found on some English millstones of Late Medieval date (Watt 2002, 100, 102), which may suggest that these stones are not Early Medieval. The excavator considered it unlikely that they came from a horizontal-wheeled mill, primarily on the grounds of their large size, having diameters of 1.06m and 95cm respectively. In the light of more recent research, there is no special reason to support this opinion, and Rynne (1997, 89) comments that they could easily have been turned by a horizontal wheel. Unfortunately, the mill to which they belonged has not been located, but the name of the site, Rathmullan, is of interest and can probably be translated as the 'Rath of the Mill' or 'Mill Rath'. Both the upper and lower millstones from Nendrum, with their diameters of 84.3cm and 82cm respectively, are currently the next largest known.

A fragment of an upper stone (stone C) found at the horizontal-wheeled mill at Mashanaglass, Co. Cork (Fahy 1956, 27–30) gave an estimated original diameter in the range of 85cm to 1.02m, while that of a fragment of a lower stone (stone A) was estimated to be in the range of 76.2cm to 1.02m. However, because of the small sizes of the fragments, some caution is necessary in accepting uncritically the upper end of the estimate. In the graveyard of Trinity Church at Glendalough, Co. Wicklow, a part of a millstone measuring 94cm in diameter was found (Inv. Wicklow, 201). As two unfinished millstones were found nearby, indicating millstone production in the locality, it is possible this stone may not have been completely finished and may been destined for a final dressing involving a reduction in size. Another Wicklow graveyard, Dunboyke, has produced a large granite millstone measuring 87cm in diameter (Inv. Wicklow 201).

The figures shown on Table 7.1 indicate clearly that early millstones show great variation in thickness and that the diameter-to-thickness ratio is an important feature.

Table 7.2: Diameter-to-thickness ratios of upper and lower millstones

Site	Upper stone Diameter/thickness ratio	Site	Lower stone Diameter/thickness ratio
Rathmullan, Co. Down, (Lynn 1982, 111, 114-115, 136-138)	**U 21.2:1**	**Ballinderry, Co. Westmeath** (Henken, 1936, 162-163)	**L 10:1**
Glendalough (Brockagh td), Co. Wicklow (Inv Wicklow, 201)	**U 13.4:1**		
Ballynarry, Co. Down (Davison 1962, 72-74)	**U 11.1:1**	**Nendrum, Co. Down**	**L 7.5:1**
Nendrum, Co. Down	**U 10.5:1**	**Glenwood, Co. Cork** (Fahy 1956, 57)	**L 4.5:1**
Rathmullan, Co. Down, (Lynn 1982)	**U 9.5:1**	**Caherolickane, Co. Cork,** (Inv. Cork 1, 406-407)	**L 3.9:1**
Cloontycarthy, Co. Cork (Rynne 1988, 2, 314-316	**U 9.3:1**	**Drumard, Co. Derry** (Baillie 1975, 29)	**L 3.7:1**
Curraghgorm, Co. Cork (Rynne, 1988, 1 79)	**U 8.1:1**	**Newton, Co. Tipperary** (Lucas 1986 24, Rynne, 1990, 26)	**L 2.7:1**
Connor, Co. Antrim (SMR 7/Ant 38:30)	**U 7.1:1**	**Ballinderry, Co. Westmeath** (Henken, 1936, 162-163)	**L 2.45:1**
Cronavan, Co. Cork, (Inv Cork 2, 165-167)	**U 6.1:1**	**Glenwood, Co. Cork** (Fahy 1956, 57)	**L 2.14:1**
Timaconway, Co. Derry, (Day and McWilliams 1993, 119)	**U 5.6:1**		
Brahalish, Co. Cork (Inv Cork 1, 406)	**U 5.5:1**		
Mashanaglass Co. Cork (Fahy 1956, 27-30)	**U 5.1:1 (C)**		
Glenwood, Co. Cork (Fahy 1956, 57)	**U 5:1:1**		
Castlefreke, Co. Cork (Inv. Cork 1, 290)	**U 5:1**		
Arundelmills, Co. Cork (Inv Cork 1, 289)	**U 4.3:1**		
Rathruane More (Inv. Cork 1, 290)	**U 4.2:1**		
Inishrush Co. Derry (Day and McWilliams 1993, 95, 120-121)	**U 4.1:1**		
Shannacashel, Co. Cork (Byrne 1851, 161)	**U 3.2:1**		

Site	Upper stone Diameter/thickness ratio	Site	Lower stone Diameter/thickness ratio
Cloonamore, Co. Galway, (Inv Galway 1, 169)	**U 2.8;1**		
Kilnagross, Co. Cork (Byrne 1851, 160)	**U 1.6:1**		
Not identified as upper or lower			
Timaconway, Co. Derry, (Day and McWilliams 1993, 119)	**5.6:1**		
Dunboyke, Co. Wicklow Inv. Wicklow, 201	3.5:1		

Key as for Table 7.1

Table 7.2 shows the diameter-to-thickness ratios of upper and lower stones. High ratios represent thin stones with large diameters, and those with small ratios thick stones of small diameter. Visually, this represents the contrast between large disc-like millstones and small dome-like ones. Both the upper and lower stones from Nendrum stand out as having high diameter-to-thickness ratios and are very near the top of the presently known range of early Irish millstones. Millstone B from Rathmullan stands well outside the normal range (Lynn 1982, 111, 114–115, 136–138), with a diameter of 1.06m and a thickness of 5cm giving a ratio of 21:1, a fact which again appears to underline the probable late dating of the millstones from there to the 12th century or later.

Few of the millstones shown on both Tables 7.1 and 7.2 are closely datable, with the exceptions of Nendrum of late 8th or 9th century date, Drumard of similar date and Cloontycarthy, Co. Cork of the 9th century, all of which are dated by associated mills. The upper millstones from Nendrum and Cloontycarthy have similar ratios (Nendrum 10.5:1 and Cloontycarthy 9.3:1) and indicate millstones of this design were in use in the late 8th and 9th centuries. However the lower millstone from Nendrum and that from Drumard horizontal-wheeled mill, the timbers from which were dated to AD 782 (Baillie 1975, 32; 1979, 82), a few years before Nendrum 2 at AD 789, provide an interesting contemporary contrast. The Drumard stone is of small diameter at 55cm and is 15cm thick, one of the two smallest currently known, while the lower stone from Nendrum, at 82cm in diameter and 11cm in thickness is amongst the largest. Nendrum and Drumard provide examples, therefore, of millstones of similar date but having very different designs. It seems obvious that this is not chronological, and in this case it is possible to see the variance in socio-economic terms. Drumard may represent an example of a small rural mill serving a community of a few households, while the Nendrum mill was constructed to service a large and prestigious monastery. It can be argued that the making of a large and thin millstone required greater skill than a smaller and thicker one.

It can also be suggested that as this type may have been more susceptible to damage from poor milling management, it belongs to technically superior mills. Indeed, in the absence of other information, it may be possible to use the size and quality of a surviving millstone as an index of the scale and sophistication of the mill from which it came.

Table 7.1 provides 20 upper stone eye diameters, with measurements ranging from 6cm–18cm. The measurement of 6cm is from a stone recorded by the Ordnance Survey Memoirs at a mill site at Inishrush, Co. Derry (Day and McWilliams 1993, 95, 120–121) and seems excessively small. Since it may be inaccurate, it is discounted here, leaving 18 of the remaining 19 eye diameters between 10cm and 16cm. Nendrum, at 16cm is at the upper end of the normal range of eye size. The Cloontycarthy stone and Rathmullan stone A, show a variation from the normal treatment of the eye, having conical-shaped eyes. In the case of Cloontycarthy, the eye is 19cm wide at the top, narrowing to 10cm at the base, and the Rathmullan one narrows from 18 to 14cm. These must have acted like miniature hoppers. The only obvious evidence of a damsel – a rod inserted into the upper surface of the upper stone, which during the rotation of the stone activates the hopper to release the grain – was found in the form of a hole 3cm wide near the rim of the Rathmullan stone B (Lynn 1982, 111, 114–115, 136–138).

On most other Irish millstones, the perforation on the lower stone has a bottle-neck constriction or hour-glass profile. The latter would seem to indicate that that the hole for the aperture was bored from both sides. Rynne (1990, 26) takes this observation further, and considers it to be a distinctive feature of Irish millstones and the earliest evidence in Europe for the use of bushings in watermills. He sees the hour-glass profile as a deliberate design feature to ensure a tight fit for the bearings, and suggests that separate bushings were inserted on either side of the constriction. The cylindrical profile of the perforation in the Nendrum lower stone (see Fig. 7.3B) therefore differs from most other Irish examples and, by virtue of the rare survival of the bearing, shows that other designs were used.

No spindle or rynd has survived from any early Irish mill site. However, the Ordnance Survey Memoirs for the parish of Tamlaght O'Crilly (Day and McWilliams, 1993, 120) recorded in 1836 the interesting discovery of a spindle with a cruciform-shape rynd at a horizontal-wheeled mill in Inishrush townland. In describing the millstone it stated:

> There was a groove [i.e. the rynd socket] in which stood an iron spindle when in the process of grinding ...

In the absence of surviving rynds, sockets provide an indication of their shape. Those found on Irish millstones show that a number of different forms were used. The most common is a T-shaped bar consisting of two arms, or wings, facing each other on either side of the eye. The Nendrum rynd socket is of this form. Variation in the shape of the arms is found among those of T-shaped form. Some are dovetail-shaped as in the

Mashanaglass stone C and others. Some are linear or almost square as in the Nendrum example. The examples from Connor and Inishrush have cruciform sockets indicating the use of four-armed rynds, and those on the probably later-Medieval stones from Rathmullan are also four-armed, but these are slightly curving and arranged in an X-shaped configuration. The socket on the millstone from Castlefreke, Co. Cork (Inv. Cork 1, 290) is also four-armed and the arms have a D-shaped profile.

The recorded depths of the sockets vary from 1.4cm to 3cm and provide an indication of the thicknesses of the rynds. The lack of dates for the millstones makes it impossible to ascertain at present a dating sequence for the different forms. It is possible, however, to state that the two-armed, T-shaped bar form was found on the Nendrum and Cloontycarthy stones and was therefore in use in the late 8th and 9th centuries, while the curving four-armed, X-shaped configuration on the Rathmullan stones appears to be late 12th or 13th century.

THE SOURCE OF THE STONE FOR THE NENDRUM MILLSTONES AND EARLY MILLSTONE MANUFACTURE

Rynne (1990, 25) states that the vast majority of Irish millstones were carved out of some type of sandstone. However, it is clear that granite was also widely employed. The Nendrum millstones have been identified as being of Mourne granite. It has long been clear that there were production sites in the Mournes where rotary querns were manufactured in the Early and Late Medieval periods. Jope and Ivens (1998, 111) mapped the distribution of sixteen Early-Medieval querns and five of Late-Medieval date, all made from Mourne granite. As expected, most are concentrated in eastern Co. Down, but examples have also been found in south Antrim, with one outlier as far away as the monastic site at Devenish, Co. Fermanagh. Such a distribution testifies to the popularity in Medieval times of Mourne granite for grinding stones. Nendrum provides the first recognised Early-Medieval example of its use to make millstones. However, excavation of a rath at Ballynarry, Co. Down produced what was interpreted as a large quern of Mourne granite of Early-Medieval date that had been re-used to make the lower stone of a smaller quern (Davison 1962, 72–74). The original stone, which exhibited a rynd socket, had a diameter of 71cm and is clearly an upper millstone refashioned into a quern with a diameter of 30.5cm.

Evans (1967, 165–166) documented the manufacture of Mourne granite millstones in the 18th and 19th centuries. Unfinished millstones have been found around 'Millstone Mountain', including one example measuring 1.52m in diameter (*op. cit.* 165). He recorded that in recent centuries, some of the general stoneworking exploited surface granite boulders rather than material quarried out of the rock face. However, it is of considerable interest that petrographical examination of the Nendrum stones suggests strongly that they were quarried from a granite outcrop and not worked up from a glacial

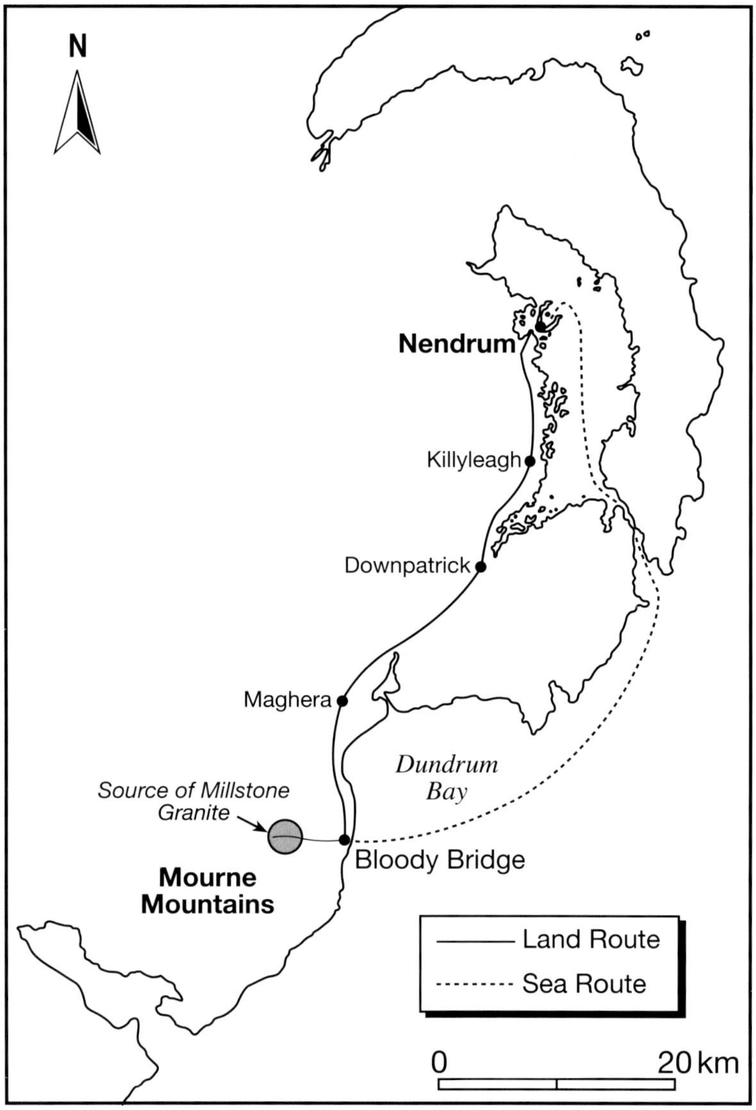

Fig. 7.8
The location of the source of the granite in the Mourne Mountains used to manufacture the millstones and the possible routes of transport to Nendrum

erratic boulder (see Meighan p. 204). Meighan's study suggests that a specific source for the millstones is in the upper reaches of the Bloody Bridge River (Fig. 7.8). This is located on the eastern slopes of the Mournes, close to the coast and approximately 25 miles (40km) as the crow flies, to the south-west of the monastery. In the 8th century this was a considerable distance to transport such heavy items without damage. Overland, a possible coastal route would have gone northwards, passing close to the early monastic site of Maghera, then over the sands in Inner Dundrum Bay at low tide or over a ford at the Blackstaff Bridge further to the north, and so to Nendrum via a route past Downpatrick and Killyleagh. However, it would have been much more convenient to bring the stones by sea, over Dundrum Bay and through the Narrows into Strangford Lough. This route would have involved the minimum of transport over land and, as the granite source lies near the shore, this can be considered a possibility.

The discovery of three unfinished granite millstones on a rocky hill-slope between 700m and 900m OD in the Wicklow Mountains near Lachan, pinpoints another production site (Inv. Wicklow 201). These stones had diameters ranging from 1.05m to 1.08m and central borings of 16cm. Their sizes suggest strongly that they were being made for an early watermill. Other examples of unfinished millstones in the Wicklow Mountains have been found around Glendalough (Inv. Wicklow 201, 202). One example measured 1.32m in diameter and was between 18cm and 34cm thick. The large size of the stone suggests it was being manufactured for a more modern mill.

An episode in the mid-7th-century *Life of St Brigit* by Cogitosus (Connolly and Picard 1987, 24–25) is of great interest in documenting some of the problems encountered in the manufacture of Early Medieval millstones. This work is probably the earliest hagiographic text to have survived and predates Adomnán's *Life of Columba* by several decades (*ibid.* 5). The 'millstone' story is the longest section in the text and tells how a millstone was brought to one of Brigit's monasteries, perhaps Kildare itself, by the miraculous intervention of the saint. The source of the stone possibly was the Wicklow

Mountains, not too far distant from Kildare. The story tells how stonecutters and workers were sent to obtain a suitable stone to make a millstone for the monastery, eventually finding one on the summit of a high and steep mountain. The stone was duly fashioned into a circular and perforated millstone. When a party arrived with oxen and workers to bring the stone back to the monastery, they found it impossible to get the oxen to the top of the mountain. Even if they had been able to do this, it would have been impossible for the oxen to pull the stone down the steep slope. It seemed as if the work would have to be abandoned until the monastic superior invoked the power of Brigit. Under her intercession, the stone was thrown over the cliffside and rolled, undamaged, over rocks and wet ground at the bottom of the slope where the oxen could not venture. From here it was safely brought to the monastic mill to join its matching stone.

The millstone was imbued with miraculous properties. Once a pagan, a druid, surreptitiously sent grain to the mill to be milled, but when it was put between the stones they refused to rotate. Later when the mill was entirely destroyed by fire, the only thing to survive was the special millstone, the other having been lost. After this it was placed at the entrance to the monastic enclosure where it was venerated as a holy object and, by touching it, many were cured of diseases and afflictions (Connolly 1987, 24). This story is of great value in illustrating the practical problems in the 7th century of transporting heavy millstones from mountain sources to mill sites and the effort involved in finding a suitable rock type from which to make them.

THE MILLHOUSES OF MILL 1 AND MILL 2

The millstones were housed in the millhouse and are the only certain artefacts belonging to it to survive. Unfortunately no trace of the millhouses belonging to the first and second mills survived *in situ*, although their location immediately above the deep wheelhouse can be firmly established. Presumably the millhouse of Mill 1 was dismantled when the new mill complex was constructed towards the end of the 8th century.

In the case of Mill 2, one is faced with the situation where the wheelhouse has survived almost complete, but there is practically no evidence of its millhouse. The original ground level of the area where it stood has been considerably lowered by tidal erosion so that all trace of its footprint has been destroyed. As no Irish Early Medieval horizontal-wheeled mill site has produce evidence (apart from stray timbers) of what its millhouse looked like, one is therefore left to speculate on their possible character. Attempted reconstruction drawings are largely based on recent surviving examples from elsewhere.

The representation of the millhouse of Mill 2 shown on Fig. 7.9 is to a great degree speculative, unlike that of the wheelhouse, which is based on solid evidence of surviving remains. The representation shows a rectangular building partially built in stone and partially in wood with thatched roof but other types of building are possible of course.

Fig. 7.9
Conjectural reconstruction drawing of Mill 2 (J. Patience)

In attempting a reconstruction of the millhouse of Mill 2 the fundamental questions are whether it was rectangular or round in plan and whether its was built in wood or stone. The presence of a rectangular wheelhouse would seem to imply that the mill building above was of the same form. In the 7th and 8th centuries, the predominant Irish domestic building tradition was of round wooden buildings. This underwent a transition, probably complete by the end of the 10th century, to rectangular houses (Lynn 1978a). Churches on the other hand appear always to have been rectangular and it seems probable that millhouses comprised a class of building that was always built in rectangular form also, and may be viewed as belonging to the same architectural tradition.

One of the possible pieces of evidence that the first mill building was made of wood is the many mortised beams found in the dam. Most of these, however, were probably originally destined for well-jointed timber buildings within the monastic enclosure, but instead were utilized in making the dam (see p. 251 for this interpretation). Since the wheelhouse of Mill 2 was stone-built, it may seem logical to conclude that its millhouse was too. Documentary evidence for stone buildings in Ireland only commences in the late 8th century. Indeed the earliest reference to a stone church in the annals occurs in AD 789 (*AU*), the year of the dating of the construction of Mill 2 when an *oratorii lapidei* (stone oratory) is mentioned at Armagh. In theory, therefore, it is possible that the mill-house of Mill 2 was built in stone, but the excavation produced no compelling evidence that this was so, but some evidence that part of it may have been in wood. If the building had been of stone, one might expect a sizeable amount of fallen masonry within the primary silting of the wheelhouse, which there was not. The large number of offcuts and other small fragments of wood, and the remains of wattle panelling, found in the base of the wheelhouse and millpond of Mill 2, suggest that the millhouse had at least a major wooden component in its structure. The presence of offcuts may suggest the salvaging of timber from a wooden building and its systematic dismantling after it went out of use. This also may account for the absence from the floor of the wheelhouse below of any structural timbers belonging to the millhouse, which might have been expected. However, one very important piece of evidence — a beam with a tenon, which had grooves along its side into which planks would have been fitted (see Fig. 9.15 and pps 245-246) — was found in the primary fill of the penstock. This timber was probably a discard from the salvage of the millhouse, and presumably was thrown into the millpond, being carried by the flow into the penstock. Similar members were found at Morett, Co. Laois. (Lucas 1953, 15, 22), suggesting that part of the millhouse at least, may have been plank–built.

The depositional context of the large amount of wattle debris present in the wheelhouse silt strongly supports the interpretation that it was derived from the mill building above, perhaps originally forming internal panelling within the building, or a part of the roof structure. Reconstruction drawings of horizontal-wheeled mills almost invariably show a small millhouse, for instance the detailed depiction by Rynne of Cloontycarty mill, Co. Cork is good example (Rynne 1989b, 22). Ideas of the size of the millhouse may be strongly influenced by the size of the wheelhouse below and by descriptions of the very small millhouses of horizontal-wheeled mills of 19th-century date, especially those of the Shetland Islands (Goudie 1886). However, the dimensions of the wheelhouse do not limit those of the millhouse, since only the grinding floor had to be located over the wheel-house. Thus, it is possible to envisage that many of the Early Medieval millhouses, especially those attached to a monastery, may have been sizeable structures. In the case of Mill 2 the dam at the back of the wheelhouse is about 5m wide, and the adjacent platform to the north is about 6m wide and therefore there would have ample space for a sizeable building.

Direct archaeological information on non-domestic timber buildings is very sparse, and most of our current knowledge comes from the documentary sources relating to churches. Two oft-quoted 7th-century references to the appearances of wooden churches are available. They occur in Cogitosus' *Life of Brigit* (Connolly and Picard 1987) and the *Hisperica Famina* (Herron 1974). An architectural interpretation of the *Hisperica Famina* description has been attempted by Brady (1997, 327–335), who notes the terms 'candle-shaped beams', 'sides joined with four-fold fastenings', 'square foundations', 'solid beam work of massive enclosure', 'vaulted roof' 'squared beams' and 'an assembly of planks' (Herron, 1974, 108–109; Brady 1997, 328). The description indicates the existence of accomplished timber-framed buildings in the 7th century.

SOURCING THE NENDRUM GRANITE MILLSTONE MATERIAL
I.G. Meighan

Petrographic examination

This has been undertaken on Nendrum Mill 2 millstone material comprising (1) the lower and upper millstones, and (2) a number of relatively small fragments from elsewhere on the site. It is confirmed that all of the material is granite in the strictest petrological sense.

The two millstones appear to be lithologically identical, being a relatively fine-grained granite with abundant dark (smoky) quartz crystals and a low ferromagnesian mineral content (colour index). The rock is unfoliated — i.e. there is no directional fabric — and is totally devoid of enclaves, that is, inclusions of other rock types. Drusy (gas) cavities are sparse. Given the thickness of these millstones, it is apparent that their source was probably a granite outcrop, as opposed to glacial erratic boulders, where the principal natural fractures (the main or master joints) have a relatively close spacing, and that it was possible to remove 'platy' slabs of large area but perhaps less than 20cm in thickness (the upper millstone is 8cm and the lower stone 11cm in maximum thickness).

The small fragments, some rather superficially weathered, seem to be similar to the actual millstones, with drusy cavities observable in certain specimens. However, in high-level (near surface) granite intrusions, the presence or absence of such cavities can be somewhat variable on a local scale. Overall it is concluded that all the material examined is probably from the same rock outcrop.

General sourcing

The most obvious potential granitic sources for the Nendrum material are (1) the Caledonian (425 million years) Newry granodiorite complex (which extends from Slieve Croob to Slieve Gullion), and (2) the Tertiary (56 million years) Mourne Mountains central complex which is subdivided into an eastern and a western centre.

A Newry granodiorite source can be precluded with confidence on mineralogical and textural grounds. Typical Newry granodiorite has a relatively high ferromagnesian mineral content (colour index), a mineral alignment (foliation), inclusions of darker rock (enclaves) and an absence of drusy (gas) cavities. As described above, the Nendrum material has none of these diagnostic features.

The mineralogy (e.g. dark quartz) rock type (granite as opposed to granodiorite) and texture of the millstone material are thoroughly compatible with a single source in the Mourne Mountains. These comprise five separate granite intrusions (G1–5 inclusive) with G1, G2 and G3 in the eastern centre and G4 and G5 in the western one. Each individual granite can be identified on a combination of mineralogy and texture (Meighan *et al.* 2002): there are also mappable textural and mineralogical variants within each (excluding G1: Meighan *et al.* 1984).

The relatively high content of dark (smoky) quartz in the millstone material is very suggestive of G2, the second and most extensive granite of the eastern centre. Mourne granite G2 has been subdivided into several mappable variants (Harry and Richey 1963; Hood 1981; Meighan *et al.* 1984). Harry and Richey (1963) identified a fine-grained facies of G2 in the northern and western parts of this body, the presence of which was confirmed during the detailed field mapping of Hood (1981). It is this fine-grained facies of G2 which is definitely represented in the Nendrum material.

Specific sourcing

Evans (1967) mentions the quarrying of millstones in the vicinity of Millstone Mountain in the north-eastern part of the eastern Mourne centre. Similarly Kirk (2002) discusses and illustrates an abandoned millstone in the Slievenaglogh area in the northern part of the eastern Mourne centre. Significantly, both of these areas are in the fine-grained facies of G2. However, this activity almost certainly relates to more recent exploitations than those relevant to Nendrum.

Outcrops in relatively accessible river valleys are likely to have been favoured in early millstone quarrying activities in preference to elevated, 'open hillside' localities such as Millstone Mountain, from where the transport of large granite slabs would have been more awkward. In the upper reaches of the Bloody Bridge River there are two adjacent (now disused) quarries in the fine-grained facies of G2 (grid reference J 363267). Significantly the main (master) joints here are gently inclined and closely spaced — a series of measurements in the upper quarry indicated a mean spacing of approximately 20cm (range 11–35cm). These planar fractures appear to be parallel to the land surface and are thus probably 'pressure release' rather than cooling joints. Regardless of origin, their relatively close spacing and sub-horizontal attitude would have presented a highly favourable aspect to early stone workers in search of suitable and extractable millstone material.

The fine-grained granite in these quarries can be slightly drusy and, overall, appears to match well the Nendrum stones. Thus, it is suggested somewhat tentatively that its millstone material was taken from an outcrop of fine-grained G2 in the upper reaches of the Bloody Bridge River in the eastern Mourne Mountains. The proposed locality (J 363267) was subsequently developed into the existing (but now abandoned) quarries. Finally, it is interesting to note that the Nendrum millstones constitute evidence for the earliest major quarrying of Mourne granite in the upper reaches of the Bloody Bridge River.

Chapter 8

An Examination of Extractable Energy and Milling Capacity of Mill 2

Max Browne

Chapter 8
An Examination of Extractable Energy and Milling Capacity of Mill 2

Max Browne

INTRODUCTION AND SUMMARY

This chapter considers quantitative aspects of milling at Nendrum for Mill 2 in its final configuration as revealed by excavation. Unfortunately as Mill 1 was partly destroyed to build Mill 2, it has not been possible to obtain the key measurements needed for a similar analysis of it. Evidence for the following assumptions is discussed below: first, that tidal amplitudes in Strangford Lough at the end of the 8th century AD were similar, and had a similar pattern, to those at the end of the 20th century, and second, that mean sea level was approximately the same for each period. Typical daily tidal curves for 12 lunar months in the late-8th century were simulated using modern data for the Standard Port of Belfast, with corrections for the location of Nendrum.

After studying aspects of the design and mounting of the Nendrum waterwheel, the tidal data, the levels and other dimensions of the millpond, penstock and orifice, a computer model was set up to calculate the annual energy — the energy using all tides which theoretically could have been imparted to the water jet as it entered the waterwheel. Parts of the millpond dam have been eroded considerably and there is no firm archaeological evidence to show how the intake sluice gate to the millpond was sited. It is postulated, therefore, that its sill was at 1.4m OD. This assumption reduces the maximum annual energy that could have been imparted to the water jet by 21%, to about 2.8 megawatt-hours (Table 8.4).

Output figures for milled grain from two other horizontal-wheeled mills, together with efficiency data from scale-model tests for both flat and shaped blades, were used to obtain a figure of *c.* 39kg of coarsely-milled barley per kilowatt-hour of net water jet energy. When applied to the energy potentially available at Nendrum Mill 2, this figure gives a theoretical potential annual output of 50 tonnes of barley. Only a fraction of this potential could have been realised in practice however. Corresponding output figures for other milled products are also indicated. The difficulties of assessing what fraction of gross available energy might have been used in practice are discussed. It is suggested that the calculations of gross annual energy that could have been imparted to the water jet are fairly reliable, but that the further calculations to arrive at the gross potential output of milled grain require some assumptions that may be less certain.

THE WORKING CYCLE OF MILL 2

The interval between one high tide and the next is roughly twelve and one third hours, and the operation of the tide mill would have fallen into three phases, each very approximately of equal duration (Fig. 8.1).

Phase 1

At high tide, when the millpond had filled, the intake sluice gate and penstock sluice gate were closed.

Phase 2

When the water level in the wheelhouse and tailrace had fallen below the waterwheel (about four hours later), the penstock sluice gate was opened, allowing the jet to commence driving the waterwheel and continue until the rising tide in the wheelhouse reached the wheel once more. This working period would, again, have been about four hours.

Phase 3

Waiting, with the millpond intake sluice gate open, until the rising tide had filled the millpond again

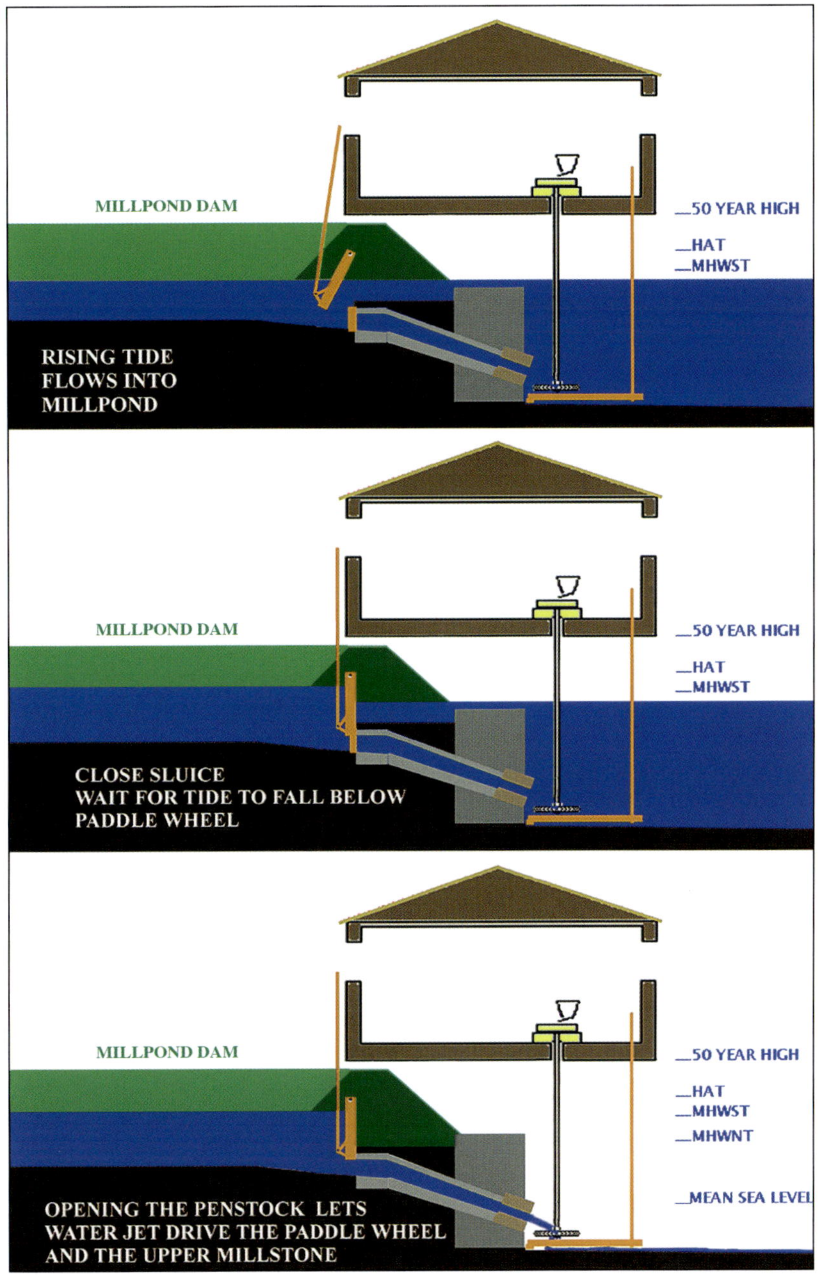

Fig. 8.1
The working cycle of Mill 2
Note: Fig.ure 8.1 shows an intake sluice gate controlled from the millhouse, but this is only diagrammatic. It is also possible that the intake sluice gate was sited more remotely in the dam and controlled from there.

SEA LEVEL AND THE TIDAL REGIMEN IN THE LATE 8TH CENTURY

The greatest possible astronomical tide-raising forces would occur if the moon and the sun were to come into exact mutual alignment with the earth at their closest respective distances. For this to happen, four conditions are required: proximity to syzygy, closeness to perigee, a node and perihelion. The most critical is the proximity to syzygy, a term that refers to either new or full moon, hence maxima in tidal strength occur twice in the synodic month of 29.5 days (the 'fortnightly' spring tides). The next most critical condition is the closeness of the moon to perigee, the point on its elliptical orbit closest to the earth. When an analysis is made to find the times when all four conditions are most closely met, the 1,800-year cycle becomes apparent with progressive weakening and then strengthening of successive centennial maxima in tidal forcing. The last maximum occurred in AD 1425 (Keeling and

Whorf 2000), and an inspection of the combined effect of the cycles indicates that in the late-8th century, the pattern of tidal forcing would have been very much as it was at the end of the 20th century.

Changes in mean sea level in Northern Ireland since the 8th century have been of the order of a few centimetres. To a certain extent, however, this will have been offset by the glacial rebound of Northern Ireland after the last Ice Age (the reason why, for example, Scandinavia currently is rising with respect to sea level). The combined result of these two small effects acting in different directions would be very small indeed (J.E. Jones, Proudman Oceanographic Laboratory, *pers. comm.* 2000). Tide tables for 1999 are therefore appropriate as a source of statistics for an analysis to approximate the performance of the tide mill in the late-8th century.

TIDAL HEIGHT STATISTICS AND OBSERVATIONS

In order to translate published data for the Standard Port of Belfast into statistics for the Nendrum site, observations of high tide levels on a tide gauge at the site were recorded through May and June 1999, to include several spring and neap periods. When the differences were plotted the trend was a straight line, which correlated spring high-water levels of 1.90m OD for Nendrum to 3.5 CD (chart datum) for Belfast, and neap high-water levels of 1.40m OD for Nendrum to 3.0 CD for Belfast. This was compared to published data from the Strangford Lough Admiralty chart No. 2156. Chart datum (CD) is a local datum used by Admiralty Charts that often approximates to the lowest astronomical tide in the area covered by the chart. Ordnance datum (OD) on the other hand is related to mean sea level and is countrywide in its application.

Table 8.1: Tidal heights at Nendrum relative to the Standard Port of Belfast

	MHWS	MHWN	MLWN	MLWS
Belfast	3.50 CD	3.00 CD	1.10 CD	0.40 CD
Killyleagh	3.80 CD	3.30 CD	--	--
Quoile Barrier	3.70 CD	3.20 CD	0.80 CD	0.30 CD
Nendrum	3.76 CD*	3.26 CD*		
Nendrum	1.90 OD	1.40 OD	-1.06 OD	-1.56 OD

*from observations at site.

Thus, observations confirm that Nendrum heights of high water do not differ significantly from those within the Lough at the Quoile Barrier and at Killyleagh and hence, that high water predictions for the site can be obtained readily from the Standard Port of Belfast by applying the same corrections as for the Quoile Barrier. The assumption has been made that low water at Nendrum is also the same as low water at the Quoile Barrier.

THE POTENTIAL FOR ANNUAL ENERGY GENERATION BY THE MILLPOND AND ORIFICE

With the exception of the intake sluice gate, it was possible to measure all of the essential elements of the tidal mill system as they existed when it was in operation, some time after AD 789.

Table 8.2: Key data

Area of millpond	2000	Sq. m.	measured
Orifice mean diameter	15.50	centimetres	measured
Level of the orifice	-0.12	metres OD	measured
Level of penstock intake sill	+0.95	metres OD	measured
Level of the wheelhouse floor	-0.75	metres OD	measured
Top of waterwheel	-0.40	metres OD	deduced
Water level for operation	-0.60	metres OD	deduced
Coefficient of velocity (C_v)	0.96	dimensionless	calculated
Coefficient of contraction (C_c)	0.99	dimensionless	calculated

The coefficient of velocity (C_v) has been calculated from the dimensions and material of the penstock and orifice using an estimated friction value of 0.01 (*cf.* 0.005 for smooth and 0.01 for rough pipes). The coefficient of contraction (C_c) derives from the degree of taper in the orifice. The coefficient of discharge (C_d) is 0.95 (the product of C_v and C_c).

Table 8.3: Computed annual energy from all useable tides - no restriction to pond filling

1 Height of layer above Ordnance Datum (OD)	2 Volume of 10 cm layer Cu. M.	3 Number of tides filling layer	4 Hours workable per tide of this height	5 Velocity at orifice from this layer m/s	6 Discharge time for this layer (hours)	7 Number adjusted for time workable	8 Layer Energy mega-joules	9 Gross energy to jet kWh
2.2	200	4	3.81	6.44	0.46	4	4.9	5
2.1	200	32	4.07	6.31	0.47	32	4.7	42
2.0	194	77	4.03	6.17	0.46	77	4.4	95
1.9	188	146	3.99	6.02	0.46	146	4.1	167
1.8	183	236	3.91	5.87	0.46	236	3.8	251
1.7	177	357	3.77	5.72	0.46	357	3.5	352
1.6	172	456	3.70	5.57	0.45	456	3.3	416
1.5	167	552	3.58	5.41	0.45	552	3.0	464
1.4	158	623	3.55	5.24	0.44	620	2.7	471
1.3	150	675	3.37	5.07	0.44	670	2.5	457
1.2	143	683	3.17	4.90	0.43	648	2.2	397
1.1	136	683	2.99	3.53	0.54	588	1.4	225
1.0	129	683	2.63	1.04	1.73	306	0.8	67
		Total gross energy of the jet for 12 lunar months, kilowatt hours					=	3408
		Total gross energy of the jet for a calendar year, kilowatt hours					=	3514
		Includes energy from all tides with High Water levels of + 1.0 OD, or more						

Table 8.3 shows the gross energy that the system could have imparted to the water jet in a year, as computed from the key data from the site and the tidal statistics. For the waterwheel to have operated, tide level must have been below -0.60m OD to adequately clear the underside of the waterwheel. By interpolation of the tide curves, working periods of about four hours at springs and 3.5 hours at neaps can be seen as typical. But as part of an overall computer model of tidal energy generation at the site, individual working times for a range of tide heights have been calculated and these are tabulated in column 4 against the height of the preceding tide shown in column 1. For an individual tide, however, column 4 is an approximation because the working period depends on the height and range of both the preceding and the following tide. Nevertheless, the height of the preceding tide gives a sufficiently accurate indication of the working period, when considered over the year.

In the computer model, the millpond has been considered as a series of horizontal layers, each 10cm deep, as shown in Table 8.3.

Column 1 of the Table shows Ordnance Datum levels in decimetre increments.
Column 2 shows the estimated volume of the ten-centimetre layer whose base is at the level indicated in column 1.
Column 3 shows the average number of tides in twelve lunar months that reach or exceed the level in column 1.
Column 4 shows the average hours per tide below -0.6m OD, following the high water level of column 1. This is the average available working time for a tide of that height.
Column 5 shows the mean velocity of the jet from the water layer indicated by column 1.
Column 6 shows the hours required to discharge the pond volume specified by column 2.
Column 7 shows the number of times in the period that the layer in column 2 can contribute its potential energy, allowing for the restriction imposed by the available working time corresponding to the high-water level specified by column 1.
Column 8 shows the potential energy (in mega-joules per tide) imparted to the jet before entering the waterwheel by the layer specified in column 2, when unrestricted by working hours.
Column 9 is the total energy (in kilowatt hours) that could be imparted to the jet by each layer in 12 lunar months whilst the waterwheel is above water level.

Individual high-tide levels and working times are influenced by atmospheric pressure and surface winds. For example, a low-pressure weather system might raise the water level by say 30cm but at the same time decrease the working time, so that the extra energy available could not be fully utilised. A high-pressure weather system would have the opposite effect, and it has been assumed that in considering energy availability over a long period, the net effect of weather may be ignored.

Table 8.3 is based on all available energy from useable tides having been exploited to the full, and also on the assumption that the millpond intake sluice gate imposed no restriction on the entry of water to the millpond at any level, although in practice this would not have been the case.

To obtain a figure that may be closer to what, potentially, could have been achieved by the actual system, it is postulated, in keeping with the intake gate configuration suggested below, that only those tides which reached or exceeded 1.6m OD would have been worth impounding. It is also postulated that when the pond level fell below 1.1m OD, the jet velocity would be insufficient for effective milling. When the pond level falls below 1.19m OD the control of flow passes from the orifice to the weir at the penstock sill, and soon after this a hydraulic jump begins to form in the penstock. As the depth over the penstock sill decreases further, the power of the jet falls off rapidly with decreasing pond level. The formulae used by the model reflect this.

The effects of these restrictions are shown in Table 8.4, with the annual gross energy at the jet reduced to 2778 kilowatt hours.

Table 8.4: Annual energy from useable tides – *pond filling restricted by intake sluice level*

1 Height of layer above Ordnance Datum (OD)	2 Volume of 10 cm layer Cu. M.	3 Number of tides filling layer	4 Hours workable per tide of this height	5 Velocity at orifice from this layer m/s	6 Discharge time for this layer (hours)	7 Number adjusted for time workable	8 Layer Energy mega-joules	9 Gross energy to jet kWh
2.2	200	4	3.81	6.44	0.46	4	4.9	5
2.1	200	32	4.07	6.39	0.46	32	4.7	42
2.0	194	77	4.03	6.24	0.46	77	4.4	95
1.9	188	146	3.99	6.10	0.45	146	4.1	167
1.8	183	236	3.91	5.95	0.45	236	3.8	251
1.7	177	357	3.77	5.80	0.45	357	3.5	352
1.6	172	456	3.70	5.64	0.45	456	3.3	416
1.5	167	456	3.58	5.48	0.45	456	3.0	384
1.4	158	456	3.55	5.31	0.44	454	2.7	344
1.3	150	456	3.37	5.14	0.43	452	2.5	309
1.2	143	456	3.17	4.96	0.42	426	2.2	261
1.1	136	456	2.99	3.53	0.54	368	1.4	70
1.0	129	456	2.63	1.04	1.73	111	0.8	0
	Total gross energy of the jet for 12 lunar months, kilowatt hours						=	2695
	Total gross energy of the jet for a calendar year, kilowatt hours						=	2778
	Tides with High Water levels less than 1.6 OD are not used.							
	Between 1.1 and 1.2 OD only jet velocities > 4 metres per sec. are used.							

THE MILLPOND AND ITS INTAKE STRUCTURE

The highest tide level observed at Mahee Island in the last half century was 3.16m OD on 1 February 2002, caused by a high spring tide coinciding with a very deep depression. The highest astronomical tide (HAT) that was predicted for the year 1999 was 2.2m OD. The height of the millpond dam, at its highest surviving point located at its north-eastern end, is 2.6m OD. It is highly probable that the original bank was at least 2.6m OD over its full length and that it continued across the north-eastern end at the same level, over the buried part of the penstock.

No evidence has been found to confirm how or where the intake of water was controlled. A rectangular aperture with a gate that was 40cm deep and 1m wide, with its lower edge at 1.2m OD would have served. But a sill as low 1.2m OD poses a problem because the northern dam appears to be undisturbed at that level and the present height of the existing stone wall of the wheelhouse is 1.5m OD.

A high sill shortens the time available for water to be impounded. For higher tides this limitation can be overcome by making the sill longer, but tides with a lesser range will still be restricted. The larger the aperture the higher the proportion of lesser range tides that will be stored, but a large aperture is more difficult to close and to seal against leaks. Computer modelling suggests that a sill at 1.4m OD and 2.8m wide, and with an aperture 25cm deep, is a reasonable compromise. For the calculation of Table 8.4 this is the configuration that has been postulated.

In Table 8.4 the discounting of tides that did not reach 1.6m OD is a simplifying approximation, since for tides between 1.5m and 1.6m OD there would have been partial filling of the millpond, providing a small amount of additional potential energy. But this has been neglected, and may be considered perhaps as compensation for leakage which has not been allowed for otherwise.

The selection of an appropriate sill level was largely a matter of assessing probabilities. Only the foundations of the dam survive behind the retaining wall of the wheelhouse. The lowest part of the top of this stone wall at present is 1.5m OD, but it is semi permeable and if the closing dam had been set back a little from the face of the wall, allowing water to enter laterally as well, a multiple gate system, partly with a lower sill, could not be ruled out entirely. However, there is no positive evidence for this.

Whatever configuration was actually used, one can be sure that it was a practical and effective design, in keeping with rest of the mill. It would have been constructed of timber in part at least, but after long exposure to tidal erosion and weathering, no parts have survived.

The penstock

Where the difference in level between the headrace and the waterwheel is nearly constant, as is the case for many river- and stream-fed mills, a flume with a free water surface can be arranged to work very satisfactorily. On the other hand, for a tide mill the working head usually varies significantly during the cycle, so a penstock, which runs full and under positive pressure, is needed.

Many Post-Medieval horizontal-wheeled mills on rivers carry the water from the headrace to the millwheel through an open flume with a free water surface, but at the Nendrum tide mill the penstock was totally enclosed. Surprisingly, all of the early horizontal-wheeled mills in Ireland that have been excavated to date had either a penstock or a flume with a lid (running full for some part of its length perhaps). This means that if small horizontal-wheeled mills with open flumes did exist in Ireland in the early period, they have not survived.

Fig. 8.2
The penstock and waterwheel

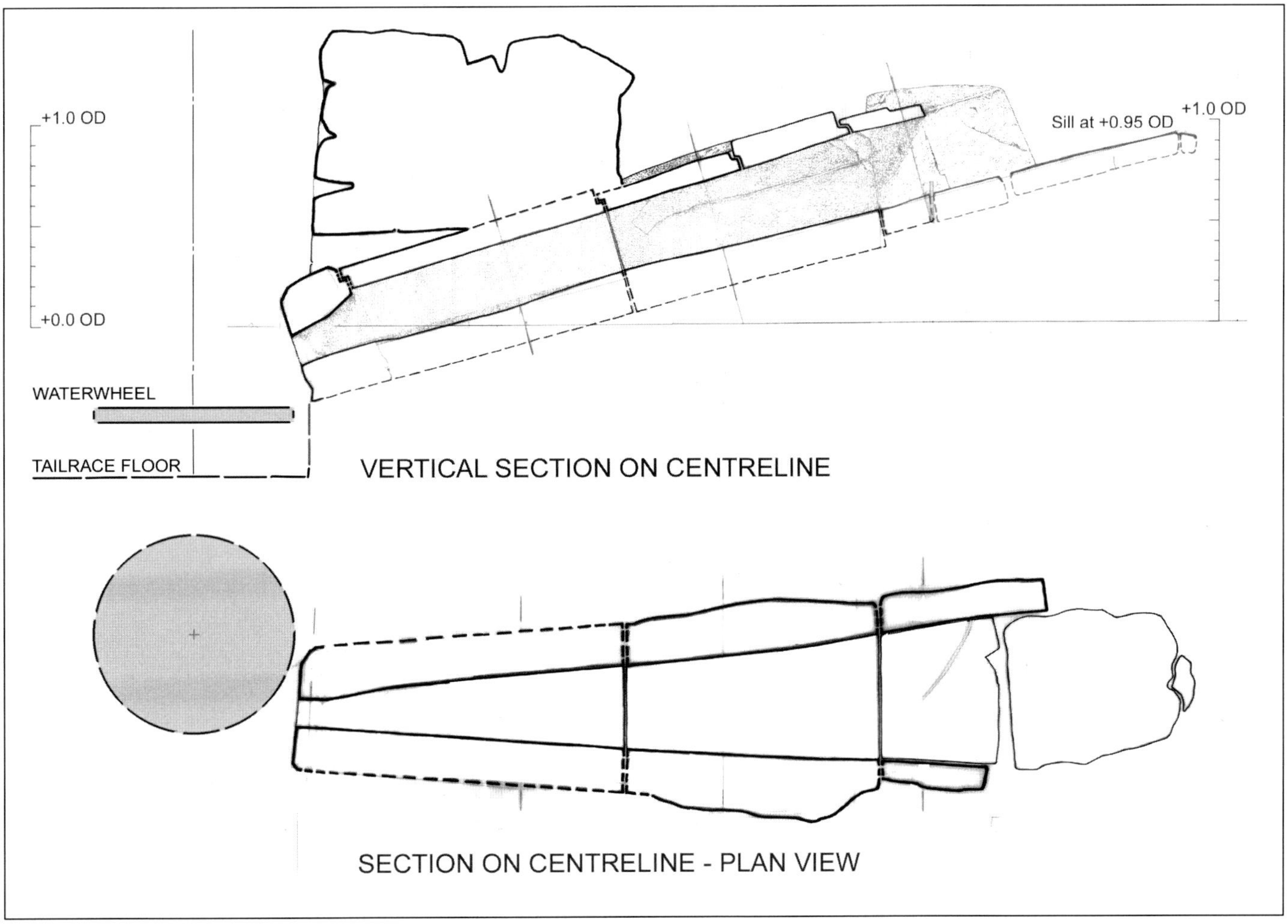

The penstock found at Nendrum is unique, being constructed of stone instead of timber. There is a gradual reduction of cross-sectional area from the millpond to the orifice, an efficient design that gives rise to minimal loss of energy (Figs 8.2 and 5.10).

It is assumed that the flow was turned on and off by a wooden sluice gate at the millpond end, and there is some archaeological evidence that this was the case. For the flume and orifice as a unit, a value was calculated for the coefficient of velocity. This allows for friction losses in the flow. The coefficient of contraction, on the other hand allows for the change of dimensions of the jet at the vena contracta, after it has left the orifice, but for an orifice of the shape found at Nendrum this contraction is very slight.

The waterwheel

The longest of the three wooden paddles, recovered at the bottom of the wheelhouse is 40.5cm in overall length. The angle of taper at the base is 15°, which might possibly indicate a waterwheel of twenty four blades and imply an overall diameter of 97–98cm (see p. 176, Fig. 8.3). On the other hand, there may have been fewer blades, but if the number were considerably less, the spacing between the blades at the working radius would have been too large to ensure that all of the jet reacted efficiently with them.

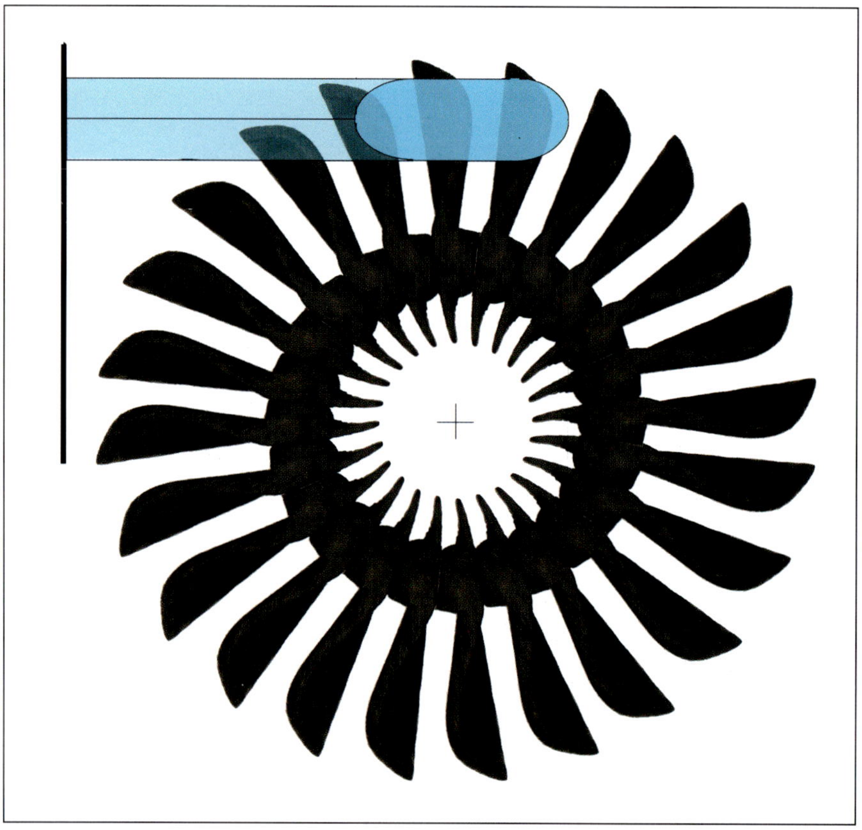

Fig. 8.3
The waterwheel and water jet

Assuming a 24-blade wheel, if the tops of the blades were 28cm below the centre of the orifice, the footprint of the jet on the top of the wheel, throughout its working range, would have fallen comfortably upon a wheel of 97cm diameter, its centre 50cm out from the orifice and offset laterally by 40cm. The area covered by the jet between maximum and minimum working head as it fell on the tops of the blades would have been about 15cm wide and some 30cm long (Fig. 8.3).

Had the diameter of the waterwheel been greater, the proximity of the wall below the orifice would have required it to have been further out, and lower, in order to have the jet fall efficiently upon it. But height is restricted because clear flow to the tailrace needs to be maintained. The offset from the centerline of the jet would also have been greater. Had the wheel been smaller and with fewer blades, it would have been less effective.

SCALE MODEL TESTS ON HORIZONTAL WATERWHEELS

Tests by Hawkesly (Hawkesley 2000, 25 and 26) on models at roughly one-tenth scale showed that when running at their optimum blade speeds, the efficiencies shown in Table 8.5 could be achieved. The blade speed for maximum efficiency is in the region of half the jet speed, but it is also affected by the shape of the blade and the angle of incidence. Thus the miller, having set the tentering for the fineness required, must control the speed of the stone by adjusting the feed rate of the grain.

Table 8.5: Efficiencies of blade designs from model tests

A. Flat blades (open tips), fed from an open flume	24%
B. Flat blades (shrouded tips), fed from a penstock and orifice	38%
C. Shaped blades carved from solid, fed from penstock and orifice	43%
D. Shaped blades (Nendrum pattern), fed from a penstock and orifice	46%

Comparison of Nendrum with other horizontal-wheeled mills to estimate its potential output of milled grain

The relationship between the power applied to, and the output of milled grain from, water-driven mills is not easily determined from the published literature. Descriptions of mills usually lack either sufficient information to make a reasonable assessment of the power that was used, or else the conditions relating to the production figures are uncertain. In addition, the type of grain, the extent to which it had been dried and the fineness of the final product, all affect the energy requirement. For example, coarsely ground barley for animal feed may need only one fifth of the milling work needed for very finely-ground barley (Jones D H, *pers. comm.* 2000). An assessment, however, has been made based on experiments carried out by D. H. Jones at the Hellumylnan mill in the Faeroes in 1955 (from 'Hellumylnan DK-4501 Grinding tests', a privately circulated, but unpublished report by Jones D H, 1955), and from information provided by de Iturribarria (*pers. comm.* 2000) on his horizontal-wheeled tide mill in the Basque Country.

The Faeroes mill is typical of small mills with flat blades situated on a stream, that were once prevalent in the area. The Basque horizontal-wheeled tide mill dates from 1683, and its mode of operation is essentially the same as for the Nendrum mill. For both the Faeroes and the Basque mills, figures are available for the rates at which grain was ground, and gross power has been assessed from their known dimensions. In both cases, however, there are factors that affect the assessment. In the Faeroes experiment the profile of the water flow in the flume is not defined with enough precision. In the historical figures from the Basque mill, 50 to 80kg per hour of barley is the quoted output, but it is not clear whether 80kg per hour was the average over a spring tide or the rate at the start of discharge from a spring tide height. Because of these uncertainties, it would be useful to analyse further suitable examples if they can be found.

In Table 8.6 below, the efficiency for Hellumylnan 24%, has been taken from Table 8.5, Case A: flat blades with open tips fed from an open flume. The Basque waterwheel is cut from solid stone and could be regarded as Case B, but the blades are curved in plan, which gives it a small degree of similarity to Case C. As a compromise, an efficiency of 39% has been estimated. The Nendrum blades have been taken as similar to Case D with an efficiency of 46%.

Table 8.6: Grain milled as a function of energy applied

		Hellumylnan, Faeroe Islands	Portu Errota, Basque Mill
Gross head	metres	1.03	2.65
Flow	litres/s	77	198
Gross Power	Watts	775	5241
Efficiency	%	24.0%	39.0%
Net Power	Watts	186	2044
Milled barley	kg/hr.	7.9	80
Milled barley	kg/kWh	42.5	39.1
		Nendrum mill	
Net annual energy	kWh	2778	from Table 4.
Efficiency	%	46.0%	
Coarse barley	kg/kWh	**39.1**	from Portu Errota above.
Potential output: Coarsely milled barley		**50.0**	**Tonnes per year**

The milled barley produced at Hellumylnan and at Portu Errota may well have been slightly different products, with the similarity between the number of kilograms per kilowatt-hour at the two sites, largely a coincidence. However, the 39 and 43kg per kilowatt-hour found in Table 8.3 are probably reasonable figures for coarsely-milled barley, bearing in mind that 36kg per kilowatt-hour, or one bushel of wheat per hour per horsepower has been mentioned by Hawkesley, presumably for bread flour, although to what stage of the process the horsepower related, is uncertain (Hawkesley *pers. comm.* 2003). In addition, figures from Denmark indicate an accepted figure there of 50kg per kilowatt-hour for barley (Jespersen 1994), but neither the British nor the Danish information is first-hand, and both lack supporting details.

The upper millstone at Nendrum was concave to match the lower stone, which was convex on top. At 83cm diameter, the stones were relatively small compared to many Post-Medieval millstones. The assumption that output per kilowatt-hour is independent of the size and shape of stones, within an appropriate range, seems reasonable, but has not been verified.

Table 8.7: Typical parameters at Nendrum, two cases

		minimum useful head	mean spring head
Water jet:			
Gross head at orifice	m	1.22	2.02
Jet velocity at orifice	m/sec	4.89	5.98
Orifice angle to horizontal	Deg.	24	24
Coefficient of velocity (Cv)		0.95	0.95
Orifice area	sq. m	0.019	0.019
Flow	litres/sec	91	111
Density	kg/litre	1.02	1.02
Fall to paddle wheel	m	0.28	0.28
Vertical velocity (jet)	m/sec	3.07	3.38
Horizontal velocity (jet)	m/sec	4.47	5.47
Power of jet, gross	Watts	1258	2347
Horizontal waterwheel:			
Speed of waterwheel	rpm	75	87
Working radius	m	0.40	0.40
Blade velocity	m/sec	3.14	3.64
Relative water velocity	m/sec	3.35	3.84
Power from blades	Watts	586	1061
Millstone diameter	m	0.83	0.83
Milled barley	kg/kW.hr	39	39
Milled barley	kg/hr.	23	42

Table 8.7 above shows typical values of several variables, including the power output and the output of milled grain from the Nendrum mill for two conditions:

1. Where the head corresponds to the millpond being almost empty but with the flow still controlled by the orifice, and hence there is tranquil flow in the penstock.
2. Where the millpond has been filled to the level of a mean spring tide and the penstock runs full throughout.

The gross annual energy shown in Table 8.4, on which potential output in Table 8.6 depends, is a theoretical maximum and it is difficult to assess how much might have been used in practice. Not all of the useable tides would have been worked and, for those that were, the operators would not have maintained optimum efficiency at all times. Much depends on the extent to which night tides were used. The drag stick was invented at a very early date, but precisely when is unknown. If it had been available at Nendrum, the automation of the feed rate of grain from the hopper could have allowed semi-unattended operation, and if that were the case, night tides are more likely to have been utilised. It was usual in many watermills to run with the feed rate a little below the optimum to prevent the stones from binding. If night tides were being worked, adequate illumination would have been needed.

THE COMPUTATIONS

The calculation of gross annual energy that theoretically could have been imparted to the water jet is probably reasonably reliable, being based on measurements of the exceptionally well-preserved tidal mill system, as it existed when it was in operation some time after AD 789. However, bearing in mind that output quantities vary by a large factor according to the fineness of the grinding and the dryness of the grain, any calculations to arrive at the potential output of milled grain must obviously allow for a substantial margin of uncertainty. Looking beyond the calculated potential to try to estimate the probable output that might actually have been achieved soon becomes highly speculative; nevertheless it can be a useful exercise to highlight areas that need further research. Questions arise about, for example, crop yields, grain consumption for various needs including the brewing of ale, how the grain was dried, milling organized and how it all fitted into the routine of the monastery.

Conclusion

The well-balanced nature of the hydraulic design, built in stone, leaves a strong impression of millwrights at Nendrum who thoroughly understood and coped with the complex challenge of harnessing tidal energy as well as the niceties of an efficient horizontal waterwheel.

Chapter 9

Wood and Woodland

The worked wood from Mills 1 and 2

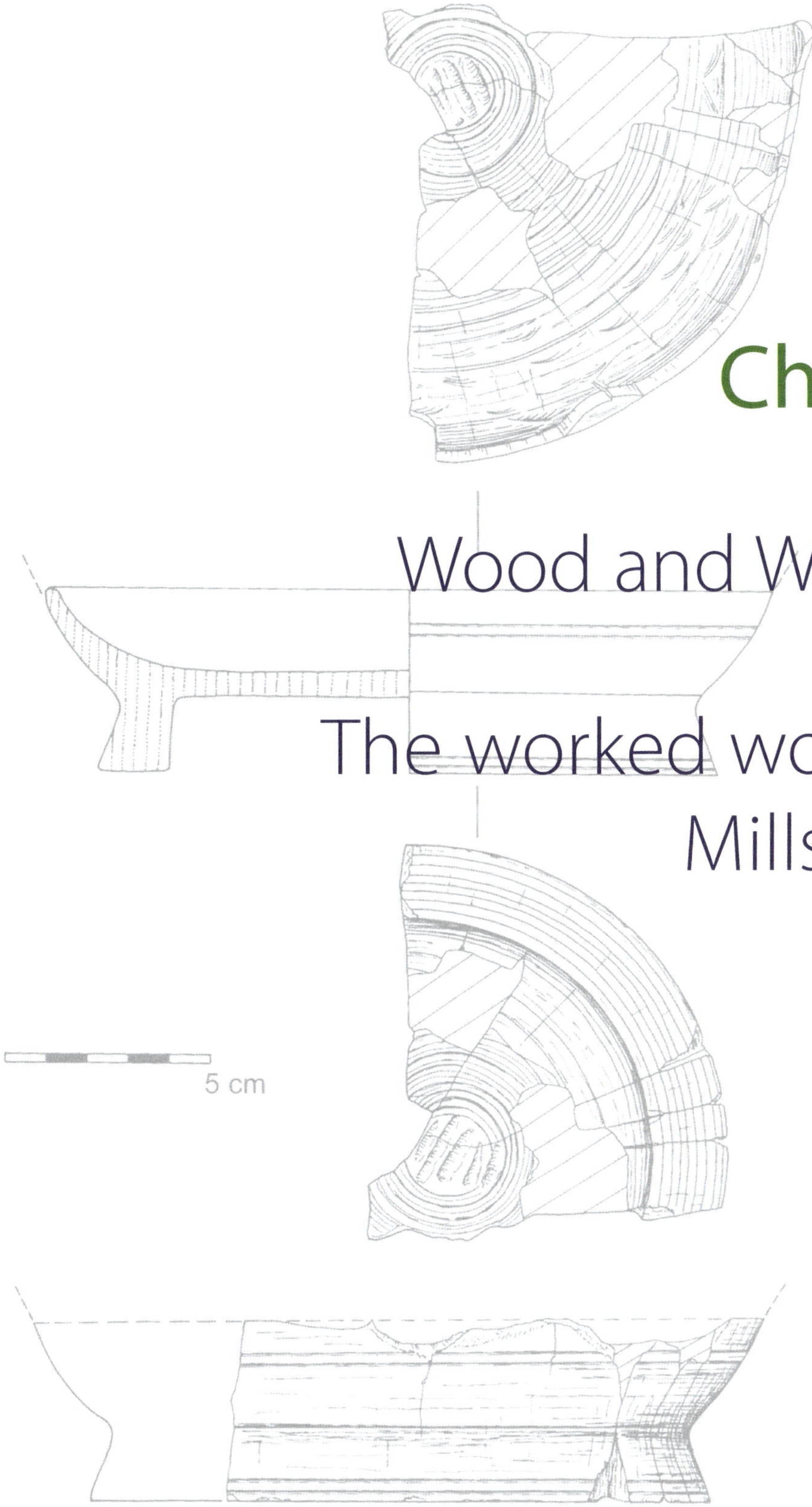

Caroline Earwood

Chapter 9
Wood and Woodland
The worked wood from Mills 1 and 2

Caroline Earwood

THE WOOD CATALOGUE

Over 1800 pieces of wood were recorded from the excavations between 1999 and 2001.Where many fragments came from the same context, they were grouped into one record and a wood catalogue with a total of 1029 records was created. Of these, 228 were for unworked wood, some 15% of which was roundwood almost all derived from rods used in hurdling or retaining woven walls. The total also includes 313 records covering worked wood and roundwood which was fragmentary and of no clearly recognisable form. Much of this wood had only a few cut marks or shaped ends. Additionally, parts of three large tree trunks with minimal woodworking were recorded.

The remaining 485 records include a considerable number of beams, planks, stakes and piles which formed part of the dam and the timber platform of the first mill or were possibly derived from the superstructure of one or both of the mills. A proportion of these large timbers may have been made for other structures and re-used on the mill site. Various components of two waterwheels were identified, and are described and discussed in Chapter 6. Direct evidence for on-site woodworking includes a collection of 200 offcuts. A small number of wooden artefacts was recorded including 46 pegs, two possible handles, an oar, a tiny wooden nail, a pin beater or spindle, parts of two stave-built tubs or buckets, the remains of two turned wooden bowls and a fragment of basketry. Reference numbers cited after individual pieces of wood refer to the wood catalogue which forms part of the Nendrum excavation archive in EHS. For ease of cross-reference the context number is also given for wooden pieces that have been previously mentioned in the text, and in the case of dated timbers their sample number is also provided.

NATURE AND CONDITION OF THE WOOD

The condition of much of the wood from the excavations in 1999 is poor, with many pieces being highly degraded. However, a significant proportion of the larger structural timbers lifted in the 2000 and 2001 seasons have well-preserved tool marks. Many of the roundwood stakes retrieved in these seasons were also in good condition. In 1999, a far higher proportion of the wood was lifted and sent for further study and conservation than was the case in 2000 and 2001, when a more rigorous selection process was instigated. As a result, many of the pieces from the 1999 season were relatively small, broken fragments and, owing to their poor condition, it was sometimes difficult to determine if they had been worked. Virtually all of the unworked wood and broken fragments of worked wood recorded in the catalogue were excavated in 1999.

The general impression gained from the nature and condition of the wood and from its context is that much of it belongs to *in situ* structural components of the dam of Mill 1. Some of it can be taken to represent casual deposition while the mills were being constructed or when in use or, in some cases, to reflect the salvage of timber after the mills had gone out of use. The remains fall into four main categories:

- recognisable parts of the mills, including parts of the waterwheels of Mill 1 and 2 and structural timber from the dam and the timber platform of Mill 1
- a small number of wooden artefacts from both phases
- debris, some of which may have derived from structural parts of both mills after they went out of use
- offcuts and other worked wood which was discarded by carpenters working on or around the mills.

WOOD SPECIES

Eighty-five per cent of the wood was identified as oak (*Quercus* sp.) with eight other species — hazel *(Corylus avellana)*, holly *(Ilex sp.)*, birch *(Betula sp.)*, willow *(Salix sp.)*, ash *(Fraxinus excelsior)*, alder *(Alnus sp.)*, yew *(Taxus baccata)* and elm *(Ulmus sp.)* — being noted. Oak was generally used for the larger structural timbers and parts of the mill wheels but was occasionally used for making roundwood stakes and pegs. Given the predominance of the use of oak for planks, beams and large piles, it not surprising to find that the majority of the offcuts were also oak. Presumably many of the large structural timbers were prepared or modified on the site of the mill, with the debris being casually dropped onto the foreshore. Tree-ring analyses indicate that, with the exception of one timber, all of the oak timbers sampled for dendrochronology were from Mill 1 and had felling dates largely falling between AD 619 and 621. The analyses also indicate that the timbers were from trees with at least 130–190 years' growth, while a small number came from trees with more than 250 years' growth.

Holly and hazel were the next most common species; holly being used extensively for the posts in the palisade and in the uprights and wands of the wattlework (see p. 438). Apart from being used in the wattlework, hazel was also used for making handles, pegs and stakes. Birch, willow, ash and alder were also used in very small quantities to make stakes and wattle. The turned bowls were, as is typical of this period, made from alder while the staves were split from yew. A single elm peg was found. Not surprisingly, given its supple qualities, ash was used to fashion the oar but otherwise appears not to have been used except for a single stake. The species of around 7% of the total amount of wood recorded was not identified.

With the possible exception of yew, it is likely that all of these species could be found growing in the immediate vicinity of the site. The considerable number of large oak timbers suggests that an oak forest was being cleared in the vicinity, and it is probable that the land immediately around the monastic settlement was being brought into cultivation in the early 7th century. It is likely, given the size and quantity of oak timbers, that some were towed by boat or rafted from nearby islands or the shores of the lough.

WOODWORKING TECHNIQUES

Analysis was constrained by the poor preservation of many of the pieces. However, examination of the tool marks that have survived indicates that the axe was by far the most common tool used for a variety of purposes. Where it could be determined, the majority of the oak timber was split, most commonly radially, with secondary shaping with an axe or occasionally, as in the case of planks and beams, an adze. The impression left by axing is generally deeper and more pronounced than that resulting from adzing (Darrah 1982, 219–229). The adze is used to produce a smooth surface, the axe for shaping where the final finish is less important. More than one size of axe and adze appears to have been used. Unusually for the period, one piece of plank has a series of parallel scores that have been identified as saw marks (Fig. 9.11). They indicate the use of a saw, probably a bow saw, of some considerable size.

A small number of pieces showed circular, drilled holes, some with wooden pegs or dowels still in place. Many of these are not sufficiently large or complete to allow identification of their function. None can be assigned with complete confidence as deriving from a part of the superstructure of either mill. Others were large beams which can be demonstrated to derive from the dam of Mill 1. Rectangular holes were cut in some of the planks, beams and piles. These were usually fairly crudely cut using a small axe, but in one example, a curved, chisel-like tool had been used. Most of these holes were made in a similar fashion. The timber was axed from one side across the grain at either end of where the hole was to be formed. The loose wood would then have been prised out, tearing along the grain. Next, the timber would have been turned over and cut similarly from the other side. This method resulted in a hole with a profile where the ends were almost straight whereas the sides were often distinctly stepped with the width of the hole being considerably less midway down than at the top or bottom. Although tending to be rather irregular in shape, the holes are competently made with only one example being found of cut marks on the surface of the timber where a mistake had been made.

Much of the worked wood had been cut or pointed at one or both ends. In some cases, roundwood or split timber was shaped into stakes or pegs, in others the pieces appear to have been offcuts from shaping some larger timber object or structure. Points on pegs, stakes and piles were commonly chisel- or wedge-shaped, although the roundwood stakes often have pencil-shaped points. A considerable number of the large beams had been re-used with one or both ends being crudely cut into a chisel shape.

Further, more detailed, comments on the woodworking methods may be found in the following sections.

DESCRIPTION AND ANALYSIS OF THE WORKED WOOD

Parts of waterwheels

Pieces of two waterwheels were identified from the 1999 excavation, including three, or possibly four, scoop-shaped paddles from Mill 2, and a damaged hub from Mill 1. These are discussed in Chapter 6. All waterwheel parts were made from oak. The fragmentary remains of three badly-eroded hubs were excavated during the 2000 season, but unfortunately the state of these is so poor that little or nothing can be ascertained regarding their true form. A wooden bearing or bush was found *in situ* in the lower millstone of Mill 2 (see Chapter 7).

Turned bowls

Substantial parts of two turned, alder bowls found in the primary silting of the stone penstock of Mill 2 were identified (493, 858, and 552; Figs 9.1 and 9.2) and are therefore of probable 9th-century date or slightly later. Several large pieces of the smaller of the two bowls (493, 858, Fig. 9.1) survive including part of the base, footring and lower side. Additionally there are three other pieces of footring from the same bowl and five small fragments from the side of this or another similar bowl. No rim fragments survive.

The smaller of the two bowls (see Fig. 9.1) is *c*. 8.6cm diameter across the outside of the base and *c*. 9cm across the bottom of the footring. The sides, which are a maximum of 8mm thick, survive to a height of 4.9cm. It is estimated, by comparison with similar bowls of this period, for instance that from Ballinderry crannóg 1 (Hencken 1936 Fig. 13b, Fig. 1, Earwood 1991/1992, 54–55, 154–159), that the finished bowl would have stood some 9cm high. There are numerous concentric cuts around the inside and outside of the bowl consistent with it having been turned. In addition, there are a number of deeply incised lines cut around the outer circumference to create decorative patterning. These are arranged in pairs, one just above the bottom of the footring and a second *c*. 1.3cm above the junction between the footring and the side of the bowl. Less well-defined lines are cut at and just above this junction.

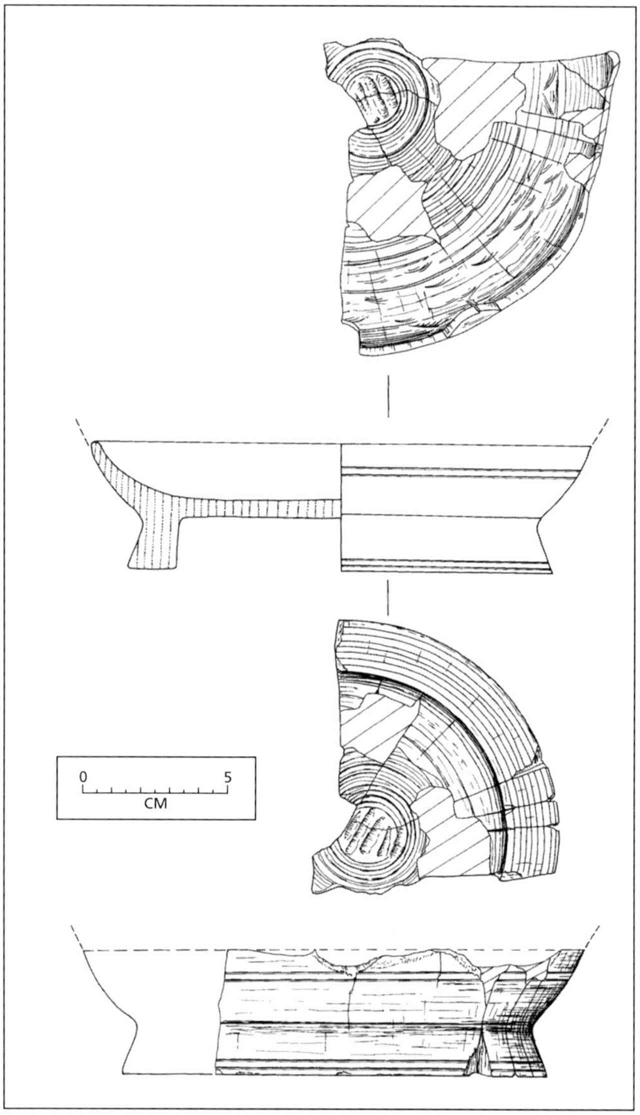

Fig. 9.1
The smaller of the two turned bowls (493 and 858) (G. Gilmour)

The fragment from the centre of the bowl (see Fig. 9.1) is irregularly broken and varies in thickness from 2mm at the edges to 4mm in the middle. It has deeply scored cut marks, made during turning on both sides. On one side these form four parallel cuts with slightly rounded ends, 2–4mm wide and 1.4–2.2cm long. On the reverse the cuts form a pattern somewhat like a W, one side of which is partially missing. Beyond the central portion of the fragment numerous concentric turning marks can be seen on both sides. The parallel cuts appear to have been made with a small gouge or chisel and are consistent with the removal of the core after turning. The W-shaped mark is, however, more difficult to explain in this way and has the appearance of a maker's mark.

The larger bowl (552, Fig. 9.2), which survives to a height of 8.3cm, had a thick base and short footring. It is *c.* 9.7cm in diameter across the outside of the base and *c.* 10.6cm across the external diameter of the bottom of the footring. Damage to its upper part makes it difficult to be certain whether any rim survives. However, the thinness of the bowl at this point (only 3mm) indicates that if the rim has not survived it is unlikely to have been more than a few millimetres above this point. The centre of the base has slight scoring, both internally and externally, where the cores were removed after turning was complete. In addition to numerous turning marks, there is a series of deeply incised, concentric lines around the exterior circumference. The highest of these decorative lines is a pair about 4cm from the surviving top of the bowl, with a further eight lines between this point and the bottom of the footring.

Both turned bowls from Nendrum are closely comparable to examples from contemporary sites in Ireland. The most complete bowl of this type is from Ballinderry crannóg 1, (Hencken 1936, Fig. 13B). Other more fragmentary examples have been recorded from Deer Park Farms (Lynn and MacDowell *forthcoming*). These bowls are similar in form to pottery A ware, imported from the Mediterranean, and were copies in wood of what was considered to be prestigious tableware (Earwood 1992, 154).

Stave-built containers

Two fragments of wooden hoop were identified from the 1999 excavations and the remains of three broken staves were excavated during the 2000 season (985, 986, 987). These were found together in the silt and gravel layer immediately above the destroyed

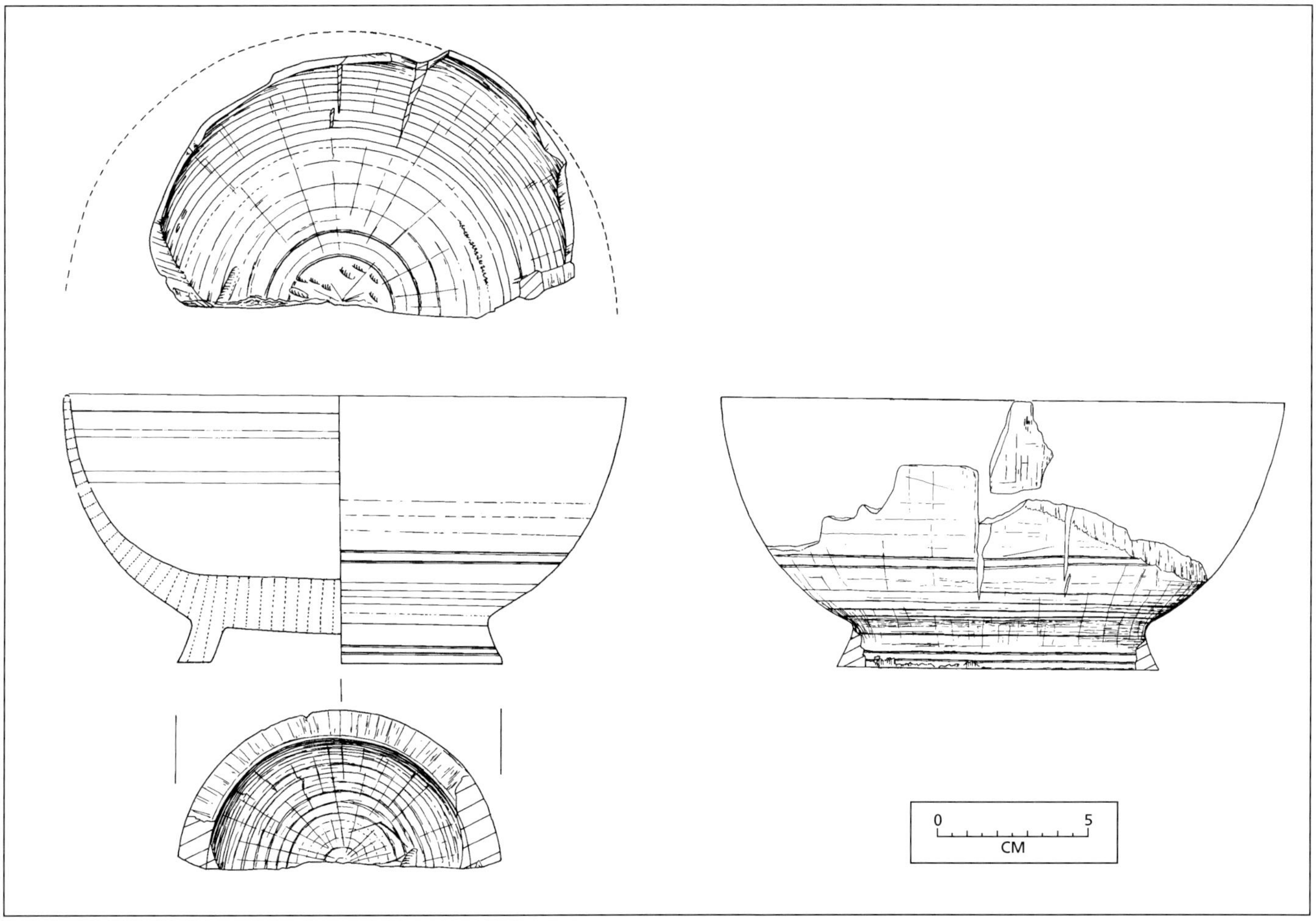

Fig. 9.2
The larger of the two turned bowls (552) (G. Gilmour)

surface of the dam of Mill 1 (C402) and are derived from at least two tubs. In 2001, a fragment of stave, part of the base of a container and a broken hoop were found in the same context.

Container 1

Although the upper part of the best-preserved stave (868) is damaged, it is intact across its width (6.6cm) and it is therefore possible to estimate, from the curvature, that the diameter of the container was in the region of 30–32cm. The height remains conjectural but, given the width and thickness of the stave, a height of some 40cm would be likely, based on comparison with other stave-built containers of this period in Ireland (Earwood 1993, 80–90). A groove 4mm wide, where the base would have been inserted, was cut from side to side of the inner face of the stave, 2.6cm from the bottom edge. Sufficient of the stave survives to see that it tapers from the bottom towards the top, thus that the container was narrower at the rim than at the base. For this reason it is most unlikely that it was a bucket as these are invariably wider at the rim than the base.

The broken hoop (987) was made of roundwood split in half with the flat side turned towards the surface of the container that it encircled. The ends were tapered and pegged to each other with three wooden pins. As none protrudes beyond the inside of the hoop, it is clear that they were not used to attach the hoop to the container. Although the hoop is incomplete, sufficient remains to suggest that it would have fitted a container measuring between 30cm and 32cm in diameter. It is likely therefore, that it was part of the tub represented by the stave (868). The two further hoop fragments are similar. Part of a composite base with the remains of a wooden dowel in the straight edge is also almost certainly from the same tub.

Container 2

The lower part of a second stave (869) (identified as the lower part because of the presence of the groove for the base) has been badly damaged so that only 13cm of the length survives. Although the stave has a carefully made, bevelled rim, the condition of the wood is so poor it is impossible to calculate the diameter of the container to which it belonged. However, at 3.5cm in width it is considerably narrower than 868 and has parallel sides indicating it came from a vertical-sided container. A third fragment (867) is too badly damaged to determine whether it was from the same container.

All of the staves were identified as being of yew, a wood that was commonly used in Early Medieval Ireland for making stave-built containers. Although it is difficult to determine accurately the original sizes of the Nendrum examples, they are directly comparable to examples from such sites as Ballinderry and Lagore crannógs. Indeed, container 1 may have been similar to a narrow-mouthed example from Lagore (W139) that had a base diameter of around 36cm and a height of 42cm (Hencken 1950,152–156, Earwood 1993, 85).

Oar

Although broken into three pieces, the oar (225, C161, Fig. 9.3,) is virtually complete. The oar was found re-used as a bracing member for one of the wattle revetments in the core of the dam of Mill 1 (see p. 59) and therefore dates to the early 7th century. It was made from split ash and was smoothly finished, so that no tool marks are visible. The blade, which is 9.6cm wide, is straight-sided with a pronounced ridge on either side and has a neatly curved end. At the shaft end it tapers to an elliptical section where it is now broken. The shaft, which is 4.4cm in diameter, has a circular section for most of its length but then widens to a squared section, 5.6cm square and 37.5cm long. When excavated, the oar was found standing vertically, blade down in the core of the dam of Mill 1 and the damage on the end of the shaft is almost certainly due to tidal erosion and wear when it was in this position. It is likely therefore that the oar was slightly longer than the surviving 1.725m, around 2m in total length, and it is probable that the shaft ended in a smooth handle of circular section to prevent the oarsman getting splinters on the hand.

There are no exact contemporary parallels in Ireland, but oars of this type were not uncommon in modern times. They are well-recorded in use on lake boats in Finland —

generally small, clinker-built boats with a high pointed bow and stern, suitable for one or two people — during the 1950s. They are not unlike the 'oselver' boats from Norway and Shetland. The oars in the Finnish lake boats were used in a variety of ways. Some lay in U-shaped crutches that were pinned into the top strake, while some pivoted against a single upright thole (pin) to which the oar was attached with a smaller horizontal pin. In a further type, the oar was held in place with a grommet (strap or tie). In all cases, the squared part of the oar shaft was inboard of the side of the boat and this shaping prevented the oar from slipping out through the crutch or grommet (Greenhill 1995, 126–7, 130, 208).

Comparisons can be made between the 'oselver' boats, the Finnish lake boats and the 9th- century boat from Årby, Sweden. This small rowing boat was some 4m in length, with a beam of about 1m. According to McGrail (1998, 214–216), the beam gives an '... ideal oar length of c. 2 metres' and the Årby oar is, in fact, 2.04m in length. The Årby oar is the only example from the Early Medieval period that is comparable in size and shape to the oar from Nendrum. A reconstruction of the Årby boat was described as being strongly constructed, but light enough to be easily beached.

> She could be propelled with little effort over the distances one might expect in a lake. The boat is small and suitable for one person only – a personal means of transport.... Indeed, for a lake dweller this little boat may have represented the same convenience and capability as one would these days expect of a bicycle. (Greenhill 1995, 207).

While the vast majority of Irish logboats found to date were propelled by paddling and many examples of logboat paddles have survived, there is evidence that some were equipped for rowing (Fry 2000, 21, 64, 105) making it a possibility that this oar was used to propel a logboat. It seems more probable, however, that the Nendrum oar represents the use of a small rowing boat of perhaps of the skin-covered currach type, or a wood-built craft employed by the monastery around the shores and islands of Strangford Lough.

Possible boat paddle fragments

Two fragments from possible boat paddles (1015, 1019) both found in the timber platform of Mill 1, were identified. The larger of these (1019), which is 1.06m long, may be the back of the blade. There is a definite ridge along the central line and the piece then tapers down to a nearly circular section where the shaft has broken away. The other fragment (1015) is similar but is in very poor condition, making positive identification impossible.

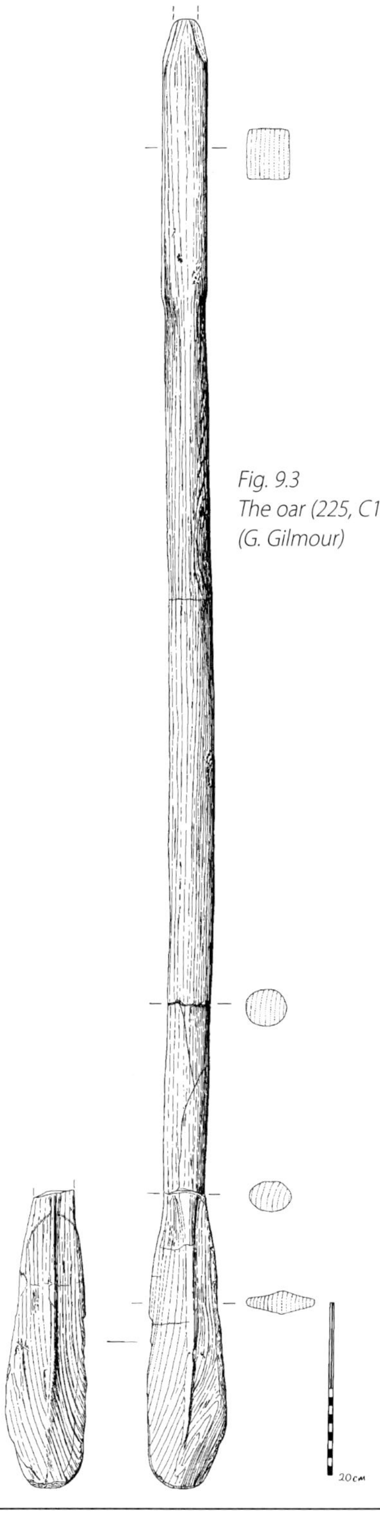

Fig. 9.3
The oar (225, C161)
(G. Gilmour)

An irregularly shaped piece of oak wood, a possible rowlock

An irregularly shaped piece of oak wood (982) clearly torn from a larger piece, has one side carefully shaped to form what appears to be a rowlock. Two pointed knobs, set *c.* 13cm apart, separate a carefully smoothed curve some 6.5cm deep. Although the piece is damaged and fragmentary, it is possible that this is a rowlock cut into the side of a logboat. A similar but much smaller fragment (1026) may be from the same object. This type of rowlock is not directly comparable to some of the rowlocks that have been found in Irish logboats (Fry 2000, 21, 94, 101, 103) but is broadly similar to the type defined by McGrail as a U-shaped opening worked in the top strake of a rowing boat (McGrail 1998, 212).

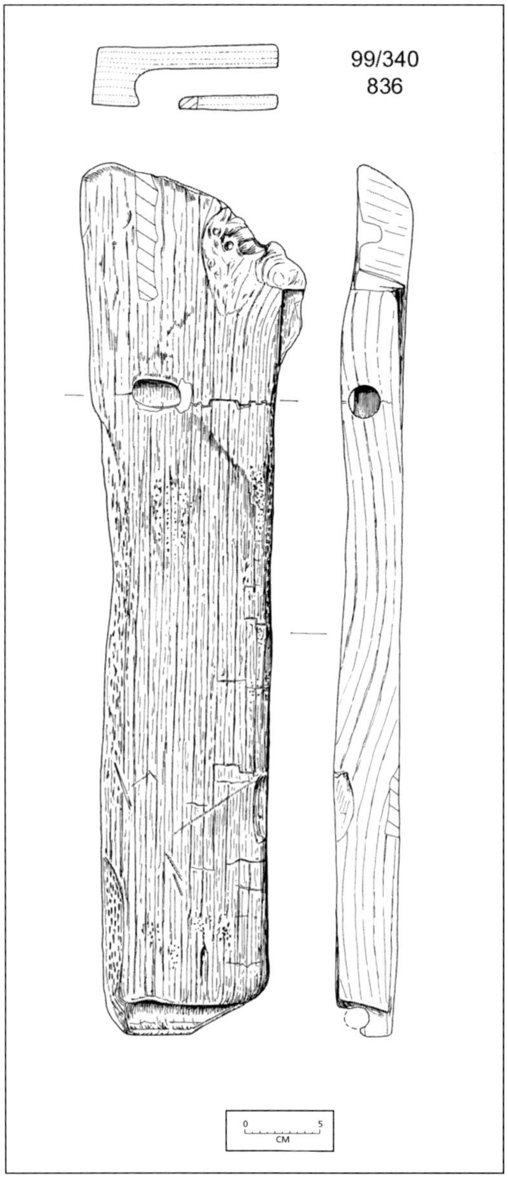

Fig. 9.4
A shaped board (836)
(G. Gilmour)

A shaped board

A shaped board (836, Fig. 9.4), roughly rectangular, 56.1cm in maximum length, 10.5cm wide and 3.3–3.9cm in average thickness, found in the foundation layer of Mill 2's millpond (C40), was made from a piece of split oak that was then adzed across its width. One end of the board is slightly damaged, but appears to have the remains of a slight step and a small, protruding, wedge-shaped flange. The other end is cut at an angle so that the length is 56.1cm on one side but only 48cm on the other. On the top of the board there is a slight L-shaped ledge, 6.2cm long by 2.6cm wide but only 8mm thick. The board widens to 12.3cm at this point. A circular hole (1.9cm diameter) has been drilled into the edge of the board inside this ledge. The hole, which is 6.1cm long, is angled so that it emerges in the face of the board.

It is tempting to suggest that the shaped board is another example from Nendrum of a flat horizontal waterwheel paddle. However, this seems unlikely on a number of grounds. From the evidence of the first waterwheel from Nendrum and from analysis of a number of similar waterwheels of more recent date, the indication is that the paddles were invariably flat boards inserted into mortise holes in the hub without any further fastening. This object is considerably longer on one side than the other, which would make it unsuitable for use as a paddle.

Moreover, there are two other features that cannot be explained. The slight flange at one end would serve no useful purpose in fastening the board into a hub. If it had been a waterwheel paddle, there is no explanation for the slight ledge and associated dowel hole. The possibility of this being a fixing point for a shroud or outer rim, as recorded in Shetland (Wilson 1960, 3), has been discarded. The lip at the back of the ledge is of insufficient thickness to withstand any great pressure and, indeed, it is now cracked.

A possible lever for adjusting the lightening-tree of the mill

A possible lever (622) for adjusting the lightening-tree of the mill has been identified (Fig. 9.5). It was found in the silt of the millpond of Mill 1 and therefore may be associated with the tentering system associated with the first mill. Made from split oak, this is the end of a pointed object that is rectangular in section at the broken end but which is tapered along one side in a smoothly cut curve (see Fig. 9.5). It survives to a length of 28.6cm, has a maximum width of 5.4cm and the thickness varies from 2.3cm to 2.5cm. The pointed end is slightly damaged.

A similar 'lever' was recorded from Mashanaglass (Fahy 1956, 32 Fig. 9). It was suggested that it had been attached to the lightening-tree, the lower end of which was fastened to the bridge-tree beam, the upper end passing through the floor of the upper millhouse (see p. 14). The lever would have been adjusted to allow the lightening-tree to move up or down to lower or raise the bridge-tree and thus adjust the gap between the millstones as shown on Fig. 1.6.

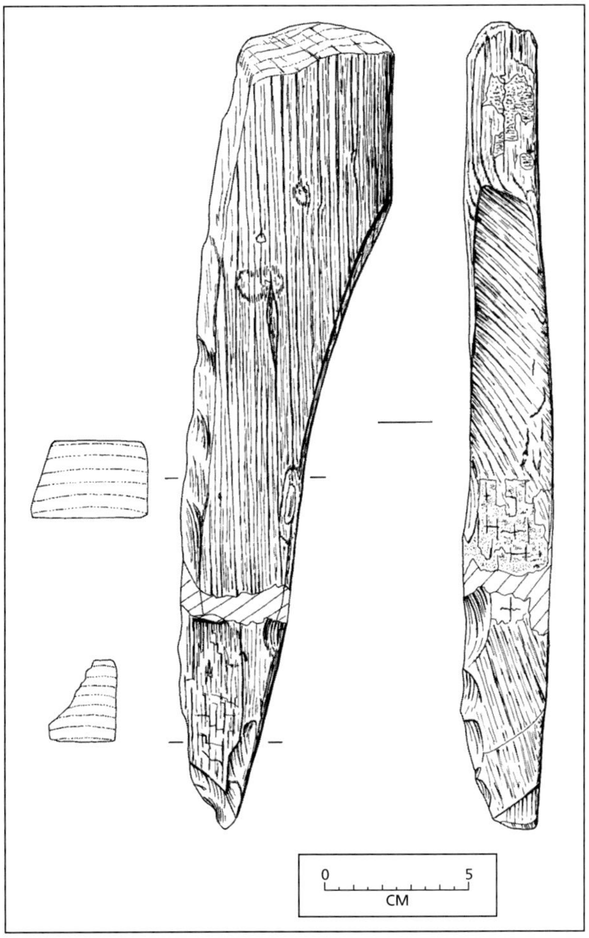

Fig. 9.5
A possible lever for adjusting the lightening-tree of the first mill (622) (G. Gilmour)

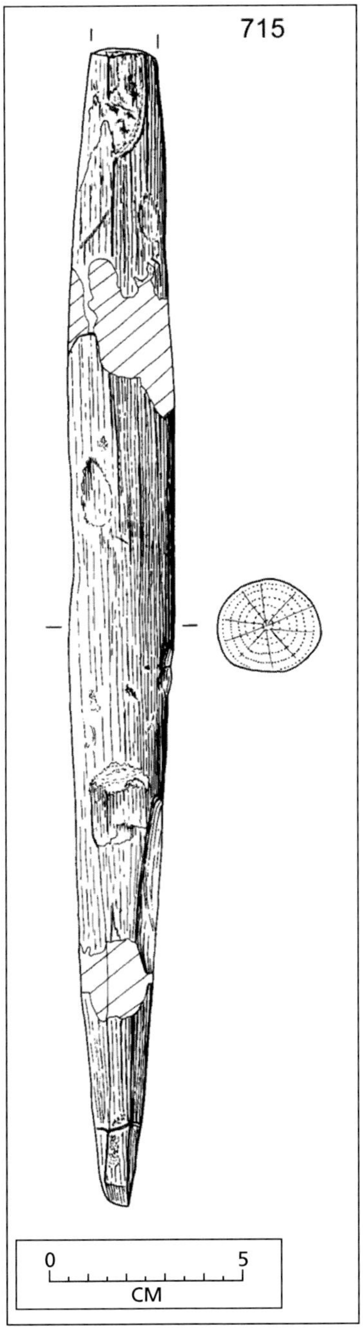

Fig. 9.6A
A probable pin beater or spindle (715) (G. Gilmour)

A probable pin beater or spindle

A probable pin beater or spindle (715, Fig. 9.6A) was found in the foundation layer of the millpond of Mill 2 (C40). It was carved from a length of roundwood, both ends of which have been tapered to carefully finished pencil points, one of which is broken. The diameter in the middle is 2.7cm and the original length was *c.* 34–35cm, although only 30.5cm survives. The wood species was not identifiable.

Fig. 9.6B
A fragment of basketry (856)

This object is closely similar to examples of pin beaters and spindles found on other Early Medieval sites in Ireland and to Viking examples from Haithabu (all largely unpublished). The closest parallel is the largest of three examples, which is 16.5cm long, from Deer Park Farms rath in Co. Antrim (Earwood 1993, 134–136).

Wooden nail

A nail (423), which is 11.4cm long and 4mm in diameter, was perfectly shaped tapering from a nearly flat head to a sharp point. It was found in the back filling of the cut made for the insertion of the stone penstock (C32). The tree species has not been identified.

A fragment of basketry

A fragment of basketry (865, Fig. 9.6B) was found in a context associated with the millpond of Mill 1. It is *c.* 70cm in diameter, however, owing to the intrusion of other material the portion lifted measures only *c.* 52cm in diameter. Seven roundwood uprights, 7–10mm in diameter, are set about 5.8–6cm apart, between which are woven roundwood rods 4–8mm in diameter. The rods appear to be arranged in pairs but are now slightly distorted, perhaps due to compression while buried.

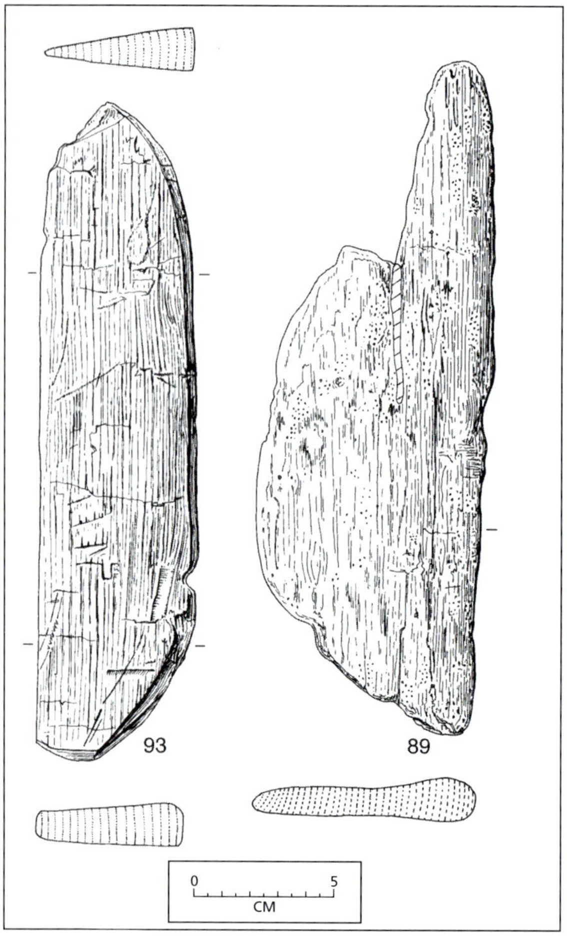

Fig. 9.7
D-shaped piece (93) and D-shaped object (89) (G. Gilmour)

Miscellaneous objects

A number of broken pieces of worked wood have shapes that suggest they may have been part of an artefact or broken structure. Unfortunately it has only been possible to identify a function for a small number of these finds.

A D-shaped piece

A D-shaped piece (93, Fig. 9.7) of split oak with smooth edges was found at the base of Mill 2's penstock intake channel. One corner is damaged but otherwise the object is intact and is 24.6cm long, 6cm wide and 4–13mm thick.

A D-shaped object

A D-shaped object (89, Fig. 9.7), one end of which is badly broken, may be the remains of a flat oak handle. It was found in the back filling of the cut made for the insertion of the stone penstock (C32, see Fig. 2.8). It is 8.3cm in maximum width and its remaining length is 24.6cm and thickness 1.1cm.

A possible handle

A possible handle (709, Fig. 9.8a) was made from a short piece of hazel roundwood with a curved top formed from the junction between the main stem and a side branch. It was found in the primary silt at the base of Mill 2's stone wheelhouse. The top and sides of the head have been carefully shaped into a finger-sized notch, the lower end is broken. The remaining length is 7.6cm and the diameter is between 1.8cm and 3.1cm.

Another possible handle

Another possible handle (683, Fig. 9.8b) found in the silt of the stone penstock, was also carved from a length of hazel roundwood, one end of which is cut at right angles to the length, while the other end is broken. At *c.* 3cm from the finished end, one side is cut into a flat face, tapering in width from 2.2cm to 1.5cm. The piece is smoothly finished with no visible tool marks other than a series of very small steps on the flat face that may be the result of shaping with a small hand adze. It survives to a length of 55.1cm and has a diameter which varies from 2.4cm to 2.8cm.

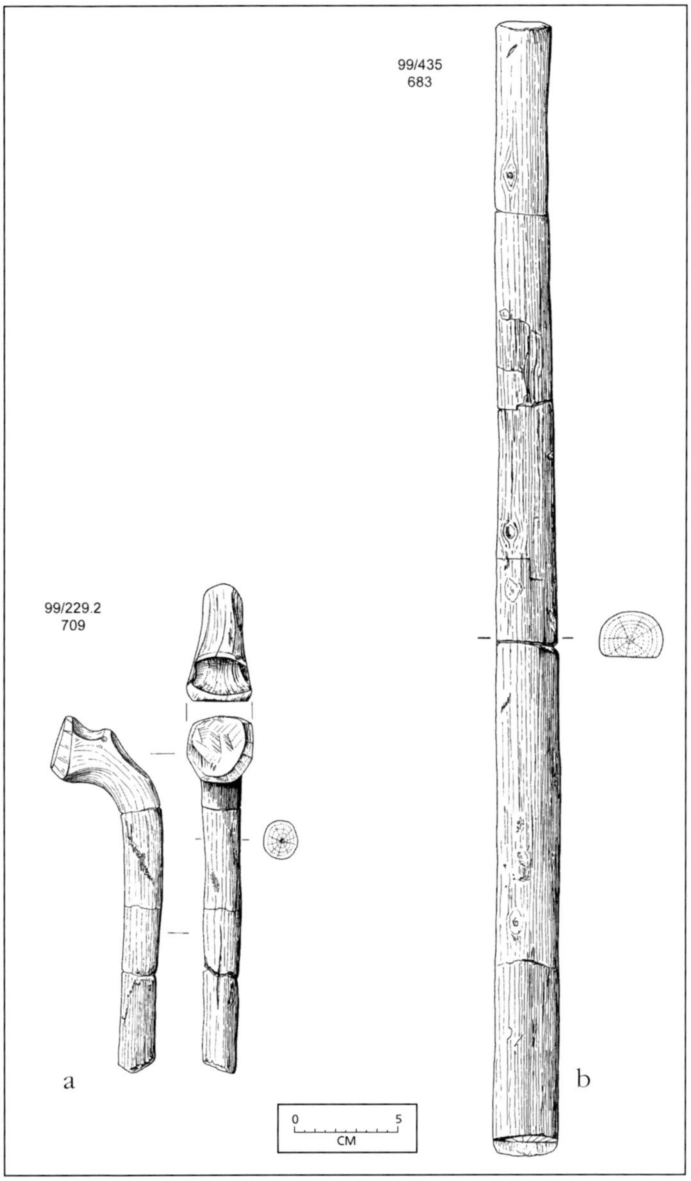

Fig. 9.8
Possible handles 709 and 683 (G. Gilmour)

Two large cylindrical blocks of oak

Two large cylindrical blocks of oak (841, 864) are of unknown function. The better preserved of these (864) is 64cm in height and was shaped from a whole tree trunk, so that some of the sapwood is still intact. The lower part, which is *c.* 46cm in diameter, has roughly vertical sides with a sloping step *c.* 15cm wide, above which is a shaft-like part that has been carefully shaped into a rectangular block *c.* 17.5cm by 20.5cm in section. The 'shaft' has vertical sides for about 25cm and then slopes inwards neatly to a flat top. A sub-rectangular hole, 18cm by 9cm, was cut through the narrower side of the 'shaft' and a second, smaller hole off-centre from the top. No tool marks survive as the wood is badly eroded. The object is not symmetrical and gives the appearance of not having been completed.

The second, less well-preserved example (841) was cut from part of a tree trunk that has two centres of growth. In other words, this must be a tree that had suffered some kind of damage such as by animal browsing or was subject to pollarding. The lower part is nearly circular, with a diameter of *c.* 45cm. Above this is a roughly rectangular block with a large elliptical hole from side to side. The object is so badly degraded that it is impossible to be sure that it is worked. However, its similarity to 864 strongly suggests that it was comparable in form, if not identical.

There is no possibility that either of these blocks could have formed part of a horizontal-wheeled mill. Further, the incomplete nature of the better-preserved example suggests that perhaps they were never used. The contexts of these finds do not suggest any possible function.

Pegs

A total of 47 pegs was recorded, the majority of which were made from split oak timber. Nine roundwood pegs, however, were shaped from other species including hazel with one example of elm. In a small number of cases, there are strong similarities between crudely cut pegs and offcuts. However, most of the pegs are fairly well made and are considerably longer than they are wide or thick. Not all survived complete, with over one third lacking a point and several having badly damaged heads.

Broadly speaking there are three main types of pegs (Fig. 9.9A).

1. Rectangular in section with either a chisel- or a wedge-shaped point. Most have a flat-topped head, i.e. cut at right angles to the length, but a few are slightly domed or cut into the shape of an inverted and truncated cone. Over half of all the pegs are of this type .
2. Triangular in section with a flattish top. Points were made by tapering each side or by cutting a chisel-shaped or wedge point. There are only eight examples.

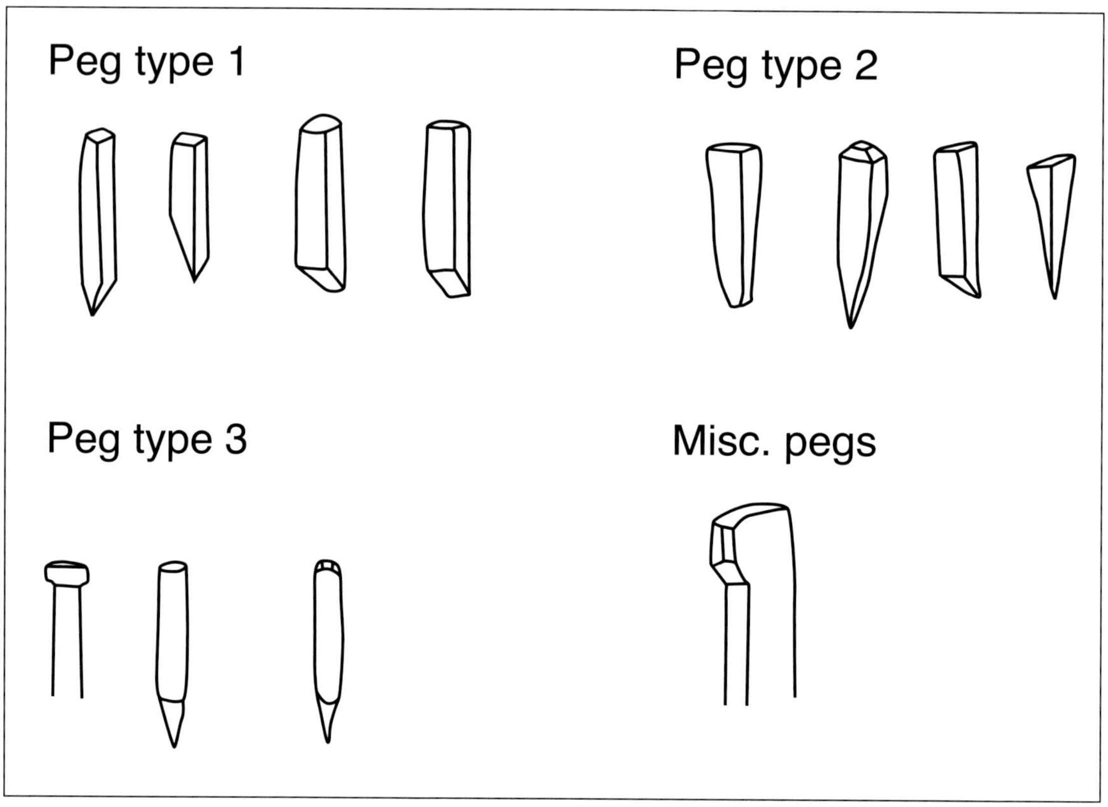

Fig. 9.9A The main peg types (G. Gilmour)

Peg type 1

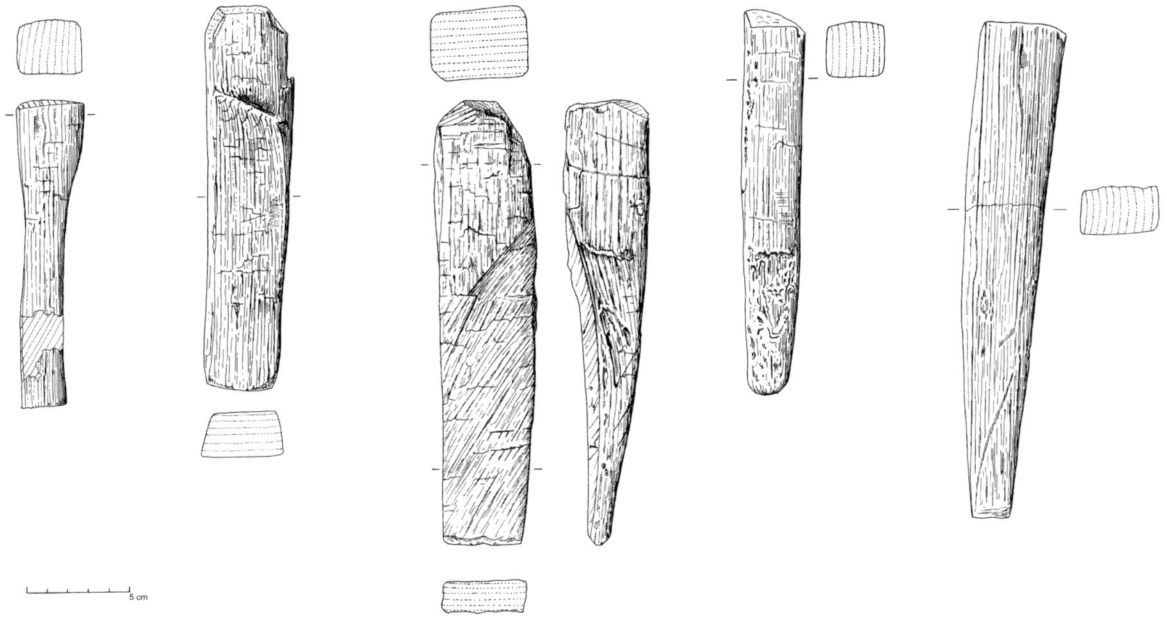

Peg type 2 Peg type 3

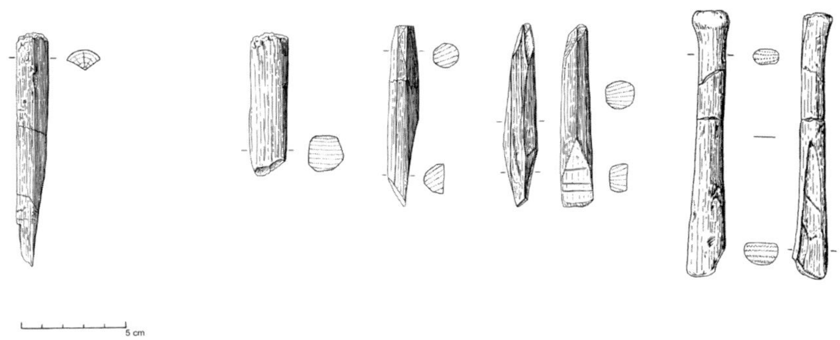

Misc. pegs

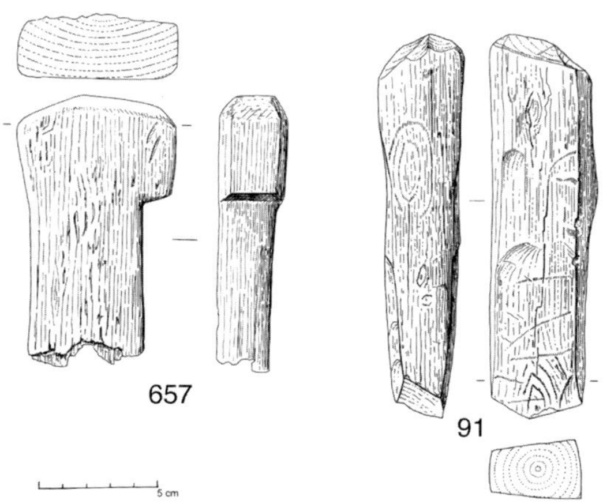

Fig. 9.9B
Examples of peg types (G. Gilmour)

3. Circular in section, the point may be wedge-shaped, chisel-shaped or tapering on all sides like a pencil. This type of peg, which was made from split oak or unshaped roundwood, may have a top that is flat, in the form of a truncated cone or stepped out from the shaft i.e. of greater diameter. Considerable variations of style have been noted in the ten examples of this general type. In particular one short, split oak peg, which has a flat top and blunt pencil point, is highly likely to have been a dowel used to secure a structural timber. Similar dowels have been noted in beams and planks from Nendrum.

In addition to these three broad types, there are a small number of pegs that show other variations. These include one (657), found at the bottom of the Mill 2 wheelhouse, with an asymmetric head on a rectangular shaft, and another made of roundwood (91) found in the foundation lining of millpond 1 (C69), crudely cut on two opposing faces, to form a roughly rectangular section tapering to a wedge-shaped end.

There is no direct correlation between the shape of the shaft, i.e. the section, and the type of head or point. No specific shape of peg was made from roundwood, various types of head and points were used. Pegs vary considerably in size, from 3.6cm long (183), a roundwood peg with blunt pencil point, to 42cm long (198), a split oak peg with rectangular shaft and chisel point. The latter example is curved along its length and crudely cut with the remains of bark still *in situ*. The majority of the pegs, however, are between *c.* 10cm and 20cm in length.

Offcuts

Records were made for 200 offcuts, although in four cases, the condition was so poor that accurate measurements were not possible. In one instance, 16 poorly preserved specimens were included in one record and in another, three possible offcuts have been recorded together. The majority (97%) are split fragments of oak that were discarded during the shaping of larger timbers such as beams and planks. There is some difficulty in distinguishing between offcuts from on-site woodworking and small fragments broken from larger pieces of worked wood. The most apparent difference is that both ends of offcuts are usually cut, but there is little other sign of working, although most have one or more split faces. Similarly, there can be some confusion between offcuts and irregularly-made pegs.

Analysis of the shapes and sizes of offcuts indicates that there are four principal types (Fig. 9.10A), with internal subdivisions. Whereas Fig. 9.10A shows these as regular shapes with flat surfaces, in reality they are usually more irregular in shape with their ends commonly cut in a series of steps, rather than a smoothly finished shape. Tool marks, usually the result of axing, are common on the ends and no attempt has been made to carry out any further shaping, naturally enough, as these pieces are the waste from woodworking. Actual examples are illustrated in Fig. 9.10B.

Type A is usually rectangular or nearly rectangular in section, although it may be also trapezoidal, each face being split but not further worked. The ends of the offcut may be cut in four different ways.

- A1 – one end cut at 90° to the length and the other a chisel shape cut from front to back i.e. through the thickness of the piece – 40 examples
- A2 – chisel ends sloping down from the front – five examples
- A3 – chisel or chisel-shaped ends but cut parallel to each other – two examples
- A4 – one end cut at 90° to the length and the other a chisel shape cut from side to side i.e. across the width of the piece – two examples

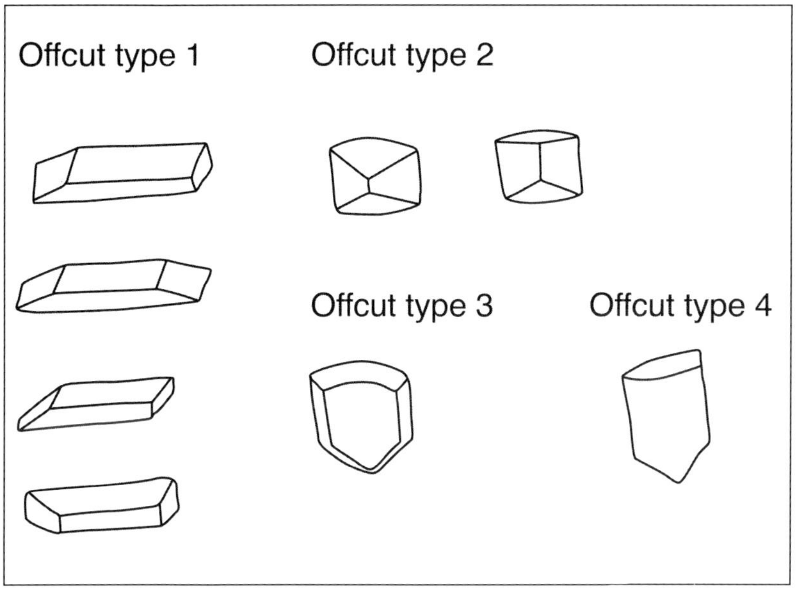

Fig. 9.10A
The main offcut types
(G. Gilmour)

It is most likely that these types of offcut were produced during the shaping of split timber to produce the beams or planks that may have been used in the main structure of either or both mill buildings. These would have been worked in the immediate vicinity of the building during its construction. The majority appear either to have been split from a larger timber, perhaps to remove excess wood, or to have been short lengths cut from a longer timber. In the latter case, the crudely cut, chisel-shaped end was probably cut when the length was first shaped, whereas the neater end (at 90° to the length) was cut when the finished length was trimmed to size.

Type B is roughly triangular in section, but with the longest side of the triangle (the back) often being slightly curved, following the natural curvature of the tree. The two remaining faces are split with no other sign of working. The rays of the tree invariably run from the curved side towards the point of the triangle opposite — i.e. the pieces are radially split. Two variations have been identified.

- B1 – the ends are each cut into a chisel shape – six examples
- B2 – one end is cut roughly at 90° to the length, the other in a chisel shape – 11 examples

Exactly what type of woodworking was involved in the creation of these offcuts is unclear. However, the curved back and the two cut ends indicate that these pieces were cut from the outer part of a tree or branch, perhaps as a means of removing the sapwood.

Type C has many variations, but consists of an irregularly-shaped piece of sapwood that is often considerably thinner than it is wide and which is curved following the natural

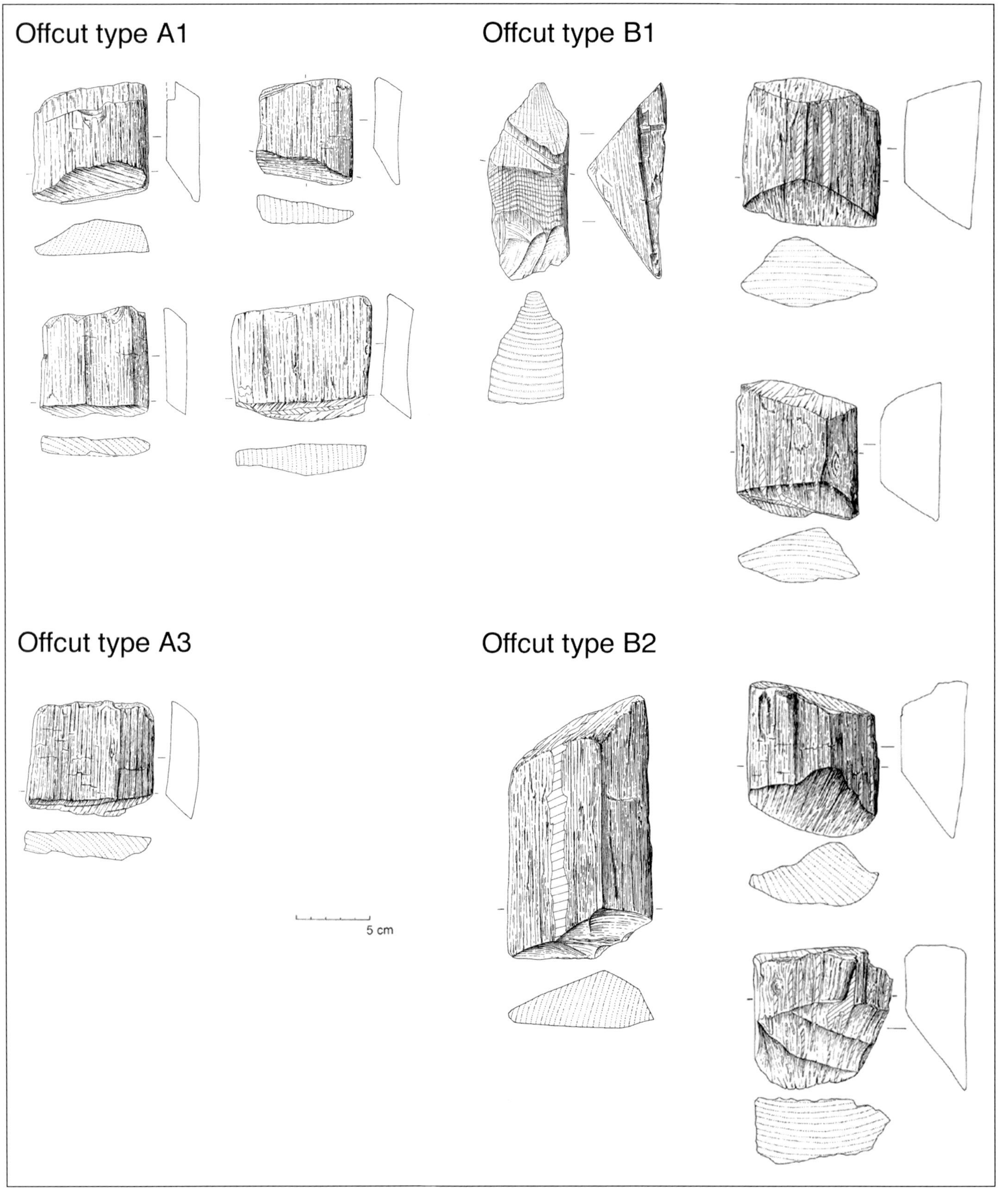

Fig. 9.10B
Examples of offcut types (G. Gilmour)

form of the outer part of the tree. In some cases, the inner and/or outer bark remains *in situ*. The ends of the offcut may be cut either at 90° to the length, or into crude chisel or wedge shapes. There are sometimes signs of working on the sides but rarely on the curved back. These pieces, of which 14 were recorded, are the result of splitting or axing away the unwanted sapwood prior to the shaping of timber into beams and planks.

Type D produced seven examples. Each piece has one end cut at 90° to the length, the other into a wedge shape – i.e. cut from either side. This form is similar to the end of a stake or pile, the only difference being that, ranging from 6.2 to 7.9cm in length, the offcuts are far too short to fulfil the function of a stake. It is unclear why they were made.

Planks

Parts of 37 planks, all but one (542) being made from split oak, were identified. Almost all were from contexts associated with Mill 1, the majority forming components of the dam with a small number found overlying the millpond lining (see Fig. 2.4). They ranged from tiny pieces to six planks of over 1m in length, the largest (979) measuring 1.8m long by 25.8cm wide and 5.2cm thick. The majority of the planks were excavated during the 1999 season and, in many cases, only one edge of plank survived, so that the original width can rarely be ascertained. The condition of these plank fragments was generally very poor, all being broken and many highly-degraded by exposure to the atmosphere and, no doubt, periodic waterlogging and drying out during the tidal cycle. As a result, very few tool marks have survived. It is clear, however, that the great majority were radially split and then shaped with an axe. In one instance, the surface had been adzed flat (80), in a few other cases axe marks were visible on the cut ends. The five planks recorded from the 2000 season were very much better preserved. With the exception of one fragmentary example (962), the surviving lengths of the planks were from around 1m to considerably longer.

The smallest fragments are broken pieces from very thin planks, the most slender being only 2–4mm in thickness. Only a fragment of the latter survives (235) consisting of the finished edge of a plank, which is 11.6cm by 7.6cm by *c.* 2–4mm thick, with a circular hole 1.9cm in diameter, drilled through the thickness immediately adjacent to the edge. Four plank fragments are under 1cm thick, with fifteen being only 1–2cm in thickness.

The unbroken ends of the planks are sometimes cut neatly at 90° to their length and in these cases, tool marks rarely survive. In a small number of instances, the ends have been cut either into a shallow chisel shape or a shallow wedge. It is possible that a few of these pieces (e.g. 194) are the discarded waste produced when a plank was cut to the desired length. However, these chisel- or wedge-shaped cuts have been recorded on some long planks. It seems most likely that the ends of the planks were not finished to a smooth surface as they were not intended to be part of the mill building, but were used as retaining components in the core of the first dam.

One plank, 854 (C19), found placed upright in the core of Mill 1's dam, has been cut in this way. It has one end broken while the other is roughly axed into a short chisel shape. It is 1.11m long, *c.* 40cm wide and tapers in thickness from side to side from 8.8cm to 4.5cm. This variation in thickness is almost certainly the result of radial splitting. Near to the chisel-shaped end a sub-rectangular hole, 16cm by 14.3cm, has been cut through the plank, about 13.5cm from the thinner edge. A second hole, roughly oval in shape, 4.2cm in maximum width, was cut about 15.3cm from the same edge but near to the broken end. On the opposite edge of the plank, nearly half way along, a circular hole *c.* 3cm in diameter, now incomplete, was cut through the thickness. Beyond this are two small dowel holes drilled into the edge of the plank and separated by a small notch. The original function of this plank is unclear, but it must have been prepared for, or been part of some large structure prior to its use as a strengthening element in the core of Mill 1's dam.

Fig. 9.11
Plank fragment (323) with parallel score marks most probably made by a saw (G. Gilmour)

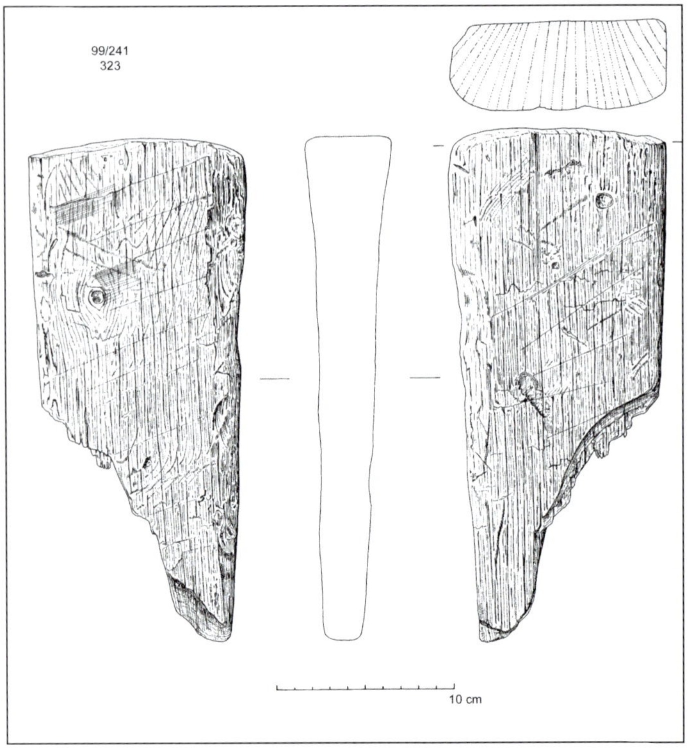

Another plank (872, C129) used as an upright in the timber revetment of Mill 1's dam and dated to AD 513±9 (Q9915), but probably from the inner section of a tree felled about AD 619 (see p. 71), shows signs of originally being derived from some other structure. It had a slightly rounded end and two circular holes *c.* 3.5cm diameter bored through from side to side, one still with a split wood peg *in situ*. A third hole appears to have been started but not finished. The plank was just over 1m long and between 2.2cm and 3cm wide.

One of the largest planks (859, C151), over 1.3m in length, used as a bracing member of outer wattle revetment, was found with a stake driven through a mortise hole (see Fig. 2.33) cut near one end. It was dated to late AD 618 or early AD 619 (Q10013). One end of the plank was axed at about 45° to the sides, the other was weathered and broken. It was radially split leaving sapwood on the thicker edge. Generally, the surfaces were poorly finished and had suffered considerably from weathering and infestation by boring creatures. A similar, but longer plank, 1.83m in length (979) also had a mortise hole cut, this time 8.3cm from one end.

The only other plank fragment of note (323, Fig. 9.11), found in the foundation layer of Mill 2's millpond (C40)), was a neatly made piece, 28.6cm long, with one smoothly finished end, 12.4cm wide by 4.6cm thick, cut at 90° to the length. Its other end is broken. Both faces have a number of parallel score marks running from side to side at a slight angle to the edges, and these are almost certainly the result of sawing. This appears to be the first example of sawn timber from this period in Ireland.

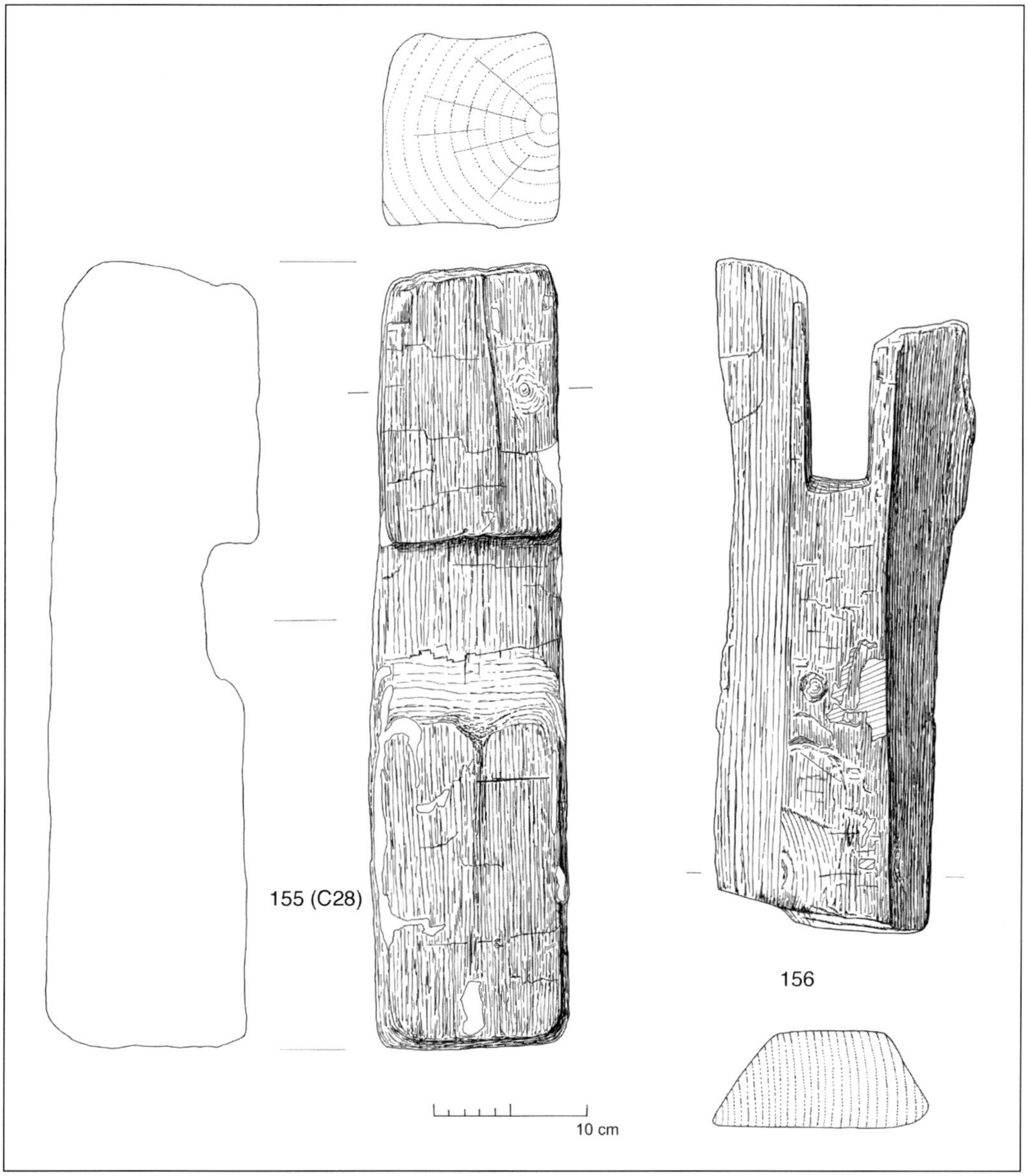

Fig. 9.12
Beams 155 (C28) and 156
(G. Gilmour)

In addition to the plank fragments, there are three fragments of very thin split oak which may be broken pieces of laths such as might be used in making woven walls. The longest of these is 13.6cm in length, has one broken end, and the other cut into a chisel shape. The thickness of these pieces is around 1.4–1.9cm except towards the ends where they are slightly tapered. In width they vary little being around 3.2–3.5cm wide.

Beams

The split timber included 48 beams, all but one of which (the species not identified) were of oak. Beams are distinguished from planks by being considerably thicker in relation to their width. Many of the beams are only small pieces broken from larger timbers, but others are considerably bigger, the largest being nearly 3m long.

Many of the smaller fragments are in very poor condition; their surfaces being heavily eroded and devoid of tool marks. The smallest is only 2.1cm long by 11cm wide and 6.5cm thick, but more typically the fragments are 20–30cm in length by *c.* 8–10cm wide

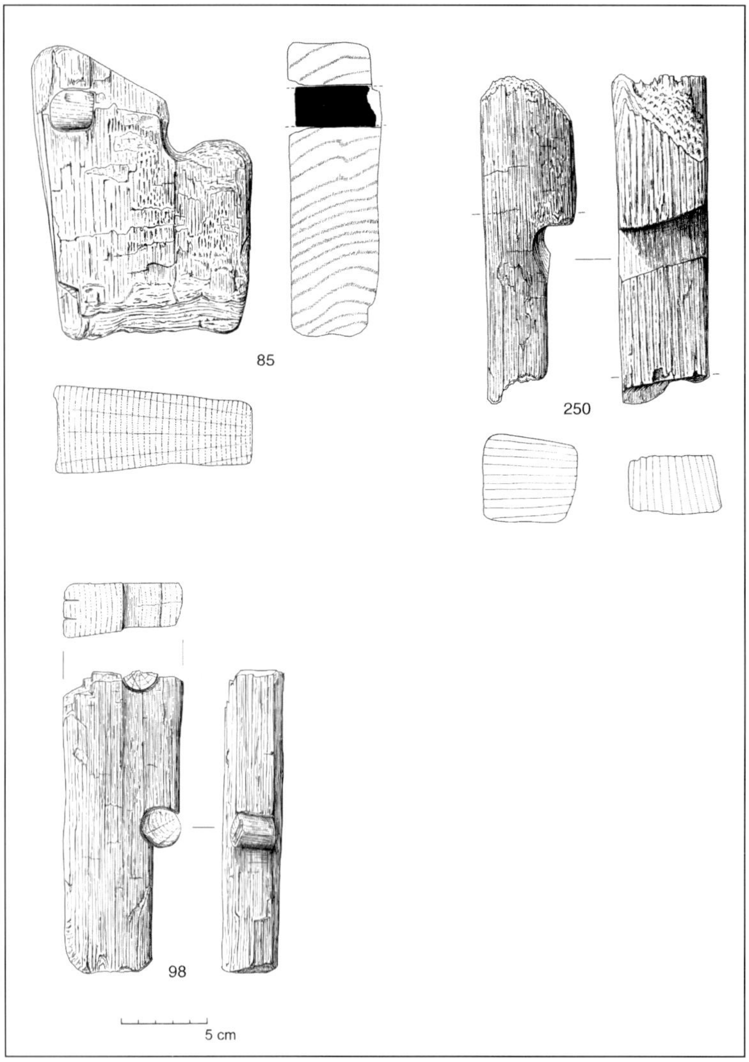

Fig. 9.13
Beams 85, 250 and 98
(G. Gilmour)

and between 4cm and 7cm thick. Of those where the splitting method could be determined, nine had been split radially and five tangentially. Most of the beam fragments were rectangular in section, but four were roughly triangular.

Two of these fragments, both found together at the base of Mill 1's millpond, were split tangentially, and may be part of the same beam. The better preserved of these is convex on one side, reflecting the natural curvature of the tree and one end has been cut at a slight angle to the length. The other piece has two distinct cut steps on one side where it has been shaped. Other examples show signs of special shaping, such as a notch, 11.5cm wide by 4.5cm deep, cut into one face of a short length of radially split timber (C155, C28, Fig. 9.12) used in the core of Mill 1's dam measuring 52cm by 10cm by 11cm, which was finished at both ends. Another beam (156, Fig. 9.12) found at the base of Mill 2's wheelhouse, is 45cm long by 14cm by 8.5cm and trapezoidal in section. It has one end cut more or less at 90° to its length, the other broken across a mortise hole which is 4.4cm wide. Three smaller beam fragments (85, 250, 98) have circular holes, *c.* 2.5cm in diameter, drilled through them, some with wooden dowels still *in situ*. These pieces are too fragmentary to determine their original function.

The larger beams show a variety of working, some of which suggests that they may in fact, be re-used timbers derived from some other structure or building. Most of the woodworking, such as the mortise holes and occasional dowel holes, appears to have no function in relation to how the beams have been used in the structures excavated. It was noted that few, if any, of the rectangular mortise holes show any sign of wear, which appears to preclude them having been used for any length of time elsewhere prior to deposition. Beams of this type were used in the retaining structure of the dam and in the wooden platform of Mill 1 where they were found in a horizontal position.

Beams with mortise holes

Twelve examples (861, 863, 871, 976, 981, 989, 1003, 1005, 1008, 1011 1013, 1022) of large beams with rectangular mortise holes positioned near one end were lifted and recorded. In two cases (1008, 1011) the beam was broken across the mortise. Beams 861

(C477, see Fig. 2.23B) and 981 (C151, see Fig. 2.33) were used as bracing members for the inner and outer wattle revetments in Mill 1's dam. Example 861 was dated to AD 616±9 years (Q10015) and 981 to late 618 or early 619 (Q10014), while 871 (C133, see Fig. 2.22B) came from the core of the dam and was dated to spring AD 619 (Q9917). The largest of the beams, 863 (C154, Q10017, see fig. 2.22B) from the timber revetment is nearly 3m in length, the smallest just over 1m long. All were split radially and their sections vary from roughly triangular to almost rectangular. The ends of some beams were cut at 90° to the length, while in other cases, one or both ends were crudely cut into a chisel-shaped point. The manner in which these chisel points were made is in strong contrast to the overall quality of workmanship, as the beams generally were carefully split and finished. It is likely, therefore, that the pointed ends are the result of reuse. There is no uniformity in the size of the mortise holes as these vary from 7.9cm by 7.6cm to 42.5cm by 20cm. Again in some cases the nature of the holes suggests that they were not an original feature of the beam.

The condition of these beams is rarely good and tool marks usually survive only in and around the mortise holes. However, the largest beam (863), dendrochronologically dated to AD 603±9 years (Q10017) and part of the timber revetment of Mill 1's dam, had adze marks along the entire length of one surface. Each tool mark was cut from the middle of the beam towards the edge at approximately 45°, creating a ridge between each cut. The adze marks vary slightly but are around 4.8cm wide. Similar shaping can be seen on 871, but in this case the cuts run parallel to the side of the beam in two bands, each tool mark being approximately 7.5cm by 3cm.

Beams with tenons

There are four examples (C1022, C620, C1004, C1018, see Figs 2.40 and 9.14 A-F) of large oak beams with tenons projecting from one end. All were from the timber platform of Mill 1, and three (C1018, C1022 and C620) were dated to AD 619/620 (Q10446, Q10445 and Q10226). In each case, the beams were split from the heartwood of substantial oak trees and were then further shaped by adzing the surfaces and shaping the tenons with axes. Initially it appears that there is not a close uniformity in the size of these beams. However, this apparent difference may be the result of one end being cut during secondary use, or in the case of (C1004), which is in poor condition, being broken. The surviving lengths of three of the beams are between 1.24m and 1.25m, the fourth being 1.48m. The lengths of the tenons of two of the beams are identical at 26cm, while the other two are slightly different at 31cm and 31.8cm respectively. In all cases, the tenons were cut so that they are slightly offset from the centre line of the beam.

At some time after their initial shaping, the beams appear to have been re-used. In all cases, a roughly rectangular mortise hole was cut a short distance from the end having the tenon. In three instances, the other end was crudely axed into a point, in two others a chisel shape and in the third a wedge shape. This secondary woodworking is quite out of character with the carefully split and adzed faces of the primary working of all four beams, in being crudely executed. The holes were more carefully cut, although they are somewhat irregular in outline and vary in size from 19.5cm by 15cm, to 30.5cm by 18.5cm.

Fig. 9.14A (left)
Beam with tenon, C1018), a possible door jamb from the bottom layer of the timber platform with a felling date of AD 619 or early AD 620 (Q10446)

Fig. 9.14B (right)
Detail of the tenon on beam C1018

Fig. 9.14C (right)
Detail of the mortise on beam C1018

Fig. 9.14D (right)
Beam with tenon, C1004 a possible door jamb from the top layer of the timber platform

Fig. 9.14E (below right)
Detail of the tenon on beam C1022 from bottom layer of timber platform with a felling date of AD 619 orAD 620 (Q10445)

Fig. 9.14F (right)
Detail of the tenon on beam C1022 (reverse side of view on 9.14E)

It would appear that the four beams represent two pairs of similar, although not identical, components of a large, timber-framed structure. In their original state, the main body of the beams were probably just over 1m in length, plus a projecting tenon of either 26cm or 31.5cm giving a total length of between 1.3m and 1.5m. The closest parallel, in shape and manufacturing detail is with the door jambs from Deer Park Farms (Lynn and McDowell *forthcoming*). However, the Deer Park Farm door jambs had holes in the tenons and a groove on the side, into which were inserted the ends of the woven house walls. These features are lacking from the Nendrum examples although, in both cases, the tenons were set slightly to one side of the beam. The Nendrum beams are slightly shorter by *c.* 25cm than those from Deer Park Farms, but they are more substantial being between 23cm and 28cm wide by 5.5cm to 19.5cm thick, as against the Deer Park Farms' examples which are less than 18cm wide. Similar beams with tenons, referred to as "tusked mortice and tenon joints", were recorded at the 7th-century horizontal-wheeled watermill at Little Island, Co. Cork (Rynne 1998, 97–99). The four beams from Nendrum may have originally been made as parts for two sets of door jambs for a building. However, as two of them had either bark or complete sapwood they may have never been used for the purpose for which they were designed, and were employed as part of a general collection of wood in the timber platform.

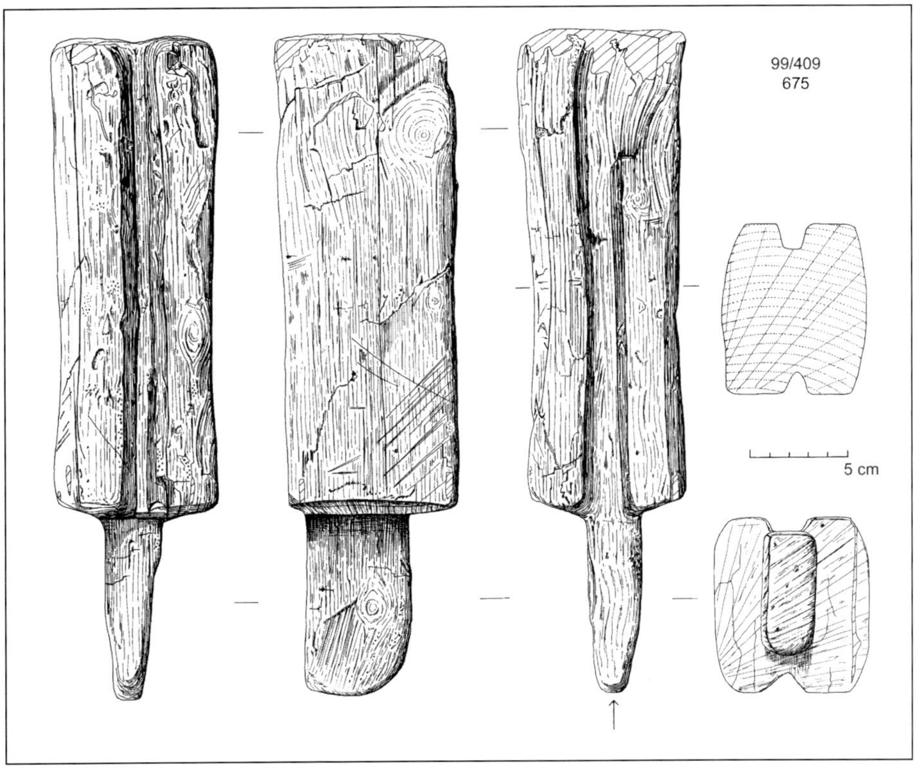

Fig. 9.15
Possible beam or post from mill building of Mill 2 (G. Gilmour)

Possible beam or post from the millhouse of Mill 2

Another beam or post (675, Fig. 9.15), found in the primary silt of the stone penstock, for which a function can confidently be suggested, is rectangular in section, measuring 8.3cm by 7.4cm, although the two opposing faces, one of which has a slight ridge along the middle, are slightly convex. Two U-shaped grooves have been cut from end to end of the flat faces. These vary in depth from 1.2cm to 1.6cm at the ends, to 2.6cm in the middle. The ends of the beam are cut at 90° to the length, but at one end a tenon, 5.5cm by 2.2cm long and with a curved end, protrudes 10.3cm beyond the cut face. The tenon has smooth surfaces but the main part of the beam is less carefully finished with many tool marks still visible. It has been positioned asymmetrically so that it is much closer to one groove than the other. Very similar short posts or beams were found during the excavation of a vertical-wheeled watermill at Morrett, Co. Laois. These formed part of the structure of the lower wheelhouse and were used to hold the plank sides in position (Lucas 1953, 15 and 22). It is highly likely that the post or beam from Nendrum, which is 34.3cm in length, was utilised in a similar way. However, as Nendrum had a stone wheelhouse, the beam is probably from the mill-house itself.

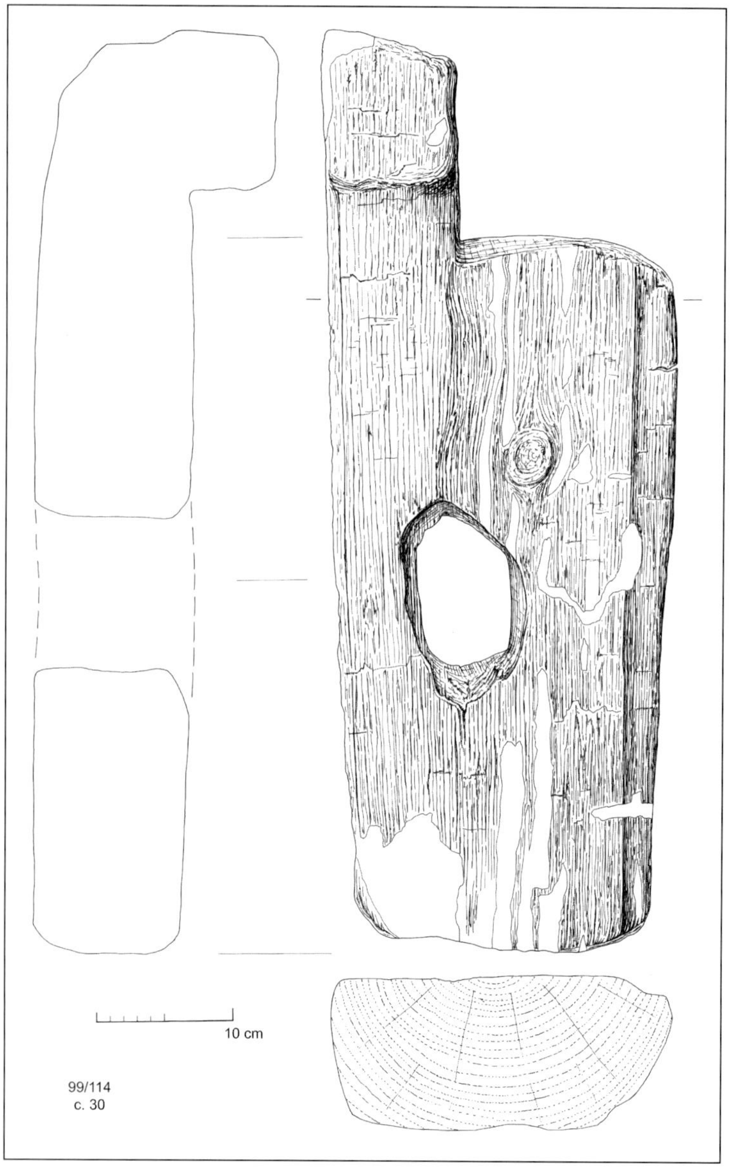

Fig. 9.16
Beam 856 (G. Gilmour)

Other large structural beams

The remaining large beams have characteristics that are difficult to understand in relation to their use in the excavated structures. These include one (855) with a roughly L-shaped section, which is 1.06m long and has one finished end that is cut approximately at 90° to the length. About 12cm from this end, which is at the top of the 'L', a rectangular hole 8cm by 7cm was cut from side to side, the tool marks suggesting the use of a chisel-like tool with a blade *c.* 1.2cm wide. The bottom edge of the 'L' has the remains of an asymmetric protruding piece that is now broken. A shallow notch or groove 22.5cm wide, has been cut from side to side into one face of the beam. Below this, a raised band of wood 18cm wide runs from side to side. On the reverse side are three circular holes, 9cm, 17cm and 22.5cm respectively from the top of the 'L'. The beam was tangentially split, with the centre of the tree being slightly offset from the middle of the beam. On one edge there is a considerable amount of sapwood remaining, with the result that this is less well-preserved and now slightly curved. The diameter of the tree from which this beam was split was considerably more than 52.5cm allowing for missing sapwood.

Another large beam (856), which is 66cm long by 26.4cm, tapering to 24cm wide, and *c.* 11.8cm thick, was split from a tree with a minimum diameter of around 30cm. It was more crudely fashioned than beam 855, with the underside being distinctly convex following the natural curvature of the outer part of the tree. The narrower end is broken and eroded, the other was cut into a curve 17.2cm wide, beyond which protruded a rectangular piece ending in a knob *c.* 12cm long by 9.5cm wide and 17cm thick. A crude, irregularly-shaped hole (see Fig. 9.16) had been cut through the thickness of the beam roughly in line with the knob. Owing to the weathered condition of the beam, few tool marks survive. On one edge, however, there were a number of tool marks *c.* 4cm wide by 5.5cm long, cut with a curved tool, possibly a concave bladed axe.

Other noteworthy examples include an incomplete length of beam (866) measuring 59cm long and 9.2cm wide and 4.9cm thick, rectangular in section, with a handle-like end that is almost elliptical in section. The other end is damaged but is slightly tapered, with the remains of a circular hole or slot 2.5cm across, cut through the thickness near one side. An unusual piece of structure is a beam (1021) that is markedly curved along its length and which has a carefully cut notch 23.5cm by *c.* 3.5cm at one end.

Stakes and piles

The difference between 'stakes' and 'piles' is largely one of size and, to a lesser extent, of function. Stakes from Nendrum were made either from lengths of split-oak timber, 6–8cm wide, or of pointed roundwood. Most came from the wattle revetments in the core of Mill 1's dam. Very few survive intact, the upper end usually being broken or weathered due to exposure to the atmosphere and tidal attrition. Piles were usually made from split oak often several metres in length and up to 28cm wide at the top end. Most were used as the larger retaining components in the dam of Mill 1.

Fig. 9.17
Stake 670 (G. Gilmour)

Stakes

Of the 102 stakes, 63 examples were fashioned from roundwood, while the remainder were made of split oak, typically around 6.5–8cm wide, usually with wedge-shaped points.

Just over half of the roundwood stakes were cut from hazel rods the rest being a mix of birch alder, willow, ash and oak. The ends were cut into a variety of different shapes, but with a predominance of chisel points, the rest being almost equally divided between wedge-shaped and pencil points. The diameters of the roundwood stakes range from 2.1cm to 8.8cm, but are typically between 4.5cm and 5cm. Interestingly, the roundwood stakes are generally better preserved and show greater detail of tool marks than those made from split oak. One of the best preserved examples (948) is 72cm long, with a weathered top and a wedge-shaped point that is slightly damaged due to compression where it was driven into the ground.

The non-roundwood stakes were all made from split lengths of oak. The ring and ray patterns indicate that these were made from trees or branches of considerable size, so that the section of each stake represents only a small part of the radius of the tree. The patterns also show that all such stakes were radially split so that usually two of the sides are split faces running parallel to the rays.

None of the tops of the stakes survive, all are either broken or heavily eroded by tidal attrition. Indeed, some are so badly damaged and decayed that it is impossible to determine their precise shape. Of those that are better preserved, 14 are rectangular in section and 16 are triangular. In the case of the triangular-sectioned stakes, the third side, which is sometimes slightly curved, lies closest to the outer part of the tree and has been split or axed (e.g. 692). The rectangular-sectioned stakes may differ only in that the point of the triangle has been split or axed away and one or more sides may have been further worked to produce a more regular section. In a few cases, however, they were split from a large timber so that the rays lie almost parallel to one another, thus providing the opportunity to split a rectangular-sectioned stake without further trimming on two opposing faces.

Where the split oak stakes were sufficiently preserved to allow observation, it was noted that 10 had chisel points, 12 had wedge-shaped points while one had been cut into a double-wedge point (i.e. cut from both sides) and one had a pencil point. Generally, the quality of preservation was so poor that individual tool marks have not survived.

Piles

A total of 23 piles in varying degrees of preservation were recorded. Most were used as strengthening uprights in Mill 1's dam. These were made from split oak either derived from large trees or, more commonly, from small trunks or branches split into halves or quarters and then further shaped.

Four of the split-oak piles (862, 975, 1007, 1010), have rectangular mortise holes cut near their tops. The two best preserved piles (862, 1007), are both nearly 2.7m long, are rectangular in section with a point that is cut on four sides to form a shape between the shape of a double wedge and a pencil end. The slighter of the two (862) measures 16.7cm by 6.7cm near the weathered top, but tapers to 9cm by 5cm just above the point. The wood on one side is totally untrimmed, with bark and sapwood still *in situ,* but the other three sides have been split and then axed into shape. The other pile is larger in section, and varies in width between 17.5cm and 20cm and is about 11.5cm in thickness. Similarly one side follows the natural curvature of the tree with little or no modification.

Another pile similar to 862 and 1007 is 977, which is just over 1.6m long. It does not have a mortise hole, but around 63cm from the top there is a series of shallow grooves that may be the result of chafing by a rope. Two of the other split-oak piles are roughly triangular in section, having been made from a segment of tree so that one side has sapwood and, in one case, part of a side branch still attached.

Four other piles (295, 298, 296, 297) survive to something close to their full length. The longest of these (296, C170) is 2.86m in length, the other three being 2.3m, 1.72m and 1.6m long, and was dated to late AD 620 or early AD 621 (Q9932). It was made by splitting a small tree trunk (*c.* 22cm in diameter), the pile being formed from just over one quarter of the trunk. Much of the sapwood and bark is still intact, except on the lower 22.5cm where the pile has been trimmed in a series of steps. Two of the piles (295 and 298) were made from half a tree (*c.* 12cm and *c.* 21–28cm in diameter), split longitudinally. The end of one was cut into a crude chisel point, the other into an asymmetric wedge. The fourth pile (295), 1.72m, long was also made from half a tree, but the sapwood was then trimmed off to create a roughly rectangular section 18cm by 19cm, tapering to 8cm. It is now in three pieces with a break across a mortise hole (7.6cm wide) cut towards the top end. The lower end, which is wider, was trimmed to a wedge-shaped point.

Fig. 9.18
Pile 975 (C135, see Fig. 2.22A) with an estimated felling date of AD 625 ± 9 years (Q9919)

Timber and woodland

Thomas McErlean

THE RE-USED WOOD, PROBLEMS OF INTERPRETATION

The early 7th-century wood assemblage from the first mill complex has provided a very rich archive of Early Medieval woodworking. It is beyond the scope of the present work to fully research the information it contains, but hopefully it will be fully exploited in future years. The assemblage and its context have raised a number of important issues, which are discussed in this section.

A significant content of wood encountered in the structure of the dam of Mill 1 and its associated landing stage has the appearance of having been re-used or recycled from other structures. The clearest manifestation of this is the presence of mortise holes in many of the piles, beams and planks used in the dam and the landing place, which did not have any function in the way the timbers were employed, and in examples of planks and beams converted into piles by making a point at one end. A simple interpretation of this is that it represents a gather-up of easily obtained timber to complete a job in hand and constitutes clear evidence of the recycling of timber from pre-existing buildings associated with the monastery and probably from structures situated within the monastic enclosure.

There are, however, problems with this interpretation. Many of the worked pieces had complete sapwood and in some cases, bark. As bark and sapwood is fragile and prone to damage, their survival would seem to indicate that it was unlikely they were re-used from an earlier structure, or at least that the structure from which the timber was derived was of very recent construction. Apart from a very small number of cases, there is little indication of worked pieces having been used prior to their use in the construction of the mill complex. Many of the mortise holes are in very fresh condition and apart from the odd example where a mortise was used as a convenient hole to drive a stake through, appear unused. These observations make the classification of most of the worked pieces encountered as 're-used wood' in need of modification to that of 'prepared wood', that is timber which has been worked into planks and beams and so on, but not actually used for the purpose it was intended. If valid, this interpretation raises a number of pertinent questions. Why were they using timber finished as planks and beams in this way when much simpler woodworking would have sufficed? What was the wood being prepared for and why was it used in the dam and landing place rather than being reserved for its original function?

The evidence, in the small portion of the site excavated, for the employment of re-used and prepared timber would seem to imply a shortage of the resource and that the builders had to turn to the prepared stock or ransack recent monastic buildings to complete the project. However, the presence of the large volume of oak used in the dam (see below), would seem to favour the interpretation that there was an abundant oak woodland resource of mature timber to be exploited. An explanation, however, may be forthcoming when the nature of the project is considered. The construction of a tidal dam in the intertidal zone presents particular problems. One of the major challenges being that once started it had to be completed within a very short period as a half-finished dam would be very vulnerable to tidal action. Unless the structure was swiftly executed and fully consolidated, previous work would have been in danger of being quickly eradicated. It is very possible that during the construction of the dam the builders may have faced a shortage of felled wood, and to finish the job in hand as quickly as possible had to raid a stock of wood prepared for other uses.

STOCKPILE OF PREPARED TIMBER

This explanation which envisages the existence of a stockpile of relatively finished timber suggests a scenario where workers were felling timber in an oak wood, immediately preparing it for use by the reduction of round wood into beams, planks and piles including detailed working such the making of mortises and building up a stockpile of prepared wood consisting of different types of worked pieces needed or anticipated to be needed. Further it suggests that the tree felling which took place from late AD 618 to AD 621 was carried out not solely for the construction of the mill complex but was part of the preparation of a much larger building project constituting a major re-development of the monastery. Indeed given the present lack of archaeological evidence of a 6th century date one may speculate that it is possible that this may represent the actual foundation of the monastery itself.

The utilization of recycled wood has dating implications with its potential to cast doubt on the precise dating of the construction of first mill to the years AD 619–621 established from the dating of major felling operations in AD 618, 619 and possibly 620. If much of the wood was derived from previously existing buildings, then the dating obtained from them dates their construction rather than that of the mill complex. The interpretation that the wood was prepared for but not actually used in other structures removes this problem and allows their dating to be accepted as the construction date for the mill complex. Additional evidence to support the interpretation that the wood encountered from the mill complex was employed immediately after felling comes from examples of unworked logs among the dated examples belonging to the AD 619–621 horizon. It is also strengthened from the context of dated timbers in the mill complex, which fits a logical construction sequence with the earliest timbers being found in the dam and the latest in the millpond and timber platform (see p. 70) suggesting the immediate use of felled timber rather than the use of wood derived from a felling horizon detached from the building of the mill complex.

THE LOCAL WOODLANDS IN THE EARLY 7TH CENTURY

The wood evidence allows some observations of the character of the local woodlands in the vicinity of the site in the early 7th century. An impression of the composition of the local woodland cover is provided by the identification of the wood species exploited. A wide range of the species is present, alder, ash, birch, elm, hazel, holly, oak, willow and yew and examples of the *Pomoideae* group which covers possible samples of pear, apple, hawthorn or rowan (see Davis, Appendix 1). Some of these species, including ash, alder, birch, elm and yew occurred only in very small quantities and made a negligible contribution to the wood used in the construction of the mill complex. This leaves oak by far the most important wood for large structural elements, with holly the most important one for the wattle work and the posts of palisade/breakwater. The range of tree types selected for use are, firstly, presumably a reflection of what was available in the local woodlands, and secondly, a deliberate choice of the best type suitable for its intended use and cannot be taken as a straightforward representation of the relative strength of each species in the locality. A direct indication of the relative economic value of the range of wood species in the Irish Early Medieval environment is supplied by the tree list in *Bretha Comaithchesa,* 'the laws of neighbourhoods' (Kelly 1997, 380–381) which divides them into four classes, 'nobles of the wood', 'commoners of the wood', 'lower divisions of the wood' and 'bushes of the wood'. Oak as might be expected is among the six noble trees listed and no doubt first choice as hard durable timber for constructional purposes and for foreshore conditions and if available would not have been substituted for anything inferior. Holly is also among the seven 'nobles of the wood' and appears to have been present in abundance. The local sheltered maritime environment with its lack of frost would have favoured its growth. Its wood is hard and durable and according to the documentary sources was used for chariot shafts (Kelly 1997, 382). It can be pollarded but there was no evidence forthcoming that this was the case among the sample. Ash, also one of the 'nobles', is poorly represented with only two examples present, the oar and a single stake/upright. As it may have been reserved for more specialist use it may be unrepresented, and it can be noted that today there are a number of ash growing on the monastic site and in surrounding hedges. The presence of yew, another of the nobles, is limited to the turned bowls and hoops representing the very specialised use of this wood. However, it spite of the fact that the wood recovered reflects the selective use of certain species it seems clear because of the large volume of oak and holly present, a woodland rich in these two species existed in the locality of the site and the immediate impression is of an oak woodland with an under story or fringe of holly. The nearest similar study is the species identification of wood used to construct the Early Medieval fish traps across the Strangford Lough from Nendrum (Deevy 2002, 389–595), which in contrast, species selection points to Fen-Carr type woodland dominated with alder and hazel.

The sheltered and mild coastal conditions around Nendrum, where the temperature rarely falls below 2° C, favours tree growth. The congenial conditions for tree-growth on

Mahee Island today is demonstrated by the fact that in the 1960s, the western end of the island was planted by Mr Paddy Mackie, who included many exotics which have thrived. In summary the evidence suggests that at the beginning of the 7th century, there was rich woodland in the vicinity of the site. This is further underlined by analyses of the mosses (see Hall, Appendix 3) a very large quantity of which was used in both dams, clearly demonstrating that much of it was gathered from nearby woodland. Some idea of the age of this woodland is supplied by dendrocronological information where it was possible to construct a tree-ring chronology of almost 300 years from AD 322–620/21 (see Table 2.2). The dated samples contained many trees, which started growth in the 5th century as well as a small number of older trees with one, which started growth in the 4th century AD and two in the 3rd century AD. This evidence points to the existence in the locality of a mature indeed possibly quite ancient oak woodland. Indeed the poem of Mo-Choí and the bird in the martyrologies of *Óengus* and *Donegal* (see p. 293) which is suggested serves as the foundation story of the monastery embodies the atmosphere of a forested environment and its exploitation with its picture of Mo-Choí and a work-force of 140 young men cutting wood to build a church.

Some 1,000 years later at the beginning of the 17th century, the area was one of the most densely forested in the country (McErlean 2002, 115–117). Raven's *c.* 1625 survey map of Mahee and the adjacent area shows Island Reagh, which overlooks the site from the north, as partially wooded (see Fig. 9.19). While palynological evidence for the imme-

Fig. 9.19
Map of the Reagh Island and Mahee Island portion of the Hamilton estates by Thomas Raven c.1625 showing woods on Reagh Island and Cross Island (courtesy of the North Down Heritage Centre, Bangor)

diate area is presently lacking it is not beyond reasonable speculation that a similar forested environment existed in the local landscape in the early years of the monastery, and was to become radically altered by the building programmes of the monks.

Although only a small part of the dam of Mill 1 was excavated it is possible to estimate roughly the amount of wood needed for the whole structure from its established dimensions and structural composition. The palisade or breakwater was traced for 26.5m and represented by 63 posts (Figs 2.1 and 2.38), its total length is in the region of 110m and a rough estimate may suggest that it required about 300 holly posts. Taking this figure with the amount used in the wattle work and to line the bottom of the external ditch underlying the dam it represents the clearance of a considerable stand of holly.

Turning to oak a similar estimate can be made. The timber revetment in the core of the dam composed of two courses of plans and beams used as shuttering may consist of something in the region of 220m of oak timber. To this can be added the many piles used in the dam and the timber in the landing stage. While no timbers that could be associated with the structure of first mill building itself were retrieved, it also is likely to have required a significant amount of oak. It seems apparent therefore that the volume of oak needed to build the mill complex must have been considerable and have necessitated the felling of oak woodland of considerable extent. If as has been suggested above, this was linked to a much larger building programme the case for a major horizon of forest clearance in the locality can be entertained. Apart from the need for timber this clearance may be coupled with a programme to bring more land into cultivation by the conversion of woodland into arable and pasture with the resulting increase in corn yield ultimately going to the mill to be ground.

The evidence would seem to support the interpretation that a large stand of oak trees was present in the vicinity in the early 7th century, which was subsequently cleared by monastic exploitation. The excavated evidence of the second mill with its relative absence of oak as a constructional material may imply that by the late 8th century it was becoming a locally exhausted resource, but as this is largely based on negative evidence more information is required before this can be demonstrated as being so.

Chapter 10

Osteological Report on the Mammal Bones from the Excavations

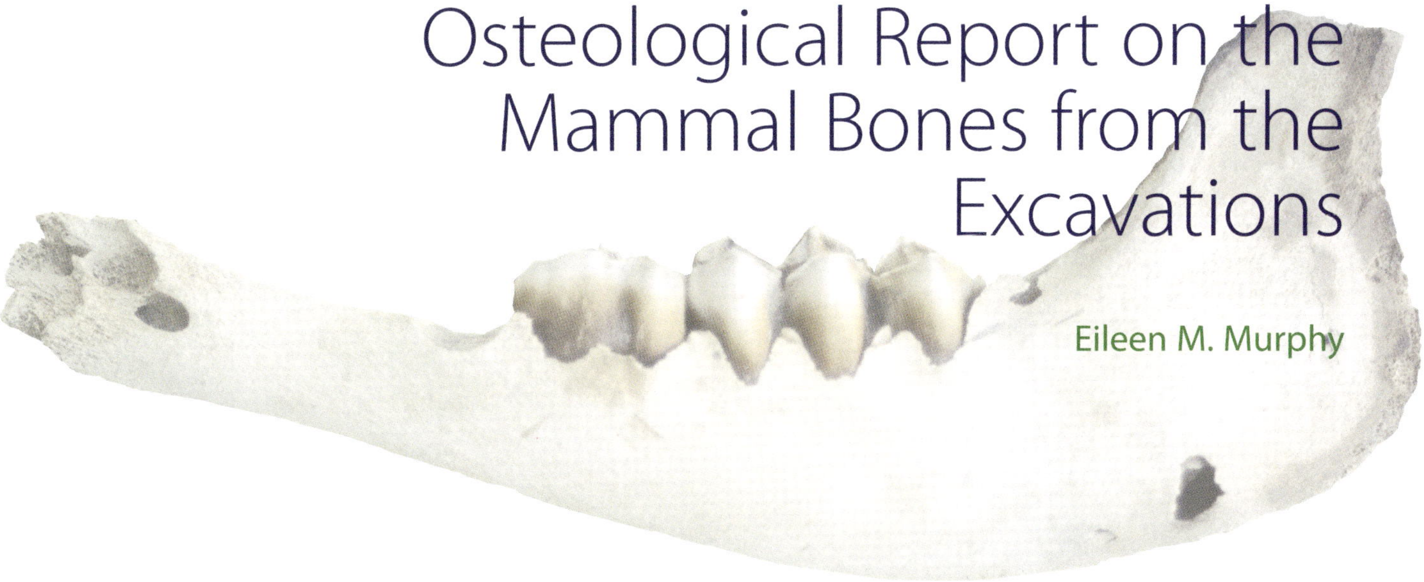

Eileen M. Murphy

Chapter 10
Osteological Report on the Mammal Bones from the Excavations

Eileen M. Murphy

INTRODUCTION

A small, but interesting, assemblage of animal bone, as well as a single fragment of human bone, was retrieved from 79 contexts, all of which were associated with the two mills and their associated millponds. The majority are considered to date to *c*. AD 600–900, with the exception of a near-complete dog skeleton (C176) found in the upper silts of the millpond of Mill 2, the skeleton of a calf (C689), a lamb or kid skeleton (C1073) from surface silt over the dam of Mill 1 and a small amount of disarticulated bone recovered from Post-Medieval horizons (see Chapters 2 and 3). Each of the contexts was analysed individually, but only a few produced sufficient quantities of bone. Consequently, the research strategy adopted for the purposes of this report has been to group the bone obtained from all contexts into a single *corpus* for each of the two periods. It is considered that this approach has enabled the most meaningful interpretation of the general economy. Occasional references to BO numbers relate to the Nendrum bone catalogue.

HUMAN

An unfused humeral proximal epiphysis was recovered from Early Medieval context 40/61. This part of the skeleton fuses at the age of 16–25 years (Brothwell 1981, 66), and it is probable that the bone came from a younger adolescent individual.

FAUNAL METHODOLOGY

The proportions of the different species present in the sample groups were quantified using the fragmentation and minimum number of individuals (MNI) methods advocated by Chaplin (1971, 64–67 and 69–75). The metrical analysis of all species was undertaken following the system of von den Driesch (1976). The estimated shoulder-height values of most species were calculated using the multiplication factors quoted in von den Driesch and Boessneck (1974), while the multiplication factors of Harcourt (1974, 154) were used to estimate the approximate shoulder-height values of the dog remains. Differentiation between sheep and goat was undertaken on the basis of the morphological characteristics of the horn-cores (Boessneck 1969, 354–355).

Sex determination of cattle was undertaken on the basis of metrical analysis of the distal metacarpals (McCormick, 1987) and the distal metatarsals (Murphy *forthcoming* a). The shape and size of the canine was used as a guide for the sex determination of pigs (Schmid 1972, 81). Age-at-death values of cattle, pigs and ovicaprids were calculated on the basis of tooth eruption and attrition data (Higham 1967, 104–106; Grant 1982), and the state of epiphyseal fusion (Silver 1969, 285–286). Age-at-death estimates for dogs were calculated on the basis of the state of epiphyseal fusion (*ibid.*), while those for cats were based on the epiphyseal fusion data of Habermehl (1961).

INTRODUCTION TO THE MAMMALIAN FAUNA

A list of the domesticated and wild mammalian species represented in the Nendrum assemblage is presented in Table 10.1.

Table 10.1: A checklist of the mammalian fauna species present in the faunal assemblages

Mammalian fauna species present
Cattle *(Bos taurus)*
Sheep *(Ovis aries)*
Goat *(Capra hircus)*
Pig *(Sus domesticus)*
Horse *(Equus caballus)*
Dog *(Canis familiaris)*
Cat *(Felis catus)*
Red deer *(Cervus elaphus)*

EARLY MEDIEVAL ASSEMBLAGE

The MNI and bone-fragment distributions for the *corpus* of Early Medieval animal bone are presented in Table 10.2. Despite the small sample size, it is apparent that cattle were the predominant species, with ovicaprids and pigs being of secondary importance. The remains of horse, dog, cat and red deer were represented in very small numbers only.

The bones displayed a variety of states of preservation, with some fragments in an excellent condition, while others were poorly preserved and displayed extensive surface erosion and flaking. In addition, some of the bone fragments displayed clear evidence of gnawing by rodents. A number of contexts contained fragments of burnt bone. In all cases this was grey or white in colour which may indicate that it had been burned at temperatures in excess of 525 °C (Mays 1998, 217).

Table 10.2: Fragment counts and MNI values for the Early Medieval assemblage. The MNI values for each element are included in brackets.

	CATTLE	HORSE	SHEEP/ GOAT	PIG	DOG	CAT	RED DEER
HORN	1	-	1	-	-	-	8
SKULL	63 (2)	-	-	20 (2)	1	-	1
MANDIBLE	28 (2)	3	8	12 (2)	1	-	-
TEETH	35	5	11	22 (5)	1	-	-
ATLAS	7	-	1	-	-	-	-
AXIS	-	-	-	-	-	-	-
SCAPULA	53 (11)	-	14 (5)	11 (4)	-	-	-
HUMERUS	61 (8)	-	3	12 (2)	1	-	-
RADIUS	39 (5)	-	6 (3)	3 (2)	-	-	-
ULNA	4 (2)	-	1	6 (4)	-	1	-
METACARPAL	16 (3)	-	3	3	-	-	-
PELVIS	40 (5)	-	13 (6)	13 (5)	-	-	-
FEMUR	37 (3)	-	7 (2)	11 (4)	-	1	-
PATELLA	2	-	-	1	-	-	-
TIBIA	53 (6)	1	7 (3)	1	-	1	-
FIBULA	-	-	-	1	-	-	-
ASTRALAGUS	7 (4)	-	-	-	-	-	-
CALCANEUS	12 (7)	-	-	2	-	-	-
METATARSAL	13 (3)	-	2	-	1	-	-
TAR/CAR	8	-	-	-	-	-	-
PHALANX 1	5	-	-	-	-	-	-
PHALANX 2	5	-	-	-	-	-	-
PHALANX 3	3	-	-	2	-	-	-
SACRUM	4	6	-	2	-	-	-
TOTAL	496	15	77	122	5	3	9
TOTAL %	68.2	2.1	10.6	16.8	0.7	0.4	1.2
MNI	11	1	6	5	1	1	1
MNI %	42.3	3.8	23.2	19.3	3.8	3.8	3.8

Small ribs - 5
Medium ribs - 101
Large ribs - 253

Small vertebrae - 2
Medium vertebrae - 41
Large vertebrae - 91

Caudal vertebrae - 9
Unid. frags. - 273
Burnt bone - 2

CATTLE

Representation of skeletal elements

Bones associated with both prime and poor quality cuts of meat were represented among the *corpus* of cattle bones. The preponderance of bones from higher quality meat joints, such as scapulae, pelves and femora, would tend to suggest that there was some preferential selection of these cuts. Nevertheless, bones from lower-quality joints, including the skull, metapodia and tarsals were also represented in the assemblage, indicating that all parts of the carcass were exploited.

Age-at-death

The cattle age-at-death profile based on the state of epiphyseal fusion is shown in Table 10.3.

Table 10.3: Cattle age/slaughter estimates for the Early Medieval assemblage based on the state of epiphyseal fusion (Silver 1969, 285–286)

Bone	Age of fusion (mths)	AD 600 – 900	
		Fused	Unfused
pelvis, scapula	7 – 10	23 (77%)	7 (23%)
distal humerus, proximal radius	10 – 18	21 (95%)	1 (5%)
distal tibia, distal metacarpal, distal metatarsal, distal phalanx I	24 – 36	18 (62%)	11 (38%)
proximal femur, calcaneus, ulna	36 – 42	7 (64%)	4 (36%)
proximal humerus, proximal tibia, distal radius, distal femur	42 – 48	17 (68%)	8 (32%)

Despite the small sample size, it would seem that cattle of all ages were being slaughtered. Only a small number of young animals, however, less than 7 to 10 months in age, were identified (n=7). A number of neonatal calf bones – a right frontal bone from the primary silt over the dam of Mill 1 (C404), right and left scapulae from the late 8th-century landing place (C697), a tarsal, an astralagus and a metacarpal from the tailrace of Mill 1 (C856) – were recovered. None of the neonatal long bones displayed cut marks and it is difficult to ascertain if the animals had been deliberately slaughtered or had died of natural causes. The majority of cattle appear to have been slaughtered between 10 and 36 months, although quite a number of animals with an age-at-death greater than 42–48 months were also represented in the *corpus* (n=17). The age-profile is quite characteristic of a dairying economy, and the older cattle may have been females which were not slaughtered until they were no longer able to bear calves and produce sufficient milk.

It was only possible to determine the age-at-death for five cattle mandibles. A mandible from a young calf (BO 96), recovered from the primary silt of the wheelhouse of Mill 2, had an age-at-death estimate of 1–4 months. This specimen displayed cut marks and evidence of burning, which may indicate that the animal had been deliberately slaughtered (Fig. 10.1). Another mandible, retrieved from the primary silt over the dam of Mill 1, (C404) provided an age-at-death estimate of 8–13 months, while one (C43) recovered from the bottom of the millpond of Mill 2 had an approximate age-at-death of 15–16 months. A specimen from the core of the late 8th-century landing place (C690) came from an animal with an approximate age-at-death of 15–18 months. In addition, one recovered from the same structure (C886) had an age-at-death of around 40 months (Higham 1967, 105; Grant 1982).

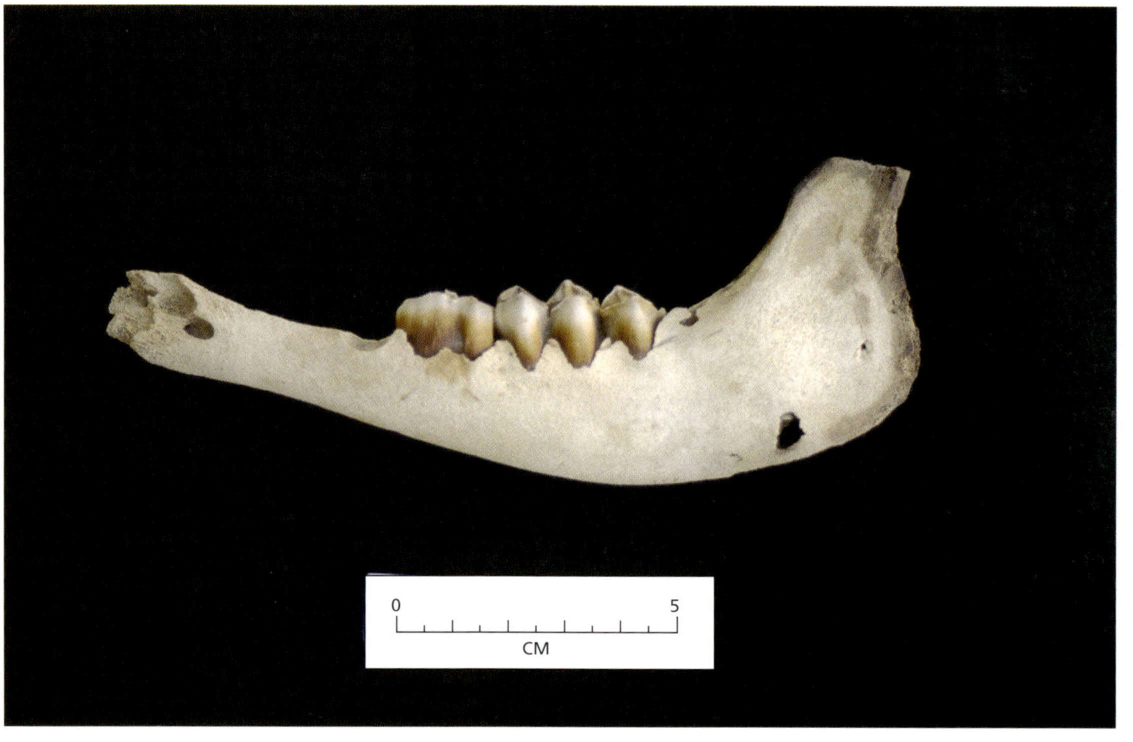

Fig. 10.1 Calf mandible (BO 96) with evidence of cutmarks and burning recovered from the primary silt of the wheelhouse of Mill 2

The typical Early Medieval cattle age/slaughter pattern, such as that recorded for Moynagh Crannóg, Co. Meath, displays a very low frequency of young calves (McCormick 1997, 822). In addition, a peak in age/slaughter occurs between the ages of 12 and 24 months, and a high frequency of cattle with an age-at-death greater than 36 months may be observed also. This form of profile has been considered indicative of a dairying economy. The age/slaughter pattern characteristic of a Late Medieval urban assemblage, such as that recorded for Waterford, displays a notable peak in slaughter at the age of 36 months or greater. This has been interpreted as indicative of a beef economy, in which the principal objective of the stockrearers was to exploit the lucrative urban meat market. The animals were not slaughtered until they reached full size, since they would yield the greatest quantity of meat at that time (McCormick 1997, 822). Although the age data for cattle obtained from the Nendrum assemblage is limited, the age/slaughter profile would appear to mirror that expected in a dairying economy.

Sex

Sex determination of cattle was undertaken on the basis of metrical analysis of the metapodia (McCormick 1987; Murphy *forthcoming a*). Multivariate analysis of a large sample of cattle metacarpals recovered from Viking levels at Fishamble St., Dublin, indicated that animals with distal breadths of less than 55.5mm were probably female, while those with distal breadths greater than 57.5mm were most likely to be male (McCormick 1987). Analysis of 46 cattle metatarsals from Late- to Post-Medieval contexts from Carrickfergus indicated that the distal breadths of metatarsals from females were generally less than 52.5mm, while those greater than this value were most likely to be male (Murphy *forthcoming a*). It should be remembered, however, that metrical analysis of cattle metapodia can only be undertaken on animals with age-at-death values greater than 24 months, since the bones do not fuse until this time (Silver 1969, 285–286).

One male and two female metacarpals and a single female metatarsal were identified from the assemblage, while the right and left pelvis from a single cow were recovered from the upper silt in the wheelhouse of Mill 2 (BO 168). In addition, single female pelves were retrieved from the bottom of the millpond of Mill 2 (C61) and the associated landing place (C697), while a male pelvis was recovered from the same structure (C690). Although the number of individuals of identifiable sex is small, the findings would tend to suggest that more adult females than males were maintained, and this again would tend to support the interpretation that a dairying economy was in operation.

Size and type

The metrical data and the estimated shoulder height values obtained from the cattle bones are presented in Table 10.4.

Table 10.4: Cattle metrical information (mm) for the Early Medieval assemblage (von den Driesch 1976) and estimated shoulder height values (cm) (Fock 1966 and Matolcsi 1970 as quoted in von den Driesch and Boessneck 1974, 336)

Bone	GL	Bp	Bd	BT	GLI	SD	LAR	LA	GBP	Sex	ESH (cm)
Scapula	-	-	-	-	-	-	-	-	54.1	-	-
Scapula	-	-	-	-	-	-	-	-	58.4	-	-
Scapula	-	-	-	-	-	-	-	-	58	-	-
Scapula	-	-	-	-	-	-	-	-	64.1	-	-
Scapula	-	-	-	-	-	-	-	-	61	-	-
Scapula	-	-	-	-	-	-	-	-	57	-	-
Scapula	-	-	-	-	-	-	-	-	55.2	-	-
Humerus	-	-	69.2	58.7	-	-	-	-	-	-	-
Humerus	-	-	81.1	68.6	-	-	-	-	-	-	-
Humerus	-	-	86.5	69.7	-	-	-	-	-	-	-

Bone	GL	Bp	Bd	BT	GLI	SD	LAR	LA	GBP	Sex	ESH (cm)
Humerus	-	-	72.6	62.9	-	-	-	-	-	-	-
Humerus	-	-	-	73.8	-	-	-	-	-	-	-
Humerus	-	-	86.9	71.6	-	-	-	-	-	-	-
Radius	-	71	-	-	-	-	-	-	-	-	-
Radius	-	-	63.9	-	-	-	-	-	-	-	-
Radius	-	-	67.6	-	-	-	-	-	-	-	-
Metacarpal	212	-	60	-	-	32.7	-	-	-	M	132.5
Metacarpal	174	48	47.5	-	-	26.5	-	-	-	F	104.4
Metacarpal	-	52.5	-	-	-	28.1	-	-	-	-	-
Metacarpal	-	-	49.9	-	-	-	-	-	-	F	-
Pelvis	-	-	-	-	-	-	40.6	53	-	F	-
Pelvis	-	-	-	-	-	-	40.1	-	-	F	-
Pelvis	-	-	-	-	-	-	43.5	63.6	-	F	-
Pelvis	-	-	-	-	-	-	45.7	54.6	-	F	-
Femur	-	-	73.2	-	-	-	-	-	-	-	-
Tibia	374	95.8	61.7	-	-	40.7	-	-	-	-	129
Tibia	-	90.7	-	-	-	-	-	-	-	-	-
Tibia	-	-	56.5	-	-	32.9	-	-	-	-	-
Tibia	-	-	56.1	-	-	-	-	-	-	-	-
Tibia	-	-	54.2	-	-	-	-	-	-	-	-
Tibia	-	-	49.6	-	-	-	-	-	-	-	-
Tibia	-	-	56.5	-	-	33.7	-	-	-	-	-
Astralagus	-	-	34.2	-	57.1	-	-	-	-	-	-
Astralagus	-	-	39.2	-	63.3	-	-	-	-	-	-
Astralagus	-	-	35.9	-	55.9	-	-	-	-	-	-
Astralagus	-	-	36.1	-	58.1	-	-	-	-	-	-
Astralagus	-	-	41	-	66.6	-	-	-	-	-	-
Calcaneus	115.5	-	-	-	-	-	-	-	-	-	-
Calcaneus	114.7	-	-	-	-	-	-	-	-	-	-
Calcaneus	112.6	-	-	-	-	-	-	-	-	-	-
Calcaneus	113.9	-	-	-	-	-	-	-	-	-	-
Metatarsal	192	-	-	-	-	21.5	-	-	-	-	104.6
Metatarsal	196	38.2	45.2	-	-	22.4	-	-	-	F	104.9
Metatarsal	-	38	-	-	-	21.8	-	-	-	-	-

The estimated shoulder height values for cattle ranged from 104.4cm to 132.5cm, with a mean value of 115.1cm. The three smaller Nendrum cattle (shoulder heights 104.4cm, 104.6cm, 104.9cm) would have been of similar small stature to animals represented in other Irish Early Christian assemblages. At Moynagh Crannóg, Co. Meath, for example, cattle had shoulder heights that ranged from 106.3cm to 118.3cm, with a mean of 112.8cm (McCormick 1997, 827). Cattle from Early Medieval contexts at Drumcliffe, Co. Sligo, had a range of shoulder height values of 102.3cm to 109.8cm, with a mean value of 105.5cm (Murphy and McCormick 1994). The two larger animals from Nendrum (shoulder heights 129cm, 132.5cm) appear to have greater shoulder height values than animals generally encountered in Irish Early Medieval assemblages. One of these was definitely male and it is probable that both beasts were large males. It is also possible that the occurrence of these larger cattle indicates that the inhabitants of the site were undertaking a degree of selective breeding. Since the number of measurable bones was so small, however, this interpretation is tentative.

Fig. 10.2
Near-complete cattle cranium (BO 168) with clear evidence of having been pole-axed recovered from the upper silt of the wheelhouse of Mill 2

Butchery

While the cattle bones retrieved from the Nendrum tide mills were generally in a very fragmentary condition, a large proportion of the better-preserved bones displayed evidence of deliberate butchery.

A near-complete cranium, recovered from the upper silt of the wheelhouse of Mill 2 (BO 168), displayed clear evidence of having been pole-axed (Fig. 10.2). A square-shaped depressed fracture, measuring approximately 4cm medio-laterally by 5cm antero-posteriorly, was evident at the midpoint of the frontal bone medial to the orbits. (Fig. 10.3). The bone at the posterior aspect of the perforation had been cleanly broken through, while that of the more anterior aspect displayed a crushed appearance. After the animal had been killed by pole-axing it was decapitated. A large chop mark was evident on the basioccipital region where the instrument had cut through the right and left occipital condyles and the left paramastoid process (Fig. 10.4). The horn-cores had been removed from the cranium and a number of crude cut marks, which ran obliquely, were evident where their bases would have been (Fig. 10.5). The

Fig. 10.3
Detail of the perforation that was attained during pole-axing in the cattle cranium (BO 168) retrieved from the upper silt of the wheelhouse of Mill 2

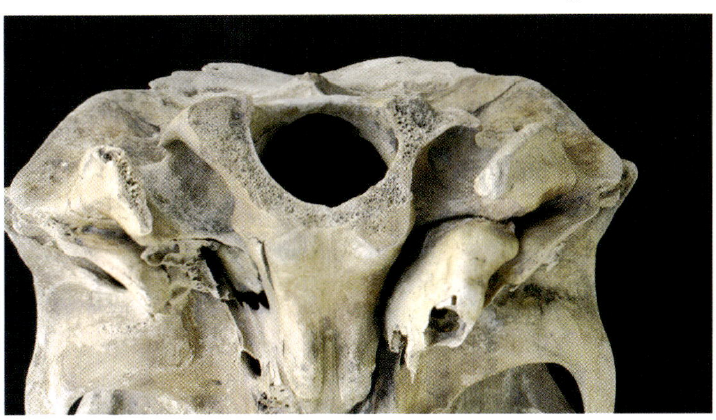

Fig. 10.4
Evidence of decapitation in the cattle cranium (BO 168) retrieved from the upper silt of the wheelhouse of Mill 2

Fig. 10.5
Crude chop marks indicative of the removal of the horn-cores on the cattle cranium (BO 168) retrieved from the upper silt of the wheelhouse of Mill 2

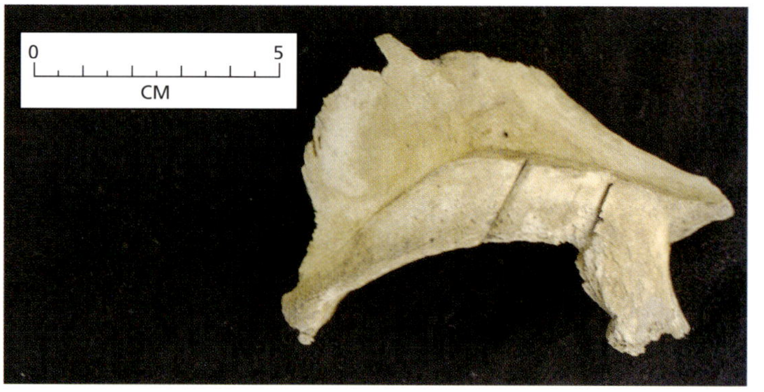

Fig. 10.7
Cutmarks on the margins of a cattle orbit recovered from the silt in the stone penstock (C16)

Fig. 10.6
Cattle cranium which displayed evidence for the removal of its horn-cores and possible evidence of having been pole-axed recovered from the primary silt over the dam of Mill 1

horn-cores had also been chopped off the remains of a cranium recovered from the primary silt over the dam of Mill 1 (C404), and a perforation, which may have been made during pole-axing, was evident on the superior aspect of the cranium (Fig. 10.6). An atlas recovered from the initial silting of the millpond of Mill 2 (C513) also displayed a large chop mark, which is again indicative of the animal being decapitated. An orbit recovered from the silt in the stone penstock (C16) displayed a number of cut marks on its margins

(Fig. 10.7) and it is possible that these were made during the removal of the eye, or when the animal was skinned.

Bones from both poor and high-quality meat cuts displayed butchery marks. First and second phalanges (very poor meat joints) retrieved from the primary silt over the dam of Mill 1 (C404), for example, displayed cut marks on their shafts. A scapula (high quality meat joint) recovered from the primary silt over the dam of Mill 1 (C90), displayed evidence of having been chopped and burnt at its neck. In addition, a number of fine cut marks were evident on its posterior surface (Fig. 10.8). Two scapulae recovered from the core of the late 8th-century landing place (C690) appear to have had perforated blades, which may have resulted from hanging the shoulder-joints of meat on hooks that penetrated the bone.

A number of large vertebrae had been chopped in half in a cranial-caudal direction (Fig. 10.9). This may indicate that the carcass was split in two longitudinally through its middle. A large proportion of the long bones had been deliberately chopped at their extremities, and a number had been chopped in two longitudinally. These practices may be indicative of the division of the carcass into meat joints, and the extraction of marrow from the interior of the bones. A number of metapodia displayed fine knife cuts on their proximal and/or distal metaphyseal regions, probably made during the severing of the ligaments at the joints. A number of ribs displayed cut marks and many had been deliberately divided into short, rectangular

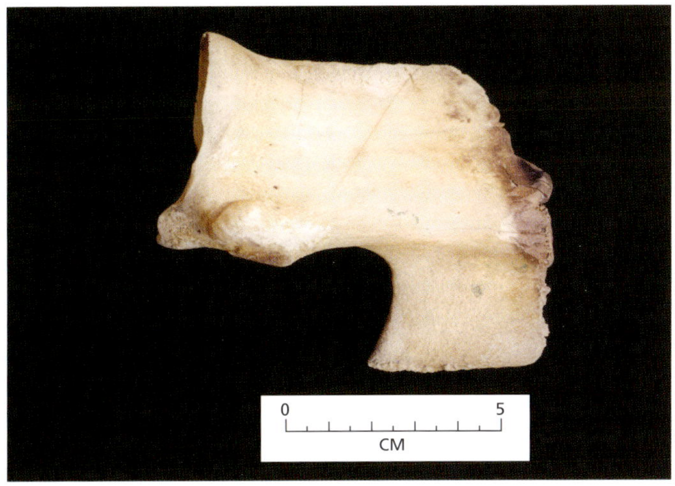

Fig. 10.8
Cattle scapula with evidence of having been chopped and burnt at its neck recovered from the primary silt over the dam of mill one. In addition, a number of fine cutmarks were evident on its posterior surface

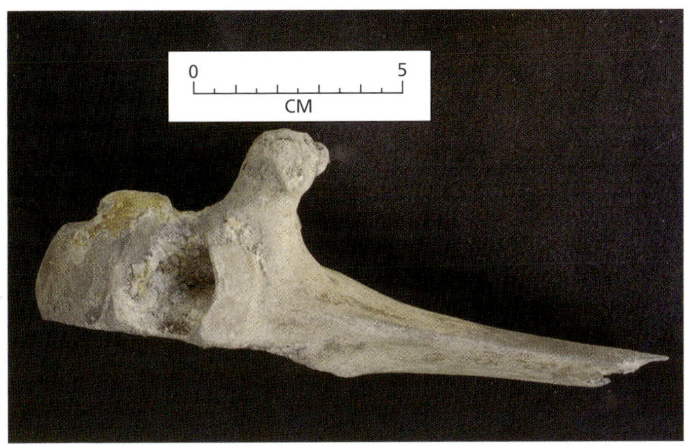

Fig. 10.9
A cattle thoracic vertebra which had been chopped through its middle in a cranial-caudal direction

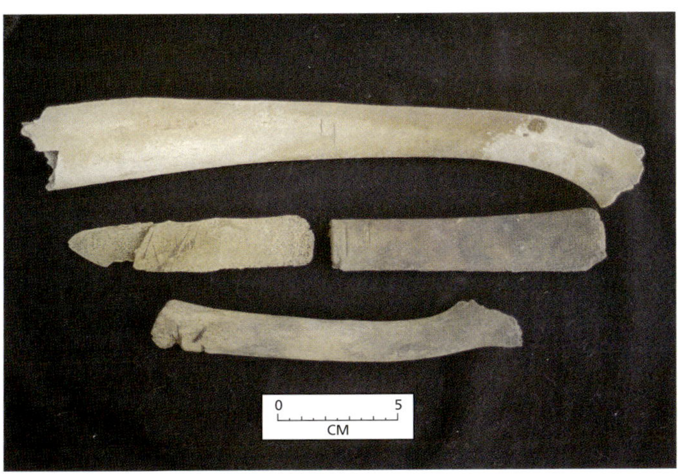

Fig. 10.10
Cattle ribs which displayed cutmarks

sections (Fig. 10.10). It is probable that this form of butchery would have occurred during the secondary processing of the thorax.

The occurrence of a mandible from a calf with an age-at-death of 1–4 months, which displayed butchery marks and evidence for burning, may indicate that young animals were deliberately slaughtered, at least occasionally (see Fig. 10.1).

Palaeopathology

A male acetabulum recovered from the core of the late 8th-century landing place (C690) displayed an abnormally large foramen at its medial margin and this may have been due to a developmental anomaly.

A fragment of acetabulum recovered from the primary silt over the dam of Mill 1 (C402) displayed an area of eburnation and porosity on its surface. The bone had been chopped through, so it is not possible to ascertain the full extent of the affected area, but such lesions are indicative of degenerative joint disease. Two centroquartal bones retrieved from bottom of the millpond of Mill 2 (C61) and the primary silt over dam of Mill 1 (C151) displayed porosity and slight marginal osteophytes on their medial inferior articular surfaces (Fig. 10.11). A first phalanx recovered from the core of the late 8th-century landing place (C697) displayed marginal osteophytes at its proximal end. Again, such lesions are indicative of degenerative processes.

A fragment of cattle long-bone metaphysis, recovered from the basal silt of the millpond of Mill 1, displayed evidence of extensive remodelling (Fig. 10.12). Unfortunately, the

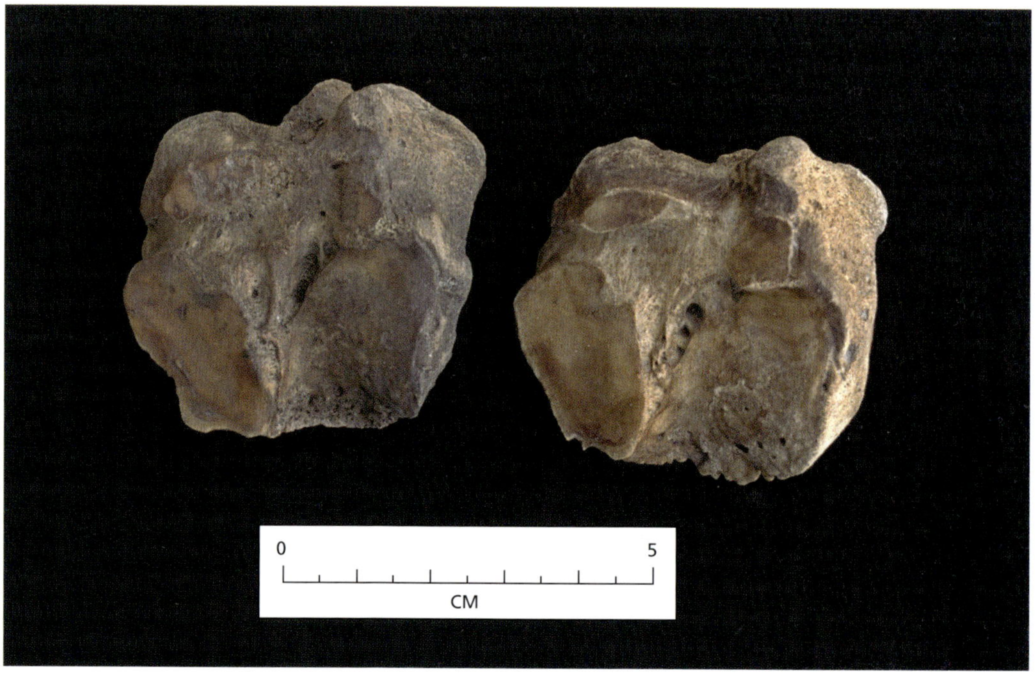

Fig. 10.11
Two cattle centroquartal bones which displayed porosity and slight marginal osteophytes on their medial inferior articular surfaces retrieved from the bottom of the millpond of Mill 2 and the primary silt over the dam of Mill 1

disease processes prevented attribution of the metaphysis to a specific bone. The cortical surface was irregular and pitted and appeared to comprise woven bone that was in the process of remodelling into lamellar bone. It is possible that this new bone formation was the result of either inflammatory or infectious processes (Murphy 2004). Maxillary first and second molars, presumably from a single bovid, displayed coral-like roots. Similar lesions were observed on a number of ovicaprid teeth from the site (see below). Roots with a similar morphology have been observed on the teeth of cattle and sheep from Late Medieval contexts at Porchester Castle (Baker and Brothwell 1980, 151), Galway City (Murphy 2004) and Maynooth Castle, Co. Kildare (Murphy 2000a). Cattle molars, with what are described as 'coral-like' outgrowths at the root apices, have also been recovered from Mount Pleasant, Dorset (Siegel 1976, 371). She considered that such abnormal root morphology is due to chronic low-grade infection.

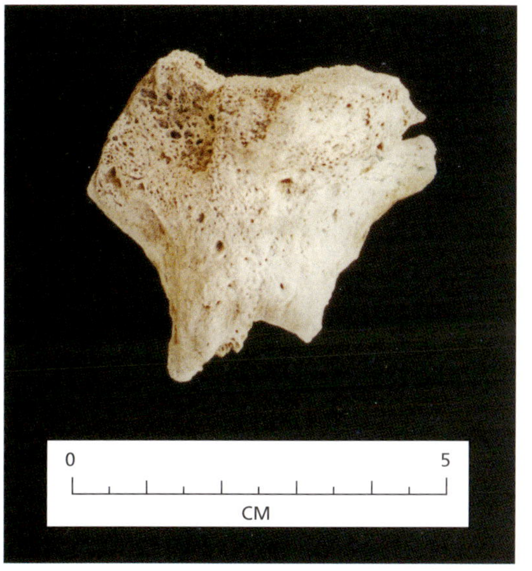

Fig. 10.12
A fragment of cattle long-bone metaphysis which displayed evidence of extensive remodelling recovered from the basal silt of millpond of Mill 1

The near-complete superior aspect of a cattle cranium, retrieved from the primary silt over the dam of Mill 1 (C404), displayed a number of perforations on the caudal surface of the parietal, between the frontal

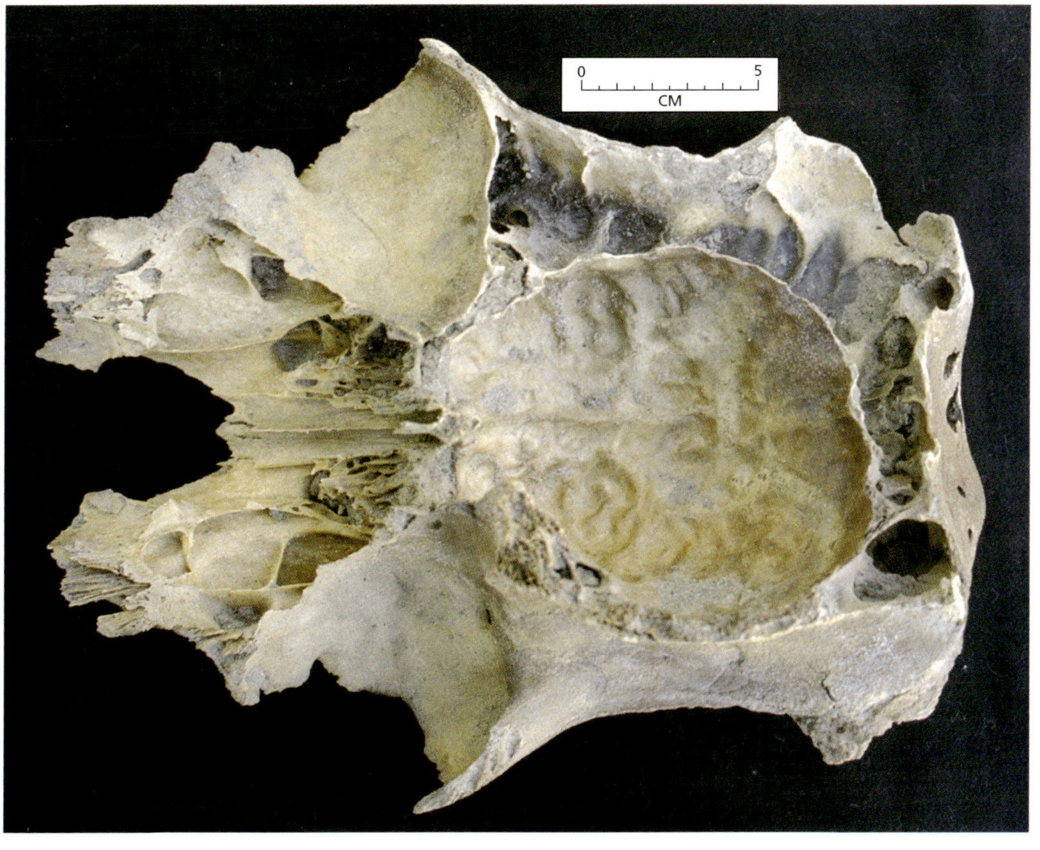

Fig. 10.13
A near-complete superior aspect of a cattle cranium which displayed a number of perforations on the caudal surface of the parietal between the frontal eminence and the linea nuchae retrieved from the primary silt over the dam of Mill 1

eminence and the *linea nuchae* (Fig. 10.13). Two large, irregularly-shaped perforations, measuring 6mm medio-laterally by 13mm supero-inferiorly, and 8mm medio-laterally by 15mm supero-inferiorly, were present at the medial aspect of the parietals. In addition, two small perforations, both with diameters of approximately 2–3mm, were present on the right parietal. A further large perforation appears to have been situated on the left parietal, but the lesion was obscured by post-mortem damage. The aetiology of such perforations is unknown, but is currently considered to be related either to the use of yokes for draught purposes or to be a developmental anomaly (Brothwell *et al.* 1996, 485–486). Examples of similar lesions have been recorded in cattle crania from a number of Late Medieval sites in Dublin (McCormick and Murphy 1997, 201; Murphy 1998), Carrickfergus (Murphy *forthcoming* a) and Post-Medieval Belfast (Murphy 2000b). An indentation was evident in the glenoid fossa of a scapula recovered from C90. It is possible that this is indicative of wear and tear on the joint and it may be related to the use of the animal for draught.

The historical sources provide further evidence that cattle were used for draught in Early Medieval times. In the Life of Saint Hogue of Ferns, for example, it was said that when he was studying under Saint David he performed a number of miracles, one of which involved the recovery of a beer-laden wagon and its draught oxen when they tumbled down a cliff (Flanagan 1990, 21). In another episode, Saint Hogue had a vision of one of the monks of Ferns slipping and falling in front of the plough he was using. The saint raised his hand and the oxen immediately stopped in their tracks, thereby saving the monk from injury (*ibid.* 21).

SHEEP/GOAT

Representation of skeletal elements

Ovicaprids were of secondary importance to cattle in the assemblage in terms of MNI, but of tertiary importance (10.6%) in terms of the fragment count (see Table 10.2). The majority of ovicaprid bones recovered appear to have been associated with prime meat cuts, and included scapulae and pelves which are associated with the shoulder and hip cuts respectively.

Proportions of sheep and goat remains

The analysis of ovicaprid material from archaeological contexts is notoriously difficult due to the problems of differentiating between sheep and goat remains, and the majority of bones thus were classified simply as sheep/goat, although a single ram horn-core was identified from the lower silt of the millpond of Mill 2 (C38). As a consequence of the small sample size, it was not possible to determine the roles which sheep and goats would each have played in the economy.

Age-at-death

Determination of age/slaughter profiles for ovicaprids from archaeological contexts is problematic due to the presence of both sheep and goat remains in an assemblage. Bearing this in mind, and following the example of other researchers (e.g. Payne 1973), it is still possible to gain important economic information from examination of the combined age/slaughter profiles of these animals. The ovicaprid age/slaughter profile, based on the state of epiphyseal fusion, is presented in Table 10.5.

Table 10.5: Ovicaprid age/slaughter estimates for the Early Medieval assemblage based on the state of epiphyseal fusion (Silver 1969, 285–286)

Bone	Age of fusion (mths)	AD 600 – 900	
		Fused	Unfused
pelvis, scapula	6 – 10	15 (88%)	2 (12%)
distal humerus, proximal radius	10	4 (100%)	0
distal metacarpal, distal tibia	18 – 24	5 (100%)	0
distal metatarsal	20 – 28	0	2 (100%)
distal radius, ulna, calcaneus, proximal femur	30 – 36	2 (25%)	6 (75%)
distal femur, proximal tibia, proximal humerus	36 – 42	0	4 (100%)

Despite the small sample, the epiphyseal fusion data would seem to indicate that few very young animals were slaughtered and that the majority of animals were killed between the ages of 24 and 36 months.

It was possible to determine age-at-death from four mandibles present in the *corpus*. A mandible recovered from the early 7th-century core of the first millpond dam (C27) had an age-at-death of 10–11 months. A specimen retrieved from the bottom of the millpond of Mill 2 (C61) provided an age-at-death estimate of 12–21 months, and one recovered from the primary silt over the dam of Mill 1 (C404) indicated that the animal had been slaughtered at the age of 25–26 months. In addition, a mandible that contained teeth with extensive wear was recovered from the redeposited silt used in the core of the dam of Mill 1 (C3b) and it is probable that this animal was old (stage 18) when it died (Higham 1967, 105; Grant 1982).

In sheep and goat husbandry, it is generally the case that, under most conditions, the prime economical meat yield is achieved if the animal is slaughtered in its second or third year of life, with the optimum point occurring between 18 and 30 months (Payne 1973, 281–282). If wool production is the principal aim of sheep husbandry, the animals are allowed to reach adulthood, although the quality of wool provided by older animals will deteriorate and, as a result, they are usually killed at approximately six to eight years of age as opposed to being allowed to live into old age, usually 8–10 years (*ibid.* 281

and 284). Sheep will not yield their first fleece until after approximately 18 months (Maltby 1979, 45).

The nature of the small sample of ovicaprid remains recovered from the Nendrum tide mills makes it impossible to determine precisely the nature of the economic exploitation of ovicaprids. The scant ageing evidence, taken in conjunction with the secondary economic importance of ovicaprids to cattle, in the economy, would tend to suggest that they were predominantly exploited for their meat. It is possible that the old animal recovered from C3 may have been a ewe that was used for breeding and providing milk and wool until she was too old and was slaughtered.

Sex

A ram horn-core (Fig. 10.14) was retrieved from the lower silt of the millpond of Mill 2 (C38), while a pelvis from a female ovicaprid was recovered from the bottom of the same deposit (C40/61).

Fig. 10.14
A ram's horn-core which had been cleanly chopped at its base recovered from the lower silt of the millpond of Mill 1

Butchery

Only a small proportion of the ovicaprid bones displayed clear evidence of butchery. A mandible recovered from the bottom of the millpond of Mill 2 (C61) displayed a perforation in its ramus, which may have been made by a hook when the head was suspended for drying or salting. Alternatively, it is possible that the entire carcass had been suspended by a hook through the head during the initial butchery process. Scapulae retrieved from the primary silt over the dam of Mill 1 (C404) and the core of the late 8th-century landing place (C690) displayed similar perforations in their subscapular fossae regions (Fig. 10.15). It is again possible that these perforations were made by hooks, but in these cases they may have been used to suspend shoulder joints of meat.

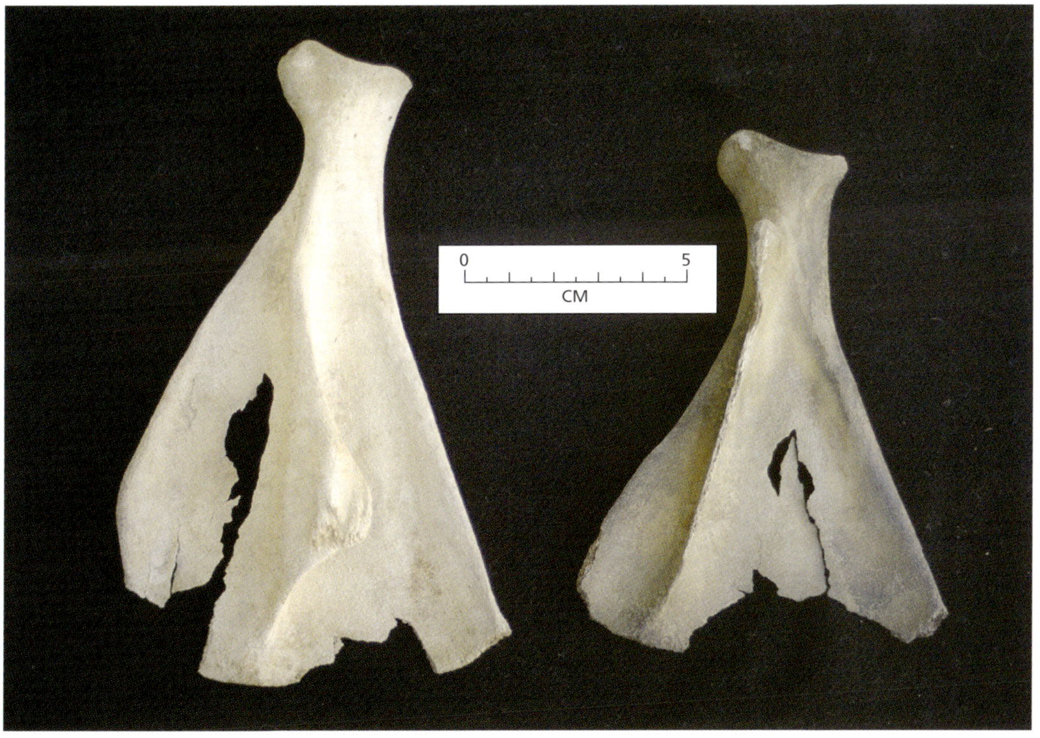

Fig. 10.15
An ovicaprid and a pig scapula which displayed perforations that may have been caused as a consequence of having been hung from hooks

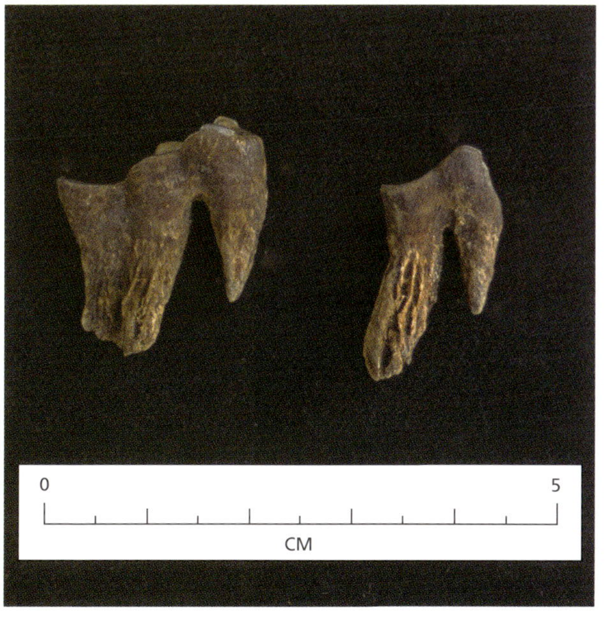

Fig. 10.16
The roots of ovicaprid second and third mandibular molars which displayed an enlarged appearance with a pitted and irregular surface recovered from the redeposited silt used in the construction of the dam of Mill 2

A number of long bones appear to have been chopped at their midshaft or metaphyseal regions. These butchery practices may be indicative of the division of the carcass into meat joints, and the extraction of marrow from the interior of the bones. The ram's horn-core recovered from the primary silt of the millpond of Mill 2 (C38) had been cleanly chopped at its base (see Fig. 10.14). It is probable that the horn had been removed from its core for some form of industrial processing.

Palaeopathology

The roots of the second and third mandibular molars recovered from C3b displayed an enlarged appearance, with pitted and irregular surfaces (Fig. 10.16). The teeth also displayed extensive attrition and were considered to have originated from an old animal (Higham 1967, 105; Grant 1982). It is probable that the root lesions were due to a low-grade infection and this may have been related to the extensive tooth attrition (see p. 269).

PIG

Representation of skeletal elements

Pigs were of secondary importance to cattle in terms of fragments count (16.5%), but in terms of MNI values they occurred less frequently than either cattle or ovicaprids (see Table 10.2). Most of the pig bones recovered appear to have been from prime meat cuts, including scapulae, humeri, pelves and femora, which are associated with the shoulder and hip cuts. Very few metapodia, tarsals, carpals and phalanges, the poorest meat cuts, were present.

Age-at-death

The age/slaughter profile for pigs based on the state of epiphyseal fusion is presented in Table 10.6.

Table 10.6: Pig age/slaughter estimates for the Early Medieval assemblage based on the state of epiphyseal fusion (Silver 1969, 285-286)

Bone	Age of fusion (mths)	AD 600 – 900	
		Fused	Unfused
distal humerus, proximal radius, pelvis, scapula	12	20 (83%)	4 (17%)
distal metacarpal, distal tibia	24	0	0
calcaneus, distal metatarsal	24 – 30	0	1 (100%)
ulna, proximal tibia	36 – 42	1 (20%)	4 (80%)
proximal humerus, distal radius, proximal femur, distal femur	42	1 (9%)	10 (91%)

Table 10.7: Pig age/slaughter profiles for the Early Medieval assemblage based on the state of tooth eruption and wear (Higham 1967, 105 and Grant 1982)

Higham eruption stage	Approx. age (mths)	AD 600– 900
1 – 6	0 – 4	0
7 – 9	4 – 8	1
10 – 13	8 – 12	0
14 – 16	12 – 16	1
17 – 19	16 – 21	3
20 – 23	21 – 29	1
24 – 27	30+	0

The peak in age/slaughter appears to have occurred when the animals were between 12 and 42 months of age, although a small number of younger and one older animal were also represented in the *corpus*. In general, pigs would have been exclusively exploited for their meat, and logic dictates that it is most economical to slaughter the animals as they approach, or reach, full size. Indeed, modern practice is to fatten pigs for slaughter during their first year of life (Maltby 1979, 55). Consequently, the presence of near-mature or mature pigs in the Nendrum assemblage is not unexpected.

The single animal with an age-at-death greater than 42 months may have been a breeding sow past her prime. Pig age/slaughter profiles, based on the state of tooth eruption and wear, are displayed in Table 10.7.

The age-at-death profile obtained from the small sample of teeth tends to suggest that the majority of pigs were slaughtered between the ages of 12 and 29 months, thereby supporting the results of the analysis of the state of epiphyseal fusion.

Sex

Sex determination of pigs was undertaken on the basis of the morphological characteristics of the mandibular canine teeth. Canines are large, have an open root and continue to grow throughout life in males, while in females they are small and with a closed root (Schmid 1972, 80). The canines erupt between the ages of 6 and 12 months in the majority of pig breeds (Bull and Payne 1982, 56), and it is therefore only possible to determine the sex of animals with an age-at-death greater than 6–12 months. A total of five male and three female canines were represented in the assemblage.

Size and type

Measurements derived from the pig bones are presented in Table 10.8.

Table 10.8: Pig metrical information (mm) for the Early Medieval assemblage (von den Driesch 1976)

Bone	Bp	Bd	BT	SD	LAR	GBP
scapula	-	-	-	-	-	31.8
scapula	-	-	-	-	-	30.9
scapula	-	-	-	-	-	30.9
scapula	-	-	-	-	-	31.4
scapula	-	-	-	-	-	33.1
scapula	-	-	-	-	-	29.1
scapula	-	-	-	-	-	30.2
humerus	-	34.9	28.2	-	-	-
humerus	-	37.6	29.9	-	-	-
radius	25.4	-	-	14.7	-	-
radius	27	-	-	-	-	-
radius	-	23.6	-	17.1	-	-
pelvis	-	-	-	-	28.9	-
pelvis	-	-	-	-	28.5	-
pelvis	-	-	-	-	27.5	-
pelvis	-	-	-	-	28.1	-
pelvis	-	-	-	-	28	-
pelvis	-	-	-	-	29.5	-
pelvis	-	-	-	-	25.7	-
pelvis	-	-	-	-	29.7	-
tibia	-	27.7	-	17.6	-	-

The pig metrical information derived from Nendrum indicates that the animals were of similar size to those recovered from other Irish Early Medieval assemblages including Drumcliffe, Co. Sligo (Murphy and McCormick 1994), Market Street, Armagh, Co. Armagh (Murphy 2000c) and Moynagh Crannóg, Co. Meath (McCormick 1987). Since no complete pig bones were present in the assemblage, it was not possible to obtain estimated shoulder height values.

The native Irish pigs of the 18th century were referred to as 'razorback' or 'greyhound' pigs, terms which derive from the physical characteristics of the animals, which included long legs, a straight snout and a narrow back. It is probable that the pigs of Early Medieval and Late Medieval Ireland would have been similar in appearance to the greyhound pig, prior to the widespread introduction of Siamese or Chinese pigs to the British Isles during the 18th and 19th centuries (Boden 1998, 403).

Butchery

The majority of pig bones appeared to have been deliberately smashed at either their proximal or distal ends. A number of medium-sized (pig and ovicaprid) rib fragments displayed cut marks, and most of these fragments had been deliberately divided into short, rectangular sections. It is probable that this form of butchery would have occurred during the secondary processing of the thorax. In addition, a number of medium-sized vertebrae had been chopped longitudinally (dorso-ventrally) through their midpoints. This pattern of butchery is indicative of the longitudinal division of the carcass into two approximate halves.

A scapula recovered from the bottom of the millpond of Mill 2 (C61) displayed two perforations in its subscapular fossa region, while a single perforation was evident in the subscapular fossa region of a scapula (see Fig. 10.15) retrieved from the foundation layer of the same millpond (C40). These perforations suggest that the shoulder joint had been hung from a hook, possibly during salting or drying. A third metacarpal recovered from bottom of the millpond of Mill 1 (C69) was white in colour, which indicates that it had been subject to burning at temperatures in excess of 525 °C (Mays 1998, 217). A hyoid retrieved from bottom of the millpond of Mill 1 (C69) displayed a number of small knife cuts which are indicative of butchering of the throat region of the animal.

HORSE

Horse remains were only occasionally encountered among the assemblage (see Table 10.2). The morphology of a fragment of tibia midshaft recovered from C2 may indicate that the bone had been deliberately broken during butchery. In addition, a possible cut mark was visible on the proximal aspect of the midshaft fragment.

Irish church law forbade the consumption of horse flesh. The thirteenth rule in the 7th-century Canons Hibernenses of the Irish Penitentials states that the penance for eating horseflesh was four years living on bread and water only (Bieler 1963, 161). In *Adomnán's Life of Columba,* the eating of horseflesh is depicted as a practice fitting only for thieves (Anderson and Anderson 1961, 251–253). Horse bones with evidence of butchery have, however, been recovered from Early Medieval monastic assemblages including Drumcliffe, Co. Sligo (Murphy and McCormick 1994).

A very poorly-preserved right mandible recovered from the bottom of the millpond of Mill 2 (C61) came from a young horse in which the roots of the deciduous teeth were still developing. A mandibular permanent third or fourth premolar with thick deposits of calculus, retrieved from primary silt in the wheel house of Mill 2 (BO 3), had a cheek-tooth height of 7cm, which may indicate that it had been derived from an animal with an age-at-death of approximately 4.5 to 7.5 years (Levine 1982, 250).

DOG

Dog bones were encountered in small numbers in the Early Medieval assemblage (see Table 10.2). The metrical information derived from the humerus recovered from the primary silting over the dam of Mill 1 (C404) is provided in Table 10.9.

Table 10.9: Dog metrical information (mm) for the Early Medieval assemblage (von den Driesch 1976) and estimated shoulder heights (ESH) based on the multiplication factors of Harcourt 1974, 154

Bone	Dp (mm)	Bd (mm)	SD (mm)	GL (mm)	ESH (cm)
Humerus	23.0	20.0	8.0	117.9	37.8

Metrical information derived from Irish Early Medieval contexts has indicated that there were two types of dog present in Ireland during this period – those which had shoulder heights of 26–40cm, and those with shoulder heights of 48–72cm. The former group may be considered to have been lap dogs (McCormick 1991, 8–9), and it is from this group that the dog humerus from Nendrum could have originated. A third metatarsal retrieved from the primary silt over the dam of Mill 1 (C402) had a greatest length of between 8.5cm and 9.5cm. As such, this bone would have been derived from a larger animal, which would probably have been of a size more in keeping with McCormick's larger group of dogs. None of the dog bones displayed either marks or breakage patterns indicative of butchery.

Metrical information obtained from the dog mandible retrieved from the core of the dam of Mill 2 (C527) is presented in Table 10.10.

Table 10.10: Dog mandible measurements (mm) for the Early Medieval assemblage (von den Driesch 1976)

Measurement	von den Driesch number	AD 600– 900
Total length	1	c. 160
Height of vertical ramus	18	65
Height of mandible behind M1	19	27.9
Length of cheektooth row: M3-P1 along alveoli	8	80.8
Length of molar row: along alveoli	10	38.8
Length of premolar row: P1-P4 along alveoli	11	41.4
Length of premolar row: P2-P4 along alveoli	12	37.1
Length of P1 at alveolus		3.1
Length of P2 at alveolus		10
Length of P3 at alveolus		11.5
Length of P4 at alveolus		10.3
Length of M1 at cingulum	13	22.3
Length of M1 at alveolus	14	21.8
Length of M2 at alveolus		8.2
Length of M3 at alveolus		4.7

The first premolar appears to have been lost ante-mortem. The teeth displayed moderate wear, and it is probable that they come from a middle-aged, adult animal.

CAT

A right cat ulna was recovered from the primary silting over the dam of Mill 1 (C642), while a left femur and left tibia were retrieved from the core of the landing place of Mill 2 (C886). It is probable that the latter two bones came from the same animal. The proximal end of the ulna was fused, which indicates that it derived from an animal with an age-at-death greater than 10 months. The distal end of the bone had been broken post-mortem. The proximal and distal ends of the femur were fused, suggesting that they belonged to an animal aged greater than 8.5 months, while the proximal and distal ends of the tibia were fused, which may indicate an age-at-death greater than 11.5 months (Habermehl 1961).

The bones were all extremely eroded and it was only possible to obtain limited metrical information from them – ulna (GL = *c.* 105.6mm), femur (Bd = 15.6mm, SD = 7.8mm) and tibia (GL = *c.* 103.4mm, SD = 5.9mm). It was not possible to assess the bones for cut marks due to their poor condition.

RED DEER

Seven fragments of very poorly-preserved red deer antler were recovered from the base of dam of Mill 1 in Trench 1 (BO 171). The fragments all originated from an antler tine which had been sawn at its inferior aspect. A piece of red deer cranium (Fig. 10.17), which included the base of an antler, was recovered from the bottom of the millpond of Mill 2 (C40/61). The antler had been sawn from the cranium and a chop mark was visible on the cranium. It is therefore possible that the antler and this region of the cranium had been deliberately separated from the remainder of the cranium before the antler was detached.

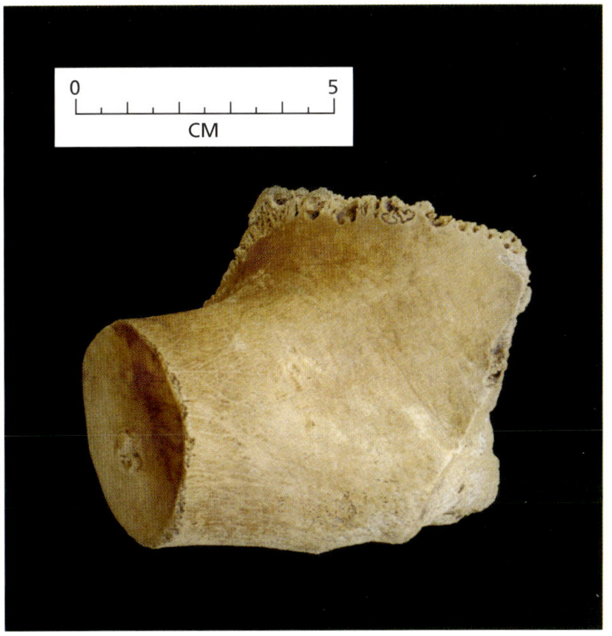

Fig. 10.17
A piece of red deer cranium which included the base of an antler recovered from the bottom of the millpond of Mill 2

WORKED BONE

A pig fibula with an unfused proximal end, retrieved from a depression in the wheelhouse floor of Mill 2, displayed evidence of having been worked. The object had a greatest length of 99.2mm. The distal end had been worked to form a point, while the proximal end remained unworked and formed a natural head. The cortical surface displayed a glossy appearance that may be indicative of wear. Pig fibula pins are generally considered to have been mundane, everyday objects. They appear to have been commonly used in Early Medieval Ireland, with 131 having been recovered from Lagore Crannóg, Co. Meath (Hencken 1950), while 82 were retrieved from Cahercommaun, Co. Clare (Hencken 1938). It is possible that the pins were used for fastening clothes or as hair pins (MacGregor 1985, 113–114).

POST-MEDIEVAL ASSEMBLAGE

Quantification

In addition to a number of semi-complete animal skeletons, a small quantity of disarticulated animal bone was recovered the upper foreshore silt and is considered to be Post-Medieval in date (C689, C1072, C1073). The details are provided in Table 10.11. It is evident that the majority of fragments had originated from cattle (72.5%), which had an MNI value of 2. Small numbers of ovicaprid, pig, dog and cat bones were also represented in the assemblage.

Cattle

Due to the small sample size, it was not possible to determine the cattle age/slaugher profile for the assemblage. Fragments of a metatarsal and a scapula recovered from C1072, however, appear to have been derived from a neonatal calf. The only metrical data that could be attained was the proximal breadth (Bp) of a metatarsal retrieved from C1073, which measured 41.6mm.

Table 10.11: Fragment counts and MNI values for the Post-Medieval assemblage. The MNI values for each element are included in the brackets

	CATTLE	S/G	PIG	DOG	CAT
HORN	-	-	-	-	-
SKULL	-	-	1	-	-
MANDIBLE	-	-	-	-	-
TEETH	-	1	-	-	-
ATLAS	-	-	-	-	-
AXIS	-	-	-	-	-
SCAPULA	2	-	-	-	-
HUMERUS	2	-	-	1	1
RADIUS	1	-	-	-	-
ULNA	1	-	-	-	-
METACARPAL	-	-	-	1	-
PELVIS	1	-	-	-	-
FEMUR	-	-	-	-	-
PATELLA	1	-	-	-	-
TIBIA	1	1	-	1	-
FIBULA	-	-	-	-	-
ASTRALAGUS	-	-	-	-	-
CALCANEUS	3 (2)	-	-	1	-
METATARSAL	3	-	-	-	-
TAR/CAR	2	-	-	-	-
PHALANX 1	2	-	-	-	-
PHALANX 2	1	-	-	-	-
PHALANX 3	1	-	-	-	-
SACRUM	-	-	-	-	-
TOTAL	21	2	1	4	1
TOTAL %	72.5	6.9	3.4	13.8	3.4
MNI	2	1	1	1	1
MNI %	33.2	16.7	16.7	16.7	16.7

Medium ribs - 2 Large ribs - 5 Unid. frags. - 6 Large vertebrae - 4

Semi-complete calf

The near-complete skeleton of a calf was recovered from C689. The remains comprised 13 fragments of skull, the mandibles, the scapulae, the right humerus shaft and epiphyses, the radii and two epiphyses, the ulnae, the left metacarpal, the iliae, the ischiae, the pubes, the femora and three epiphyses, the tibiae and two epiphyses and the left metatarsal. In addition, fragments of 20 ribs, one cervical vertebra, ten thoracic vertebrae, one lumbar vertebrae, five vertebral bodies, two vertebral epiphyseal plates and four caudal vertebrae were recovered. The bones were in an excellent state of preservation and the remains of hair were evident on one of the long bones.

The first permanent molars were unerupted and the third deciduous molars displayed primary wear. These findings would tend to suggest that the calf had died at the age of approximately 1–4 months (Higham 1967, 104). No signs of butchery were apparent on the bones and it is possible that it died of natural causes and was dumped close to the mill.

Sheep/Goat

A very large ovicaprid left tibia was recovered from C689 (SD = 18mm). On the basis of size, it is possible that the bone had originated from a goat or a large ram.

Semi-complete lamb/kid

The near-complete skeleton of an immature ovicaprid was recovered from C1073. Unfortunately, it was not possible to determine if the animal had been a lamb or a kid. The remains comprised 20 fragments of skull, the mandibles and seven loose teeth, the hyoid, the left scapula, the humeri, the ulnae, the radii and one epiphysis, the metacarpals and one epiphysis, the pelves, the femora, the tibiae, the metatarsals, two tarsals/carpals, six first phalanges, two second phalanges and a single third phalanx. In addition, the majority of the ribs, two fragments of atlas, the axis, four cervical vertebrae, six thoracic vertebrae, three lumbar vertebrae, one caudal vertebra and seven vertebral epiphyseal plates were recovered. The bones were in an excellent state of preservation.

The mandibular first permanent molars were in secondary eruption and primary wear was apparent on the deciduous second, third and fourth premolars. These characteristics would tend to suggest that the animal had died at the age of approximately four months (Higham 1967, 106).

The animal had clearly been butchered and knife cuts were apparent on the hyoid, three ribs, a thoracic vertebra, a caudal vertebra, the proximal metaphysis of the right humerus, the metaphyses of the femora, the superior surface of the ischio-public ramus of the right innominate and the superior surface of the left pubis. In addition, both of the horn buds displayed charring. The butchery pattern is more characteristic of dismemberment for meat rather than skinning, although the possibility that its skin was also used cannot be excluded. The semi-complete nature of the skeleton, despite the butchery, may indicate that the carcass had been dumped close to where it had been butchered.

Dog

A small number of disarticulated dog bones were recovered from Post-Medieval contexts. These comprised a left humerus, a left tibia and a right fifth metacarpal recovered from

C1072 and a left calcaneus retrieved from C1073. On the basis of size, it is quite probable that the bones had all originated from the same animal. Metrical information obtained from the bones is provided in Table 10.12.

Table 10.12: Post-Medieval dog metrical information (mm) (von den Driesch 1976) and estimated shoulder heights (ESH) (cm), based on the multiplication factors of Harcourt (1975, 154). *The measurement Dp is only applicable to humeri.

Measurement	GL	Bp/Dp*	BD	BT	SD	ESH (cm)
Humerus	195	45.3	39.1	27.7	16	64.2
Tibia	c. 225	41.2	-	-	15.1	66.6
Calcaneus	57.1	-	-	-	-	-
MCV	71.2	-	-	-	-	-

It is evident that the dog would have been quite large, with an estimated shoulder height of 64–67cm. The remains of dogs of similar stature have been recovered from Post-Medieval contexts at Carrickfergus, Co. Antrim (Murphy *forthcoming a*). Marginal osteophytes were visible at the proximal end of the humerus, tibia and calcaneus and these were probably due to degenerative joint disease. Their presence may suggest that this was an older animal. No butchery marks were apparent on any of the bones.

Semi-complete dog skeleton

A near-complete dog skeleton was recovered from a Post-Medieval horizon (see Fig. 2.6 and Fig. 10.18). The animal was contained within a sack, which would tend to suggest that it had been deliberately deposited. A visual inventory of the bones that were present is provided in Fig. 10.18.

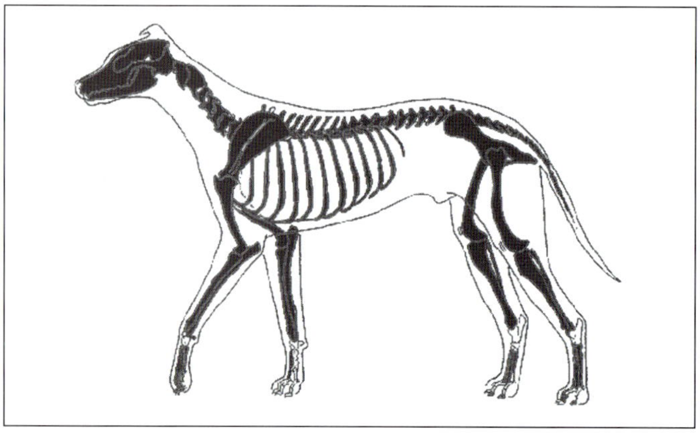

Fig. 10.18
Visual inventory of the near-complete Post-Medieval dog (not to scale), retrieved from the upper silt of the millpond of Mill 2 (C176). The bones present are coloured in black.

All of the bones were fused, which indicates that the animal was mature at death. In addition, the occurrence of extensive tooth attrition, dental disease and slight spinal degenerative joint disease may indicate that the animal was middle-aged to old when it died.

The post-cranial measurements are provided in Table 10.13, while the metrical data obtained from the cranium and mandibles are presented in Tables 10.14 and 10.15.

Table 10.13: Near-complete dog metrical information (mm) (von den Driesch 1976) and estimated shoulder heights (ESH) (cm), based on the multiplication factors of Harcourt (1975, 154). *The measurement Dp is only applicable to humeri.

Measurement	GL	Bp/Dp*	BD	BT	SD	ESH (cm)
Humerus						
Right	122.2	33.1	28.4	11.8	-	39.3
Left	122.3	33.6	28.1	10.7	-	39.3
Radius						
Right	121.4	15.4	21	10.7	-	40.6
Left	121.2	15.5	21.2	11	-	40.5
Ulna						
Right	144.7	-	-	-	-	40.8
Left	145.5	-	-	-	-	41.1
Femur						
Right	134.5	33.2	27.6	10.8	-	40.9
Left	135.1	33.4	26.8	10.7	-	41.1
Tibia						
Right	138.5	29.9	19.7	10.1	-	41.4
Left	138.4	29.6	19.6	10.5	-	41.4
Fibula						
Right	128.6	-	-	-	-	-
Left	127.5	-	-	-	-	-
Scapula						
Right	-	-	-	-	24.7	-
Left	-	-	-	-	24.8	-

Table 10.14: Near-complete dog cranial measurements (mm) (Harcourt 1974; von den Driesch 1976)

Measurement	von den Driesch number	Harcourt number	Post-Medieval
Total length	1	I	155
Occipital protuberance to nasion		II	87.2
Condylobasal length	2		145.1
Viscerocranium length	8	III	75.2
Greatest mastoid breadth	23		56.1
Greatest neurocranium breadth	29		51.6
Greatest diameter of the auditory bulla	22		21.0 (R) 20.7 (L)
Maximum zygomatic breadth		IV	84.3
Palatal length	13a	IX	72.4
Palatal width between PM4 and M1		X	47.7
Least palatal breadth	35		33.9
Breadth at the canine alveoli	36	XII	29.1
Length of the cheektooth row	15	XI	52.1 (R) 52.1 (L)
Length of P1 at alveolus			4.8 (R) 4.4 (L)
Length of P2 at alveolus			7.9 (R) 8.4 (L)
Length of P3 at alveolus			9.1 (R) 9.6 (L)
Length of P4 at alveolus	19		14.8 (R) 15.2 (L)
Length of M1 at alveolus			9.6 (R) 8.4 (L)
Length of M2 at alveolus			5.7 (R) 6.0 (L)
Cephalic index (IV x 100/I)			54.4
Snout index (III x 100/I)			48.5
Snout width index (XII x 100/III)			38.7

Fig. 10.19 Ante-mortem loss of the maxillary incisors in the Post-Medieval dog retrieved from the upper silt of the millpond of Mill 2 (C176)

Table 10.15: Near-complete dog mandible measurements (von den Driesch 1976)

Measurement	von den Driesch number	Post-Medieval	
		Right	Left
Context			
Total length	1	118.1	117.1
Height of vertical ramus	18	43.1	43.9
Height of mandible behind M1	19	15.5	17.6
Length of cheektooth row: M3-P1 along alveoli	8	63	65
Length of molar row: along alveoli	10	31.2	32.9
Length of premolar row: P1-P4 along alveoli	11	32.7	32.3
Length of premolar row: P2-P4 along alveoli	12	26.7	29.4
Length of P1 at alveolus		3.5	4.2
Length of P2 at alveolus		5.5	6.1
Length of P3 at alveolus		8	9.1
Length of P4 at alveolus		9.4	10.2
Length of M1 at cingulum	13	16.3	16.8
Length of M1 at alveolus	14	15.8	15.6
Length of M2 at alveolus		7.2	6
Length of M3 at alveolus		3.8	4.2

The shoulder-height value was estimated to be approximately 39cm to 41.5cm, suggesting that the Nendrum dog would have been similar in size to McCormick's (1991, 8–9) lap dogs. The bones were quite robust, however, and it is possible that the animal may have been similar to a terrier. The remains of small, sturdy dogs have also been encountered in Late- and Post-Medieval assemblages from Carrickfergus, Co. Antrim (Murphy *forthcoming* a) and Bishop Street, Derry (Murphy 2000d).

A couple of minor palaeopathological lesions were evident in the remains. A number of the transverse processes of the thoracic vertebrae displayed porosity and marginal osteophytes, while a number of rib heads displayed corresponding lesions. In addition, a number of the upper coccygeal vertebrae displayed marginal osteophytes on their superior and inferior body surfaces.

The teeth of the animal were not in a good condition and periodontal disease was evident. This was particularly severe at the base of the right maxillary fourth premolar, which also displayed deposits of sub-gingival and gingival calculus. The teeth generally displayed extensive attrition, but this was particularly severe on the canines and the surviving incisor teeth. All of the mandibular incisors and the four central maxillary incisors had been lost ante-mortem (Fig. 10.19). The alveolar bone displayed an extremely pitted appearance, which suggested that the tooth sockets were still in the process of remodelling. This would tend to suggest that the teeth had been lost not long before the animal died.

Cat

A left cat humerus from C1072 came from an adult animal and it was possible to take a number of measurements – GL = 94.4mm, Dp = 18.9mm, Bd = 14.9mm and SD = 7.4mm. The bone displayed marked surface erosion.

SUMMARY

Despite the nature of the small sample size, the Early Medieval animal bones recovered have produced some interesting results. Cattle contributed most to the economy, with ovicaprids and pigs being of secondary importance. The cattle appear to have originated from a predominantly dairying economy. Two of the cattle bones had been derived from notably large animals, which may indicate that a degree of selective breeding was in operation at the site. A number of interesting examples of butchered animal bone were represented in the *corpus,* including a cattle cranium with evidence of pole-axing and decapitation.

The other species represented in the Early Medieval assemblage included horse, dog, cat and red deer. The occurrence of a small number of fragments of sawn red deer antler may indicate that, in addition to cattle and sheep horn-cores, antler was at least occasionally processed at the site. A pin that had been made from a pig fibula was the only worked bone represented in the assemblage. A single human proximal humeral epiphysis was also present in the *corpus.*

A small amount of disarticulated animal bone was recovered from Post-Medieval horizons at Nendrum, but the remains of three near-complete animals were of particular interest. These comprised a one to four month old calf, a four month old lamb or kid, which had clearly been butchered, and a near-complete dog. The dog appears to have been contained within a sack and was an adult of a small breed. Its remains displayed evidence of slight degenerative joint disease and dental disease. The discovery of these three near-complete animals during the excavations would tend to suggest that animal carcasses must have been dumped in close proximity to the mill during Post-Medieval times.

Chapter 11

The History of Nendrum

Thomas McErlean

Chapter 11
The History of Nendrum

Thomas McErlean

INTRODUCTION

This chapter brings together the documentary sources relating to the history of Nendrum. There are two main interconnected aspects, that which has a bearing on St Mo-Choí and his cult and that which relates to the history of the monastery, and it is convenient to treat these separately. The historiography of Nendrum can be said to have begun with the rediscovery of the site by Reeves in 1844 (Reeves 1902 and 1847) and continued by O'Laverty (1878, 1895). It was brought to a new level by Lawlor (1925a) who attempted to write a historical narrative about Nendrum based on the integration of the historical and archaeological sources. Further commentary has been supplied by Towill (Towill 1964) and Hamlin (1997) and a fresh appraisal of the cult of St Mo-Choí has been carried out by Fitzsimons (2000). The archaeological archive has been augmented quite dramatically with the discovery and excavation of the tide mills, while the historical sources have not. However, some new perspectives can be extracted from them in the light of modern scholarship and are reviewed below. The chapter concludes with a comment by Etchingham on coverage of Nendrum in the annals and the significance of recorded bishops at the monastery in the 7th and 8th centuries, and while inevitably covering some of the material already discussed in the main section provides a change of perspective.

SAINT MO-CHOÍ/CÁELÁN OF NENDRUM

Almost nothing is known about the original individual who became known as Mo-Choí of Nendrum and like all saints he was probably more powerful in death than in life. The suggestion by Hamlin that he may have been a 5th-century missionary working in the East Ulster region is at present a plausible speculation (Hamlin 1997, 48–49). Sadly, no dedicated life of Mo-Choí has survived, if such ever existed. Like most Irish saints there are no primary sources, and the dossier on the saint is slim. What we know about him is derived from a number of different secondary sources of various dates, none of which is contemporary. Putting all these together, it would be possible to write a brief life in similar vein to those of many other early Irish saints compiled from similar sources by medieval hagiographers. The sources relating to Mo-Choí can be easily summarised. His death is recorded in the *Annals of Ulster (AU)* as having take place in either AD 497 or AD 499, although this source admits some doubt stating at AD 497 'Mo-Chaí of Naendruim rested,' and at AD 499 'or here, Mo-Chaí of Naendrum according to another book' *(Annals of Clonmacnoise (AC)* AD 487, *Annals of the Four Masters (AFM)* AD 496, *Annals of Ireland*

(AI) at AD 498). These entries are not contemporaneous and cannot be regarded as reliable, since they could well have been added to the annals in the 10th century or later. His conversion, ordination and his elevation to the status of a bishop or abbot by Patrick is recorded in the *Tripartite Life of Patrick,* which mentions his major relic, the *Etech* or the 'flying crozier of Mo-Choí of Nendrum' (Stokes 1887, 36–41; Mulchrone 1939, 25–26). The *Martyrologies of Tallaght* (Best and Lawlor 1931, 51), and *Óengus* (Stokes 1905, 142), as well as the later collections, *Gorman* (Stokes 1895, 123) and *Donegal* (O'Donovan *et al* 1864, 176–178) give his feast day as June 23rd. They also contain glosses (notes) giving additional biographical information, most notably a story of his miraculous reawakening after a 150-year sleep induced by the singing of an angelic bird.

The name Mo-Choí is a hypocoristic form (a familiar or pet name version of his original name) and *Tallaght,* as well as a gloss in *Gorman,* provide the valuable information that his real or original name was Cáelán (also rendered as Coelan, Coelán, Caolán among others). He is included in the Litany of Irish Saints which is of possible 8th-century date. Genealogical statements in *Corpus Genealogiarum Sanctorum Hiberniae* (CGSH) give him a maternal lineage as the son of St Brónach, daughter of Patrick's old master, Míliucc, and brother of five other saints. The same source gives him and the other associated saints a paternal genealogy linking them to the ancestors of the Conaille Muirthemne of northern Co. Louth. Further information on the saint is contained in the 14th-century Latin lives of two neighbouring saints, St Colman of Dromore (Heist 1965, 357–360) to the west and St Finnian of Movilla (Sperber 1997, 91) across the Strangford Lough on the north-east. The latter suggests a possible link between Nendrum and St Ninnian, and with Whithorn, a short distance across the North Channel in Galloway in Scotland. In summary, although the evidence is slim there is sufficient to show that his cult was of some significance in Early Medieval Ireland.

MO-CHOÍ IN THE *TRIPARTITE LIFE OF PATRICK*

The single most important work giving information about the saint best known as Mo-Choí is the *Tripartite Life of Patrick* (Stokes 1887 36–41, Mulchrone 1939, 25–26). In this, Mo-Choí figures as a young contemporary of Patrick, thus placing him in a 5th-century context and among the first generation of Irish saints. The background to the story begins with Patrick landing in the Quoile estuary in Strangford Lough in the territory of Mag nInis of the Dál Fiatach (the Ulaid). Here he encounters Díchu son of Trichim, who was baptised and became the first convert among the Ulaid and who gave him 'the barn' (Saul, near Downpatrick). Patrick then departs to attempt an unsuccessful conversion of his old master Míliucc of the Dál mBúain in the Slemish area of Mid Antrim. He returns to Díchu in Mag nInis and carries out missionary work there.

In carrying out his missionary activity in Mag nInis, Patrick leaves Saul and goes to the south of Downpatrick to a district called Derlus to preach to Ross, another son of

Trichim. The *Tripartite Life* states that this was located at Bright and notes that there was once a Bishop named Loairn there. On this journey he meets a young man called Mo-Choí who is herding swine, and to whom he preaches. Subsequently, Patrick baptises and tonsures him, and gives him a gospel and *meinistir,* a word normally translated as 'credence-table'. However, *meinistir* is probably a term which covers the whole range of altar vessels such as a chalice, paten and other items necessary for the celebration of the Mass and communion (Ryan 2000, 10).

Some time later they meet again, and God drops a crozier from heaven, the head of which lands in Patrick's breast and the foot on Mo-Choí's, this becoming known as the *Etech* (variously translated as the 'the winged-thing', 'the 'flying staff' or 'flying crozier') of Mo-Choí of Nendrum. Mo-Choí promised that a shaven pig should be given every year to Patrick, and it is noted that this tribute is still being paid. The same story is given in the early 15th-century *Leabhar Breac Homily on St Patrick* (Stokes 1887, 453).

Jocelyn, a Cistercian monk of Furness Abbey in Cumbria wrote a life of Patrick in the late 12th century, probably at the instigation of John de Courcy to further the claims of Downpatrick to the Patrician cult. His account is based on that given in the *Tripartite Life*, but provides a slightly more narrative account of the episode (Swift 1809, 50–51). It states that after primary instruction, Patrick sent Mo-Choí away for further education, but that within a year he had acquired great learning. Sometime later Patrick and Mo-Choí were conversing at Bright when the crozier, which Jocelyn remarks the Irish call the 'flying staff', fell between them. Patrick later made him a bishop and placed him over the church of *Edrum* where the relic was said still to be preserved. Jocelyn recounted that as Mo-Choí was a swineherd, a pig was paid yearly from Nendrum to the church of Down.

The story probably has many layers of meaning which are now lost to us. Clearly the major point of this part of the narrative is that Mo-Choí had a direct connection with Patrick. Within the context of the rest of the text of the *Tripartite Life*, in which numerous churches and estates all over Ireland are claimed for Patrick and Armagh, Mo-Choí is given a small walk-on part to lay claim to the monastery of Nendrum. During the first encounter with Patrick, Mo-Choí is converted, baptised and ordained a priest and given the essential equipment for his ministry, a gospel and a *meinistir.*

At the second encounter with Patrick, Mo-Choí receives the heaven-sent crozier or pastoral staff. As the latter is part of the insignia of a bishop, it would seem to imply that Patrick made him one. However, Mo-Choí is not specifically given this status here or in other early documentation, but is by Jocelyn in the late 12th-century. Alternatively, as a crozier is also part of the insignia of an abbot it may indicate Mo-Choi's perceived status as a monastic founder. The symbolism of the head of the crozier in Patrick's breast and its foot in Mo-Choí's is a representation of the position of church of Nendrum as subservient to that of Patrick's at Armagh. The annual tribute of the shaven pig, echoing Mo-Choi's early life as a swineherd, is viewed by Charles-Edwards as similar to a peppercorn-rent and largely symbolic, and represents a weak claim by the church of Armagh (or Down according to Jocelyn) as its superior (Charles-Edwards 2000, 28, 31). It may be of relevance that the saint was a swineherd, Patrick was also a swineherd during the years of his captivity and swineherds were prominent in early Irish literature.

A secondary sub-theme is the placing of Mo-Choí within the context of Mag nInis (the Lecale peninsula) of the Dál Fiatach, and an association with the Uí Trichim and the Uí Díchon, (the families descended from Trichim and his son Díchu). The Uí Trichim and the Uí Díchon were an important ecclesiastical family of the Dál Fiatach who controlled the monasteries of Saul and nearby Down, and whose lineage is given to a number of saints by the genealogists.

The important point to be observed is that there is no mention of Mo-Choí in the earlier Patrician information in Muirchú's Life of Patrick or Tírechán's Collectanea in the Book of Armagh (Bieler 1979) of late 8th-century date. Its absence in Muirchú may be particularly telling as it does devote much space to Patrician episodes set in Mag nInis and among the Ulaid (Bieler 1978, 78–81) which the account in the *Tripartite Life* follows quite closely. The absence of Mo-Choí in Tírechán may not be that surprising as Charles-Edwards (2000, 67) notes that Tírechán in his account steered well clear of the principal churches of the Dál nAraide and the Dál Fiatach, Nendrum, Bangor and Movilla. The dating of the *Tripartite Life* is uncertain and is open to debate, with a range from *c.* AD 900 to *c.* AD 1100 being suggested (Dumville 1993, 255–258). This would leave the first documentation of Mo-Choí's association with Patrick and to the Uí Trichim and the Uí Díchon and Mag nInis, open to the suspicion that it may be a late addition to the Patrician story.

It is possible — but highly unlikely — that the Mo-Choí story is based on a genuine tradition, and therefore one must look for the motivation or agenda behind its formulation and insertion into the Patrician narrative in the *Tripartite Life*. Apart from the claim on Nendrum bestowed on Armagh (or Down) by the supposed Patrician connection of Mo-Choí, his association with Patrick would have raised the prestige of the cult of Mo-Choí and been of benefit to the monastery. It would also have suited the Dál Fiatach to bind the traditions of the monastery to their own history, and in this regard it is possible to see an Uí Díchon dimension at work. It has been noted that the Míliucc story does not reflect well on the Dál mBúain (Charles-Edwards 2000, 64–67), and is in contrast to the high esteem bestowed on the Dál Fiatach and especially their Uí Trichim and the Uí Díchon lineages in Muirchú's life and in the *Tripartite Life*. This high esteem is evidenced in Muirchú by Díchu of Saul being given the status of Patrick's first convert among the Ulaid, that Díchu gives Saul to Patrick, and that his descendants are specially blessed by Patrick. The family are similarly treated in the *Tripartite Life* and given very high distinction as it is stated that among the four requests of the dying Patrick was one that the descendants of Díchu ' shall find mercy and shall not perish'. In contrast the Dál mBúain are given unsympathetic treatment, Míliucc of the Dál mBúain was

Patrick's master when he was a slave, he burned himself to death rather than being converted and his lineage was cursed by Patrick so that they would lose kingship.

While part of the motivation behind the story may a device to explain the reasons for the political decline of the once important Dál mBúain at a later date, Charles-Edwards sees the whole Míliucc and Slemish story as fiction motivated by a wish to denigrate Míliucc's people, the Dál mBúain (Charles-Edwards 2000, 64–67). He points the finger at the monks of Saul, the monastery controlled by the Uí Díchon, as the possible originators. He would see the motivation for the story lying in a rivalry between the Uí Díchon controlled monasteries of Down and Saul, and the monastery of Inis Causcraid (Inch). The patron of Inis Causcraid, Mo Bíu (or Do Bíu) whose feast day is on July 22nd in *Tallaght* (which refers to Dobhi Inis Causcraidh), is given Dál mBúain lineage in the genealogies (CGSH 152, 662.185) and presumably was controlled by a Dál mBúain family. All three monasteries functioned in close proximity to the Dál Fiatach royal centre at Down and Charles-Edwards interprets the Míliucc story as a part of an attempt by the monasteries of Saul and Down to undermine the prestige of Inis Causcraid in case it achieved the status of the principal monastery associated with the royal seat. In addition, it may well proceed from a general antipathy of the Uí Díchon towards Dál mBúain lineage at Inis Causcraid, as another prominent local ecclesiastical family. There is further interleaving in other sources between the Dál mBúain and the Uí Díchon concerning Mo-Choí and Nendrum. Mo-Choí is given a maternal Dál mBúain ancestry in the genealogies and the Uí Díchon express a claim on Nendrum in a genealogical statement (Table 12.3).

MO-CHOÍ IN THE MARTYROLOGIES

The martyrologies (calendars of feast days) of the Irish saints, especially the early 9th-century *Tallaght* (Best and Lawlor 1931) and its metrical version, *Óengus* (Stokes 1905), are a tremendous source of information on the early church. By plotting, for instance, the location of the churches mentioned in *Tallaght* it is possible to compile a very full map of the churches and monasteries in existence in late 8th-century Ireland. The martyrologies are a prime source of study of the cults of the individuals considered as saints, made up of early bishops, men and women who founded monasteries, ascetics, hermits and Irish missionaries abroad. *Tallaght* and *Óengus* are approximately contemporary and have been dated to *c*. AD 828–833 (Ó'Riain 1990, 38), *Gorman* (Stokes 1895) is dated to the second half of the 12th century and *Donegal* (O'Donovan *et al*. 1864) to the first half of the 17th century.

Mo-Choí's feast day is listed in all four martyrologies on June 23rd. The entry in *Tallaght* gives the brief notice *Mocoe sac. Ab Noendrome* (holy Mo-Choí, Abbot of Nendrum) and also records the saint under the day of the octave (the eighth day after his feast day) on June 30th as Coelan, Dachoe. This is an important entry as it gives the original name of the saint, Coelan (Cáelán), along with a hypocoristic form, in this case Dachoe using personal prefix *da* or *do* meaning 'thy' or 'you' instead of the more usual form, Mo-Choí, with *mo* meaning 'my'. Also found very commonly among saints names is the use of a diminutive form, again to convey a sense of affection or endearment created by the addition of a suffix like *án* or *óg* meaning 'little'. It is possible that the Mo-Choí root name Cáelán incorporates the diminutive suffix 'án' and that his original name was Coel/Cáel.

The use of pet names for most of the early Irish saints has been described by Ó'Riain (1982, 147) as the most 'complicating feature of early Irish hagiography'. The practice appears to belong to the 6th century, the so-called 'Age of the saints' and may have become moribund by the early 7th century (Ó'Riain 1982, 147), having caused confusion of identification of saints for later commentators. The process of development of hypocoristic forms, each stage being at a further remove from the root form, has frequently rendered the original name of the saint quite incomprehensible and extremely difficult to ascertain (Russell 2001).

Lawlor had considerable problems accepting the identification of Mo-Choí and Cáelán as the same person. He devoted approximately eight pages (Lawlor 1925a, 46–64) to its discussion, coming to the conclusion that Cáelán was a separate person who succeeded Mo-Choí at Nendrum. He was unaware, apparently, of the entry in *Tallaght* for June 30th that gives the real form of the name. While not addressing the problem of the hypocoristic form directly, Lawlor argued that the gloss in *Gorman* which reads 'Coelán was his own name' (Stokes 1895, 123) is unsound, and claimed that this late commentary was followed uncritically by most later sources and writers. Some of Lawlor's opposition to Cáelán being Mo-Choí is based on chronology. A saint called Cáelán (Coelan) of Nendrum occurs in the lives of Ss Colman of Dromore (Heist 1965, 357–360) and Finnian of Movilla (Sperber 1997, 91). As Mo-Choí is supposed to have died in AD 499 and Finnian in AD 596, Lawlor argued that it is highly unlikely that Mo-Choí could have taught him and that this strengthens the argument that Cáelán mentioned in the life of St Finnian was a separate person and not Mo-Choí. He cites Ware and Ussher who mentioned a bishop of Down called Coelan of around AD 520 who was previously abbot of Nendrum, but for whom there is no other authority. However, he pleaded that they had access to many documents now lost. It is clear that Lawlor placed more faith in the historical value of the saints' lives than that placed by modern scholarship. But despite his pleadings, there seems no doubt that Mo-Choí and Cáelán are the same saint.

The entry in the metrical calendar of *Óengus* (Stokes 1905, 142) reads.

> Commemoration of my Coe, there is nothing that escapes us:
> May the famous happy champion from Oendruim protect us.

It is glossed

> Mochóe who is in Nóendruim in Ulster i.e. Nine ridges which are in the island wherein his church is. Or Oendruim, i.e. one hill in the whole island; and Loch Cuan it is.

and gives the following verse

> A sleep without fading of flesh Mochoe of Oindruim slept
> (of) the folk of the congregation in which the saga above he found none save their great grandsons
> To Mochoe the beautiful sang the little bird from the skies
> Three strains from the tree-top, fifty years in each strain.

Another gloss in *Óengus* displays an element of confusion as to which saint the entry refers to. It states 'Mochua of Luachair if he be from Lismóre Mochutu' (Stokes 1905, 158). Both *Óengus* and *Tallaght* establish that by the early 9th century and presumably for a considerable period before this, the centre of the cult of St Mo-Choí was at Nendrum.

Gorman gives 'my Coe gentle, sad' and is glossed, 'abbot of Noendruim: Coelán was his own name' (Stokes 1895, 123) thus providing another clear statement of the saint's original name. In *Gorman* (and in *Donegal*) the octave entry on June 30th is given as 'Caolán and Failbhe of Cill-eo'. This coupling does not occur in *Tallaght* where 'Falbe o Chill Eó' forms a separate entry and is presumably scribal error.

The entry in early 17th century *Donegal* gives a synthesis of information on Mo-Choí derived from the earlier martyrologies, the *Tripartite Life,* genealogies and other sources and therefore is worth quoting in full. The story of Mo-Choí and the bird behind the poem in *Óengus* is given in much fuller form and may, in a sense, be regarded as the foundation tale of Nendrum.

> Mochaoi, Abbot of n-Aondruim, in Uladh. Caolán was his first name. Bronagh, daughter of Miliuc, son of Buan, with whom Patrick was in captivity, was his mother. He went with seven score young men to cut wattles to make a church. He himself was engaged at the work, and cutting timber like the rest. He had his load ready before the others, and he kept it by his side. As he was so, he heard a bright bird singing on the blackthorn near him. He was more beautiful than the birds of the world. And the bird said: "this is diligent work, O cleric" said he. "This is required of us in building a church of God" said Mochaoi. "Who is addressing me?" said Mochaoi. "A man of the people of my Lord in heaven is here" said he, "i.e., an angel of God from Heaven." "Hail to thee," said Mochaoi, "and wherefore hast thou come hither?" "To address thee from the Lord, and to amuse thee for a while." "I like this" said Mochaoi. He afterwards fixed his beak in the feathers of his wing. Three hundred years did Mochaoi remain listening to him, having his bundle of sticks by his side in the middle of the wood, and the wood was not the more withered, and the time did not seem to him any longer than one hour of the day. The angel afterwards bade him farewell. He went then to the church having his wattles with him, and he saw an oratory in the church which had been erected for his soul by his people. He wondered at the church which he saw. He went to the residence, and none of them knew each other, until he himself told his stories

to them, and how he was treated by the bird. When they heard this they all knelt to him; and made a shrine of the wood, and they afterwards built the church at that place, i.e. the place where he was listening to the bird. Of this the following was said:

A sleep without decay of the body
Mochaoi of Aendruim:
Of the people of the congregation where the sage was,
He did not find but the descendants.
Three melodies of delightful music
The angel, in the shape of a bird, sang
In the middle of the wood at the foot of the tree,
Fifty years each melody lasted.

AD 496 Mochaoi was the first man of the saints of Erin to whom Patrick gave a crozier, i.e *Eiteach Mochaoi,* which came from Heaven, as is related in the life of Patrick, lib. chap.16.

It is to be noted that the poem in *Óengus* and the version in the entry above gives the length of Mo-Choí's sleep as 150 years, while the prose text above states 300 years. Taking *Óengus* because of its early 9th-century date rather than *Donegal* of 17th-century date as the more reliable, the 150-year gap obviously represents the original story. Another version survives in a manuscript in Brussels (Grosjean 1929, 41–42). The full significance and meaning behind the story of Mo-Choí and the bird is now probably lost. The miraculous sleep of Mo-Choí, as suggested by Hamlin (1997, 49), may represent a break in the traditions of the monastery between a presumed foundation date in the early 6th or late 5th century, with the 7th century which resulted in a loss of its early history. Alternately, it may have been invented at a later date to bridge a chronological gap and link the traditions of a saint called Mo-Choí with a new monastic foundation at Nendrum in the early 7th century.

The story provides an interesting picture of timber cutting portraying Mo-Choí with 140 workers felling timber in a wood to build a church. Two churches are mentioned — the church in the monastery to which Mo-Choí returned after his sleep, and where an oratory had been erected for his soul (presumably Nendrum), and the church that was afterwards built on the site in the wood where he listened to the bird. The latter may refer to an actual church whose location has been lost, though one might conjecture that it was in the locality of Nendrum. The story as told in the martyrology of *Donegal* seems to imply that a shrine was fashioned from the wood he brought back. However, as the sense in this translation is not entirely clear, it may mean that the wood itself wherein the bird sang became a shrine, and that later a church was built in it. But the Brussels version seems to clear up this ambiguity by explicitly stating that the shrine was made from the wood Mo-Choí brought back (Grosjean 1929 41–42). It seems probable that this refers to a wooden shrine which was venerated at Nendrum as one of the objects associated with the cult of Mo-Choí.

A new approach to the study of the martyrologies has been pioneered by Ó'Riain in various papers (Ó'Riain, 1975, 1977, 1982) and further research using his methodology may expand the number of entries which relate to Mo-Choí/Cáelán of Nendrum and the saints with which he was associated. Interesting results along these lines have been proposed by Fitzsimons (2000) some of which are incorporated in the discussion below.

Among the main features of the martyrologies is the repetition of a saint's name on different feast days, and of saints with the same name attached to different churches as seemingly different and separate individuals. Ó'Riain has commented (1982, 152) that

> The notion that there existed hundreds of SS Colmán, scores of SS Mochua and Molaisse and dozens of other denominations within one relatively small area by European standards, in the course of a very limited period of time, again by European standards, flouts the most basic rules of common sense not to mention historical criticism, no matter which gloss is put on the word saint.

Ó'Riain has highlighted the extent of cloning of a saint into many separate individuals in different localities, as his cult spreads and fragments, leading to the duplication of entries in the martyrologies. The localisation of the cult of a saint leads to a separate identity with stories, lineage and other features tailored to the local milieu. A number of other factors also contributed to this 'multiplication'. Careless copying and interpolation by scribes is one factor. Confusion over the hypocoristic forms of the saint's name also contributed to the creation of a separate identity of the original saint. Another factor is the date on which the feast day of the saint is celebrated, as this may have varied in different churches dedicated to his cult. The date of his feast day in the martyrology may record his genuine death-day, or it may be the date on which his relics were translated to that church from the centre of the cult. Alternatively, as is seen for Mo-Choí, the feast day recorded may be the octave or indeed within the octave period when it was permissible to celebrate his feast day in the regulations of the Church.

Multiplication of entries for Mo-Choí and Cáelán

There are a number of Mo-Choí/Cáelán or similar names listed in the martyrologies which constitute possible variations of Mo-Choí and Cáelán of Nendrum. The June 23rd entry *Mocoe sac. Ab Noendrome (Tallaght)* and that of June 30th *Coelan, Dochoe (Tallaght),* though the latter does not specify an affiliated church is obviously an example of the celebration of the saint's feast day on the octave of its original date and refers to Mo-Choí/Cáelán of Nendrum and not to a separate saint of the same name. Among other possible entries in *Tallaght* are, *Coelain Inis Celtra* on July 29th, Caelen on September 25th and *Caelani o Thig na Manach* on October 29th. The Caelen of September 25th is regarded as identical to Mo-Choí/Cáelán of Nendrum by Ó'Riain (Ó'Riain 1977, 69). He is not specified to a church by *Tallaght,* but is assigned to one called Ech-Innis in *Gorman* and *Donegal,* and this is probably the church site in Aughnish Island and Aughnish parish near Ramelton, Co. Donegal. No trace of this church has survived, but its location on a tidal island in the estuary of the river Swilly in Lough Swilly is reminiscent of the location of Nendrum. It is possible that further research may reduce these entries and other similar name forms to one original saint, Mo-Choí/Cáelán of Nendrum, and by so doing contribute to tracing the extent of his cult beyond Nendrum.

Interrelated group of saints

Another feature of significance in the martyrologies highlighted by Ó'Riain is the presence of a pattern or clustering of interrelated groups of saints associated by feast days occurring on or near the same date. Ó'Riain has commented on the group of saints whose feast days are celebrated on September 25th, the same feast day as Caelen of Aughnish and on the 24th and 26th (Ó'Riain 1977, 69). Apart from the latter Caelan, it includes three other saints with probable East Ulster associations — Finnbarr of Cork (originally Finnbarr/Finnean of Moville), Imchad who is associated in *Gorman* and *Donegal* with a church called Chille Droichit in the Ards peninsula Co. Down, and Colman Comraire who is named as a brother of Mo-Choí in a genealogical statement discussed below. It is difficult to interpret this pattern of associated saints but it may be assumed that it meant something to the compilers of the martyrologies and it follows that if its significance is understood it may provide information on their cults. For instance, Ó'Riain has suggested that the clustering of East Ulster saints around September 25th may indicate that the cult of Mo-Choí spread in association with those of the others (Ó'Riain 1977, 75).

MO-CHOÍ/CÁELÁN IN THE GENEALOGIES

In Early Medieval Ireland, the genealogies of the saints were as important as those of members of secular society. A saint's lineage could be used to raise the status of his cult, justify claims to churches and their lands and strengthen territorial identity to individual churches. It could also provide a basis for linking churches. As a source of information on the early saints, the genealogies supply a complementary source to that supplied by the martyrologies, lives of saints and the annals. However, they present considerable problems of interpretation and often incorporate many inconsistencies and chronological improbabilities. The earliest *corpus* of genealogies of the saints largely survived in 12th-century manuscripts such as Rawlinson B505 or the Book of Leinster (CGSH), but most of the information from which they derive is based on earlier material. Ó Corráin has observed that the early Irish genealogies are primarily the product of a professional genealogist working in a literary medium rather than based on oral sources transmitted into writing (Ó Corráin 1998). While some constitute a genuine record of descent many have been tailored to produce a desired result and are patent fabrications. The collections contain many examples of saints having more than one version of their descent and these conflicting pedigrees present major problems for interpretation.

There are two genealogical statements on Mo-Choí/Coelin contained in the CGSH (722.92 and 702.1–5) relating to his maternal descent. In the tract 'On the mothers of the saints' in the Book of Leinster, Mo-Choí is provided with an identity as the son of Brónach, the daughter of Patrick's old master Míliucc Moccu Bóin (CGSH 722.92), and has four brothers and one sister, all of whom were saints (see Table 11.1, below), attributed to him. In another version, an additional brother, Manchán of Liath, is added (CGSH 702.1–5).

Table 11.1: Mo-Choí and the children of Brónach

CGSH 722.92	CGSH 702.1–5	Identification
Brónach ingen Milchon m. Buin	Ingen Milcon	Bronagh of Kilbroney Co. Down and Clonbroney Co. Longford
Children		
Mochae Noendromma oc Loch Cuan	Mochoe	Mo-Choí of Nendrum
Colmain Chomraire oc Uisniuch	Colman Comraire	Colman Comraire of Uisneach
Colmain Mulind oc Daire Chaechain i nDal Riatai	Colman Mulind	Colman of Derrykeighan, Co. Antrim
Epscuip Meic Erca o Domnuch Mór Maige Coba	Epscop Mac Erca o Domnuch Mór in Maige	Bishop Mac Erca of Donaghmore, Co. Down
Damnatan Slebe Betha	Damnat chonnalb Chonaillech	Damnat of Tedavnet Co. Monaghan
Fursu Craibdig in Perona		Fursa of Peronne in Picardy
	Manchan do Liath	Manchán of Lemanaghan Co. Offaly

Information on his paternal side is found in the Book of Leinster (CGSH 159) which makes Mo-Choí (under the name Coelan) the son of Luachain, son of Roire, son of Laga, son of Conaill, the eponymous ancestor of the Conaille Muirtheime (CGSH 158). To this pedigree can be added a number of others linking him again to the saints named as children of Brónach. (CGSH 157.1, 157.2, 158, 159 and 188), but not as a sibling but as a cousin of varying degree, with all being descendants of Laga Lethanglas, son of Conall

Anglonnach (see Table 11.2 below). These entries make him a first cousin of Bishop Meic Erca and of a bishop named Luachan (CGSH 159). Manchán's father Sillain is described as a second cousin of Coelan (CGSH 188). Colmán Mulind is the most distantly related of all, his great-grandfather being a second cousin of Coelan (CGSH 158). Some of these statements contradict the identity of Brónach as their mother. Thus, Fursu's mother is given as the Gelges, daughter of Aeda Find (CGSH 157.1) and Machán's mother is given as Mella (CGSH 188). Another element of confusion is to be found in a statement, where Coelan the son of Luachain, mentioned in CGSH 158, is replaced by a saint called Colman, son of Luachain, in CGSH 662. 216.

Table 11.2: Coelan and related saints of Conaille ancestry

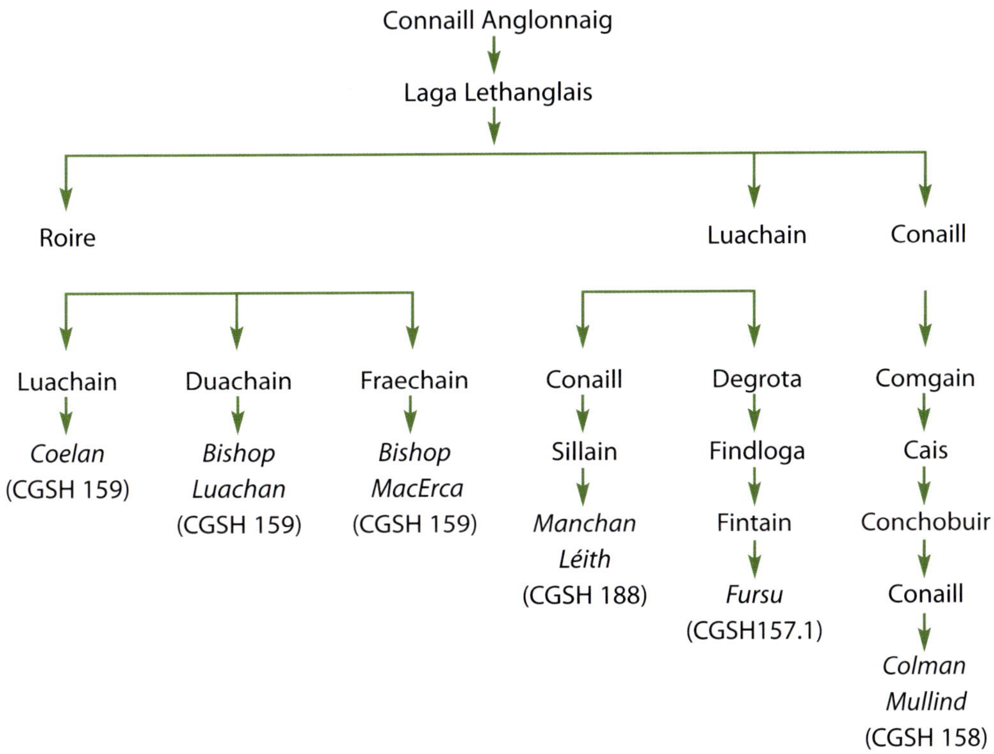

The association of Mo-Choí/Cáelán with this group of saints is of interest, but its significance is unclear. The group are both geographically and chronologically diverse. Fursu is probably the most prestigious in the list, and an historical figure about whom something is known. He was a 7th-century missionary active in East Anglia and in Northern France and famous for his visions. Bede devotes a chapter to him in his *Ecclesiastical History of the English People* (HE) and refers to his noble blood (HE 111.19; Sherley-Price 1990, 172–176). He died *c.* AD 655 and was buried in the monastery of Péronne on the river Somme in Picardy, becoming the subject of an early Latin life (Richter 1999, 126–133). This work mentions his two brothers, Fóillán and Ultán who were also missionaries.

Manchán is probably the second best known one of the group and was a bishop and founder of Líath Mancháin (Lemanaghan, Co Offaly), dying in the great plague of AD 665 *(AU)*. His monastery is located on a bog island to the north-east of Ferbane, Co Offaly, and has a number of early grave slabs and a stone oratory called St Mella's Cell (presumably taking its dedication from his mother) among other early features (Fitzpatrick and O'Brien 1998, 12–13). His feast day is recorded in *Tallaght* as January 24th, and there he is called Manchan Leith, son of Indach.

Colman Comraire of Uisneach, Co.Westmeath is one of 'the three colmans of Meath' and as has been seen, he is also associated in *Tallaght* with Caelan through having joint feast days on September 25th. The remaining three children of Bronagh: Colman Mulind, Bishop MacErca and Damnat, are minor localised saints about whom there is little known information. Colman Mulind, 'Colman of the Mill' of Derrykeighan, Co. Antrim (O'Laverty 1887, 127–129) in Dál Riata whose feast day is January 1st *(Tallaght),* is so nicknamed from the fact that he used to receive his brother monks in a mill *(Donegal),* which may indicate a tradition that he was a monastic miller. Nothing further is known about Bishop MacErca apart from his feast day, September 17th *'Herci episcopi o Domnuch Mór Maigi Coba' (Tallaght),* and his association with Donaghmore in Maige Coba in western Co. Down, in Uí Echach Coba. The early placename element *domnach* in his church suggests he may belong to a Patrician horizon (Flanagan 1984, 31), and have been a bishop of Maige Coba or Western Down. Damnat is associated with the church of Tedavnet in Co. Monaghan, and is described in the genealogical statement and in *Tallaght* as of *Slieb Betha* (Slieve Beagh), a mountain straddling the boundaries of Cos Monaghan, Fermanagh and Tyrone in Airgialla. The cult of Damnat has been categorised as being local to Co. Monaghan by Charles-Edwards (2004, 79–81), who comments that the connections claimed by the genealogists for Damnat are typical of a pattern of relatively insignificant saints with localised cults being given connections to the more important ones.

Brónach, the mother of the six saints, is associated with two churches, Kilbroney near Rostrevor, Co Down, on the northern side of Carlingford Lough and Clonbroney, Co Longford. Her feast day is given in *Tallaght* as April 2nd. Kilbroney has some early archaeological material including an important cross. A reference in the *Swain Register* in 1428 (Reeves 1847, 116) mentions the 'keeper of St. Brónach's *bachall'* (crozier) and in the 19th century a bell was found in the graveyard. It is now known as 'St. Brónach's bell' and is kept in the local Catholic church in Rostrevor. While Brónach gave her name to Clonbroney Co. Longford the main saint associated with this church is Samthan whose death is recorded in *AI* at AD 739 and whose feast day is given in *Oengus* as December 19th. In the genealogies she is given an Uí Díchon/Uí Trichim ancestry and described as being descended from Díchu son of Trichim (CGSH 185, see Table 11.4).

What little information exists about this group of saints renders the maternity of Brónach for most of them impossible on chronological grounds, and thus it all appears to be genealogical fiction. Brónach and Mo-Choí are connected with the Patrician story and therefore presumably belong to a 5th- or early 6th-century AD context. On the other hand, Fursu who died in AD 650 *(AU)* and Manchín who died in AD 665 *(AU)* belong largely to the 7th century. To reconcile all the strands of chronological and genealogical information would require Brónach to have had children by at least five different fathers of the Conaille in the 5th, 6th and probably 7th centuries!

Chronologically, the Conaille genealogical statements hang together somewhat better, with the 7th-century Manchán and Fursu being one to two generations removed from the 6th-century Mo-Choi and Mac Erca.

While it seems probable that the confusing genealogical documentation on Mo-Choí/Cáelán is largely fictitious, it cannot be ignored as a possible source of information on him or his cult. It is extremely difficult, however, to ascertain its significance. There are two main aspects. The first is the grouping of Mo-Choí/Cáelán with the other saints furnished by two separate genealogical schemes. This can be read as a deliberate attempt by the genealogists to group these saints together, possibly indicating that the churches or monasteries where they were venerated were linked in some way. If true, this would suggest a connection between Nendrum or the cult of Mo-Choi/Cáelán, and the churches of Donaghmore, Co. Down, Derrykeighan, Co. Antrim, Tedavnet, Co. Monaghan, Kilcomereagh, Co. Westmeath, Lemanaghan, Co. Offaly and, through Brónach, a connection with Kilbrony, Co. Down and Clonbroney, Co. Longford.

The second aspect is the provision of Mo-Choí/Cáelán (and of the other saints) with a connection to the Dál mBúain on the one hand and to the Ui Laga of the Conaille Muirtheime on the other. The association with the Dál mBúain is intriguing. The territory and people known as the Dál mBúain, like many others, occupy a somewhat hazy zone in the historical evidence. As a result of the story of Patrick's captivity, the most famous member of the Dál mBúain is Míliucc Moccu Boin, Patrick's master, named by Muirchú's 'life' as a king, but in Tírechán's *Collectanea* as a druid. Both accounts place the location of Patrick's servitude under Míliucc in the Slemish area of Co. Antrim. Tírechán refers to Slemish as Slíab Miss of Bónrige (Bieler 1963). The Bónrige being another form of the name of the tribe to which Míliucc belonged, and Bieler suggests that perhaps Bón may have been a pre-Christian god. From the story it would seem the territory of the Bónrige consisted of, or included, the Braid valley to the east of Ballymena in mid Co. Antrim. Dál mBúain continued to be used as the name of a minor territory down to the 12th century. It is mentioned as one of the constituent sub-kingdoms in the Book of Rights in apparent geographical order with sub-kingdoms Uí Erca Céin on the north-east and Uí Blathmeic on the south-east (Dillon 1962, 85, 89). *AFM* records the death of Gillapatrick Mac Sherry, Lord of Dal Buinne as AD 1130. In the Late Medieval period it was also used to form one of the rural deaneries of the diocese of Down. Its extent, as outlined by the parishes in the deanery of the name in the *c.* 1306 papal taxation (Reeves 1847, 23–234), would place it as covering part of southwest Co. Antrim and a small part of northern Co. Down. This therefore locates it much further to the south than the mid-Antrim area indicated in

Muirchú and Tírechán. It is possible therefore to speculate that at an early period, Dál mBúain may have been of much greater extent than the later rural deanery of the name and may have contracted as a result of the expansion of the Dál nAraidne and Dál Fíatach. Indeed it may have once covered much of south Antrim and eastern Down.

Durthech of Oendruim

Probably the most intriguing aspect of the genealogies of Mo-Choí is that no overt attempt appears to have been made by Dál Fiatach genealogists to provide him with a Dál Fiatach lineage, unlike, for example, that given to Uinniau/Finnean of Movilla (CGSH 136.1, see Table 11.4, below) since, by at least the mid-8th century, it is apparent that Nendrum was within their territory (see p. 306). However, what might be interpreted as an overt claim to Nendrum by the Dál Fiatach and their leading ecclesiastical lineage, the Uí Díchon, is contained in a genealogical statement (CGSH 136.2) listing, the seven saints who were sons of Trichim (the father of Dictú who gave Saul to Patrick in Muirchú and the *Tripartite Life*). In this statement, the seven sons are listed with associated churches. They are Laegaire at Down, Aillill at Movilla, Dictú at Saul, Durthech at Nendrum (Oendruim), Eoghan and Niall at Kilclief and Rus at Dun Da Lethglass (Down). The purpose behind this genealogical statement can be interpreted as a clear attempt by the Uí Díchon to claim most of the major monasteries in Dál Fiatach —Nendrum, Downpatrick, Saul, Kilclief and Movilla — by stating that theses saints, seemingly claimed as the original founders, were of their family.

Table 11.3: The sons of Trichim (CGSH 136.2) and their six associated churches

Trichim

Laegaire	Ailill	Dictú	Durthech	Eoghan	Niall	Rus
ic Dún	*i mMaig Bile*	*ic Sabull*	*ic Oendruim*		*Cill Chlethi*	*ic Dun Da Lethglas*
(Down)	(Movilla)	(Saul)	(Nendrum)		(Kilclief)	(Down)

Apart from the seven sons of Trichim, further genealogical information gives a wider network of saints with Uí Trichim or Uí Díchon pedigrees (CGSH 150, CGSH 184, CGSH 185 and Mac Fhirbhisigh 723.9), as shown in Table 11.4 below.

If Durthech of Oendruim, whom the genealogical statement assigns to a Patrician horizon, was a real historical figure he is of considerable interest in that along with Mo-Choí he is the only other potential late 5th- or early 6th-century cleric associated with Nendrum in the historical sources. A Dearthucht occurs in Mac Fhirbhisigh's mid 17th-century *Book of Genealogies* which states 'Dearthucht and Eóghan were two sons of Treitheamh who were not full brothers. From Dearthucht were Corca Ansa among the Ceinéal Eóghain' (Mac Fhirbhisigh 496.11) but no association with Nendrum is given. Durthech does not occur in any other documentation relating to Nendrum but a saint called Duthracht is mentioned without an associated church, on May 16th in *Tallaght*. In *Gorman* the glossed entry associates him with a church called *Liathdromma* or *Líathdruima* but a marginal note speculates he may be of *Aentroma* and may be the individual recorded in the genealogies as a son of Trichim. *Donegal* also follows the speculation that he is probably the son of Trichim and brother of Dictú and belongs to a church called *Caon-druim,* which it suggests is probably at or near Tara. This somewhat tentative identification of Duthracht in both *Tallaght* and *Donegal* leads one to speculate that the church called *Liathdromma* in *Gorman* or *Caon-druim* in *Donegal* may have been in origin a scribal error for *Oendruim* or *Naendruim* (Nendrum).

The existence of a saint called Durthech of Oendruim in the history of Nendrum is open to serious question and may well be a fabrication of the genealogists. This may also be true of genealogical information on Mo-Choí. In spite of the fact that the value of the genealogies are difficult to interpret they cannot be ignored as they open up an avenue of research which may eventually shine more light on the history of the monastery and of the cult of its patron saint.

Table 11.4: Saints (names in bold) with Uí Trichim, Uí Díchon and Dál Fiatach ancestry

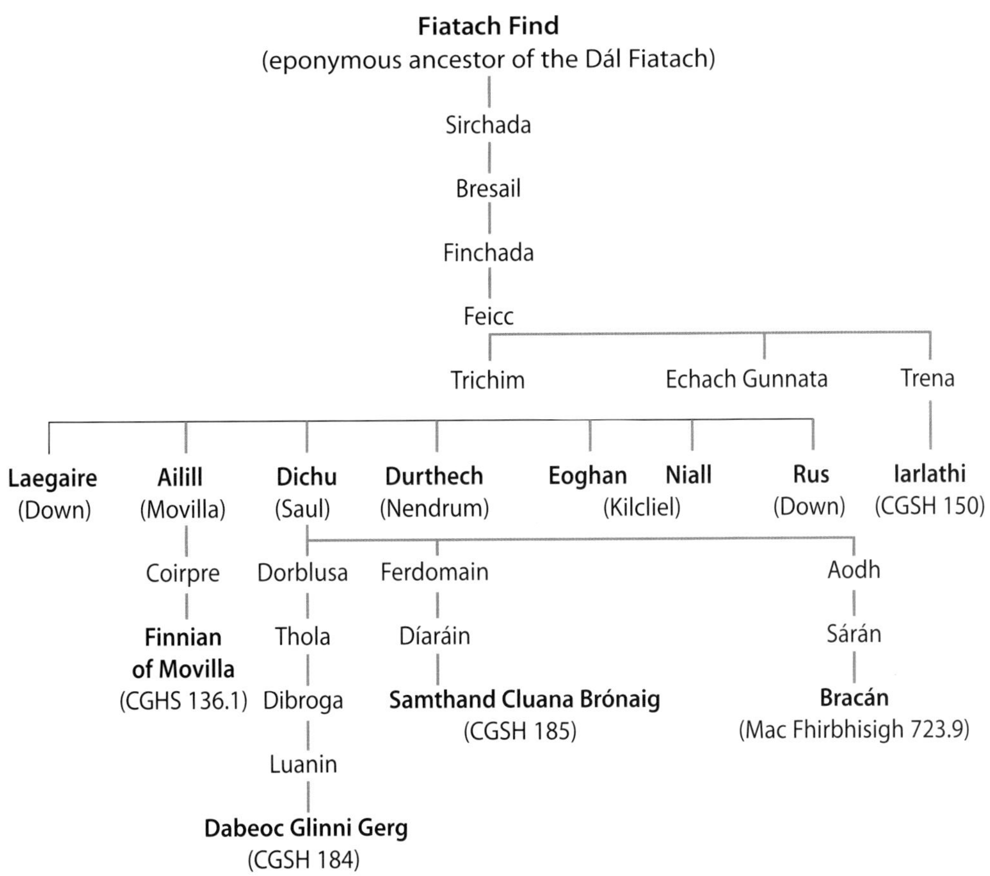

MO-CHOÍ/CÁELÁN IN THE LIVES OF COLMAN OF DROMORE AND FINNIAN OF MOVILLE

The life of St Colman of Dromore in 14th-century *Codex Salmanticenis* gives the saint as having received his early education at Nendrum (Heist 1965, 375-360) under Coelán (Cáelán). The 'life' contains some miraculous incidents in which the saint was involved when at Nendrum. One day after Colman had finish his studies, he asked Coelán what he should do next and was commanded to break a large stone on which the monks often tripped on their way to matins. Colman blessed the stone, which broke into many fragments and Coelán then commanded him to throw the pieces into the sea. This he accomplished with the help of angels and the fragments came together to form Colman's stone. The story relates that Colman revisited Nendrum in later life where he found that the community had become lax, and he exhorted them to reform. The location and tradition of Colman's stone, which must have been a landmark in the sea around Nendrum, has been lost. However, Lawlor points out that the name of the little bay on Rainey Island opposite the southern side of the monastery was called Colman's Bay (Lawlor 1925a, 54 and Plate 3).

The link between St Finnian of Movilla and Nendrum is found in the brief life of Finnian in the collection of saints lives compiled by John of Tynemouth in the mid 14th century (Sperber 1997, 91). This gives Finnian (whose death is recorded by *AU* at AD 579) as having studied first at Colman's monastery at Dromore. But after a certain time, Colman felt himself unworthy to teach him further and sent him to Coelán (Cáelán) at Nendrum *(Coelanum Noendrumsem)* who felt the same. On telling Finnian this, Coelán foretold that someone was coming whom he should follow, whereupon 'some ships from Britain, carrying a most holy bishop by the name of Nennius' (Sperber 1997, 91) arrived at the landing place in front of the monastery. Nennius agreed to take Finnian back to 'the great monastery' where he completed his studies. It is possible that Nennius can be identified with St Ninian and the 'great monastery' with Whithorn.

The value as sources of genuine historical information of the lives of these saints (or indeed, that of the vast majority of those of other saints) is very dubious, and most should be read as historical fiction of hagiographical genre. Both lives survive in 14th-century manuscripts but are based on early sources. The material in the Colman's life connects two of the principal East Ulster monasteries, Dromore in Uí Echach Cobo and Nendrum in Dál Fiatach and their saints, Coleman and Mo-Choí. The life of Finnian goes further and links three of the local principal monasteries by adding Finnian of Movilla, also in Dál Fiatach. Of special interest is that it links all three with St Ninnian and to Whithorn in Galloway, if the identification is correct, a short distance across the North Channel from East Down. Both lives portray Coelán as a reputed teacher and Nendrum as a place of learning somewhat superior to Dromore, but secondary to Whithorn.

THE EVIDENCE FOR THE CULT OF MO-CHOÍ AND CÁELÁN

The relics of St Mo-Choí

In the Early Medieval Irish church the burial place and relics of saints were of enormous significance and the central focus of the cult of the saint. The story of Mo-Choi and the bird would seem to imply that his burial place was at Nendrum. The relics of saints were used for a wide variety of functions, including the raising of revenue, swearing of oaths and gifting success in battle (Lucas 1986). Their bones and any artefacts associated with their lives were venerated as relics, and the pastoral staff or crozier was often regarded as the most important symbol. The historical sources from about the 10th century make it clear that the principal relic of St Mo-Choí was his heaven-sent crozier, the *'Etech'* or 'flying crozier' and it is strongly implied that it was kept at Nendrum. The *Etech* has not survived and is not mentioned in any later documentation, presumably like many other famous Early Medieval relics, having been lost or destroyed at some period. It is not specifically mentioned in the great mustering of the relics of the North of Ireland, but may well have been pressed into service along with the croziers of the other three East Ulster saints, Comgal of Bangor, Finnian of Moville and Ronan of Mageralin in the counter-offensive by Ruaidrí Mac Duinn Sléibe, King of Ulaid or Dál Fiatach following the seizure of Down by John de Courcy in 1177. The account contained in the notes of the martyrology of *Donegal* mentions that Mac Duinn Sléibe's forces were slaughtered and that '... the staff of Finian and the staff of Ronan Finn, and many other reliquaries were left in that slaughter' (O'Donovan 1864, xxx-xxxii). Individual mention of the staff or crozier of St Finnian of Moville and that of Ronan of *Lann Rónain Fhinn* (Mageralin), in north-western Co. Down would seem to imply that they were regarded as being among the most important relics of the Ulaid. Magheralin, for instance, is described in an entry in the *Miscellaneous Irish Annals* (Ó hInnse 1947) for 1178 when it was plundered by John de Courcy as 'chief sanctuary of all Ulaidh'. A second attempt to win back Down by Mac Duinn Sléibe, with the assistance of the Cinel Eoghain followed. They were accompanied by 'Giolla-an-Coimghe O'Ciaran, Comarb of Patrick', with 'the reliquaries of the North of Eirenn' including the 'Canon of St Patrick' (the Book of Armagh), the *Finnfaidhech of Patrick* (a bell), the bell of the circuit of Armagh, the staff of Comgal, the *Ceolan* of Tighernach (a bell), the staff of Dachiarog of Arcail (Errigal Keeroge, Co. Tyrone) the staff of Mura, and 'many other reliquaries'. The staff of Mura was an important relic (Ó'Floinn 1995, 113–116), and his monastery at Fahan in Inishown, Co. Donegal one of the principal monasteries of the Cenél Éoghan. The Comarb of Patrick was captured and later released with the Canon of St Patrick and the *Ceolan* of Tighernach, but was stated that 'the English have all the other reliquaries to the present time'.

Among some 26 relics mentioned in the possibly 8th-century poem *A maccucáin, sruith in tiag* contained in the Book of Leinster (CGSH 714) is the head of St Mo-Choí (Carney 1983, 35). The list of relics mentioned include those of many of the eminent saints of the early church such as Patrick, Bridget, Columba, Cainnech, Enda of Aran and others. The inclusion of Mo-Choí would seem to imply that the importance of his cult at this period made him worthy in the mind of the poet of association with the others. Whether the relic of his head really existed — or is the creation of poetic licence — is unclear, but the fact that many of the other relics referred to are known to have existed, suggests that it did.

The extent of the cult of Mo-Choí/Cáelán beyond Nendrum

There is sufficient evidence, outlined below, to demonstrate that the cult of Mo-Choí extended beyond the immediate vicinity of Nendrum to other parts of the Strangford Lough region and probably much further afield in Ireland and Scotland (Fitzsimons 2000). A church dedication probably to Cáelán or Mo-Choí is to be found a few miles to the south of Nendrum, in Rathgorman townland in the parish of Killinchy, where the ruins of a church beside a motte is probably to be identified with the church of Kilscalan mentioned in the 'Regal Visitation Book' in 1633 (O'Laverty 1878, 345).

Caelan of Kilclief

Kilclief is located on the coast of Lecale (Mag nInis) at the entrance of the Irish sea into Strangford Lough, some 20km to the south of Nendrum. It was raided by Dublin Vikings in 1101 *(AFM)* along with *Inis Causcraid* (Inch) and many people were carried off, but otherwise the annals are silent about its history. However, it does figure in two genealogical statements (CGSH 238 and CGSH 136.2). As previously discussed the monastery is included among those claimed along with Nendrum by the Uí Díchon branch of the Dál Fiatach in the genealogical statement on the sons of Trichim where brothers Eoghan and Niall *i Cill Chlethi* are mentioned (CGSH 136.2). A further genealogical statement documents a 'Caelan Cilli Clethi' (CGSH 238) who had a royal pedigree, being descended from the Eóganacht Caissil Kings of Munster (see Table 11.5 below), and was a brother of St Mac Tail of Kilcullen, Co. Kildare.

Table 11.5: The Eóganacht Caissil genealogy of Caelan of Kilclief (CGSH 238)

Lugdech
|
Cuirc
|
Nadfraich
|
Oengusa
|
Cronain
|
Coluimb
|
Derggain
|
Echdach
|
Caelan of Cilli Clethi — MacTáil Cilli Culind

Another version replaces Cáelán with a saint called Colman of *Chill Chleiticch* (CGSH 662.224) in a somewhat similar fashion to Cáelán of Nendrum being replaced by Colman in the Conaille pedigree. Evidence from the mid-15th century Archbishops of Armagh registers of Prene (Prene 398) and Mey (Quigley and Roberts 1972 170) show that the church at Kilclief was dedicated to a St Kelani, a name obviously derived from Cáelán. Reeves was in some doubt as to whether Caelan of Kilclief was the same as Cáelán of Nendrum or was to be identified with Cillan of Achadh-chaill (Reeves 1847, 39, 217; O'Laverty 1878, 205). However, given the close proximity of Kilclief and Nendrum, it seems highly probable that they are in origin the same saint who, as a result of the fragmentation of his cult, developed different identities. Fitzsimons (2000, 26) suggests that the shrine or church connected with the story of Mo-Choí and the bird relates to Kilclief, which translates as 'the wattle church', and within the parish of Kilclief is the townland of Loughkeelan which also may preserve the name of the saint. A possible trace of a St Cáelán is suggested by O'Laverty (1878, 143) in the name of the church of Kilschaelyn in Ballynoe townland, near Bright in Lecale, on lands granted to the Benedictine cell of Nendrum in the late 12th century. Across The Narrows from Kilclief, at the southern tip of the Ards peninsula, is the site of Templecooey with its holy wells which are still venerated. It seems probable that the saint here is Mo-Choí of Nendrum, and it seems obvious that the cult of Cáelán had a firm base in the Dál Fiatach heartland of Mag nInis and the Ards peninsula of Co. Down.

Slightly further afield in south Antrim in Dál nAraide, it has been suggested that a church in Kilmakee townland, near Templepatrick, described in the 13th century as '... the chapel of Hugh de Logan's town ...', and referred to as a possession of the benedictine cell of Nendrum, may derive its name from Cill Mo-Choí (Lawlor 1925, 42). The evidence of the martyrologies suggests also his veneration at Aughinish on Lough Swilly in Co. Donegal.

Traces of Mo-Choí/Cáelán in Scotland

Watson proposed that Kirkmahoe in Dunfriesshire and Kilmahoe in Kintyre are dedications to Mo-Choí of Nendrum, noting the personal name Gillemachoi and the surname Mc Gilmocha recorded in 15th century Scotland as derived from his name (Watson 1926, 161–162). Knight adds Clashmahew near Stranraer and a number of others (Knight 1933, I, 188). Given the close proximity of eastern Down to south-western Scotland, especially Galloway, it is not surprising that some evidence of his cult may be found there. Towill (1964) further suggests strong links between Whithorn and Mo-Choí.

The study of the cults of the saints is still in its infancy, and new insights are likely to be made as research progresses. It is not entirely clear what the link shared by churches united by common devotion to a saint meant in practical terms in Early Medieval Ireland. For some monasteries, devotion to a particular saint may have entailed following the same rule. There seems little doubt, however, that the promotion and spread of the cult Mo-Choí, which appears to have been extensive at least in the 7th and 8th centuries, would have raised the status and prestige of Nendrum and that it, as the centre of his cult, would have been a place of pilgrimage by his devotees.

THE HISTORY OF THE MONASTERY FROM THE 6TH TO 12TH CENTURY

In general, the sparse historical information which has survived regarding the monastery is in contrast to the relatively rich archaeological sources discussed in Chapter 12. The historical sources relating to the history of the monastery, as distinct from those to the cult of St Mo-Choí, consist almost entirely of entries in the annals giving the terse death notices of important clerics. From these, a very slim outline of the history of the monastery can be constructed. Frustratingly, there is no annalistic information or other historical material regarding the possible 6th-century or earlier origin of the monastery, and this corresponds with the lack of archaeological information retrieved so far for the same horizon. The earliest archeologically-attested phase of the monastery to date is the AD 619–621 tree-ring dated horizon for the construction of Mill 1, while the earliest historically-dated information is the *AU* entry recording the death of Cridán of Nendrum in AD 639. Thus, both strands of evidence show broad chronological agreement that the earliest known phase of the monastery dates to the first half of the 7th century. It seems valid therefore, based on present knowledge, to doubt the existence of Nendrum before the 7th century, having due caution regarding the value of absence of evidence. Until earlier material is recovered it is adopted as a working assumption that the monastery was founded in the early 7th century.

The 7th century

Territorial context of the monastery in the 7th century

Given the very strong territorial identity of monastic institutions in Early Medieval Ireland the first issue to be tackled is the territorial context of the monastery in the early 7th century. The context of Nendrum during the 7th and, possibly, early 8th centuries is obscure unlike, for example, neighbouring Movilla with its clear Dál Fiatach identity or Bangor (in its early stages) and the Dál nAraidi. It would appear that until perhaps as late as the second half of the 8th century, the Kingdom of Dál Fiatach was confined to Lecale/Mag nInis, the Ards peninsula, the Mournes area in Co. Down and possibly North Louth (Byrne 1973, 118). During the reign of Fiachnae Mac Aedo Roin, king of Dál Fiatach and over-king of Ulaid (AD 750–789), the kingdom commenced an expansion northwards to take over former Dál nAraidi territory in north-eastern Down (Byrne 1973, 110). Its kings started to patronise Bangor in the early 10th century (Byrne 1973, 119), as noted in a genealogical statement in Mac Fhirbhisigh (510.2, p. 361), which claims that Aed mac Eochacán († AD 919 *AU*) was the first Dál Fiatach king to render service to Bangor. This suggests that the territorial expansion northwards was completed and consolidated by the early 10th century. The implications, therefore, are that in the early 7th century, and for a century or so after, Nendrum probably lay outside Dál Fiatach territory. It may have been in Dál nAraide or indeed, though less likely, have been located in an eastward extension of Uí Echach Cobo, the kingdom to the west. It is also possible that in the 7th century it lay in a previously much more extensive Dál mBúain kingdom. If so this may explain why Mo-Choí is not given a Dál Fiatach lineage in the genealogies and is given a Dál Búain and Conaille connection rather than a Dál Fiatach one.

The newly acquired Dál Fiatach lands to the north of the Dál Fiatach heartland of Mag nInis constituted the sub-kingdom of Uí Blathmeic (McErlean 2002, 57–64) taking its name from the descendants of Bathmac, son of the Ulaid king Aodh Róin († AD 735) whose lineage held it. The Uí Blathmeic was the leading branch of the Dál Fiatach supplying many kings of both Dál Fiatach and of Ulaid. The sub-kingdom of Uí Blathmeic is mentioned in the early 12th-century *Book of Rights*, where its king is listed as receiving a stipend from the King of Ulaid of eight slaves and horses with silver bridles (Dillon 1962, 85). The sub-kingdom itself would appear to be an amalgam of a number of smaller territories mentioned in the *Book of Rights* and the genealogies.

The boundaries of ancient Uí Blathmeic may have been fossilised in Late Medieval territorial units, making possible their reconstruction. In the 13th century, the sub-kingdom formed the basis of the Anglo-Norman administrative bailiwick of *Blathewic* (McNeill 1980, 12) and, in the 14th century, it gave its name in ecclesiastical organisation to the deanery of *Blaethwyc,* one of the subdivisions of the see of Down (Reeves 1847, 9–16, 360–363). The evidence from the location of the list of parishes in the deanery in the taxation roll of *c.* 1306 (Reeves 1847) would place Nendrum on the southern boundary of Uí Blathmeic. This boundary position was perpetuated in the Late Medieval period when Nendrum was on the southern boundary of Upper Clandeboye and the northern one of Dufferin. Projecting backwards in time it seems probable, therefore, that in the early 7th century, Nendrum was on the boundary of Dál Fiatach and the territory lying to the north and if so, would conform to the pattern of many early Irish monasteries being founded in boundary zones (Ó Riain 1972).

The foundation of Nendrum

A major issue in the history and archaeology of Nendrum is the question of when, and by whom, the monastery was founded. It is possible to interpret the archaeological evidence to propose a model that the monastery was established as a major project in a single phase rather than growing over a period from small-scale beginnings (further discussed at p. 426) and to speculate this took place in the early 7th century. From this perspective the enclosure walls and sophisticated tide mill can be seen as part of an initial phase of development and datable to around AD 619. Present behind most grand projects there was one great driving force or personality and it seems probable that this was the case at Nendrum. History is silent concerning who this individual may have been, but Cridán of Nendrum as the first named cleric of Nendrum, whose death is recorded in AD 639 *(AU),* is a possible candidate. The length of Cridán's authority at Nendrum is unknown but it lasted more that twenty years, up to his death. This would have him contemporary with — and possibly responsible for — the major works of which Mill 1 was a part in AD 619–621.

It seems also inconceivable that a monastery could be founded without the direct input or patronage of the local temporal lord or territorial king, or leading local lineage. The king of Ulaid at the time of the construction of Mill 1 was the powerful Fiachnae Mac Báetain (Fiachnae Lurgan) of the Dál nAraide who ruled AD 588–626 (Byrne 1973, 111–112), and it is possible that it was under his patronage that the monastery was founded.

7th-century entries in the annals
639 *(AU)* Repose of Cridán in Naendruim

643 *(AU)* Repose of Crónán bishop of Naendruim

644 *(Tig)* Mo Cháe Naendroma rested

659 *(AU)* Cuiméne bishop of Naendruim died

684 *(AU)* Death of Maine, abbot of Naendruim

684 *(AI)* Repose of Mórann, bishop of Naendruim

Little is known about Cridán, who died in AD 639 — his probable feast day is given in *Tallaght* as May 17th. In *Gorman,* the entry reads Critan and is glossed 'bishop of *Oendruim'*, and similarly treated in *Donegal.*

The feast day of Crónán who died in AD 643, is given in *Tallaght* ('*Cronani Episcop*') as January 7th. In *Gorman* the entry is glossed '*Becc* ('Little Cronán') and 'I epscop Naondroma' and similarly in *Donegal.* He has been identified as one of the recipients of the papal letter of AD 640 discussed below. The entry which mentions Mo Cháe of AD 644 is found only in the *Annals of Tigernach* (Tig., Stokes 1896). Lawlor, who rendered the name as Mochua interpreted it as a variant form of Mo-Choí (Lawlor 1925a, 66) and Etchingham (p. 316) suggests that this is a misplaced entry for Mo-Choí/Cáelán. It may be observed, however, that the name Mochua is a hypocoristic form of Cronán, and the entry may be a duplication for Crónán of AD 643. The feast day of *Cuiméne episcopus Naendruma,* whose death is given by *AU* as occurring in AD 659, is listed under the hypocoristic form Do Chumma Noindruim (glossed 'or *Mo Chumma*') in *Tallaght* for January 31st. The two entries for AD 684 — for Maine, abbot of Nendrum in *AU* and Mórann, bishop of Nendrum in *AI* — may be a confusion of the same person. Alternatively, they could refer to two separate individuals, one who held the abbacy and the other who acted as bishop. It has been suggested tentatively that Ballymorran townland on the mainland opposite the monastery takes its name from abbot Mórann (Lawlor 1925a, 67).

A primary feature of interest in the 7th-century annalistic documentation for Nendrum is the mention of bishops at the monastery, and its significance is discussed by Etchingham below (see p. 315). Their documented presence raises the status of the monastery to that of an episcopal church. The Nendrum bishops can be put into context by considering references to bishops as a whole in the 7th- and 8th-centuries annals (Etchingham 1999a, 99–100 and map 2). Bishops are recorded at 22 churches or monasteries in Ireland in the period between AD 601 and AD 740 (23 if Iona is included). In the great majority of locations, some 18 of the total, only one or two bishops are recorded. Standing out by virtue of greater numbers of recorded bishops are Nendrum and Armagh each with five, and Clonard and Ferns each with four.

This seems to imply that Nendrum in the 7th century was an episcopal centre of some note. Indeed, it is possible that for much of the 7th century, the annals provide a complete succession list of the bishops of Nendrum, from Cridán to Mórann. If this is an unbroken succession, it can be deduced that the length of the episcopacy of Crónán was four years, that of Cuiméne sixteen years, and that of Mórann twenty-five years.

It is evident that bishops in the early Irish church often combined their office with that of abbot, and an example of this at Nendrum occurs in the 9th century where the death is recorded in AD 873 *(AU)* of Colmán, who is styled both as bishop (and scribe) and abbot of Nendrum. However, it is clear that often the two roles were separate, and that a monastery may have had a resident bishop as well as an abbot. It is unclear, therefore, whether the sequence of clerics given for the 7th century can be taken also as a sequence of the abbots of the monastery.

For most of the 7th century, the only known bishops in the region were at Nendrum. The only other contemporary bishops recorded for Co Down were at Movilla, where obituaries for bishops are recorded in AD 603 *(AU)* and AD 621 *(AI)*. Apart from these, the only other 7th-century bishop recorded in the annals for eastern Ulster (Cos Antrim and Down) is *Dímma Dub,* Bishop of Connor (Co. Antrim), who died in AD 659 *(AU)*. The dates for the Movilla bishops are interesting, in that the latest occurs just when it seems likely that the sequence of bishops at Nendrum begins, and it is possible that Nendrum took over from Movilla as the seat of the regional bishop. However, as discussed by Etchingham (p. 319), this interpretation requires caution as there may well have been other contemporary bishops in the region whose names have not been recorded.

The territorial extent of the sphere of jurisdiction of the early bishops of the Irish church is difficult to ascertain, but it may have been co-extensive with that of the *túath* or minor kingdom. Charles-Edwards (2000, 260) suggests that Nendrum was the principal episcopal church of the Ulaid in the 7th century and, given the apparent absence of other recorded bishops in the region during that period, the bishops of Nendrum may have commanded a see that extended over all of the kingdom of Ulaid.

Crónán, Bishop of Nendrum and the papal letter of AD 640 on the dating of Easter

It is of considerable interest that Crónán, Bishop of Nendrum, if the identification is correct, is included among the addressees of a letter from Rome to the Irish clergy in AD 640. The content of the letter, which has been much discussed (Reeves 1847, 149; Kenny 1979, 221–223; Harrison 1984; Richter 1999, 211–213; O Cróinín 2003, 87–98 and see Etchingham, p. 316), is concerned with conformity regarding the date on which Easter, the day of the Resurrection of Christ, was to be observed. The dating of Easter was a major preoccupation of 7th-century Christianity, and that a different calculation system was employed by the Irish church from that adopted by Rome and most of western Christendom was a matter of concern.

The letter was written in AD 640 from Pope-elect, John IV and three members of the Roman curia, to some of the leading Irish clergy in response to a letter from them (which has not survived) to Rome asking for guidance on the dating of Easter. It is preserved in Bede's *Historia Ecclesiastica* (*HE* 11.19; Sherley-Price 1990, 138–139, 367). It has been remarked that the speed of reply to the letter implies that a request was made to specifically confirm the dating of the Easter that was to fall in AD 641 (Richter 1999, 211-213). The letter, as quoted by Bede, is stiff in tone and admonishes them for their persistence in calculating the dating of Easter in contradiction to the method employed by Rome. In Bede's description, the letter also contains the accusation that the Pelagian heresy has taken root in Ireland and urges its eradication. It is addressed in particular to eleven individuals — five bishops, five presbyters (priests, although most of latter are identifiable as abbots), one other whose clerical status is not specified, and in general to 'the other Irish teachers and abbots'. The assumption to be made is that the sequence of names is the same as that of the original letter, and that the order in which they occur may have some significance. Identification of at least some of the clerics in the list can be attempted from their obituaries in the annals (Reeves 1947, 149; Kenny 1929, 221–223). Those given by Kenny are below.

Bishops	
Tomianus	Tóiméne, bishop of Armagh, † AD 661 *(AU)*
Columbanus	Colman moccu Telduib, bishop and abbot of Clonard, † AD 654 *(AU)*
Cromanus	Cronán, bishop of Nendrum, † AD 643 *(AU)*
Dinnaus	Dímma Dub, bishop of Connor, † AD 659 *(AU)*
Baithanus	Baethán moccu Cormaicc, bishop and abbot of Clonmacnoise, † AD 664 *(AU)*

Presbyters (priests)

Cromanus	Crónán, abbot of Movilla, † AD 650 *(AU)*
Ernianus	possibly abbot of Tory † c. AD 650 (Reeves 1847, 149)
Laistranus	possibly Mac Laisre, abbot of Bangor † AD 648 (AU) or Laissen Mac
Nesca	Abbot of Ard-mac-Nasca (Hollywood, Co. Down, (Reeves 1847, 149)),
Scellanus	possibly Sillan of Devenish, † AD 661 *(Chronicum Scotorum)*
Segenus *and*	Ségéne, abbot of Iona, † AD 652 *(AU)*
Saranus	possibly Sarán ua Crítán Sapiens of Tech Sarán near Banagher, Co. Offaly, † AD 662 *(AU)*

The inclusion of Crónán, bishop of Nendrum, if the identification is correct, in such distinguished company as the bishop of Armagh and bishops or abbots of Iona, Clonmacnoise and Clonard, would seem to place him among the leading movers and thinkers in the mid-7th-century Irish church. It argues also for the prominence of the monastery at a national level during this period and for it being the seat of an influential bishop.

The 8th century

Eighth-century annal entries

735 *(AU)* Oígedchar, bishop of Naendruim rests

755 *(AU)* Snédcheist, abbot of Naendruim died

In contrast to the 7th-century, notices of Nendrum in the annals notably decline in the 8th, and consist of the two entries above, one for a bishop and one for an abbot. It is frustrating that no leading cleric can be associated, from the historical record, with the phase of development represented by Mill 2 of *c.* AD 789. To meagre annalistic information can be added a mention in the Litany of the Irish Saints of probable late 8th- or early 9th-century date, which refers to '…nine times fifty monks under the yoke of Mochoe of Nendrum' (Plummer 1925, 67). The figure of 450 monks at Nendrum seems large, but pales in comparison to Bangor to which the same source attributes 4000 monks. In a similar vein, a quatrain in marginal notes in *Tallaght* gives figures of 900 for Bangor, 600 for Antrim and 500 for Connor (Best and Lawlor 1931, 113). These figures, if not poetic exaggeration, may well include the monastic tenants or clients (the *manaigh*) living on the monastic estates as well as the monks living within the enclosure of the monastery.

The 9th and 10th centuries

Ninth- and 10th-century annal entries

873 *(AU)* Colmán, bishop, scribe and abbot of Naendruim rested

917 *(AFM)* Máelcoí, abbot of Oendruim

976 *(AU)* Sétna ua Demán, superior (*Airchinnech*) of Naendruim was burned to death in his own house.

There is one entry in the annals for the 9th century and two for the 10th century. Colmán, who died in AD 873, combined the roles of both abbot and bishop as well as being a scribe, and is the last recorded bishop of Nendrum, and its only recorded scribe. The office of scribe does not refer to a copyist of texts, but to someone who — as an expert in canon law — acted as an ecclesiastical judge and legal authority (Etchingham 1999a, 174) and as such was an important figure. The record of the obituary of Máelcoí, only found in *AFM*, bears a personal name derived from Mo-Choi, with the prefix *Máel,* which encompasses the sense of 'devotee' or 'servant' of the named saint.

The entry for AD 976 is the last mention of Nendrum in the annals. Apart from speculation on the reason for the fire, it is of interest in that it implies that the *Airchinnech* had his own separate residence within the monastery and was not housed communally with the rest of the monks. Such an arrangement is demonstrated by frequent references in the annals, such as those of AD 824 *(AU)* when 'the abbot's mansion' in Armagh was burned, and AD 917 *(AFM),* which records that 'Innreachtach, Abbot of Trefoil, was slain in his own abbatical house'.

The title *airchinnech* (anglicised erenagh) has a number of levels of meaning at this period, generally centering around 'lord of the monastic estate', 'governor' or 'church head' (Sharpe 1984, 259; Etchingham 1999a, 50–63, 65–67, 71–74). The surname of the *airchinnech* of Nendrum in the late 10th century, Ua Demán, is of special interest. It provides the name of the family who controlled the monastery and its estate in the 10th to the 12th centuries, something that has not been recorded elsewhere. The surname would appear to identify him as a member of the Dál Fiatach line known as the Cenél Demmáin (O'Brien 1962 330c 30–46; Mac Fhirbhisigh 495.1, 508.1), who claimed descent from Demán, King of Ulaid and Dál Fiatach who died in AD 572 *(AU).* The control of monasteries and their estates by segments of the local royal line is a frequently found feature of the period. In Bangor for instance, some of the later coarbs of Comgal belong to Dál Fiatach families. The Ua Demán do not appear to have continued in occupation in the Later Medieval period. It is probable that they were removed by John de Courcy, clearing the church lands of their previous controllers as a logical step before the granting of these lands to his followers and to the new religious orders, which he introduced. This surname, anglicised as O' Diamond, is found among Late Medieval *erenaghs* in the parish of Kilrea, Co. Londonderry.

Nendrum and the Viking in Strangford Lough

In AD 824 and 825 the comparatively peaceful world in which Nendrum existed was violently shattered by devastating Viking raids on its nearest monastic neighbours Bangor, Movilla and Downpatrick. In AD 824 *(AU)* the Viking raid on Bangor 'destroyed the oratory and shook the relics of Comgal from their shrine', and a poem appended to the entry states that the bones of the saint were sent to the inland monastery of Antrim for safety. In AD 825 Down and Movilla were plundered, and at Movilla 'its oratories' were burned. This Viking targeting of the monasteries of Dál Fiatach appears to have been brought to an end by their defeat in Mag nInis later in the year by the Ulaid, when many of them were killed. Nendrum is not specifically mentioned as being raided in this campaign, or at any other time during the Viking period, but given its coastal location exposed to seaborne attack, it is likely that it was. This campaign, almost the first of the Viking wars in Ireland, ushered in a period of warfare, which was to last for a considerable time. Irish monasteries, previously, were not strangers to occasional acts of warfare but these attacks by foreign heathens were of a different order of violence and outrage. The Viking onslaught continued with unrelenting intensity during the following decades with attacks recorded at most of the major monasteries of Ireland. Armagh for example, was plundered three times in one month in AD 832 *(AU)*. In the same year, Maghera (Co. Derry) and Connor (Co. Antrim) were raided, Clondalkin (Co. Dublin) in AD 833 *(AU)*, Glendalough (Co. Wicklow) in AD 834 *(AU)*, Ferns (Co. Wexford) in AD 835 *(AU)* and Kildare (Co. Kildare) in AD 836 *(AU)* and Devenish, (Co. Fermanagh), Clones (Co. Monaghan) and Inis Celtra (Co. Clare) in AD 837. In AD 840 *(AU)*, the Vikings of Lough Neagh raided Co. Louth and took away 'bishops, priests and scholars, and put others to death'.

In AD 842 *(AU)* Clonmacnoise, Birr and Saigher Co. Offaly were plundered and in the same year the first reference is found to a possible Viking *longphort* in Dál Fiatach at an unidentified place called *Linn Sailech (AU)*.

It is clear that the Vikings were targeting monasteries as the main centres of population, since they were rich in booty and potential captives. While there are no direct references to Viking aggression against Nendrum in the annals, they demonstrated strong Viking activity during the 9th, 10th and early 11th centuries in the Strangford Lough region (McErlean 2002, 78–87). There are 19 references in total, eight from the 9th and 11 from the 10th and early 11th centuries. The first is the two-year campaign of AD 823–825, which seems to have been brought to a close by a successful Dál Fiatach counter-offensive. A second phase appears to have commenced in AD 842 with the establishment of the Viking *longphort* at *Linn Sailech*, and continued at least until AD 853 when Cathmal, joint-king of Ulaid, was killed by them. There are no entries between this date and AD 877, when it is recorded that a battle between the Danish and Norse Vikings took place on Strangford Lough. Again, there is another hiatus between AD 877 and AD 924 *(AU)*. In the period between AD 924 and AD 943, the entries clearly demonstrate that there was a resident Viking group somewhere around the Lough, sufficiently well established to be referred to as the 'Vikings of Lough Cuan' (Strangford Lough). The arrival of their fleet is announced in AD 924 and they are recorded as having plundered the monastery of Downpatrick in AD 942. The capture of their 'island' and expulsion by the Leth Cathail branch of the Dál Fiatach in a decisive victory is recorded in AD 943 *(AU)*, and the victory over them, which included the killing of their king, 'was gained with the help of God and Patrick'. After this period, although a number of raids and one military alliance in AD 970 *(AU)* when the king of Ulaid joined with them in raiding Connor, are recorded, there is no strong evidence to suggest the presence of a Viking settlement in the region. Thus, a summary of the evidence highlights the period between AD 924 and 943 as a time of probable Viking settlement in the area. While the entry of AD 976 was taken by Lawlor as referring to a Viking raid resulting in the burning of the *airchinnech* in his residence, there is no supporting evidence for this interpretation and in any case, the annals demonstrate that fires at monasteries were frequent occurrences.

It seems highly unlikely that Nendrum, as a relatively rich and prominent monastery, should have escaped attention by the Vikings at some period during the 9th and 10th centuries though historical documentation for such an event is lacking. It is probable that excavation would be not be able to produce recognisable evidence for a specific Viking raid in spite of Lawlor's arguments and interpretation of the contrary. If a raid did occur it is instructive to speculate on its possible long-term effects. The short-term impact would have been severe. It may well have included the destruction of buildings and of cultural resources such as the monastic library with its precious manuscripts and the destruction of relics. It would have entailed the loss of people including key personnel. All this would have led to a short-term impoverishment. However, there is little evidence that any monastery was effectively wiped out and ceased to exist as a result of sustained Viking aggression. Indeed the resilience of Irish monasteries in the face of attacks is a characteristic trait. This resilience would have been partly based on their landed wealth and continued patronage by the local community. It would be facile to blame the apparent decline of Nendrum in the 11th and 12th centuries on Viking violence of the 9th and 10th centuries, therefore other reasons need to considered.

The 11th and 12th centuries

The end of monastic life at Nendrum

From the last entry in the annals for Nendrum in AD 976 until the Anglo-Norman invasion, the historical sources are silent about the monastery. Its great days appear to belong to the 7th and 8th centuries as witnessed both by the historical sources and the tide mills. The construction of a round tower is evidence that the community was still flourishing in the 10th century, but in the light of present knowledge, there is no convincing evidence — either archaeological or historical — for the monastery functioning in the 11th or 12th centuries. Indeed, in the 12th century, its main monastic neighbours were being revived. That vigorous reformer of the Irish church, St Malachy, both as Archbishop of Armagh and Bishop of Down, was responsible from *c.* 1124–1148 for the introduction of Augustinian Canons to Bangor and Downpatrick, also probably to Movilla and Saul. This may indicate that at these sites, monastic communities of some sort still existed on which to base the new foundations. If such had been the case at Nendrum, it seems probable that Malachy would have established an Augustinian community there also. All that may have survived there was the church and perhaps a small associated settlement of some sort and the estate, the latter in the hands of the *erenagh* family.

Thus, the central questions are when and why regular monastic organisation ended at Nendrum. The evidence from the 1922–1924 excavations yielded no clear indication of when this situation may have come about. However, occupancy of the site, but not by a monastic community, may have continued down to the founding of the Benedictine priory by John de Courcy in the late 12th century. The excavation shows that at some point in time, Mill 2 was destroyed and not repaired. When this happened has not, unfortunately, been ascertained. It is possible to link the demise — or at least the decline — of community life with the history of the mills, as a flourishing and organised monastery needed a mill and its abandonment may be taken as an indication community life had ceased or at least diminished considerably.

It is possible to look for reasons for the decline of Nendrum in the history of its monastic neighbours, Movilla, Bangor and Downpatrick. In the 9th century, all four were in the small, but politically important and powerful kingdom of Dál Fíatach in eastern Down. In terms of royal and other forms of patronage, the existence of four major monastic houses within the same territory, and within a relatively small geographic area, must have meant at least one would have lost out. Thus, it is possible that by the 11th century, Nendrum experienced a loss of royal patronage and prestige that resulted in a gradual decline. The others continue to receive mention in the annals and occasionally, at least in the case of Down, have associated bishops, while Nendrum fades from view historically

THE BISHOPS OF NENDRUM: A NOTE
Colmán Etchingham

The record of Nendrum in the annals is of interest for several reasons. One is that it is better documented in the 7th century AD than in any subsequent period. This is the reverse of the usual pattern, for most Irish churches with an appreciable profile in the annals enjoy fuller coverage after the mid-8th century. In the case of Nendrum, however, following at least four and perhaps as many as six genuine records for the 7th century, there are two notices in the 8th-century annals, one in the 9th and two in the 10th. Nendrum disappears altogether from the annals after AD 976, when its *airchinnech* or leading official died in a fire 'in his own house'. H. C. Lawlor, the original excavator of the site and author, eighty years ago, of the only extended account of Nendrum, assumed that this was a Viking attack. 'At this date all our documentary history of Nendrum as a Celtic monastery ends ...', he declared, but proposed that it may have continued as a settlement of the 'Danes' (Lawlor 1925a, 68–70, 133). A noteworthy feature of the annalistic dossier of Nendrum, and the one with which this note is chiefly concerned, is the prominence of bishops among its recorded ecclesiastics.

The earliest mention of Nendrum is the obituary notice or 'obit' of its founder, Mo-Choí, which is reported in *AU* for AD 497, where he is given no title. Annalistic 'records' of this era, the so-called 'Age of the Saints', are not, in their present form, contemporary and are suspect. Generally we have no means of knowing whether any particular event found in the annals for the conversion period reflects more or less reliable tradition, guesswork or deliberate fabrication. Ninth- or 10th-century Armagh propaganda claims that Mo-Choí was a convert and religious initiate of Patrick's (Stokes, 1887, 41; Mulchrone 1939, 25–26). Obviously, there would have been an incentive for later chroniclers to synchronize Mo-Choí with the chronology of the 'National Apostle', one version of which has Patrick die in the 490s. (On recent scholarship relating to Patrick, including the question of his dates, see conveniently Etchingham 1999c). Scepticism, or at any rate caution, seems in order therefore, regarding Mo-Choí. That is not necessarily to question the existence of Nendrum as an early Christian centre in the 5th century, but we ought to resist the temptation to accept non-contemporary 'traditions' as evidence of the history of any such church in the 5th century.

One point that may tell against the authenticity of early 'records' of saintly founders is that they are often isolated. To take the parallel case of Kildare, early 6th-century obituaries of both Brigit and Bishop Conláed do not initiate a continuous 6th-century record, but are followed by over a century of silence, after which plausible references to historical *personae* of Kildare commence in the 7th century (Etchingham 2000a, 8–9). By contrast, Nendrum's Co. Down neighbours, Bangor and Movilla, are first noticed only in the second half of the 6th century (*AU* 555, 579). In both cases, these early references seem to be genuine opening records in a comparatively regular chronicle of Bangor and Movilla churchmen that continues through the 7th century and the first half of the 8th. The record of Nendrum is more like that of Kildare. After AD 497 we must wait well over a century until the obituary of the first of a series of 7th-century officials of Nendrum is reported in 639 *(AU)*. With this begins in reality the early annalistic record of the monastery. Whether a certain Cáelán of Nendrum was identical with Mo-Choí, or was his successor, is a question with which Lawlor grappled (Lawlor 1925a, 46–64). In connection with this, we can be clear about one point — the annals provide no evidence of a distinct ruler of Nendrum of that name.

The coverage of Nendrum in the annals may be briefly surveyed. It consists almost exclusively of the obituaries of its leading ecclesiastics (all *AU*), beginning with Bishops Cridán (†639), Crónán (†643) and Cúmméne (†659). The 'record' of the death of a 'Mo-Cháe' of Nendrum in 644, to which Lawlor gave credence (1925, 57 and 66), may be dismissed as no more than a misplaced duplicate of the 'record' of the founder confined, among the early annals, to the 'Clonmacnoise-version' texts, *AT* and *CS*. It has been suggested that Crónán may be the same as Cromanus, a bishop, who was among the leading northern Irish ecclesiastics to whom Rome in AD 640 addressed a letter concerning the Easter controversy (Kenney 1929, 222). This is a unique survival, the first intimation that Rome was in contact with Irish Christianity since Pope Celestine's dispatch of Bishop Palladius, two hundred years earlier, in AD 431. In AD 662, *AU* reports the death of one Sarán nepos Critáin, a master of learning *(sapiens)*, whose affiliations are not disclosed. Perhaps he was a grandson *(nepos)* of Bishop Cridán of Nendrum, given the interest shown by the annals in that church, but this is no more than conjecture. In AD 684, *AU* reports the death of Maine *abbas* 'abbot' of Nendrum. *AI*, apparently for the same year, reports instead the death of Mórann bishop of Nendrum. It is not clear whether two distinct officials of Nendrum died in this year, or whether one of these records is a mistaken variant of the other. For Nendrum in the 8th century we have the obituaries of Bishop Oígedchar in AD 735 (*AU*) and Abbot Snédcheist in AD 755 *(AU)*, while for the 9th century there is only the obituary of Colmán, 'bishop and *scriba,* abbot of Nendrum', in 873 (*AU*: for the meaning of *scriba*, see conveniently Etchingham 1999a, 174). For the 10th century, there is the obituary of Máelcoí, abbot of Nendrum, in 919 (*AFM* 917) and then the record of the *airchinnech* Sétna Ua Demán's death by fire in 976.

Bishops dominate this brief catalogue of the officials of Nendrum. Four of the five or six individuals of 7th-century date were bishops, as were one each in the 8th and 9th centuries. There is also reference to an abbot in the 7th century and to another in the 8th, while the 9th-century bishop is also termed an abbot. Only in the 10th century is the episcopal title not used: one official is called an abbot and another an *airchinnech*. This latter title is more explicitly indicative of governorship or rulership, with an emphasis on his function in managing the church as a worldly institution (Etchingham 1999a, 50–63, 65–67, 71–74).

Until relatively recently, most accounts of the early Irish church had little to say of bishops after the era of conversion. That church was portrayed as essentially and distinctively monastic in character. For an example we need look no further, in the present context, than Lawlor. The title of his study and references, such as one already quoted referring to Nendrum as a 'Celtic monastery', illustrate the point of view. He is anxious to dispel any notion that comparatively frequent mention of Nendrum's bishops implies it was

> ... a regular diocesan see...This is of course misleading, as in the early centuries the Irish Church was almost, if not entirely, a monastic church. The position or status of the bishops of the early Celtic Church, as compared with that of the Roman Church and with modern ideas, is involved in a certain amount of obscurity ...' (Lawlor, 1925a, 21*n*)

In recent years, a root-and-branch reassessment of the organisation of the early Irish church has, among other things, denied the validity of the 'Celtic Church' concept and restored the bishop to a more central role. Bishops were indispensable — for the church in general and for specific settlements of any consequence — to ordain clergy, minister confirmation and confer the highest status on a church, and often acted as judge at the highest level within the ecclesiastical sphere. The bishop was the essential overseer of the pastoral role of the churches, albeit that regular pastoral care seems to have been supplied only to select groups and not to the lay community generally. Moreover, the bishop was expected to have jurisdiction within a spatially defined sphere and the existence of such spheres is clear by the 10th century at the latest.

This latter point requires us to revise the generally held view (implicit in Lawlor's remarks) that diocesan sees were introduced to Ireland by the 12th-century reform. In the pre-12th-century Irish church, the episcopal role might be either combined with, or distinct from that of effective day-to-day management of the settlement. This latter role was designated either by the term 'abbot' or by the title *airchinnech/princeps*, which more explicitly acknowledged his function as 'executive director', 'governor' or 'leader'. Major church settlements thus had a multi-faceted and flexible leadership structure, of which various permutations were possible in practice. The most common, it seems, was to separate the episcopal and executive roles. In this case, the non-clerical church head would appoint a clerical functionary at the level appropriate to the status of the church in question, be it episcopal, priestly, diaconal or lower (Etchingham, 1991, 1993, 1994, 1999a, 1999b, 2000a, 2000b).

The annalistic record of church affairs is dominated by the obituaries of church officials who performed the executive role. Bishops are much less frequently recorded in the annals. In the case of very well documented churches, such as Kildare, bishops are recorded, together with various categories of subsidiary officials. Bishops are also recorded in the cases of those churches whose chief executives or managers were also bishops, which was generally true of Armagh up to the late-8th century and sometimes thereafter (Etchingham, 1999a, 87–90, 99–101). It would seem that 7th-century Nendrum was, for the most part, in this latter category and that, from the 7th to 9th centuries, the functions of bishop and of effective governor were usually performed by the same person. This was a relatively unusual, but by no means exceptional, permutation of a system of organisation that was multi-faceted and flexible, as has been observed. This system allowed for the performance of a variety of functions, both monastic and non-monastic, by the leading churches.

The record of bishops of Nendrum is, of course, positive evidence that it enjoyed that high status among ecclesiastical settlements that only a bishop could bring. In the case of other prominent churches in the East Ulster region, where such positive evidence is limited or entirely lacking, the conclusion to be drawn is not so obvious. Two or three early officials of Movilla are explicitly credited with episcopal orders (*AU* 579, 603; *AI* 621). The title does not occur again, however, among the records of Movilla down to the 12th century, which consist mostly of a sequence of its executive heads. These are designated 'abbots', *princeps/airchinnech* or, from the 10th century onwards, 'coarbs' or successors of Finnian, the founding saint. It seems improbable that Movilla forfeited an early status as an episcopal church, given the continuing prominence indicated by its relatively frequent mention in the annals. More likely is that the episcopal and gubernatorial functions were first combined but later separated, after which the individual bishops were of insufficient interest to the annalists to merit separate record. Some such interpretation would also seem appropriate to Bangor, none of whose early leaders is accorded episcopal orders. Yet the existence of bishops among its officials is revealed sporadically in the annals for the 9th and 10th centuries (*AI* 823, *CS* 929 [928], *AU* 953). Again, the relative prominence of Bangor in the annalistic record for the 7th and 8th centuries tells against any possibility that Bangor originally did not have bishops, or did not enjoy the high status that only bishops could bring to a church.

In short, positive evidence of bishops associated with a church, as in the case of early Nendrum, speaks for itself, but the reverse is not true. In this, as in so many other aspects of the annalistic record, absence of evidence cannot be assumed to be evidence of absence. This, of course, greatly complicates the problem of determining the geographical extent of episcopal spheres in East Ulster (or, for that matter, anywhere else in Ireland). It can be shown that the annalistic record is, in various respects, partial and incomplete (*cf.* Etchingham 1996), and it cannot be expected to supply us with the data needed to map episcopal spheres over time. The author has attempted elsewhere to map Irish episcopal seats known from the annals and tentatively to identify the most significant centres in the best documented region, the central east (Etchingham 1999a, 477–484). However, the evidence is not available to do more than conjecture at the spheres of jurisdiction involved.

In the case of Nendrum, we can be confident that it was the seat of at least a local bishopric in the 7th century and perhaps also in the 8th and 9th centuries, after which the situation becomes unclear. It seems likely that Movilla and Bangor also housed bishops, as already noted. Further afield in East Ulster, there are occasional indications in the annals that Downpatrick (*AFM* 825 [823], 1043; *AU* 956), Dromore (*AFM* 974 [972]) and Connor, Co. Antrim (*AU* 659, 726, 1038), had bishops before the 12th-century reform. Partial and incomplete though the evidence is, we can form some impression of very small spheres of jurisdiction associated with the basic level of local bishop. It is also possible that, on the analogy of secular political hegemony, there was a pecking order among such local bishoprics, so that one might on occasion subordinate the others in a loose and fluid system of episcopal hierarchy.

A model proposed by the author is for an organic, bottom-up development of episcopal hierarchy in Ireland before the 12th-century reform (Etchingham 1999a, 177-194; 2000b). While no direct, positive evidence for this in East Ulster is apparent, an indirect indication of such a development may be found in the genealogies of the local ruling dynasty of much of Co. Down, the Dál Fíatach. These show that, from the 8th to the early-11th centuries, the dynasty distributed its ecclesiastical members and patronage chiefly between Downpatrick and Bangor, with interests also in the likes of Movilla and Saul. Bangor was also linked with other local noble families (Dobbs 1921, 346—347, 350–351; 1923, 72–73, 80–87, 93–95, 109). Both Bangor and Downpatrick housed bishops in that century, as we have seen. Should we detect evidence of the precedence of Downpatrick in the 11th century, when only Downpatrick of the two of them has a bishop recorded in the annals? The patchy character of the annalistic evidence will scarcely allow such an inference to be drawn.

By the same token, it is difficult to feel confident about interpreting the absence of recorded bishops of Nendrum after the 9th century or, indeed, the complete disappearance of that church from the annalistic record after AD 976. Perhaps Nendrum did lose out in competition for lay patronage with other churches of the region. Its cult is not referred to in the genealogies of the Dál Fíatach and other local nobility, mentioned above. Perhaps Nendrum fell victim to developments in native Irish secular politics or perhaps, as Lawlor conjectured, it fell victim to Vikings. In the nature of the evidence, however, one can never rule out the possibility that the explanation is simply textual: one of those myriad developments in the textual history of the annals that allow various churches, great and small, to move in and out of the sights of the chroniclers over the centuries.

One aspect of the profile of Nendrum in the annals is surely to be attributed to a feature of the textual history of the annals that is well known. There is no doubt that a key element of the contemporary record up to the 730s is a chronicle that was written on Iona (Bannerman 1968). Given the relative proximity of Nendrum to Iona, this may account for comparatively regular notices of Nendrum in the 7th century and the first half of the 8th. The early records of Bangor and Movilla may also be explained thus. A more sporadic record of the leaders of Nendrum after AD 755 must be attributed to diminished interest on the part of annalists/compilers after the Iona chronicle ceases to be a key component of our surviving compilations of annals. By comparison, coverage of Bangor continues after the period of the Iona chronicle. The case of Movilla lies somewhere in between for, although there is a substantial break between AD 749 and 825, a record of its leading figures, albeit a more sporadic one, resumes thereafter. It is tempting to conjecture that the complete disappearance of Nendrum from the annals after AD 976 is, therefore, explicable on textual grounds — a longer-term failure to sustain the interest of Irish-based annalists/compilers after the transfer of the core-chronicle from Iona.

In that event, the violent death of the last recorded leader of Nendrum in AD 976 may be no more than coincidence. Certainly Lawlor's view that he was a victim of Vikings is mere conjecture and is supported by no positive evidence. It has been maintained elsewhere that the Vikings had an appreciable impact in the Ards peninsula, the native dynasty of which, Uí Echach Arda, is supposed to have succumbed to them in the 9th century (Byrne 1973, 108). This is no more than an inference, however, for which there is no positive evidence. It is at least a plausible conjecture, nevertheless, given that the 9th century is a period of demonstrable Viking pressure in East Ulster, pressure that continues in the early 10th century.

Less plausible, on the face of it, is Lawlor's assumption that Nendrum succumbed entirely to the Vikings as late as the last quarter of the 10th century. By that stage, the peak of substantial church raiding by Vikings had long passed and the Vikings in Ireland were to a greater or lesser degree Christianised (for detailed consideration of Viking raiding in the 9th century, see Etchingham 1996 and, for the 9th and 10th centuries, Etchingham, *forthcoming* 2007). Indeed, four years after the incident of AD 976 at Nendrum, Áleifr (Amlaíb Cúarán), king of Dublin, died in ecclesiastical retirement on Iona *(AT)*. On the other hand, a brief spurt of renewed raiding broke out in the 980s and targeted locations on both sides of the Irish Sea, including Derry. The perpetrators are called 'Danes' in the Irish annals, 'pirates' in the Anglo-Saxon chronicles and 'Black Gentiles' (apparently synonymous with Danes) in the Welsh annals. A few years earlier, in AD 975, *Rechru*, probably in this case Rathlin Island, was raided by Vikings described as 'heathens' *(gentiles)*, a description not commonly applied to Insular Vikings by Irish annalists since the 920s. It is possible that this was an early precursor of the Danish campaigns of the 980s but, alternatively, the raiders may have been Orkneymen (Etchingham 2001, 175–179).

Could the burning of the *airchinnech* of Nendrum 'in his own house' in AD 976 be related to the probable attack on Rathlin in the previous year? A difficulty with such a conjecture is that the annals do not attribute the incident at Nendrum to a Viking raid. Such reticence would be unusual and not obviously explicable and would point, rather, to an incident involving the native Irish that the reporter was reluctant to detail or, just as likely, to an accidental fire involving no culpability. The annals, then, provide no positive evidence for Lawlor's supposed Viking attack, still less any warrant for his conjectural period of subsequent Viking occupation.

As regards the postulated demise of Nendrum as a church settlement after AD 976, the silence of the annals must be treated with caution, as argued above. There is, nevertheless, possible circumstantial evidence that Nendrum was indeed no longer a going concern of any consequence in the middle of the 12th century. In 1149 *AFM* report an extensive raiding campaign in East Ulster by the Derry-based Muirchertach Mac Lochlainn (McLoughlin), by then the most powerful king in Ireland. The annals name several churches in the vicinity of Strangford Lough targeted by his forces, including Iniscourcey, Cell Áedáin (precise location unknown), Movilla, Bangor and 'all churches of the country besides'. It is added that Downpatrick and Saul were exempted from attack. The absence of Nendrum from this list may indicate that it was defunct, or of so little consequence as not to merit mention. On the other hand, one should not exclude the possibility that it escaped the raiders along with Downpatrick and Saul, both churches connected with the cult of Patrick. Nendrum too was associated with the Patrick cult, as we have seen, and such places may have been preserved from attack in AD 1149 in deference to the then archbishop of Armagh, Gilla Mac Líag, who hailed from Mac Lochlainn's backyard at Derry. Concerning this, like other aspects of the history of Nendrum, one cannot be quite sure.

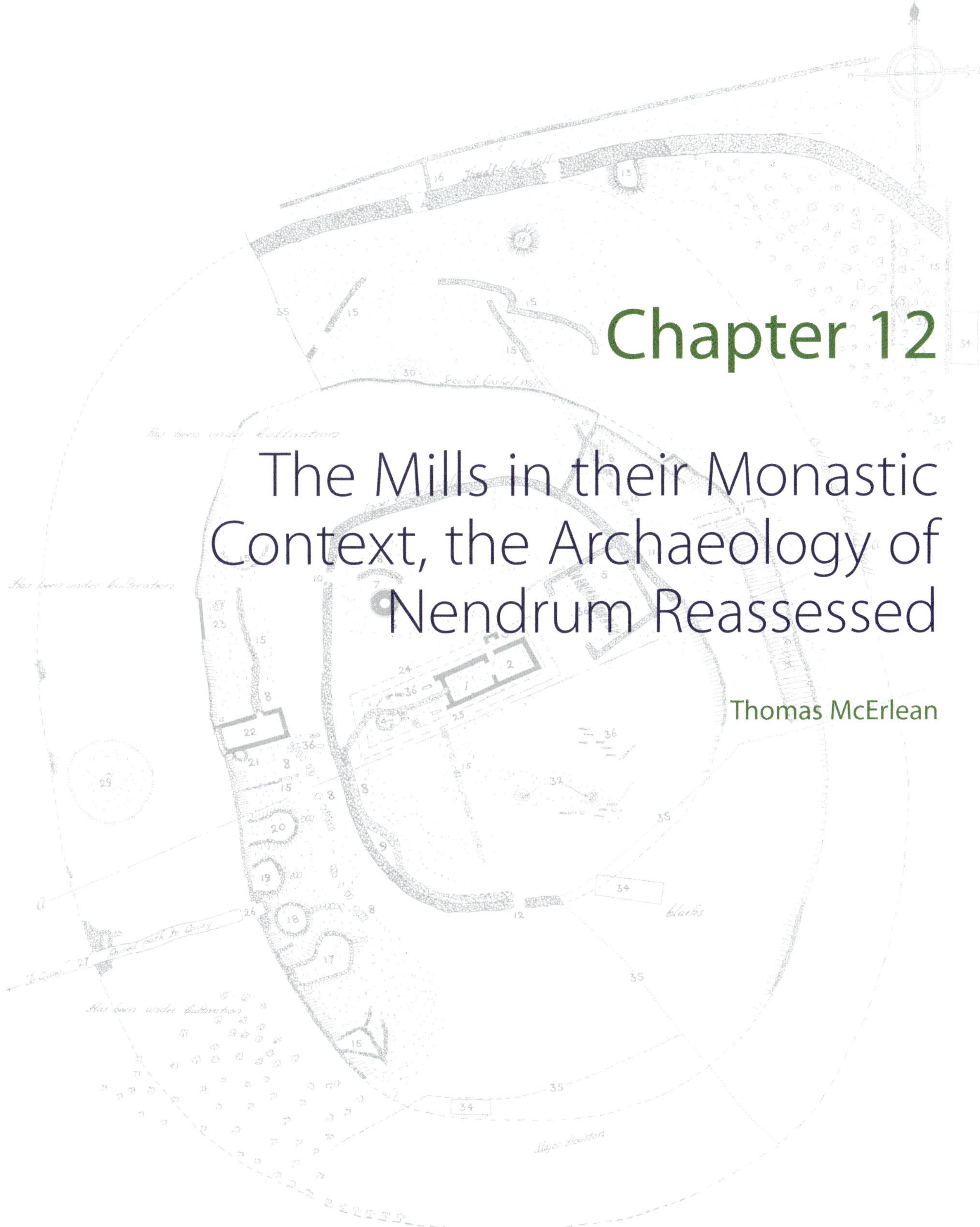

Chapter 12

The Mills in their Monastic Context, the Archaeology of Nendrum Reassessed

Thomas McErlean

Chapter 12
The Mills in their Monastic Context, the Archaeology of Nendrum Reassessed

Thomas McErlean

INTRODUCTION

The discovery and excavation of the tide mills have provided a major expansion of our knowledge of the archaeology of Nendrum. Not least among the new evidence are the dating horizons which they have provided, establishing that the monastery went through a strong building phase in AD 619–621, and another one towards the end of the 8th century. The new evidence demands integration with that from the excavated monastic site, of which the mills were an integral functional component.

This chapter aims to place the mills in their monastic context by providing a description of the existing ruins, and attempts a review of Lawlor's findings, incorporating subsequent research and reassessment of his interpretations. It incorporates important contributions in this direction made by ASCD, Phillips (1960), Hamlin (1976), and Matthews (1995). Lawlor's excavation produced a rich range of artefactual evidence and Bourke (Chapter 13) provides a re-evaluation of this in the light of subsequent research.

THE REDISCOVERY OF NENDRUM 1844

In 1843 William Reeves commenced work to edit the Papal Taxation Roll for the dioceses of Down and Connor of *c.* 1306. His efforts went far beyond documentary research and included an attempt to locate any physical remains of the churches and monastic houses mentioned in the taxation list, as well as any other known ecclesiastical sites in the united dioceses. One of the many problems of identification that he encountered was a parish church called 'Nedrum', valued at seven marks, and which occurred in the list between the churches of Kilwyinchi (Killinchy) and Kilmode (Kilmood), in the deanery of Blaethwyc in the diocese of Down (Reeves 1847, 10, 11). As the listing of churches in the document followed an approximately topographical order, his search was directed to the area between the latter two churches.

Following the suggestion that an old stone structure, possibly a ruined lime kiln, on Mahee Island might be of antiquarian interest, he visited the island and easily identified the ruin as the stump of a round tower. Further investigations located the church site near

Fig. 12.1A
The monastic ruins and the tide mills from the north (Gail Pollock, 1999)

Fig. 12.1B
A view of the millponds and dams from inside the monastic enclosure. The area occupied by the car has been largely reclaimed from the foreshore.

the round tower, and identified a surrounding triple-walled enclosure. From these ruins, and from name of the Island, 'Mahee', he quickly realised that he had rediscovered the lost monastic site mentioned in the annals and martyrologies, whose patron was named as Saint Mo-Choi, publishing his discovery in 1845 (re-published in Reeves 1902).

Fig. 12.2
Reeves' plan of his discoveries at Nendrum in 1844 (Reeves 1902)

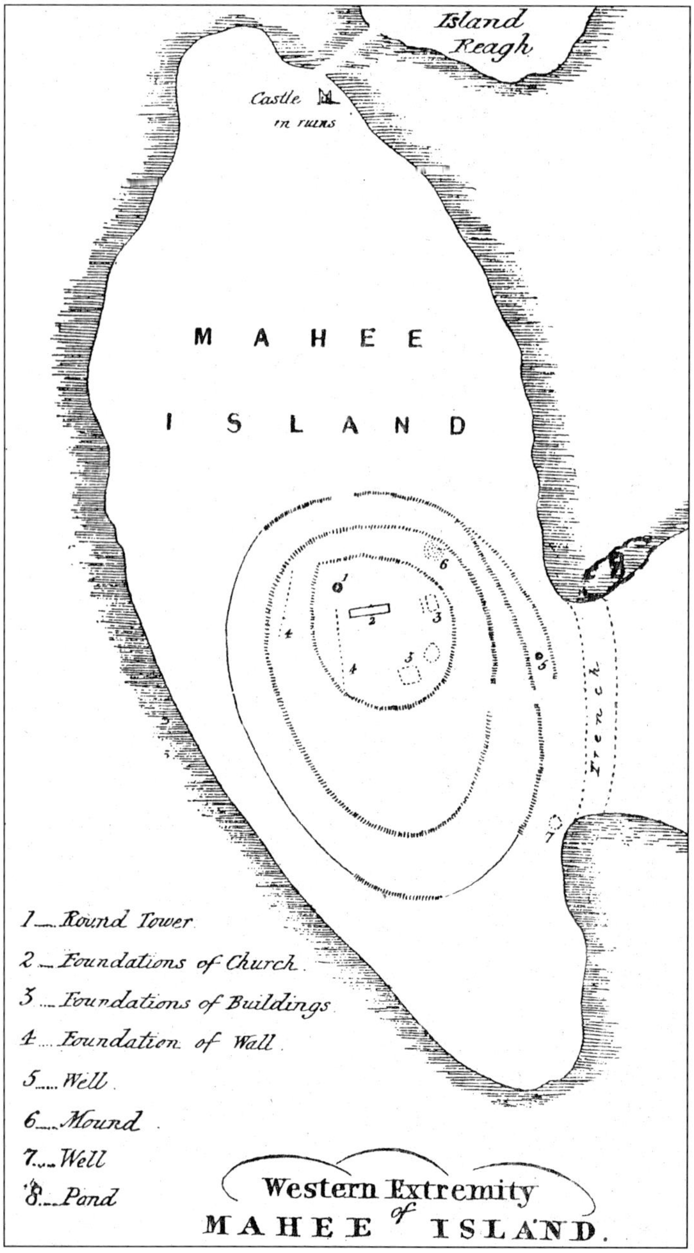

THE EXCAVATION OF NENDRUM, 1922–1924

In 1922, H.C. Lawlor, under the auspices of the Belfast Natural History and Philosophical Society, commenced excavation of the site on an ambitious scale, with a small workforce, which varied from four to 12 workmen. The work was carried out over 14 months during 1922, 1923 and 1924 and the results published promptly in interim reports in 1922 (Lawlor 1922) and 1923 (Lawlor 1923) and in final form in 1925 (Lawlor 1925a). As an excavation report, Lawlor's book is somewhat disturbing for the modern archaeologist. Its narrative style and the presence of many throwaway lines, which reveal glimpses of features of great interest, create frustration. A large part of the annoyance for the archaeologist is that, if the great richness of the material uncovered had been excavated using modern standards of recording and techniques not available then, the results would have been outstanding.

The recovery of artefacts appears to have been the priority of the excavation method. This is not to say structures were not respected, but Lawlor provided only one section drawing and left no clear record of what he reconstructed. The lack of reliable stratigraphic information for such a multi-period site is a severe handicap to sound interpretation. One great failing of his publication is that it does not seem to have been edited properly. Observations are spread all over the book, vital stratigraphic information is given in a haphazard manner and some figure numbers in the text do not correspond to those on the map.

In general, succeeding generations of archaeologists have been very unkind to Lawlor, one going as far (fortunately not in print) as describing his excavation

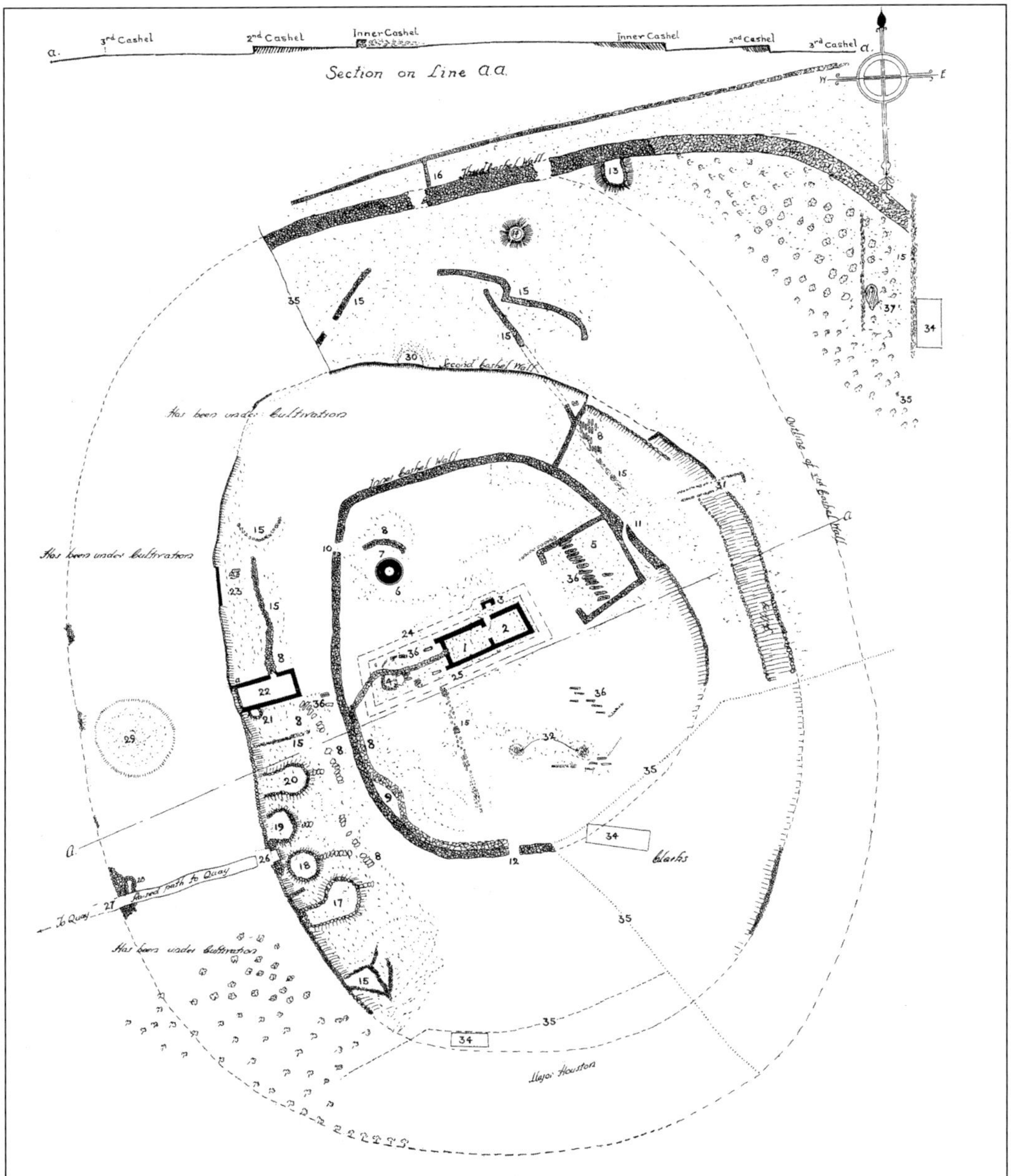

KEY TO PLAN.

1. Church Nave.
2. Church Chancel.
3. Exedra.
4. Site of Cell (?)
5. Foundation of Walled-in Square.
6. Round Tower Stump.
7. Site of very early Pottery.
8. Remains of Paved Paths (or floors).
9. Site of Monks' Seat (?)
10. }
11. } Gates of Inner Cashel.
12. }
13. Remains of Circular Building in Hollow.
14. Circular Cell (?)
15. Fragments of very Ancient Walls.
16. Angle of Walls where Bell was found.
17. }
18. } Sites of Circular or Oval Buildings.
20. }
19. The Brazier's Workshop.
21. Deep Oven or Sweathouse (?)
22. The School.
23. Remains of Square Building.
24. Protecting Dyke built round Church (Modern).
25. Sundial.
26. West Gate of 2nd Cashel.
27. West Gate of 3rd Cashel, Leading to Quay.
28. Foundations of Janitor's Cell.
29. Circular Hollow.
30. Large Midden.
31. Causeway.
32. Mounds of Bones.
33. Monks' Well.
34. Modern Bungalows.
35. Modern Fences.
36. Graves.
37. Large Stone.

The Monks' Well, in transcribing a somewhat indistinct figure 3, appears in the plan as 35. It should read 33.

For a further correction in the plan, see p. 95 note a.

Fig. 12.3
Lawlor's plan of his discoveries in 1922-1924 (Lawlor 1925a)

technique as similar to digging a field of potatoes. Sadly, his rightful position of one of the founding fathers of Northern Irish archaeology has been undermined by sometimes unnecessarily harsh judgement of his excavation at Nendrum. Stressing the positive side of his work, he should be congratulated for his swift publication of the results within a year of completion, and for presenting the site to the public in a way that excited interest, and stirred the imagination, two achievements that modern archaeologists and heritage mangers aspire to achieve but seldom do!

Admiration is also due for the scope of his vision. At an early stage of archaeology in Ireland, he attempted to place his findings within a wider context. It can be said that the platform he created, both for the study of the site and for an approach to the excavation of early monastic sites, has not been fully exploited. Many of Lawlor's ideas were seminal at the time, and he provided the first clear indications of the potential archaeological richness of Irish Early Medieval monastic sites and what excavation could achieve, and attempted to integrate this approach with historical research. If there had been a continuity of effort following on from his work, much could have been achieved. In the meanwhile, many other very important monastic sites have been destroyed by development. Nendrum's near neighbour, the great monastery of Movilla, across the lough to the north, illustrates this point well. During the second half of the 20th century most of the archaeology of the area within its probable large enclosure boundary has been destroyed by a combination of a heavily-landscaped housing estate, road improvement and extended municipal cemetery. Some very limited excavation, which took place after most of the damage was done, has demonstrated relatively intense occupation (Yates 1983; Ivens 1984). Writing in 1990 Edwards observed that in spite of the poor excavation techniques, the 1922–1924 excavations at Nendrum remain of crucial importance because they were the only large-scale Irish monastic excavations to have been published to date (Edwards 1990, 101) though adds that the results are now almost impossible to interpret (Edwards 1990, 107). To a certain extent this observation is true. However, it can be claimed that it is possible, from a re-examination of the findings, to gain much more information.

Condition of the site before excavation

The condition of the site before Lawlor's excavation is shown on the sequence of OS 6-inch maps of 1833, 1859 and 1920 (OS Six-inch survey, Co. Down, sheet 17: see Figs 12.4 ABC). The 1833 map shows that nearly all of the north-eastern half of the site was under relatively dense scrub vegetation. The remaining south-western half, including parts of the middle and outer enclosures, are shown as cleared and presumably under cultivation. The 1859 map shows a very similar picture and marks and designates the round tower and church for the first time. By the 1920 OS survey, completed some two years before the excavation commenced, the area covered by the inner enclosure and part of the middle enclosure on the north-east are shown as clear of vegetation. The map sequence also documents the progressive small-scale reclamation of shoreline below the monastery on the north-east in the area of the present car park and where the dam of

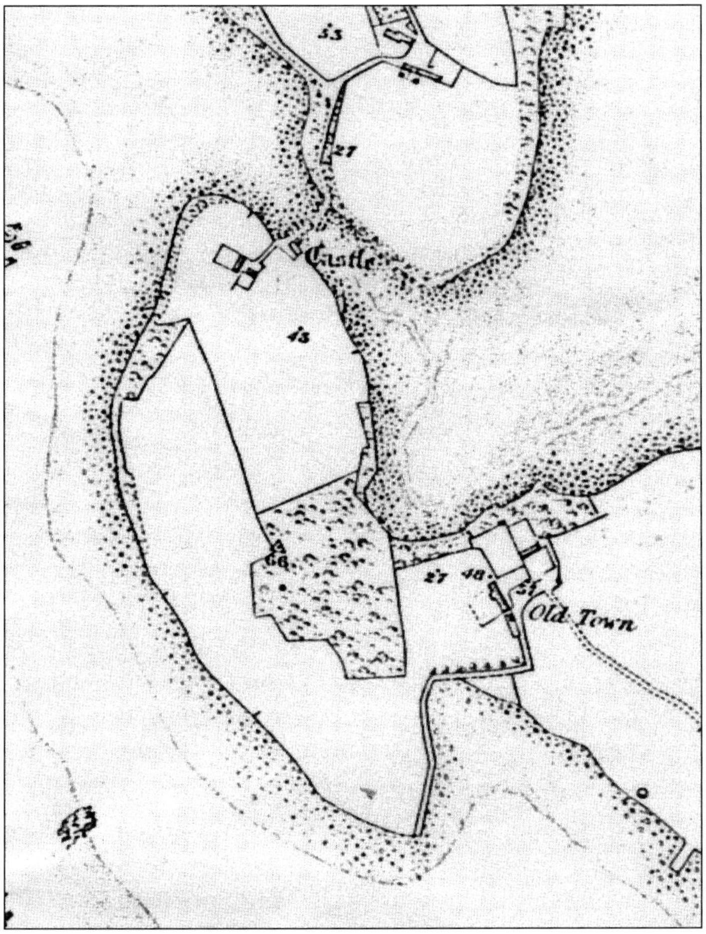

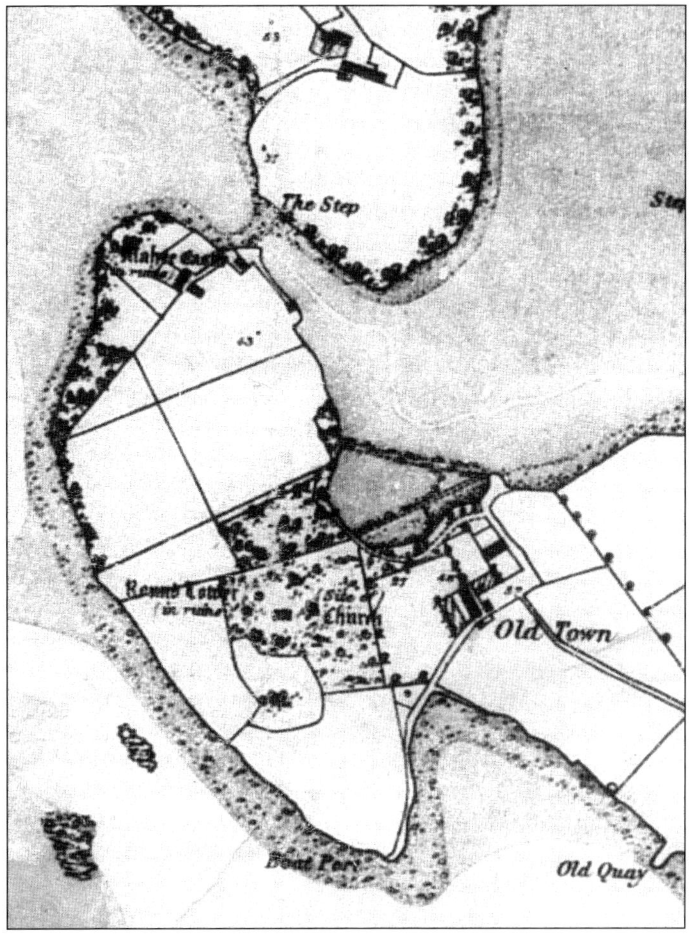

Fig. 12.4A
Nendrum as shown on the OS 6-inch surveys (County Down Sheet 17) of 1833 (Fig. 12.4A) 1859 (Fig. 12.4B) and 1920 (Fig. 12.4C)

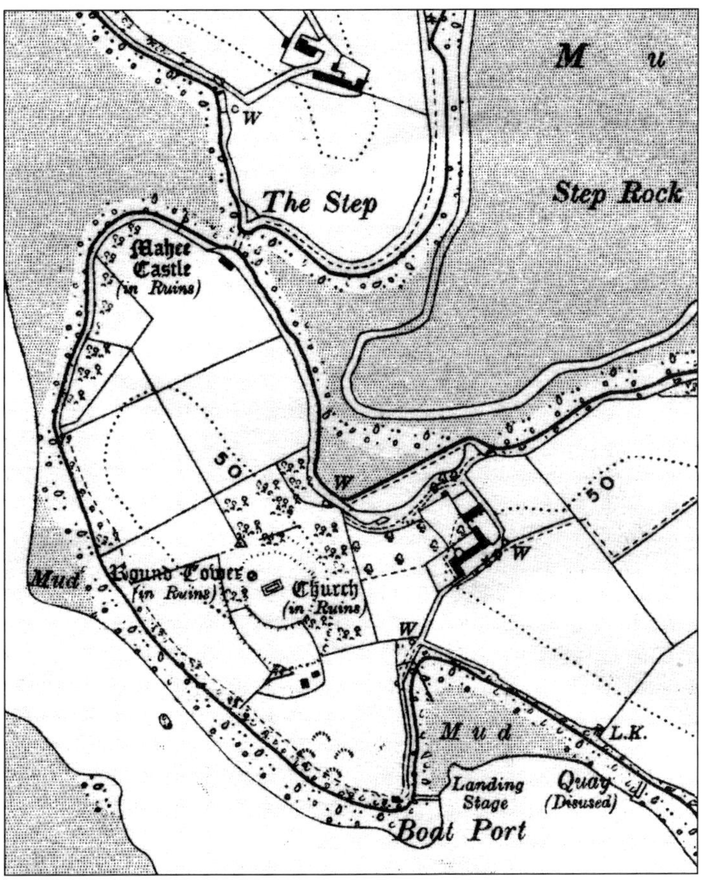

Fig. 12.4 B
1859

Fig. 12.4 C
1920

Mill 2 connects with the shore. The impression given by all three maps is that the north-eastern half of the site had been relatively free of cultivation, at least in recent centuries, while the other part had been subject to agricultural use. Cultivation in the north-east would have been inhibited by the relatively steep sloping nature of the terrain rather than any reverence to its archaeology or religious association.

Lawlor's plan and text gives further information on the extent of cultivation and confirms that almost all of the western half of the outer enclosure and much of the western half of the middle one had been under cultivation. As he made no specific reference to the presence of rigging or 'lazy beds', the inference is that the cultivated area had been under the plough rather than the spade. In reference to the part of the site under scrub vegetation, he described its clearance during June 1922 before excavation, as involving '... the removal of the clumps of briars and thorn which almost completely covered the site ...' which were '... torn out by means of chains drawn by horses ...' (Lawlor 1922, 94). The north-eastern part of the outer enclosure (not investigated until the 1923 season) was described as 'a wilderness' (Lawlor 1925a, 96).

Areas excavated 1922–1924

Unfortunately Lawlor has not left us with a clear plan of trenches outlining precisely where he excavated, and this is frustrating. However, he did indicate the areas he investigated on the published site plan by a somewhat vague dot stippling, and this does supply a good indication of where his main areas of activity were concentrated (see Fig. 12.5)

It can be seen that although the investigation was on a large scale, it was by no means exhaustive. The impression is sometimes given that his work rendered the site to some degree archaeologically sterile but, as Fig. 12.5 shows, large areas remain relatively untouched and much yet remains to be discovered.

Lawlor's restoration work

The appearance of Nendrum today owes much to Lawlor's presentation of the site after his excavation. He did not see his work as restoration but 'repair', and claimed that the only work of restoration carried out was the rebuilding of the western gable of the church. This is perhaps an understatement as he carried out extensive work in rebuilding the enclosure walls. Based on subsequent research, some criticism of his wall reconstruction can been made, most notably in the stretch around the middle of the western segment of the middle enclosure. Here the original line can be observed as a scarp some 4m to the west of that reinstated.

Further excavations

Since the completion of Lawlor's work in 1924, a number of small-scale excavations have taken place, none of which has been published. The purpose of these was largely to check on the accuracy of his reconstruction and to gain more knowledge of the stratigraphy. The sum total of the information gained was very small and, with one or two

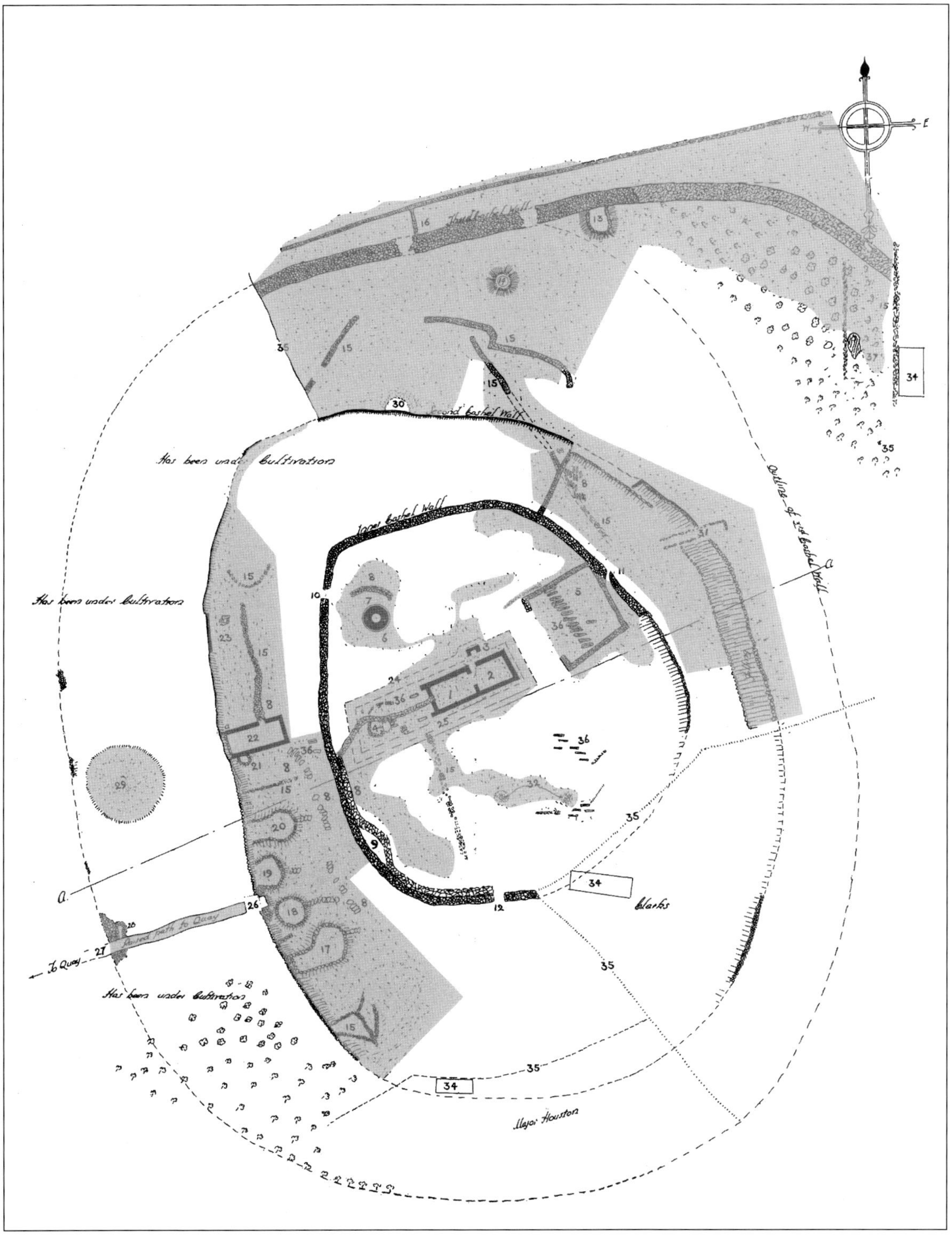

Fig. 12.5
Areas investigated by Lawlor 1922–1924. Areas originally stippled with dots have been shaded

exceptions, no new areas were investigated. A very significant limiting factor was the extremely small size of the trenches excavated. In contrast to Lawlor's large, open-area method, later work took a pixel-like approach, which greatly limits its contribution to our understanding of the site.

Between July 21st and August 13th, 1954, Charles Thomas excavated 14 very small trenches or cuttings, almost exclusively within areas previously investigated by Lawlor (Matthews 1995, 53–77; SMR Dow 17:8). Six of the cuttings were located around 'the graveyard' in the central enclosure, while others were positioned to check the accuracy of Lawlor's reconstruction of the middle enclosure wall in the area of the 'school'. A small cutting was made at the western end of the church and another on the possible line of the outer enclosure. The results were disappointing, something which is not totally surprising given the small scale of the work and the location of the trenches. The main finding was that Lawlor's reconstruction of parts of the middle enclosure wall might not be precisely on their original line.

Waterman excavated two small trenches on the south-western periphery of the middle enclosure at an unknown date, but probably after 1966, but again these were on such a small scale that little of significance was found (Matthews 1995, 55–56; SMR Dow 17:8). Brannon carried out very limited excavations on the site in 1979 and 1982 (Brannon 1979, 1982; Matthews 1995, 78–82; SMR Dow 17:8). Fifteen small trenches were excavated — again almost entirely within areas investigated by Lawlor. Matthews (1995) has carried out a very useful analysis of the later unpublished excavation work which has been incorporated into the discussion below.

Lawlor's interpretations

Later research has made many of Lawlor's interpretations redundant, although it seems a shame that some of the romance and drama has been taken out of the narrative he created from the excavated evidence. He proposed a pre-monastic, secular origin for the enclosure walls, but there is no evidence to support this. He believed he had discovered strong evidence to support the interpretation of a 'conflagration' and a 'Viking massacre' which he dated to AD 976, based on the reference in the annals *(AU)* for that year to the *airchinnech* being burned 'in his own house' (Lawlor 1925a, 73, 149–150, 155). There is no compelling reason to the blame the fire, which destroyed the abbot's house, on the Vikings. Indeed the excavated evidence of a fire seems isolated to the 'school' building and when it occurred is not known.

The two mounds of bones in the central enclosure, which he took as evidence of a Viking raid, are probably late in the history of the site and produced no firm dating evidence. In short, there is now little evidence to support the existence of a Viking destruction horizon. The 'massacre' was supposedly followed by a 'Danish Christian settlement' of unknown duration (Lawlor 1925a, 155). This was based on the identification of 'Viking skeletons' (Lawlor 1925a, 73) and a Christian grave slab with a 'runic' inscription. It was believed then that it was possible to identify a specific ethnic skeleton type from bone measurements, and he thought he had at least one clear example of a 'Viking' skeleton. We now know that this is not valid. His strongest piece of 'Viking' evidence was the fragment of grave slab with 'runic' writing. Further research considered it to be a very doubtful example and described it as '... a typical example of a common practice: identifying as runes any incised symbols made up of intersecting straight lines. ...' (Barnes *et al.* 1997, 2). More excitingly, it has recently been identified as a very rare Irish example of a Latin inscription using Insular display capitals and probably dates to the first half of the 8th century, well before the Viking incursions (see p. 396).

The precision of tree-ring and radiocarbon dating would have been beyond the imagination of Lawlor's generation of archaeologists and he was working under the severe limitations of the dating techniques available to archaeologists in the early 20th century. In the present excavation, dendrochronology has fixed the dating of the construction of the first tide mill as taking place between AD 619 and AD 621, and has provided Nendrum with its earliest securely dated horizon discovered so far. It has established that the monastery was undergoing a major development phase during these years. Indeed it is possible that the existing layout of the monastery may belong to this horizon. Somewhat ironically, Lawlor, though lacking scientific dating techniques, suggested that '... about the year AD 620 the monastery was reorganised and replanned ...' (Lawlor 1925a, 113). He based this interpretation and choice of date on the information of the annals where there is a gap of nearly century and a half between the death of Mo-Choí, in AD 497/499 *(AU)* and mention of the death of Bishop Cridán, in AD 639 (see p. 316). This was interpreted as possibly implying that the monastery had declined or ceased to exist, and was refounded with Cridán as its first bishop in the early 7th century. Lawlor arrived at the date of *c.* AD 620 for the start of the new phase. Excavation some 74 years later, aided by dendrochronology, supports the probable validity of part of this speculation.

The 'Benedictine phase'

De Courcy established a small Benedictine priory at Nendrum in the late 12th century (Lawlor 1925a, 75–88), but this appears to have been abandoned sometime in the 13th century. Lawlor and ASCD have interpreted evidence of late 12th- and 13th-century activity on the site as representing the 'Benedictine phase' at the site. However, very few structures, if any, can be dated with confidence to this horizon. The chancel addition to the church, the sundial and 'the fishpond' all have been cited as evidence of this phase. In fact, 'the fishpond' is the millpond of Mill 2, the chancel could be an addition to the small monastic church when it became a parish church before *c.* 1306, and the sundial could easily predate the late 12th century, so that evidence for the 'Benedictine phase' is getting slimmer. However, the discovery of a significant number of Late Medieval glazed wares of probable 13th-century date, as well as other wares (Waterman 1958; McCorry 2001), provides evidence of activity on or near the site at this period.

The question remains, however, why no built structures can be identified from this phase given the relatively good survival of those belonging to before this date. The monastic ruins are shown on Raven's map of Mahee Island and surrounding area, part of his survey of the Hamilton estate of *c*. 1625–1626 (Fig. 12.6). Of considerable interest is that two separate ruins are shown on the western end of the island, in addition to Browne's tower house of *c*. 1570 (ASCD 244, McErlean *et al*. 2002, 114). At the approximate location of the site of the monastery, a ruined building with two standing gables is shown. Presumably this represents the remains of the church, and the representation suggests that the gable ends were still substantial in the early 17th century. Towards the northern end of the drumlin ridge on which the monastery is situated, is depicted another substantial ruin of a building with two gables. Nothing is visible above ground today at this location, but O'Laverty (1878, 365) reported the finding of pottery in this area, and there is some geophysical survey information indicating below-ground structures.

The site of the portrayed ruin is located on the end of the ridge, commanding panoramic views northwards over Ardmillan Bay and eastwards over Strangford Lough. It is possible that this is the missing Benedictine Priory and if so, Raven's map indicates that it was not located on the site of the earlier monastery, but some 150m to the north. This would account for the lack of any definite structures found on the old site during excavation. The de Courcy charter and that of Malachy, bishop of Down, (Reeves 1847, 190—196, O'Laverty, 1878, 360–381, Lawlor 1925a, 76–88) stress the division of the Mahee island into three parts, two being granted to the Benedictines, with the bishop retaining the

Fig. 12.6
Detail from the map of the Reagh Island and Mahee Island portion of the Hamilton estates by Thomas Raven c.1625 showing two ruined buildings, one on the site of the monastery and another to the north of it (courtesy of the North Down Heritage Centre, Bangor)

third. In the implementation of these grants on the ground, the bishop may have retained the site of the monastic church to serve as a parochial church, while the Benedictines chose a new site nearby to the north.

THE LAYOUT OF THE MONASTERY, THE TRIPLE ENCLOSURE PLAN

The site occupies the southern end of the north-south drumlin ridge and has an overall diameter of about 190m north-south by 159m east-west and an enclosed area of approximately 2.46ha (6.08 acres). Three plans of the monastic ruins exist — Reeves' plan of 1844, Fig. 12.2 (Reeves 1902), Lawlor's plan, Fig. 12.3 (Lawlor 1925a) and that in ASCD (1966) Fig. 12.7. To these can be added a new survey carried out for the present work (Fig. 12.8). All four plans highlight what can be considered as the leading feature of the layout of the monastery, that it was enclosed by three roughly oval and concentric stonewalls. The walls define three zones consisting of a central enclosed area, surrounded by a middle area which was, in turn, enclosed by a large outer one. The central enclosure is 0.38ha (0.94 acres) in size, the middle 0.76ha (1.88 acres) and the outer one 1.32ha (3.26 acres). The archaeology of the central enclosure with its church and burial evidence, suggests it constituted a ritual zone; the middle enclosure with evidence of industrial and other activities suggests a living and working zone; the outer enclosure, the archaeology of which is largely to be established, was probably used for agricultural activities. The tide mills and their ponds can be regarded as an extension of the outer enclosure onto the foreshore. The significance of the use of a triple-enclosure plan at Nendrum, which can be taken as providing evidence of the organisation and division of space into three distinct activity zones, is discussed later (pps 390-396).

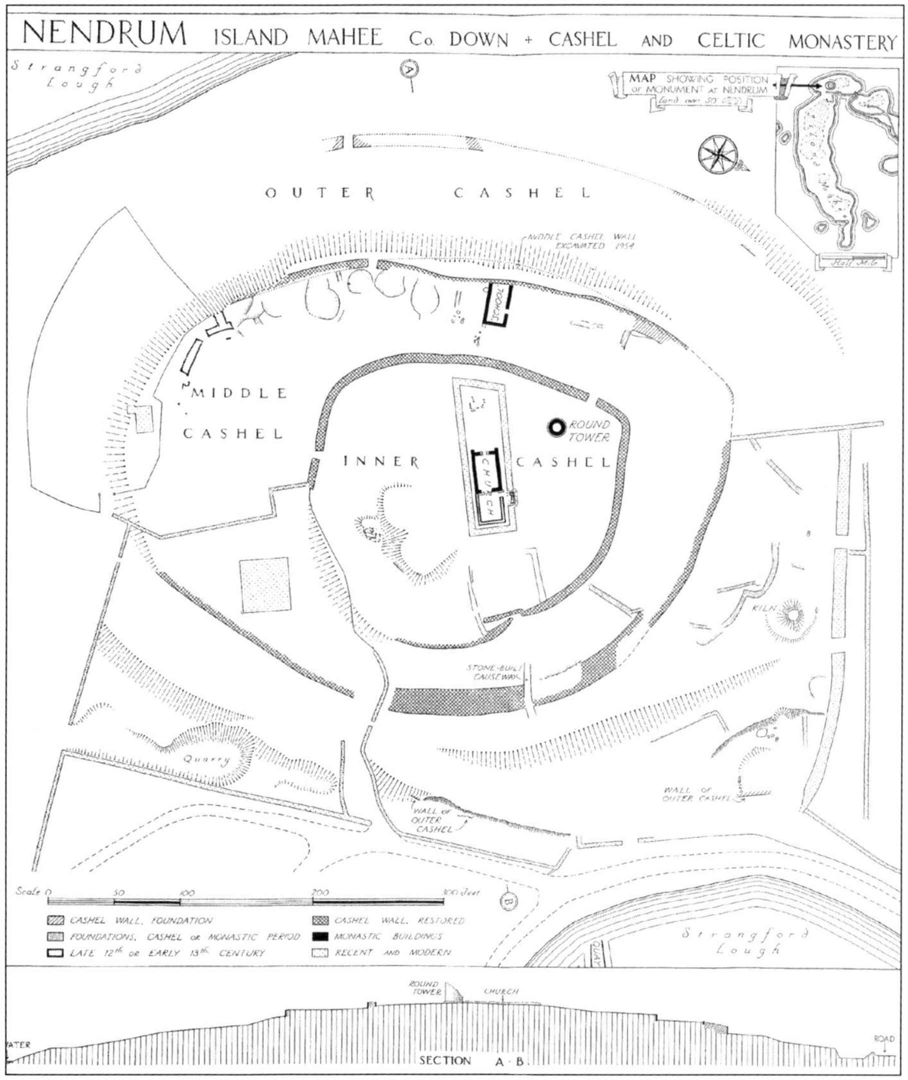

Fig. 12.7
ASCD's plan of 1966 (ASCD 1966)

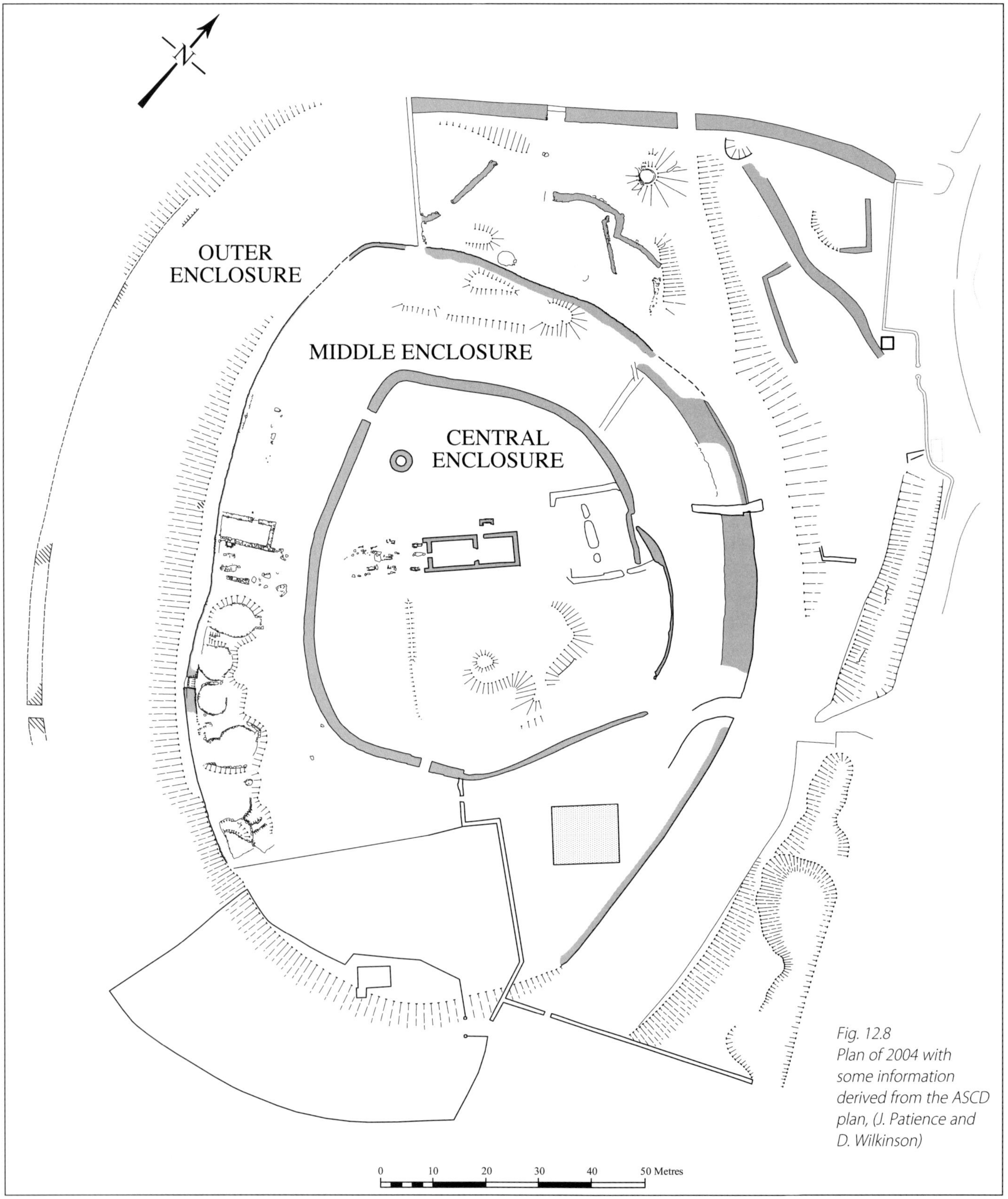

Fig. 12.8
Plan of 2004 with some information derived from the ASCD plan, (J. Patience and D. Wilkinson)

THE CENTRAL ENCLOSURE

The central enclosure is roughly circular, measuring approximately 78m north-south and 67m east-west and has an area of *c.* 0.38ha. The ground slopes down relatively gently from the north-west to the south-east. Lawlor considered that some artificial platforming had been carried out in the latter area (Lawlor 1925a, 26). Its present topography is the result of centuries of burial, occupation debris and may indeed have contained an element of ancient landscaping. As restored by Lawlor, the central enclosure is bounded by a free-standing, dry-stone wall on average *c.* 1.95m thick and 1.25m high, with entrances on the south, north-west and east. The east entrance may not have been original.

The main features of the central enclosure are the stone church, burials, the round tower, cross-slabs and other decorated stones, a 'graveyard' enclosure, two burial mounds, a sundial, paved pathways, a possible *leacht* or stone shrine, and trace of a rectangular mortared stone building (Figs 12.3, 12.7 and 12.8).

Lawlor's main areas of activity in the central enclosure were in the interior of the church and surrounding it to the west and north, the area of the round tower, and the parts of the north-eastern, southern and south-western portions of the central area. However, if the stippled areas representing where he excavated (Fig. 12.5) are taken at face value, a considerable part remains untouched and should have relatively undisturbed features and stratigraphy.

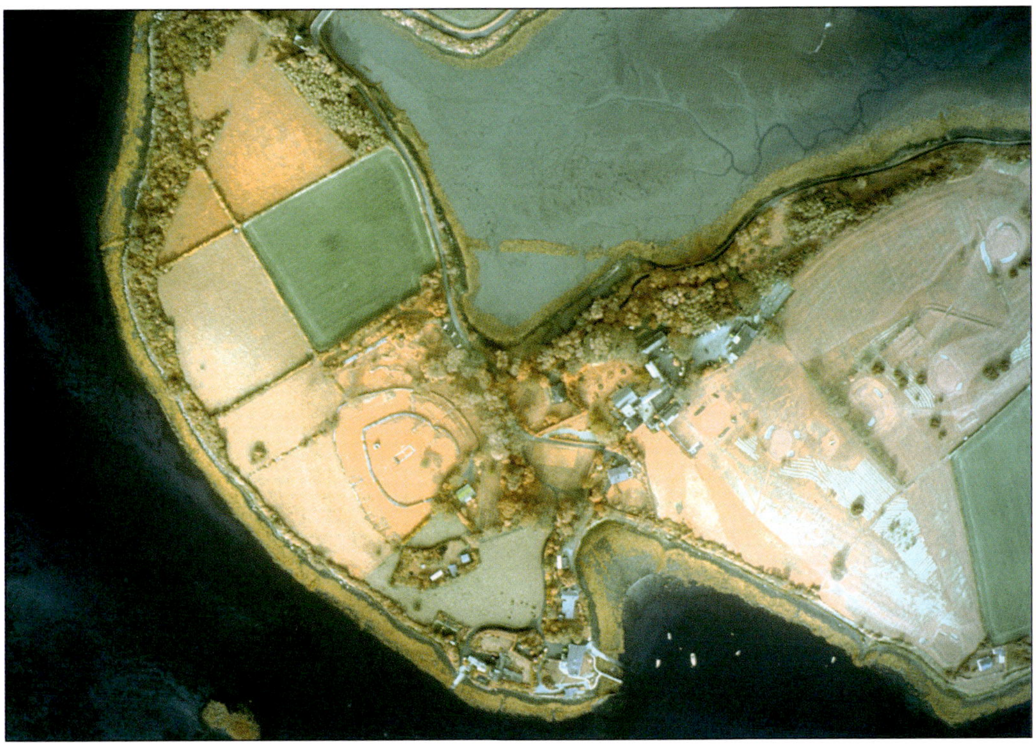

Fig. 12.9A
Vertical infra-red photograph of the monastic ruins and tide mills (1998 courtesy of the University of Ulster)

Fig. 12.9B
View from north of the central and middle enclosures and part of the outer enclosure (Gail Pollock, 1999)

Fig. 12.9C
View from south-east of the central and middle enclosures and part of the outer enclosure (Gail Pollock, 1999)

Fig. 12.9D
View from the west of the monastic enclosures and the dams of the tide mills (Gail Pollock, 1999)

Fig. 12.9E
View from the north-west of the monastic enclosures and the dams of the tide mills (Gail Pollock, 1999)

The church

The foundations of a mortared stone church of simple nave-and-chancel plan, first discovered by Reeves in 1844 under a bramble-covered mound, are located near the middle of the central enclosure, indeed of the whole monastic complex. On clearance, Reeves found the outline of a rectangular building, described as measuring 54 feet 4 inches (17.78m) by 22 feet 4 inches (6.81m), of which only the foundations survived (Reeves 1847, 196). Its orientation tends slightly to the north-east rather than east-west.

Lawlor commenced his excavations at the church in 1922, and revealed it to be a two-phase building consisting of a nave 7.98m by 4.88m (Lawlor 1925a, 116) giving it an internal area of 38.94m^2 onto which a chancel had been built. This extended the building by 6.78m to the east, adding a further approximately 33.09m^2 to it, almost doubling its size. The dividing wall was taken to be the eastern gable of the original church. On the northern side of the chancel was a small porch or sacristy, with entrances on the east and west. The western gable is approximately 84cm thick and has antae or extensions of the lateral walls, which are relatively deep, projecting *c.* 75cm beyond the gable. The position of the centrally-placed west door was identified from the presence of a large flag, on which lay a massive door lintel approximately 1.5m long by 37cm high and 47cm wide.

The long walls are approximately 74cm thick, and all of the walls rest on a plinth which projects externally round both parts of the building. Within the debris of the church were found three fragments of round-headed windows (Lawlor 1925a, 123). One of the window fragments, measuring approximately 18cm wide, has survived (ASCD 294) and has been cut from a single block of red sandstone. A few fragments of mullions, presumably of later Medieval date, were also found. Lawlor claimed that the state of the ruins indicated deliberate destruction at some period (Lawlor 1925a, 117). If this interpretation is correct, it must have taken place sometime after 1625/6, as the Raven map shows substantial standing remains (see Fig. 12.6).

Writing of the clearance of the mounded debris covering the church ruins, Lawlor mentioned the discovery of the bones of children (Lawlor 1925a, 129). This suggests that the site was being used after abandonment for the burial of unbaptised infants. On the floor of the church were a number of largely undisturbed burials, arranged in seven regular rows, with approximately eight skeletons in each row and one skeleton in each grave. Lawlor noted that the skeletons were well preserved (*ibid.* 132) and that all of the graves were of shallow depth (*ibid.* 133) being about '24 inches deep' [61cm]. One of the rows lay underneath the chancel wall, suggesting that at least some of the burials predated the extension and possibly the stone church. There were three burials at the eastern end, which Lawlor interpreted as being focused around the probable position of the altar. Two were orientated north-south on either side of the probable altar position, and one with a normal east-west orientation in front of it. The latter contained a skeleton of a large male identified as 'Nordic' (*op. cit.* 133). As the chancel is considered a later addition, of probable 12th-century date or later, these burials, if the interpretations concerning their focus on the probable site of the altar is correct, must date to this period or later. Lawlor estimated that there were around 60 burials inside the church (*ibid.* 134). Sometime in the past, a pony or foal had been buried in the doorway of the cross-wall between the chancel and nave, disturbing an earlier burial (*op. cit.* 133). A small portable slate sundial (identified by Lawlor as a clock face) was found in the debris of the interior (Lawlor 1925a, 152).

Fig. 12.10A
Plan of the church (J. Patience)

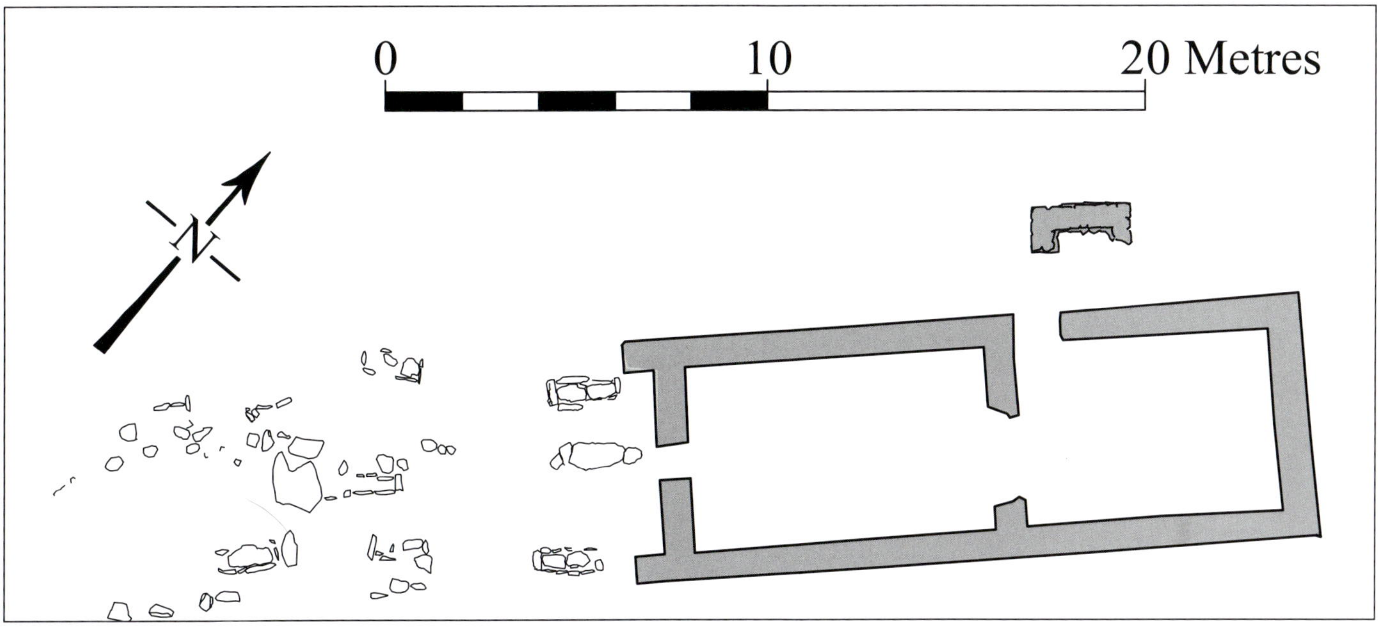

Fig. 12.10B
The restored west gable of the church showing antae

Fig. 12.10C
The nave and chancel of the church from south west

Fig. 12.10D
View of the east end of the church

Fig. 12.10E
The north wall of the church and anta

A straightforward interpretation of the church ruins is that they represent a simple one-cell, pre-12th-century stone church to which a chancel and small sacristy were added, perhaps in the 12th or 13th centuries. As previously mentioned these have been interpreted as features of the 'Benedictine phase' of the site (ASCD 264; Hamlin 1976, 1, 134) but this is by no means certain and the chancel and sacristy may have been added when the small monastic church became a parish church in the late 12th or 13th century. The nave, therefore, as constituting the stone church of the monastic period of the site, is of special interest. It has an internal length-to-breadth ratio of 1.62:1. Very similar length-to-breadth ratios can be found at the small number of other early churches in Co. Down suggesting that a conventional architectural ratio may have been in use. Raholp church is 1.65:1, St John's Point is 1.54:1 and Temple Cormac, at 1.62:1, is the same as Nendrum (Hamlin 1976, 1, 130).

The dating of the Nendrum church

The first recorded stone church (*daimliac*) in the annals is one at Armagh in AD 787 *(AU)*. Annalistic references suggest that the building of stone churches may have begun in the 9th century, have become more common in the 10th century and standard by the 11th century (Harbison 1970, 49), replacing the previous tradition of building churches in wood. The relatively small *corpus* of early Irish stone churches presents great difficulties of more precise dating other than from 9th to the 12th centuries, as most are of a simple, single-cell form and generally devoid of closely dateable features. The problem is compounded at Nendrum, as the ruin has survived to near ground level only.

The church at Nendrum is one of only seven in north-eastern Ireland which Hamlin considered as being probably pre-12th century, the others being the Derry North and

South churches, St John's Point, and Raholp, all in Co. Down, Killevy West Church, Co. Armagh, and Inismacsaint, Co. Fermanagh (Hamlin 1976, 1, 130). Manning (1998, 76) has summarised the relatively small number of features commonly found in Irish pre-Romanesque churches, and the Nendrum church possesses most of these. They include the antae (the projecting side walls), the massive lintel over the west door, externally-projecting plinth at ground level and possible small round-headed windows. It should, however, be pointed out that the plinth extends around the later chancel foundations as well as the nave, although it can be argued that the retention of this feature may have been influenced by its presence on the earlier part of the structure.

Most early churches have an internal length-to-breadth ratio of around 1.5:1 and Nendrum, at 1.62:1, comes close to this. Manning (*ibid.* 93) argues that deep antae may indicate an early date in the sequence of Irish stone churches and, in comparison to many others, the Nendrum antae, projecting *c.* 75cm, can be considered as deep. The length of their projection is almost the same as those of the cathedral at Clonmacnoise (Manning 2003, 63), which has been dated to the early 10th century (Manning 1998 71, 76), perhaps suggesting a similar date. The Nendrum church was built with lime mortar and, as mortared stone churches were probably rare before the 10th century, further suggests that it probably does not pre-date the 10th century. It is therefore possible to tentatively suggest that the church may belong to the early 10th century.

It can be assumed that the stone church succeeded at least one and probably a number of previous churches built in wood and dating to the 7th, 8th and 9th centuries, either on the site of the present church or somewhere within the inner enclosure. As no post-holes were observed anywhere during the 1922–24 excavations, it is extremely unlikely that the footprint of a wooden church would have been recognised. Post holes or beam slots of a substantial wooden building are likely to have penetrated into the subsoil and therefore below the probable depth of Lawlor's excavation and may await discovery by further excavation. The abundant oak used in the construction of the first mill dam demonstrates that suitable timber for building churches and other major buildings was easily available in the vicinity in the early 7th century.

Multi-church sites are a feature of Irish Early Medieval monasteries. Clonmacnoise and Glendalough are sites where these are still visible and documentary evidence shows that Armagh, Derry and Down, amongst others, each had a number of churches. An entry in the annals concerning the Viking raid at Nendrum's near neighbour Movilla in AD 825 *(AU)* mentions the destruction of its *dertech* (literally oak houses and normally translated as 'wooden oratories'). Given the scale and status of Nendrum, it is probable that it had more than one church. If any existed, it is highly probable that they would have been situated in the inner core and may yet be found by excavation. It is possible that the traces of a mortared stone building found under one of the mounds of bones towards the south of the enclosure (Lawlor 1925a, 73), may have been the remains of a small church or oratory.

The enlarged church, taken to represent the post-12th-century parish church, is approximately 62.03m^2. This may seem small but Ó Carragáin has pointed out than many early churches which later achieve parochial status have a typical average of 59m^2 (Ó Carragáin 2006, 108) and Nendrum is very close to this figure. In estimating the number of people a church could accommodate a formula of three people per square metre has been suggested (Ó Carragáin 2006, 114–115). Using this would suggest that the nave alone at Nendrum could hold a packed parochial congregation of about a hundred people. Similarly, taking the nave as representing the latest monastic church on the site it would have been capable of accommodating a sizable community of monks.

Burials

The 1922–1924 excavations uncovered a large number of graves, most of probable early date, but unfortunately they were very poorly recorded. Indeed in his otherwise laudatory introduction to the 1925 publication, R.A.S. Macalister (Lawlor, 1925a, viii) singled out the lack of recording of skeletal material for criticism. This comment can also be extended to the lack of description of the form of burial. As regards the distribution of the burials, Lawlor's plan (Fig. 12.3) shows graves located to the west of the church, within the square enclosure to the east of the church and two groups in the south-eastern sector of the central enclosure. However, in addition to those shown on the plan, his text makes clear that the areas to the north and south of church had many burials (*ibid.* 135). Burial on the site as whole appears largely confined to the central enclosure, however, three were found in the middle enclosure, and outside the site on the south-east, to the south of the Johnson farmhouse, human bones had been found, perhaps indicating a small cemetery (*ibid.* 81).

Nendrum may have been used as a burial ground from the early 7th to 16th centuries, a period of nearly 1000 years, and therefore it is to be expected that differing grave forms should be present. Three appear to have been encountered — stone-lined graves, unlined graves and burial mounds. Lawlor did not specifically mention the presence of simple dug graves, but their existence may be inferred by his singling out of the stone-lined graves for comment. He mentioned a number of 'stone topped graves' in reference to those to the west of the church (Lawlor 1922, 99). The present appearance of these shows them to belong to the long cists with lintels type of grave. The stone-lined graves to the west of the church contained multiple burials, while those within the church held single ones. The latter were regularly spaced and tightly packed, '... the feet of one row touching the skulls of the next ...' (Lawlor 1925a, 132).

Given that it is highly probable that burial continued on the site in the Late Medieval period some of the graves which he encountered must have belonged to this later period, but it has not been possible from Lawlor's descriptions to differentiate a Late Medieval burial form. Later burials may include the three in the church, which Lawlor interpreted as being arranged around the altar of the added chancel that must date to the 12th century or later. Another late grave may have been one on the southern side of the church, which contained three French monastic tokens of 16th-century date (*ibid.* 152). The last burials on the site would appear to be those of young children, probably unbaptised, found in the mounded ruins of the church (Lawlor 1922, 94–95).

The lintel-cist graves.

The lintel-cist graves (Lawlor's 'stone-topped graves') appear concentrated in the area to the west of the church where some are still visible on the surface today (Fig. 12.10A). Lawlor noted that much of the fallen debris or stone from the church was concentrated in this area (Lawlor 1925a, 120). This material, probably derived from the collapse or destruction of the western gable of the church, shown as intact on the 1625 Raven map (Fig. 12.6), may have contributed to their well-preserved state. Frustratingly, Lawlor did not provide any clear description of these, apart from referring to them as 'stone covered graves' or 'stone-topped graves' and mentioned that after they were examined '... everything was put back as found ...' (*ibid.*120). It is not clear if this statement refers only to the bone material, or if includes the repositioning of the stone surrounds.

Brannon re-excavated this area (SMR Dow 17:8) and produced a plan which shows six well-preserved, stone-lined graves — two to the north of the path and four to the south (see Fig. 12.11A) — as well as a number of less well-defined ones. A number of the graves still contained bones. The two best-preserved graves, visible on the surface at present (Fig. 12.11A, nos 1 and 2), lie about 1m out from the western gable of the church and on either side of the entrance path. Grave 1, situated to the north of the entrance path to the church, measures externally 1.83m long by 89cm wide. Its long sides and eastern end are formed by thin slabs of local shale set on their edges. At the western end, a larger sub-rectangular stone with an inward sloping face forms 'a pillow stone' type feature. There are two large slabs which seem to form a base to the grave, but these are not bottom stones and are considered to be collapsed lintels (Brannon *pers. comm.* Oct 2004). Grave 2, to the south of the entrance path, is practically identical in form but slightly different in size. It measures 1.8m long and 62cm wide. It has a similar 'pillow stone' and two collapsed lintels. Both graves share a common, slightly south-west/north-east orientation in line with that of the church. In contrast, grave 3 (see Fig. 12.11A) has a different orientation, somewhat more to east-west. It is 1.62m long by 68cm wide. In general, the character of the graves to the west of the church can be described as short, narrow and shallow. Lawlor noted that each grave in this area contained several skeletons, the lower ones being found about 3 ft down and the upper ones just below the surface covering (Lawlor 1925a, 135). Two graves had their covering of cross-inscribed slabs *in situ* (*ibid.* 128–9).

In reference to the stone-topped graves to the west of the church, Lawlor (1922, 100) stated that

> ... these are all much shorter than human adults and investigation showed that the stone tops were only surface markings of full length graves, not stone lined, some 18 to 24 inches deep. Most of the graves appear to have been disturbed at some time, as bones in many case were in confusion, In every case care was taken to leave the grave exactly as exposed.

Lawlor provided no information regarding the form of the graves situated to the north and south of the church and as no mention is made of a stone component and none had been retained on the surface in his presentation of the ruins, it may be tentatively concluded that they were simple dug graves.

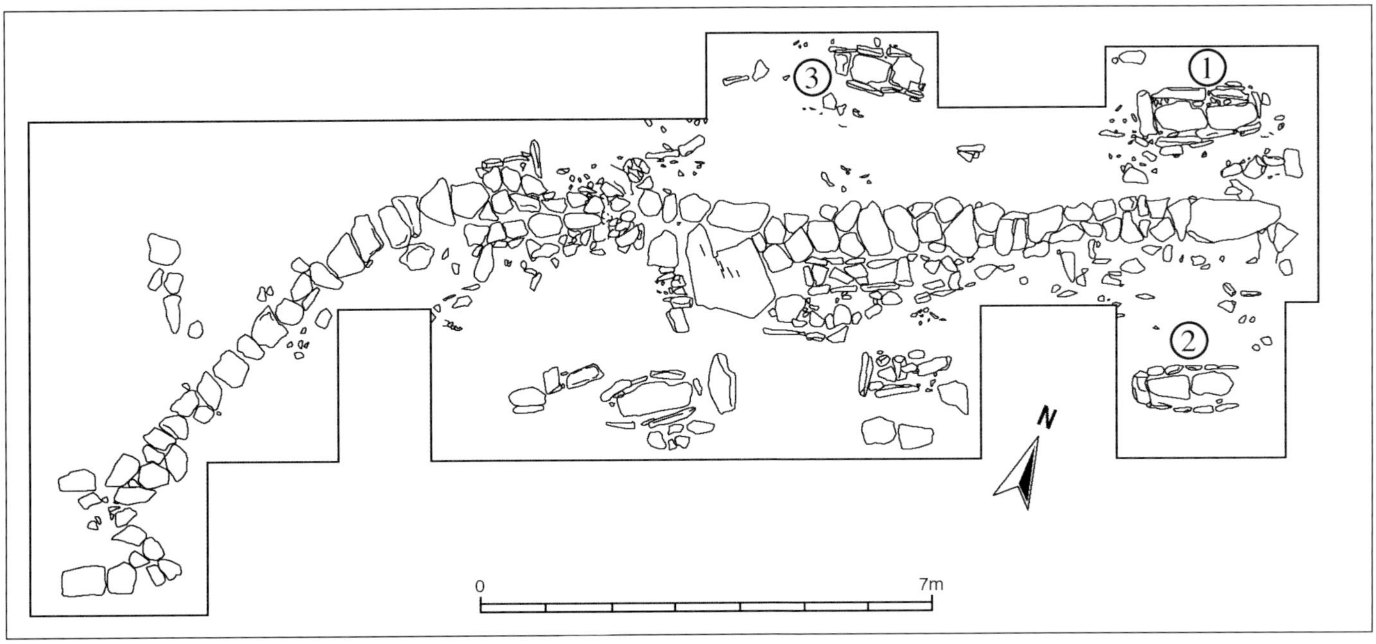

Fig. 12.11A
Plan of the stone pathway and burials to the west of the church re-exposed during N. Brannon's excavations in spring 1982 (SMR DOW 17:5)

Fig. 12.11B
The stone pathway to the church and adjacent graves (looking west) re-exposed during Brannon's excavation in spring 1982 (SMR DOW 17:5/39). Grave no 1 in foreground

Fig. 12.11C
Grave 1 as re-exposed during Brannon's excavation in spring 1982 (SMR DOW 17:5/57)

Fig. 12.11D
View (from the north-west) of the continuation of the stone pathway to the church as it turns to the south west re-exposed during Brannon's excavation in spring 1982 (SMR DOW 17:5/52)

The stone-lined graves to the south-east

Another group of stone-lined graves was discovered beneath the two mounds on the south, and extended '... a considerable distance to the south and east. ... ' (Lawlor 1922, 98–99). These are described as closely-packed and '... regular graves lined with rough stones ...' and orientated '... with their feet to the south east ...'. Presumably this description includes reference to the two clusters of graves in the south-east shown at this location on his plan. The slight north-west/south-east orientation of this group of graves differs from the slight south-west/north-east orientation of the church and of the other graves in the central enclosure.

The 'graveyard' enclosure

Prominently shown on Lawlor's plan (Fig. 12.3) to the east of the church and abutting the enclosure wall is a square enclosure designated as 'foundation of a Walled-in Square'. Most of the western side is shown as open or missing. Within the enclosure is shown one row of burials composed of 13 or possibly 14 graves along with a single burial adjacent on the east. The burials share the same orientation as the church and are described by Lawlor as being '... covered with rough stones ...' (Lawlor, 1922, 97–98). The stones are still visible on the surface today (see Fig. 12.8). Lawlor expressed difficulties in differentiating between the stone rows which mark graves and those which may be the remains of walls, suggesting that he did not excavate to any great degree in this area,

Fig. 12.11E
The scarp in the south-east sector of the central enclosure with the remains of a stone revetment (from south). The area above the scarp is the approximate site of the burial mounds recorded by Lawlor (1925a 73-74)

and it is not clear if more than one row was found. Charles Thomas re-excavated parts of this area in 1954 but the results were difficult to interpret but would seem to suggest that the square enclosure does not have any clear relationship to the burials and that it cannot be regarded as a graveyard enclosure.

The two burial mounds

Some 19m to the south of the church, Lawlor excavated two circular 'mounds of bones' (Lawlor 1925a, 73, 74), on which, largely, he based his interpretation of a Viking massacre in AD 976. These were about 9m apart and were around 2.3m in diameter. Their height is not recorded. Although not mentioned by Lawlor, the mounds were apparently situated on two small knolls of natural rock outcrops or boulder concentrations from 1–1.5m above the ground level on the south. A short length of wall revetting the scarp on this side is visible (Fig. 12.11E).

As described by Lawlor, the mounds had central depressions on their tops, which he interpreted as the result of body decay. Both contained the heaped skeletons of men, women and children without any order or uniform orientation to their deposition. One female skull showed evidence of trepanning (*ibid.* 73). Another female skull was associated with an amber bead (see p. 406), which seemed to have been worn around the neck (*ibid.* 73, 152–153). The mounds overlay stone-lined burials and below, among the graves, was found '... a fragment of the foundations of a building of stone and lime mortar ...' (*ibid.* 74).

The lack of dating evidence and Lawlor's somewhat vague description renders interpretation of the significance of the mounds very difficult. The form of collective burial devoid of conventional Christian treatment is in stark contrast to the rest of the burial evidence on the site. They could conceivably be a very late feature of the site and date to long after the decline of the monastery, an interpretation receiving some support from the underlying stratified burials and possible lime-mortared building. A possible interpretation is that they may be a feature of the clearance of the old abandoned graveyard prior to a possible phase of cultivation at some time in the past. However, as Lawlor gives the impression that some of the skeletons were articulated, this renders this interpretation less plausible.

The form of deposition does seem to indicate haste, perhaps after a violent episode or during a period of plague. The presence of a male skeleton with evidence of a sword cut may be seen as further proof of a possible massacre. The general description of the two concentrations of bodies does indeed stimulate the interpretation of a bloody event of wholesale slaughter of a community and adds drama to the reconstruction of the narrative of Nendrum.

The cross-carved grave slabs

Nendrum has produced 16 examples of cross-carved stones constituting the largest collection found so far from any northern Irish ecclesiastical site. Nearly all were found during the 1922–1924 excavations. They were subsequently displayed for many years on the walls of the church but are now in the visitors centre. Nine were illustrated by Lawlor (1925a, plate V111) and some more by ASCD and have been discussed by Lionard (1961, 114–117, 150–151), and in more detail by Hamlin (1976, 665–668) but have not been fully published before. Only two were found remaining *in situ* and were located over graves to the west of the church (cross numbers 2 and 3). In addition to this area they were found in various parts of the central enclosure, including among the debris of the church and the enclosure wall (Lawlor, 1921–1922, 100, 130–131). One was found in the late 19th century in a field boundary outside the site to the south-east (cross no. 1). Only four of the slabs are in a complete or nearly complete condition (nos. 1–4). Lawlor considered that the remaining had been deliberately smashed (Lawlor 1925a, 117). Most (if not all) can be regarded as recumbent slabs placed on the surface of graves. Four cross forms are present in the *corpus*. The first form and constituting the most common cross type is a ringless Latin outline cross, with hollows at the intersections of the arms and shaft. Eight examples of these were found (crosses 1–8), leading Hamlin (1976, 1, 243) to name it 'the Nendrum type' and suggest that the monastery may have been a production centre for them (Hamlin, 1976, 2, 279). The second type represented by one damaged example (no. 9) is a plain Latin outline cross without the hollows at the intersections. The third type also represented by one example is a simple linear cross with bifurcated (forked) terminals (no 10) and the forth, represented by three examples is a simple incised linear cross (nos 11-13). In addition there are two other examples of possible linear crosses of uncertain form (nos 12 and 13). The site has produced two other carved stones, 'the marigold stone' and the so-called 'runic stone' and it is possible to place these from the form of decoration on them into the class of arciform crosses, thus adding a fifth form represented at Nendrum. However, it is not entirely clear whether the symbolism behind the decoration is intended to represent a cross. These stones are discussed separately.

'The Nendrum type' outline Latin cross with hollows at the intersections

Cross no. 1 (Fig. 12.12A) Outline Latin cross with hollows at the intersections and edge-border
This is the largest cross-carved stone in the collection and the most finely executed. The slab (shale/greywacke) measures 83cm long and tapers in width from 38cm at the top to 10cm at the base and is 15cm in maximum thickness. Except for some damage at the top of the shaft the slab is complete. The cross has a long shaft and short arms and is outlined in low relief by a pecked-backed background. The surface of the cross is smooth and forms a pleasing contrast to the rough surface of the background. The smooth surface on the cross would seem to reflect the original surface of the shale/greywacke stone rather than a finishing technique. A border formed by a thin incised or finely pecked line highlights the edges of the cross. The tapering base may suggest that it was originally placed upright, but this is by no means sure. It was found in the late 19th century outside the site to the south-east in a field fence near Mr Johnson's house and published by Patterson (1870–74, plate X1, Fig. 8). It was missing in Lawlor's day but subsequently found and placed in the visitors centre (Lawlor 1925a, 130, Plate V111, no. 9, Hamlin (1976, 665, no. 1, Fig. 60 no. 1).

Cross no. 2 (Fig. 12.12B) Outline Latin cross with hollows at the intersections and edge-border
Cross no. 2 is a roughly sub-rectangular to long-oval-shaped slab (shale/greywacke) measuring 49cm by 25cm by 6cm thick. The stone is complete but the surface at the top of the shaft of the cross is slightly damaged. The cross is in low relief formed by pecking back the background and has an edge border (as cross no. 1). It was found *in situ* over one of the graves to the west of the church; which one is not specified by Lawlor.
(Lawlor 1925a, 130, Plate V111, no. 1, (Hamlin 1976, 667 no. 10)

Cross no. 3 (Fig. 12.12C) Outline Latin cross with hollows at the intersections
This is a roughly sub-square slab (shale/greywacke) measuring 45cm by 39cm by 7cm thick. It is complete and undamaged. The cross is in low relief and has no edge border.

Fig. 12.12A
Cross no. 1 (Tony Corey)

Fig. 12.12B
Cross no. 2 (Tony Corey)

Fig. 12.12C
Cross no. 3 (Tony Corey)

Fig. 12.12D
Cross no. 4 (Tony Corey)

It was found *in situ* over one of the graves to the west of the church; which one is not specified by Lawlor.
(Lawlor 1925a, 130, Plate V111, no. 4, Hamlin 1976, 667, no. 9)

Cross no. 4 (Fig. 12.12D) Outline Latin cross with hollows at the intersections and edge-border
Cross no. 4 is a sub-square slab (shale/greywacke) surviving in two pieces. It measures, when rejoined, 31cm by 29cm and varies in thickness from 5cm to 10cm and is almost complete. The cross is in low relief created by a pronouncedly pecked background and has an edge-border. There is a roundel in false relief in the middle of the crossing formed by a pecked circle. The lower part of the slab was found in the debris inside the church while the upper part was found in the debris of the central enclosure wall on the north-east.
(Lawlor 1925a, 130, Plate V111, no. 8, Hamlin 1976, 667, no. 11)

Cross no. 5 (Fig. 12.12E) Outline Latin cross with hollows at the intersections with edge-border (fragment)
This is a small broken slab (shale/greywacke) measuring 19.5cm by 13cm and 3cm in thickness, containing the carving of one arm of outline Latin cross with hollows at the intersections and with an edge-border. It was found in the rubble of the central enclosure wall.
(Lawlor 1925a, pl. V111, 7 and 131, Hamlin 1976, 666, no. 8))

Cross no. 6 (Fig. 12.12F) Outline Latin cross with hollows at the intersections
Cross no. 6 is a fragment of a broken sub-rectangular slab (shale/greywacke) measuring 28.5cm by 23cm by 8cm thick. The cross is in false relief created by a wide pecked

Fig. 12.12E
Cross no 5. (Tony Corey)

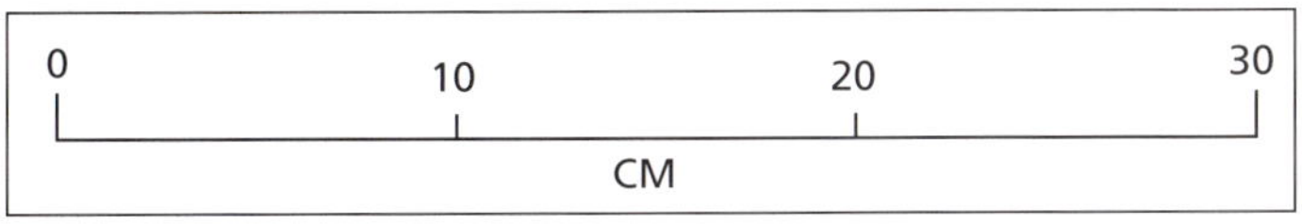

Fig. 12.12F
Cross no. 6 (Tony Corey)

groove and has no edge-border. The work seems somewhat cruder than the others. It was found in debris inside the church.
(Lawlor 1925a, 130, pl. V111, no. 2, Hamlin 1976, 667, no. 12)

Cross no. 7 (Not illustrated) Outline Latin cross with hollows at the intersections with edge-border (fragment)
This is a fragment of slab measuring 16.5cm by 15cm (thickness not known) with part of the central area of a cross surviving, carved in relatively high relief. There is a triangular interlace knot at the centre of the crossing. It was found near the platform to the west of the church and recorded by Lawlor and Hamlin, but its present location is not known and was not inspected.
(Lawlor 1925a, 131, pl. V111, no. 5, Hamlin 1976, 667–668, no. 14)

Cross no. 8 (Not illustrated) Outline Latin cross with hollows at the intersections
Although not listed by Lawlor and not located during the present survey, cross no. 8 was described and drawn by Hamlin as a 'rather battered' rectangular slab with part of the shaft and arm of 'the Nendrum type' of cross in false relief.
(ASCD plate 77, top left and to left of no. 8, Hamlin 1976, 666, no. 6 and fig. 60, no. 6)

Most, if not all, of the slabs are of the local shale or greywacke and a ready source is to be found on the foreshore below the monastery which abounds with naturally formed slab-like stones, which would require little secondary working to achieve the desired shape. Where it can be ascertained, it seems that the edges of the natural slab were left unworked and irregular. Carving is confined to one side of the slab. The main technique used in making the 'Nendrum type' was to dress one side of the naturally flat surface of the stone by pecking back a background to produce a cross standing out in low relief. In general the crosses further stand out by virtue of a contrast between the rough pecked background and the smooth surface of the cross. It is unlikely that the smooth surface of the cross was the result of polishing, and more likely that it reflects the original smooth surface of the stone left untouched. The main variation in treatment of the cross is an additional definition by an edge-border created by a shallow pecked or incised line around its outline and present in five crosses (nos 1, 2, 4, 5, 7) or its absence on three crosses (nos 3, 6, 8).

Another example of variation on the standard design is found on two slabs: cross no. 4 has a circle or roundel at the crossing (Fig. 12.12D) and cross 7 has a small triangular interlaced knot. Apart from these a defining feature of these crosses is their lack of elaboration. None of the crosses is placed in a frame and none has an inscription. Only four of the eight appear to be relatively complete, allowing the probable original dimensions to be ascertained. Cross no. 1 (Fig. 12.12A) is the largest measuring 81cm by 38cm in maximum width and 15cm thick. The others are considerably smaller. Cross no. 2 (Fig. 12.12B) is approximately 49cm long by 25cm wide and 6cm thick, no. 3 (Fig. 12.12C) is 45cm long by 39cm wide and 7cm thick, and no. 4 (Fig. 12.12D) is 31cm by 29cm and

5–10cm thick. The relatively small size of the slabs would imply that they would have covered only part of the surface of the grave. The small size of the Nendrum slabs can be contrasted with the relatively large size of many of the Clonmacnoise recumbent slabs with average dimensions of 50cm to 1m in length and 75cm in width (Ó Floinn 1998, 89, 92).

Examples of ringless crosses with hollowed angles and unenclosed in frames on slabs like the Nendrum type are not common in Ireland (Lionard 1961, 115–117). Only two other examples have been found in the north-east, both in relative proximity to Nendrum — one at Saul and one at Derry South church, both in the Strangford Lough region (Hamlin 1976, 1, 259). Further afield, there is a strong concentration at Inishcealtra, Co. Clare where over half of the 67 slabs are of this form (Lionard, 1961 148). Eighteen of these, like the Nendrum examples, occur without surrounding frames. At St Berrihert's Kyle (Kilberrihert) Co. Tipperary, there are 18 examples mostly on erect slabs (Ó nÉailidhe 1967, 125), and at Gallen Co. Offaly there are 16 in circular frames (Lionard 1961, 116, 147). Three examples have been found at High Island, Co. Galway (Marshall and Rourke 2000, 146, 150–151, 156, 163–164). Apart from these, a few single examples occur at Clonmacnoise Co. Offaly, Glendalough, Co. Wicklow, Ahenny, Co. Tipperary and St Patrick's Dublin (Hamlin 1976, 1, 259). At present, therefore, Nendrum and Inishcealtra have the main concentrations of the form in the country. However, the cross form is very common in Northumbria, with 23 examples being found at Whitby and sizeable numbers occur also in Scotland (Lionard, 1961, 116–117) including a few examples at Iona (RCAHMS 1982, 184). Three examples on cross-slabs have been found during excavations at Dull, Perthshire (Will *et al* 2003), one of which had an inscription, most probably of a personal name. Examination of the palaeography of inscription by Gifford Charles-Edwards (Will *et al.* 2003, 69), suggests a date in the first quarter of the 8th century.

Fig. 12.12G
Cross no. 9 (Tony Corey)

A Northumbrian origin has been proposed for the Irish examples, and the form may have appeared in Ireland at least as early as the 8th century (Marshall and Rourke 2000, 163). From comparison with the Northumbrian examples, some of which can be dated to the late-7th or the first half of the 8th century AD, Hamlin (1985, 294) suggested a possible dating of 8th or 9th centuries for the Nendrum examples, but a date of late 7th or early 8th seems quite acceptable. As both of the only two cross-inscribed slabs found *in situ* over graves, found to the west of the stone church, were of the Nendrum type, it may be possible very tentatively to date the graves at this location to the same date range.

Simple outline Latin cross

Cross no. 9 (Fig. 12.12G) Simple outline Latin cross

Cross no. 9 is a broken slab of probable original rectangular form (colour light brown but probably shale/greywacke). The maximum surviving length is 31cm and maximum breadth (at base) 13.5cm and thickness 7.5cm. This damaged slab retains the carving of part of the lower shaft and one arm of a plain outline Latin cross, without hollows at the intersections and without an edge-border. The surviving arm of the cross splays out slightly from the crossing point. At the latter it is 5cm wide expanding to 5.5cm at its termination. The drawing in Lawlor (1925a, 131, pl. V111, no. 3) showing a much more pronounced splay is misleading. The carving is in relatively higher relief than the other examples and made by the same techniques used in the manufacture of 'the Nendrum type' by pecking back a background. It was found in the rubble of the central enclosure wall. (Lawlor 1925a, 131, pl. V111, no. 3, Hamlin 1976, 666, no. 5, Fig. 60, no. 5)

Plain outline Latin crosses have a wide distribution in Ireland. Nearby an example occurs at Saul (Hamlin 1976, Fig. 61 no. 2). Thirteen examples of the type occur at Inishcealtra (Lionard, 1961, 105). One at Clonmacnoise has been dated by inscription to AD 709 (Lionard, 1961, 109). Lionard suggests a possible inspiration for some are wooden crosses and that they were used from the early 8th century onwards.

Simple linear cross with bifurcated terminals

Cross no. 10 (Fig. 12.12H) Simple linear cross with bifurcated terminals with triangular hollows

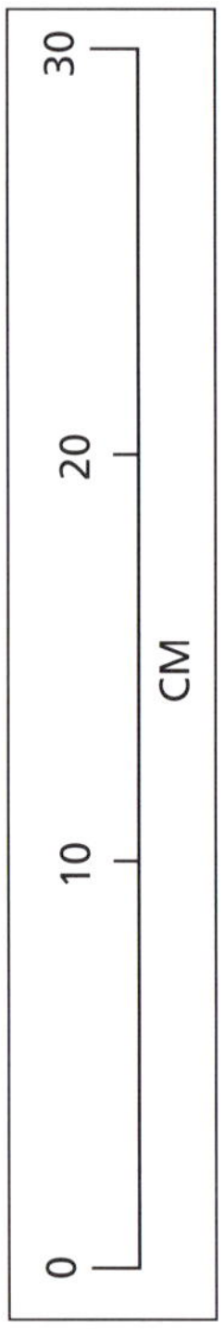

Fig. 12.12H
Cross no. 10
(Tony Corey)

This is a broken angular slab fragment (shale/greywacke) measuring approximately 30cm by 21.5cm in maximum width, and 6cm thick. The arms of the cross end with bifurcating terminals formed by triangular-shaped hollows carved out relatively deep (about 2mm) extended with shallow incised lines. The surviving end of the shaft (the other end is missing) is similar but is surmounted with an incised triangle. On both sides of this is a shallow hole. This appears to be the stone referred to in ASCD (295 no. 3) as a 'fragment of foliated head probably of Medieval coffin-lid' but clearly now identifiable as a fragment of an Early Medieval cross slab, (not illustrated by Lawlor, Hamlin 1976, 665, no. 2, Fig. 60, no. 2)

This cross would appear to belong to the class generally described as a cross with bifurcating terminals. Crosses with bifurcating terminals were the single most common cross form at High Island Co. Galway and are generally thought to be early, with a dating to the 7th to 9th centuries being suggested (Marshall and Rourke, 2000, 163). One of very similar form to the Nendrum example was found there (Marshall and Rourke, 2000, 155, 163 and Fig. 112) on a slab, which had been turned on its side and reused as a side stone for a later burial. This cross is ringed but the treatment of the terminal top end of the shaft, which has an additional bifurcation, closely resembles no. 10 above.

This type of cross has a wide distribution in Ireland but few have been found in the north-east part of the country. There is an example at Iona for which a 9th-century date has been suggested by an inscription (RCAHMS 1982, 181), but see p. 414.

Simple incised linear crosses

Fig. 12.12I
Cross no. 11 (Tony Corey)

Cross no. 11 (Fig. 12.12I) Simple incised linear cross
Cross no. 11 is a small irregular-shaped slab, roughly sub-rectangular, measuring approximately 27cm by 14cm and which is 4cm thick. The stone is light brown in colour but is probably shale/greywacke. The right side is missing. It has a shallow incised simple Latin linear cross and was found near the platform to the west of the church.
(Lawlor 1925a, 131, pl. V111, no. 6, Hamlin 1976, 667, no. 13)

Fig. 12.12J
Cross no. 12 (Tony Corey)

Cross no. 12 (Fig. 12 12J) Simple incised linear cross
This is a slab (shale/greywacke) measuring 29cm by 18cm by 7.5cm thick. (Not illustrated by Lawlor, Hamlin 1976, 666, no. 4, Fig. 60, no. 4)

Cross no. 13 (Not illustrated) Simple incised linear cross
Cross no. 13 is an irregular-shaped, thin, broken slab (shale/greywacke) measuring 24cm by 15cm by 2.5cm thick with a lightly scratched linear cross. (Hamlin 1976, 668, no. 16)

The extreme simplicity of these linear crosses renders them almost impossible to date and they were probably in use over a long time period.

Possible crosses of uncertain form

Possible linear cross no. 14 (Fig. 12.12K)
This is a fragment of angular broken slab (shale/greywacke) approximately 20cm by 11.5cm by 3.5cm thick containing an L-shape carving with a cross-bar, made by pecked lines. It is a possible cross of uncertain form, perhaps part of a swastika-shaped cross. (Not illustrated by Lawlor. Hamlin 1976, 665–666, no. 3, Fig. 60, no. 3)

Fig. 12.12K
Cross no. 14 (Tony Corey)

Possible linear cross no. 15 (Not illustrated)
Cross no. 15 is listed by Hamlin (668, no. 15) as a slab fragment measuring 4cm by 12.5cm, which may be part of the arm of a cross of uncertain form. It has not been possible to trace this stone (Hamlin 1976, 668 no. 15).

Possible linear cross no. 16 (Not illustrated)
This is an irregular-shaped, thin, broken slab (shale/greywacke) measuring 9.5cm by 7.5cm by 2cm thick. It contains lightly scratched lines, two of which appear to form a linear cross, but also has additional lines that blur definite interpretation as such. The slab has relatively recent incised graffiti consisting of the letter H and the date '5 April'.

Discussion
Presumably the collection of 16 crosses represents the random survival of the range of cross types used on burial markers over graves in the central enclosure. The absence of certain cross types commonly found on other monastic sites of the period is to be noted. There are no ringed crosses of any type, and no highly decorated forms or free-standing crosses or high crosses. There are no clear examples of vertical grave slabs. There is only one stone with an inscription (discussed below). This limited range of cross types and their relative simplicity may have dating implications. It may imply that most of the graves on which they were placed belong to 8th and 9th centuries and possibly the 7th if an early date for some of the cross types is accepted. It seems probable, however, that the use of the site for burial continued during the later part of the Early Medieval period, but no example of definitely later cross types has been found. This apparent fact and the lack of dedications may suggest that the later users of the cemetery were of low status and did not commission carved grave slabs.

On present evidence, it seems clear that the main form of grave marker at Nendrum was the recumbent slab. The origin and duration of use of the recumbent slab in Ireland is under researched but Lionard (1961, 156) has tentatively suggested that it was introduced into Ireland in the 7th century, and was the predominant type of grave marker through to the 12th century.

Pillar stone with multiple marigold design

This stone (Fig. 12.13A), (Lawlor 1925a, 130, Fig. 4; ASCD 295, plate 78) was found in a secondary context in a modern field fence near Clarke's bungalow (the present visitors centre) within the middle enclosure (see Lawlor's plan, Fig. 12.3). The stone (shale/greywacke) is sub-rectangular to wedge shape in section with its thickness varying from 33cm on the left side to 23cm on the right side. Its width at the base is 29cm which expands to 32cm at the top. Both the top and bottom sections of the stone have been broken off so it is impossible to estimate its original height. The surviving piece is 29cm high. It seems acceptable, because of its shape, to interpret it as a fragment of a pillar stone. On one face is an accomplished carving based on compass-work that has been termed the 'multiple marigold design' (Lionard, 1961, 110–112). Above this, along the

Fig. 12.13A
The marigold stone (Tony Corey)

Fig. 12.13B
Broken top face of the marigold stone, (decorated face on top side) (Tony Corey)

Fig. 12.13C
Broken bottom face of the marigold stone, (decorated face on top side) (Tony Corey)

damaged top part of the stone, is a small surviving part of an interlace design. Lawlor's published drawing of it (Lawlor 1925a, 130, Fig. 4), is a mirror image and not accurate.

At some period a small hole has been drilled into the stone at the top. This is approximately 3.8cm wide and 2.6cm deep. There is a lower section of a similar hole at the opposing point at the back of the stone (Fig. 12.13B), the upper section of this having been removed when the stone was broken. The presence of the remains of the hole at the back suggests that an attempt was made at some time to bore a hole right through the stone. The purpose of the hole is not clear but it is possible to speculate that perhaps at some time the pillar was used as a gatepost and the hole was made to receive the drawbar of a gate.

The carving consists of a finely-executed complex design of seven compass-drawn intersecting circles and additional arcs forming interconnected 'six-leaf (hexafoil) marigold' motifs contained within a framing larger circle (diameter 28cm). The circles are arranged in an upper row of two, a middle row of three, and a bottom row of two and have diameters of 13cm. The centre points of the six peripheral circles in the group are all equidistant of one radius (3.5cm) from the centre of the central circle in the composition and therefore are all on its circumference. The arcs forming 'petals' or 'leaves' around the periphery of the circles were drawn from points outside the main composition. Presumably the compass work design was marked out on the stone and the lines carefully pecked out. About 6cm of the design has been lost to damage at the bottom.

There are two examples of the single (as opposed to multiple) six-leaf marigold design among the *corpus* of the stone motif pieces from Nendrum (O' Meadhra, 1979, 102: 144A2 and 144 A11. ASCD plate 81). Motif piece 144A2 preserves the compass dot corresponding to the arc centres lying outside the motif field. The existence of the six-leaf marigold design on these two motif pieces and also on the marigold stone is of interest as it provides one example at the monastery of a trial design being worked out on motif pieces being used on a stone carving. Of considerable interest is the presence of the much rarer multiple marigold composition among the possibly early 9th-century motif pieces found during the excavation of Gransha Mound (Lynn 1985, O' Meadhra, 1979, 72 and 75 : 76 A1) a few miles north of Nendrum and on lands associated with Bangor abbey (McErlean *et al.* 2002, 77–78). This is a miniature version of the design on the Nendrum stone with an outer circle of 6cm diameter and the seven smaller circles having diameters of 3cm. It was obviously laid out using a very small compass capable of drawing circles of 1.5cm. A possible compass arm was found at Gransha (Lynn 1985, 88) and Lawlor believed an iron object found in the 'school' was one arm of a compass (Lawlor 1925a, 146) but Phillips (1960, 6–7) cast doubt on this identification.

Crawford (1926, 20–24) places the marigold motif as a part of his 'star patterns' classification and designates the six-leaf form as 'the six-ray pattern', while Lionard in his classification scheme places the motif as belonging to his 'crosses of arcs' group (Lionard

1961, 110) and suggests four-leaf form can be viewed as a Maltese cross. That said, it is clear that examples of the motif with six or eight leaves are less recognisable as cross forms, but they may have had a similar religious symbolism. It has been suggested that the six-leaf form may have its origin in the Chi Rho symbol embodying the Greek initials I and X placed in a circle. It is possible that the fragment of the design of arcs on the 'runic stone' discussed below may be another example of the motif at Nendrum. There is little precise dating evidence in general for the 'crosses of arcs' group but Lionard very tentatively suggests that most of the Irish examples may date to the 8th century (Lionard 1961, 112).

Multiple marigold designs are very rare. One has been found on a broken grave slab at Clonmacnoise (Macalister 1909, 16, no. 82, plate X1, Crawford 1926, 21 no. 22, see Fig. 12.33) which Lionard regarded as 'identical even to the irregularities' to the Nendrum example (Lionard 1961, 110). The Clonmacnoise slab fragment measures approximately 44.5cm by 35.5cm and is 4.5cm thick. The enclosing circle framing the design has a diameter of 35.5cm. So the design is similar in scale to the Nendrum example. A very similar one is present on a slab at Maughold, Isle of Man (Lionard 1961, 110). At Whitorn, Galloway a very similar design of seven interlocking circles occurs on a slab but only the central circle has the six-leaf marigold, the other circles being left blank (Hill 1997, 438 Fig. 10.108: no. 17, 439). The diameter of the circles is 15.2cm and is therefore similar in size to those on the Nendrum stone. A very similar compass-work design lies behind the layout of the decoration on the Donore disc 1 (Ryan 1995, 27, 30 Fig. 3) and no doubt lies behind many of the other complex designs seen on both the metalwork and manuscript illumination of the period. The function of the pillar is not clear, it may have been a burial marker or alternatively a free-standing pillar serving some other function.

Slab with inscription in Insular display capitals (formerly the 'runic stone')

The most interesting carved stone discovered at Nendrum to date is that previously referred to as the 'runic stone', which was found immediately to the north of the sacristy or porch (Lawlor 1925a, 70 and plate 11) of the church and is now in Down County Museum (Fig. 12.25). Macalister, who interpreted the inscription as runic, hailed its discovery as opening 'a new door in North European epigraphy' (*ibid,* vii) and made a tentative translation of the nine incised symbols of the top line as meaning 'Brimabota' or 'Brimobata', a word he took as Old Norse for 'of the chief abbot' (Lawlor 1925a 70–71). The bottom line was impossible to decipher. Barnes *et al.* (1997, 2) state that only one of the symbols coincides with a runic graph, with the slight possibility of one other, while the rest are 'pretty clearly not runic' and in addition, the word 'primábóta' is not found in any of the dictionaries of Old Norse. They regard it as a typical example of misidentifying as runes 'any incised symbol of intersecting straight lines'. Very recently this long-neglected and potentially very important stone has been reassessed by Gifford Charles-Edwards (discussed at p. 396) who has identified it as a Latin inscription in Insular display capitals. The stone is of special significance as the only slab found at Nendrum with an inscription and a very rare example of the use of Insular display capitals on stone in Ireland. Early Medieval grave slabs with inscribed names are relatively common at a small number of monastic sites, but are absent or have not survived at the great majority.

The round tower

The Nendrum round tower is one of four known from ecclesiastical sites in Co. Down, the others being at Downpatrick, Drumbo and Maghera. No towers have yet come to light at Nendrum's great monastic neighbours of Bangor and Movilla. The extensively-restored stump of the tower is located approximately 15m to the north-west of the church and on the highest part of the enclosure. It is rubble-built using the local shale/greywacke stone. When discovered by Reeves in 1844, the external face had eroded away leaving the mortared wall core and internal face intact. Fortunately, two stones remained to indicate the original thickness of the outer face. These provided Lawlor with the necessary information on which to base his restoration of the external face with the tumbled stone which had accumulated around the base (Lawlor 1925a, 114). The stump stands to a maximum height on the north-west of *c.* 4.27m, sloping to 1.22m on the south-east. It has an external offset projecting 23cm out from the base and 62cm high above present ground level. The external diameter above the offset is 4.33m, the internal diameter 2.06m, and the external circumference is 13.32m.

Fig. 12.14A
The round tower (from the west)

Fig. 12.14B
The round tower and the north-west entrance into the central enclosure from the middle enclosure

Among the approximately 65 remaining examples of Irish round towers (Barrow 1979; Lalor 1999) the Nendrum example stands out by virtue of the small size of its base dimensions. Only two towers, Rams Island in Lough Neagh (external diameter 4.16m) and Clondalkin, Co. Dublin (external diameter 4.04m) have smaller (Barrow 1979; Lalor 1999, 105, 135). This suggests that the Nendrum tower was a shorter and slimmer tower than most of the extant examples (Barrow 1979). Lawlor conjectured that its original height may have been 15–18m (Lawlor 1925a, 113, 114). The height of surviving complete towers ranges from 25–35m (Barrow 1979, 13) which, according to Lawlor's conjecture, would leave the Nendrum tower considerably lower. The suggestion by Stalley (2000, 39) that the ratio between the basal circumference and height used by the builders of round towers may have been 1:2, would give a possible estimated height (the circumference is 13.32m) of *c.* 26.64m. It is instructive to consider the very well-preserved Clondalkin tower, which stands some 27.5m high but whose external diameter is smaller than Nendrum's. It is possible (if not probable) therefore, that the Nendrum tower was much higher than envisaged by Lawlor and others. Whatever the case, the siting of the tower on the top of a drumlin ridge whose sides drop to surrounding sea level would have made it a prominent feature of the local landscape and visible from a considerable distance.

The excavational history of the round tower is extremely unsatisfactory. Prior to its discovery by Reeves in 1844, someone digging for treasure found a large human skeleton near to its north-western base, which may indicate burials below it. Reeves carried out some excavation and ascertained that the floor was at the same level as the present ground surface outside, and dug deep into the internal foundations, finding some animal bones (Reeves 1902, 19).

The dating of round towers is still largely dependant on the evidence of the annals, which contain some 25 references (O'Keeffe 2004, 18, Barrow 1979, 15; Lalor 1999, 91–93) to a *cloicteach* (belfry or 'bell house'). The earliest entry records the burning of the tower at Slane, Co. Meath, in AD 950 *(AU)* by the Vikings of Dublin, and the last is of the destruction of the tower at Rosscarbery, Co. Cork by a strong wind in AD 1285 *(AI)*. The latest recorded entry of the construction of a round tower occurs for Annaghdown, Co. Galway in AD 1238 *(AFM)*. This suggests that their construction started in the first half of the 10th century and that they survived as an architectural form into the 13th century. Lawlor proposed that the round tower was destroyed at the same time as the 'school' and huts and suggested construction in AD 850 and destruction in AD 974, based on annalistic evidence (Lawlor 1925a, 113). In the absence of any independent dating evidence for the Nendrum example, a 10th century or later date seems probable on current information. Though imprecise, this wide dating bracket is of value as it suggests that the monastery was still functioning and sufficiently affluent in the 10th century or later to build one, and goes a certain distance to counter the silence of the annals.

Where it can be ascertained, the great majority of round towers are located to the west, and in many cases a short distance to the north-west, of the principal church. This location pattern can be observed at Armagh, Clonmacnoise, Glendalough, Kildare and Monasterboice (Lalor 1999, 33), and it is interesting to observe that Nendrum conforms to this. At Downpatrick and other sites, where the tower is situated to the south-west of the present church site, it may well indicate the latter was not the original church. The reasons behind the placing of towers to the north-west of churches are unclear and may be liturgical. Stokes (1875) suggested that this area may have been relatively free of burials. Barrow (1979) has suggested that the towers were built by specialist builders who moved around the country and used variations on a standard design. Round towers, especially during the winter months, would have cast long shadows and acted as a type of giant sundial.

The primary function of Irish round towers — apart from making a monumental architectural statement — was to act as bell towers but it is clear that they also acted as treasuries for valuables and for keeping relics. A link to the round tower may be provided by the discovery of an iron hand bell in the wall of the outer enclosure at Nendrum, (see p. 412). It has been assumed that hand bells were used in round towers as many examples have survived from the period, but it has been speculated that hung bells may also have been employed but as yet the evidence is lacking (Stalley 2000, O'Keeffe 2004, 96–97). The ringing of bells was central to the regulation of monastic daily life and the preoccupation with time-keeping is shown also by the sundial. Bells would have been rung to mark the canonical hours and calls to prayers as well as marking the working day. As members of the community would have been spread over a considerable distance around the various parts of the enclosures and the surrounding fields, the bells would have been necessary to summon them to prayer. Some sensation of the bell ringing of monastic days is present today in the normal silence of Nendrum by virtue of the adjacent golf course bell, which, at frequent intervals, echoes across the western end of the island.

The sundial

Popular interest in ancient time measurement instruments has made the reconstructed vertical sundial attached to the south-western gable of the church, among the notable features for visitors to Nendrum. Eleven fragments of this were discovered during Lawlor's excavation. The base and some of the dial were found to the south of the western gable of the church, suggesting that it originally stood in this area, while other smaller fragments were recovered over a wider area, thought mostly to the west of the church (Lawlor 1922, 101). In 1985 an additional fragment was found in the roots of a fallen tree in the vicinity of the visitors centre in the middle enclosure, bringing the total number of surviving fragments to 12. These consist of two fragments of the dial, nine fragments of the decorated shaft, and a relatively complete base. The fragments (with the exception of that found in 1985) were assembled and set in concrete in an attempted reconstruction by Lawlor and placed against the south-western gable of the church. The reconstruction is open to criticism especially in the treatment of the shaft and is overdue for dismantling and reconsideration. However, it seems evident that the fragments are parts of a one-piece free-standing rectangular pillar of the local shale/greywacke stone consisting of a base, shaft and dial. The reconstructed height is 1.92m making it, as observed by Harbison (1991, 214), the tallest surviving example among the small number of early sundials in the country. However, because of the incomplete nature of surviving parts an accurate estimate of the original height is a matter of conjecture. Only 1.41m of the reconstructed height can be verified from extant fragments, the remainder being made up by concrete. Therefore 1.41m is the minimum possible height and 1.92m a maximum possible height.

Fig. 12.15A
The sundial as reconstructed (C. Bourke)

Fig. 12.15B
The dial of the sundial (C. Bourke)

Fig. 12.15C
Detail of the surviving decoration on the side of the shaft

The dial

The reconstruction of the dial, largely based on the larger of the two fragments of the dial face, can be regarded as reliable. It is U-shaped and of very similar dimensions to the shaft and base. (see Fig. 12.15A). Its features are carved in low relief. From the hole for the gnomon, (the latter not recovered), five main rays with stirrup-shaped terminals radiate. Further subdivision is present in the form of four minor rays placed approximately midway between the main ones. These have terminals in the shape of small circles. The five main rays indicate dawn, dusk, noon and the times of mid-morning and mid-afternoon and a division of daylight into four periods. The four minor rays indicate intermediate intervals between the five main rays. Taken together the nine rays provide a division of daylight into eight periods and show nine time markers. The duration of the number of hours in each division would vary according to the time of the year and consist of quite long periods during the long hours of daylight in summer, contrasted with quite short periods in winter. The approximate angle of the rays has been estimated by Hamlin (1987, 35) and are (main rays indicated by italics) at *10° (dawn),* 30°, *51° (mid-morning),* 70°, *90° (noon),* 110°, *130° (mid-afternoon),* 146° and *172° (dusk).* Arnaldi (2000, 29) estimated the angles to be set slightly differently at 5°, 27°, *45° (mid-morning),* 65°, *85° (noon),* 108°, *132° (mid-afternoon),* 150° and *132° (dusk).* Above the gnomon hole is a horizontal line with small circle terminations and it is unclear if this is purely decorative or had some functional purpose. The dial is framed by a triple roll moulding; the outermost roll has traces of cable decoration.

The divisions of the dial have been discussed by Lawlor (1926) and Hamlin (1987) and Arnaldi (2000). Among the small *corpus* of Pre-Norman Irish sundials and the larger *corpus* of Anglo Saxon examples, the most common division of time is into four periods defined by five rays in a similar manner to that represented by the major rays on the Nendrum dial. The consensus is that each of the five rays marks the times of the canonical hours when prayers were said. From left to right therefore, the major rays mark the time of prime, terce, noon, nones and vespers. Further, the division of daylight into four periods, and a presumed complementary division of night time into another four parts, represents the octavial system division of the day. It has been suggested that this was the prevalent system before the 11th or 12th century. The additional subdivisions on the Nendrum dial, giving the division of daylight into eight parts and therefore the day into 16 parts, represents a further refinement of this. The division of the Nendrum dial into major and minor divisions is a refinement that is not found on any other of the Irish examples.

The base

Practically all of the base was recovered. It is rectangular in section, measuring 36cm wide by 48cm high and 16cm thick. It is undecorated and plain. Presumably much of the height of the base would have been set below ground level. A small portion of a corner of the shaft framing decoration survives at the top of the base (see Fig. 12.15A).

The decorated shaft

The shaft appears to be the same width as the base. Its thickness cannot be accurately ascertained as eight of the fragments are set in concrete and the remaining one has been broken longitudinally, but it appears to have been thinner than the base. The nine fragments consist of six pieces which include parts of the face and sides (three of the right side and two of the left as reconstructed, and one whose position is uncertain) and three pieces constituting part of the panel on the face of the shaft. Only part of the character of the relief ornamentation can be established. It seems clear that the shaft had a panel defined by a rectangular frame formed by a triple roll moulding of which only fragments of the decoration inside the panel (also formed by roll moulding) survive. The present reconstruction presentation is probably unreliable. Harbison (1991, 214) suggests that it contains 'a narrow cross with a hammer-headed terminal to the uppermost limb' but this is by no means certain.

The sides of the shaft have a diagonal fret design framed by roll mouldings (see Fig. 12.15C). The backs of the stones have been hidden from view since its reconstruction making it impossible to ascertain if this face of the shaft was decorated. It is probable that if any decoration existed it would have been noted by Lawlor. However, it is to be observed that the fragment found in 1985 has been split longitudinally and that one face is missing, and some of the other fragments may be similar. The possibility exists that some of the decorated pieces may belong to the back of the shaft.

Discussion
The Nendrum sundial is one of 10 probably Pre-Norman examples known in Ireland. The other examples are at Bangor Co. Down (Hamlin 1987), Clogher (Lawlor 1931, Hamlin 1987) Co. Tyrone, Clone, Co. Wexford (Way 1868, 217) Inishcealtra, Co. Clare (Macalister 1916, 167–168, plate XX1V), Kilmalkedar, Co. Kerry, Kilcummin, Co. Mayo, Monasterboice, Co. Louth, Toureen Peakaun, Co. Tipperary and Saul Co. Down (Hamlin 1987). Aspects of the Northern Irish examples, Bangor, Clogher, Nendrum and Saul have been discussed by Hamlin (1987) while Harbison (1991) has commented on the group in general.

All the Irish examples share some features in common. They are all freestanding, one-piece pillars or slabs. All are of similar height, from *c* 1.20–2m, perhaps designed so the dial was near eye level. They can be divided into two groups according to whether they have a five or twelve time division system on the dials. The five time division is more frequent but Bangor and Clone have 12 divisions.

The dating of the Nendrum sundial is problematic. On art historical grounds the diagonal fretwork pattern could be at home in a 9th or 10th century context, but was popular over a long time span. A local East Ulster example in stone carving is found on the base of the High Cross at Dromore Co. Down. Hamlin, though considering the sundial to be Pre-Norman, noted that the treatment of the mouldings on the shaft, with their fillets, seems more similar to 13th-century work than Early Medieval (Hamlin 1987, 39) and dated it and the examples at Saul and Bangor to the 12th century.

Perhaps the closest parallel to the Nendrum dial is that from Kilmalkedar, Co. Kerry (Lawlor 1926, 53). This lacks the subsidiary rays, but has five main rays defining the four-part division of the daylight hours, each ray terminating in a semi-circular moulding. A very small portable sundial (considered originally to have been a clock face) of probable 14th- or 15th-century date was found in the debris of the church (Lawlor 1925a, 152 and plate XV). It is of slate and has 24 rays radiating from a hole for the gnomon, with the hours designated by the Roman numerals 1 to 12 for the two divisions of the day. One may speculate that its use was in connection to the parish church. The sundial with its fine low relief work roll mouldings and diagonal fret decoration is the most accomplished surviving example of stone carving from Nendrum and is probably the most sophisticated early sundial in Ireland.

Possible leacht or stone shrine

Lawlor described a slightly raised, stone-enclosed platform, located a short distance to the west of the church, and marked no. 4 on his plan (Fig. 12.3), and designated ' Site of cell (?)' suggesting that this was the foundation of a small, rectangular building (Lawlor 1925a, 120). The feature overlay some undisturbed burials (*ibid.* 135). By virtue of its prominent position, near to the entrance to the church, it is possible to suggest that it may be the remains of a stone *leacht,* a feature present at many early monastic sites. There are examples at Innismurray (Wakeman 1893), Co. Sligo, Omey Island (O'Keeffe 1994), Co. Galway, Skellig Michael, Co. Kerry (Bourke 2005) and Illaunloughan, Co. Kerry (Marshall and Walsh, 1998, 105–106) and many other sites. O'Keeffe (1998, 116) sees them as part of the Memoria class of free-standing funerary monuments over the graves of, or containing the relics of, saints. Some may have served as outdoor altars or pilgrimage prayer stations (Herity 1995, 91–143). It is tempting to suggest that given the cult of Saint Mo-Choí was a strong part of the identity of the monastery, the structure may mark his grave or where his relics were housed. The presence of a founder's tomb or shrine was considered by Rynne (2005, 88) as one of the typical features of an Early Medieval monastic enclosure, and the existence of one at Nendrum is to be entertained. This feature may be the site of the wooden shrine associated with Mo-Choí and Nendrum referred to in a story in the *Martyrology of Donegal* (see pps 293-294).

Mortared stone building

Lawlor's brief reference to '... a fragment of the foundations of a building of stone and lime mortar ...' (Lawlor 1925a, 73, 74) encountered beneath the two burial mounds to the south-east of the church, provides tantalising but vague evidence that other major built structures, apart from the church and round tower, may have existed within the central enclosure and remain to be discovered by future work. As previously mentioned, this may have been the remains of a small church or oratory.

Paved pathway from the church to the south entrance

Lawlor's plan (Fig. 12.3 no. 8) shows a narrow flagged pathway leading from the western door of the church towards the enclosure wall, and then running around its south-western perimeter to the entrance from the middle enclosure on the south. Lawlor described it as being found *c.* 25–30cm below the surface (Lawlor 1925a, 53, and plate VII). At present some of the large flags are exposed to view, but most lie buried just underneath the sod. Part of it was re-exposed during Brannon's excavation in 1982 (see Figs 12.11A-D).

Another possible fragment of paved pathway is shown as an arc of stones on Lawlor's plan (Fig. 12.3) to the north of the round tower and included under no. 8 in his key as, 'Remains of Paved Paths (or floors)'. Without further information it is impossible to tell if this is a pathway, although its location near the north-west entrance makes it plausible.

The north-south wall

This is shown on Lawlor's plan (Fig. 12.3 no. 15) and described as extending from near the south-western corner of the church to very near the southern entrance to the enclosure. It was interpreted as demarcating the western boundary of the burial ground from the open and level space with its pathway on the western side of the enclosure (Lawlor 1922, 99). Some of the line of this wall is still visible on the surface as a linear band of rough ground with some surface stone.

'Site of very early pottery'

Immediately north of the round tower, Lawlor discovered what he interpreted as a 'primitive pottery' for souterrain ware (Fig. 12.3 no. 7, 1925a, 166). The feature was found 'about twelve inches' (30.5cm) below the surface and described as a large and dense deposit of 'half fired' wasters of souterrain ware, in association with lumps of clay with finger and thumb marks. The latter had been fired and he surmised that they discarded clay which had been casually thrown into the fire. The deposit also contained several stone chisel-like artefacts, which he speculated might have been used in decorating the pots. If Lawlor's interpretations are correct, it seems puzzling that such an industrial activity was carried out within the central enclosure and a short distance from the church. Unfortunately, as with so many other features encountered during the 1922–1924 excavations, its significance is difficult to assess. It is possible that the wasters and associated material were brought from elsewhere to fill a hole or even-up the ground. It is also possible that the pottery, if that is what it was, dates to the post-monastic phase of the site (see p. 421, note 89).

What the structures in the central enclosure were like during the early, and probably most vigorous phase of the monastery in the 7th and 8th centuries, when the tide mills were built, is a matter for conjecture. Some of the main known features would not have formed part of the layout belonging to that horizon. The nave of the present stone church probably dates to the 10th century and replaced an earlier wooden church on the same site, while the round tower must belong to the 10th century or later. The stone-lined burials to the west of the church, on either side of the pathway are not closely dateable, but could belong to the 8th century and may constitute features contemporary with the life of the two mills. In addition they seem to demonstrate that parts of the central enclosure were being used as a cemetery in the 7th and 8th centuries. Lawlor's report provides no good evidence of wooden structure but at various places in his text tantalisingly refers to, without further comment, traces of wooden buildings and surviving timber and wattle. The large content of timber prepared for building purposes, including some possibly reused pieces found in the dam of Mill 1, along with wattle work and the evidence for

Fig. 12.16A
The north-western entrance from the central enclosure into the middle enclosure

competent woodworking skills and the availability of good oak, adds considerable weight to the interpretation that there existed many wooden buildings within all three enclosures in the 7th and 8th centuries.

Fig. 12.16B
The southern entrance into the central enclosure from the middle enclosure

Fig. 12.17
A portion of the south-western part of middle enclosure and the central enclosure wall showing the terrace topography which characterises most of the middle enclosure

THE MIDDLE ENCLOSURE

The middle enclosure is surrounded by an external stone revetment, except for a short section on the east where there is a free-standing, dry-stone wall. It is approximately 0.76 ha (1.88 acres) in area and largely takes the form of an extensive terrace, in places up to 60m wide. Lawlor excavated relatively intensively in the western sector and in parts of the north-eastern sector. However, large areas on the north-west and south-east remain untouched and should retain relatively undisturbed deposits (see Fig. 12.5). The southern sector is wide and Lawlor (1922, 97) speculated that this area may have been the location of some of the principal accommodation buildings.

Lawlor interpreted the terraced appearance of the middle enclosure as being largely created by deliberate land-scaping and, based on this interpretation, divided the development of the site into pre- and post-terrace phases (Lawlor 1925a, 137). Most pottery from the pre-terrace phase was souterrain ware (Lawlor's type A), but very few other types of artefact — with the exception of a few objects — could be related with confidence to this phase (*ibid.* 141). There are problems regarding Lawlor's interpretation about the formation of the terrace, which only further excavation is likely to elucidate. He stated that the main component of the make-up of the terrace was midden material (*ibid.* 138), which poses the question of whether or not some areas of it may be the result of accumulation of material rather than deliberate infill. What remains to be resolved is whether the terrace form of the middle enclosure represents a major phase of landscaping when most of the middle enclosure was transformed from inconveniently sloping ground to a level surface suitable for buildings, or whether it represents a centuries-long accumulation of occupation material which eventually assumed terrace form. This cannot be determined at present, although it is possible that the terrace was formed by a combination of both processes.

Only two burials are shown in the middle enclosure on Lawlor's plan, and these are located to the east of the 'school' and near the inner enclosure wall. In addition another burial was found beneath the floor of the 'school' (Fig. 12.18A, no. 8). No details are provided about these burials, and it is not known if they were of stone-lined type or of other form. The plan indicated that they were oriented approximately east-west, and it may be observed that they are located in the area of the middle enclosure nearest to the church.

The house platforms

The main features of significance uncovered in the middle enclosure were the foundations of possibly nine buildings or house platforms, set against or close to the boundary wall with the outer enclosure, and mainly concentrated in the south-western sector. Neither Lawlor nor ASCD have provided detailed discussion concerning them, which leaves their existing, post excavation or 'restored' presentation the main source of information. With the exception of the 'school' they survive mainly as low stone revetted circular or oval platforms from *c.* 35cm to 55cm in height or of short arcs of stones. In the discussion that follows, the house numbers refer to Fig. 12.18A, but for ease of cross-reference to Lawlor's plan (Fig. 12.3) and text (1925a) his reference numbers are given in brackets.

Seven of the structures were circular or sub-circular (Fig. 12.18A nos 1-7: Lawlor's plan, Fig. 12.3, nos 15, 17–20) and two were rectangular (Fig. 12.18A nos 8 and 9, Lawlor's plan, Fig. 12.3, nos 22 and 23). Little of significance appears to have been found within nos 1–4, 6 and 8, but no. 5 produced evidence (see below) that led Lawlor to interpret it as a 'bronze foundry/brazier's workshop' (*ibid.* 141–143). The finds from rectangular house no. 8 were extremely interesting and from these, Lawlor concluded it was the monastic 'school'.

Circular or sub-circular platforms

Circular or oval platform no. 1 (Lawlor's plan, Fig. 12.3 no. 15)

Lawlor marks a number of stone features on his plan under the number 15 on the south-west of the middle enclosure, and these are still visible today. His representation, and that of the plan in ASCD, is somewhat confusing but tends to make more sense on the ground (see Fig. 12.18A) where it is seen as consisting of two arcs of stone revetting and a length of relatively straight wall. It is difficult to interpret the latter, but it seems clear that the arcs provide evidence of two house platforms of circular or oval form, one partially overlying the other and both extending over part of the top of the enclosure wall. No. 1 is represented by a short arc of revetting stones, the end of which appears to underlie no. 2 to the north and therefore would appear to be of earlier date (see Fig. 12.18A). It has a short length of a stone-lined entrance path and ramp *c.* 1.2m wide, on the east. The only finds recorded were a large fishhook and a bronze ring pin, which were found near the surface, and souterrain ware at a lower depth (Lawlor, 1923, 68).

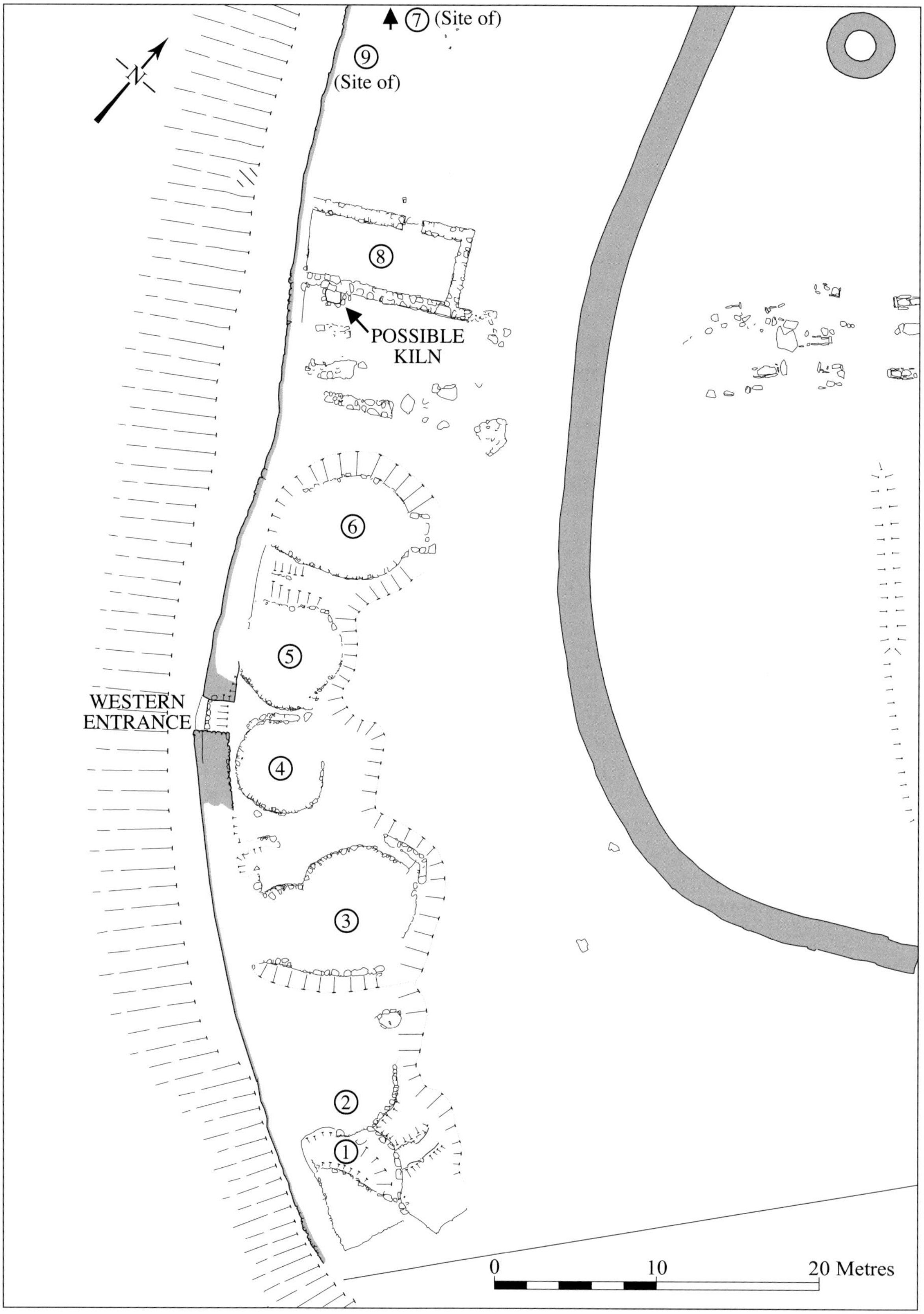

Fig. 12.18A

Plan of the house platforms and other features on the south-western sector of the middle enclosure (James Patience and David Wilkinson, 2004)

Circular platform no. 2 (Lawlor's plan, Fig. 12.3 no. 15)
The remains of this circular platform are substantial. It is *c.* 7m in diameter and stands 45cm high. If the line of the arc is extended, it indicates that this platform is closely contiguous to no. 3 on the north.

House platform no. 3 (Lawlor's plan, Fig. 12.3 no. 17)
As left (or as restored by Lawlor) this platform is shaped like a pear or light bulb and stands 35cm high. It is possible that it represents a roughly oval house with an annex. If so, the oval portion measures approximately 8.1m north-south and 6.7m east-west, while the annex portion measures 5m north-south and 3.1m east-west. On the north-east, and 1.1m out from the platform and at a slightly lower level, is an arc of stones which seems to represent an earlier house below this one. Lawlor's plan shows a flagged pathway and entrance ramp on east. Finds associated with this house included a possible decorated bronze book clasp (no. 80) a bronze pin and two ring pins (Lawlor 1925a, 141).

Fig. 12.18B
View of the south-western part of the middle enclosure looking north showing in sequence from bottom houses platforms nos 1, 2, 3, 4, 5 and 6 ending with no. 8 the 'school house' at the top right of the picture

Circular platform no. 4 (Lawlor's plan, Fig.12.3 no 18)
This almost circular house platform measures approximately 5.5m north-south by 5.7m east-west. The stone revetment of the platform stands to a maximum height of 55cm. It is only 35cm out from the inner cashel wall as restored. Lawlor shows a flagged pathway and entrance ramp slightly to the north of east. Finds associated with this house were an iron adze and stone axe (Lawlor 1925a, 141).

House platform no. 5 (Lawlor's plan, Fig. 12.3 no. 19, 'The bronze foundry' or 'the Brazier's workshop')
This platform is roughly horseshoe-shaped and abuts the middle enclosure revetment wall. It measures 6.5m north-south and 6.2m east-west, and is *c.* 40cm high. Because of the character of the finds in and around this house, which included 'innumerable fragments of crucibles' for bronze-working (Lawlor 1925a, 142), Lawlor named it the 'bronze foundry'. Lawlor's plan shows a flagged pathway entrance ramp on the east side.

House platform no. 6 (Lawlor's plan, Fig. 12.3, no. 20)
This takes the form of a stone-revetted platform *c.* 40cm high and of roughly horseshoe-shaped outline. It measures 7.4m east-west by 6.3m north-south. There is indication of a flagged pathway *c.* 2.3m wide and an entrance ramp on the east side. The shape may indicate a round or oval house with an annex structure at the rear.

Possible round house no. 7 (Lawlor's plan, Fig. 12.3 no. 15, to north of nos 22 and 23)
This is shown on Lawlor's plan as a large semi-circular arc of stones, which he describes as '... traces of another circular hut site of which only a few stones remain, nothing was found ...' (Lawlor 1925a, 108–109). There are no visible above-surface features at this location at present.

Given the rather crude techniques employed by the 1922–1924 excavation, information on the round house structures represented by the platforms is severely limited. No post holes, hearths or constructional material are mentioned as being encountered. Therefore it is difficult to ascertain the type of house plans present beyond the fact that they appear to belong to general round house tradition for domestic structure prevalent in the early part of the Early Medieval period in Ireland. It is possible, however, to ascertain the approximate size of five of the platforms from their diameter measurements.

From these a range of house sizes from 5–8m seems apparent. This compares quite closely to the size range of domestic round houses encountered from ringfort excavations (Lynn 1978a). The shape of platforms 3 and 6 may possibly represent the round house with an annex plan. Five have evidence that their entrances faced east into the centre of the enclosure and that they were approached by stoned flagged paths. These pathways running east-west would seem to connect with a north-south stone-lined path shown on Lawlor's plan (no. 8) near the middle of the enclosure.

Rectangular houses

Rectangular house no. 8, (Fig. 12.18C, Lawlor's plan, Fig. 12.3, no. 22 'The school')
The surviving foundations or basal courses of this stone building measure internally 14.33m long by 3.96m wide, with walls *c.* 75cm thick and are described by Lawlor as being cemented with puddle clay (Lawlor 1925a, 107–108). A doorway *c.* 1.1m wide is located in the northern wall, towards the eastern gable from which a stone pathway going a considerable distance northwards is shown on Lawlor's plan. The building has a similar orientation as the church. In terms of size this building with a ground area of approximately 56.75m^2 is larger than the pre-chancel church in the central enclosure which is approximately 39m^2. The structure may have extended further to the west as it appears truncated on this side.

Fig. 12.18C
The 'school' from the east

This was by far the best-preserved structure in the middle enclosure and Lawlor interpreted its function, on the basis of finds, to be the monastic school. This interpretation, suggesting evidence for the monastic scriptorium, has attracted considerable interest. Before excavation, the feature consisted of '... a rectangular mound overgrown with vegetation ...' (Lawlor 1925a, 143), and had been untouched by cultivation. Apart from stones, the mound consisted of earth with a high content of charred wood, half-burnt roof beams, roofing nails and burned straw (*ibid.* 143). Lawlor's observations serve to stress that the survival of organic material was excellent. He was able to identify the remains of the doorway, which had '... nailed planks 1$^1/_4$ inches thick ...' and recovered the door hinge and handle (*ibid.* 148). Beneath the debris, the stone walls, which were cemented with clay, survived to a height of between 30cm and 60cm.

Some of the most interesting artefacts from the excavations were found on what was interpreted as the floor of the structure. These include 30 slate motif pieces (O' Meadhra, 1979), described as '... cracked by fire ...', three of which had traces of lettering (Lawlor

1925a, 144). The other artefacts found were four iron styli for use on wax tablets, four short knife blades, probably for bone and wood carving, approximately 13 stone discs, some perforated and perhaps gaming pieces, 16 bone beads found together, some ornamented, and one bronze and one iron needle (*ibid.* 144–149). From the range of finds, especially the motif pieces with lettering and the styli, Lawlor concluded that he had discovered the monastic school. The apparent evidence of burning formed one of his strongest arguments for a general 'conflagration' caused by the Vikings in AD 976 (*ibid.* 149–150).

The well-preserved nature of the ruins of the building and of the organic material, as well as its rectangular form and size, throw up some suspicion regarding its antiquity. Some doubt must be expressed about the connection between the building and the great richness of artefact material found in apparent association with it, given Lawlor's level of stratigraphic observation. It is possible that the artefacts relate to an occupation layer or structure below the rectangular building. (see, also p. 420 note 42)

The building may be considerably later than the adjacent round houses and constructed well after the monastery had a functioning scriptorium or 'monastic school' and other

Fig. 12.18D
View from the south-west showing house platforms in the middle enclosure (Gail Pollock 1999)

functions need to be considered. One possibility is that it is of Late Medieval date and was the house of the parish priest. Domestic occupancy of the middle enclosure in the post 12th century is demonstrated by the discovery of a sizable amount of 13th- and 14th-century pottery found during Lawlor's excavation and that of Waterman (1958, 67–70).

Possible rectangular building no. 9 (Lawlor's plan, Fig. 12.3, no. 23)
Lawlor describes some features encountered to the north of the 'school' which might be interpreted as another rectangular structure. These consist of a fragment of wall on top of the enclosure wall, similar in character to the walls of the 'school', and another wall fragment parallel with it some 20 ft (6.1m) away 'apparently of much more ancient type' (Lawlor 1925a, 108). Midway between the two walls was a stone-lined hearth-like feature. While the walls were considered to be of different date, Lawlor interpreted them as somehow associated and 'evidently a building was at sometime erected here, in which an anciently existing wall was used, and a newer one put up…'. His plan shows a linear section of wall more or less in line with the outer face of the enclosure wall (no. 23) and, to the east, a long section of slightly meandering wall (no. 15). Brannon put a small trench through this to ascertain its antiquity, which seemed to be genuine. Below the wall, *c.* 80cm of occupation soil, overlying the sub-soil and containing bone and souterrain ware, was encountered.

Discussion
In broad terms two building traditions are represented in the middle enclosure, the round house and the rectangular house. The possible presence of both round and rectangular house forms during the monastic phase at Nendrum has potentially important chronological implications as Lynn has proposed that there was a change in house-building tradition, from round to rectangular, in the Early Medieval period, possibly taking place in the 9th century and being largely complete by the end of the 10th century (Lynn 1978a). Unfortunately, we have no stratified relationship between the two forms at the site, but the two possible rectangular houses do appear to be nearer to the surface than the round forms, and it seems probable that the round house platforms belong to the earlier phase of the site.

While there is little evidence to demonstrate how many of the houses were in contemporary use, the density of house structures in the south-western sector is nonetheless impressive. Most of the platforms lie very close to each other and to the enclosure wall and in some cases appear to, at least partially, overlie it. There is evidence also of platforms overlying earlier ones. A segment of the north-east part of the middle enclosure was excavated, but no houses are reported as having been found. However, this may have been the result of a number of factors such as the depth of excavation, eradication by cultivation, or failure to recognise them, in which regard, Lawlor is frank about not being able to make sense of many of the wall features encountered (1925a, 103–104). There are therefore no good reasons to assume that this density did not occur all around the approximately three-quarters of the middle enclosure that was untouched during the 1922–24 excavations. It is tempting to see the cluster of house platforms on the south-west as providing a glimpse of a wider pattern of high building density inside all of the middle enclosure.

Possible kiln

Partially underlying the southern wall of the 'school', and adjacent to the middle enclosure wall, was an oval, stone-revetted pit superficially resembling a stone-lined well (Fig. 12.18A.: Lawlor plan Fig. 12.3 no. 21). It would seem to pre-date the 'school' building, and measures *c.* 1.9m deep and *c.* 95cm by *c.* 80cm (Macdonald 2003, 1). The top of the feature may have been partially arched over. At the bottom was a deep layer of 'fire remains', with some fragments of animal bone (Lawlor 1925a, 104). It is difficult to ascribe a function to this feature. It may pre-date the formation of the terrace as Lawlor thought, and have been set in a mound subsequently covered by the terrace build-up. Lawlor considered that it resembled somewhat the corn-drying kiln in the outer enclosure (see below), and it is possible that interpretation as a corn-drying or other type of kiln or oven is correct.

Industrial zone in south-western middle enclosure

Lawlor's interpretation of house platform no. 5, on the basis of finds, as a 'bronze foundry/brazier's workshop' (*ibid.* 141-143) was taken, along with other evidence, as indicating the existence of an industrial zone in the south-western sector of the middle enclosure. The other evidence of metal-working found in the south-west, was a circular bronze ingot weighing 8oz, some crucibles and 'nodules of ironstone' found near the site of Major Houston's bungalow (Fig. 12.3 no. 34, to the south of no. 15, Lawlor 1925a, 140), suggesting that both iron- and bronze-working were being carried out in this area. The low level at which these were found, possibly on the pre-terrace surface, allowed Lawlor to conclude that they much pre-dated the evidence from the 'the bronze foundry'.

The western entrance

This was found 'in a fairly complete state' and consisted of an opening 5' 6" (1.68m) wide (Lawlor 1922, 98). It obviously pre-dates the two house sites (Figs 12.18A nos 4 and 5: Lawlor's plan, Fig. 12.3 nos 18 and 19), as these block access to it and are at a higher level suggesting quite strongly that it had gone out of use at a comparatively early date in the history of the site (see Fig. 12.18E).

THE OUTER ENCLOSURE

In an anti-clockwise direction, the outer enclosure (Figs 12.7 and 12.8) is defined on the north-west, west and south-west by a low scarp with traces of stone revetting visible in places. For a small section on the south little surface trace has survived, while on the south-east it is enclosed by a deep and wide ditch. The area enclosed is approximately

Fig. 12.18E
The western entrance between the middle and outer enclosures (looking west from inside the middle enclosure). Visible in the foreground are house platforms no. 4 (on left) and no. 5 (on right, Lawlor's 'bronze foundry' or 'Brazier's workshop') almost blocking the approach to the entrance on this side. The townland of Ballydorn is shown on the top of the picture across the c. 336m of water at high tide separating Mahee Island from the mainland at this point.

1.32 ha (3.26 acres) in size. The north-eastern segment of the boundary is somewhat complex and problematic and is discussed below. As restored, it consists of a free-standing linear dry-stone wall *c.* 2m thick, which runs down the slope to terminate near the shore with a gentle curve to the south east.

The terrain enclosed by the outer boundary is generally sloping, but contains small areas of level ground on the north and south. Lawlor noted on his plan (Fig. 12.3) that parts of the north-western and south-western areas had been under cultivation in the past, and that part of the relatively steeply sloping north-eastern sector was a wilderness of bushes. His excavations in the outer enclosure were very limited and, to a large extent, it remains untouched. Excavation appears to have been concentrated on a relatively small area on the north, and on the north-east and extended a short distance outside the enclosure at this location (see Fig. 12.3). In the western sector he excavated a small area around the western entrance and paved pathway leading to it, and around a circular hollow. Along with the hollow, the main features uncovered in the outer enclosure were a large corn-drying kiln, a midden and, in the northern sector, some stone walls. Referring to these Lawlor notes that ' ... for the most part they took the form of arcs of circles; they were in places so close together, however, that the circles could not be completed without intersecting each other; so that, apparently, they were not the foundations of circular hut sites. ...' (1925a, 103–104).

The north-eastern sector

The north-eastern sector of the site contains a number of features which are difficult to interpret and are discussed in relation to Figs 12.3, 12.7, 12.8 and 12.19). The external boundary as marked on Lawlor's plan (Fig. 12.7) is confusing and shows a dotted line to the east of the middle enclosure wall designated '... outline of the 3rd cashel wall ...'. As explained in the text, however, the plan was finished for publication before clearance of the wilderness in the north-eastern corner of the site was carried out (Lawlor 1925a, 96, 97). It was discovered subsequently that the enclosure wall continued eastwards down almost to the shore and this additional portion was subsequently added to the published plan. The feature he originally followed as the outline of the enclosure is a prominent scarp which runs through most of the north-western sector (Fig. 12.19 no. 1). Reeves' plan of 1844 (Fig. 12.2) also shows this. Although it is possible that at an early stage of the development of the site this scarp may have defined the outer enclosure, it is much more probable that it is simply an internal division and the result of terracing to create more level space. There is another prominent scarp to the east and down slope of the above mentioned scarp which has visible traces of a stone revetment (Fig. 12.19 no. 2). It commences near the part of the outer enclosure to the north-east of the kiln (see below) and slopes down to the south-east to terminate at the well near the present entrance to the site from the car park. In spite of its prominence, it is not shown on Lawlor's plan (Fig. 12.3) and only a small segment is marked on that in ASCD (Fig. 12.7).

A third enclosing feature is present in the form of a short, linear stone revetment roughly parallel to the shore and at 90° to the north-eastern section of the outer enclosure wall (Fig. 12.19 no 3). Lawlor (1923, 57) mentions this feature in his 1923 interim report

> ...behind the tea house may be seen fragments of a wall running at right angles; if our investigations continue, much may yet be laid bare in this direction.

He shows it on his plan as abutting the western side of the teahouse (Fig. 12.3 no. 34). It is also shown on the ASCD plan (Fig. 12.7) and designated 'wall of outer cashel'. The wall is still visible and forms a revetment to a roughly level area behind. It survives to a height of *c.* 70cm and is 5m long and contains some very large boulders. At its southern end is a possible right-angled return going for a short distance eastwards. A small trench was excavated through this revetment by Brannon in 1979 and demonstrated its antiquity (SMR Dow 17:8, Hamlin 1997, 49). Stratified below the revetment was an occupation layer approximately 14cm deep with charcoal and slag, which produced a 6th-century radiocarbon date, (1375 +45 BP, UB-3265) demonstrating activity in the area before it was constructed. While this sample may be of limited application in dating the whole of the outer enclosure, in the current absence of other dating evidence it provides an indication of a possible 7th-century date for construction of the enclosure boundary. Without further excavation it is impossible to work out the relationships between, or chronology of these various features. It is possible to suggest that they represent a progressive expansion eastwards of the original outer enclosure boundary down to the shore. Alternatively, they may all be contemporary. The car park occupies ground reclaimed from the foreshore in the mid-19th century, and therefore part of the eastern boundary of the enclosure must have originally been just above the high water mark. The east-west dam of the second millpond may have originally touched the enclosure boundary at this location, and it is possible to envisage that both it and Mill 1 could be considered as part of the monastic enclosure.

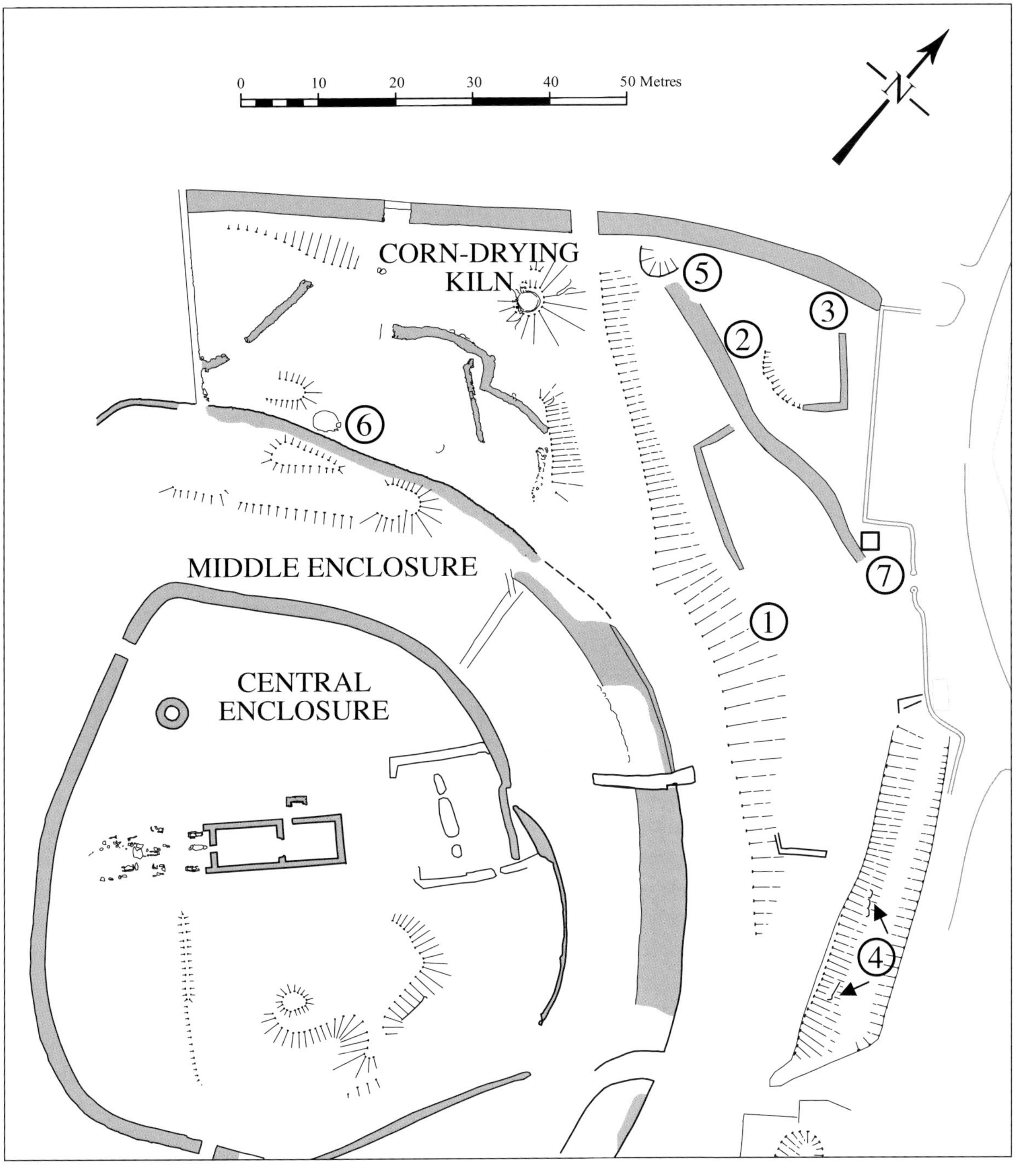

Fig. 12.19 Features within the north-eastern sector of the outer enclosure

Entrances

The 1922–1924 excavations uncovered an entrance to the outer enclosure on the south-west, which seems to have connected with the western landing place on the shore below. A possible northern entrance was also located. It is probable that there was an eastern entrance near the termination of the dam of Mill 2. It is highly probable also that there would have been an entrance on the south, but almost all surface trace of the outer enclosure at this location has been eradicated.

The ditch

It is somewhat curious that the impressive ditch (see Figs 12.8, 12.20A and B) which forms part of the south-eastern boundary of the outer enclosure has been largely ignored in previous discussions of the site. Reeves (1902) shows it prominently on his plan first published in 1844 (Fig. 12.2), but it was not shown by Lawlor (Fig. 12.3), but is in ASCD (Fig. 12.7). Reeves' plan, which can be regarded essentially as a sketch, depicts it as detached from the main enclosure complex. However, it is clear that it formed a major enclosing element around part of the outer enclosure and also served to almost separate the monastic western part of the island from the remaining area.

Fig. 12.20B
View from north of the ditch (presently obscured by vegetation) forming part of the outer enclosure boundary

The ditch extends over a narrow neck of land from very near the shoreline on the north to *c.* 100m from the shoreline on the south (Fig. 12.2). It is *c.* 10-15m wide in places and up to 3m deep, with a short length of revetment walling on its inner face (Fig. 12.19 no. 4). There is no obvious evidence of a bank where the material extracted during its digging may have been dumped, and it is tempting to speculate that it may have been a major source of the constructional material of one or both mill dams.

The corn-drying kiln

This feature is situated on the north-east sector of the outer enclosure and near the external enclosure wall (Fig. 12.19). It takes the form of a mound of stone and earth built against the sloping terrain, with a dry-stone chamber in its centre (Figs 12.21A and B). The chamber is almost circular, measuring *c.* 2.86m east-west and 2.63m north-south, and has a surviving height of *c.* 1.1m. The sides are vertical and there is no indication of corbelling. From the floor of the chamber, three 'vents' or 'flues' radiate in straight lines through the mound on the north-east, south-east and north-west. The one on the north-west had been reduced to ground level and was originally interpreted by Lawlor to be an entrance into the chamber. The two flues on the north-east and south-east survive well and their openings into the chamber are approximately square measuring 25cm by 28cm. That on the north-east can be traced for *c.* 2.4m to where it emerges on the exterior face of the mound.

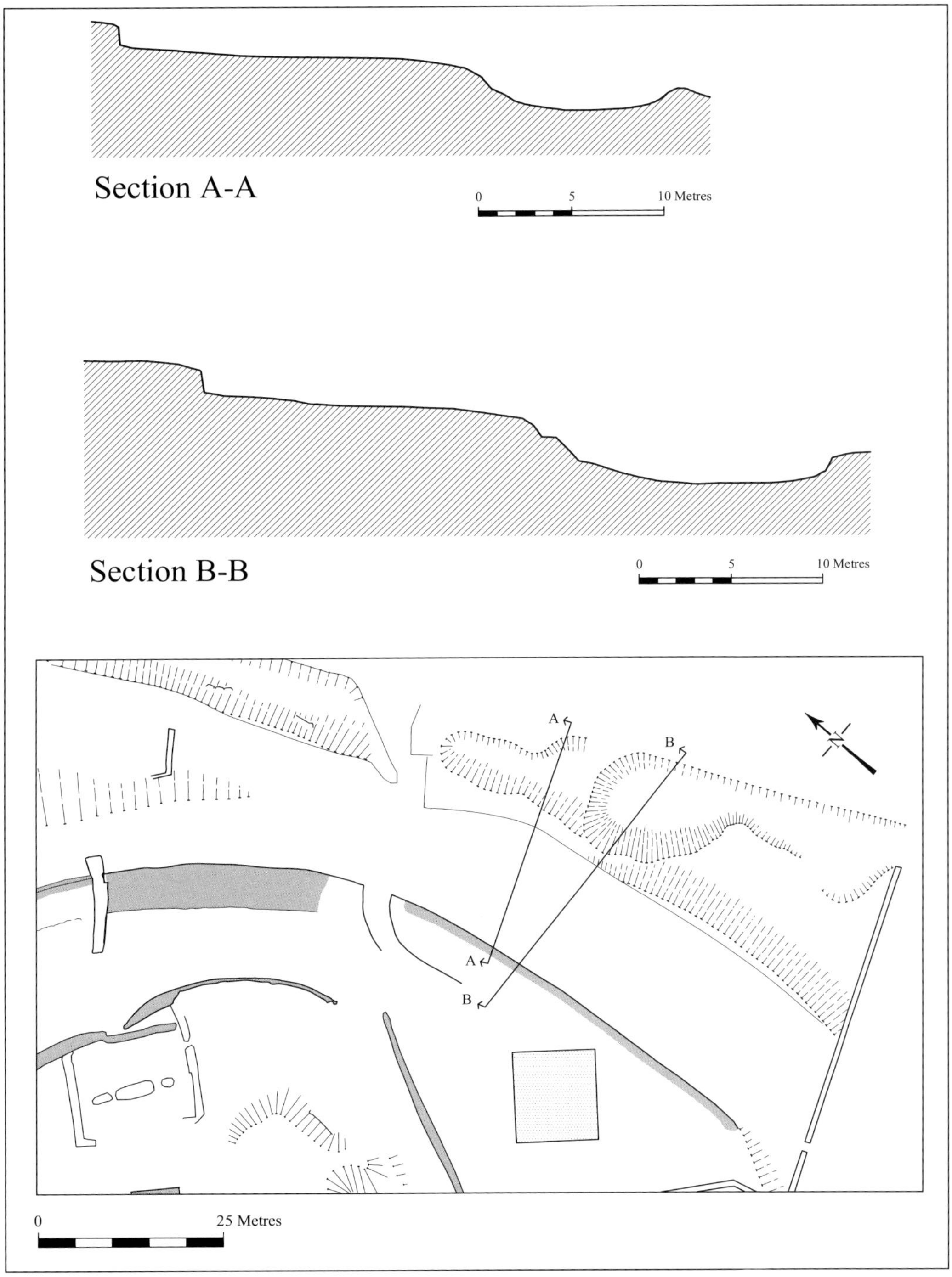

Fig. 12.20A
Sections across the ditch forming part of the outer enclosure boundary on the south-east

Lawlor designated the feature a 'circular cell (?)' (Fig. 12.3 no. 14) on his plan, but noted in the text that the 'drains' (the flues) seemed to indicate a structure with some special purpose (Lawlor 1925a, 102). On the floor of the chamber he found '... slight traces of burned lime and charcoal ...' (Lawlor 1923, 59), but rejected interpretation as a lime kiln

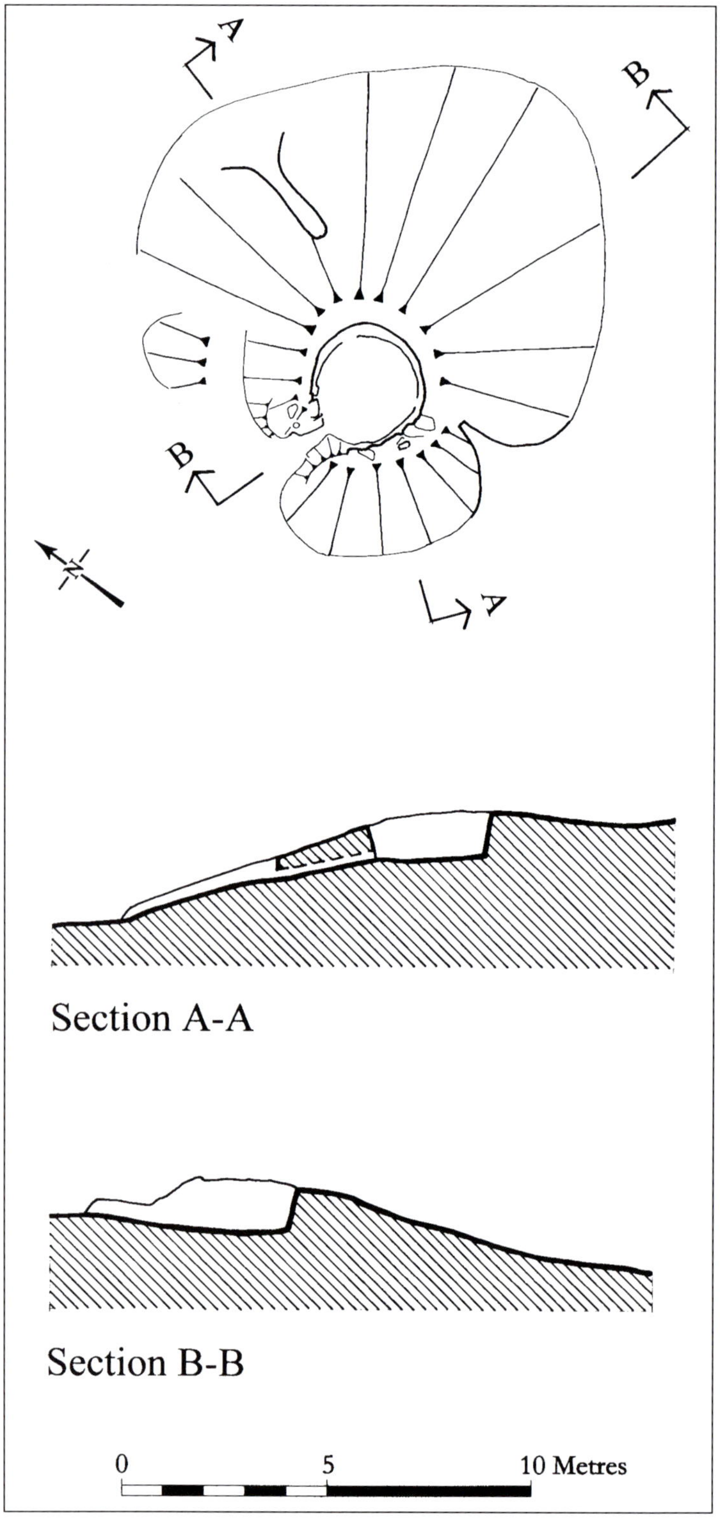

Fig. 12.21A
Plan of the kiln with sections (J. Patience)

perhaps built to construct the round tower because of the absence of any signs of fire on the chamber walls (Lawlor 1925a, 102). A small trench was excavated through the north-western flue by Brannon 1982 (SMR Dow 17:8 Brannon's trench X1V), which confirmed that it was not an entrance but a third flue. The excavation revealed that the basal courses of the structure rested on subsoil and were not underlain by earlier deposits. A Late Medieval sherd and some 'mortar debris, sand and charcoal' were found.

The nearest parallel to the structure is one found in a Late Medieval context at the Early Medieval monastery of Tullylish, Co. Down (Ivens 1987 62–64), and identified as a corn-drying kiln. The most plausible identification of the Nendrum structure is that it is also a large corn-drying kiln. The Tullylish structure has a similar circular, stone-revetted chamber and an arrangement of three flues. Its chamber, with a diameter of 2m, is smaller in size than the Nendrum structure while its flues are wider (*c.* 50m wide as they enter the chamber) and shorter in length. The Tullylish example is relatively well dated by coin evidence to the late 14th or 15th centuries (Ivens 1987, 62), suggesting a similar date for the Nendrum example (*op. cit.* 64).

With its triple-flue arrangement and greater size (the kiln would have had a drying floor of approximately 5.91m^2) compared to other known Irish Early Medieval examples, a later date for the Nendrum structure sounds plausible as at present there are no other comparable Irish Early Medieval corn-drying kilns of this type known. Known Irish Early Medieval corn kilns conform to the small 'keyhole' type, consisting of a heating chamber, single flue and fire-bowl or pit. However, one documentary reference suggests the presence of corn-drying kilns of large size (Kelly 1997, 365) during the period and, with the discovery of a very sophisticated late 8th-century mill at Nendrum, it is tempting to suggest it was matched with a similarly sophisticated kiln. The Nendrum

Fig. 12.21B
The corn-drying kiln in the outer enclosure from the north-west. The millpond of Mill 2 is visible on the top left

example may be a type of Early Medieval corn-drying kiln not previously discovered or recognised, and be contemporary with Mill 2.

Corn-drying kilns are becoming one of the most common features to be discovered on Early Medieval excavations (Bennett 2004, *v*), although, at the time of writing, very few have been published. Grain harvested at the end of damp Irish summers normally has a high moisture content and requires artificial drying in a corn-drying kiln before storage or milling. The importance of the corn-drying kiln in Irish cereal processing is reflected by frequent references in early Irish documentary sources (Kelly 1998, 241). Damage to a kiln incurred a penalty, and in *Críth Gablach* for instance, it is stipulated that the self-sufficient farmer of *bo-aire* status is expected to have his own, while the *ocair*, a less-affluent farmer, was expected to have share in one. It is obvious that a monastery like Nendrum would have at least one. A corn-drying kiln can be also regarded as a necessary ancillary building to a mill. Cereal drying kilns were not only needed to prepare the grain for storage and milling, but were required as part of the malting process for the production of ale and beer which were an important part of the early Irish diet.

Possible second kiln

Lawlor briefly describes a feature a short distance to the north-east of the kiln (shown on his plan, Fig. 12.3, as no. 13 with the key stating 'remains of Circular Building in Hollow') as 'a similar, though larger structure' and as being 'deeply buried' (Lawlor 1925a, 102). Unfortunately this structure has been re-buried and its features cannot be ascertained. It is situated against the outer enclosure wall, in relatively steeply sloping ground (Fig. 12.19 no. 5). It is possible that it was a second kiln and that this part of the outer enclosure was given over to cereal processing.

Circular hollow

This feature (Lawlor's plan, Fig. 12.3 no. 29 'Circular Hollow') was described by Lawlor as '... a circular saucer-shaped depression, in the grass ...' and, on excavation, produced some souterrain ware, nails and stones. He was uncertain about its significance, but suggested that it may have been a building. The feature is not marked on the ASCD plan, but is still visible as a roughly circular and shallow depression about 14m in diameter. There seem no grounds to suggest that it represents the site of a building. The depression is surrounded by higher ground on the north and east and constitutes a break in otherwise sloping terrain. Given its topographical position and shape, it is possible to suggest that it may have been an artificial pond for cattle, horses and other livestock kept in the outer enclosure, and supplied by rain water flowing down the surrounding slopes.

The midden

In the northern sector of the outer enclosure, and against the exterior of the middle enclosure revetment, '... a large heap of kitchen midden refuse ...' was found (Lawlor 1925a, 136: Fig. 12.19 no. 6, Lawlor's plan, Fig. 12.3 no. 30). The main contents were animal bone, charred wood, oyster and other sea shells, souterrain ware and wheel-turned wares. In addition to this was some other interesting material, including a motif piece (*ibid.* plate XII no. 115), a large cube of 'pig iron' and 'iron slag' and a number of rubbing stones (*ibid.* 136–137). The finds would seem to suggest that the midden accumulated over a long period of time. Its location, in the outer enclosure but up against the exterior of the middle enclosure revetment wall suggests the dumping of refuse from the middle enclosure.

The well

Just outside the exterior of the enclosure on the east, and just above the original shore, is a stone-lined well which was still in use in recent times (Fig. 12.19. no. 7): Lawlor 1925a, 19–20, 106, marked on Lawlor's plan, Fig. 12.3 as no. 35, but corrected to no. 33 in the accompanying key and designated 'Monks' well'). Lawlor's conjecture that this spring supplied the monastery with its fresh water seems correct. There was another stone-lined well, recently filled in, above the shore to the south of the site, with stone steps leading down into it (shown on Reeves' plan, Fig. 12.2 no. 7)) and Lawlor mentions a third spring above the shoreline on the north-west of the island.

In summary, it should be clearly stated that very little is known about the archaeology of the outer enclosure. However, within the zoning of activities in the monastic complex, with the central enclosure acting as the ritual core and the middle enclosure functioning as an industrial and domestic area, it is tempting to see the outer enclosure as acting as a type of estate farmyard with the range of activities that would have been associated with it. One might envisage a part of it used as a place where the monastic dairy herd was brought in for milking, with areas devoted to processing dairy products. It is highly probable that there would have been a large granary to store the annual cereal crop, which was processed in the kiln and tide mill. Some of it may have been given over to kitchen gardens. Given the density of buildings revealed in the middle enclosure, it seems probable that by the late 8th century some building may have spilled over into this area.

Fig. 12.22A
View (looking north) over part of the eastern sector of the outer enclosure with part of the middle enclosure on top left

OUTSIDE THE ENCLOSURE

The farmscape

Present information on features belonging to the Early Medieval phase outside the enclosure is very limited and constitutes a challenge for future research. It is clear that early Irish monasteries were directly involved in farming, and the immediate landscape around the monastery would have been subject to quite intensive agricultural activity. Unfortunately this is unlikely to have left very much above-ground traces. It is possible to envisage the land around Early Medieval monastic enclosures as constituting agricultural units very similar to those, which in the Late- and Post-Medieval periods, constituted a home farm or demesne. It is very probable that these agricultural units were subject to a high level of management and relatively efficient agricultural technology.

Fig. 12.22B
View (looking east) of the millponds and dams of Mills 1 and 2 from the boundary wall of the middle enclosure

In terms of cereal processing, the tide mills are a fine representation of this and it is likely that other aspects of monastic farming were similarly sophisticated. Kelly (1998) has provided a general overview of the level of farming technology in the 7th and 8th centuries, based mainly on the evidence of the law texts and it is probable that the monasteries of the late 6th, 7th and 8th centuries may have been at the forefront of agriculture improvement. The size of these units or farms attached to early Irish monasteries

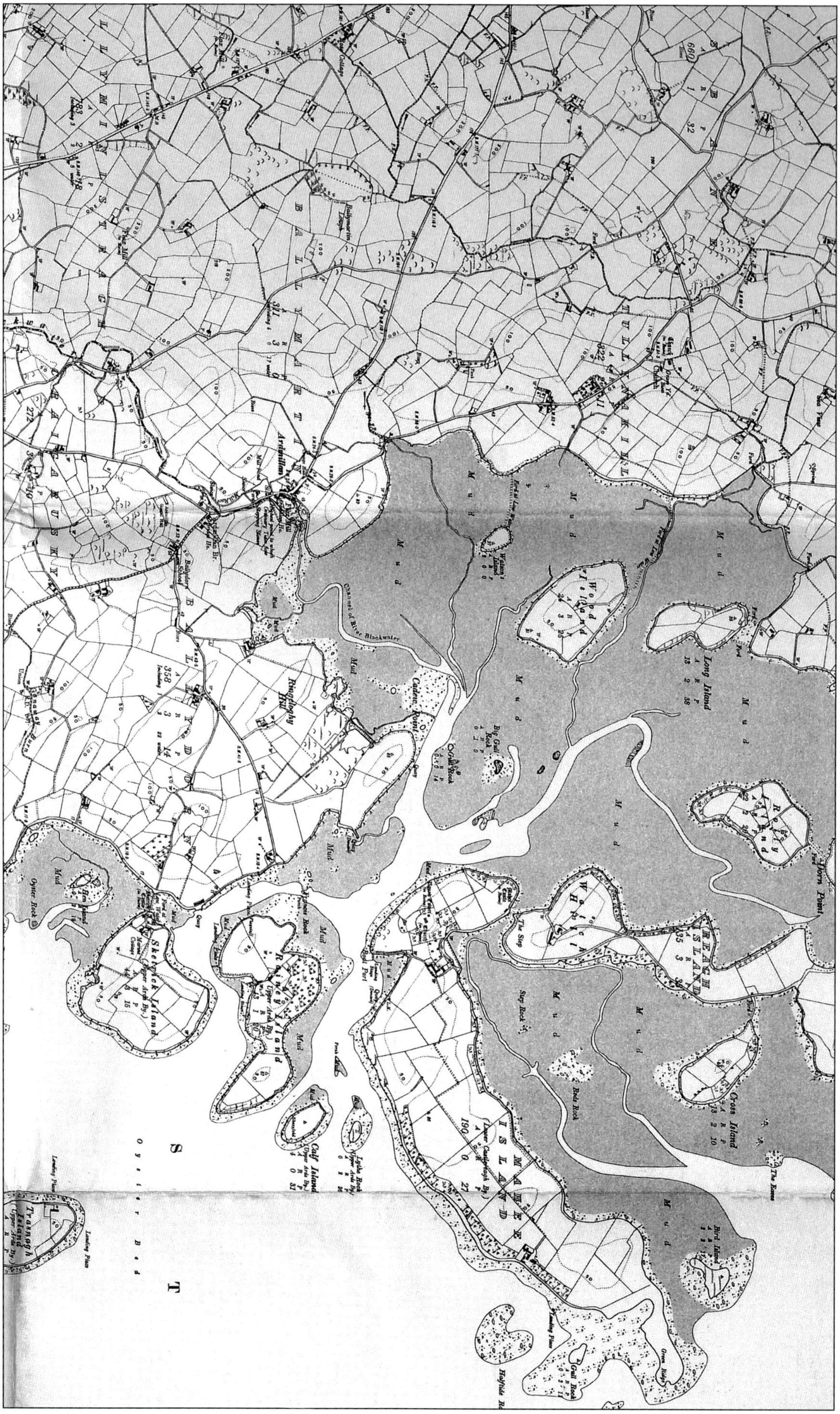

Fig. 12.23 Nendrum, Mahee Island and surrounding area (OS Six-inch survey, 1920, Country Down Sheet 17, edition of 1933)

is difficult to assess and has received very little attention. On Iona, the impression is given in Adomnán's *Life of St Columba* (Sharp 1995) that the monastery was farming the whole island. At Nendrum, the home farm is likely to have encompassed all of Mahee Island and the closely adjacent Reagh Island, and probably included Rainey Island (see Fig. 12.22). The present field system on Mahee and neighbouring islands is Post-Medieval and at present, no trace of the monastic field system has survived above ground, although geophysical survey may yet reveal much.

THE MONASTERY AND THE OUTSIDE WORLD

The land approach via fords

There is a strong local tradition amongst some of the residents of Mahee Island that, before the construction of the causeway linking Ringneal townland on the mainland to Reagh Island in the 1870s, Nendrum was accessed from the mainland by a ford at low water over the mud and sand flats to Rolly Island and from there by a ford to Reagh Island and from the latter to Mahee Island over the short ford formerly known as 'the step' and now spanned by a causeway (see Figs 12.4B and C, Fig. 12.23). These fords are not marked on the OS maps of 1833 or 1856, and so far have not shown up on air photographs. But since the building of the Ringneal to Reagh Island causeway, Ardmillan Bay has considerably silted up and all trace of the fords are now probably covered by accumulated mud. That they once existed is highly probable, and they would have served at low tide as the main land access route to the monastery.

The landing places

Given its island location, it is clear that boats would have played a big part in the life of the monastery. So far the only archaeological evidence for watercraft recovered on the site is the early-7th-century oar found in the dam of Mill 1 (p. 228). Evidence exists for landing places at a number of different locations around the shore in the vicinity of the enclosures, and probably represents those in use during the Early Medieval period. The choice of which landing place to use for craft arriving or leaving the monastery would have been determined by the state of the tide and direction of arrival, or destination.

The western landing place

On the foreshore, below the western side of the enclosure and roughly in line with the entrances on this side, are two curving stone walls forming a somewhat enigmatic crescent-shaped feature (McErlean *et al.* 2002, 528). The southern wall of the feature is *c.* 25.5m long and 1m wide and extends from the upper shore to the low water mark. It consists of a curving wall of double-boulder construction and contains some very large boulders. The northern wall is less well preserved. It is *c.* 13m long and is of similar width to the southern wall. The crescent-shaped space defined by the two walls is *c.* 5m wide and largely free of boulders, with the exception of a massive boulder located on the upper shore in a roughly central position. A probable interpretation of the feature is that it was a landing and beaching place for small craft, the large boulder serving as a navigational marker. Some sherds of Late Medieval pottery have been found in the vicinity in recent years, and excavation may produce more information on its significance and may possibly reveal a wooden component. Lawlor's interpretation (1925a, 18, 105) as the remains of a landing place dating to the time of the monastery seems probably correct. Its location at the point nearest to the mainland in Ballydorn townland on the opposite shore would seem to suggest that it was the main landing place at high water for traffic to and from the monastery and the mainland. Interestingly, at the point opposite in Ballydorn are the remains of a quay of 18th-century date (McErlean *et al.* 2002, 497). Its presence at this location demonstrates its suitability as a landing place and it is possible to plausibly speculate that it is on the site of an early landing place which corresponds with the probable monastic landing place on the opposite shore.

Other probable landing places in the vicinity of the site used in monastic times are the 'boat port' to the south and the site of the old quay to the south-east (McErlean *et al.* 2002, 528). It is probable, however, that the main landing place for craft arriving at the monastery from the open lough was the wooden landing place adjacent to both the 7th- and 8th-century mills (see p. 65).

NENDRUM AND THE TRIPLE ENCLOSURE PLAN

The most impressive feature of Nendrum, is the survival, albeit aided by restoration, of much of the enclosure element of the monastery. It is this defining component of the site, which makes the greatest impression on the visitor and contributes most to the power Nendrum possesses in conveying something of the aura of an early monastic site. Thanks to aerial photography, an increasing number of examples of monastic enclosures have come to light in recent decades (Norman and St. Joseph 1969; Swan 1983; Hurley 1980, 1982). Field survey, especially geophysical survey, and excavation are providing more information about them. Their significance has been discussed by various authors (Edwards 1990, 105–112, Bitel 1990, 57–82, Mytum 1992) and the stage has now been reached where the existence of an enclosure is now to be regarded as one of the most diagnostic features of an Early Medieval ecclesiastic site. Much, however, remains to be discovered about the nature of the monastic enclosure and the organisation of space within it.

The monastic enclosure, *the vallum monasterri*

There has been a tendency to regard monastic enclosures as primarily a feature of Irish monastic sites and view them within the strong tradition of enclosed settlement sites of the Irish Early Medieval period abundantly represented in the Irish landscape by the many thousands of ringforts. It is important to point out, however, that the enclosure was not only a characteristic of insular Irish monasticism but also a fundamental feature of all Christian monasteries. The monastic Rule compiled by St. Benedict of Nursia (McCann

1952) in the mid 6th century contains some direct information on the centrality of the enclosure in monastic life and helps put the Irish enclosures in their European context. Benedict's Rule was not an original work but was heavily influenced by existing practice of coenobitic communities and became the basis for much of the subsequent development of Western monasticism.

Regarding the enclosure, Benedict's Rule states that:

> ...the monastery should, if possible, be so arranged that all necessary things, such as water, mill, garden, and various crafts may be within the enclosure, so that the monks may not be compelled to wander outside it, for that is not at all expedient for their souls. (chapter 66)

Chapter 4 describes the space defined by the enclosure as the 'workshop' where all the spiritual life outlined by the Rule was carried on, and chapter 66 states that a punishment is to be imposed on any monk who goes outside the enclosure without the permission of the abbot. This latter stricture is also found in Penitentials of St. Columbanus where penance is imposed on any monk who leaves the enclosure without permission during the day or night (Bieler, 1963, 106, 107), and also in the Rule of Ailbe, which restricts the monks from leaving the enclosure (O'Neill 1907, 105). The importance of the entrance into the enclosure is also highlighted in Benedict's Rule (chapter 66), which is devoted to the porter or doorkeeper of the monastery and states that his cell should be near it which serves to emphasise the importance of controlled access into the enclosure. Statements from Irish and continental sources emphasise the importance of the enclosure as clearly defining the space within which monastic life was to be followed. Their prime purpose was to define the monastic precinct in which the regulations of the rule of discipline governing the spiritual life of the enclosed monastic community were observed. There has been a tendency in the past to view monastic enclosures as defensive structures but their defence role may have been largely limited to defining the boundary of sanctified and legally protected spiritual space in the landscape separated from the external secular world beyond the enclosure. The monastic enclosure — *the vallum monasterii* — is a recurrent feature in many of the lives of the Irish saints. The *Life of St Mochuda,* for instance, mentions the digging of the enclosure at Lismore (Plummer 1922, 299) and the enclosure at Clonmacnoise is mentioned in Adomnán's *Life of Columba* (Sharpe 1995).

It can be claimed that Benedict's instructions mentioned above can be seen to be carried out at Nendrum, where the church, the cemetery, the workshops, the well and other 'necessities', including the mill were within the enclosure.

Irish monastic enclosure plans

Swan has suggested Irish ecclesiastical enclosures range in size from 30–400m in diameter with a national average of between 90m and 120m (Swan 1983, 274). Thus Nendrum with an overall diameter of 190m north-south by 159m east-west lies well outside this

Table 12.1: The area of Nendrum and some other large Irish ecclesiastical enclosures

Site	Approximate overall area
Bright, Co Down	1.6ha
Nendrum	2.46ha
Fanobbus, Co. Cork (Hurley 1980, 59, 59, 1982, 314–317)	3.24ha
Kilmacoo, Co. Cork, (Hurley 1980, 61, 1982, 314–319)	4.05ha
Bawnatemple, Co. Cork (Hurley 1980, 53,1982, 318–320)	4.05ha
Duleek, County Louth, (Swan 1973, 13, 1973, 17, Clinton 2005, 155)	6.07ha
Iona, Argyll, Scotland (Sharpe 1995, 332)	8.08ha
Killeigh, Co. Offaly, (Hurley 1982, 323)	8.1ha
Armagh (Bradley 1998, 44)	11.4ha
Seirkieran, Co. Offaly, (Edwards 1990, 107, Murphy 2003, 20)	12ha
Clonmacnoise, (Murphy 2003, 22)	13ha
Monasterboice, Co. Louth, (Murphy 1993, 23, Murphy 2003)	24ha
Dromin, Co. Louth, (Murphy 1993, 23, Murphy 2003, 22)	28ha

average and can be considered in the larger category of ecclesiastical enclosures in the country. It is to be noted that it is on much the same scale as the important site of Whithorn, in Galloway (Hill 1997). However, comparison with the areas of some of the other ecclesiastical enclosures where details are known from published sources (table 12.1) show it to be considerably overshadowed in terms of size by many other sites.

Irish enclosure plans vary. Most are circular or oval but rectangular, sub-rectangular or curvilinear forms occur. The enclosing element can be formed by a bank and ditch or stone wall. Classified according to the number of enclosure elements, three main types seem evident: sites with a single enclosure, sites with double, roughly concentric enclosures and sites like Nendrum with three concentric enclosures.

The single enclosure

The single enclosure plan is the most common and the number of examples runs into large figures. Most of the small sites, some around 0.4ha (0.99 acres), are of this form but the examples also include some very large enclosures. The most consistent plan is that consisting of a circular or oval enclosure with a church site or cemetery placed approximately at the centre. At many sites internal divisions can be detected, some like Kiltiernan Co. Galway or Moyne, Co. Mayo (Norman and St Joseph 1969 102–105) subdivided by roughly radial banks or walls dividing the interior into a large number of smaller enclosures. Good examples have survived at many of the islands on the west coast of the country like Inishmurray, Co. Sligo, High Island, Co. Galway or Illauntannig Co. Kerry (Marshall and Rourke, 2000, 47, 128, 178, 179) and at sites like Reask, Co. Kerry (Fanning 1981, 71).

The double enclosure plan

The double enclosure plan is present at a large number of sites including some of the more historically important monasteries like Armagh, Cashel, Downpatrick, Glendalough, Kells, Kildare, Killala, Lorrha, Lusk, Monasterboice, Tuam (some plans conveniently given in Aitchison 1994) as well as at non-historically documented sites like Dundesert, Co. Antrim (Reeves 1847) and others. Further afield, a double enclosure system of oval form has been proposed for Whithorn, at least in the period around AD 700 (Hill 1997). A double enclosure is seemingly represented in the possible monastic plan in the *Book of Mulling* colophon (Nees 1983). A recurrent pattern at many double enclosure sites, both large and small, is the separation of the ritual area containing the church within the central enclosure.

The triple enclosure plan

Few other clear examples of the multiple boundary system, of which the triple enclosure plan at Nendrum is a splendid example, have been found. The most similar is Kilmacoo, near Kanturk in north Co. Cork (Norman and St. Joseph 1969, 66; Hurley 1980, 61–62, 1982, 314–319), which has, like Nendrum, three roughly concentric enclosures. The recent discovery of a hitherto unknown ecclesiastical site with a triple enclosure plan at Oldtown, Co. Dublin (Baker, 2004, 14–15) of similar size to Nendrum provides another clear example. Traces of three enclosures have been observed at Faughard, Co. Louth though the outer one is not concentric to the others (Norman and St Joseph 1969, 111, Murphy 2003, 23). The dearth of clear examples of the triple enclosure plan may be a result of poor survival as outer enclosures are much more prone to destruction and many may have been obliterated in the past by encroachment of cultivation. The more ritually important inner enclosure, the ritual core, with its church site and often having a continued use for burials tends to survive to a greater degree. Discovery of more examples of the triple enclosure plan are likely to emerge from further field surveys and excavation.

Symbolism of the triple enclosure plan

A multiple boundary system at ecclesiastical sites is outlined in the early 8th-century *Collectio Canonum Hibernensis* (Wasserschleben 1885). In this details are given on legislation pertaining to the *termini* (boundaries) around religious sites. These vary in number between two and four but three appears to be the implied norm, and defined spaces of increasing sanctity, *sanctus, sanctior* and *sanctissimus,* holy, holier and holiest, (Doherty 1982, 302, MacDonald 2001, 29, Aitchison 1994, 339). The presence of a strong symbolic or cosmic dimension to the ecclesiastical enclosure has been proposed by many commentators who would see in it a reflection of the biblical *'civitas refugii',* a city of refuge (Doherty 1982, 302, MacDonald 2001). The heavenly city in *Saltair na rann,* a text also probably heavily influenced by the account in Ezekiel, is described has having three walls (Carey 1986, 87).

Working from Adomnán's *Life of Columba,* MacDonald has interpreted the symbolic significance of the triple enclosure plan, and proposes the concept of a 'sacred' or 'spiritual triple-boundary' system in the layout of early monasteries and sees it as ultimately derived from the description of the ideal temple in Ezekiel. He suggests that Adomnán's perspective of a monastic layout envisaged that 'a system of progressively more sacred enclosures was usual around seventh-century monastic — perhaps more broadly ecclesiastical — sites' (MacDonald 2001, 29–30). In the discussion of the plan in reference to Iona, he envisages the outer enclosure there as the foreshore around the island. This defined the space where agricultural and domestic activities took place and, although it was a closely controlled zone, it was not an actively restricted area. The middle zone was defined by the enclosure boundary and was more strictly controlled. The central zone containing the church was a highly controlled space, with entry restricted to those of sufficient religious status.

What may be underlying Adomnán's concept, if MacDonald's interpretation is correct, and to a certain extent implicit in *Collectio Canonum Hibernensis* is the model of how a 7th-century monastery should be laid out. It can be claimed that the archaeology of Nendrum, perhaps much more than any other Irish Early Medieval monastery investigated so far, demonstrates the reality of this model of monastic planning.

Function of the triple enclosure plan: patterns of zoning

The excavated evidence from Nendrum and from other Irish monastic sites shows that 'the various crafts', referred to in Benedict's Rule and carried out within the monastic enclosure, were diverse in nature and impressive in their range and underline that Early Medieval monasteries whether Irish or European were complex institutions. These factors would have necessitated effective organisation of space incorporating the zoning of the different activities to differentiate the sacred dimension from the practical, social and economic ones. The adoption of a triple enclosure plan can be seen to be a highly efficient layout in a functional sense to fit Benedict's strictures on 'best practice', on how a monastery should be planned. Although the information on activities and structures within each enclosure is far from complete there is sufficient evidence to propose a zoning of activities in spatial planning with each of the three spaces being functionally different. Comparable in date (later 6th to 8th century) to much of the Nendrum evidence the zoning of activities within a D-shaped enclosure has been well demonstrated at the excavations of the Early Medieval monastery at Portmahomack, Tarbat Ness (Carver 2004) which also includes evidence of a horizontal-wheeled mill site in the form of a dam and a mill pond (Carver 2004, 19–21). It can be observed that at Nendrum the plan also makes sense topographically. The three concentric enclosures following the contours of the site and modified with some degree of terracing to provide much-needed level ground were best suited to the ridge-top setting of the monastery with relatively steep slopes on the east and west. Much has still to be learnt about the pattern of the internal organisation within the enclosure of Irish monasteries and future work at Nendrum has much to offer in this regard.

Dating of the triple enclosure plan at Nendrum

Excavation has demonstrated that the enclosure element may not have been static during the lifetime of a monastery and at some sites it underwent change. Banks and ditches once dug were abandoned or re-cut. The Whithorn excavations, for example, provide a good example of an ever-changing ecclesiastical site (Hill 1997). The lack of sound stratigraphic information from Lawlor's excavation precluded the making of meaningful observations on this score in relation to Nendrum. However, he interpreted that the middle enclosure wall was allowed at an early stage to go to ruin and was subsequently repaired at some time. It also seems evident that the original western entrance in the middle enclosure may have gone out of use at an early period. The dating of the enclosures at Nendrum is problematic and resolution of this problem should be a target for future research. Although Nendrum is a multi-period site, present dating evidence suggests that the enclosures are early in the development of the site if not a primary feature. Certainly there is no evidence at present to negate a possible, if not probable, early 7th-century date for the enclosure system. The construction of a large tide mill in AD 619 demonstrates that centralised organised planning capable of a large-scale building project existed at the monastery at that early date. It is possible, therefore, to speculate that the

Fig.12.24
Imaginative reconstruction of Nendrum viewed from the north-east (source EHS guide card, 1997)

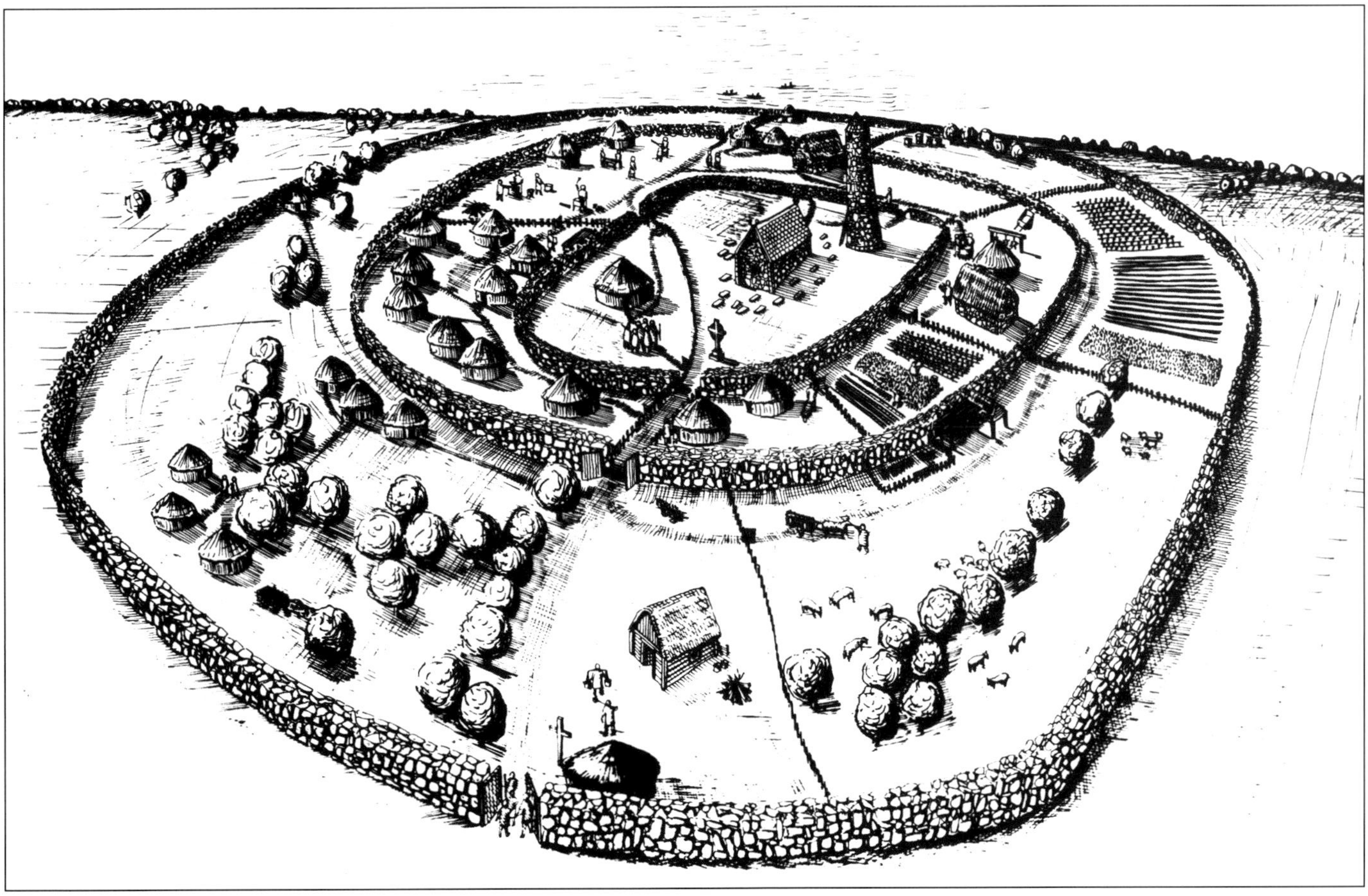

triple-enclosure plan was in existence then or was laid out at the same horizon following a contemporary monastic model of the organisation of space. The plan of the monastery may have become fossilised in its 7th-century form. Any subsequent development required only minor adjustments to the original plan.

Conclusion

In terms of size or of presently established archaeological information Nendrum cannot be considered a monastic town. There is no evidence there of the complexity of settlement and layout evidence with numerous churches, division into trians (thirds) or precincts as found at Armagh or Downpatrick and possibly present at its neighbours Bangor and Movilla in the 11th and 12th centuries. The term 'monastic village' suggested by Bradley for some of the smaller monastic settlements may be more appropriate. However, even this may be a misnomer for Nendrum, as it may never have developed a significant secular function as a settlement, unlike many other monasteries had by the 10th century, if not before.

Although much remains to be discovered at Nendrum, its outstanding feature is the relatively full picture it has provided, relative to other monastic excavations, to which the discovery of the mills has contributed a major component. There remain, however, many features known only from the documentary sources outlined by MacDonald (1984) and Hamlin (1985). These include the *Magna domus,* the *Platea,* communal buildings like the refectory, and others such as the abbot's house and guest house, which may reasonably be expected to have left traces and are still to be discovered. At least two composite imaginative reconstruction drawings roughly have been attempted (Hamlin and Hughes 1977, 46–47 and the EHS guide card 1997) and a large-scale model is on show in the visitors centre. These need updating in the light of the new discoveries.

READING THE NENDRUM 'RUNESTONE'?

G. Charles-Edwards UWB

In H.C. Lawlor's excavations a fragment of a slab was found with unusual angular letter-forms (Lawlor 1925a, 70 and plate 11); to interpret them Lawlor asked for the advice of the expert in the field of inscriptions, R.A.S. Macalister, who read what he supposed were 'runes' as 'of the chief abbot' in Old Norse. When Macalister had first seen an inscription in this style from the 1909 Toureen Peacaun excavation in Tipperary he felt a similar assurance that he was seeing Runic characters; in Professor Duignan's 1944 excavation at the same place yet another was found, on a small slab (Macalister 1949, 213; Waddell and Holland 1990, 165–86). In the 1949 Volume II of *Corpus Inscriptionum Insularum Celticarum,* Macalister included a notice of this new find and the east cross-shaft from Toureen Peacaun, Co. Tipperary (Macalister 1949, no. 924b; Lawlor 1925a, 70–1). At this stage he admitted in a footnote that he had at first taken the cross-shaft lettering to be an inscription in Runic, but had been corrected later by H.G. Leask, and convinced otherwise (Macalister 1949, 101). Nevertheless, the initial Macalister label of 'Runic' has been difficult to detach from the Nendrum inscription. John Higgitt was the first to suggest in print that it could be, in fact, what H.G. Leask had suggested, an inscription in a style of Insular geometric capitals (Higgitt 1994, 216). In 2001 Anne Hamlin made it quite clear that the Runic theory was doubtful, and closed her comments with: 'It would be interesting to know if any epigrapher would be prepared to attempt a reading of this puzzling stone.' (Hamlin 2001, 56–7)

Only a fragment of the original slab was recovered (see Figs 12.25, A,B,C). This is roughly triangular and measures *c.* 43cm high by 30cm wide and approximately 3cm thick and is of the local shale/greywacke. Lawlor estimated an original width of *c.* 68cm but this may be an under estimation and it may have been up to *c.* 90cm wide. It is not possible to estimate its original length. In spite of the fact that a considerable portion is missing it is obvious that when complete it would have been a very large slab and indeed a major monument. The surviving expertly designed decoration consists of a small segment of a circular frame defined by three groves apparently cut or rather abraded with mechanical aids enclosing a design composed of arcs, probably part of a 'cross of arcs' pattern. Crosses of arcs are found in Insular manuscripts and stone carving from the early-to-mid-sixth century (Milan Bibliotheca Ambrosiana MS D.23 sup. f.1v; Henry 1965, pl.14; Nash-Williams 1950, no. 388; Allen and Anderson 1903, 496). Below this are two incomplete lines of lettering, previously taken by Macalister as being Runic. It can be seen that the last character in the topmost line is indeed 'rune-like'. But there is an alternative explanation for the apparent 'rune'. The line may be read, in Insular display capitals, as PRIM[um]OPUS I[nter]; on the lower line may be SACR, employing the S-form that consists of a vertical and two short horizontals (Higgitt 1994, 214). The symbol of a downstroke, crossed from right to left by a downwards diagonal, represents the Celtic scribal abbreviation for inter (Dumville 2004, 3, 14, 18, 21). The rune for N consists of a downstroke with a diagonal crossing downwards from left to right. Hence they look very similar, except that the diagonal stroke is different. Rather than constructing a theory that involves Viking or Anglo-Saxon craftsmen appearing at Nendrum in the second half of the eighth century and creating a major monument, decorated with a cross-of-arcs pattern previously associated with the native population on both sides of the northern Irish Sea, (Hamlin 2001, 60, pl.23; Craig 1997, 439, no.16), this article discusses an alternative explanation. Nendrum's connection with foundations facing it across the Irish Sea in Galloway and on the Isle of Man have been discussed by Professor Bowen. Fiona Edmunds has recently completed a re-examination of these ecclesiastical links (Bowen 1969, 191–6; Edmunds *forthcoming*).

Figs 12.25 A,B,C
The geometric display-lettered inscription (formerly 'the runestone') from Nendrum (Courtesy of Down County Museum, photograph, A, Down County Museum, B and C, Dr Betty O'Brien)

Geometric lettering in Insular epigraphy: why it might be used for a grand 'opus'

Fig. 12.26
The Cummene and Ladcen inscription from Toureen Peacaun (after Okasha and Forsyth 2001, Toureen Peacaun no. 16)

H.G. Leask persuaded Macalister that the angular style of the Toureen East Cross lettering was that of: 'the decorative form of Roman capitals which we may see on the cup commonly called the Ardagh chalice, or in the opening pages of the Lindisfarne Gospels', cut in stone (Macalister 1949, 101). Indeed, the third example in this style mentioned above, excavated by Duignan in 1944 (Wadell and Holland 1990, 165–86), demonstrates, beyond a shadow of doubt, that the 'rune-like' angular characters are the display capitals employed by 8th-century Insular scribes to accompany high-grade half-uncial pen letters (Okasha and Forsyth 2001, Toureen Peacaun no.16; see also nos 8, 22, 37, 39). Here we see the name CUMMENE in display capitals above another name, in half-uncial, LADCEN (Fig. 12.26). The same contrasting of angular capital forms with curvilinear half-uncial occurs in the East Cross inscription where the Latin is above and the Irish below.

A further critical issue is whether, in using these display letters, scribes copied the style of lettercutters, or lettercutters copied the style of scribes: Nash-Williams thought that lettercutters were emulating scribes (Nash-Williams 1950, 12–13), but Julian Brown believed that the angular display letters betrayed origins in cut letters on stone or wood (Brown 1956–60, 75). The dazzling quality of late 7th- and 8th-century Insular manuscript examples has tended to obscure the existence of protoforms of the geometric alphabet cut in stone as early as the late 6th century (Charles-Edwards 2002a, 114–126). The failure to recognise angular epigraphic lettering, particularly of Early Christian Monuments of Wales (Nash-Williams 1950), as a specific alphabetic subsection in the Group I mixed-alphabet period of *c.* 400–600, has over-simplified both epigraphic and palaeographic analysis of Insular monuments and manuscripts (Charles-Edwards 2002b, 27–45). The fact that the earlier monuments, simply inscribed, are aesthetically unquantifiable to the modern eye has contributed to their neglect, so that Nash-Williams' major classification of the Welsh monuments (Nash-Williams 1950), using the high-grade manuscripts of an 8th-century scriptorium as comparanda for the plainer cut letters of the monuments of Group I and transitional Group II, has remained undisturbed until recently.

Carlo Tedeschi, a pupil of Petrucci, began a serious revision of the relationship between cut letters on stone, and written letters on animal skins (Tedeschi 2001, 16–25; 2005, 43–63). On account of the loss of manuscripts, it has always been acknowledged that our Insular epigraphic evidence predates our earliest surviving palaeographic material; our revised conception of how epigraphic forms evolved suggests that they were not necessarily dependent on the book arts of a scriptorium. Contemporary with Nash-Williams Group I, three inscriptions from

Fig. 12.27
Schematic diagram of angularised minuscules from Welsh Ogham/Latin inscriptions (pre. 600 AD) (drawing G. Charles-Edwards)

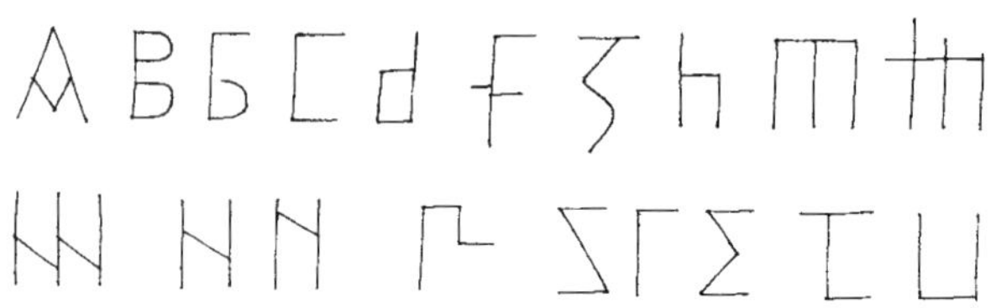

Kirkmadrine, all with a circular rim and a Latin cross with open-rho, show in themselves the evolution towards angular display capitals (Macalister 1949, nos 516, 517, 518; Thomas 1992, 3–13). In them we see the boxed ET ligature that will appear later as a decorative ampersand in the Book of Kells; these squared pairings of ET, LI, and FI are cloned from the common epigraphic versions of FILI seen in ECMW Group I. Crudely as these angular letters were cut, there is a discernible continuum in their evolution; the Nendrum inscription sits firmly in it. Within Group I of Early Christian Monuments of Wales (ECMW, Nash-Williams 1950), in the mixed-alphabet inscriptions, we find almost the entire alphabet reduced to simplified angular form (Fig. 12.27). Nash-Williams was the first to define those Group I debased capital inscriptions in which some letters were displaced by minuscules as 'mixed-alphabet' (Nash-Williams 1950, 12).

Moving into ECMW Group II, in the Catamanus inscription from Anglesey of *c.* AD 625, (Nash-Williams 1950, no. 13) we find a lettercutter who uses a grander display form of lettering in his opening title, but who downsizes to a minuscule form for the concluding section. Notice particularly the Greek-style three-bar A, and the two forms of M: three-bar display above and angular minuscule below (Fig. 12.28). As far as it is possible to judge from survivors, apart from the three-bar A used in the Cathach, in its titling style the Catamanus inscription has no connection with the manuscript practice of the time. On the Llanlleonfel, Breconshire, inscription of the second half of the 7th century (Nash-Williams 1950, no. 62; Thomas 1999, 7–9), we find strongly angularised minuscules, (Fig. 12.29A) massed in a close pattern.

Fig. 12.28
The Catamanus inscription from Anglesey (after ECMW, Nash-Williams 1950, no.13)

Fig. 12.29A
The Llanlleonfel, Breconshire, inscription (after ECMW, Nash-Williams 1950, no. 62)

Fig. 12.29B
The Caldey Island, Pembrokeshire, inscription (after ECMW. Nash-Williams 1950 no. 301)

Fig. 12.30
Diagram showing the use of four-line and two-line display letters. A, a two line layout, and B, a four line-layout (G. Charles-Edwards)

Geometric capitals do not appear in manuscripts until the late 7th century: when they do appear they use upgraded minuscules, lined up in combination with capital letters, in the same two-line system as used by the earlier inscriptions (Fig. 12.30).

This would accord with Julian Brown's theory above that the manuscript display letters are modelled on earlier epigraphic forms (Brown 1956–60, 75). On the other hand, by the early 9th century we find inscriptions, like the one from Caldey Island, Pembrokeshire, (Fig. 12.29B, Nash-Williams 1950 no. 301) that are clearly versions in stone of the massed geometric capitals of the 8th-century Gospel books. The fragmentary inscription to Saturnbiu, found on Ramsey Island (Fig. 12.31), off the Pembrokeshire coast in 1967, is of a type closely related to the Nendrum inscription, which possibly uses the same rare angular form of S and seemingly is scored in the same manner of execution (Okasha 1970, 68–70).

Fig. 12.32
Enlarged detail of the Nendrum inscription, showing bored line-ends (photograph copyright Ulster Museum)

Fig. 12.31
The Saturnbiu inscription from Ramsey Island, Pembrokeshire, (G. Charles-Edwards drawing from a rubbing in the National Museum Wales)

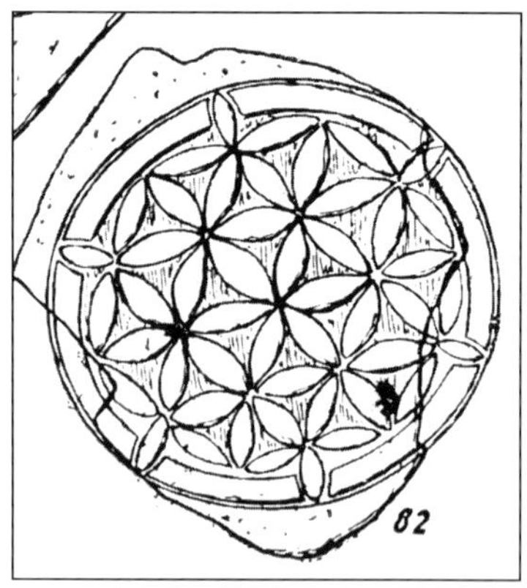

Fig. 12.33
An incised multiple hexafoil device from Clonmacnoise (Macalister 1909, plate XI, no 82)

The Nendrum 'runestone' does, then, have – as it were – a kindred of related inscriptions, and its style of lettering, peculiar to a certain time, is deliberately chosen for a grand memorial. In its manner of cutting, the inscription has more in common with some Breton examples in light angular letters that are scored in a friable slate, with bored line-ends (Fig. 12.32) to guard against any accidental elongation of the down-strokes (Davies *et al* 2000, 258–66). The manner of cutting or scoring of the elaborate design on the Nendrum fragments, to which the lettering appears as a form of caption, is tightly controlled, with the use of a compass-like instrument to score the triple band that bounds the design. If the suggestion that there was a multiple pattern of hexafoils is correct, Macalister noted a design at Clonmacnoise (fig. 12.33) that may be related (Macalister 1909, 81–2).

The design and language of the opus

An attempt to reconstruct the design, by extending the arcs present on the fragments, produced an inconclusive result; it may have had an equal-armed cross on a ground of hexafoils, the line ends being bifurcated (Fig. 12.34). It certainly appears to be a variation on the cross-of-arcs, quatrefoil or hexafoil and may be of a cross-type, known from the Isle of Man and Clonmacnoise, having a multiple hexafoil as an overall ground (Kermode 1907, 111; Macalister 1909, no. 82 see above). This is made more likely since the style of lettering, use of elaborate language and a design utilising hexafoil arcs within a triple rim, link the Nendrum example to a memorial to a pre-Viking Bishop of Man at Maughold (Kermode 1907, 112).

Fig. 12.34 An attempted reconstruction of the Nendrum design of lentoid arcs (G. Charles-Edwards)

Insular cross-of-arcs designs are found on early stones in the Western Isles, at Whithorn and Kirkmadrine in Galloway, in Wales, in Ireland, and on the Isle of Man (Fisher 2001, 12, 169; Trench-Jellicoe 1998, 495–513). If it can be shown that the Nendrum fragments employ the rarer hexafoil design then there may be a link with the inscription from Maughold. Here we find a similar scored triple rim, containing a sharply defined hexafoil design. It is much smaller than the Nendrum slab, and its less accomplished lettering is set vertically in relation to the design, rather than horizontally. However, its phraseology is grander than the execution of its letterforms, which is of a similar geometric style, but uses more minuscule forms. At Nendrum we have capital A (Uncial), P and R (Roman) whereas the Maughold inscription uses squared minuscule a, d, r and p.

When Insular craftsmen created a memorial they might use elaborate, formulaic Latin to record the fact that they executed their work as a tribute, or offering, to God or Christ. We find expressions like 'in honore' (Okasha 1971, no. 29), 'in commemoratione' (Allen and Anderson 1903, no. 10), or 'in nomine dei' (Nash-Williams 1950, no. 223) in these dedicatory inscriptions, with the cross or slab referred to as signum (Okasha 1971, no. 21), imagenem [sic] (Kermode 1907, no. 27) and opus (Okasha 1971, no. 68). In the Nendrum slab the use of the expression prim[um] opus may be a reflection of the Irish use of the word prím with the sense of 'chief' or 'most important'; such hybridising might be compared to the bi-alphabetic inscription on the East Cross at Toureen Peacaun where a mixed Latin/Irish inscription uses half-uncial for the Irish and geometric capitals for the Latin. In other words the monument, as a work, exemplified the highest quality and complexity of which the craftsman was capable.

Interchange between scriptorium and workshop

As we have seen, at the beginning of the 7th century, although lettercutters showed no interest in replicating high-grade scribal half-uncial, they do, however, use non-scribal display letters and heightened language showing knowledge of florid Latin vocabulary. A grandly expressed epitaph such as that for Catamanus/Cadwallon (Nash-Williams 1950, no. 13) King of Gwynedd, was obviously designed in an acceptable manner thought appropriate to that language and to his status. It raises questions about the written literacy of the patron of the work. Whatever model was in mind, it was not that of a high-quality Gospel book. Nash-Williams' contention that high-grade scribes had a hand in the laying out of such inscriptions on the stone, as the model for the lettercutter to follow, is not demonstrable during the period of his Group I, or the period shading into Group II. But at some point in Group II, *c*. AD 600–800, we begin to see the use of manuscript terminology, contractions and ligatures in inscriptions. It may be a coincidence that it was also about this time, the late 7th century, that scribes begin to adapt geometric letters for use as display capitals. If this interchange arose from a newly established closeness between workshop and scriptorium, it might be that major monastic houses had so grown in size that they had come to include a settlement of lay craftsmen dependent on the monastery, who interacted with the existing personnel of the scriptorium (Edwards 2001, 33–38).

It is rare to find an inflected scribal half-uncial rendered on stone; especially in Wales, lettercutters continued to use a minimalist uninflected monoline for their letterforms. When we see an Insular symbol that represents an abbreviated word, as we do in the Nendrum inscription, it tells us that it comes from the period of Irish, and presumably Welsh, pocket book production that used many such symbols, as well as angular display capitals such as we see in the Book of Dimma (TCD MS 59). On the mixed-alphabet Llanwnnws inscription, in Cardiganshire (Nash-Williams 1950, no. 125), for example, we find the abbreviation of q with a suprascript i for qui, h with a suprascript dot for hoc and no with a suprascript bar for nomen. Although the layout is four-line, with provision of space for ascenders and descenders, some of the letterforms are squared minuscule: h, u and, critically, a. Its simplified 'half-uncial' is much less grand in style than a geometric capital inscription like the Toureen or Nendrum examples which employ the geometric display capitals. These letters must have been, in comparison, an arcane alphabet used by an educated elite practising high-grade book arts. We might expect that it was only to be found at the grandest of monastic establishments.

The dating of the Nendrum inscription

If we associate geometric display letterforms with the highest book arts of the 8th century, we must do so in the knowledge that, for a much longer period, such angular letterforms were used by lettercutters before scribes utilised their sharply architectural forms to contrast with the full curves of the Phase II half-uncial hand. For about a century there may have been a period of overlap between epigraphic and calligraphic practice, when we see a range of scribal knowledge shown in cut lettering: there might be inscriptions with an overall scribal 'half uncial cast' but including angularised minuscules like the Llanwnnws inscription above; more tightly organised and angular layouts like those of Llanlleonfel and Caldey, and most ambitious, the strongly banded style of the Toureen Peacaun East Cross and the Tarbat inscription from north east Scotland (Higgitt 1982, 300–321).

But by the end of the 9th century scribes had allowed the geometric capital form to become decadent, and angular letters fall out of favour. Increasingly, as is clear from the great sequence of stones at Clonmacnoise, lettercutters were able to render, well-spaced, the calligraphic forms of pen lettering on stone (Petrie 1872; Macalister 1909 and 1949). The geometric capital, with its tight massing of forms, goes out of fashion. It is last seen, used competently, in Welsh inscriptions in mixed-alphabet compositions like that on Eliseg's pillar at Valle Crucis Abbey in Denbighshire, from the first half of the 9th century, in perhaps a deliberate antiquarian attempt to compose an inscription in 'old style' (Nash-Williams 1950, no. 182). When we see an inscription composed entirely in a homogeneous geometric alphabet, with elaborate Latin and signs of scribal knowledge, as for example we see at Toureen Peacaun and probably at Nendrum in the misnamed 'rune-stone', it should date from a period when the alphabet was a live tradition, of use and interest to lettercutters and scribes alike.

Acknowledgements

I would like to thank Cormac Bourke and Katherine Forsyth for encouraging me to attempt an account of the Nendrum inscription and commenting on an early draft; Betty O'Brien for hospitality, transport to Downpatrick Museum and the digital photography of the fragments, from which I attempted to reconstruct the design; and Mike King and the staff of the Downpatrick Museum for their helpfulness and enthusiasm. I have benefited greatly from discussions with my present supervisor Nancy Edwards and my past supervisor John Higgitt.

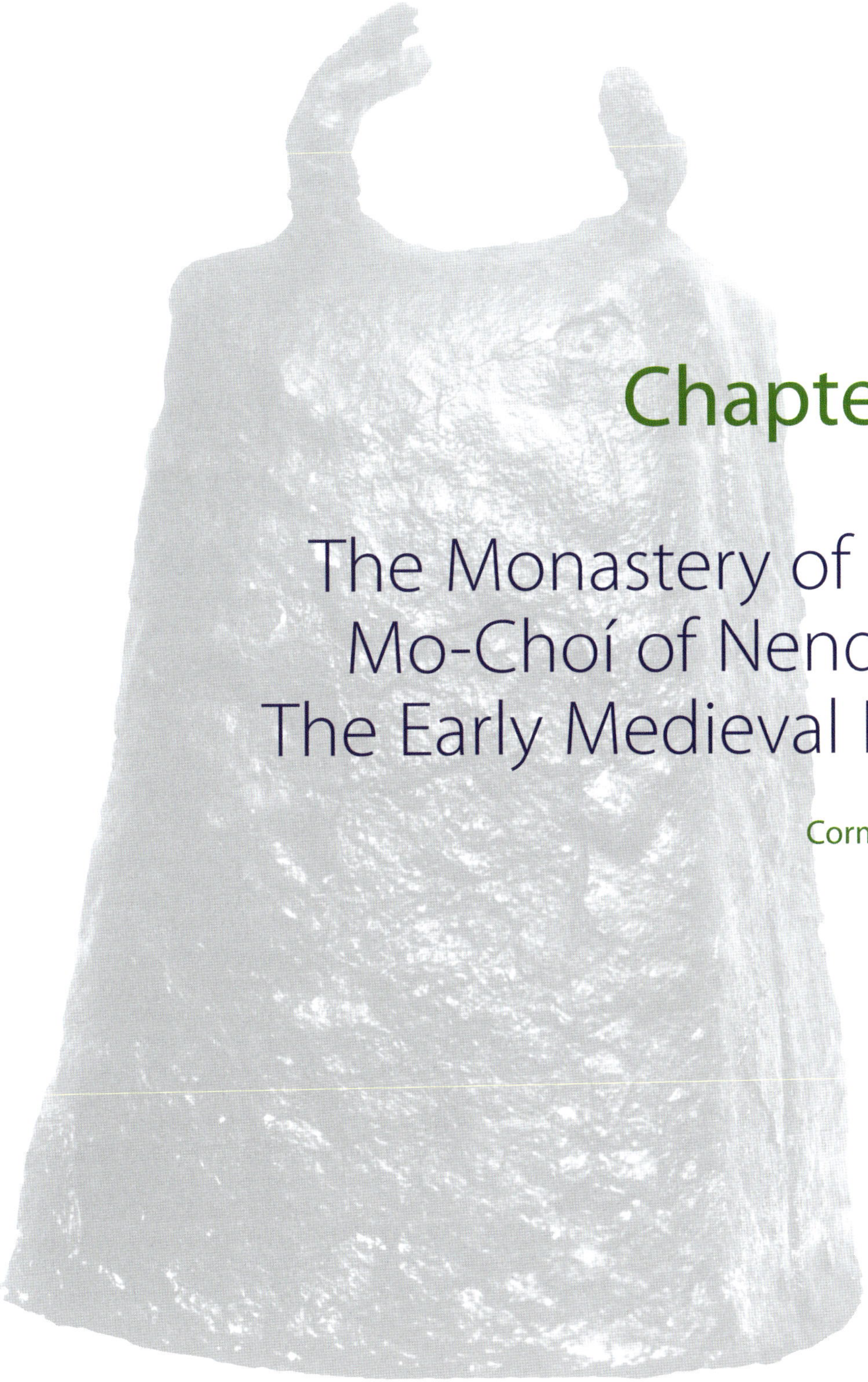

Chapter 13

The Monastery of Saint Mo-Choí of Nendrum: The Early Medieval Finds

Cormac Bourke

Chapter 13
The Monastery of Saint Mo-Choí of Nendrum: The Early Medieval Finds*

Cormac Bourke

For Nendrum, as for Ireland, one might enumerate lost treasures. The gospel-book and *meinistir,* perhaps a reliquary,[1] bestowed by Patrick on Mo-Choí belong to hagiographical convention but represent realities, and the *Etech* or 'winged' staff of Mo-Choí, although heaven-sent, might have had mundane existence.[2] Neither need the wooden *cretair,* 'shrine', of Mo-Choí mentioned in the *Martyrology of Donegal* be wholly fictional.[3] We cannot doubt the existence of material accessories to the cult of the founder, even if all trace of them is lost. Nor can we doubt, given resources sufficient to build mills and a round tower, that books, fine metalwork and free-standing crosses once existed. Lawlor expressed his regret that

> Of relics of intrinsic value, such as chalices, flagons, vessels of bronze or even iron, ornaments of gold or silver, nothing whatever was found.[4]

Fig. 13.1
Polished stone axe-head; quoit-shaped amber bead; bone plaque

But archaeology deals with the tangible, and the Nendrum assemblage is worthy of a detailed reassessment to which this short chapter might be preliminary.

The institution manifested in the standing remains and material culture of Nendrum is monastic, given the record of the deaths of four abbots (interspersed with those of bishops) between AD 684 and 919,[5] and the tradition of Mo-Choí as a monastic founder, even if in episcopal orders.[6] A 9th-century litany mentions 'nine times fifty monks under the yoke of Mochoe of Noendruim'.[7] The personnel and/or the wider community of Nendrum are revealed in their physical remains,[8] although none of the many burials is dated and the site was a Christian cemetery for perhaps a thousand years. Lawlor referred to burials of men, women and children, some in ordered rows, others disarticulated within at least partially stone-built graves, others disarticulated under mounds.[9] One was associated with a polished stone axe-head of prehistoric date,[10] a second with what Lawlor called 'a small pierced and polished stone', in fact a quoit-shaped amber bead,[11] a third with a pierced bone plaque with dot-and-circle ornament (Fig. 13.1).[12] Taken at face value, this is rare evidence for the inclusion of minor personal possessions in Early

Medieval graves.[13] One of the Nendrum skulls had been trepanned and another showed a sword or axe cut.[14]

Fig. 13.2
Iron tongs; copper-alloy ingot; copper-alloy waste

The monastery would have sustained practitioners in both generalised and specialised fields. Adomnán mentions scribes, blacksmiths and (by implication) boat-builders on Iona,[15] while the presence of wood-turners and of leather-, glass- and bronze-workers is archaeologically attested.[16] Nendrum, another island monastery, must have had such personnel, as well as stonemasons; many projects were interdisciplinary and there is archaeological evidence in some cases. Boat-builders were carpenters and thus potentially, *inter alia,* house- and mill-builders and makers of the floors in the round tower, of its internal ladders and of the external timber staging by which its door was reached. Boats of the currach class called for carpentry and tanned hides, but also for sail-cloth and ropes. Leather products also included footware, belts, bags and vellum for scribal use,[17] while working clothes and liturgical vestments were further products of the textile industry.[18] The use of wax tablets for ephemeral jottings is a likelihood, and bee-keeping is accordingly inferred. Tools themselves tend to mix media, if only in having iron and wooden parts.

Fig. 13.3A
Ceramic crucible in stone stand

Iron and copper alloy are the only metals certainly represented in the Early Medieval assemblage, although the separate use of gold, silver, tin and lead is a probability. Evidence for in-house metalworking, derived in the main from the 'hut circles' inside the middle enclosure wall,[19] includes 'lumps of iron slag' and what Lawlor inaccurately termed 'a large cube of pig iron',[20] a disc-shaped copper-alloy ingot[21] and 'innumerable little nodules of bronze, droppings from the crucibles' (Fig. 13.2),[22] as well as crucibles and stone crucible stands (Figs 13.3A and B).[23] The crucibles, with visible copper-alloy residues, are typical of the Early Middle Ages in form and size, being triangular at the mouth or, less commonly, oval with pinched handles.[24] A pair of iron tongs (Fig. 13.2) was both the product and the adjunct of metalworking.[25] A small clay mould is said to have had a matrix for a glass or metal stud.[26]

Fig. 13.3B
Ceramic crucible in stone stand

A series of copper-alloy brooches includes what appears to be the earliest metal object in the whole assemblage (Fig. 13.4).[27] Of diminutive if not miniature proportions, the brooch lacks its pin and has no exact parallel, but the form and profile of the terminals recall the zoomorphic penannular brooches of Kilbride-Jones' Group D, a late 6th-century type.[28] A second small penannular (Fig. 13.5) has cusped, disc-shaped terminals,[29] a form represented by moulds from 7th-century contexts at both Dunadd, Argyll,[30] and Mote of Mark, Kirkcudbright,[31] although 8th- or 9th-century versions include brooches from Ervey, Co. Meath,[32] and Smulan, Nord-Trøndelag.[33] The terminals of the

Fig. 13.4
Copper-alloy penannular brooch (lacking pin)

Nendrum brooch bear reversed S motifs which, it seems, were originally reserved in enamel and a 7th- or 8th-century date is arguable. A third, pseudo-penannular, brooch (Figs 13.6A and B) is probably of the 9th century.[34] Squared terminals with round cells and traces of marginal decoration, together with a round-sectioned hoop, suggest an affinity with more elaborate pseudo-penannular brooches such as that from Lough Ravel, Co. Antrim,[35] and the pair (made of silver) from Scattery Island, Co. Clare.[36] The in-house manufacture of brooches is suggested by a slate motif-piece,[37] one of a well-known series,[38] on which a sophisticated brooch and a related shape are sketched in outline (Fig. 13.7). The illustration of a (semi-) finished artefact is unusual, and motif-pieces typically bear patterns which are realised in two dimensions as surface ornament. The only analogy is a motif-piece from Dunadd which also shows a brooch in outline.[39]

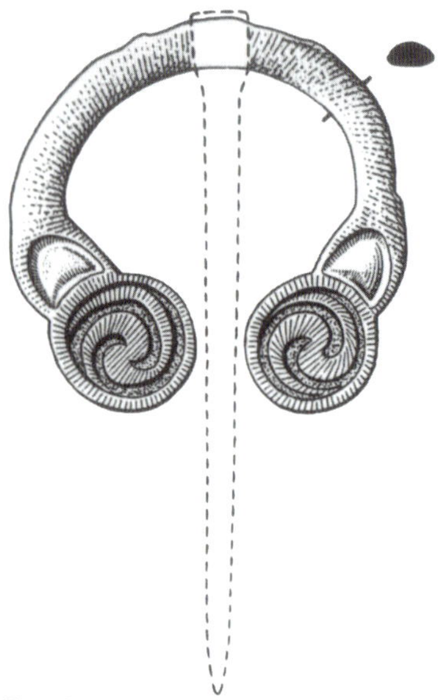

Fig. 13.5
Copper-alloy penannular brooch (lacking pin) (after ASCD 1966)

Fig. 13.6A
Copper-alloy pseudo-penannular brooch

Fig. 13.6B
Copper-alloy pseudo-penannular brooch

Fig. 13.7
Stone motif-piece with incised outline of pseudo-penannular brooch

The working-out, or trying-out, of interlace and other patterns at Nendrum is witnessed on several other stone motif-pieces which are likewise relevant to the production process (Fig. 13.8).[40] They derive, with two exceptions,[41] from the building which Lawlor termed the 'school' and are said to have been found '[o]n the floor'.[42] None qualifies as a master from which moulds might have been made and they are uniformly shallowly engraved, perhaps with the iron styli recovered in the same place, although one of these has a spatulate top suggestive of use with wax tablets (Fig. 13.9).[43]

Fig. 13.8 Stone motif-piece with incised knots

Fig. 13.9
Iron styli

A 'brooch-pin', in effect a ringed pin modelled on a brooch, is represented by a corroded fragment consisting of part of the ring and a round cell at the apex of one terminal (Fig. 13.10).[44] The cell contains decolourised enamel set with a square of blue and ostensibly yellow chequer-pattern millefiori. An important find, recognised by Phillips, but not by Lawlor, is a clay mould for a similar ring which, though formally appropriate to the 'brooch-pin' class, is more appropriate to a ringed pin in terms of scale (Fig. 13.11a).[45] Analogies, as Phillips pointed out, are provided by open

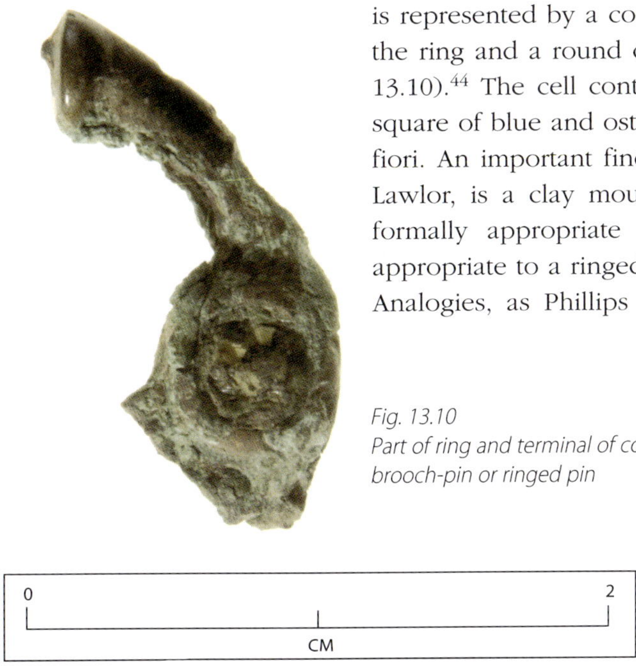

Fig. 13.10
Part of ring and terminal of copper-alloy brooch-pin or ringed pin

Fig. 13.11
Clay mould for ring of brooch-pin or ringed pin; a (dia. 2.4cm), with modern impression; b (after Phillips)

Fig. 13.12
Copper-alloy baluster-headed pin with incomplete spiral ring

moulds for glass studs such as those found at Lagore,[46] and the same site produced half of a two-piece mould for a cognate ring.[47] In use the Nendrum matrix must have been provided with an integral, free-standing 'core' to create the opening within the ring, and the loss of such an element appears to be in evidence. A lead model for a ring from Moylarg crannog, Co. Antrim, was probably used to impress a clay mould in which the final product was cast.[48] Such a model may be presupposed by the Nendrum mould. The 'brooch-pin' fragment, by contrast, is the product either of a two-piece mould or of a one-piece mould made on a wax original, as shown by the expansion of the ring on both faces at the point of breakage. Such dress-fasteners are taken to be of 8th- or 9th-century date.[49]

The manufacturing of pins is evidenced by the mould already mentioned and a series of ringed pins and stick pins, mainly of copper alloy, form part of the assemblage. The earliest is likely to be a baluster-headed spiral-ringed pin, a type current in the 7th and 8th centuries (Fig. 13.12);[50] a later type, of the 10th or 11th century, is a robust specimen with loose kidney ring (Fig. 13.13).[51] Phillips documented a clay mould for an oval ring,[52]

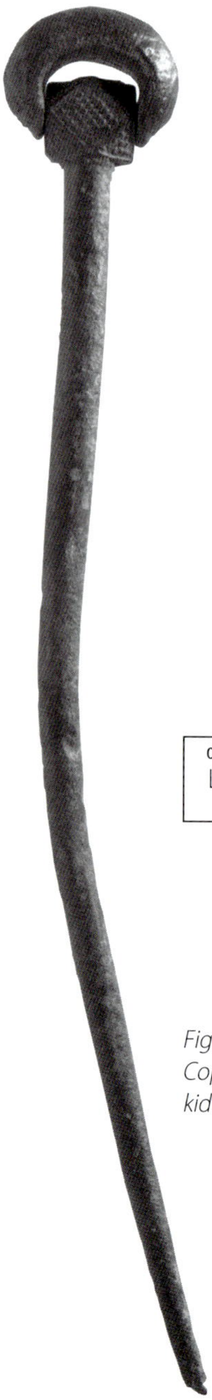

Fig. 13.14
Copper-alloy buckle frame

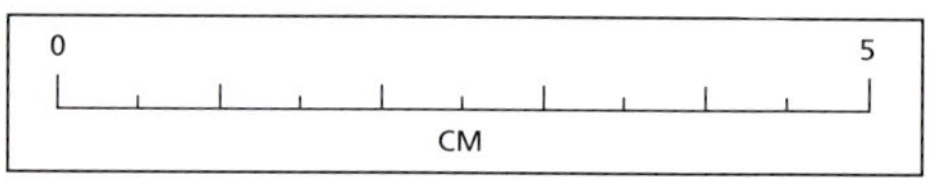

Fig. 13.13
Copper-alloy pin with kidney ring

Fig. 13.15
Incomplete ringed pins; a, b copper alloy; c iron

but the ring cited in comparison is a buckle frame which Lawlor associated in error with the shank of a pin (Fig. 13.14, 13.15b).[53] A third, probable, ringed pin lacks its ring and appears to have been loop-headed (Fig. 13.15a).[54] A fourth example is made of iron, a rare survivor of what must have been a numerous class; its looped head holds a fragment of the vanished ring (Fig. 13.15c).[55] Stick pins include one with non-functional kidney ring (Fig. 13.16b),[56] and two club-headed examples (Fig. 13.16a, d);[57] a fourth pin is undifferentiated (Fig. 13.16c)[58] and a fifth is perhaps box-headed (Fig. 13.17).[59] All four types saw varying periods of popularity from the 10th to the 13th century.[60] Three modified off-cuts of long bone may be pin-heads (Fig. 13.18),[61] although an identification as gaming pieces has recently been suggested.[62] All three are D-sectioned and smoothed as though from handling; a hole in the flat facet in two cases retains a vestigial iron insert. The type is best paralleled in the Orkneys at Burrian and, in an 8th- or 9th-century context, at Brough of Birsay, although some Irish finds are comparable.[63] Three bone pins (Fig. 13.19A and B) complete the tally.[64]

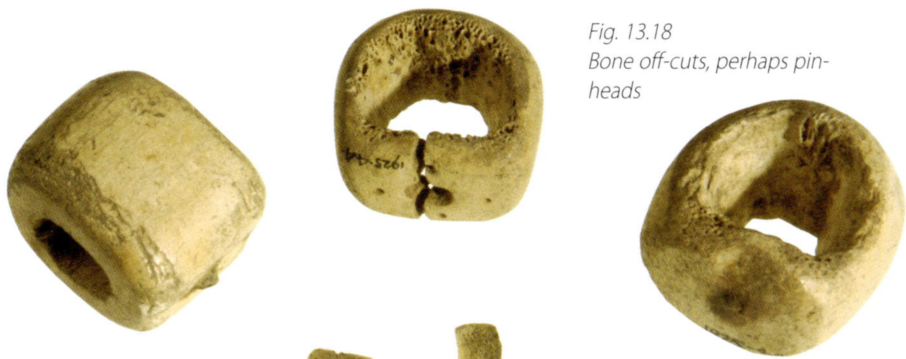

Fig. 13.18
Bone off-cuts, perhaps pin-heads

Fig. 13.16
a, b, c, d Copper-alloy stick pins

Fig. 13.17
Copper-alloy stick pin

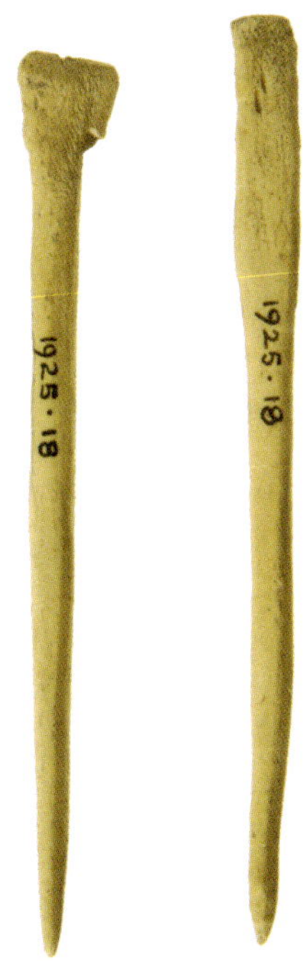

Fig. 13.19A
Bone pins

Fig. 13.19B
Bone pin

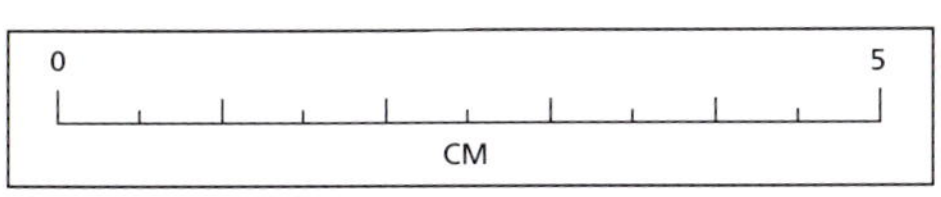

The term 'high-quality' legitimately attaches to a strap-end with an animal-head terminal (Fig. 13.20) which is less canine (as Lawlor argued) than calf-like, and reference to the symbol of St Luke may be intended.[65] Gospel-books would have had closing and carrying straps to which such a casting might have belonged, and there is an equal-armed cross on both faces. The animal head compares in its shape and plastic modelling with that on the 9th- or 10th-century Clonmacnoise kite brooch,[66] although comparison can also be made with the head on the primary (11th-century) suspension fitting of the *Soiscél Molaisse*.[67] The piece as a whole compares in outline and in some of its surface detail with a strap-end found recently not far from Nendrum at Strangford, Co. Down (Fig. 13.21).[68] The latter, exceptionally among strap-ends, has chip-carved ornament and shows two bird-like creatures which compare with the marginal animals on one of the Scattery Island brooches already referred to.[69] A 9th-century date therefore seems appropriate and the Nendrum piece could be contemporary. A further casting, a stud with a plain centre in a ring of interlace, has a pierced lug at the back and might have belonged to an 8th- or 9th-century tomb-shaped shrine (Fig. 13.22).[70]

Fig. 13.20
Copper-alloy strap-end

Pride of place in the catalogue of Nendrum metalwork goes to the iron hand-bell, despite its poor condition when found and subsequent deterioration (Figs 13.23 and 13.24).[71] Bells are the accessories *par excellence* of monastic regulation and the Nendrum example is typical of the iron series with copper-alloy coating; its date probably lies between the 7th and 10th centuries. Bells were used to mark the canonical hours and to call communities to assembly, and apotropaic bell-ringing on monastic boundaries is

Fig. 13.22
Copper-alloy
stud

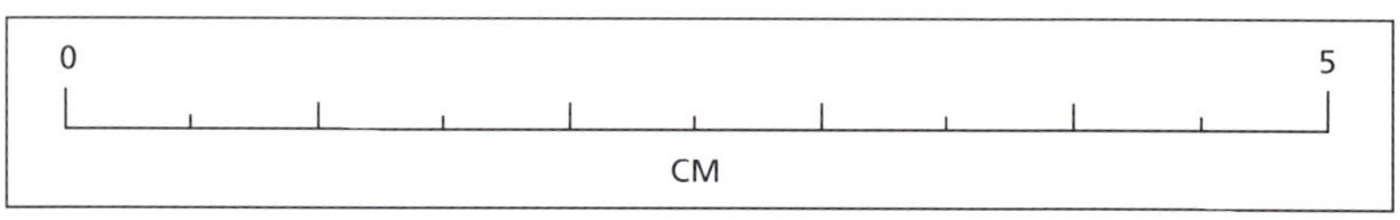

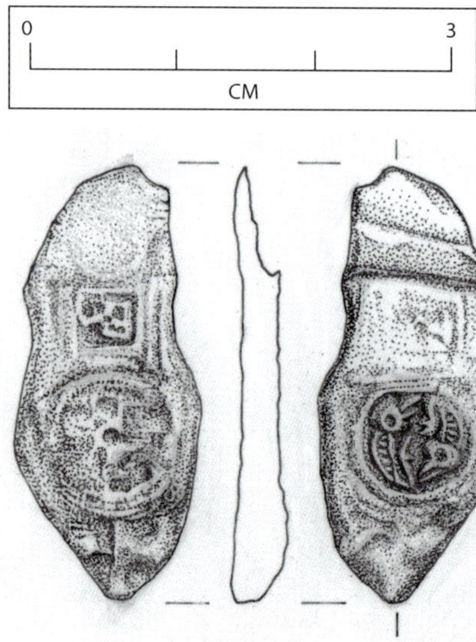

Fig. 13.21
Copper-alloy strap-end; Strangford, Co. Down

attested. The bell termed *Clog Timchill Arda Macha*, 'the bell of the circuit of Armagh', must owe its name to this practice.[72] The hagiographical association of bells with the cults of individuals has inflated their primary significance, but there is no reason to suppose that the Nendrum bell had achieved trophy status within the lifetime of the Early Medieval monastery, despite evidence for its careful concealment. As Lawlor reported, the bell was found on 17 May 1923[73] 'in the angle of two walls outside the north of the outer cashel'.[74] It was described as having been

> ... sunk about one-third of its height in the normal surface, ... the upper two thirds covered with stones fallen from the cashel, and vegetable soil which permeated this debris.[75]

Fig. 13.23
Iron hand-bell with copper-alloy coating (now lacking handle) (height c. 20cm)

Doubt has been expressed as to the antiquity of the walls to which Lawlor referred,[76] and the concealment of the bell (for whatever reason) might well have followed its accidental discovery during clearance or grave-digging in recent centuries.[77] The *corpus* of insular bells includes examples long preserved in the open at early church sites, as well as several found by chance in such places in the 18th and 19th centuries. The famous copper-alloy bell of Bangor was found 'in the ruins' of the abbey *c.* 1790.[78]

Lawlor reported of the Nendrum bell that

> The site where it was found was afterwards carefully turned over and riddled, with the result that a portion of the handle was found; a small section is still missing.[79]

Fig. 13.24
Iron hand-bell with copper-alloy coating, photographed by R J Welch in the 1920s

Lawlor's plate, here reproduced (Fig. 13.24), shows the partially reconstructed handle. While the handle is now wholly unaccounted for,[80] the issue is complicated by the existence in the Ulster Museum of the cross-piece of a handle, attributed to Nendrum, which is inappropriately big for the Nendrum bell and which cannot be identified with any of the reconstructed parts (Fig. 13.25).[81] Charles Thomas confirms (*pers. comm.*) that the cross-piece was not found in his excavation in 1954 and its history remains unknown. While it now appears that two bells are evidenced at Nendrum, it is not clear that there is any necessary connection between hand-bells and round towers, albeit that Nendrum is a site (one of the few) where the phenomena coincide. The suggestion that round towers accommodated bigger, suspended bells is unsupported,[82] given a lack of unambiguous documentary evidence and the fact that neither bells, moulds nor casting pits have yet been recognised.

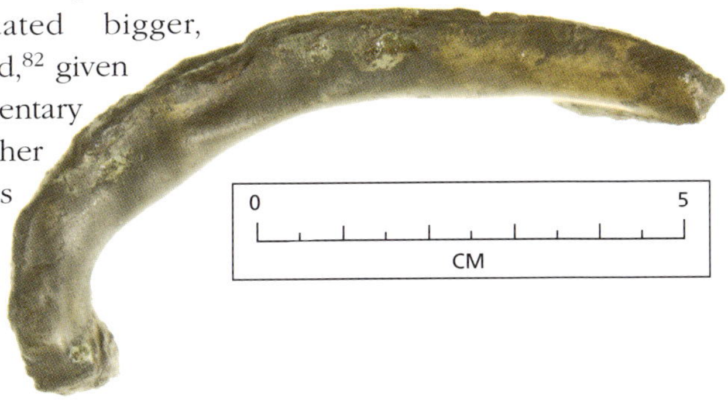

Fig. 13.25
Incomplete iron bell handle with copper-alloy coating

Fig. 13.26
Stone motif-piece with incised lettering (c 7.5 x 4cm)

The monastery, occupying an island site, was itself an island of literacy in a largely illiterate world. Its books are lost, but trainee scribes or students must have been responsible for a stone motif-piece bearing parts of the alphabet (Fig. 13.26),[83] and for some other pieces with rudimentary letters. The other testament to literacy is the inscription on a grave-slab,[84] which Macalister took to be runic[85] but which recent scholarship has shown to consist of Insular display capitals.[86] The world of letters is recalled by another exceptional slab bearing part of an incised footed cross with forked terminals (pps 356-357 and Fig. 12.12H). This has been compared with crosses in the 6th- or 7th-century manuscript psalter known as the *Cathach,* as well as with other equally early carvings.[87] A further series of uninscribed Nendrum slabs suggest a local preference for crosses of unringed form.

Fig. 13.27
Part of souterrain ware cooking pot

The art of the potter is manifested at Nendrum in crucibles and souterrain ware.[88] The former have already been described; the latter is a representative range of this everyday type and no distinction can be made between the Nendrum assemblage and the ware found on secular sites (Fig. 13.27). It might have been made by members of the community, by monastic tenants or by independent specialists.[89] But given the 'universal' nature of the clerical calling, and the tendency of monastic *paruchiae* to transcend political boundaries, it is noteworthy that souterrain ware is largely confined to north-eastern Ireland in both secular and ecclesiastical spheres. On the other hand, that the use of souterrain ware could be transmitted selectively by inter-church communication is illustrated strikingly by its appearance on Iona.[90]

As mentioned above, the Nendrum finds include two pins and three possible pin-heads of bone. The latter were part of a group of 16 bone or antler cylinders, of which 'several crumbled to pieces on exposure', reportedly found in association with a burial beneath the 'school'.[91] Eight cylinders, apart from the 'pin-heads', can now be accounted for and show varying degrees of modification (Fig. 13.28).[92] One, although unperforated, is D-sectioned like the pin-heads and one has an incised triquetra which is paralleled on a slate motif-piece (Fig. 13.8). Groups or sets of such cylinders are known from Dublin and Waterford, in the latter case mainly from late 11th- or early 12th-century contexts, although their function is a matter of speculation.[93] On the other hand, the Nendrum series can be compared equally validly with bone and antler beads, interpreted as components of a necklace, from an ostensibly late prehistoric context at St Ninian's Isle, Shetland.[94] Phillips suggested of the Nendrum pieces that they might be abacus beads.[95] Two further bone objects are a fragment of a double-sided comb (Fig. 13.29)[96] and a tubular handle, perhaps for a knife, bearing an incised bird head (Fig. 13.30).[97]

Fig. 13.28 Bone cylinders

Fig. 13.29
Part of tooth-plate from double-sided bone comb

A decorated bone plaque has already been mentioned, together with an amber bead, and two other beads form part of the assemblage. One is an incomplete annular bead of 'brownish ... dark glass with dark red streaks, with a white design marvered into it' (Fig. 13.31),[98] which compares with an example (though differently coloured) from a ringfort at Garryduff, Co. Cork.[99] The other is a segmented blue glass bead of a type familiar in Early Medieval contexts.[100] A dumbbell-shaped stone is perhaps a toggle (Fig. 13.32).[101] Another stone (Fig. 13.33), shaped to a rectangular section and perforated for suspen-

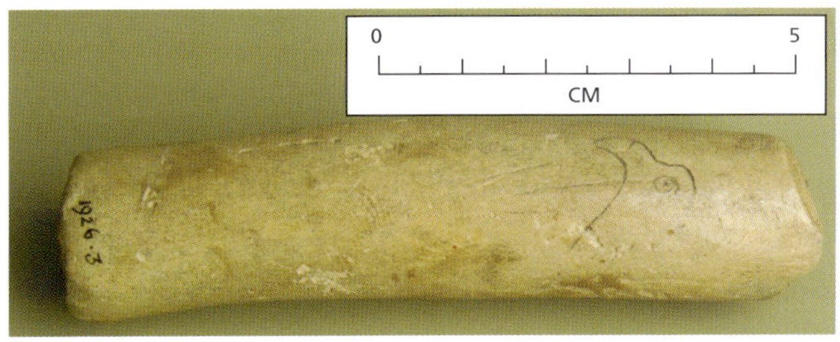

Fig. 13.30
Bone handle with incised bird head

Fig. 13.31
Incomplete glass bead (dia. 2.5cm) (after Phillips)

Fig. 13.32
Dumbbell-shaped stone toggle

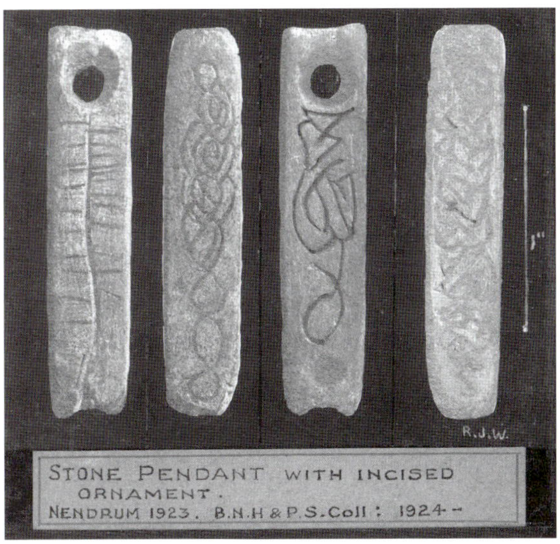

Fig. 13.33
Perforated stone with incised markings

Fig. 13.34
Part of rotary grindstone

sion at one end, was interpreted by Lawlor as a charm or fishing weight and by Phillips as '[p]erhaps a charm for personal adornment'.[102] It bears incised, but not necessarily ancient, markings.

The range of stone artefacts from Nendrum includes part of a rotary grindstone (Fig. 13.34)[103] and numerous hones[104] and querns.[105] The use of querns is surprising in view of the provision of tide mills, but there was probably no alternative after the 9th century when Mill 2 had ceased to be maintained. Cross-decorated slabs, already mentioned, are suggestive of a local school, probably of the 8th century,[106] and the reconstructed sundial is an accomplished carving (Fig. 12.15A-C). Its use (weather permitting) in conjunction with bell-ringing is to be envisaged; the 'horizontal' line and three main radii presumably indicate prime, terce, sext, none and vespers, five of the 'hours' of the octaval system to which at least some Irish churches adhered.[107] A 10th-century date is possible.[108] That free-standing high crosses once existed is very likely, and it is a matter of regret that the most probable location – immediately to the west of the church – has been thoroughly disturbed (see below). It is worth asking, in this regard, whether the name of nearby Cross Island might commemorate the former presence of such a monument marking one line of approach to Nendrum.

The chronology of the evidence calls for consideration, as does the extent of any Viking influence, even in the absence of meaningful stratification. Nothing suggestive of pre-monastic occupation has been recognised and the enclosure walls themselves remain undated.[109] One brooch belongs to the late 6th or, arguably, the early 7th century[110] and might be contemporary with the building of the first tide mill (Mill 1) in the years between AD 619 and 621, and the same can be said of the exceptional cross-decorated slab (p. 414). Occupation in the 8th and 9th centuries is indicated by, *inter alia,* the other brooches, the decorated stud, the strap-end, the motif-pieces and the inscription in Insular capitals, while activity, and presumably occupation, is witnessed for the 10th to 12th centuries by the kidney-ringed pin and stick pins.

The last reference to Nendrum in the annals records the death of the *airchinnech* or 'superior', Sétna ua Demáin, in a fire in AD 976,[111] and was taken by Lawlor to mark the end of monastic life as the result of a Viking raid.[112] But that Sétna was burned 'in his own house' – which Lawlor equated with the round tower – need imply no more than individual misadventure, and the silence of the annals is no proof of the demise of Nendrum.[113] Evidence for a conflagration was confined to the 'school', and burning evidenced elsewhere can be explained in terms of industrial processes and domestic occupation.[114] Nor can the round tower, which was surely non-residential, have been the *airchinnech*'s house. The tower could post-date AD 976 and was scarcely commissioned by a community in decline.

The extent of Viking influence, if any, is uncertain. Hamlin has recently referred to the strap-end, the 'runic' inscription, 'one trial-piece with a Viking-type design' and an iron axe-head as 'distinctively Viking material'.[115] But the first two, as we have seen, are of Insular character; it is not clear which motif-piece is referred to and the axe-head (Fig. 13.35), although of Viking ancestry, is probably Late Medieval.[116] However, a second iron axe-head (Fig. 13.36), discovered in the 1970s, is a rare type represented in Dublin in the 10th and 11th centuries and might have seen service at Nendrum in Viking hands.[117] But it might, equally, have been in general circulation, and the same can be said of a 'Norwegian silver coin of ... about the year 930' which it seems was not preserved.[118] Contrary to what Lawlor believed, monastic life probably continued throughout the 11th and 12th centuries, and de Courcy might have drafted his personnel into a still-functioning institution.

Fig. 13.35
Iron shaft-hole axe-head

A final question, imponderable for now, is the extent to which the whole of Mahee Island was a monastic precinct, given that the place-name preserves the name of the founder.[119] Iona, like Nendrum, has its enclosure, but the whole island partook of a sacral character; as Adomnán records, it was blessed in its entirety by Columba on the eve of his death.[120] Inishmurray likewise is sanctified in its entirety by a series of *leachta* which mark the stages of the pilgrimage round. That such evidence is lacking for Mahee Island should not blind us to the possibilities; Lawlor cited a reference from Primate Fleming's Register to the theft of cattle in 1410 'in a certain holy island in the County of Down', and Mahee might have been intended.[121] He speculated that a hollow near a well in the north-west of the island might

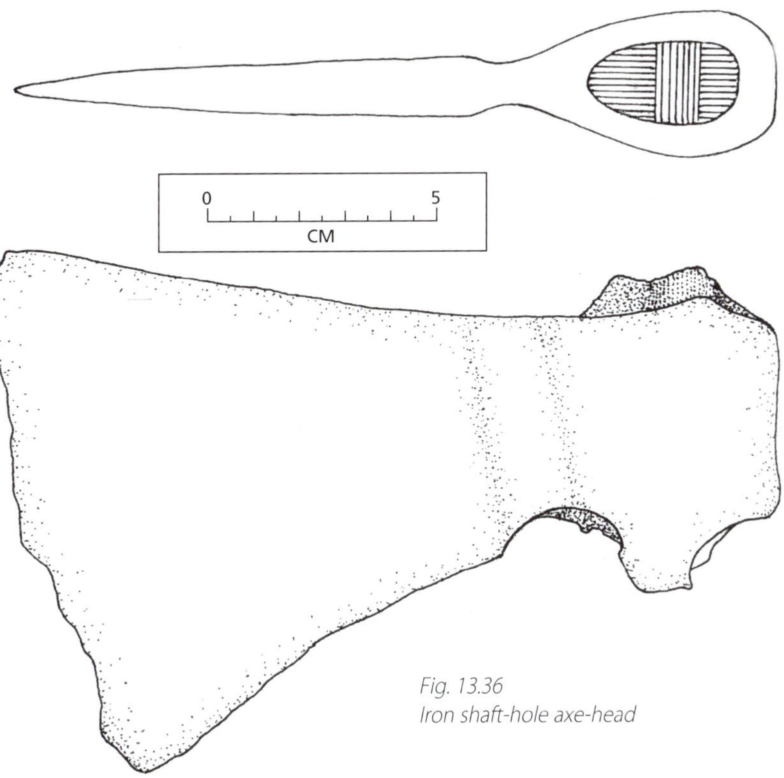

Fig. 13.36
Iron shaft-hole axe-head

have been a *díseart* or retreat dependent on the Early Medieval monastery.[122] He also recorded the discovery of human bones to the south of the landowner's house, suggesting that the Benedictine monastery lay in the vicinity.[123] A cross-decorated slab, lost even in Lawlor's day, had been recorded in a nearby 'fence', but need not necessarily have migrated from within the triple enclosure.[124] Tullynakill (*tulaigh na cille,* 'hill of the church'), on the adjacent mainland, which, as Reeves established, gave its name to the Late Medieval parish (in succession to Nendrum), was probably the site of 'some ancient sacred building' as Lawlor supposed.[125] This may well have been a satellite church of the Early Medieval monastery and is conceivably identifiable with that built, as the *Martyrology of Donegal* records, on the reputed site of Mo-Choí's miraculous sleep of 150 (or 300) years.[126]

But the greatest potential for the enlargement of our understanding lies inside the monastic enclosure. This assertion will perhaps surprise, given the widely held view, because of Lawlor's intervention, that the archaeology of Nendrum has been forever compromised. But such a view fails to take account of Lawlor's statement made in a preliminary report *à propos* of the same ground-plan which appeared in the final publication. Referring to its stippled shading, Lawlor remarked that 'the places excavated are marked with small dots'.[127] This is crucial, given that most of the plan is not stippled (see Fig. 12.5).[128] I conclude, optimistically, that much potential evidence remains.

Acknowledgements

I am grateful for their advice on specific points to Thomas McErlean, Tom McNeill, Paul Mullarkey, Norman Patton, Brian Scott, Lesley Simpson and Charles Thomas, and to Niamh Whitfield who commented on this chapter in draft.

* The basic sources are Lawlor 1922, 1923 and 1925a; the plates in the 1925 monograph are referred to here although first published with the 1923 paper. Reference will also be made to Phillips 1960, an unpublished BA thesis by Stephen Phillips submitted to Queen's University, Belfast. Phillips describes and illustrates several Nendrum pieces which are now unlocated, some of which, it seems (despite the explicit scope of his thesis), were found independently of Lawlor's excavation; Phillips' Plate 11 afterwards appeared as figure 80 in Jope 1966, for which publication it was doubtless prepared. The bulk of the material from Lawlor's excavation was accessioned by the then Belfast Museum and Art Gallery (now the Ulster Museum) in 1923, 1925 and 1926, but Lawlor specifies (1923, 79) that the landowner, A G Johnston, retained some material for exhibition in the Nendrum tea house, and Macalister was careful to note (in Lawlor 1925a, xi) that the excavator '*So far as possible* [my italics], with the generous co-operation of the proprietor, … has secured the preservation of the finds in a public museum' (see also Blakiston Houston 1925, 12). Charles Thomas (*pers. comm.*) recalls seeing original material in the Nendrum tea house in the 1950s, and Waterman, in a paper published in 1959, referred to 'a small collection [of Nendrum finds] in the club-house of the Island Mahee golf club' (1958, 67, note 2). Some, at least, of this material must equate with the then unregistered finds which Phillips documented in the Ulster Museum in 1960, although no record of their receipt has been found. The cross-decorated slabs discovered in the course of Lawlor's excavation are a separate case, being at first set in the internal face of the reconstructed church gable but transferred to the Nendrum exhibition centre in the 1980s.

[1] DIL 1983, s.v. *meinistir;* Ó Floinn 1990, 54.

[2] All three are referred to in the 10th-century *Tripartite Life* of Patrick (Stokes 1887, 40–41).

[3] O'Donovan J.H. Todd J.H. and Reeves, W. (eds and trans.) (1864) *The Martyrology of Donegal, a Calendar of the Saints of Ireland*. Dublin (Irish Archaeological and Celtic Society).

[4] Lawlor 1925a, 156.

[5] Gwynn and Hadcock 1970, 42; see Etchingham this volume.

[6] Ryan 1931, 103–4.

[7] Plummer 1925, 66–67; Hamlin has suggested (1997, 54) that Nendrum 'may have been a complex settlement, the seat of a bishop as well as housing a community of monks ruled by an abbot'.

[8] These are now largely unavailable for examination; see Murphy this volume.

[9] Lawlor 1925a, 73, 132–135.

[10] Ulster Museum accession number A39.1923; Lawlor 1925a, 135, Plate x, 38; Ulster Museum accession numbers are hereafter identified solely by the prefix A.

[11] A43.2.1923; Lawlor 1925a, 73, 152–153, Plate xi, 97. The bead was reportedly found under the neck of a female skeleton in the more westerly of two mounds south of the church; its identification as amber was first made in Phillips 1960, 22

[12] A43.1.1923; Lawlor 1925a, 152, Plate xi, 88.

[13] On Early Medieval burial see O'Brien 1992; Conway 1999.

[14] Lawlor 1925a, 73.

[15] *Vita Columbae* i. 23, ii. 29, ii. 45: Anderson 1991, 50–51, 136–137, 174–175; the smiths and scribes are specifically identified as monks; carpenters are so identified at Durrow in *Vita Columbae* i. 29, iii, 15: Anderson 1991, 56–7, 202–3.

[16] Barber 1981; Graham-Campbell 1981; McCormick 1993; 1997.

[17] Lawlor (1925a, 17) suggested that 'a large number of polished rubbing stones' found in the vicinity of the round tower were indicative of leather-working.

[18] Lawlor (1925a, 149) mentioned two needles from the 'school', 'one of iron, broken off at the eye, and one of bronze, perfect (No. 75)'. These are A25.2.1925 and A25.1.1925; his earlier reference in similar terms (1923, 72) to 'two bronze needles' seems to be a mistake. Some pierced stone discs may be spindle-whorls, e.g. Lawlor 1925a, Plate x, 7, 18 (both now unlocated), 9 (A55.6.1925); the detached head of a cattle femur found in the course of excavations by Charles Thomas in 1954 (A26035) might be a roughout for a whorl.

[19] Ryan (1988) has shown that metalworking is characteristically evidenced outside the inner sanctum at Early Medieval monasteries, citing Nendrum, Armagh, Downpatrick and Movilla in illustration.

[20] Lawlor 1925a, 136, cf. 17, 140. This material is now unlocated, but slag was again found in the course of excavations by Charles Thomas in 1954 (e.g. A12327). I am indebted to the Editor, Brian Scott, for the information that the so-called 'pig iron' was probably a piece of hypoeutectoid steel like an ingot from an Early Medieval context at Lissue, Co. Antrim: see Scott 1990, 9–10, 162, 217.

[21] A17.1925; Lawlor 1925a, 140, Plate xi, 89; for a similar ingot from Lagore, Co. Meath, see Hencken 1950, 86, fig. 22, A.

[22] Previously un-numbered, now A7812; Lawlor 1923, 69.

[23] e.g. A53.1.1925 and A54.1.1925; Lawlor 1925a, Plate xi, 99, 98; Youngs 1989, no 175. Lawlor (1925a, 142) referred to three stands, but only two were accessioned (A54.1–2.1925; Lawlor 1925a, Plate xi, 98, 101). The third (Lawlor 1925a, Plate xi, 100) is unaccounted for.

[24] Lawlor (1925a, 142) referred to 'six almost or quite perfect examples', but only four were accessioned (A53.1-4.1925). Seventy-two fragments survive in addition; previously numbered sequentially, they are now A7550–7622. Vitrification is commonly evidenced externally and is present on both surfaces in some cases. There are variations in size and wall-thickness; while one triangular crucible (A7550) was *c.* 2.3cm high, another (A7551) was *c.* 8cm high and comparable in scale with examples from Moynagh Lough, Co. Meath, and Garranes, Co. Cork (Youngs 1989, no 158a; Ó Ríordáin 1942, 134–9). The larger crucible can never have been used because the sherd, of well-fired grey fabric, is unvitrified. A handled crucible lid (now A7840), with specks of vitrification externally, is of coarser grey-brown ware. A unique fragment (now A7839) derives from a shallow dish *c.* 6cm in diameter with a thick, flat base and with traces of vitrification internally. Such forms may not be crucibles but 'parting vessels for separating precious metals' (Lane and Campbell 2000, 134).

[25] A35.1925; Lawlor 1925a, 143, Plate xiii, 65; Youngs 1989, no 226.

[26] Now unlocated; Phillips (1960, 18) gave the diameter of the matrix as 0.4 inches (*c.* 1cm) and described the piece as 'long and thin as if it were held in tongs while the metal or glass was run in'.

[27] Previously un-numbered, now A7823; Jope 1966, fig. 80, 3.

[28] Kilbride-Jones 1980, 65–67; Warner 1989; that the Nendrum brooch is a miniature and a variant might be indicative of relative lateness.

[29] This brooch, lacking its pin, was described as 'lost' by Phillips (1960, 32, Plate 11, 1; see also Jope 1966, fig. 80, 1; Laing 1976, 16–17) and appears never to have been received by the Museum.

[30] Lane and Campbell 2000, illus 4.27.

[31] Laing 1975, Fig. 3, d, e.

[32] Youngs 1989, no 86.

[33] Wamers 1985, 111, Liste 1,4, Taf 36,3.

[34] A21.1925; Lawlor 1925a, Plate xi, 84; Phillips 1960, Plate 11, 2; Jope 1966, Fig. 80, 2; Laing 1976, 15–16. Lawlor (1923, 69) referred to this brooch as 'the larger of the two penannular brooches', apparently in distinction to a Late Medieval ring brooch (A20.1925; Lawlor 1925a, 149, Plate xi, 85) which he called (1923, 71) 'a small penannular [sic] brooch', as though to imply that no other brooches had been found at the time of writing. Lawlor's silence in the final report in relation to the lost brooch (Note 29 above) and the miniature D brooch suggest that both were found subsequent to his excavation.

[35] Graham-Campbell 1974, Plate iii, a.
[36] Youngs 1989, nos 87–88; the brooches were found near the Early Medieval monastery on Scattery (*Inis Cathaig*).
[37] A51.1.1925; O'Meadhra 1979, no 150; Youngs 1989, no 154.
[38] O'Meadhra 1979; 1987.
[39] Youngs 1989, no 155.
[40] O'Meadhra 1987, 71–74.
[41] Lawlor 1923, 73.
[42] Lawlor 1925a, 144. It is worth considering the possibility that the so-called 'school' is a Post-Medieval dwelling house, and it may be significant that 'when first seen it was overgrown with a very luxurious crop of nettles, a weed which was not remarkably prevalent except in this neighbourhood' (Lawlor 1923, 70). Nettles are more characteristic of thatched houses in the first decades of their abandonment than of long-vacant Medieval sites. The roof (?and walls) of the structure had evidently been destroyed by fire, and Lawlor found 'charred wood and straw' and 'half burned roof beams' (1925, 143–144). That such material would have survived in this elevated and dry position for up to a thousand years seems unlikely, and the Medieval finds may have been sealed beneath the floor. None seems to be fire-damaged, contrary to what Lawlor suggested. There is no reason to suppose that Lawlor's workers will have recognised the floor level or appreciated its stratigraphic significance, given his assumption that the structure was ancient. He recorded, further (1923, 71), the finding of a burial 'about eighteen inches below the probable surface of the floor' and was evidently not present at the time.
[43] A52.1–4.1925; Lawlor 1925a, 146, Plate xiii, 40–43.
[44] Previously un-numbered, now A7821; Phillips 1960, 47; compare Armstrong 1922, fig. 3, 1.
[45] A50.1925; Phillips 1960, Plate 8, 92; Lawlor 1925a, 153, no 24, Plate x, 24; Phillips (1960, 30) gives the diameter of the matrix as 0.4 inches, equivalent to *c*. 1cm. The piece, now unlocated, is unprovenanced within the site, having been recovered from redistributed soil.
[46] Hencken 1950, 129–32; Youngs 1989, no 209.
[47] Hencken 1950, 126, fig. 60, 1517.
[48] As suggested by Ó Floinn (1989). The diameter of the Moylarg model is 1.3cm; a comparable lead model is reported from Lagore (Comber 1997, 107).
[49] *Cf.* Youngs 1989, nos 90–92, 95, 186–7; the incidence of millefiori is unusual if not exceptional in this category of dress-fastener.
[50] A23.1925; Lawlor 1925a, Plate xi, 82; Jope 1966, fig. 80, 12; Fanning (1994, 13–14) mentions the Nendrum example and suggests that such pins 'had largely gone out of fashion by the early Viking period'.
[51] A5943; the pin was found in 1992, reportedly on the ground surface inside the pedestrian gate from the car park (Bourke 2002). For the type see Fanning 1994, 36–41.
[52] Phillips 1960, 17, Plate 5, 52; now unlocated.
[53] The loop and shank are respectively A22.1.1925 and A22.2.1925; Lawlor 1925a, 141, Plate xi, 80; Jope 1966, fig. 80, 6.
[54] Previously un-numbered, now A7819; the pin was shown in conjunction with a penannular ring (A7820) by Lawlor (1925a, Plate xi, 81; cf. Jope 1966, fig. 80, 5), but an original association seems implausible. The non-appearance of these specimens among the material accessioned by the Museum in the 1920s rules out a simple equation of the latter assemblage with specimens accorded numbers in Lawlor's publications.
[55] Previously un-numbered, now A7861; the ring might have been a spiral.
[56] Previously un-numbered, now A26207; Jope 1966, fig. 80, 7.
[57] (i) previously un-numbered, now A7817; Jope 1966, fig. 80, 10; (ii) A24.1925; Lawlor 1925a, 141, Plate xi, 83; Jope 1966, fig. 80, 11. Lawlor (1923, 60) described a 'bronze pin' from the vicinity of structure 14 as 'similar to one found later in the hut sites [i.e. structure 17] on the west side. (No. 83) [i.e. A24.1925]'. The first pin found might plausibly be identified with A7817; although they differ in size, Lawlor might have had these pins in mind when he stated (1923, 69) that 'two of the pins found in other places seemed to fit' one of the matrices in a stone mould (A8.1925; Lawlor 1925a, Plate x, 20) from structure 19. He referred elsewhere (1928, 72) to the finding in structure 19 of 'many bronze pins and moulds for casting them', and to 'a stone mould for casting pin heads or buttons' (1925, 143). However, with the exception of the lost mould A50.1925 (Note 45 above), for casting a ring, no moulds for pins (or parts thereof) can be identified. The mould A8.1925 is best associated with Late Medieval (or more recent) button-making (*cf.* Ryan 1988, 43). Lawlor recorded (1923, 69) that 'two other stones with similar moulds were also found in other places'; one is evidently the related piece A9.1925 (Lawlor 1925a, Plate x, 22); the other, with unaccomplished herring-bone decoration, is bigger and may be a journal stone (previously un-numbered, now A26209; Lawlor 1925a, 147, note p). A further stone was implausibly identified by Lawlor (1925a, 135, Plate x, 19) as a 'mould' for crusie lamps (see also Ó Ríordáin 1942, 109) but might itself be a lamp *sensu stricto,* and another possible lamp can be identified (A11.1925; Lawlor 1925a, 154, Plate x, 35). The first was formerly set, together with the cross-decorated slabs, in the internal west gable of the church and is now in the Nendrum exhibition centre.
[58] Previously un-numbered, now A7937; Phillips 1960, Plate 11, 9; Jope 1966, fig. 80, 9.
[59] Previously un-numbered, now A7818.
[60] I follow the terminology and dating in O'Rahilly 1998.
[61] A44.9–11.1925.
[62] Newman 2002, 111, interpreting iron inserts as remnants not of pin-shanks but of pegs. That four pits, as on a die, frame the perforation of A44.9.1925 (Fig. 13.18b) may lend support to Newman's view.
[63] Stevenson 1955, 292–3; MacGregor 1974, 76, 102; Curle 1982, 62.
[64] (i-ii) A18.1.1925 and A18.2.1925; Lawlor 1925a, 140, Plate xi, 90, 91; (iii) previously un-numbered, now A11179, with a triple moulding at the head. A bone peg found in excavations by Charles Thomas in 1954 (A12332) might be a roughout for a pin.
[65] A26.1925; Lawlor 1925a, 141, Plate xi, 86; Jope 1966, fig. 80, 13.
[66] Whitfield 1997, Plate 40.
[67] Ryan 1983, no 75; a parallel pointed out to me by Paul Mullarkey.
[68] A26114, previously unpublished and acquired by the Museum in 2002 with the co-operation of Harry Quee.
[69] Youngs 1989, no 88; *cf.* also the sub-zoomorphic details on the hoop of an 8th- or 9th-century penannular brooch from near Clunie Castle, Perthshire (Youngs 1989, no 110).
[70] A44.1923; Lawlor 1925a, 154, Plate xi, 87; Jope 1966, fig. 80, 8.
[71] A32.1923; Lawlor 1925a, Plate xiv. See Andrews 1969 for an interesting fictional account of the monastery in which the bell has a prominent role.
[72] Ó hInnse 1947, 66-67, s.a. 1178.
[73] Lawlor 1923, 61.
[74] At a point marked 16 in Lawlor 1925a, Plate i.
[75] Lawlor 1925a, 149.
[76] Jope 1966, 293.
[77] Lawlor recorded (1922, 94–5) the discovery of burials '[a]mong the raised heaps of the debris of the church …, including many of young children, probably unbaptised infants, which up to a couple of centuries ago, or in places, recent times, were buried in some otherwise disused holy place'.
[78] Reeves 1853, 179.
[79] Lawlor 1923, 62.
[80] The date of its loss cannot be established with accuracy; Jope (1966, Plate 83) reproduced the early photograph (by R G Welch) and I am unaware of any other illustration. Lawlor noticed, further (1923, 62; 1925, 150), the survival of the suspension loop for a clapper, but only a detached fragment is now identifiable.

[81] Previously un-numbered, now A26208; the piece seems not to be referred to in Phillips 1960.
[82] Stalley 2000, 16, 33; Moss 2002.
[83] The first (part of the group A51.1925; Lawlor 1925a, 144–5, Plate xii, 108; O'Meadhra 1979, no 157), is now unlocated and was described as 'lost' by Phillips (1960, 39); see also O'Meadhra 1979, nos 136, 137, 153. O'Meadhra 1979, no 154 (previously un-numbered, now A11343) bears an irregular grid and is identified by Breen (2003, 45) as an incomplete gaming board. Breen *(ibid)* equates the latter piece in error with the larger stone, A26209, mentioned in Note 57.
[84] A6.1925; Lawlor 1925a, Plate ii.
[85] Macalister in Lawlor 1925a, 70–71.
[86] Higgitt 1994, 216; see also Barnes *et al* 1997, 2 and Charles-Edwards this volume.
[87] Herity and Breen 2002, 30–36, fig. 15a; Jope 1966, Plate 77.
[88] The single sherd of imported E ware attributed to Nendrum by Thomas (1959, 109; 1981, 23) and Jope (1966, 133) is now unlocated and accordingly left out of account; the identification of an A ware vessel was set aside by Waterman (1958, 69) and Jope (1966, 133).
[89] Pieces of fired clay with finger impressions (A33.1923; Lawlor 1925a, 166–7, Plate xvii, 128) were found with souterrain ware to the north of the round tower; they might relate to pottery production, as Lawlor supposed, but might equally pertain to an unrelated activity, as Tom McNeill (*pers. comm.*) points out. On the other hand, Lawlor referred to 'countless fragments of half baked broken pots' from the same place (1923, 76; see also 1925, 166); some of these might have been genuine wasters, but none is now identifiable.
[90] Lane and Campbell 1988, 211.
[91] Lawlor 1925a, 148, Plate xvii, 122–132; *cf.* Lawlor 1923, 70–71, where fifteen are referred to.
[92] A44.1–8.1925. The eleven accessions correspond to the eleven illustrated in Lawlor 1925a, Plate xvii, 122–32.
[93] Hurley 1997a, 263–66, fig. 108; 1997b, 685, fig. 17:9. An isolated example from Dublin in the Ulster Museum (A12412) was found 'in a wall' of Christ Church Cathedral in 1874; an additional set of seven (A12413–9) is probably of Dublin origin.
[94] Small *et al.* 1973, 7, fig. 6.
[95] Phillips 1960, 5.
[96] Previously un-numbered, now A7105; Phillips 1960, 26, Plate 7, 73.
[97] A3.1926; Lawlor 1925a, 145, Plate xii, 112. The site has yielded nine single-edged iron knives (A42.1–5.1925 and A43.1–4.1925; Lawlor 1925a, 147, Plate xiii, 46–54), one of them now unlocated.
[98] A45.1925; Lawlor 1925a, 153, Plate x, 25; Phillips 1960, 27, Plate 8, 76; the bead is now unlocated and Phillips' description is quoted.
[99] O'Kelly 1962, fig. 13, A.
[100] This bead derives from Nick Brannon's excavations in the late 1970s and is now on loan to Down County Museum; for similar beads from Lagore see Hencken 1950, fig. 67. 51, 680.
[101] A40.1.1923; Lawlor 1925a, 154, Plate x, 31.
[102] A7.1925; Lawlor 1925a, 109, 139, Plate xii, 116; Phillips 1960, 45–46; now unlocated.
[103] A7834; Lawlor 1925a, Plate x, 10; for similar grindstones from Lagore see Hencken 1950, 173, fig. 90. Lawlor also referred (1925a, 137) to a 'circular grindstone, 15 inches in diameter ... apparently of Ballygowan free-stone'; the object was described as 'lost' by Phillips (1960, 44) and appears never to have been received by the Museum.
[104] e.g. A51.1–9.1923.
[105] Lawlor reported (1925a, 18) that 'a great many fragments of querns were found'. All were said to have been of granite, one having a cross carved in relief; one lower stone only was unbroken (Lawlor 1925a, 137). No querns were accessioned by the Museum in the 1920s and only one possible quern fragment (previously un-numbered, now A7649), which is made of sandstone, is now identifiable.
[106] The date suggested in Hamlin 1985, 294.
[107] Stokes 1887, cxcii-cxciii; Best 1912; Ryan 1931, 333–45, at 341; Hamlin 1987, 33, 36–7.
[108] Hamlin, however (1987, 39), allowed for the possibility of a later, Benedictine, context in view of the elaborate framing of the shaft; see also Arnaldi 2000, 28–9.
[109] Note, however, a single radiocarbon date of 1375 ±45 b.p. cited by Brannon (1988), obtained from charcoal from beneath the outer cashel wall. On dating the enclosing walls of monastic sites see Marshall and Rourke 2000, 175–82.
[110] See Notes 27–28 above.
[111] Mac Airt and Mac Niocaill 1983, 412–3.
[112] Lawlor 1925a, 68–69, 72, 149–150, 155, adhering to the Four Masters' date of 974.
[113] This is also the view expressed in Hamlin 1987, 39.
[114] *Cf.* Lawlor 1923, 67, 70.
[115] Hamlin 1997, 58.
[116] A28.1925; Lawlor 1925a, 154, Plate xiii, 78. For the type see Bourke 2001, 87–88.
[117] A17.1988; Bourke 2002.
[118] Lawlor 1925a, 75; he recorded that the coin 'got broken into small pieces by the blow of a pick axe'; see also Lawlor 1925a, 149.
[119] Reeves 1847, 10, 187.
[120] *Vita Columbae* ii, 28: Anderson 1991, 134–135.
[121] Lawlor 1925a, 89; he suggested either Nendrum or 'Inis Loughan' (?Loughinisland), favouring the former; see Lawlor 1913, 133–134.
[122] Lawlor 1925a, 20.
[123] Lawlor 1925a, 81.
[124] Lawlor 1925a, 130.
[125] Reeves 1902, 15–17; Lawlor 1925a, 93.
[126] O'Donovan J.H. Todd J.H. and Reeves, W. (eds and trans.) (1864) *The Martyrology of Donegal, a calendar of the Saints of Ireland.* Dublin (Irish Archaeological and Celtic Society).
[127] Lawlor 1923, 65, cf. 58, 66, 77. The plan (Lawlor 1923, Plate facing p 81; 1925a, Plate i; Blakiston Houston 1925, frontispiece) was drawn up before the final season, but the tenor of Lawlor's reports suggests that little digging was done in 1924. Fourteen months in all were devoted to the excavation (Lawlor 1925a, xxv), four in 1922 (Lawlor 1923, 94, 96), seven and a half in 1923 (Lawlor 1923, 56, 77), the balance in 1924. The find-spot of the axe-head A17.1988, as recorded in Ulster Museum files, is within the unstippled area.
[128] The non-excavation of the unstippled area is confirmed by Lawlor's further statement (1925a, 106; cf. 95, note a), with reference to the house- or hut-sites in the western sector, that 'were investigations continued on the S. and S.E., it is probable others would be found'. The location of the graves numbered 36 outside the stippled area on the plan is the only apparent inconsistency.

Chapter 14

Conclusions

Thomas McErlean

Chapter 14
Conclusions

Thomas McErlean

INTRODUCTION

This chapter summarises the major themes that have emerged from the excavation of the tide mills and a re-evaluation of Lawlor's work at Nendrum. These include aspects of the chronology of the monastery, its economy, the organisation of space and the role of the mill within monastic organisation, and the significance of the Nendrum mill evidence to early Irish and European mill archaeology.

THE CHRONOLOGY OF NENDRUM

Tree-ring dating

The large number of dated timbers from Mill 1 makes it the most firmly dated horizontal-wheeled mill in Ireland so far, and perhaps also one of the most reliably dated structures of the Early Medieval period in the country. The precise chronological positioning achieved by tree-ring analysis of timber from the two mills has made a fundamental contribution not only to Nendrum itself, but also to the chronology of Irish monastic archaeology in general. The history of nearly all Irish Early Medieval monasteries spans a period of approximately six centuries — from their main foundation horizon in the mid to late 6th century though to the 12th-century reform and introduction of the continental orders. Over this period of 600 years, monasteries underwent considerable change, but much of our current archaeological information — the stone churches, high crosses and round towers for example — date mostly from the 10th century or beyond, and therefore belong to the later part of this period. Archaeological knowledge of the late-6th century is practically non-existent, and extremely poor for the 7th. Indeed, information on the 8th and 9th centuries is not appreciably better. Thus, the well-dated early-7th and late-8th centuries' horizons from Nendrum, as represented by the mills, provide a considerable advance. The delineation of a major development phase at the monastery during the years from AD 619 to AD 621 is of particular significance, in that it provides the first clear archaeological evidence of an Irish monastery going through an early major stage of development.

Historical dating

Etchingham in Chapter 11 has highlighted the significant coverage of the monastery in the 7th-century annals in contrast to the pattern at most other monasteries, which receive more notice in succeeding centuries. This fact, and the presence of bishops at the monastery, suggests that during the 7th century AD, Nendrum had a greater prestige than many of its contemporaries. This apparent prominence of the monastery in the annals in the 7th century agrees well with the archaeological interpretation of the significance of Mill 1. Its construction demonstrates clearly that, in the early part of the century, the monastery had the need for — and possessed sufficient resources to undertake the building of — a tide mill involving the construction of a large dam. The historical sources would seem to imply that the monastery continued to have a significant status through the 8th and 9th centuries, but notably declines from the 10th century onwards. It is to be remarked therefore, that there is extremely good correspondence between the dendrochronological dating of the mills and the historical dating supplied by the annals. Both independent dating sources appear to underpin each other and confirm the importance of the monastery in the 7th and 8th centuries.

Dating from the evidence from the 1922–1924 excavations

While much of the structural evidence from Lawlor's excavation would appear to be of the 10th century or later, a re-evaluation of some of the evidence in Chapters 12 and 13 has served to place more material earlier than previously thought. The cross forms on the grave-slabs and the stone with the inscription in Insular display capitals, can be probably dated to the first half of the 8th century or possibly to the late 7th century. Similarly the roundhouse forms in the middle enclosure probably belong to before the 10th century. The review of the artefactual evidence by Bourke (Chapter 13) concludes that one brooch may be of late-6th century, or possibly early-7th century date, and therefore possibly contemporary with Mill 1. But in general most of the material belongs to later centuries and therefore it can be claimed that to a certain degree the early 7th-century horizon clearly established by Mill 1 is not, as yet, matched with material from within the monastic enclosure. At present therefore, there is an apparent marked lack of correspondence between the dating evidence from both the mills and the historical sources, with that from the 1922–1924 excavations. Reconciling the apparent discordance is an issue that needs to be addressed.

As many of the buildings within the enclosure during the 7th and 8th centuries would have been of wood, lack of evidence of structures belonging to this horizon from Lawlor's excavation may be accounted for, to a great degree, by his excavation methodology with its concentration on stone structures and non-recognition of features such as post holes and beam slots. Also, excavation seems to have focused on the top layers of the site. Thus, many of the earlier structures contemporary with the mills and annalistic references may have been left undisturbed and may still survive below ground.

Problems of chronology

In spite of the new information there remain many chronological problems, which can only be solved by further excavation concentrating in the areas untouched by Lawlor. More information is needed on the early archaeology of the site especially to ascertain if an earlier horizon predating the first mill in the early 7th century can be detected. Information that might establish a foundation date for the monastery is of prime importance for the interpretation of the site. The dating of the construction of the enclosure walls would be of particular relevance to test the suggestion that these are contemporary with Mill 1, and that both belong to the primary foundation phase and that this may have occurred in the early 7th century.

Bound up with consideration of the foundation date of the monastery is consideration of the mechanisms involved in the establishment of a monastic community in 6th- or early 7th-century Ireland. The Lives of the Saints provide some models of origin or the foundation process of some of the Irish monasteries that grew to prominence in the 7th and 8th centuries. One version portrays the founding saint going off to a remote location to seek the spiritual life in isolation and how gradually a great monastery grew around the simple cell of the saint. Other versions hint at the positive interaction of local kings and the founding saint, who was endowed with lands and people to found a monastery. While the first version in some instances may be an authentic historical account of the foundation of a particular monastery, its use as a general model for the origins of most of the Early Medieval Irish monasteries appears too simplistic. It is highly probable that the foundation of a coenobite community, a large and complex institution, in most cases did not simply evolve on an *ad hoc* basis, but was the product of deliberate planning and decision-making. Such projects must have involved a high level of organisation and should be seen in most cases as well-planned enterprises. As early monasteries were closely associated with the minor kingdom or territory in which they were located, their foundations must have involved a high level of interaction between the local temporal ruler and the ecclesiastical one represented by the local bishop.

The foundation process would have encompassed the endowment of resources in land and people in the form of the granting of an estate by the local king or landholding family. It would have involved a major building programme, which would have gone through a major initial phase of development, probably on a large scale, subsequently followed by other smaller scale phases of renewal, and periods of redevelopment and expansion.

In considering the origin and early development of Nendrum the question arises as to whether its origin should be viewed as resulting from the organic growth of the simple cell or church of a founder, or viewed as a grand territorial project. In favour of the first are the traditions and cult of St Mo-Choí. This narrative implies the monastery grew from a church founded in the late 5th or early 6th century by a historically shadowy holy man. In support of the second there is the archaeological evidence of a major building project taking place in the early 7th century, with the building of a large and sophisticated tide mill, the felling of oak woods and preparation of a large stockpile of timber for buildings together with the possibly, contemporaneous construction of the enclosure walls.

Another major chronological problem at Nendrum lies in ascertaining how long communal monastic life lasted in any meaningful sense. One hypothesis is that a community following a strictly monastic rule was present in the 7th, 8th and 9th centuries, but gradually a more lax regime developed in later centuries and the monastery declined in vigour and vitality. A hint of decline in monastic life at Nendrum is contained in the 14th-century life of St Colman of Dromore (see p. 302), which preserves traditions of the occurrence of a period of laxity which was subsequently followed by revival of religious life. The annal entries suggest that Nendrum was still functioning in the early 10th century but their silence regarding the monastery during the 11th and 12th centuries, although negative evidence — of somewhat dubious value — may suggest that it had ceased by this period. It seems clear that by the late 12th century, the monastery no longer existed as an independent unit and its lands had passed to the bishop. Occupation of a religious nature may have continued on the site but not of a monastic nature. The chronology of this decline and cessation of monastic life has still to be charted by archaeology.

THE MONASTIC ECONOMY

Evidence from both excavations has supplied information on the monastic economy and demonstrates that it was organised for self-sufficiency and economic independence. A wide range of economic activities is represented, including agriculture, milling, and industrial and craft operations like working metal and stone. There is direct evidence that the monastery, like Early Medieval Irish society in general, practised a mixed farming system consisting of crop growing and animal husbandry. The tide mills highlight the arable side of the mixed agriculture system, an aspect often overlooked because of the low level of retrieval of cereal remains from excavation in contrast to that of animal bones. The sheltered coastal location of the monastery and its local landscape, with its low rate of frost and a relatively long growing season would have favoured cereal growing. To produce the crop, enclosed fields were needed and draught animals to pull ploughs. Grain was stored in granaries and dried in kilns within the monastic enclosure and brought down to the mill for grinding to produce the daily bread required by the community, or converted into malt to make ale and beer. Other crops included flax, grown to make linen. Vegetables were grown in the monastic gardens and there is little doubt the monastery would have had an apple orchard.

The small bone assemblage found around the mills, which is discussed in Chapter 10, provides evidence of the importance of animal husbandry in the monastic economy. This small but significant assemblage is particularly valuable because of the absence of bone analyses carried out on the large amount of bone material encountered during Lawler's excavations in 1922–1924, which resulted in the loss of a large body of information. Cattle, sheep (or possibly goats) and pigs were kept. Cattle were the most important and kept primarily for milking, but they were also an important source of meat and leather. The monastery would have required a substantial dairying herd, which would have been milked on a daily basis, during the summer months at least, and would have needed herding. The probable presence of oxen bones and evidence of the use of oxen for draught agrees with the documentary sources for the period, which show that they were used for ploughing and other heavy work such as moving felled timber. Flocks of sheep figure prominently in many of the saints' lives and these, like the cattle, required herding and a substantial amount of pasture. The discovery of a probable pin-beater or spindle provides evidence for the weaving of wool, and demonstrates that sheep were kept for their wool as well as a source of milk and meat. Pigs were fattened for meat, and some of their bones were used for making pins. The pig herd may have grazed in surviving oak woodland and scrub or, as sties are mentioned in the law texts, may have been penned perhaps within the outer enclosure and fed on waste food.

The bone evidence provides some information of slaughter and butchery techniques, which included poleaxing, followed by the division of the carcase into joints that were then hung on hooks. The bone collection from the mills also shows the presence of dogs and cats around the monastery. The cat would have been a desirable, if not necessary, presence around the mill to control rodents attracted by the cereals and meal. And the presence of rodents in the vicinity is demonstrated by the marks of their gnawing on some of the bones.

It is possible to see part of the outer enclosure functioning as the farmyard where many of the hands-on farming activities took place: the milking, slaughtering and butchering of animals and the drying and storage of cereals. However, the evidence for the presence of domestic animals and their husbandry and of cereal culture opens up a vision of the world beyond the monastic enclosure to a local landscape of herding and cultivation of crops in field divisions. It is possible to envisage the monastery as a major farming enterprise comprising not only activities which took place within the enclosure but also embracing a wider farmscape composed of arable fields, pasture and woodland. In assessing the organisational character of this farming unit, the model of a demesne or 'home farm' under direct management of the monastery within the wider context of the estate and land seems appropriate. Given the maritime setting of the monastery it is highly probable that the marine food resources were important in its domestic economy and the oar found in the core of the first millpond dam and the provision of a landing place attached to both mills provides a tantalising link to this aspect.

Fish and shellfish would have formed an important component of the diet especially during the frequent days of abstinence in the Christian calendar. Direct evidence for fishing from the 1922–24 excavations was slight, which is hardly surprising given the standards of small bone retrieval at the time. However, among the artefacts found were a fish-hook and possible sinker (Lawlor 1925a, 39). Fine sieving was carried out during the mill excavation, and this resulted in the retrieval of a small sample of fish bones from the naturally-deposited silts in the millpond and from the silts used in the construction of the dams. Their presence, however, cannot be taken as direct evidence of human exploitation, but reflects rather the presence of the natural fish population in the lough (McErlean 2002, 132–136) deposited by normal processes. Occasionally fish may have become trapped in the millpond and picked up after the impounded water was released, but it is highly probable that the monastery possessed a network of purposely built wooden foreshore fish traps. A significant number of these was discovered during the Strangford Lough Survey (McErlean and O'Sullivan, 2002, 144–185). Two stone fish traps dating to the Later Medieval period, located on the foreshore of Island Reagh and Ringneil on lands associated with the monastery, may overlie wooden ones dating to the Early Medieval period. Lawlor mentions that a large amount of shell material was present in the midden and occupation layers within the enclosure (Lawlor 1925a, 137), with oysters being particularly abundant. The monastery is situated in an area of the lough that in the past was surrounded by rich oyster beds, and today is still used for the commercial production of the Pacific oyster (McErlean *et al* 2002, 187–189). The monastery may have managed these beds to prevent over-exploitation.

The excavation of the first mill clearly demonstrates the importance of wood as a resource in the monastic economy. The utilisation of a large amount of oak and other wood species in the construction of the dam of Mill 1 establishes that the monastery possessed important resources of timber, at least in the early 7th century. Judging by the quality of the oak and the joinery techniques used to construct the mill complex, it is possible to envisage that the wooden buildings within the enclosure were of a high constructional standard. Wood was also used for the manufacture of a wide range of small functional everyday objects from the finely turned alder bowls, to the yew stave-built containers for carrying milk, water and other liquids. The amount of oak, holly and other species used in the construction of Mill 1 constitutes evidence for wood clearance in the vicinity. It is highly probable that the former woodland was converted into arable land and pasture. In the absence of any local pollen study it is not possible to speculate on how long the woods in the vicinity lasted and whether some were managed as a renewable resource or if they were eradicated by over-exploitation.

Probably the single greatest and stable economic resource possessed by an Early Medieval monastery was its landed estate. At Nendrum there exists good information of what constituted the bulk of this in the form of the Late Medieval episcopal manor on the adjacent mainland. This is some 1,183 ha in extent and consists of eight modern townlands, and as a unit was used to form the Late Medieval parish of Nendrum or Tullynakill. The relationship of Early Medieval monasteries to their estates is a largely unexplored area. It is unknown to what degree an active policy of estate management was followed along the lines of the Later Medieval monastic estates of the Cistercians for instance. Many questions are posed for future research, including whether the archaeology of a monastic estate differs from a secular one in terms of settlement character and density of population. Is it possible that monastic estates were more economically and agriculturally developed, perhaps having a higher component of arable cultivation than secular ones? There is considerable evidence about the status of the tenants of monastic estates, the *Manaig*

(Etchingham1999a). The *Manaig* class appears to have had a contractual relationship with the monastery and in return for farming the lands and paying rent in food renders, received close pastoral care.

Nothing survives of the intellectual achievements of the monastery in terms of learning, but mention of Crónán, Bishop of Nendrum in the papal letter of AD 640 on the paschal controversy would place the monastery among the important centres of ecclesiastical authority in the country in the mid 7th century. Undoubtedly Nendrum in the 7th and 8th centuries was a place of learning and scholarship. It probably had, like many of its contemporaries, a monastic school. The artefacts from the 'schoolhouse', which include iron styli, suggest the presence of a scriptorium whose main function, as in other Irish monasteries, was to copy holy writ. Direct evidence for literacy is present in the inscribed stone in Insular display capitals, while art is represented by the motif pieces, metalwork and the stone carving. What has been recovered must represent an extremely small residue of the output of the workshops of the monastery in the 7th to 9th centuries but its importance is enhanced when one considers how little is known archaeologically about the work of its great monastic neighbours Bangor, Downpatrick and Movilla. Competence in stone-working is displayed in the stone penstock of Mill 2 and in the cross slabs, the inscribed stone, the sundial and the 'marigold' stone. Evidence for brooch manufacture and other craft products poses the question regarding its nature. Some of it may have been for monastic personnel but much must have been traded.

Interaction with the secular world was strong. The cult of a saint had a pilgrimage dimension, which would have brought many people to the monastery. A significant element in the economy of many Early Medieval monasteries were revenues from a saint's cult. There is sufficient historical evidence to show the importance of the cult of St Mo-Choí in the identity of Nendrum. Some information has survived on some of the principal relics of his cult: the heaven-sent crosier, the *Etech* or 'flying crosier', the wooden shrine and possibly the relic of his head (see p. 303). Monasteries function as cemeteries for the lay population as well as for the monastic community and great prestige was attached to burial in the sanctified ground of an important monastery. It is probable therefore that donation from pilgrims and fees for burials would have been a valuable source of revenue (Etchingham, 1999, 73).

An aspect of Nendrum which needs consideration is the historical record of the presence of bishops in the monastery in the 7th, 8th and 9th centuries (see p. 315). Bishops enjoyed considerable status in early Irish law. In the law text *Críth Gablach* the status of a bishop is equated to that of the king of a *túath* and in *Hibernensis,* the presence of a bishop or even his grave in a church raises it status relative to others (Etchingham 1999, 49). By the late 9th century, Nendrum may have lost its episcopal status to Down and Bangor where bishops are recorded after they disappear from Nendrum. The episcopal dimension to Nendrum poses the question of whether a monastery with a resident bishop differed in its organisation and economy from those without this status and, if so, if it is reflected in the archaeology. It is possible that in the 7th and 8th centuries, the monastery, with its resident bishop with pastoral responsibilities, functioned as a form of minister or collegiate church with a number of priests carrying out a pastoral role to a number of 'proto-parish' units in the local kingdom.

MONASTIC PLANNING

The archaeological evidence makes it clear that Nendrum, like other Irish monasteries and those in the rest of Christendom, were complex organisations within the bounds of which a range of quite diverse activities were carried on, apart from the religious activities pertaining to the communal monastic life with its strict ordering.

Buildings — including churches, oratories and shrines, sleeping and eating quarters, workshops and farm buildings — and space were needed for these varied and often conflicting activities. Such settlement complexity demanded some rational organisation of space and a practical division of the sacred from the profane, the functional from the ritual. The answer at Nendrum was to adopt a tripartite zoning system of concentric enclosures. It is possible that this system of planning may be predominantly a monastic feature of the 7th and 8th centuries incorporating, along with its obviously practical dimension, the concept and symbolism of a cosmological monastic ideal of the use of space. At present Nendrum probably provides the clearest example of this in Ireland, although examples of the double system abound. The later history of the monastery, with its lack of further development, may have been a factor that has helped preserve this pattern more clearly in comparison to other monasteries where development from the 10th century onwards tended to blur any sharp delineation of zonal organisation. Further excavation may produce a clearer indication of how other buildings and activity areas were arranged at the monastery and how they relate to each other within the zoning system.

The island location of the monastery – a place apart
It is important to consider the island location of the monastery in any discussion of its organisation. Islands were a popular choice for the founders of Early Medieval monasteries both in Ireland and abroad. Island monasteries abound around the Irish coastline, and in its inland lakes, and most have their origins in the 6th century. Perhaps the most famous example of an island monastery is Iona, off the coast of Argyll, which was founded by Columba sometime in the late 6th century. The west coast of Ireland has a large number of sites, such as Tory Island and Rathlin O' Birne, Co. Donegal, Inishbofin and Inishmurray, Co. Sligo, High Island and the Aran Islands, Co. Galway, Scattery Island, Co. Clare and Sceilig Mhiceal, Co. Kerry amongst others. On the lakes on the Shannon, island monasteries such as Inis Cealtra, Co. Clare, are particularly plentiful and most of the inland lakes in Ireland have their major monastic settlements, like Devenish on Lower Lough Erne. There are also numerous examples of monasteries on bog islands — such

as Clonmacnoise and Derry. Nendrum, situated on the large tidal island of Mahee, is a fine example of this strong preference for an island location.

The reasons behind the location of many of the Early Medieval monasteries are worth considering. No doubt monasteries were founded primarily in locations that were granted to the founding saint by a local king or land-owning family, but some choice must have been exercised, and it would appear that island locations were very desirable from the 6th century onwards. It seems much too simplistic to view this merely as the church — as a new institution in Irish society — filling a marginal space in a landscape previously little exploited and available for settlement, and other factors should be considered. The most obvious one is that in the monastic ideal, the island offers 'a place apart', providing a location for spiritual isolation, where a semi-enclosed religious rule could be observed away from the secular world and with a degree of independence from local rulers. Islands provided a landscape that could be defined and controlled, where order could be maintained and outside interference minimised. Nendrum, located on a tidal island, must have offered a particular appeal, being for half of each day cut off from access by foot from the outside world, while retaining a link to it for the other half.

As a maritime monastery the use of boats must have been an everyday activity at Nendrum. Its coastal location would have facilitated contact with monasteries and places around the Irish Sea and further, and given it an outward-looking perspective. That it may have been a port of call for visiting overseas traders and functioned as a trading station seems plausible, but it has yet to be established by solid evidence and disappointingly, there is no reflection of this presumed cosmopolitan aspect among the artefactual evidence. Apart from a single sherd of possible E-ware, (p. 421, n. 88) no other exotic material has yet come to light and this aspect has yet to be demonstrated archaeologically.

THE MILL AND THE MONASTERY

The discovery and excavation of the tide mills provide a point of entry into many aspects of monastic organisation as it is possible to view them as occupying a central position in cereal production and processing, food organisation and economic planning.

The documentary sources suggest strongly that bread composed a large content of the daily diet of monks (Sexton 1998). It is to be envisaged that when the monastery was fully functioning as a community in the 7th, 8th and probably the 9th centuries, the monastic mill would have been in daily operation, tides permitting, producing meal and flour for daily consumption of bread for a sizable group. The prime source of the cereals ground at the mill would have been the arable fields of the monastic 'home farm'. It seems probable, however, that the tenants on the monastic estate would have owed food rents, some of it rendered in the form of grain, and that this was also processed at the monastic mill. The question arises as to whether the tenants on the estate were compelled to grind at the monastic mill, foreshadowing the model of the manorial mill. Indeed the discovery of large numbers of hand querns in raths, crannógs and monasteries may indicate the practice of confiscating hand mills from clients or tenants to enforce the use of an estate mill and thus allow a tax to be levied on the grain harvest.

A clear statement of the place of the mill in the practical organisation of early Irish monasteries is given in the law tract *Bretha Nemed,* which, in addition to the seven grades of clergy, lists the seven officers or 'functional grades' of the church. In hierarchical order from top is the monastic superior *(airchinnech),* prior *(secnap),* cook *(coic),* quest-master *(ferthigis),* gardener *(lubgortóir),* doorkeeper *(doirsaid)* and millar *(muilleoir)* (Breatnach 1987, 84–85; Etchingham 1999, 384–385; Kelly 1988, 66). Etchingham has attempted to calculate the honour price of the miller who is at the bottom of the hierarchy, and suggests that it was one third of an ounce of silver or two thirds of a *sét,* the equivalent of a *colpdach,* a two-year-old heifer (Etchingham 1999 384–385). Although in this lowly position, his inclusion in the list establishes him and the mill as an essential component of the monastery.

The inference from the Nendrum evidence is that the mill, like the enclosure, should be seen as a characteristic component of an early Irish monastery. Specific mention of the mill in the Rule of Benedict gives a clear indication of its importance in European monastic organisation, and indeed it is possible to see it as an essential feature of all but the smallest of Irish monastic communities. At Nendrum it is possible to equate the history of its mills with the general history of the monastery. When the community life of the monastery was in full vigour the mill was an essential part of its organisation, and the ultimate abandonment of milling on site may be linked to the economic and cultural decline of the monastery.

The excellent survival of many of the features of Mill 2 made it possible to make a reasonably reliable assessment of its annual energy capacity and more speculatively estimate a figure for its annual output of milled grain (see p. 217). If the mill worked at full capacity a figure in the region of 50 tonnes of coarsely milled barley is suggested. The amount of more finely milled flour would have been below this figure but still substantial. There is little difficulty in accepting, therefore, that Mill 2 was more than capable of supplying a sizable monastic community with all its milled grain requirements for bread and other cereal based foodstuffs. Furthermore it can be entertained that it was capable of producing a surplus above what was consumed at the monastery and therefore if production went beyond subsistence level it opens up the possibility that the monastery was engaged in trading meal and flour. Mills were a significant source of revenue for monasteries in the later Medieval period. Indeed Brady in a stimulating paper, and partly based on the Nendrum evidence, argues the case of a wider distribution network for cereals in 7th- and 8th-century Ireland (Brady 2006) than has been previously thought. Indeed he goes further and suggests that Nendrum may have been a dependency of Armagh and served as a specialised centre to provide grain to support the population of

Armagh (Brady 2006, 52). The latter link is presumably based on the reference to the token tribute of a shaven pig to Armagh recorded in the *Tripartite Life of Patrick* (see p. 287). However, apart from the weakness of the historical evidence for Nendrum having a tributary relationship with Armagh it seems highly improbable that it was supplying it with milled grain as the overland distance to Armagh is considerable and this monastic centre had extensive estates and a large number of satellite churches near to hand to supply its needs. However, it is conceivable that the monastery may have been the centre of a small distribution network for meal and flour on a scale that was largely confined to the population on its estate and immediate landscape, but whether there is sufficient evidence of the presence of a large scale production centre for milled grain is open to debate.

NENDRUM AND MILL TECHNOLOGY AND CHRONOLOGY

The Nendrum evidence demonstrates that early Irish mill technology was not static. Solid evidence has been produced of an important technological advance in horizontal waterwheel design between the early 7th and late 8th centuries, when the horizontal waterwheel was transformed from one with simple flat-blade paddles, to a much more energy-efficient form with scoop paddles. Further, it is possible, using the evidence of the two types of waterwheel found at Nendrum and the paddle form from Ballykilleen, Co. Offaly, to propose an Irish development sequence in this transition. Since the time of MacAdam in the mid-19th century, students of the horizontal-wheeled mill — and water power in general — have been preoccupied by the distribution of the two main types of horizontal waterwheel (the flat paddle type and scooped paddle type), a distribution previously regarded as mutually exclusive. The existence of both types at Nendrum has shown this conclusion to be erroneous and demonstrated that the flat-blade type preceded the scoop type, so that the relationship appears chronological rather that geographic. It further suggests that the scoop form was unknown in early 7th-century Ireland and that when the horizontal-wheeled watermill was introduced into the country in the 6th century or earlier it had a waterwheel with flat paddles. Other advances in milling technology in the 7th and 8th centuries evident at Nendrum are improvements in the millpond and dam design and the transformation of the penstock from wood to stone.

The Nendrum evidence has also contributed significantly to Irish mill chronology, by clearly establishing archaeologically that the horizontal-wheeled mill and the tide mill were in existence in Ireland in the early 7th century. This confirms the evidence of the Little Island discovery (Rynne, 1988) and pushes the dating of Irish mills back to nearer a 6th-century horizon. The firm chronological platform it has established sets an agenda for future research. Main issues on the research agenda include the discoveries of 6th-century or earlier examples of mills in the country. Others include obtaining more information from excavation to throw light on the dating and source or sources concerning the introduction into the country of both the horizontal-wheeled and vertical-wheeled mill and the technology of the tide mill. It should be noted, however, that the problems of sourcing origins for early Irish mill technology are greatly compounded by the lack at present of early dated examples beyond Ireland. Regarding the ultimate origin of horizontal-wheeled mill technology, Lucas has neatly summarised the current level of interpretation from present evidence, which suggests a Middle East or North African origin during the first half of the 4th century (Lucas 2006, 37, 41). The evidence of the law texts suggests that milling technology and millwrighting was a specialised skill which had become embedded in Irish secular society by the end of the 6th century. The active role of the monasteries or the church in general as an agent in the introduction of mills, given their cosmopolitan contacts, their ownership and exploitation of large estates and their communal settlements, would seem plausible.

Regarding the origin of the application of tidal power for milling it is tempting to claim that Ireland, as it has produced the two earliest known examples of the tide mill, is its place of invention. However appealing this interpretation would be to an Irish audience, it would be premature to make it, given the lack of research along other coastlines. A working hypothesis based on their later distribution (Fig. 1.8), would suggest the Atlantic coastline of western France and the Iberian Peninsula as the zone of primary adoption of tidal energy. Trade contact between Ireland and the western coast of France in the 6th century is well attested in E-ware, and strong contacts in Christianity with the same area and with Spain around the same period are also evident in the transmission of texts and general influence. It is possible to see the diffusion of tide mill technology and mill technology in general being part of an intellectual and technological exchange between the two areas.

The participation of the University of Ulster in the European Union's *Cultura 2000* project on the *Tidemills of Western Europe* (Ecomuseu, Seixal, 2005 Portgual) has served to place Nendrum in its European context. Its status as the earliest scientifically dated tide mill found so far anywhere and its importance for the chronology of mill technology has been recognised and discussed in the most recent synthesis on European tide mills (Litoral Atlántico, 2005). Indeed the reconstruction of the horizontal waterwheel from the second mill has been used as a frontispiece to this work.

CONCLUSIONS

The richness of the Nendrum evidence is remarkable: the enclosures, the church, the round tower, the early burials and artefacts and now the tide mills. Added to this is the documentary evidence of some of its early clerics and its cult of Mo-Choí. This means that study of Nendrum still has the potential to continue to make an important contribution to Early Medieval monastic archaeology. There are many old unresolved problems and many new ones to resolve and some aspects of the research agenda for the future have been outlined. In addressing these problems there is the reassurance that the site itself constitutes an invaluable underground archive of future knowledge of the past and has the potential to answer many questions and pose many more about an important and exciting formative phase of Irish and European civilisation when the foundations of the western Medieval world were taking shape. The story of Nendrum is just beginning and hopefully future generations will return to the site with the latest archaeological techniques and follow in the footsteps of Reeves in 1844 and Lawlor in 1922–1924 as we had the privilege of doing between 1999 and 2001.

Appendices

APPENDIX 1

Identification of the wood in the wattlework
Anne Davis

Introduction

Approximately 321 worked wood samples were received for species identification. Fifty-one came from uprights and wands from the inner wattle revetment (C167, C585), 73 from uprights and wands from the middle wattle revetment (C166) and 51 from uprights and wands from the outer revetment C168. Forty samples came from the posts of the palisade on the seaward side of the dam of Mill 1, five from the north-south post line near the termination of this dam and wheelhouse and four from the adjacent north-west/south-east post line. Forty-eight samples came from the wattle panel (C533) and 25 from the probable wickerwork basket (C541), both found in Trench 5. A further 22 samples of probable wattle derived from contexts associated with the Mill 1 dam, but were not *in situ* and could not be assigned to a definite structural component of the dam. All samples with their context and identification, are listed in Table App 1.1.

Method

Thin sections of the transverse, tangential, longitudinal and radial-longitudinal sections were taken for each piece of wood and examined through a transmitted light microscope at magnifications between 40x and 200x. Diagnostic features of each section were recorded, and identifications made using criteria listed by Schweingruber (1978).

Results

Preservation was generally very good, and identification was possible for 278 of the samples. The majority of unidentifiable pieces were narrow wands, which were badly decomposed with few diagnostic features surviving. A few small, badly-decomposed samples could not be identified because they had dried out. The identifications are summarised by feature in Table App 1.1.

Table App 1.1: Summary of wood identification by structure

Structure	Uprights	Wands	Miscellaneous
Inner wattle revetment (C167 and C585) of Mill 1 dam	13 holly 1 oak 1 pomoideae	31 holly 4 willow 1 indeterminate	
Middle wattle revetment (C166) of Mill 1 dam	13 holly 1 willow 1 oak 1 pomoideae	36 holly 15 willow 1 hazel 1 alder 2 indeterminate	
Outer revetment (C168) of Mill 1 dam	41 holly 1 oak 1 elm 1 willow	3 willow 2 holly 2 birch	

Palisade/breakwater of Mill 1 dam	29 holly 8 oak 1 willow 1 ash 1 birch		
North-south post line	3 hazel 2 holly		
Short north-west/ south-east post line	4 holly		
Wattle panel (C533)	3 hazel 1 pomoideae	32 hazel 10 indeterminate	
Possible wicker basket (C541)		22 hazel 3 indeterminate	
Isolated stakes	1 holly 1 hazel		
From Mill 1 dam, (not *in situ*)			7 holly 10 oak 1 hazel 1 ash 1 indet, coniferous 2 indeterminate

Holly *(Ilex aquifolium)* was the most abundant wood sample among the samples. It predominated among both uprights and wands of the inner, middle and outer wattle revetments, although a significant number (22) of examples of willow *(Salix sp.)* was used to make wands. Holly is an evergreen tree or shrub, which will grow in a wide range of conditions and produces hard, dense wood. It is particularly suitable for carving and turning, but posts of holly have been recorded in a Saxon waterfront structure at Ipswich and in Medieval pit-lining in London (Gale and Cutler 2000, 139).

The samples identified from wattle panel C533 and possible wickerwork C541 were almost all of hazel *(Corylus avellana)*, although several of the wands were too badly decomposed for identification. Long, straight rods and poles of hazel, suitable for wattle, could have been produced by coppicing.

Oak *(Quercus sp.)* was used occasionally for some of the uprights and posts, and in several of the samples not *in situ*. Birch *(Betula pendula/pubescens)*, ash *(Fraxinus excelsior)*, alder *(Alnus glutinosa)*, elm *(Ulmus sp.)* and *Pomoideae* (a large group including pear, apple, hawthorn and rowan) all appear very occasionally. Altogether, 60% of the identified wood was holly, 21% hazel, 9% willow, 7% oak and 3% other species.

APPENDIX 2

Notes on some aspects of the woodworking from the wattle structures

Damien Goodburn

Introduction

The examination of the cut ends of roundwood found in prehistoric wetland excavations has become standard practice, and patterns of the introduction and use of different tool types are beginning to be discerned and dated in Britain and Ireland (Goodburn 2003, O'Sullivan 1997). Much less attention has been paid to such details in waterlogged Early Medieval woodwork, but the assemblage from Nendrum provided an opportunity for study, particularly as the roundwood is large enough for fairly complete tool marks to be preserved.

Methods

Thirteen stake-ends were washed and examined in oblique light to highlight toolmark features. Basic information, such as maximum diameter, point form and very approximate annual ring numbers (although hard to see), was recorded for all of the stakes. As most of the cut ends were extremely well preserved, with the fine detail of the original tool marks surviving, the total assemblage was viewed together. The key interest here was to ascertain whether or not distinctive 'signature' marks from an individual tool could be seen on more than one worked stake-tip. The ends of the stakes clearly had all been cut with an axe or hachet, rather than with a billhook, as some of roundwood workers used in recent times, and which goes back possibly as far the Iron Age. 'Signatures' were made by unique patterns of small nicks in the edges of the axe blades, and two clear and one possible signature matches were found in stakes from the same structure, showing that they were worked at the same time and with the same axe (see below).

Results

1 Stake-ends from the north-south post line (C651 and C1023–1026)

Diameters ranged from 3cm (C651) to 5.5cm (C1024), and the tips were formed with one 'chisel'-type facet for C1026, two for C651 and C1023 and three for C1024 and C1025. The axe-marks preserved were the result of cutting at a low angle with a tool that had a fairly straight edge.

The stake-ends were also fairly smooth, with some signatures surviving, but only some small portions of the blade edges left marks due to the size of the rods used. No matching marks could be found. Although the rings were difficult to see, it was possible to carry out very rough ring-counts which showed that the material was of varying age from *c.* 7 years (C1023) to *c.* 18 years (C1025).

2 Stake ends from short post line orientated north-west/south-east at wheelhouse end of the Mill 1 dam (C1027–1029)

Diameters ranged from 5.2cm (C1029) to 8.2cm (C1028), and stake-ends C1027 and C1028 had 'pencil'-type types formed of many facets, while stake-tip C1029 had a point formed by two adjacent facets. Stake-points made with 1–3 adjacent facets indicate that the base of the growth used had a curve, which is common in coppiced wood. However, the spread of ages from *c.* 12 years (C1029) to 44 years (C1028) shows that the woodland harvested was not managed on an intensive, short-rotation system of coppicing where the vast majority of rods and poles are of closely similar ages when cut.

The axe marks preserved were over 5cm wide and had a pair of clear signature marks, the largest of which was *c.* 2mm wide and composed of two clear lines. This distinctive mark showed up clearly on the stake tips C1027 and C1028 and probably on C1029. The matching of the general form of the mark and the specific signatures showed that both stake-tips C1027 and C1028 (and probably C1029) had been hewn to points with the same axe at the same time. If the same signature marks were to occur on all of the other stakes of this feature, it would show that only one axe was used to point the stakes, probably indicating the work of one person.

3 Stake ends (C1031, C1033 and C1037) from uprights in the outer wattle revetment (C168)

These came from the south-eastern termination of the structure near the wheelhouse, and the diameters of the stake-ends varied from 5.8cm (C1031) to 8cm (C1033), and ring counts from *c.* 18 (C1037) to *c.* 36 (C1033). The point form was different in each case — a broad facet in the case of C1033, two on C1031 and three on C1037. Very importantly, several almost-complete axe stop-marks survived on the end of stake-tip C1033, clearly of holly. A stop mark is a linear mark which is left when the blade of an edge tool stops moving and forms a negative impression of the very edge of a blade on the surface of the worked wood. The longest stop-mark was 8.4cm wide, with a curve of *c.* 3mm over that length. As the corners of the edge of the tool were not present in the stop mark, the blade must have been a little wider. This shows that a comparatively wide and fairly thin-bladed axe was used for cutting the pole and had a blade that was probably around 10cm wide. In Anglo-Saxon England, such simple work as cross-cutting, felling and lopping, was carried out typically with blades 6.5–9cm wide (Goodburn 1992, 108). However, the use of wider axes for this simple work is sometimes found, and broader-bladed tools were used for truing and smoothing operations (Goodburn 1999, 49). It can be noted that in Iron Age evidence from Ireland currently available to this writer, the axe marks noted are generally smaller (O'Sullivan 1997).

4 Isolated stake ends (C697 and C899)

Stake-tip C697 was a very abraded, two-facet point with a diameter of *c.* 3.6cm and a ring count of *c.* 15 years. C899, with *c.* 13 rings, was slightly abraded and formed with one very long facet on a rod of 3.8cm diameter.

Summary and conclusions

Detailed recording of this small assemblage of early 7th-century roundwood stakes has shown the very high degree of preservation of the woodwork excavated. In some cases, the size of tool can be reconstructed. In the case of one stake, the tool used can be seen to be a noticeably wider-bladed axe than would be typical of earlier periods in Ireland on current evidence, and also wider than those used for such work in Anglo-Saxon England. In other cases, individual tool-signature marks show that several stake-tips were cut with the same tool.

The use of large quantities of holly roundwood, together with oak, is rare in Britain as a whole, but may reflect the distinctive makeup of local woodlands. Although holly is difficult to cut due to the foliage and its hardness, it is very strong, and appears, in this writer's experience, to be comparatively durable when used outside. It was also used for some Medieval riverside wattle structures along the English River Trent, (Salisbury 1991, 76) where such properties, together with local availability, may also have favoured its use.

APPENDIX 3

Assessment of the samples rich in mosses
Allan Hall

Methods
The eleven samples submitted ranged in size from 10gm of moss shoots to a sub-sample of 500gm, all taken from much larger original samples. On inspection, the larger samples were found to consist almost entirely of tangled moss shoots and small sub-samples were taken from them in turn for the assessment (weights are shown in Table App 3.1). These sub-samples were rinsed on a 300 µm-mesh sieve to remove the very small amounts of silt and fine organic debris present, and the resulting residues were examined under a low-power binocular microscope with oblique illumination. Mosses (and other remains) were recorded semi-quantitatively using a three-point scale (rare-common-abundant) and the scores were entered into a computer database.

Results
Table App 3.1: Samples examined, sub-sample weights and context information

Sample	Weight (kg)	Context
6	0.010	Stone wheelhouse, Trench 1, C1135
9	0.010	Mill pond, Trench 4, C18, approx 1m south of penstock
10	0.010	Mill pond, Trench 4, C18, approx 1m south of penstock mill pond.
21	0.050	Millpond, Trench 4, C3b.1m south of penstock
32	0.015	Penstock, below penstock sill stone
34	0.010	Packing from northern end of beam C34
35	0.015	Packing for base of northern side of penstock
36	0.010	From base of timber C19
37	0.015	Stone wheelhouse C1135
38	0.015	From among stones underlying C6
40	0.030	From among stones to west of wall C31

All of the samples consisted largely or wholly of well-preserved moss shoots and, in some cases, there were fragments which retained their green colour. Very few specimens had undergone any substantial decay. The presence of some shoots of a leafy liverwort, *Plagiochila sp.* indicates the superb state of preservation. Such plants are rarely encountered as subfossils in natural or archaeological deposits, and those previously encountered by the author (remains of *Frullania dilatata* in Early Medieval rath deposits at Deer Park Farms, Co. Antrim, Kenward *et al. forthcoming*) were of a species which is rather more robust than the *Plagiochila* seen at Nendrum.

As Table App 3.2 shows, the samples were consistently rich in the large, dendroid moss *Thamnobryum alopecurum*, often as whole plants (up to *c.* 12cm long), with the basal rhizoids still attached and, in some cases, held in clumps and clearly pulled from the ground together. One sample yielded evidence of a clump of *Thamnobryum* shoots adhering to a fragment of bark, indicating that this material, at least, had been growing on an exposed tree-root or tree-base (one of the typical habitats of this species). Moreover, the range of other taxa recorded, and the frequent presence of oak buds and bud-scales (and, in one sample, seeds of wood sorrell also) clearly points to an origin in woodland. Some taxa, such as *Pseudoscleropodium purum*, are perhaps more characteristic of less-shaded habitats, but an origin in a woodland clearing readily explains its presence with such an otherwise very characteristic woodland floor/tree-base group.

That most, if not all, of this material was recorded as packing in the fabric of the mill dams probably explains the presence of all of it at the site. Such plants certainly do not seem likely to have grown in and around the mills, especially as they were within tidal reach, since most of the taxa recorded are not found in areas subject to inundation and certainly are not particularly salt-tolerant.

It is noteworthy that many of the taxa, while widely distributed throughout the British Isles, are not recorded from the area around the western side of Strangford Lough according to the distribution maps of Hill *et al.* (1994). This seems likely to reflect a low incidence of recording of bryophytes in the area, rather than a real change in distribution, although reduction in forest cover would have certainly narrowed the range of available habitats for many of the mosses recorded here. There is no reason, therefore, to suppose the mosses were not collected from woods in the general area of Nendrum.

Table App 3.2 Mosses and other plant remains recorded. Taxonomic order and nomenclature follow Smith (1978) for mosses and Tutin (1964-1990) for vascular plants. Numbers are abundance scores on a three-point semi-quantitative scale. * indicates material which includes shoots which retain a green coloration.

Sample	6	9	10	21	32	34	35	36	37	38	40
Musci											
Polytrichum commune Hedw							2				
Polytrichum sp (p)								1			
Dicranum cf. *Majus* Sm.							2				
Mnium hornum Hedw.							1				
Plagiomnium undulatum (Hedw.) Kop.						1		2	1	2	1*
Neckera complanata (Hedw.) Hüb.								36			
Thamnobryum alopecurum (Hedw.) Nieuwl.	3*	3	3			1	2	3	1	2*	

Sample	6	9	10	21	32	34	35	36	37	38	40
Thuidium tamariscinum (Hedw.) Br. Eur.	3			1	3	2*	2	2	1	2	1
Isothecium myurum Brid.		1				2		1	1		
I. myosuroides Brid.							2				
Pseudoscleroposium purum (Hedw.) Fleisch.						1					
Cirriphyllum piliferum (Hedw.) Grout									1		1
Eurhynchium striatum (Hedw.) Schimp.	1				1	1	1	1	2	1	2*
E.praelongum (Hedw.) Br.Eur.						1*			1	1	
Rhytidiadelphus cf loreus (Hedw.) Warnst.							2		2		
Pleurozium schreberi (Brid.) Mitt.							1				
Hylocomium cf. Brevirostre (Brid.) Br. Eur.					2	1	1	1	1	2	
Hepaticae											
Plagiochila sp (p).								1	1		1
Angiospermae											
Corylus avellana L. (Buds/bud-scales)		1									
Quercus sp (p). Buds/ bud-scales)	2					1	1		1	1	
Oxalis acetosella L. (seeds)					1						
Viola sp (p). (capsule segment)											1
Lapsana communis L. (achenes)										1	
dicotyledonous leaf fragments						1					

Bibliography

Journal abbreviations

Antiq. J. – *Antiquaries Journal.*
Anatolian Stud. – *Anatolian Studies*
Archaeol. Ireland – *Archaeology Ireland*
B.A.R. – British Archaeological Reports
Bull. Ulster Place-name Soc. – *Bulletin of the Ulster Place-name Society*
Z. Celtische Phil. – *Zeitschrift für celtische Philologie*
Celtica – *Journal of the School of Celtic Studies*
Curr. Archaeol. – *Current Archaeology*
Int. J. Osteoarchaeology – *International Journal of Osteoarchaeology*
Irish Engineers' J. – *Irish Engineers' Journal*
Irish Hist. Stud. – *Irish Historical Studies*
Irish Nat. J. – *Irish Naturalists Journal*
J. Archaeol. Sci. – *Journal of Archaeological Science*
J. Down and Connor Hist. Soc. – *Journal of the Down and Connor Historical Society*
J. Cork Archaeol. Hist. Soc. – *Journal of the Cork Archaeological and Historical Society*
J. Galway Archaeol. Hist. Soc - *Journal of the Galway Archaeological and Historical Society*
J. Irish Archaeol. – *Journal of Irish Archaeology*
J. Kildare Archaeol. Soc. – *Journal of the Kildare Archaeological Society*
J. Manx Mus. – *Journal of the Manx Museum*
J. Roy. Hist. Arch. Assoc. – *Journal of the Royal Historical and Archaeological Association*
J. Roy. Soc. Antiq. Ireland - *Journal of the Royal Society of Antiquaries of Ireland*
LpoolManchr Geol. J. –*Liverpool and Manchester Geological Journal*
Med. Archaeol. – *Medieval Archaeology*
Mineralogical Mag. – *Mineralogical Magazine*
N. Munster Antiq. J. - *North Munster Antiquarian Journal*
Peritia, J. Med. Acad. Ireland – *Journal of the Medieval Academy of Ireland*
Proc. Prehist. Soc. – *Proceedings of the Prehistoric Society*
Proc. Belfast Nat. Hist. Phil. Soc. - *Proceedings of the Belfast Natural History and Philosophical Society*
Proc. Roy. Irish Acad. - *Proceedings of the Royal Irish Academy*
Proc. Soc. Antiq. Scotland- *Proceedings of the Society of Antiquaries of Scotland*
Rév. Celtique – *Révue Celtique*
Stud. Hibernica – *Studia Hibernica*
T.I.M.S. – *Transactions of the International Molinological Society*
Trans. Anglesey Antiq. Soc. – *Transactions of the Anglesey Antiquarian Society*
Trans. Dumfriesshire Galloway Natur. Hist. Antiq. Soc. - *Transactions of the Dumfriesshire and Galloway Natural History and Antiquarian Society*
Trans. Kilkenny Archaeol. Soc. – *Transactions of the Kilkenny Archaeological Society*
Trans. Newcomen Soc. – *Transactions of the Newcomen Society*
Ulster J. Archaeol. - *Ulster Journal of Archaeology*

Websites

Horizontal watermill: efficiency T 10 (2000), 82- 90 editor Leo van der Drift, Groothertoginnelaan 174 b, NL-2517 EV DEN HAAG, THE NETHERLANDS.

http://tims.geo.tudelft.nl/Publications/Publications%20Menu.htm

de Iturribarria, J. (2000) 'The Portu Errota Tide mill', **www.arrakis.es/%7eerrota/.**

Spain, R. (2005) 'A possible Roman tide mill, Paper No.005, **www.kentarchaeology.ac**, 1–64

Books, articles, reports and maps

AFM = O'Donovan, J. (ed. and trans.) (1856) *Annála Rioghachta Éireann (Annals of the Kingdom of Ireland by the Four Masters from the earliest period to the year 1616),* 7 vols, Dublin (Hodges and Smith); (reprinted 1966, New York, AMS Press)

AI = MacAirt, S. (ed. and trans.) (1951) T*he Annals of Inisfallen: (Ms. Rawlinson B. 503),* Dublin (Dublin Institute for Advanced Studies)

Aitchison, N.B. (1994) *Armagh and the Royal Centres in Early Medieval Ireland, Monuments, Cosmology and the Past,* Woodbridge, Suffolk, (Cruithne Press and Boydell and Brewer Ltd.)

Allen, R. and Anderson, J. (1903) *The Early Christian Monuments of Scotland : a classified, illustrated, descriptive list of the monuments, with an analysis of their symbolism and ornamentation.* Edinburgh (Society of Antiquaries of Scotland)

Anderson, A.O. and Anderson, M.O. (1961) *Adomnan's Life of Saint Columba,* London (Nutt Ltd.)

Anderson, M.O. (ed. and trans.) (1991) *Adomnán's Life of Columba,* Oxford (revised edn, Clarendon Press)

Andrews, J.S. (1969) *The Bell of Nendrum,* London (reprinted Belfast 1985, The Blackstaff Press)

Armstrong, E.C.R. (1922) 'Irish bronze pins of the Christian period', *Archaeologia* 72, 71–86

Arnaldi, M. (2000) *The Ancient Sundials of Ireland.* London (The British Sundial Society)

ASCD = Jope, E.M. (ed.) (1966) *An Archaeological Survey of County Down,* Belfast, (HMSO)

ASI GA *Record of Monuments and Places, County Galway, Archaeological Survey of Ireland,* issued by the Commissioners of Public Works in Ireland, National Monuments and Historic Properties Service, 1977 (Office of Public Works)

ASI Ga, *Recorded Monuments. Protected under Section 12 of the National Monuments (Amendment) Act, 1994, County Galway,* Archaeological Survey of Ireland, The Office of Public Works (Issued by the National Monuments and Historic Properties Service, 1997)

ASI Wa, *Recorded Monuments. Protected under Section 12 of the National Monuments (Amendment) Act, 1994, County Waterford,* Archaeological Survey of Ireland, The Office of Public Works (Issued by the National Monuments and Historic Properties Service, 1995)

AT = Stokes, W. (ed.) (1896) *The Annals of Tigernach: Third Fragment. Rév. Celtique* 17, 119–263 (reprinted Felinfach, 1993)

AU = MacAirt, S. and Mac Niocaill, G. (eds and trans.) (1983) *The Annals of Ulster (to AD 1131), Part 1, Text and Translation,* Dublin. (Dublin Institute for Advanced Studies)

Azurmendi Pérez, L. and Gómez Carballo, M. (2005) 'La Arquitectura y el paisaje', in *Litoral Atlántico,* 17–38

Baillie, M.G.L. (1975), 'A horizontal mill of the eighth century A.D. at Drumard, Co. Derry', *Ulster J. Archaeol.* 38, 25–32

— (1979) 'An interim statement on dendrochronology at Belfast', *Ulster J. Archaeol.* 42, 72–84
— (1980) 'Dendrochronology – the Irish View', *Curr. Archaeol.* 73, 62–63
— (1982) *Tree-Ring Dating and Archaeology,* London (Croom-Helm)
— (1986) 'A sherd of souterrain ware from a dated context', *Ulster J. Archaeol.* 49, 106–107
— (1995) *A Slice Through Time: Dendrochronology and Precision Dating,* London (Routledge)
Baillie, M.G.L. and Brown, D.M. (2003) 'Dendrochronology and the reconstruction of fine-resolution environmental change in the Holocene' in (eds) A. W. Mackay *et al.,* 75–91
Baker, C. (2004) 'A lost ecclesiastical site in Fingal', *Archaeol. Ireland* 18 (3), 14–15
Baker, J. and Brothwell, D.R. (1980) *Animal Diseases in Archaeology,* London (Academic Press)
Bannerman, J. (1968) 'Notes on the Scottish entries in the early Irish annals', *Scottish Gaelic Studies* 11, 149–170
Barber, J. (1981) 'Excavations on Iona 1979', *Proc. Soc. Antiq. Scotland* 111, 282–380
Barnes, M., Hagland, J.R., and Page, R.I. (1997) *The Runic Inscriptions of Viking Age Dublin,* Dublin (Royal Irish Academy)
Barrow, G.L. (1979) *The Round Towers of Ireland: A Study and Gazetteer,* Ireland (The Academy Press)
Barry, T.B. (1987) *The Archaeology of Medieval Ireland,* Cambridge (Cambridge University Press)
Barry, T.B., Frame, R. and Simms, K. (eds) (1995), *Colony and Frontier in Medieval Ireland,* London and Rio Grande (The Hambledon Press)
Bennet, I. (ed.) (2000) *Excavations 1998: Summary accounts of archaeological excavations in Ireland,* Bray (Wordwell)
Bennet, I. (ed.) (2004) *Excavations 2002: Summary accounts of archaeological excavations in Ireland,* Bray (Wordwell)
Bergin, O. and Marstrander, C. (eds) (1912) *Miscellany Presented to Kuno Meyer,* Halle (Niemeyer)
Berry, H.F. (1893) 'The manor and castle of Mallow in the days of the Tudors', *J. Roy. Soc. Antiq. Ireland* 2, 21–23
Best, R. I. (1912) 'The Lebar Brecc tractate on the canonical hours', in (eds) O. Bergin and C. Marstrander, 142–166
Best, R.I. and Lawlor, H.J. (eds and trans.) (1931) *The Martyrology of Tallaght,* London (Henry Bradshaw Society)
Bieler, L. (ed.) (1963) *The Irish Penitentials,* Dublin (Dublin Institute for Advanced Studies, *Scriptores Latini Hiberniae,* vol. V)
— (1979) *The Patrician Texts in the Book of Armagh,* Dublin (Dublin Institute for Advanced Studies, *Scriptores Latini Hiberniae,* vol. 10)
Binchy, D.A. (ed.) (1941) *Críth Gablach,* Dublin (reprinted 1979, Dublin Institute for Advanced Studies, Medieval and Modern Irish Series, vol. 11)
— (ed.) (1955) 'Irish law tracts re-edited', *'Coibnes Uisci Thairidne',* Ériu, 17, 52–85
— (1982) 'Brewing in eighth-century Ireland', in (ed.) B.G. Scott, 3–6
Bitel, L. (1990) *Isle of the Saints, Monastic Settlement and Christian Community in Early Ireland,* Ithaca, New York (Cornell University Press)
Blakiston-Houston, C. (1925) *Guide to the Ruins of Nendrum Monastery,* Belfast
Boden, E. (1998) *Black's Veterinary Dictionary,* London (A. & C. Black 19th edn)
Boessneck, J. (1969) 'Osteological differences between sheep (Ovis aries Linné) and goats *(Capra hircus Linné)*', in (eds) D. Brothwell and E. Higgs, 331–358
Bourke, C. (ed.) (1995) *From the Isles of the North; Early Medieval Art in Britain and Ireland,* Belfast (HMSO)
Bourke, C. (2001) 'Antiquities from the River Blackwater III, iron axe-heads', *Ulster J. Archaeol.* 60, 63–93
— (2002) 'An axe-head and ringed pin from Nendrum, Co. Down', *Lecale Miscellany* 20, 18–19
Bourke, E. (2005) 'A preliminary analysis of the inner enclosure of Skellig Michael Co. Kerry', in (eds) T. Condit and C. Corlett, 121–137
Bowen, E.G. (1969) *Saints, Seaways and Settlements in Celtic lands,* Cardiff (University of Wales)
Bowie, G.S.S. (1977) 'Tide (salt) watermills in Ireland', *Irish Engineers J.* 30 no.10, 9–10
— (1979) 'Corn drying kilns, meal milling and flour in Ireland', *Folklife* 17, 5–13
Bradley, J. (ed.) (1988) *Settlement and Society in Medieval Ireland, Studies Presented to F. X. Martin, o.s.a,.* Kilkenny (Boethius Press)
Bradley, J. (1991) 'Excavations at Moynagh Lough, County Meath', *J. Roy. Soc. Antiq. Ireland* cxxi, 5–26
Bradley, J. (1998) 'The monastic town of Clonmacnoise', in (ed.) H.A. King, 42–55
Brady, N. (1997) *'De Oratorio: Hisperica famina* and church building', *Peritia* 11, 327–335
Brady, N. (2006) 'Mills in Medieval Ireland: Looking beyond design', in (ed.) S.A. Walton, 39–68
Brannon, N.F. (1979) 'Nendrum Excavation Notes', unpublished, SMR. EHS
— (1982) 'Nendrum Excavation Notes', unpublished, SMR. EHS
— (1988) 'Life and death at an early monastery, Cathedral Hill, Downpatrick, Co. Down', in (eds) A. Hamlin and C.J. Lynn, 61–64
Breatnach, L. (ed.) (1987) *Uraicecht na Ríar,* Early Irish Law Series vol. 2, Dublin (Dublin Institute for Advanced Studies)
Breen, G. (2003) 'Board games from Medieval Cork in context', *J. Cork Archaeol. Hist. Soc.* 108, 41–50
Brothwell. D. R. (1981) *Digging up Bones,* 3rd edn, New York (British Museum and Cornell University Press)
Brothwell, D. R., Dobney, K. and Ervynck, A. (1996) 'On the causes of perforations in archaeological domestic cattle skulls', *Int. J. Osteoarchaeology* 6, 471–487
Brothwell, D. R. and Higgs, E. (eds) (1969) *Science in Archaeology,* 2nd edn, London (Thames and Hudson)
Brown, T.J. (1956–60) 'The palaeography of the Latin text' in (eds) T. D. Kendrick *et al.*
Bull, G. and Payne, S. (1982) 'Tooth eruption and epiphyseal fusion in pigs and wild boar', in (eds) B. Wilson, C. Grigson and S. Payne, 55–71
Butler, L.A.S. and Morris, R.K. (eds) (1986) *The Anglo-Saxon Church,* Council for British Archaeology Report 60, London (Council for British Archaeology)
Byrne, D. (1851) 'Ancient Irish Watermills', *Trans. Kilkenny Archaeol.* Soc. 1, 154–164
Byrne, F.J. (1973) *Irish Kings and High-Kings,* London (Batsford)

C.A. (2002) 'Ebbsfleet Saxon Mill', *Curr. Archaeol.* 16 (3) December, 193
Carey, J. (1986) 'The Heavenly City in *Saltair na Rann', Celtica* 18, 87–104
Carey, J., Herbert, M. and Ó Riain, P. (eds) (2001) *Studies in Irish Hagiography, Saints and Scholars,* Dublin (Four Courts Press)
Carney, J. (1983) 'A Maccucáin, Sruith in Tíag', *Celtica* 15, 25–41

Caulfield, S. (1977) 'The beehive quern in Ireland', *J. Roy. Soc. Antiq. Ireland* 107, 104–138
Carver, M. (2004) 'An Iona of the East: the Early-Medieval monastery at Portmahomack, Tarbat Ness', *Med. Archaeol.* 48, 1–30
Chadwick, O. (1968) *John Cassian,* Cambridge (Cambridge University Press)
Charles-Edwards, G. (2002a) 'The east cross inscription from Toureen Peacaun: some concrete evidence', *J. Roy. Soc. Antiq. Ireland* 132, 114–126
— (2002b) 'The Springmount Bog Tablets: their implications for Insular epigraphy and palaeography', *Studia Celtica* 36, 27–45
Charles-Edwards, T.M. (2000) *Early Christian Ireland,* Cambridge (Cambridge University Press)
— (2004) 'Early Irish Saints' cults and their constituencies', *Ériu* 54, 79–102
Chaplin, R.E. (1971) *The Study of Animal Bones from Archaeological Sites,* London (Seminar Press)
CIH = Binchy, D.A. (ed.) (1978) *Corpus Iuris Hibernici,* Dublin (Dublin Institute for Advanced Studies)
CGSH = Ó Riain, P. (ed.) (1985) *Corpus Genealogiarum Sanctorum Hiberniae,* Dublin (Dublin Institute for Advanced Studies)
Clarke, P. (1997) 'Lessons from Bronze Age boat-building', *British Archaeology* 24, 119–141
Cleary, R.M. (1999) 'A vertical-wheeled mill at Ardcloyne, Co. Cork (with discussion by C. Rynne)', *J. Cork Archaeol. Hist. Soc.* 104, 37–58
Cleary, R.M., Hurley, M.F. and Shee-Twohig, E. (eds) (1997) *Skiddy's Castle and Christ Church, Cork, Excavations 1974–77 by D. C. Twohig,* Cork (Cork Corporation)
Clemoes, P. (ed.) (1977) *Anglo-Saxon England,* 6, Cambridge (Cambridge University Press)
Clinton, M. (2005) 'Souterrains in potential association with church sites in Co. Meath', in (eds) T. Condit and C. Corlett, 149–169
Colfer, B. (2004) *The Hook Peninsula,* Rural Landscape 2, Cork (Cork University Press)
Comber, M. (1997) 'Lagore crannóg and non-ferrous metalworking in early historic Ireland', *J. Irish Achaeol.* 8, 101–14
Condit, T. and Corlett, C. (2005) *Above and beyond, essays in memory of Leo Swan,* Bray (Wordwell)
Connolly, S.J. (2002) *The Oxford Companion to Irish History,* 2nd edn, Oxford (Oxford University Press)
Connolly, S. and Picard, J.M. (1987) 'Cogitosus' Life of St Brigit', *J. Roy. Soc. Antiq. Ireland* 117, 5–27
Conway, M. (1999) *Director's First Findings from Excavations in Cabinteely,* Dublin (Margaret Gowen and Co. Ltd.)
Corlett, C. (2001) 'Milling around Bagenalstown', *Archaeol. Ireland,* 15 (3), 7
Costello, M.A. (1912) *De Annatis Hiberniae,* Dublin (Record Society, St. Patrick's College, Maynooth, M.H. Gill and Sons Ltd.)
Cotter, E. (2003) 'A horizontal-wheeled watermill at Crushyiree, Co. Cork', *J. Cork Archaeol. Hist. Soc.* 108, 105–116
CPRJ1 *Irish Patent Rolls of James 1st, Facsimile of the Irish Record Commission's Calendar,* Dublin (Stationery Office for the Irish Manuscripts Commission 1966)
Craddock, P. (1989) 'Metalworking techniques', in (ed.) S. Youngs, 170–174
Craig, D. (1997) 'The sculptured stones', in P. Hill, 433–441
Crawford, H.S. (1926) *Handbook of carved ornament,* Dublin (Royal Society of Antiquaries)
Crossley, D.W. (1981) *Medieval Industry,* CBA research report 40, London (Council for British Archaeology)
Cruden, S. (1948) 'The horizontal water-mill at Dounby on the mainland of Orkney', *Proc. Soc. Antiq. Scotland* 80, 43–47
CS = Hennessy, W.M. (ed.) (1866) *Chronicum Scotorum,* London
Curle, C.L. (1982) *Pictish and Norse Finds from the Brough of Birsay, 1934–7,* Society of Antiquaries of Scotland monograph series, no.1 Edinburgh (Society of Antiquaries of Scotland)
Curwen, E.C. (1937) 'Querns', *Antiquity* 12, 133–151
— (1944) 'The problem of early watermills', *Antiquity* 17, 130–146

Darrah, R. (1982) 'Working unseasoned oak', in (ed.) S. McGrail, 219–229
Davies, W., Graham-Campbell, J., Handley. M., Kershaw, P. Kock, J. LeDuc, G. and Lockyear, K. (2000) *The Inscriptions of Early Medieval Brittany,* London (University College London)
Davison, B.K. (1962) 'Excavations at Ballynarry, County Down', *Ulster J. Archaeol.* 24–25, 39–87
Day, A. and McWilliams, P. (eds) (1991) *Ordnance Survey Memoirs of Ireland Volume 18, Parishes of County Londonderry* 3, *1831–5, Roe Valley Lower,* Belfast (The Institute of Irish Studies in association with the Royal Irish Academy)
— (eds) (1993) *Ordnance Survey Memoirs of Ireland Volume 18, Parishes of County Londonderry* 5, *1830, 1833, 1836–7, Maghera and Tamlaght O' Crilly,* Belfast (The Institute of Irish Studies in association with the Royal Irish Academy)
Day, G. (1994) *Tide Mills in England and Wales,* Ipswich (Friends of the Woodbridge Tide Mill)
Deevy, M. (2002) 'Report on the wood from the wooden fish traps', in T. McErlean, R. McConkey and W. Forsythe, 589–595
de Paor, L. (1987) 'The high crosses of Tech Theille (Tihilly), Kinnitty, and related sculpture', in (ed.) E. Rynne, 131–158
— (1997) *Ireland and Early Europe,* Dublin (The Four Courts Press)
Dickinson, H.W. and Starker, E. (1934) 'The Shetland water mill', Trans. *Newcomen Soc.* 13, 89–94
DIL = Dictionary of the Irish Language, Dublin 1993 (compact edn, Royal Irish Academy)
Dillon, M. (1962) *Lebor na Cert: the Book of Rights,* Dublin (Irish Texts Society)
Dobbs, M.E. (1921) 'The history of the descendants of Ír', *Z. Celtische Phil.* 13, 308–59
Doherty, C. (1980) 'Exchange and trade in Early Medieval Ireland', *J. Roy. Soc. Antiq. Ireland* 110, 67–89
— (1982) 'Some aspects of hagiography as a source for economic history', *Peritia,* I, 300–328
Driesch, A. von den (1976) *A Guide to the Measurement of Animal Bones from Archaeological Sites,* Massachusetts (Peabody Museum of Archaeology and Ethnology)
Driesch, A. von den and Boessneck, J.A. (1974) 'Kritische Annmerkungen zur Widerristhoherberechnung ans Langermassen vor-und frühgeschichtlicher Tierknocken', *Saugetierkundliche Hitteilingen* 22, 325–348
Duignan, M. (1944) 'Irish agriculture in early historic times', *J. Roy. Soc. Antiq. Ireland* 74, 124–145
Dumville, D.N. (1993) 'The dating of the Tripartite Life of St. Patrick' in (ed.) D.N. Dumville, 255–258
Dumville, D.N. (ed.) (1993) *St. Patrick AD 493–1993,* Studies in Celtic History X111, Woodbridge (The Boydell Press)
Dumville, D.N. (2004) *Abbreviations used in Insular Script before AD 850: Tabulation based on the Work of W.M. Lindsay,* Cambridge (Department of Anglo-Saxon, Norse and Celtic, University of Cambridge)

Earwood, C. (1992) 'Turned wooden vessels of the early historic period from Ireland and western Scotland', *Ulster J. Archaeol.* 54–55, 154–159

— (1993) *Domestic Wooden Artefacts in Britain and Ireland from Neolithic to Viking Times,* Exeter (University of Exeter Press)

Edwards, N. and Lane, A. (eds) (1992) *The Early Church in Wales and the West,* Oxbow Monograph 16, Oxford (Oxbow)

Edwards, N. (1990) *The Archaeology of Early Medieval Ireland,* London (Batsford)

Edwards, N. (2001) 'Early Medieval inscribed stones and stone sculpture in Wales: context and function', *Med. Archaeol.* 45, 33–38

EHS Guide Card 1997 Nendrum

Elden, A. (1935) 'Tide-mills in New England', *Old Time New England,* 25, 117–127

Ellmers, D. (1981) 'Post-Roman waterfront installations on the Rhine', in (eds) G. Milne and B. Hobley, 89–95

English Heritage (1998) *Guidelines on producing and interpreting dendrochronological date,* London

Etchingham, C. (1991) 'The early Irish church: some observations on pastoral care and dues', *Ériu* 42, 99–118

— (1993) 'The implications of *paruchia', Ériu* 44, 139–162

— (1994) 'Bishops in the early Irish church: a reassessment', *Studia Hibernica* 28, 35–62

— (1996) V*iking raids on Irish church settlements in the ninth century: a reconsideration of the annals,* Maynooth (Maynooth monographs; series minor; St. Patrick's College, Department of Old and Middle Irish)

— (1999a) *Church Organisation in Ireland,* AD 650 to 1000, Maynooth (Laigin Publications)

— (1999b) 'Bishoprics in Ireland and Wales in the early middle ages: some comparisons', in (eds) J.R. Guy and W.J. Neely, 7–26

— (1999c) 'Preface to paperback edition', in E.A. Thompson, *Who was Saint Patrick?* 2nd paperback edn, Woodbridge (Boydell), xvii-xxxii

— (2000a) 'Kildare before the Normans: "an episcopal and conventual see"', *J. Kildare Archaeol. Soc.* 19, 7–26

— (2000b) 'Episcopal hierarchy in Connacht and Tairdelbach Uá Conchobair', *J. Galway Archaeol. Hist. Soc.* 52, 13–29

— (2001) 'North Wales, Ireland and the Isles: the Insular Viking zone', *Peritia* 15, 145–187

— *(forthcoming 2007) Viking raiders and Irish reporters: Viking attacks on Irish churches and their chroniclers AD 795-1015,* Maynooth

Evans, E.E. (1967) *Mourne Country: Landscape and Life in South Down,* Dundalk (Dundalgan Press, W. Tempest Ltd.)

Fahy, E.M. (1956) 'A horizontal mill at Mashanaglass, Co. Cork', *J. Cork Archaeol. Hist. Soc.* 61, 13–57

Fanning, T. (1981) 'Excavation of an Early Christian cemetery and settlement at Reask, Co Kerry', *Proc. Roy. Irish Acad.* 81C, 3–172

— (1994) *Viking Age Ringed Pins from Dublin,* Dublin (Royal Irish Academy)

Faul, M. and Moorehouse, S.A. (eds) (1981) *West Yorkshire: An Archaeological Survey to AD 1500,* vol. 3, Leeds (West Yorkshire Metropolitan County Council)

Fisher, I. (2001) *Early Medieval Sculpture in the West Highlands and Islands,* Monograph series 1, Edinburgh (Royal Commission on the Ancient and Historical Monuments of Scotland and the Society of Antiquaries of Scotland)

Fitzpatrick, E. and O'Brien, C. (1998) *The Medieval Churches of County Offaly,* Dublin, (Dúchas The Heritage Service)

Fitzpatrick, E. (1998) 'The early Church in Offaly', in (eds) W. Nolan and T. O'Neill, 93–130

Fitzpatrick, E., O'Brien, M. and Walsh, P. (eds) (2004) *Archaeological Investigations in Galway City,* 1987-1998, Bray (Wordwell)

Fitzpatrick, E. and Gillespie, R. (eds) (2006) *The Parish in Medieval and Early Modern Ireland,* Dublin (Four Courts Press)

Fitzsimons, E.M. (2000) *Mochae of Nendrum and his Cult,* thesis submitted for degree of Master of Philosophy, Queen's University, Belfast, Faculty of Humanities

Flanagan, D. (1984) 'The Christian impact on early Ireland: the place-name evidence', in (eds) P. Ní Chatháin and M. Richter, 25–51

Flanagan, L.N.W. (1990) *A Chronicle of Irish Saints,* Belfast (The Blackstaff Press)

Fry, M. (1989) *Grist to the Mill: A forgotten machine for grinding corn,* Belfast (DoENI)

Fry, M. and Martin, A.M. (1994) 'Logboats, horizontal mills and other large archaeological timbers from the North of Ireland', *Ulster Local Studies* 16 (1), 7–30

Fry, M. (2000) *Coití, Logboats from Northern Ireland,* Northern Ireland Archaeological Monographs: no. 4, Belfast (Environment and Heritage Service, Department of the Environment)

Gailey, A. (1970) 'Irish corn-drying kilns', *Ulster Folklife* 15/16, 52–71

Gale, R. and Cutler, D. (2000) *Plants in Archaeology,* Otley (Westbury Publishing)

Gelly, M.A. (1995) 'The Irish high cross: methods of design', in (ed.) C. Bourke, 157–166

Good, G.L., Jones, R.H. and Ponsford, M.W. (eds) (1991) *Waterfront Archaeology: Proceedings of the Third International Conference on Waterfront Archaeology held at Bristol 23-26 September 1988,* CBA Research Report: 74, London (Council for British Archaeology)

Goodburn, D. (1992) 'Woods and woodland: carpenters and carpentry', in *Timber Building Techniques in London c. 900-1400,* London and Middlesex Archaeology Soc. Special Paper:15, 106–130

— (1999) 'Summary of the evidence for Early Medieval woodwork found at Cheapside', in J. Hill and A. Woodger, 47–51

— (2003) 'Prehistoric woodwork', in 'A Later Bronze Age Well Complex at Swalecliffe, Kent', Masefield R., Branch N., Couldrey P., Goodburn D. *et al. Antiq. J.* 83, 98–104

Goudie, G. (1886) 'On the horizontal water mills of Shetland', *Proc. Soc. Antiq. Scotland* 20, 257–297

Graham-Campbell, J. A. (1972) 'Two groups of ninth-century Irish brooches', *J. Roy. Soc. Antiq. Ireland* 102, 113–28

— (1974) 'The Lough Ravel, Co. Antrim, brooch and others of ninth-century date', *Ulster J. Archaeol.* 36–37, 52–7

— (1981) 'The bell and the mould', in (ed.) R. Reece, 23–25

Grant, A. (1982) 'The use of tooth wear as a guide to the age of domestic ungulates', in (eds) B. Wilson *et al.*, 91–108

Green, E.R.R. (1963) *The Industrial Archaeology of County Down,* Belfast (HMSO)

Greenhill, B. (1995) *The Archaeology of Boats and Ships: An Introduction,* London (Conway Maritime)

Gribbon, H.D. (1969) *The History of Water Power in Ulster,* Newton Abbot (Institute of Irish Studies, Queen's University Belfast)

Grosjean, P. (1929) 'S. Caelani cum ave colloquium', in A*nalecta Bollandiana* 47, 39–43

Guy, J.R. and Neely, W.G. (eds) (1999) *Contrasts and Comparisons: studies in Irish and Welsh church history,* Powys and Keady (Welsh Religious Historical Society Powys and Church of Ireland Historical Society, Keady Co. Armagh)

Gwynn, A. and Hadcock, R.N. (1970) *Medieval Religious Houses, Ireland,* London (Longmans: republished by Irish Academic Press, Dublin, 1988)

Habermehl, K.H. (1961) *Die Altersbestimmung bei Haustieren, Pelztieren und beim jagbaren Wild,* Berlin (Paul Parey)
Haggarty, A.M. (1988) 'Iona: some results from recent work', *Proc. Soc. Antiq. Scotland* 118, 203–213
Hamlin, A. (1976) 'The archaeology of early Christianity in the North of Ireland', (unpublished Ph.D. thesis, Queen's University Belfast)
— (1977) 'A recently discovered enclosure at Inch abbey, County Down', *Ulster J. Archaeol.* 40, 85–88
— (1982) 'Using mills on Sunday', in (ed.) B.G. Scott, 11
— (1985) 'The archaeology of the Irish church in the eighth century', *Peritia* 4, 279–299
— (1986) *Nendrum, Co. Down,* Belfast (Historic Monuments and Buildings Branch, DoE)
— (1987) 'Some northern sundials and time-keeping in the early Irish Church', in (ed.) E. Rynne, 29–42
— (1997) 'The early church in County Down to the twelfth century', in (ed.) L. Proudfoot, 47–70
Hamlin, A. and Hughes, K. (1977) *The Modern Traveller to the Early Irish Church,* Dublin (reprinted 2004, The Four Courts Press)
Hamlin, A. and Lynn, C.J. (eds) (1988) *Pieces of the Past, Archaeological Excavations by the Department of the Environment for Northern Ireland,* 1970–1986, Belfast (HMSO)
Hamlin, A. (2001) 'Some little-known Ulster inscriptions', in (eds) J. Higgitt *et al,* 51–56
Harbison, P. (1970) 'How old is Gallurus Oratory? A reappraisal of its role in Early Irish architecture', *Med. Archaeol.* 14, 34–59
Harbison, P. (1991) *Pilgrimage in Ireland,* London (Barrie and Jenkins)
Hare, M. and Hamlin, A. (1986) 'The study of early churches and round towers', in (eds) L.A.S Butler and R.K. Morris, 130–145
Harcourt, R.A. (1974) 'The dog in Prehistoric and Early Historic Britain', *J. Archaeol. Sci.* 1, 151–175
Harris, W. (1744) *The Ancient and Present State of the County of Down,* Dublin (printed by A. Rielly for Edward Exshaw)
Harrison, K. (1984) 'A letter from Rome to the Irish Clergy, AD 660', *Peritia,* 3, 222–229
Harry, W.T. and Richey, J.E. (1963) 'Magmatic pulses in the emplacement of plutons', *Lpool and Manchr Geol. J.* 3, 254–268
Haverson, M. (1993) 'The mills of Medieval Iraq', *Proc. Ninth and Tenth Conferences Mill Research Group,* 15-17
Haverson, M. (2000) *Mills of the Muslim World,* London (Society for the Protection of Ancient Buildings, Mill Section)
Hawkesley, J. (2000) 'How efficient were horizontal waterwheels? An attempt to answer the question by testing a series of models', in 10th Symposium on Molinology of The International Molinological Society
HE= Sherley-Price, L. (trans.) *Bede, Ecclesiastical History of the English People,* London (Penguin Classics, revised edn 1990, Penguin Books)
Heist, W.W. (ed.) (1965) *Vitae Sanctorum Hiberniae* ex codice olim Salmanticensi nunc Bruxellensi, Subsidia hagiographica; 28, Brussels (Société des Bollandistes)
Hencken, H.O'N. (1936) 'Ballinderry crannóg I', *Proc. Roy Irish Acad.* 43C (5), 103–239
— (1938) *Cahercommaun: a Stone Fort in County Clare,* Dublin (Royal Society of Antiquaries of Ireland)
— (1950) 'Lagore crannóg: an Irish royal residence of the 7th to 10th centuries A.D.', *Proc. Roy. Irish Acad.* 53C (1), 1–247
Hennessy, W. (ed.) (1866) *Chronicum Scotorum,* London = CS
Henry, F. (1965) *Irish Art in the Early Christian Period (to 800 AD),* London (Methuen)
Herity, M. (1983) 'The buildings and layout of early Irish monasteries before the year 1000', *Early Irish Monasteries: Monastic Studies No. 14,* 247–285 (Montreal)
Herity, M. (1995) *Studies in the Layout, Buildings and Art in Stone of Early Irish Monasteries,* London (The Pindar Press)
Herity, M. and Breen, A. (2002) *The Cathach of Colum Cille; An Introduction,* Dublin (The Royal Irish Academy)
Herron, M. (1974) *The Hisperica Famina, 1: the A-Text, a new critical edition with English translations and philological commentary,* Toronto (Pontifical Institute of Mediaeval Studies)
Hickey, E. (1994) *Skryne and the Early Normans,* Meath (The Meath Archaeological Society)
Higgitt, J. (1982) 'The Pictish Latin inscription at Tarbat in Ross-shire', *Proc. Soc. Antiq. Scotland,* 112, 300–321
— (1994) 'The display script of the Book of Kells and the tradition of Insular decorative capitals', in (ed.) F. O'Mahony, 209–233
Higgitt, J. *et al.* (eds) (2001) *Roman, Runes and Ogham,* Donington
Higham, C.F.W. (1967) 'Stock rearing as a cultural factor in prehistoric Europe', *Proc. Prehist. Soc.* 33, 84–106
Hill, G. (1869) *The Montgomery Manuscripts* (1603-1706), Belfast (James Cleeland, Arthur Street and Thomas Dargan, Castle Lane)
Hill, J. and Woodger, A. (1999) *Excavations at 72-75 Cheapside/ 83–93 Queen Street City of London,* MoLAS Archaeological Studies Series 2
Hill, M.O., Preston, C.D. and Smith, A.J.E. (1994) *Atlas of the bryophytes of Britain and Ireland. 3. Mosses (Diplolepideae)* Colchester (Harley Books)
Hill, P. (1997) *Whithorn and St. Ninian: The Excavation of a Monastic Town 1984–91,* Stroud (The Whithorn Trust and Sutton Publishing)
Hodgen, M.T. (1939) 'Domesday water mills', *Antiquity* 13, no. 51, 261–277
Hood, D.N. (1981) 'Geochemical, Petrological and Structural Studies on the Tertiary Granites and Associated Rocks of the Eastern Mourne Mountains, Co. Down, Northern Ireland', (unpublished PhD. thesis, Queen's University of Belfast)
Horn, W. (1975) 'Waterpower and the plan of St Gall', *Journal of Medieval History 1,* 219–258
Hourihane, C. (ed.) (2001) *From Ireland Coming: Irish art from the early Christian to the late Gothic period and its European context,* Index of Christian art occasional papers 4, Princeton, New Jersey (Dept. of Art and Archaeology, Princeton University Press)
Howlett, D. (2006) *Muirchú Moccu Macthéni's 'Vita Santi Patricii' Life of Patrick,* Dublin (Four Courts Press)
Hughes, A.J, and Nolan, W. (eds) (2001) *Armagh History and Society: Interdisciplinary Essays on the History of an Irish County,* Dublin (Geography Publications)
Hughes, K. (1979) *Early Christian Ireland: Introduction to the Sources,* Cambridge (The Sources of History Ltd. in association with Hodder and Stoughton Ltd.)
Hull, J. (1966) 'Cáin Donmaigh', *Ériu* 20, 151–177
Hurley, M. (1997a) 'Artefacts of skeletal material', in (eds) R.M. Cleary *et al.* 237–273
— (1997b) 'Artefacts of skeletal material', in (eds) M. Hurley, O. Scully and S.W.J. McCutcheon, 650–699
Hurley, M., Scully, O.M.B. and McCutcheon, S.W.J. (eds) (1997) *Late Viking Age and Medieval Waterford Excavations 1986-1992,* Waterford (Waterford City Council)

Hurley, V. (1980) 'Additions to the map of monastic Ireland: the south-west', J. Cork Archaeol. Hist. Soc. 85, 52–65
Hurley, V. (1982) 'The early church in the south-west of Ireland', in (ed.) S.M. Pearce, 287–332

Inv. Cavan = *Archaeological Inventory of County Cavan,* Dublin 1995 (The Stationery Office)
Inv. Cork 1 = *Archaeological Inventory of County Cork, Volume 1,* Dublin 1992 (The Stationery Office)
Inv. Cork 2 = *Archaeological Inventory of County Cork, Volume 2: East and South Cork,* Dublin 1994 (The Stationery Office)
Inv. Galway 1 = *Archaeological Inventory of County Galway: Volume 1: West Galway,* Dublin 1993 (The Stationery Office)
Inv. Galway 2 = *Archaeological Inventory of County Galway, Volume 2: North Galway,* Dublin 1999 (The Stationery Office)
Inv. North Tipperary = *Archaeological Inventory of County Tipperary, Volume 1: North Tipperary,* Dublin 2002 (The Stationery Office)
Inv. Waterford = *Archaeological Inventory of County Waterford,* Dublin 1998 (The Stationery Office)
Inv. Wexford = *Archaeological Inventory of County Wexford,* Dublin 1996 (The Stationery Office)
Inv. Wicklow = *Archaeological Inventory of County Wicklow,* Dublin 1997 (The Stationery Office)
Ivens, R. (1984) 'Movilla Abbey, Newtownards, County Down: excavation 1981', *Ulster J. Archaeol.* 47, 63–70
— (1987) 'The Early Christian monastic enclosure at Tullylish Co. Down', *Ulster J. Archaeol.* 50, 55–121

Jespersen, A. (1994) 'Den Danske Mølle 1994 Nr 1', Molinological Computations
Jope, E.M. (ed.) (1966) *An Archaeological Survey of County Down,* Belfast (HMSO) = ASCD
Jope, M. and Ivens, R.J. (1998) 'The Rath at Ballymacash, County Antrim', *Proc. Roy. Irish Acad.* 98C, 101–123

Keeling, C.D. and Whorf, T.P. (2000) 'The 1800-year oceanic tidal cycle: a possible cause of rapid climate change', Scripps Institution of Oceanography, at the University of California, San Diego, *Proceedings of the National Academy of Sciences* 97 (8), 3814–3819
Kelly, F. (1976) 'The old Irish tree-list', *Celtica* 11, 107–124
— (1988) *A Guide to Early Irish Law,* Early Irish Law Series III, Dublin (Dublin Institute for Advanced Studies)
— (1997) *Early Irish Farming,* Early Irish Law Series IV, Dublin (Dublin Institute for Advanced Studies)
Kendrick, T.D. *et al* (eds) (1956-60) *Evangeliorum Quattuor Codex Lindisfarnensis,* Olten and Lausanne (Urs Graf)
Kenney, J. (1929) *The Sources for the Early History of Ireland: Ecclesiastical,* New York (Columbia University Press: reprinted 1979 by Octagon Books, New York)
Kenward, H., Hall, A. and Carrott, J. *(forthcoming) Environment, activity and living conditions at Deer Park Farms: evidence from plant and invertebrate remains,* in C. Lynn and J.A. McDowell, (forthcoming)
Kermode, P.M.C. (1907) *Manx Crosses,* London (Bemrose and Sons)
Kilbride Jones, H.E. (1980) *Zoomorphic Penannular Brooches,* London (Society of Antiquaries)
King, H.A. (1998) *Clonmacnoise Studies Volume 1, seminar papers 1994,* Dublin (Dúchas, The Heritage Service)
King, H.A. (2003) *Clonmacnoise Studies Volume 2, seminar papers 1998,* Dublin (The Stationery Office)
Kirk, D. (2002) *The Mountains of Mourne – A celebration of a place apart,* Belfast (Appletree Press)
Knight, G.A.F. (1933) *Archeological Light on the Early Christianising of Scotland, 1,* London (J. Clarke and Company)
Knox, H.T. (1906) 'Notes on gig-mills and drying kilns near Ballyhaunis, Co Mayo', *Proc. Roy. Irish Acad,* 26C, 263–273

Laing, L. (1975) 'The mote of mark and Celtic interlace', *Antiquity* 49, 98–108
— (1976) 'Penannular brooches in Ireland and Scotland', *Ulster J. Archaeol.* 39, 15–19
Lane, A. and Campbell, E. (2000) *Dunadd, An Early Dalriadic Capital,* Oxford (Oxbow Books)
Lalor, B. (1999) *The Irish Round Tower: origins and architecture explored,* Cork (Collins Press)
Lawlor, H.J. (1913) 'A calendar of the register of Archbishop Fleming', *Proc. Roy. Irish Acad.* 30C, 94–190
— (1922) 'Interim report on work of repair and preservation of the ruins of Nendrum monastery', *Proc. Belfast Nat. Hist. and Phil. Soc.,* (1921–22) 92–106
— (1923) 'Report of work at Nendrum', Proc. *Belfast Nat. Hist. Phil. Soc.,* (1922–23) 56–81
— (1925a) *The Monastery of Saint Mochaoi of Nendrum,* Belfast (Belfast Natural History and Philosophical Society)
— (1925b) 'Archaeological section, 9th session, 1924–1925', *Proc. Belfast Nat. Hist. Phil. Soc.,* 35–37
Lawlor, H.C. (1926) 'Divisions of the Nendrum sundial', *The Irish Nat. J.* 1, 53–55
Lawlor, H.C. (1928) *Ulster: Its Archæology and Antiquities,* Belfast (R. Carswell)
Lewis, S. (1837) *A Topographical Dictionary of Ireland,* 2 vols, London (S. Lewis and Co.)
Levine, M.A. (1982) 'The use of crown height measurements and eruption-wear sequences to age horse teeth', in (eds) B. Wilson *et al.,* 223–250
Lionard, P. (1961) 'Early Irish grave-slabs', *Proc. Roy. Irish Acad.* 61C, 95–169
Litoral Atlantico (2005) *Molinos de Mar y Estuarios,* Santander, Spain (Litoral Atlantico, Asociación para la conservación de la Arquitectura Tradicional, Tajamar)
Lucas, A. (2006) *Wind, Water, Work: Ancient and Medieval Milling Technology,* Technology & Change in History; no. 8, Brill (Leiden and Boston)
Lucas, A.T. (1953) 'The horizontal mill in Ireland', *J. Roy. Soc. Antiq. Ireland* 83, 1–36
— (1955) 'A horizontal mill at Ballykilleen, Co. Offaly', *J. Roy. Soc. Antiq. Ireland* 85, 100–112
— (1967) 'The plundering and burning of churches in Ireland, 7th to 16th century', in (ed.) E. Rynne, 172–229
— (1969) 'A horizontal mill at Knocknagranshy Co. Limerick', *N. Munster Antiq. J.* 10, 12–22
— (1985) 'Toghers or causeways: some evidence from archaeological, literary, historical and place-name sources', *Proc. Roy. Irish Acad.* 85C, 37–60
— (1986a) 'A two-chute horizontal mill at Newton, Co. Tipperary', *N. Munster Antiq. J.* 28, 16–27
— (1986b) 'The social role of relics and reliquaries in ancient Ireland', *J. Roy. Soc. Antiq. Ireland* 116, 5–37
Lucy, W.M. (1939) 'Tide mills worked by the inland sea between Holy Isle and Anglesey', *Trans. Anglesey Antiq. Soc.,* 109–110

Lucy, W.M. (1945) 'Anglesey tide mills', *Trans. Anglesey Antiq. Soc.*, 61–63
Lynn, C.J. (1978a) 'Early Christian period domestic structures: A change from round to rectangular plans?', *Irish Archaeology Research Forum* 5, 29–45
— (1978b) 'A rath in Seacash townland, County Antrim', *Ulster J. Archaeol.* 41, 55–73
— (1982), 'The excavation of Rathmullan, a raised rath and motte in County Down', *Ulster J. Archaeol.* 44–45, 65–171
— (1983) 'Some early ring-forts and crannógs', *J. Irish Archaeol.* I, 47–58
— (1985) 'Excavations on a mound at Gransha, County Down, 1972 and 1982: An interim report', *Ulster J. Archaeol.* 48, 81–90
Lynn, C. and McDowell, J.A. *(forthcoming) An Early Christian Settlement at Deer Park Farms, Glenarm, Co. Antrim*

MacAdam, R. (1856) 'Ancient water-mills', *Ulster J. Archaeol.* (1st series) 4, 6–15
Macalister, R.A.S. (1909) *The Memorial Slabs of Clonmacnoise, King County,* Dublin (Royal Society of Antiquaries of Ireland)
Macalister, R.A.S. (1949) *Corpus Inscriptionum Insularum Celticarum,* Dublin (The Stationery Office)
McCann, J. (ed. and trans.) (1952) *The rule of St Benedict,* London (Burns and Oates)
McCormick, F. (1987) 'Stockrearing in Early Christian Ireland', (unpublished Ph.D. thesis, Queen's University of Belfast)
— (1991) 'The dog in prehistoric and Early Christian Ireland', *Archaeol. Ireland* 5, 7–9
— (1993) 'Excavations at Iona, 1988', *Ulster J. Archaeol.* 56, 78–108
— (1997) 'The animal bones', in (eds) M. F. Hurley *et al.*, 819–853
— (1997a) 'Iona: the archaeology of the early monastery', in (ed.) C. Bourke, 45–68
— (1997b) 'Farming and food in Medieval Lecale', in (ed.) L. Proudfoot, 33–46
McCormick, F. and Murphy, E.M. (1997) 'Mammal bones', in (ed.) C. Walsh, 199–218
McCorry, M. (2001) *The Medieval Pottery Kiln at Downpatrick, Co. Down: an Investigation of its Working Life, its Products and their Distribution,* B.A.R. British series; no. 326, Oxford (John and Erica Hedges Ltd.)
McCracken, E. (1971) *The Irish Woods Since Tudor Times: Their Distribution and Exploitation,* Newton Abbot (David and Charles)
McCutcheon, W.A. (1980) *The Industrial Archaeology of Northern Ireland,* Cranbury, N.J. (Associated University Press)
MacDonald, A. (1981) 'Notes on monastic archaeology and the Annals of Ulster', in (ed.) D. Ó Corráin, 304–319
MacDonald A. (1984) 'Aspects of the monastery and monastic life in *Adomnán's Life of Columba, Peritia* 3, 271–302
— (2001) 'Aspects of the monastic landscape in *Adomnán's Life of Columba I',* in (eds) J. Carey *et al.*, 15–30
Macdonald, P. (2003) 'Data structure report: no. 16, Monitoring at Nendrum, Mahee Island Co. Down', (unpublished report for EHS by the Centre for Archaeological Fieldwork, Queen's University Belfast)
McErlean T. and Crothers N. (2001), 'Tidal power at Nendrum', in *Archaeol. Ireland* 15 (2), 12–14
McErlean T., McConkey R., and Forsythe W., (2002), *Strangford Lough, An Archaeological Survey of the Maritime Cultural Landscape,* Northern Ireland Archaeological Monographs No. 6, Belfast (Blackstaff Press)
McErlean, T. and O'Sullivan, A. (2002) 'Foreshore tidal fish traps', in T. McErlean, et al., 144–185
McErlean, T. and Williams, B. (2003) 'The Early Medieval tide mills at Nendrum Monastery, County Down, Northern Ireland', *The Bulletin of the Australian Institute for Maritime Archaeology* 27, 35–42
MacEoin, G., (1982) 'The early Irish vocabulary of mills and milling', in (ed.) B.G. Scott, 13–19
— (1982) 'The death of the boys in the mill', *Celtica* 10, 60–64
Mac Fhirbhisigh, *Leabhar Mór na nGenealach, The Great Book of Irish genealogies, compiled (1645-66) by Dubhaltach Mac Fhirbisigh,* vol. 2, edited with translations and indexes by Nollaig Ó Muraíle, Dublin (de Búrca 2003)
McGrail, S. (ed.) (1982) *Woodworking techniques before AD 1500,* B.A.R. International Series S129, Oxford (B.A.R.)
McGrail, S. (1978) *Logboats of England and Wales with Comparative Material from European and Other Countries,* B.A.R. British Series 51 (ii) Oxford (B.A.R.)
— (1998) *Ancient Boats in North-West Europe: The Archaeology of Water Transport to AD 1500,* London and New York (Longman, reissued in paperback 1998)
MacGregor, A. (1974) 'The broch of Burrian, North Ronaldsay, Orkney', *Proc. Soc. Antiq. Scotland 105,* 63–118
— (1985) *Bone, Antler, Ivory and Horn,* London (Croom Helm)
Mackay, A.W., Battarbee, R.W., Birks, H.J.B. and Oldfield, F. (eds) (2003) *Global Change in the Holocene,* London (Arnold)
McNeill, T.E. (1980) *Anglo-Norman Ulster: The History and Archaeology of an Irish Barony,* 1177-1400, Edinburgh (John Donald Publishers Ltd.)
Mallory, J.P. and McNeill, T.E. (1991) *The Archaeology of Ulster, from Colonisation to Plantation,* Belfast (Institute of Irish Studies, Queen's University Belfast)
Maltby, M. (1979) *The Animal Bones from Exeter 1971-1975,* Sheffield (Exeter Archaeological Reports vol. 2: Department of Archaeology and Prehistory, University of Sheffield)
Manning, C. (1998a) 'Clonmacnoise cathedral' in (ed.) H.A. King, 57–86
Manning, C. (ed.) (1998b) *Dublin and Beyond the Pale: Studies in Honour of Patrick Healy,* Bray (Wordwell)
— (2003) 'Some early masonry churches and the round tower at Clonmacnoise', in (ed.) H.A. King, 63–95
Marshall, J.W. and Walsh, C. (1998) 'Illaunloughan, Co. Kerry: An Island Hermitage', in (eds) M. Monk and J. Sheehan, 102–111
Marshall, J.W. and Rourke, G.D. (2000) *High Island, An Irish Monastery in the Atlantic,* Dublin (Town House and Country House, Dublin)
Matthews, G. (1995) 'Nendrum Rediscovered', (unpublished dissertation, Dept. of Archaeology and Palaeoecology, Queen's University Belfast)
Mawhinney, G. (ed.) (1992) *John O'Donovan's letters from County Londonderry (1834),* Draperstown, (Ballyinascreen Historical Society)
Maxwell, S. (1955) 'A horizontal mill paddle from Dalswinton', *Trans. Dumfriesshire Galloway Natur. Hist. Antiq. Soc.* XXXIII, 185–196
Maxwell, S. (1956) 'Paddles from horizontal mills', *Proc. Soc. Antiq. Scotland* LXXXVIII, 231–232
Mays, S. (1998) *The Archaeology of Human Bones,* London (Routledge)
Megaw, B.R.S. (1940) 'Mwyllin Beg: an account of the horizontal mills', *J. Manx Mus.* IV, 199–202
Meighan, I.G., Simpson, D.D.A. and Hartwell, B.N. (2002) 'Newgrange – sourcing of its granitic cobbles', *Archaeol. Ireland* 16 (1), 32–35

Meighan, I.G., Hood, D.N. and Gibson, D. (1984) 'Some aspects of tertiary acid magmatism in NE Ireland', *Mineralogical Mag.* 48, 351–363

Menanteau, L. and Kostrowicka, M. (2005) 'La geografía de los molinos en el litoral atlántico europro', in *Litoral Atlántico,* 89–102

Milne, G. and Hobley, B. (eds) (1981) *Waterfront Archaeology in Britain and Northern Europe,* CBA Research Report No. 41, 1981, London (Council for British Archaeology)

Minchinton, W.E. (1977) 'Tidemills of England and Wales', Trans. of the Forth Symposium of International Molinological Society , T.I.M.S., vol. 1–8, 339–353

MoLAS (2003) Museum of London, Archaeological Services, Annual Review, Selected projects 2003/3

Monk, M.A. (1981) 'Post-Roman drying kilns and the problem of function: a preliminary statement, in (ed.) D. Ó Corráin, 216–230

Monk, M.A. and Sheehan, J. (eds) (1998) *Early Medieval Munster: Archaeology, History and Society,* Cork (Cork University Press)

Moog, B. (1994) *The Horizontal Watermill, History and Technique of the First Prime Mover,* The Hague, Holland (The International Molinological Society)

Moss, R. (2002) 'Round towers', in (ed.) S.J. Connolly, 517

MRD The Maritime Record for Co Down of the Environment and Heritage Service of Northern Ireland

Mulchrone, K. (1939) *Bethu Phátraic,* Dublin and London (Royal Irish Academy)

Murphy, D. (1993) 'Monasterboice: secrets from the air', *Archaeol.* Ireland 7 (3), 15–17

Murphy, D. (2003) 'Excavation of an early monastic enclosure at Clonmacnoise', in (ed.) H.A. King, 1–33

Murphy, E.M. (1998) 'Osteological report on the mammal bones from Digges Lane, Dublin', (unpublished report prepared for ADS Ltd., Belfast)

— (2000a) 'Osteological report on the animal palaeopathological lesions from Maynooth Castle', (unpublished report prepared for Claire Walsh Ltd., Dublin)

— (2000b) 'Osteological report on the mammal bones from Gordon St., Belfast', (unpublished report produced for ADS Ltd., Belfast)

— (2000c) 'Osteological report on the mammal bones from Market St., Armagh City', (unpublished report produced for NAC Ltd., Belfast)

— (2000d) 'Osteological report on the mammal bones from Bishop's Street Without, Derry City', (unpublished report for EHS, Belfast)

— *(forthcoming a)* 'Osteological report on the mammal bones from Carrickfergus, Co. Antrim', in R. Ó Baoill *(forthcoming)*

— (2004) 'Animal palaeopathology', in (eds) E. Fitzpatrick *et al.*, 602–608

Murphy, E.M. and McCormick, F. (1994) 'The mammal bones from Drumcliffe, Co. Sligo', (unpublished report for Ms. Joyce Enright, Sligo)

Mytum, H. (1992) *The Origins of Early Christian Ireland,* London and New York (Routledge)

Nash-Williams, V. (1950) *The Early Christian Monuments of Wales,* Cardiff (University of Wales Press)

Neill, M.E. *(forthcoming) A Report with Catalogues, Diagrams and Discussion on the Use of Woodland in the Construction of Houses at Deerpark Farms Raised Rath, Glenarm, Co. Antrim,* in C. Lynn and J.A. McDowell, (forthcoming)

Nees, L. (1983) 'The colophon drawing in the Book of Mulling: A supposed Irish monastery plan and the tradition of terminal illustration in Early Medieval manuscripts', *Cambridge Medieval Studies,* 5, 67–91

Newman, C. (2002) 'Ballinderry crannóg no. 2, Co. Offaly: pre-crannóg Early Medieval horizon', *J. Irish Archaeol.* 11, 99–123

Ní Chatháin, P. and Richter, M. (eds) (1984) *Ireland and Europe: the Early Church,* Stuttgart (Klett-Cotta)

Nolan, W., Ronayne, L. and Dunlevy, M. (eds) (1995) *Donegal History and Society: Interdisciplinary Essays on the History of an Irish County,* Dublin (Geography Publications)

Nolan, W. and O'Neill, T. (1998) *Offaly, History and Society, Interdisciplinary Essays on the History of an Irish County,* Dublin (Geography Publications)

Norman, E.R. and St Joseph, J.K.S. (1969) *The Early Development of Irish Society,* Cambridge (Cambridge University Press)

Ó Baoil, R. *(forthcoming) Excavations in Carrickfergus Town 1991-95,* Belfast (*Northern Ireland Archaeological Monographs,* Environment and Heritage Service)

O'Brien, M.A. (ed.) (1962) *Corpus Genealogiarum Hiberniae I,* Dublin (Dublin Institute for Advanced Studies: reprinted 1976)

O'Brien, E. (1992) 'Pagan and Christian burial in Ireland during the first millennium AD: continuity and change', in (eds) N. Edwards and A. Lane, 130–37

Ó Carragáin, T. (2006) 'Church building and pastoral care in Early Medieval Ireland', in (eds) E. Fitzpatrick and R. Gillespie, 91–123

Ó Conlon, M.A. (1926) 'The Knockrour discovery. A watermill?', *J. Cork Archaeol. Hist. Soc* 31, 96–101

Ó Corráin, D. (ed.) (1981) *Irish Antiquity, Essays and Studies Presented to Professor M. J. O'Kelly,* Cork (Tower Books of Cork)

Ó Corráin, D. (1998) 'Creating the past: The early Irish genealogical tradition,' *Peritia* 12, 177–208

Ó Cróinín, D. (1995) *Early Medieval Ireland 400–1200,* London (Longman)

— (2003) *Early Irish History and Chronology,* Dublin (Four Courts Press)

O'Donovan, W.J. (1859) 'Note on Milverton, Co. Dublin', Trans Kilkenny Archaeol. Soc 2, 252

O'Donovan, J.H., Todd, J.H., and Reeves, W. (eds and trans.) (1864) *The Martyrology of Donegal, a Calendar of the Saints of Ireland,* Dublin (Irish Archaeological and Celtic Society)

Ó Floinn, R. (1989) 'Model of ring for brooch-pin', in (ed.) S. Youngs, 194

— (1990) 'A fragmentary house-shaped shrine from Clonard, Co. Meath', *J. Irish Archaeol.* 5, 49–55

— (1995) 'Sandhills, silver and shrines: fine metalwork of the Medieval period in Donegal', in (eds) W. Nolan, L. Ronayne and M. Dunlevy, 85–148

— (1998) 'Clonmacnoise: Art and patronage in the Early Medieval period', in (ed.) H.A. King, 187–100

Ó hÉailidhe, P. (1967) 'The crosses and slabs at St. Berrihert's Kyle, in the Glen of Aherlow', in (ed.) E. Rynne, 102–126

Ó hInnse, S. (ed. and trans.) (1947) *Miscellaneous Irish Annals* (AD 1114–1437), Dublin (Dublin Institute for Advanced Studies)

O'Keeffe, T. (1994) 'Omey and the sands of time', *Archaeol. Ireland* 8 (2), 22–24

— (1998) 'Architectural traditions of the early church in Munster', in (eds) M.A. Monk and J. Sheehan, 112–124

— (2004) *Ireland's Round Towers,* Stroud (Tempus)

O'Kelly, M.J. (1958) 'Church Island near Valencia, Co. Kerry', *Proc. Roy. Irish Acad.* 59C, 57–136

O'Kelly, M.J. (1962) 'Two ring-forts at Garryduff, Co. Cork', *Proc. Roy. Irish Acad.* 63C, 17–125

O'Laverty, J. (1878) *An Historical Account of the Diocese of Down and Connor Ancient and Modern,* vol. 1, Dublin (James Duffy and Sons)
— (1880) *An Historical Account of the Diocese of Down and Connor Ancient and Modern,* vol. 2, Dublin (James Duffy and Sons)
— (1887) *An Historical account of the Diocese of Down and Connor,* vol. 4, Dublin (James Duffy and Sons)
— (1895) *The Bishops of Down and Connor: An Historical Account of the Diocese of Down and Connor Ancient and Modern,* vol. 5, Dublin (James Duffy and Co.)
O'Mahony, F. (ed.) (1994) *The Book of Kells, Proceedings of a Conference at Trinity College Dublin,* 6-9 September 1992, Aldershot (Scolar Press)
O'Meadhra, U. (1979) *Early Christian, Viking and Romanesque Art: Motif-pieces from Ireland,* Stockholm (Almqvist and Wiksell)
— (1987) *Early Christian, Viking and Romanesque Art: Motif-pieces from Ireland 2: discussion on aspects of find-context and function,* Stockholm (Almqvist and Wiksell)
O'Neill, J. (1907) 'The Rule of Ailbe', *Éiru* 3, 92–115
O'Rahilly, C. (1998) 'A classification of bronze stick-pins from the Dublin excavations 1962–72', in (ed.) C. Manning, 23–33
O'Reilly, J.P. (1904) 'Some further notes on ancient horizontal mills, native and foreign', *Proc. Roy. Irish Acad.* 24C, 58–84
Ó Riain, P. (1972) 'Boundary association in early Irish society', *Studia Celtica* 7, 12–99
— (1975) 'The composition of the Irish Section of the calendar of Saints', *Dinnseanchas* 6, 77–92
— (1977) 'St. Finnbarr: a study in a cult', *J. Cork Archaeol. Hist. Soc.* 82, 63–82
— (1982) 'Towards a methodology in early Irish hagiography', *Peritia* 1, 146–159
— (ed.) (1985) *Corpus Genealogiarum Sanctorum Hiberniae* Dublin (Dublin Institute for Advanced Studies) = CGSH
— (1990) 'The Tallaght martyrologies, redated', *Cambridge Medieval Celtic Studies* 20, 21–38
Ó Ríordáin, S.P. (1942) 'The excavation of a large earthen ringfort at Garranes, Co. Cork', *Proc. Roy. Irish Acad.* 47(C), 77–150
O'Sullivan, A. (1997) 'Neolithic, Bronze Age, and Iron Age woodworking techniques, in trackway excavations in the Mountdillon Bogs, Co. Longford 1985–91', *Trans. Irish Archaeological Wetland Unit,* 3, 391–342
Oskamp, H.P.A. (1970) *The Voyage of Máel Dúin,* Grönigen (Wolters-Noordhoff Publishing)
Okasha, E. (1971) *Hand-List of Anglo-Saxon Non-Runic Inscriptions,* London (Cambridge University Press)
— (1970) 'A new inscription from Ramsey Island', *Archaeologia Cambrensis* 119, 68–70
Okasha, E. and Forsyth, K. (2001) *Early Christian Inscriptions of Munster: A Corpus of the Inscribed Stones,* Cork (Cork University Press)

Parfitt, K. (1993) 'The Dover Boat', *Curr. Archaeol.* 133, 4–8
Patterson, W.H. (1870–4) 'On some ancient sepulchral slabs in the counties of Down, Antrim and Donegal', *Proc. Roy. Irish Acad.* 2nd series 1, 273–278
Payne, S. (1973) 'Kill-off patterns in sheep and goats: the mandibles from Asvan Kale', *Anatolian Stud.* 23, 281–303
Pearce, S.M. (ed.) (1982) *The early church in western Britain and Ireland,* Oxford, (B.A.R.)
Petrie, G. (1872) *Christian Inscriptions in the Irish Language,* Dublin (The Royal Historical and Archaeological Association of Ireland)
Phillips, S. (1960) 'The material excavated from Nendrum Monastery, Co. Down, 1922-24', (unpublished undergraduate thesis, Queen's University Belfast)
Plummer, C. (1910) *Vitae Sanctorum Hiberniae.* vols 1 and 2, Oxford (Oxford University Press, reprinted 1968: Sandpiper Books Ltd.)
— (1922) *Bethada Náem n Érenn. Lives of Irish Saints,* Oxford (reprint 1968: Sandpiper Books Ltd.)
— (1925) *Irish Litanies,* London (Harrison and Sons)
Pollock, A. J. and Waterman, D.M. (1963) 'A Medieval pottery kiln at Downpatrick', *Ulster J. Archaeol.* 26, 79–104
Powell, T.E. (1994–1995) 'The disappearance of horizontal watermills from Medieval Ireland', *Trans. Newcomen Soc.* 66, 219–224
Proudfoot, L. (ed.) (1997) *Down History and Society: Interdisciplinary Essays on the History of an Irish County,* Dublin (Geography Publications)
Proudfoot, V. B. (1954) 'Excavations at the Cathedral Hill, Downpatrick, Co. Down', *Ulster J. Archaeol.* 17, 97–102

Quigley, W.G.H. and Roberts, E.F.D. (eds) (1972) *Registrum Johannis Mey: The Register of John Mey, Archbishop of Armagh 1443–56,* Belfast (HMSO)

Rahtz, P. (1981) 'Medieval milling', in (ed.) D.W. Crossley, 1–15
Rahtz, P. and Sheridan, K. (1971) 'Tamworth', *Curr. Archaeol.* 3, 164–168
Rahtz, P. and Bullough, D. (1977) 'Parts of an Anglo-Saxon mill', in (ed.) P. Clemoes 15–39
Rahtz, P. and Meeson, R. (1992) *An Anglo-Saxon watermill at Tamworth,* Council for British Archaeology Research Report 83, London (Council for British Archaeology)
Rankin, J.F. (1997) *Down Cathedral: The Church of Saint Patrick of Down,* Belfast (Ulster Historical Foundation)
Raven, T. (1625) 'Maps of the Hamilton Estates, County Down 1625', (unpublished, held by North Down Borough Council Office, Bangor, Co. Down)
RCAHMS (1982) *Argyll: An Inventory of the Monuments, vol. 4 Iona,* Edinburgh (HMSO)
Reece, R. (ed.) (1981) *Excavations in Iona 1964 to 1974,* London (Institute of Archaeology)
Reeves, W. (1845) *Papers read before the Down, Connor and Dromore Church Architectural Society, during the year 1844,* Belfast (printed for the Society, and sold by G. Phillips, Belfast: Grant and Bolton, Dublin: Rivingstons, London: Parker, Oxford: and Stevensons, Cambridge)
— (1847) *Ecclesiastical Antiquities of Down, Connor and Dromore,* Dublin (Hodges and Smith)
— (1853) 'The antiphonary of Bangor', *Ulster J. Archaeol.* (1st series) 1, 168–179
— (1902) 'Nendrum, commonly called Mahee Island, embracing its present condition and past history, 5th November 1845', *Ulster J. Archaeol.* (2nd series) 8, 13–22; 58–68
Reeves-Smyth, T. and Hamond, F. (eds) *Landscape Archaeology in Ireland,* B.A.R. British Series 116, Oxford (B.A.R.)
Richardson, H.G. (1961) 'Some Norman monastic foundations in Ireland', in (eds) J.A. Watt, J. B. Morrall and F.X. Martin, 29–43
Richter, M. (1999) *Ireland and her Neighbours in the Seventh Century,* Dublin (Four Courts Press)
Rivals, C. (1973) 'Tide mills in France', *T.I.M.S.* 3, 159–165
Robertson, L. (1861) 'Note', *Trans. Kilkenny Archaeol. Soc* 3, 347–348
Russell, P. (2001) 'Patterns of hypocorism in early Irish hagiography', in (eds) J. Carey *et al.*, 237–249

Ryan, J. (1931) *Irish Monasticism, Origins and Early Development,* Dublin (Talbot Press)
Ryan, M. (ed.) (1983) *Treasures of Ireland, Irish Art 3000 BC—1500 AD,* Dublin (Royal Irish Academy)
Ryan, M. (1988) 'Fine metalworking and early Irish monasteries: the archaeological evidence', in (ed.) J. Bradley, 33–48
— (1995) 'The decoration of the Donore Discs', in (ed.) C. Bourke, 27–35
— (2000) *Early Irish Communion Vessels,* Dublin (The Irish Treasures Series, Country House in association with the National Museum)
Rynne, C. (1988) 'The Archaeology and Technology of the Horizontal-wheeled Watermill, with Special Reference to Ireland', vols 1 and 2, (unpublished Ph.D. thesis, University College, Cork)
— (1989a) 'Archaeology and the early Irish watermill', *Archaeol. Ireland* 3 (3), 110–114
— (1989b) 'The introduction of the vertical watermill into Ireland: some recent archaeological evidence', *Med. Archaeol.* 33, 21–31
— (1990) 'Some observations on the production of flour and meal in the early historic period', *J. Cork Archaeol. Hist. Soc.* 95, 20–29
— (1992) 'Early Medieval horizontal-wheeled mill penstocks from Co. Cork', *J. Cork Archaeol. Hist. Soc.* 97, 54–68
— (1992) 'Milling in the 7th century: Europe's earliest tide mills', *Archaeol. Ireland.* 6 (2), 22–24
— (1997) 'The Patrick Street watermills. Their technological context and a note on reconstruction', in (ed.) C. Walsh, 81–89
— (1998a) 'Technological change in Anglo-Norman Munster', in *The Barryscourt Lectures,* 3, 65–96, Carrigtwohill, Co. Cork (The Barryscourt Trust, in association with Cork County Council and Gandon editions, Kinsale)
— (1998b) 'The craft of the millwright in Early Medieval Munster', in (eds) M.A. Monk and J. Sheehan, 85–101
— (1999) *The Industrial Archaeology of Cork City and its Environs,* Dublin (The Stationery Office)
— (2000) 'The Early Medieval monastic watermill', in (eds) J.W. Marshall and G.D. Rourke, 185–213
Rynne, E. (ed.) (1967) *North Munster Studies: essays in commemoration of Monsignor Michael Moloney,* Limerick (Thomond Archaeological Society)
— (1987) *Figures from the Past, Studies on Figurative Art in Christian Ireland in Honour of Helen M. Roe,* Dún Laoghaire (The Glendale Press and The Royal Society of Antiquaries of Ireland)
— (2005) 'Leo Swan's pet subject: enclosed early ecclesiastical sites in Ireland', in (eds) T. Condit and C. Corlett, 87–93

Salisbury, C. (1991) 'Primitive British fish-weirs', in (eds) G.L. Good, R. Jones and M. Ponsford, 76–87
Santos, L.F.R. (1992) *Os Moinhos de Maré da Ria Formosa,* Quarteira, Portugal (Parque Natural da Ria Formosa)
Sass, J. (1990) *The Versatile Millstone, Workhorse of Many Industries,* Newton, N. Carolina (Society for the Preservation of Old Mills)
Schmid, E. (1972) *Atlas of Animal Bones,* Amsterdam (Elsevier Publishing Company)
Schweingruber, F.H. (1978) *Mikroskopische Holzanatomie,* Birmensdorf
Scott, B.G. (ed.) (1982) *Studies on Early Ireland: Essays in Honour of M.V. Duignan,* Belfast (Association of Young Irish Archaeologists, Annual Seminar 1980)
— (1990) *Early Irish Ironworking,* Belfast (Ulster Museum)
Seixal (2005) *Moinhos de Maré do Ocidente Europeu 2005,* Seixal (Ecomuseu Municipal de Seixal Portugal)
Sexton, R. (1998) 'Porridges, gruels and breads: The cereal foodstuffs of Early Medieval Ireland', in (eds) M.A. Monk and J. Sheehan, 76–85
Sharpe, R. (1984) 'Some problems concerning the organization of the church in Early Medieval Ireland', *Peritia* 3, 230–270
— (1995) *Adomnán of Iona, Life of St. Columba,* London (Penguin Books)
Sheehy, M.P. (1962) *Pontifica Hibernica, Medieval Papal Chancery Documents concerning Ireland,* 640-1261, vol.1, Dublin (M.H. Gill)
Siegal, J. (1976) 'Animal palaeopathology: possibilities and problems', *J. Archaeol. Sci.* 3, 349–384
Silver, I.A. (1969) 'The ageing of domestic animals', in (eds) D. Brothwell and E. Higgs, 283–302
Small, A., Thomas, C. and Wilson, D.M. (1973) *St. Ninian's Isle and its Treasure,* 2 vols London (Oxford University Press for the University of Aberdeen)
Smith, A.J.E. (1978) *The moss flora of Britain and Ireland,* Cambridge (Cambridge University Press)
Smith, B. (ed.) (1999) *Britain and Ireland 900-1300, Insular Responses to Medieval European Change,* Cambridge (Cambridge University Press)
Smith, N.A.F. (1984) 'The origins of water power: a problem of evidence and expectations', *Trans. Newcomen Soc,* 55, 67–84
Smith, N. (1971) *A History of Dams,* London (P. Davies)
Smyth, A.P. (1999) 'The effects of Scandinavian raiders on the English and Irish churches; a preliminary reassessment', in (ed.) B. Smith, 1–38
SMR *The Sites and Monuments Record of the Environment and Heritage Service of Northern Ireland*
Sperber, I. (1997) 'Lives of St Finnian of Movilla: British evidence', in (ed.) L. Proudfoot, 85–102
— (2001) 'The life of St Monenna or Darerca of Killevy', in (eds) A.J. Hughes and W. Nolan, 63–97
Stalley, R. (2000) *Irish Round Towers,* the Irish Treasures series, Dublin (Country House)
— (2001) 'Sex, symbol, and myth: some observations on the Irish round tower', in (ed.) C. Hourihane, 27–47
Stevenson, R.B.K. (1955) 'Pins and the chronology of brochs', *Proc. Prehist.* Soc. 21, 282–294
Stokes, M. (1875) *The Early Christian Architecture of Ireland,* London (G. Bell and Sons)
Stokes, W. (1868) *The Life And Labours in the Art and Archaeology of George Petrie,* London (Longmans, Green, & Co)
— (ed. and trans.) (1887) *The Tripartite Life of Patrick, with other documents relating to that saint,* 2 vols London (H. M. Stationery Office)
— (1895) *Fílire hUí Gormáin: The Martyrology of Gorman,* London (Henry Bradshaw Society)
— (ed.) (1896) 'The Annals of Tigernach', *Rév. Celtique,* vols 17 and 18, (reprinted Llanerch Publishers, Lampeter, 1993)
— (ed.) (1905) *The Martyrology of Oengus the Culdee: Fílire Óenguiso Céli Dé,* Dublin (Henry Bradshaw Society, reprinted 1984, Institute for Advanced Studies)
— (1906) 'The birth and life of St. Moling', *Rév. Celtique* 27, 257–312
Swan, L. (1973) 'Duleek: an Early Christian site', in *The Annals of Duleek* 3, 12–20
— (1983) 'Enclosed ecclesiastical sites and their relevance to settlement patterns of the first millennium AD', in (eds) T. Reeves-Smyth and F. Hamond, 269–294
Swift, E. (trans.) (1809) *The Life and Acts of Saint Patrick, the Archbishop, Primate and Apostle of Ireland /Now First Translated from the Original Latin of Jocelyn, The Cistercian Monk of Furness,* Dublin (Hibernia Press Company)

Swift, M. (1999) *Historical Maps of Ireland,* London (Parkgate Books Ltd.)

Tedeschi, C. (2001) 'Some observations on the palaeography of Early Christian inscriptions in Britain', in (eds) J. Higgitt *et al.*
— (2005) *Congeries Lapidum: Iscrizioni Britanniche dei Secoli V–VII,* Pisa
Thomas, C. (1959) 'Imported pottery in Dark-Age western Britain', *Med. Archaeol.* 3, 89–111
— (1976) 'Imported Late-Roman Mediterranean pottery in Ireland and western Britain: chronologies and implications', *Proc. Roy. Irish Acad.* 76C, 245–256
— (1979) 'Saint Patrick and the fifth-century: an historical model explored', in (ed.) P.J. Casey 81–101
— (1981) 'A provisional list of imported pottery in Post-Roman western Britain and Ireland', Institute of Cornish Studies, Special report, no. 7, Pool, Redruth, Cornwall (Institute of Cornish Studies)
— (1990) '"Gallici Nautae de Galliarum Provinciis"- a sixth/seventh century trade with Gaul reconsidered', *Med. Archaeol.* 34, 1–25
— (1992) *Whithorn's Christian Beginnings,* First Whithorn Lecture, Whithorn (Friends of the Whithorn Trust)
— (1999) *Silent in the Shroud: a Seventh-century Inscription from Wales,* Balgavies (Pinkfoot Press)
Towill, E.S. (1964) 'Saint Mochaoi and Nendrum', *Ulster J. Archaeol.* 27, 103–121
Trench-Jellicoe, R. (1998) 'The Skeith Stone, Upper Kilrenny, Fife, in its context', *Proc. Soc. Antiq. Scotland* 128, 495–513
Tutin, T.G., Heywood, V.H., Burges, N.A., Moore, D.M., Valentine, D.H., Walters, S.M. and Webb, D.A. (eds) (1964-80) *Flora Europaea* 1–5, Cambridge (University Press)

Valante, M.A. (1998) 'Reassessing the Irish 'monastic town'', *Irish Hist. Stud.* 31(121), 1–18
Verheyen, B. (1949) (trans.) *The Holy Rule of St Benedict,* Atchisom, Kansas

Waddell, J. and Holland, P. (1990) 'The Peakaun site: Duignan's 1944 investigations', *Tipperary Historical Journal* (un-numbered), 165–86
Wailes, R. (1938–39) 'Tide mills in England and Wales', *Trans. Newcomen Soc.* 19, 1–33
Wailes, R. (1978) 'The 'Greek' and 'Norse' horizontal waterwheels', *T.I.M.S.* 4, 163–165
Wakeman, W.F. (1873) 'Note on the Rossery 'Canoe'', *J. Royal Hist. Arch. Assoc.* 2 (4th series), 16–19
Wakeman, W.F. (1893) 'A survey of the antiquarian remains on the Island of Inishmurray', Royal Society of Antiquaries of Ireland, London (Williams and Norgate)
Walsh, C. (ed.) (1997) *Archaeological Excavations at Patrick, Nicholas and Winetavern Streets, Dublin,* Dingle (Brandon Book Publishers Ltd.)
Walton, S.A. (2006) *Wind & Water in the Middle Ages: Fluid Technologies from Antiquity to the Renaissance,* Pennsylvania (Pennsylvania State University Press)
Wamers, E. (1985) *Insularer Metallschmuck in wikingerzeitlichen Gräbern Nordeuropas,* Neumünster
Warner, R. (1989) 'Brooch terminal waster', in (ed.) S. Youngs, 194
Wasserschleben, F.W.H. (ed.) (1885) *Die irische Kanonensammlung,* Leipzig
Waterman, D.M. (1958) 'A note on Medieval pottery from Nendrum and Grey Abbey Co. Down', *Ulster J. Archaeol.* 21, 67–73
Watson, W.J. (1926) *The Celtic Placenames of Scotland,* Edinburgh (republished 1993, Birlinn)
Watt, J.A., Morrall, J.B. and Martin F.X (eds) (1961) *Medieval Studies Presented to Aubrey Gwynn,* S. J., Dublin
Watts, M. (2002) *The Archaeology of Mills and Milling,* Stroud (Tempus)
Way, A. (1868) 'Ancient Sun-dials', *Archaeological Journal,* 25, 207–233
Whitfield, N. (1997) 'The Waterford kite-brooch and its place in Irish metalwork', in (eds) J. Hurley and O.M.B. Scully *et al.*, 490–517
Wikander, Ö. (1985) 'Mill-channels, weirs and ponds. The environment of ancient watermills', *Opuscula Romana* 15, 149–154
Wikander, Ö. (ed.) (2000) *Handbook of Ancient Water Technology,* Leiden, Boston and Köln (Brill)
Will, R., Forsyth, K., Clancy, T. and Charles-Edwards, G. (2003) 'An eighth-century inscribed cross-slab in Dull, Perthshire', in *Scottish Archaeological Journal* 25 part 1, 57–71
Wilde, W.R. (1857) *A Descriptive Catalogue of the Antiquities of Stone, Earthen and Vegetable Materials in the Museum of the Royal Irish Academy,* Dublin (M.H. Gill)
Williamson, K. (1946) 'Horizontal water-mills of the Faroe Islands', *Antiquity* 20, 83–91
Wilson, B., Grigson, C. and Payne, S. (eds) (1982) *Ageing and Sexing Animal Bones from Archaeological Sites,* British Archaeological Reports British Series 109, Oxford (B.A.R.)
Wilson, P.N. (1960) *Watermills and Horizontal Wheels,* Kendal (Society for the Protection of Ancient Buildings)
Windele, (1843) The Cork Constitution, 15th June 1843
Windele, (1844) The Cork Constitution, 21st Dec., 1844

Yates, M.J. (1983) 'Preliminary excavations at Movilla Abbey, Co. Down', *Ulster J. Archaeol.* 46, 53–66
Youngs, S. and Clark, J. (1982) 'Medieval Britain and Ireland in 1981', *Med. Archaeol.* 26, 164–227
Youngs, S., Clark, J. and Barry T.B. (1983) 'Medieval Britain and Ireland in 1982', *Med. Archaeol.*, 27, 161–229
Youngs, S., Clark, J. and Barry T.B. (1987) 'Medieval Britain and Ireland in 1986', *Med. Archaeol.*, 31, 110–191
Youngs, S. (ed.) (1989) *'The Work of Angels, Masterpieces of Celtic Metalwork, 6th - 9th Centuries AD,* London (British Museum Publications in assoc. with the National Museum of Ireland and the National Museums of Scotland)

Index